SCOTLAND
The Later Middle Ages

THE EDINBURGH HISTORY OF SCOTLAND

General Editor
GORDON DONALDSON, D.Litt.

*Fraser Professor of Scottish History and Palaeography
in the University of Edinburgh*

———————————

SCOTLAND

The Later Middle Ages

Ranald Nicholson

The Edinburgh History of Scotland
Volume 2

MERCAT PRESS

MERCAT PRESS
James Thin Ltd.
53-59 South Bridge
Edinburgh EH1 1YS

Hardback edition first published, 1974
First published in paperback, 1978
Reprinted in paperback, 1989, 1993

ISBN 0 901824 84 4 *paperback*

Printed and bound in Great Britain
by The Cromwell Press, Melksham, Wiltshire

PREFACE

The whole period covered by this volume has figured, and continues to figure, in many popular histories varying in merit and idiosyncrasy. Many aspects of it have been touched upon in the last half century in specialised publications that are scholarly and less popular. But scarcely since Edwardian times has there been an attempt to embody the products of accumulating research in a fresh synthesis of Scotland's history in the later Middle Ages. This is an attempt. The somewhat profuse footnotes (which can be ignored by all save the zealous) draw attention to the useful labours of many scholars, and perhaps disclose that I have occasionally supplemented their work by a little independent research.

It will be obvious that what I have produced is not harmonious in its proportions, that some parts are emaciated and others gross. This has resulted from my inclination to give to the fifteenth century a fuller weight corresponding to the increasing abundance of source material. I have also lingered longest in treating periods that are complex and have paused more briefly at those which may be understood with less detailed exposition. In all cases dates have been rendered in modern reckoning : thus medieval Scottish documents dated between 1 January and 24 March inclusive have been assigned to the year following that stated in the original.

This book would not have taken shape without the co-operation of a succession of secretaries and typists, some of whom sought other employment. Three—Mrs Frederick Law, Mrs William Pollard and Miss Gilian MacPherson—persevered to the end. The publishers, as represented by Mr A. W. R. Seward and Miss Alison Reid, have been skilful, courteous, and patient beyond belief. My present colleagues in the University of Guelph, as well as my former colleagues in the University of Edinburgh, have been helpful and encouraging. Nor should I omit to acknowledge the aid of my parents, whose enduring enthusiasm extended even to the Augean task of proof correction. To three scholars I owe a great deal: Professor Geoffrey Hand of

v

University College, Dublin, read one-third of the book in typescript; Professor A. A. M. Duncan of the University of Glasgow read half of it; and Professor Gordon Donaldson of the University of Edinburgh read the whole of it. All extricated me from pitfalls, and I am particularly indebted to Professor Donaldson's sagacity.

It need hardly be said that none of my various helpers bears responsibility for the remaining defects in this work, which are entirely my own. It is some consolation that Sir Gilbert Hay opined: 'there is na man withe out sum falt may wret'. And, for the moment, doubts and hesitations must take second place to the kind of relief that Gavin Douglas felt when he wrote: 'heir is endit the lang desparit wark'.

RANALD NICHOLSON

Note on 1978 impression (Paperback edition)

So few scholarly reviews of this book have so far appeared that I have been deprived of the feelings of contrition that might have inspired me to major revision. One exception is a review by Dr Athol L. Murray, who has rightly pointed out that the men whom I described as "commissioners for the assessment of crown lands" were primarily concerned with leasing the lands and ought properly to be styled "commissioners for the leasing of crown lands".

Another review suggested that in view of the latest research I might feel inclined to revise my general opinions regarding the relations of crown and nobility. I do not feel so inclined. I should, however, draw the attention of readers to Professor G. W. S. Barrow's interesting article on "Lothian in the First War of Independence, 1296–1328" (*Scottish Historical Review*, vol. LV, 1976, pp. 151–71), which offers an interpretation somewhat different from my own. Lastly, in view of my predilection for Scotticisms, I regret that I have written of a certain common unit of account as a "mark" rather than a "merk" and would be relieved if readers would bear in mind that the latter is the appropriate Scottish rendering.

RANALD NICHOLSON

CONTENTS

LIST OF ABBREVIATIONS USED IN FOOTNOTES

Particulars of works not cited here are given either in the footnotes (if they are of minor relevance) or in the bibliography (if they are of major relevance). In the footnotes numerals in roman type signify the number, or part, of a volume; those in arabic signify pages, unless preceded by 'No.', in which case they refer to a document. When one footnote in which two or more works are cited is followed by a footnote citing the last of those works, the title of that work has been repeated for the sake of clarity, in place of the term *ibid*.

Aberdeen-Banff Illustrations	= *Illustrations of the Topography and Antiquities of the Shires of Aberdeen and Banff* (Spalding Club, 1847–69).
Aberdeen Burgh Recs.	= *Early Records of the Burgh of Aberdeen* (S.H.S., 1957).
Aberdeen Council Register	= *Extracts from the Council Register of the Burgh of Aberdeen* (Spalding Club, 1844).
Aberdeen Fasti	= *Fasti Aberdonenses: Selections from the Records of the University and King's College of Aberdeen* (Spalding Club, 1854).
Aberdeen Registrum	= *Registrum Episcopatus Aberdonensis* (Spalding and Maitland Clubs, 1845).
A.D.A.	= *The Acts of the Lords Auditors of Causes and Complaints, 1466–94*, ed. T. Thomson (London, 1839).
A.D.C.	= *The Acts of the Lords of Council in Civil Causes*, ed. T. Thomson and others (Edinburgh, 1839 and 1918).
A.D.C.P.	= *Acts of the Lords of Council in Public Affairs 1501–1554: Selections from Acta Dominorum Concilii*, ed. R. K. Hannay (1932).
A.P.S.	= *Acts of the Parliaments of Scotland*, ed. T. Thomson and C. Innes (Edinburgh, 1814–75).
Arbroath Liber	= *Liber S. Thome de Aberbrothoc* (Bannatyne Club, 1848–56).
Ayr Burgh Charters	= *Charters of the Royal Burgh of Ayr* (Ayr and Wigton Archaeological Association, 1883).

Balfour-Melville, *James I*	= E. W. M. Balfour-Melville, *James I, King of Scots* (1936).
Barbour, *The Bruce*	= J. Barbour, *The Bruce* (S.T.S., 1894).
Barron, *War of Independence*	= Evan Macleod Barron, *The Scottish War of Independence: a Critical Study*, 2nd edn. (1934).
Barrow, *Bruce*	= G. W. S. Barrow, *Robert Bruce and the Community of the Realm of Scotland* (1965).
B.I.H.R.	= *Bulletin of the Institute of Historical Research.*
Blind Harry, *Wallace* —	= *The Actis and Deeds of the Illustere and Vailzeand Campioun Schir William Wallace, Knicht of Ellerslie* (S.T.S., 1889).
B.M.	= British Museum.
Boece, *History*	= Hector Boethius, *Scotorum Historiae*, 2nd edn. (Paris, 1574), pp. 1–384 v.
Boece, *Vitae*	= *Hectoris Boetii Murthlacensium et Aberdonensium Episcoporum Vitae* (Bannatyne Club, 1825).
Brechin Registrum	= *Registrum Episcopatus Brechinensis* (Bannatyne Club, 1856).
Brown, *Early Travellers*	= Brown, P. Hume, *Early Travellers in Scotland* (1891).
Buchanan, *History*	= G. Buchanan, *The History of Scotland*, translated J. Aikman (Glasgow and Edinburgh, 1827–30).
Burghs Convention Recs.	= *Extracts from the Records of the Convention of the Royal Burghs of Scotland*, ed. J. D. Marwick (1870–90).
Burns, *Basle*	= J. H. Burns, *Scottish Churchmen and the Council of Basle* (1962).
Cal. Close	= *Calendar of the Close Rolls preserved in the Public Record Office* (1900–).
Cal. Docs. Scot.	= *Calendar of Documents relating to Scotland*, ed. J. Bain (1881–8).
Cal. Papal Letters	= *Calendar of Entries in the Papal Registers relating to Great Britain and Ireland: Papal Letters* ed. W. H. Bliss and others (1893–).
Cal. Papal Petitions	= *Calendar of Entries in the Papal Registers relating to Great Britain and Ireland: Petitions to the Pope*, ed. W. H. Bliss (1896).
Cal. Patent	= *Calendar of the Patent Rolls preserved in the Public Record Office* (1901–).

Cal. Scot. Supp.	= *Calendar of Scottish Supplications to Rome* (S.H.S., 1934–71).
Cambuskenneth Registrum	= *Registrum Monasterii S. Marie de Cambuskenneth* (Grampian Club, 1872).
Cameron, *Apostolic Camera*	= *The Apostolic Camera and Scottish Benefices*, ed. A. I. Cameron (1934).
Chron. Anonimalle	= *The Anonimalle Chronicle, 1333–81*, ed. V. H. Galbraith (1927).
Chron. Auchinleck	= *The Auchinleck Chronicle, ane schort memoriale of the scottis corniklis for addicioun*, ed. T. Thomson (Edinburgh, 1819, 1877).
Chron. Baker	= Geoffrey le Baker, *Chronicon*, ed. E. M. Thompson (1889).
Chron. Bower	= *Johannis de Fordun Scotichronicon cum Supplementis et Continuatione Walteri Bower*, ed. W. Goodall (Edinburgh, 1759).
Chron. Fordun	= *J. de Fordun, Cronica Gentis Scotorum*, ed. W. F. Skene (1871–2).
Chron. Froissart	= *The Chronicle of Froissart translated out of French by Sir John Bourchier, Lord Berners, annis 1523–25*, ed. W. P. Ker (1967).
Chron. Knighton	= Henry Knighton, *Chronicon*, ed. J. R. Lumby (R.S., 1889, 1895).
Chron. Lanercost	= *Chronicon de Lanercost* (Maitland Club, 1839).
Chron. Melsa	= *Chronica Monasterii de Melsa*, ed. E. A. Bond (R.S., 1867).
Chron. Pluscarden	= *Liber Pluscardensis*, ed. F. J. H. Skene (1877–80).
Chron. Walsingham	= Thomas Walsingham, *Historia Anglicana*, ed. H. T. Riley (R.S., 1863).
Chron. Wyntoun	= Andrew Wyntoun, *Orygynale Cronykil of Scotland*, ed. D. Laing (1872–79).
Conway, *Henry VII*	= Agnes Conway, *Henry VII's Relations with Scotland and Ireland, 1485–1498* (1932).
Coulton, *Scottish Abbeys*	= G. G. Coulton, *Scottish Abbeys and Social Life* (1933).
Davidson and Gray, *Staple*	= John Davidson and Alexander Gray, *The Scottish Staple at Veere* (1909).
Dowden, *Bishops*	= J. Dowden, *The Bishops of Scotland* (1912).
Dumfriesshire Trans.	= *Transactions of the Dumfriesshire and Galloway Natural History and Antiquarian Society* (1862–).

Dunbar, *Scot. Kings*	= A. H. Dunbar, *Scottish Kings: A Revised Chronology of Scottish History*, 2nd edn. (1906).
Duncan, *Nation of Scots*	= A. A. M. Duncan, *The Nation of Scots and the Declaration of Arbroath* (Historical Assoc., 1970).
Dunfermline Registrum	= *Registrum de Dunfermelyn* (Bannatyne Club, 1842).
Dunlop, *Bishop Kennedy*	= Annie I. Dunlop, *The Life and Times of James Kennedy, Bishop of St Andrews* (1950).
Durkan, *Bishop Turnbull*	= John Durkan, *William Turnbull, Bishop of Glasgow* (1951).
Easson, *Religious Houses*	= D. E. Easson, *Medieval Religious Houses: Scotland* (1957).
Edinburgh Burgh Recs.	= *Extracts from the Records of the Burgh of Edinburgh* (S.B.R.S., 1869–92).
Edinburgh City Charters	= *Charters and Other Documents Relating to the City of Edinburgh* (S.B.R.S., 1871).
E.H.R.	= *English Historical Review.*
E.R.	= *The Exchequer Rolls of Scotland*, ed. J. Stuart and others (Edinburgh, 1878–1908).
Extracta	= *Extracta e Variis Cronicis Scocie* (Abbotsford Club, 1842).
Ferrerius, *Continuatio*	= Hector Boethius, *Scotorum Historiae*, 2nd edn. (Paris, 1574), pp. 385 *et seq.* (*continuatio per Ioannem Ferrerium*).
Fife Court Bk.	= *The Sheriff Court Book of Fife* (S.H.S., 1928).
Flodden Papers	= *Flodden Papers, Diplomatic correspondence between the Courts of France and Scotland 1507–1517*, ed. Marguerite Wood (S.H.S., 1933).
Foedera	= *Foedera, Conventiones, Literae . . . accurante Thoma Rymer*, 3rd edn. (The Hague, 1739–45).
Fraser, *Douglas*	= W. Fraser, *The Douglas Book* (1885).
Glasgow Registrum	= *Registrum Episcopatus Glasguensis* (Bannatyne and Maitland Clubs, 1843).
Godscroft, *Douglas and Angus*	= David Hume of Godscroft, *The History of the Houses of Douglas and Angus* (Edinburgh, 1644).
Grant, *Social and Economic Development*	= I. F. Grant, *The Social and Economic Development of Scotland before 1603* (1930).

Gregory, *Western Highlands*	= Donald Gregory, *History of the Western Highlands and Isles of Scotland from ... 1493 to ... 1625* (1881).
Hailes, *Annals*	= Sir David Dalrymple, Lord Hailes, *Annals of Scotland from the Accession of Malcolm III surnamed Canmore to the Restoration of James I*, 3rd edn. (Edinburgh, 1819).
H.B.C.	= *Handbook of British Chronology*, ed. F. M. Powicke and E. B. Fryde (1961).
Highland Papers	= *Highland Papers* (S.H.S., 1914–34).
H.M.C.	= *Reports of the Royal Commission on Historical Manuscripts* (1870–).
Innes, *Scot. Middle Ages*	= Cosmo Innes, *Scotland in the Middle Ages* (1860).
Innes, *Sketches*	= Cosmo Innes, *Sketches of Early Scotch History* (1861).
James I, Life and Death	= *The Life and Death of King James the First of Scotland* (Maitland Club, 1837).
James IV, Letters	= *The Letters of James IV* (S.H.S., 1953).
Kelso Liber	= *Liber S. Marie de Calchou* (Bannatyne Club, 1846).
Knox, *History*	= *John Knox's History of the Reformation in Scotland*, ed. W. C. Dickinson (1949).
Lesley, *History*	= J. Lesley, *The History of Scotland from the Death of King James I in the Year MCCCCXXXVI to the Year MDLXI* (Bannatyne Club, 1830).
Mackenzie, *Highlands and Isles*	= W. C. Mackenzie, *The Highlands and Isles of Scotland: A Historical Survey* (1949).
Mackenzie, *Flodden*	= W. M. Mackenzie, *The Secret of Flodden* (1931).
Mackie, *James IV*	= R. L. Mackie, *King James IV of Scotland, A Brief Survey of His Life and Times* (1958).
MacQueen, *Robert Henryson*	= John MacQueen, *Robert Henryson: A Study of the Major Narrative Poems* (1967).
Major, *History*	= J. Major, *A History of Greater Britain* (S.H.S., 1892).
Melrose Liber	= *Liber Sancte Marie de Melros* (Bannatyne Club, 1837).
Misc.	= *Miscellany* (of S.H.S. etc.).
Monro, *Western Isles*	= *Monro's Western Isles of Scotland and Genealogies of the Clans 1549*, ed. R. W. Munro (1961).

Moray Registrum	= *Registrum Episcopatus Moraviensis* (Bannatyne Club, 1837).
Morton Registrum	= *Registrum Honoris de Morton* (Bannatyne Club, 1853).
Nat. MSS. Scot.	= *Facsimiles of the National Manuscripts of Scotland* (London, 1867–73).
Nicholson, *Edward III*	= Ranald Nicholson, *Edward III and the Scots: the Formative Years of a Military Career, 1327–35* (1965).
Paisley Registrum	= *Registrum Monasterii de Passelet* (Maitland Club, 1832; New Club, 1877).
Palgrave, *Documents*	= *Documents and Records Illustrating the History of Scotland*, ed. F. Palgrave (London, 1837).
Patrick, *Statutes*	= *Statutes of the Scottish Church*, ed. D. Patrick (S.H.S., 1907).
Pinkerton, *History*	= J. Pinkerton, *The History of Scotland from the Accession of the House of Stuart to that of Mary, with Appendixes of Original Papers* (London, 1797).
Pryde, *Burghs*	= G. S. Pryde, *The Burghs of Scotland: A Critical List* (1965).
P.R.O.	= Public Record Office, London.
Pitscottie, *Historie*	= R. Lindesay of Pitscottie, *The Historie and Chronicles of Scotland* (S.T.S., 1899–1911).
Proc. Soc. Antiq. Scot.	= *Proceedings of the Society of Antiquaries of Scotland* (1851–).
Raine, *Letters*	= *Historical Papers and Letters from Northern Registers*, ed. Jas. Raine (R.S., 1873).
Rait, *Parliaments*	= R. S. Rait, *The Parliaments of Scotland* (1924).
Rashdall, *Universities*	= Hastings Rashdall, *The Universities of Europe in the Middle Ages* (1964).
R.M.S.	= *Registrum Magni Sigilli Regum Scotorum*, ed. J. M. Thomson and others (1882–1914).
Robertson, *Concilia*	= *Concilia Scotiae* (Half Title: *Statuta Ecclesiae Scoticanae*), ed. J. Robertson (Bannatyne Club, 1866).
Rot. Parl.	= *Rotuli Parliamentorum ut et Petitiones et Placita in Parliamento* (1783).
Rot. Scot.	= *Rotuli Scotiae in Turri Londinensi et in Domo Capitulari Westmonasteriensi Asservati*, ed. D. Macpherson and others (1814–19).

R.P.C.	= *Register of the Privy Council of Scotland*, ed. J. H. Burton and others (1877–).
R.S.	= Rolls Series.
R.S.S.	= *Registrum Secreti Sigilli Regum Scotorum*, ed. M. Livingstone and others (1908–).
St Andrews Acta	= *Acta Facultatis Artium Universitatis S. Andree 1413–1588* (S.H.S., 1964).
St Andrews Copiale	= *Copiale Prioratus Sanctiandree* ed. J. H. Baxter (1930).
St Andrews Univ. Recs.	= *The Early Records of the University of St Andrews* (S.H.S., 1926).
Scalacronica	= *Scalacronica, by Sir Thomas Gray of Heton, Knight* (Maitland Club, 1836).
S.B.R.S.	= Scottish Burgh Records Society.
Scot. Church Hist. Soc. Recs.	= *Records of the Scottish Church History Society* (1926–).
Scot. Legal Hist.	= *An Introduction to Scottish Legal History* (Stair Soc., 1958).
Scots Peerage	= *The Scots Peerage*, ed. Sir J. Balfour Paul (1904–14).
S.H.R.	= *Scottish Historical Review* (1903–28, 1947–).
S.H.S.	= Scottish History Society.
Sources of Scots Law	= *An Introductory Survey of the Sources and Literature of Scots Law* (Stair Soc., 1936).
Stevenson, *Documents*	= *Documents Illustrative of the History of Scotland*, ed. J. Stevenson (1870).
Stones, *Documents*	= E. L. G. Stones, *Anglo-Scottish Relations, 1174–1328: Some selected documents* (1964).
S.T.S.	= Scottish Text Society.
T.A.	= *Accounts of the Lord High Treasurer of Scotland*, ed. T. Dickson and Sir J. Balfour Paul (1877–1916).
'Trewe Encountre'	= 'A contemporary account of the battle of Flodden', *Proc. Soc. Antiq. Scot.*, VII (1866–7). 141–52.
T.R.H.S.	= *Transactions of the Royal Historical Society.*
Tytler, *History*	= Patrick Fraser Tytler, *The History of Scotland* (1887).
Vita Edwardi	= *Vita Edwardi Secundi monachi cuiusdam Malmesberiensis*, ed. and trs. N. Denholm-Young (1957).

Watt, *Fasti*

= *Fasti Ecclesiae Scoticanae Medii Aevi*, ed. D. E. R. Watt (1969).

Wigtown Charters

= *Wigtownshire Charters* (S.H.S., 1960).

Wittig, *Scottish Tradition*

= Kurt Wittig, *The Scottish Tradition in Literature* (1958).

1

SCOTLAND AT THE CLOSE OF THE THIRTEENTH CENTURY: SOCIETY, ECONOMY AND INSTITUTIONS

Despite the alarms and vicissitudes of the years between 1286 and 1296 they were years of lingering peace. Within Scotland there was discord, even civil war, but there was no armed conflict with an external foe, and little to show that the relatively golden age of the Alexanders was about to be followed by one of blood and iron. When it came, the change was unforeseen, sudden and traumatic. With the beginning of the Anglo-Scottish wars in 1296 there was an end, so far as Scotland was concerned, to the formative years of the earlier Middle Ages. Preceding centuries of rapid innovation were succeeded by others of slow and erratic development. The last decade of peace summed up achievements that coming generations had to strive to regain before attempting to surpass. What was characteristic of Scotland during that decade impressed itself as a pattern that was afterwards modified, but which was nonetheless still perceptible centuries later.

The pattern was unique. It showed some features that were common throughout western Europe, together with others that were indigenous. For though the Scots were not wholly isolated, they dwelt (so affirmed the Declaration of Arbroath) in a land 'beyond which there is no habitation', distant by two months journey from the papal court at Rome which was the centre of western Christendom.

Within Scotland itself, geography fostered diversity and particularism. Yet the physical features of the land amounted to hindrances rather than absolute barriers. By horseback the normal day's journey was one of twenty miles; but with relays of horses it was possible for a man to cover eighty. The king's highway, the *via regis*, passed from one royal burgh and royal castle to another, forming a network of recognised routes in the more developed parts of Scotland. The Tweed could be crossed by ford or by bridges at Berwick and Roxburgh. The Tay could be crossed by the bridge at Perth. The Forth could be crossed not only by the bridge at Stirling but by the ferries of Airth, Queensferry and Earlsferry. And a river might be not so much a barrier as a route of communication: the Forth was navigable by seagoing vessels as far as Stirling, the Tay as far as Perth, though the Clyde, not artificially deepened until more modern times, could take ships only as far as Dumbarton, so that Glasgow was no bustling sea-port but a sleepy inland market town and ecclesiastical centre. The importance of water-borne traffic meant that an inland loch might be the nucleus of a parish or barony. Among the sea-lochs and islands of the west, where the population was part Norse in descent, much use was made of galleys propelled by oars and fitted with an auxiliary mast and sail.

Linked together in a scheme of communications which differed from that of the present day was a population of some 400,000 whose distribution corresponded to a society that was agricultural, not industrial. Although there were over fifty burghs, they can have comprised scarce ten per cent of the population, for a typical burgh was rarely more than a street or 'gait' leading to the castle that almost invariably rose beside it. It was the existence of a cathedral which alone conferred the title of 'city' and brought distinction not only to Aberdeen, a leading burgh, but to places like Brechin and Glasgow which perhaps had a few hundred inhabitants apiece. Though townsfolk were few, the rural population was probably as large as at the present day, particularly where the land was fertile—around the estuaries of the Forth and Tay, in the lower reaches of the Tweed valley, and in parts of Moray and Galloway. Even in these areas, however, the typical rural community was not that of a 'nucleated' village, for the population was fairly evenly spread over the land that sustained it.[1] Settlements took the form of steadings (isolated farms) or 'touns' (townships) dispersed over the lands of a barony. Their inhabitants were subject to the baron's court, which had more than a

---

[1] See Lord Cooper, 'The Numbers and the Distribution of the Population of Medieval Scotland', *S.H.R.*, xxvi. 2–9; G. W. S. Barrow, Rural Settlement in Central and Eastern Scotland: the medieval evidence', *Scottish Studies*, vi. 123–44.

judicial function: it organised and supervised their labours and thereby instilled a sense of community.

The original functional basis of each township was probably the plough-team. The heavy wooden plough needed six or eight oxen to drag it. Almost as many men were needed to urge it on its way. This was reflected in the measurement of land commonly used in the Lowlands: the arable land of a township was normally one ploughgate (or ploughgang) supposedly amounting to 120 English acres or 104 Scots acres, though not necessarily in one compact tract. North of Perth, where the usual measurement was the davoch (comparable to four ploughgates) [2] the underlying concept was not area but productivity. Even the ploughgate seldom represented a measured area, but rather a notion of the amount of land a plough team could cope with. It was made up of eight oxgates (or oxgangs). A husbandman was supposed to contribute two oxen and thus be entitled to two oxgates or one 'husbandland'.[3] But a rich husbandman might possess a whole plough-team of oxen; a poor one might have only a half share in an ox;[4] a more depressed class, the cottars, owned no oxen and were enjoined to use the foot-plough.[5] It was usual for a group of between four and sixteen husbandmen to act as joint tenants and to combine their resources both in tilling the soil and in paying the rent in money, produce and labour services. The various shares in the plough-team probably determined the share that each husbandman paid in rent as well as his share in the common arable lands. These lands were from time to time re-allocated according to the practice of 'run-rig'. Although the word is not found in a written source prior to 1437,[6] the practice it described was doubtless older. The method of ploughing had the effect of dividing the arable land into strips or 'rigs', some twenty or thirty feet wide, and of separating these by shallow ditches, the upcast topsoil of the ditches both raising the height of the rigs and improving their quality.

Rig cultivation was an answer to a main problem of Scottish agriculture, that of drainage. The rigs ran downhill so that the ditches dividing them played the part of field drains. This method could not

---

[2] *E.R.*, XIII. cxxxix.

[3] An interesting entry in the Colvil MS. states: 'Anno Domini [blank] the erll of Marche causit his servand Sim Samond to divide the haill landis in the Mers in husband landis, ilk husband land xxvj akkeris quhair pluk [plough] & syth may gang.' (*A.P.S.*, I. Notices of Manuscripts, xxiv).

[4] *Ibid.*, II. 8, c. 20.

[5] *Ibid.*, I. 397; II. 8, c. 20.

[6] Grant, *Social and Economic Development*, p. 287, n. 2.

be successfully applied to the level carses or straths that bordered many a Scottish river. These potentially fertile lands were undrained bogs or were used as summer pasture while the plough-teams toiled up and down the rigs on the neighbouring slopes. These received whatever manure was available and were sown year after year with coarse barley (bere) or oats, more rarely with wheat. From time to time the cultivated 'infield' would be expanded when part of the outlying land, the 'outfield', was manured by folding cattle upon it, thereafter being ploughed and cropped until its fertility was exhausted. The higher slopes, the roughest and wettest pieces of ground, were kept for grazing. In both Highlands and Lowlands, however, there were large tracts that were unsuitable even for grazing. Vast peat bogs provided fuel but little else. The Scottish 'forests' were mostly destitute of trees and used as game reserves for hunting, hawking and fishing. These sporting pursuits played an important part in the economy and, particularly in the Highlands, might make the difference between famine and plenty.

Although the Highlands were less suited to arable farming than the Lowlands, the rearing of cattle and sheep was probably of more significance in both areas alike than was the cultivation of crops. There are traces of an official campaign to encourage tillage and to prevent earls, barons and freeholders 'wastand thair landis and the cuntre with multitud of scheip and bestis'.[7] But a sixteenth-century writer could still assert that the country was 'more gevin to store of bestiall than ony production of cornys'.[8] The agrarian difference between Highlands and Lowlands was not so much that the one region was pastoral and the other agricultural, but rather that the Highlands concentrated on cattle-rearing and the Lowlands on sheep-farming.

For mixed farming was universal. A share in the arable lands carried with it grazing rights for so many head of sheep or cattle. Both in Highlands and Lowlands, there was a migration to the summer shielings, usually, but not always, on the upper slopes. There the men guarded the herds and flocks from wolves and foxes and sheared the sheep; the women carded and spun wool and made butter and cheese from the milk of cows and ewes. By the use of summer shielings the animals were removed from the growing crops in the open fields—for the only permanently fenced enclosures were parks for the preservation of game. The practice of transhumance also helped to conserve

[7] *A.P.S.*, I. 382, 397; II. 8, c. 20; *Chron. Wyntoun*, II. 265-6.
[8] Bellenden, cited in *Scot. Legal Hist.*, p. 286.

scarce winter fodder. Even so, it was necessary around Martinmas (11 November) to slaughter most of the cattle, keeping just enough for breeding and to draw the plough. Over winter there was no fresh meat save what could be got by hunting. The population lived on the salted carcases of the 'marts', eked out with oatmeal, barley-bread and salted or dried fish. There were violent fluctuations in the food supply, and it was not easy to relieve wholesale famine by imports of corn from abroad.

In a society whose main concern was land and its produce it was natural that personal status should depend on the amount of land held and the way in which it was held. Landholding, as it affected the whole range of society from serf to king, presented a variety that almost defies classification. The essential dividing line was between the minority, the free tenants (*libere tenentes*), who held their land by homage and fealty, quit of labour service or any other 'dishonourable' burden, and the vast majority who lived and worked upon the land but enjoyed neither secure tenure nor complete personal freedom. Various terms, with different shades of meaning, were used to describe this vast servile or semi-servile class—*nativi*, *bondi*, neyfs, carls, cumlaws, *rustici*, churls and husbandmen. Some were still outright slaves, 'thai that ar of foul kyn',[9] who, if they fled from their master, could be led back by the nose.[10] Many were tied to the soil (*adscripti glebe*) and could not depart from the barony without their lord's permission. In the Gaelic areas there was also a semi-servile class, known in Ireland as *betagh*, relegated to humdrum toil while their betters engaged in the aristocratic pursuits of fighting, hunting, fishing, or steering a galley.

There was, however, a tendency for servile status to disappear, or at least to be mitigated. While the husbandman had to provide boon work, labour for stipulated periods on the demesne lands, and pay the 'heriot' and 'merchet' that signalised his semi-servile condition, he might rise in the world if these obligations were commuted into cash payments. Though this process was not completed until modern times it had already begun on the lands of Kelso Abbey and elsewhere in Scotland.[11] This development held out prospects to the husbandman with capital and initiative. Legislation attributed to

---

[9] *A.P.S.*, I. 401. See also 'A gud were of law', *ibid.*, 753.
[10] *Quoniam Attachiamenta*, *ibid.*, 655.
[11] *Kelso Liber*, II. 455–6.

Alexander II alludes to 'malaris of carls born',[12] men of base descent who paid 'maill' or money rent. Usually the husbandman paid maill for a year at a time and his tenure was secure only for that year; he might have cottars working under him who were his tenants-at-will and could be dismissed without warning from their croft and kail yard. It was possible, however, for a husbandman to obtain a 'tack' (a lease of land) for a number of years (often three or five) in return for a fixed yearly 'ferm' (*firma*) in cash. The 'fermour' (*firmarius*) might be no husbandman but someone of higher status who wished to invest in the exploitation of a large holding of land. Such a tenure might be not merely for a term of years, as in the case of a tack; it could be granted in liferent—it might even be perpetual and heritable, held 'in feu'. So came about the concept of tenure 'in feu-ferm' (*in feudifirma*). This term, already found in ecclesiastical chartularies and in the exchequer rolls, signified a heritable grant of land in return for a fixed and perpetual money rent.[13]

Nonetheless the hybrid feu-ferm tenure was still rare and undefined. It conveyed less authority and prestige than the earlier forms of feudal tenure in which land was held in return for knight-service or a token payment (blench-ferm) or prayers (*in elemosina*). These feudal tenures might be regarded as a superstructure erected over the subordinate forms of Scottish landholding that concerned the bulk of the population. A grant in feudal form, usually made by a written charter issued by the 'superior', conferred upon a vassal a fief which was heritable, held by the vassal and his heirs 'of' the superior and his heirs, and this connection was symbolised by the swearing of fealty and the performance of homage. Though families might come and go, the fiefs that they had held remained. A fief was a continuing entity, theoretically indivisible save in the circumstance of descent to co-heiresses. It was imbued with obligations that might be real or merely nominal, but were always 'honourable'. It was imbued also with inherent privileges, not least economic privileges. If the fief was a barony its holder had the right to exploit its woods, its arable and pasture lands, its fishing waters, its deposits of peat and minerals. He might take tolls from those who used the tracks that ran through it. If he built a watermill the men of the barony were 'thirled' to it and had to pay 'multure' for the compulsory facility of grinding their corn there. There was much concern over what a barony was worth,

---

[12] *A.P.S.*, I. 401.

[13] A survey of the development of feu-ferm from the twelfth century to the sixteenth is given in *E.R.*, XIII. cxiii–cxxv.

and 'extents' or surveys were often carried out to assess its rental in money and kind. The rental interested not only the holder of the fief but the superior of whom it was held: apart from any service that was stipulated, most fiefs were bound to render to the superior the customary feudal 'aids' and the 'casualties' of wardship, marriage and relief. The specific or implied conditions on which fiefs were held provided a basis for justice, administration, military service and land law. When land and its produce provided the chief source of wealth it was feudal land law that ultimately controlled economic life. Theoretically a vassal might not dispose of his fief save by limited sub-infeudation or resignation to the superior. In practice, however, land could be disposed of in any way by obtaining from the superior (at a price) a charter of confirmation to cover the transaction. Whether homage and oaths of fealty kept their pristine significance is questionable. Often they must have been looked upon only as a form of land registration, the traditional and formal method of completing, or renewing, a business bargain between landlord and tenant.

In England the statute *Quia Emptores* of 1290, drawn up in the interests of the king and the greater landholders, tended to eliminate the intermediate stages between the top and the bottom of the feudal 'pyramid'. In Scotland no such measure ever operated: the pyramid of free tenants existed with its intermediate stages intact. At its apex was the king. Those who held fiefs directly of the king were his tenants-in-chief, who in their turn might have subordinate feudal tenants. The category of tenants-in-chief was wide: it included some persons of relative obscurity and excluded others who might hold broad lands not directly of the king but of a baron. Thus a man's position on the tenurial pyramid did not in itself determine his social or political standing. Wealth, the holding of office, experience in government, administration or warfare, all these counted.

Noble birth counted most of all and was emphasised by the devices of heraldry. Scarcely yet, however, was noble birth marked by the award of titles. In the Gaelic areas illustrious descent and the formal recognition of the immediate kinsfolk was enough to make a man a chief. In the north-east there were some fifty thanes; but the word 'thane' was merely one of office applied to the holders of a particular kind of heritable stewardship. No one was created a baron: anyone who held a barony—a fief with a court in which public justice could be dispensed—simply *was* a baron. Nor were lords created: the term 'lord' could be applied to any baron; and a 'lordship' denoted nothing more than a barony, although in the Gaelic areas it might correspond more closely to the type of petty kingdom known in Ireland as a *tuath*. Knights were certainly created (not necessarily by the king) but the rank they held was military and was granted in recognition, or expectation, of service in war. On the other hand the thirteen earls of Scotland were distinguished by the fact that only they possessed a specific and heritable title of dignity; and this title, conferred by the king upon them or their predecessors, carried a social and political rank nearest to that of the king himself.

The hierarchical structure of lay society was matched by another and more clearly defined hierarchy, that of the kirk, which occupied a place in society far greater than it holds today. No one questioned the literal truth of any passage in the Bible. The saints were not remote [14] and would intervene in this world to punish those who scorned them,[15] or to reward those who venerated their name and their relics.[16] Their feast days, together with pilgrimages to their shrines, were the medieval equivalent of holidays and tourism, although they carried more serious overtones. For the bliss of heaven and the pains of hell were real, and the concept of morality was more broadly based than that of the present day when only one sin attracts attention while its six deadly companions are scarcely remembered : in the Middle Ages each of the seven could earn damnation. It was believed, however, that 'the super-abundant merits of Christ, the Virgin Mary and the Saints formed a celestial treasury, out of which the debts of individual penitents could be paid'. This treasury of merits was at the disposal of the priests who heard confession and through the sacrament of penance granted remission of ever-lasting punishment. Nonetheless the forgiven sinner had to pay the wages of his sin either on earth or in purgatory, the intermediate existence between heaven and hell. The pains of purgatory could in turn be avoided, or mitigated, by good works, by the prayers of monks, by the celebration of the sacrifice of the mass, by indulgences granted by the pope.[17]

Not surprisingly, the influence of the clergy was great. Comparable to the thirteen Scottish earls were the twelve Scottish bishops.

---

[14] Thus in 1459 an inquest found that 'the Blessed Virgin Mary, our Lady, was the last possessor of the lands of Brochton ... and Sir John Denum, chaplain, took sasine of the said lands on the part of our foresaid Lady with a portrait painted on paper' (cited in Dunlop, *Bishop Kennedy*, p. 421).

[15] See *Chron. Bower*, II. 462.

[16] *Ibid.*, 250.

[17] A. I. Dunlop, 'Remissions and Indulgences in Fifteenth Century Scotland', *Scot. Church Hist. Soc. Recs.*, XV. 153–67, at 154–5.

Comparable to the barons were the abbots, priors, cathedral deans and archdeacons. All of these prelates, together with the earls and barons, were 'magnates' and, under the king, shared in government and administration. Moreover, bishops, abbots and priors controlled the lands and property (the 'temporalities') with which their bishopric, abbey or priory had been endowed. In respect of these temporalities they were tenants-in-chief of the king. In contrast to the lay magnates, however, their position was not hereditary : they held their lands by virtue of their ecclesiastical office. They were elected to that office by the chapter of their cathedral, abbey or priory, usually after the king's approval. They had then to seek confirmation of the election by the pope, to whom they swore obedience. Bishops would be consecrated either at the papal court or by three Scottish bishops specially commissioned by a papal bull—a letter sealed with the pope's seal (*bulla*). The king then invested the new bishop in his temporalities, for which he swore fealty and did homage. Their oaths of fealty to the king and obedience to the pope sometimes involved the prelates in conflicting loyalties; and since the prelates were mostly kinsmen or clients of king or barons the appointments to the great benefices were usually conducted against a background of contesting claims, ambiguity, dispute and intervention. The last word lay with the pope. His powers were not limited to confirmation of an 'elect'. He might quash or disregard an election. In 1233 he had 'provided' a bishop of Dunblane. Of the twelve bishops in office in 1296 five had been provided by the pope.[18]

The *plenitudo potestatis* of the pope—his fulness of power in any spiritual matter—extended beyond appointments. His was the authority to give a final decision and to confer any spiritual benefit. From the decisions of diocesan courts litigants appealed to the papal court (*curia*). Dispensations from the requirements of canon law, indulgences, absolution, spiritual grace in all its forms, could be obtained from the pope. Recourse to the *curia* was costly and often had to be financed by loans from Italian bankers, whose operations extended even to Scotland.[19] Nonetheless, the obstacles of distance and expense did not stop the flow of appeals and petitions to Rome and the return flow of letters of grace and papal bulls.

The process was perhaps encouraged by conditions peculiar to

[18] For the growth of papal provisions see George P. Innes, 'Ecclesiastical Patronage in Scotland in the Later Middle Ages', *Scot. Church Hist. Soc. Recs.*, XIII. 73–83.
[19] *Rot. Scot.*, I. 6–7.

Scotland:[20] for although it was a distinct ecclesiastical 'province' it had as yet no archbishop to act as metropolitan and supervise its kirk. This anomaly had been recognised in 1192 when a papal bull had made the Scottish kirk a 'special daughter' of Rome. Two bishoprics were excluded from this privilege: the see of Galloway was part of the province of York; the see of Sodor (or the Isles) was subject to the Norwegian archbishop of Nidaros (Trondheim). The other ten bishops, however, were answerable only to the pope. A bull of 1225 allowed them to hold a provincial council at which it became the practice to choose one bishop as a temporary 'conservator of the privileges of the Scottish kirk'. This device preserved the formal parity of the Scottish bishops. But if all were equal, two, St Andrews and Glasgow, were more equal than the rest, or at least far richer.

The disparity in wealth among the bishoprics was reflected in the scale of their cathedrals (by this time mostly completed) and in the number of canons—a mere handful or more than thirty—who served them.[21] It was also reflected in the complexity or the simplicity of diocesan organisation. St Andrews had two archdeaconries (St Andrews and Lothian) subdivided into eight rural deaneries. The organisation of the diocese of Glasgow was similar.[22] But these two dioceses, with over two hundred parish kirks apiece, were exceptional in Scotland and together included almost half the total of about eleven hundred parishes.

By the end of the thirteenth century Scotland had already obtained almost the full complement of parish kirks that it was to possess down to the Reformation.[23] When a patron built a kirk he also endowed it, often with a ploughgate of land. In addition to the rents obtainable from this kirkland the parson or *rector* had the right to the teinds of the parish. The teinds (tithes) represented a tenth of all annual increase, such as the tenth sheaf in the fields after harvest, or the tenth calf that was born. Apart from the teinds there were offerings, and these, together with mortuary dues and other fees, formed a large part of the parson's income. In 1275 Boiamund de Vitia had arrived as a papal collector and had set down the revenue of each kirk in the so-called 'Bagimond's Roll' to be used as a basis of taxation by the papacy. The resources available from an aggregation of kirks are

---

[20] *Cal. Scot. Supp. 1418–1422*, p. xii.
[21] See Ian B. Cowan, 'The Organisation of Scottish Secular Cathedral Chapters', *Scot. Church Hist. Soc. Recs.*, XIV. 19–47.
[22] See Watt, *Fasti*, pp. 143–96, 289–332.
[23] See Ian B. Cowan, 'The Development of the Parochial System in Medieval Scotland', *S.H.R.*, XL. 43–55, and his *Parishes of Medieval Scotland*.

shown by the fact that over a six-year period those in the diocese of Glasgow alone produced 'tenths' amounting to £4,575 3s. 6¾d.[24]—a vast sum by contemporary standards.

While monasteries, cathedrals and episcopal households had landed revenues of their own on which to draw, it was largely by the accumulation of parish kirks that they were financed. Arbroath Abbey had been gifted thirty-three parish kirks *in proprios usus*, a term that conveyed to the abbey all the rights and revenues that pertained to the parson (*rector*) of each kirk. If a kirk was 'appropriated' in this way the abbey as *rector* uplifted most of the revenues and appointed a vicar to serve the parish. At this period the latter would normally be a 'vicar perpetual', who had some security of tenure, and his income would include a share in the teinds.[25] But although a statute of the provincial council accorded the vicars a reasonable minimum income of ten marks a year (£6 13s. 4d.)—a fair professional salary for the time—this statute was not always observed. The appropriation system held 'temptations to injustice' and 'risks of friction'.[26] There was a danger that well-qualified men might not be attracted to the sweated labour of an ill-paid parish priest and that the spiritual life of the parishes might suffer. The danger was not, however, widely realised. By 1286 appropriation had gone far and it was still to continue; in 1521 John Major remarked that it had gone 'beyond what was wise'.[27] While only about one third of the English parishes were appropriated, the Scottish parishes were eventually nearly all appropriated.[28] Over a hundred and fifty were already appropriated to five monasteries alone—Arbroath, Paisley, Kelso, Melrose and Holyrood.[29] It was often at the expense of the parishes that monasticism flourished.

By 1273, when Lady Devorgilla Balliol founded Sweetheart Abbey, monastic development in Scotland was virtually complete and all the chief religious orders save the Carthusians were represented.[30]

[24] See A. I. Dunlop, 'Bagimond's Roll', *S.H.S. Misc. VI.* 3–77, at 25, also *ibid., V.* 79–106; *X.* 1–9.
[25] Ian B. Cowan, 'Vicarages and the Cure of Souls in Medieval Scotland', *Scot. Church Hist. Soc. Recs.*, XVI. 111–27.
[26] Coulton, *Scottish Abbeys*, pp. 99, 77–80.
[27] Major, *History*, p. 136.
[28] Ian B. Cowan, 'Some Aspects of the Appropriation of Parish Churches in Medieval Scotland', *Scot. Church Hist. Soc. Recs.*, XIII. 203–22, at 205.
[29] See Ian B. Cowan, *The Parishes of Medieval Scotland*. The appendix lists the kirks appropriated to each religious institution.
[30] For details of the religious orders and their Scottish foundations, see Easson, *Religious Houses*.

These orders may be divided into two main groups—the monks and the canons regular. The monks were 'cloistered' and followed the Benedictine rule or the modifications of it that had been adopted at Cluny, Tiron, Cîteaux, or Val des Choux.[31] The Augustinian and Premonstratensian canons regular, like monks, lived according to a rule (*regula*), but one which allowed them to leave the bounds of their cloister, even to serve a parish kirk.[32] In Scotland the Augustinians were comparable in importance to the Cistercians: though the latter possessed eleven abbeys the former were established at Holyrood and Scone; their priory of St Andrews was not only the richest religious house in Scotland but its canons acted as the chapter of the cathedral of St Andrews.

By English or continental standards no Scottish religious house was particularly wealthy; yet in relation to the country's slender resources the religious houses were extremely well endowed. In the thirteenth century when the monastic population reached its peak it can hardly have been more than a thousand. Piety never wholly disappeared; but 'since so much wealth was in so few hands, the social status of the monk was high'; there were 'self-interested converts' and 'the cloister was becoming an almshouse for the nobility'.[33] This was even more true of the few nunneries that provided respectable retreats for well-born ladies whose marriage prospects were blighted.

From the thirteenth century onwards a new ecclesiastical development, the rise of the mendicant orders, supplemented the work of parish priests, monks and canons regular, and overshadowed the lingering eremitical tradition still represented by a few hermits and anchorites.[34] By 1286 the friars preachers (Dominicans or black friars) had at least twelve friaries in Scotland; the friars minor (Franciscans or grey friars) had six; the Carmelites (white friars) had three; and expansion was to continue throughout the Middle Ages.[35] The friaries were invariably established in the burghs, and their relatively small endowments came mainly from burghal rents. While the friars lived a communal life they were not cloistered. Their work (and their mendicant vocation) took them among the people. Whereas the monastic

[31] Monastic rules and monastic life are discussed in Coulton, *Scottish Abbeys*.
[32] Ian B. Cowan, 'The Religious and the Cure of Souls in Medieval Scotland', *Scot. Church Hist. Soc. Recs.*, XIV. 215–30.
[33] Coulton, *Scottish Abbeys*, pp. 35, 49, 251.
[34] See D. McRoberts, 'Hermits in Medieval Scotland', *Innes Review*, XVI. 199–216.
[35] Easson, *Religious Houses*, pp. 96–119.

orders stressed prayer, meditation, and a withdrawal from the world, and it was no part of the duty of a monk to preach, the friars preached, acted as confessors, and ministered to the poor and the sick. It was not, however, the friars alone who were responsible for charitable works. Charity was a means by which any man might acquire spiritual grace. Before the Reformation more than a hundred foundations had been made of leper-houses, almshouses, hospitals and hospices for pilgrims and travellers.[36] Almost half of these had definitely been founded before 1296 and the proportion may well have been higher. In addition, all ecclesiastical establishments were expected to relieve the poor and furnish hospitality to pilgrims and travellers (and the royal household as well).

Another social service that concerned the kirk was teaching, for 'the notion of a purely secular education was unknown'. So also was the idea that even elementary education should be available to all; no systematic attempt was made to provide it on a parochial basis. But if education was 'fostered by the church to subserve the church's ends'[37] it subserved other ends as well. The novice or song schools of the cathedrals and religious houses taught potential monks, canons, friars, vicars-choral and choristers how to sing plain-song and read (if not understand) Latin. These schools, which were probably open, at a price, to boys of the locality,[38] gave the aptest scholars the means of acquiring further learning. Moreover, the chancellor of a cathedral had responsibility for the running of a 'grammar school' in which Latin, the language of higher education, was inculcated. Such grammar schools were not confined to the cathedral precincts but were already to be found in the burghs. As yet, however, there was no *studium generale* entitled to confer a university degree. A degree had to be obtained outside Scotland, usually at Paris, or perhaps at Oxford, where Lady Devorgilla Balliol had recently founded Balliol College and where John Duns, a Scottish Franciscan, was making his mark in Merton College as a theologian and philosopher of lasting repute. It is perhaps difficult to reconcile the view that 'the standard of school education in Scotland was, as compared with England and

---

[36] *Ibid.*, pp. 134–65; John Durkan, 'Care of the Poor: Pre-Reformation Hospitals', *Innes Review*, x. 268–80.
[37] D. E. Easson, 'The Medieval Church in Scotland and Education', *Scot. Church Hist. Soc. Recs.*, vi. 13–26, at 21, 24, 25
[38] *Kelso Liber*, i. No. 173.

France, decidedly low'[39] with the fact that in thirteenth-century Scotland graduates formed 'a normal feature of the social scene'.[40]

The importance of the kirk was not limited to its spiritual and social works: in employing the resources that had been piously bestowed upon it the kirk made a direct and material contribution to the economic development of Scotland, sometimes proving itself a pastor of sheep as well as of souls. The Cistercians in particular specialised in sheep-farming and had granges and shielings on the Galloway moors, the Lammermuir hills and the glens of Angus. Those of Newbattle had even begun to exploit the nearby coal seams and to produce salt at Prestonpans by boiling the sea water. Almost every religious house owned tenements in the burghs and used them to promote its own trade, both local and overseas. Some bishops and abbots obtained royal charters allowing them to set up burghs of their own, such as St Andrews and Glasgow.

Their example was followed by the barons: Robert Bruce had a burgh at Annan, James the Steward had one at Renfrew, and there existed at least eight other baronial burghs.[41] By the late sixteenth century it could be contemptuously assumed that such burghs were 'thrallit to serve ane raice of pepill'[42]—they allegedly served a mere baronial family, whereas the community of burgesses of a royal burgh held their burgh as tenants of the king. In the thirteenth century however, distinctions among the various types of burgh—royal, baronial or ecclesiastical—were not so obvious as at later times: all burghs were 'free' (privileged) burghs,[43] at least in the sense that all burghs enjoyed the 'freedom' of burghal law. Yet distinctions were beginning to be made: the royal burgesses thought themselves by virtue of their tenure to be superior to other burgesses;[44] and they profited from the close connection between the king's burghs, the king's castles, the sheriffdoms, the royal administration and royal finance. For the royal burghs provided the king with various revenues, including 'maills' (rents), the profits of the burgh court, and the tolls or 'petty customs'[45] levied on goods entering the burgh for

---

[39] D. E. Easson, *op. cit., Scot. Church Hist. Soc. Recs.*, VI. 13–26, at 25.

[40] Donald E. R. Watt, 'University Graduates in Scottish Benefices before 1410', *ibid.*, XV. 77–88, at 77.

[41] See Pryde, *Burghs*, Section II, and *Kirkintilloch Burgh Court Book* (S.H.S.), pp. xi–xviii.

[42] *Burghs Convention Recs.*, I. 321.

[43] *Kirkintilloch Burgh Court Book* (S.H.S.), pp. xxxiv, xxxvii–xl.

[44] See *Leges Quatuor Burgorum*, cap. xiii (*A.P.S.*, I. 335).

[45] For a list of these see *Assisa de Tolloneis* (*ibid.*, 667–70).

sale in its market. These miscellaneous revenues might be assessed and the right to collect them granted each year for a stipulated sum (ferm). To the king the ferms forthcoming from his burghs represented a useful, but by no means the foremost, source of revenue : in 1264 his chamberlain accounted for burgh ferms (less allowances) amounting to £675 18s. 2½d. ;⁴⁶ as much might be obtained as feudal 'relief' from one important tenant-in-chief.⁴⁷

But distinct from the burgh ferms there was an increasingly important revenue collected *in* the burghs, though not *from* the burghs : whilst there were no import duties, save anchorage dues,⁴⁸ the king had begun to levy a 'new custom'⁴⁹ (later known as the 'maltote' or 'great custom') on the wool, woolfells (fleeces) and hides exported from Scotland. And these 'staple goods', which, together with fish, were virtually the sole Scottish exports, could be lawfully exported only from a burgh.

Of the king's burghs twenty-three out of the total of thirty-six ⁵⁰ were situated on the east coast, or had subordinate havens upon it. To these ports came vessels laden with the fine cloth and manufactures of Flanders and Lombardy, the wines of France, timber from the Baltic, oriental luxuries, and the spices that made a winter diet of salt beef palatable. A company of Lombards sought to set up a trading post at Cramond or Queensferry but was thwarted through the opposition of the merchants of Edinburgh, probably already organised in their own merchant gild. Hanseatic merchants and men from Cologne were trading in Scotland,⁵¹ while the Flemings had a trading post in the Red Hall in Berwick. But Scottish merchants were not content to do business only in their own home burghs : when their goods were arrested in Flanders in 1292 the value came to £1,459 8s. od.⁵²—a sizable figure by contemporary standards.

The enterprise of Scottish merchants was aided by the development of merchant gilds. These were brotherhoods founded upon oath

⁴⁶ *E.R.*, I. 10. This sum may be compared with the chamberlain's accounts of proceeds of the crown demesnes (£2,896 18s. 3d.) and the 'common receipts', fines and feudal casualties (£1,808 5s. o½d.).

⁴⁷ In 1293 the relief of the Scottish lands of the Earl of Buchan was put at 1,097 marks, that is £731 6s. 8d. (Stevenson, *Documents*, I. No. cccvii).

⁴⁸ See *Custuma Portuum* (*A.P.S.*, I. 671-2).

⁴⁹ Documents relating to this export duty are mentioned in a contemporary list of the royal muniments (*ibid.*, 114, 118); see also Stevenson, *Documents*, II. 487.

⁵⁰ See Pryde, *Burghs*, Section I.

⁵¹ J. W. Dilley, 'German Merchants in Scotland, 1297-1327', *S.H.R.*, XVII. 142-55.

⁵² Stevenson, *Documents*, I. No. ccxlviii.

and pledge, fostered by a gild court, common gatherings, common religious worship, and social benefits limited to the members and their families. The gild was not a national organisation : its trading privileges, such as the exclusive right to deal in staple goods, were based upon a burgh. For each burgh was the centre for a defined trade precinct which, in the case of some royal burghs, might amount to a whole sheriffdom. It was hopefully envisaged that within this trade- precinct goods, or at least staple goods, would invariably go for sale to the burgh market. And if the burgh possessed a merchant gild it was the gild merchants who profited most from this monopoly.

Even in the late thirteenth century there is evidence of the exis- tence of a gild only in the more important burghs—Perth, Aberdeen, Stirling, Dundee, Elgin and Berwick. In the case of Berwick, the most important Scottish burgh, a set of *Statuta Gilde*, rules of the gild, sur- vives, of which the last nine chapters are dated between 1281 and 1294.[53] From these statutes it is evident that the Berwick gild was both a merchant gild and a gild of burgesses, had a connection with the election of the burgh council and magistrates, and thought itself to be the 'community' of the town.[54] A list of the burgesses and community of Berwick who swore fealty to Edward I in 1291 yields only eighty- one names; a similar list for Perth gives seventy-one;[55] and a corres- ponding list for Berwick in 1333 gives forty.[56] If numbers such as these approached the sum total of the burgesses the latter must have com- posed an exclusive oligarchy among the indwellers of the burgh; and it was in the merchant gild that this oligarchy was entrenched.

For although there were craftsmen in the burghs, each burgh was first and foremost a *villa mercatoria*, a town whose chief function was trade. Even the craftsman engaged in cloth manufacture was of an inferior and almost servile status : in the mid-thirteenth century, when there was a successful attempt to prevent cloth manufacture becoming a rural industry, it was enacted that any wool-comber leaving a burgh to dwell among 'uplandmen'—countryfolk—was to be imprisoned.[57] More than a century later a man was described in the burgh court of Aberdeen as scarcely human (*semihomo*) because he was a weaver.[58] Not surprisingly, certain craftsmen—fleshers, shoe-

[53] *A.P.S.*, I. 431–38.
[54] *Statuta Gilde* (*A.P.S.*, I. 431–8), *passim*. See also 'of the breder of the Gild' (*ibid.*, 719).
[55] *Cal. Docs. Scot.*, II. No. 508.
[56] *Rot. Scot.*, I. 255–6.
[57] James Mackinnon, *Social and Industrial History of Scotland*, I. 64.
[58] *Aberdeen Burgh Recs.*, pp. 32–3.

makers and fishermen—were excluded from membership of the merchant gild unless they merely supervised the workmen under them and abjured the personal exercise of a craft that soiled their hands.[59] In any case the entrance fee to the Berwick gild was the high sum of forty shillings.[60] When a labourer's daily wage was 2d. and that of a craftsman between 3d. and 6d.[61] the entrance fee alone debarred them from the gild; the entrance fee for burgess-ship may also have debarred all but the more substantial craftsmen even from becoming burgesses.

While the inhabitants of the Scottish burghs were a small minority of the country's population, and while the burgesses were a fraction even of that minority, their influence was surprisingly great. The fact that trade was entirely in their hands had something to do with this. But in addition the influence of the burgesses owed much to the co-operation that existed among them [62] and to the distinct and complex institutions and organisations that the burgesses evolved, of which the gild was only one. The burgesses, and even the underlings in the burghs, were set apart from the rest of the population by their special courts and by the right of the bailies of the burgh to 'repledge' an inhabitant of the burgh from a non-burghal court if the case was one with which the burgh court was competent to deal.

In civil cases, however, there could be an appeal from the burgh court. As chief financial officer of the crown the king's chamberlain had a special responsibility for the king's burghs. One of his duties was to hold a chamberlain ayre, supposedly once a year, passing from one royal burgh to another. Burgh courts, and even the chamberlain on his ayre, might ask counsel from a special advisory body named 'the four burghs'.[63] This was composed of four burgesses from each of the king's burghs of Berwick, Roxburgh, Edinburgh and Stirling, who met at Haddington under the chairmanship of the chamberlain to declare the law on contested points of burghal usage and privilege.[64] Already, however, there existed a written collection entitled the

---

[59] *Leges Quatuor Burgorum*, cap. xciv (*A.P.S.*, I. 351).
[60] *Statuta Gilde*, cap. xi (*ibid.*, 433).
[61] *Cal. Docs. Scot.*, IV. 459. On the basis of such figures the purchasing power of money was about two hundred times greater than at the present day.
[62] See *A.P.S.*, I. 723.
[63] It is so styled when it first appears (*c.* 1270) in the Berne MS. (S.R.O.), similarly in a plea of 1292 (Stevenson, *Documents*, I. 380); not until the fourteenth century is it called a court.
[64] See *A.P.S.*, I. 742, c. 8.

Leges Quatuor Burgorum and a copy of these laws of the four burghs was kept among the royal muniments.[65]

Just as the burghs were administered through the burgh court, the gild court, the chamberlain ayre and the four burghs, the administration of the other communities of the land took a curial form; and the various courts made up the framework of local and central government. For the greater part of the population the court that mattered most was the baron court of their lord. This was the lowest court in which public justice could be dispensed—for proceedings in the baron court were begun in the name of the king. The court could deal with such civil actions as petty debt. In criminal actions it could pass sentence of death if a culprit was caught red-handed committing theft or manslaughter; criminal justice was always summary and there was no appeal from the gallows. But the ordinary stock-in-trade of the baron court was the variety of minor disputes, economic and administrative decisions, that comprehended 'the weill of the tenandis and the keeping of gude nichtbourhede'.[66] It was the baron (or his bailie) who presided over the baron court; but in its proceedings he theoretically took no direct part. The body of the court was made up of the baron's tenants who owed 'suit of court'. Their attendance was enforced by fines, for it was the suitors who acted as judges. If they were numerous they might choose an assize—a jury of men put upon oath (*jurati*)[67]—to declare their knowledge of the case before the court. The forespeaker of the assize announced the joint finding and the dempster of the court declared the 'doom' or judgment.

But a discontented litigant might formally declare that the doom given against him was 'fals, stynkand and rottin'[68] and appeal to the court of the sheriffdom. Scotland was divided into almost thirty sheriffdoms and it was the sheriff court that gave meaning to this territorial organisation. Although the jurisdiction of the sheriff court was not notably greater than that of the baron court the former had the greater prestige : it was a royal court, presided over by the king's sheriff, who was aided by subordinate officers—crowners, mairs and serjeants—and it was held usually at the royal castle which was the *caput*, or legal centre, of the sheriffdom ; its suitors were the barons of

[65] *Ibid.*, 114, 329–56.
[66] For the organisation, functions and procedure of a baron court see *The Court Book of the Barony of Carnwath* (S.H.S.), pp. lxxiv–cxii; *Scot. Legal Hist.*, pp. 374–7.
[67] See Ian D. Willock, *The Origins and Development of the Jury in Scotland* (Stair Soc.).   [68] *A.P.S.*, I. 742.

the sheriffdom who were the king's tenants-in-chief; its procedure linked it closely with the central government, for many civil actions could begin only when a plaintiff presented a brieve that he had bought from the king's chancery.[69] A brieve was an instruction written *brevi manu* in Latin and sealed with the king's seal.[70] It ran in the king's name and was addressed to a particular official, usually sheriff or justiciar. It outlined some alleged grievance and ordered investigation by a sworn inquest. By 1292 the royal muniments included two sacks full of rolls of inquests.[71]

Just as the process of appeal linked the baron court to the sheriff court, it linked the latter to the court of the justiciar. There were three justiciars with authority respectively over Lothian, Galloway, and Scotia—the district north of the Forth. In theory each justiciar went on ayre in the spring and in the autumn, holdng his itinerant court (to which the tenants-in-chief owed suit) at the *caput* of each sheriffdom.[72] Apart from dealing with falsed dooms from the sheriff court, the justiciar's court was one of first instance for civil actions raised by brieves. In the course of the ayre administrative matters were also dealt with : the justiciar was to enquire into the probity and efficiency of the sheriffs and other officials. But it was its criminal jurisdiction that made the court so formidable : only it could deal with the four pleas of the crown (murder, rape, robbery and arson) which were withheld from lesser courts. Since the profits of justice— in the shape of fines and amercements—were large, the justice ayre played a significant part in royal finance : the justiciar of Lothian raised almost £550 in 1266.[73] The success of the justice ayre was estimated both by the amount of the fines forthcoming for the king and by the number of criminal corpses left dangling from the gallows.

In civil cases, however, there lay an ultimate resort even higher than the justice ayre : the disappointed litigant could once more false a doom and appeal to the king and his council;[74] and that council might meet *in parliamento*.

[69] For procedure in the sheriff court, see *Scot. Legal Hist.*, pp. 350–5.

[70] For the various brieves and their use see H. McKechnie, *Judicial Process upon Brieves, 1219–1532* (David Murray Lecture, 1956), and *The Register of Brieves* (Stair Soc.).

[71] *A.P.S.*, I. 114.

[72] For a contemporary outline of procedure see *Modus Procedendi in Itinere Justiciarie* (ibid., 705–8). See also *Scot. Legal Hist.*, pp. 408–10.

[73] *E.R.*, I. 27.

[74] Sir Philip J. Hamilton Grierson, 'The Appellate Jurisdiction of the Scottish Parliament', *S.H.R.*, xv. 205–22.

In surviving Scottish documents the first mention of parliament is in July 1290 when burgesses of Berwick applied the word to a contemporary assembly of Scottish magnates at Birgham.[75] The word 'parliament' was a novel term, probably introduced from England, and it did not yet entirely displace the earlier term *colloquium* as a description of the greatest and most formal assemblies of the king and his counsellors.[76] That parliament was the centre of supreme jurisdiction may be inferred from a treatise written in French and probably composed in 1293 for the edification of John Balliol.[77] This treatise mentions occasions when the king has 'common assembly and personal speech with all the prelates, earls and barons of the realm'[78]—a description which might cover both parliament and some other type of council. But a distinction is drawn between the two : certain cases which might involve disinheritance should be decided 'in full parliament and not by a lesser council'.[79] The words 'full parliament' did not signify a parliament that had a full attendance but one that was fully competent to act as a court of law and was formally summoned on forty days' warning.[80] Thus the surviving records of the parliaments of February and August 1293 take the form of rolls of pleas— 'pleas . . . before the king and his council in his first parliament' or 'pleas of parliament . . . before the lord king and his council'.[81] From the decisions of parliament there could be no appeal. And parliament not only applied the law : it could enact new law through its statutes and ordinances.

Besides its judicial and legislative functions parliament had others. There, above all, the king acted in concert with those who by birth or office were the recognised leaders of the kingdom : to the parliament or *colloquium* held at Birgham in March 1290 came twelve bishops, twenty-three abbots, eleven priors, twelve earls and fifty barons; all were magnates; probably all were tenants-in-chief of the king and, as such, owed him suit of court. No one questioned their right to give counsel and reach collective decisions upon *ardua negocia*, the affairs of state affecting the wellbeing of the realm.

While such decisions might be made and publicised in parliament, there existed (or were soon to exist) two other types of council

[75] Stevenson, *Documents*, I. No. cix.

[76] A. A. M. Duncan, 'The early parliaments of Scotland', *S.H.R.*, XLV. 36–58.

[77] 'The Scottish King's Household', ed. Mary Bateson, *S.H.S. Misc.* II. 1–43. The editor dates the document 1305 but admits (p. 5) that it might have 'resulted from the work of Alexander III or John Balliol'.

[78] *Ibid.*, 37.   [80] *R.M.S.*, I. No. 446.

[79] *Ibid.*, 43.   [81] *A.P.S.*, I. 445, 448.

that might also make such decisions. One was the 'general council', first styled as such in the later fourteenth century [82] and described simply as a 'council' before that time. This, like parliament, was an assembly of bishops, abbots, priors, earls and barons. Unlike parliament, it scarcely ever functioned as a court: it could be summoned on shorter warning and its procedure was not hampered by judicial formalities or clogged up with litigation. Nonetheless it was just as competent as parliament to deal with any *ardua negocia*, whether administrative, financial or political. Moreover in dealing with the day-to-day problems of government the king relied not on parliaments or on full-scale councils, which might be held only on one or two occasions in the year, but on the advice of a small, informal and speedily convoked royal council, later known as the secret or privy council—secret or privy in the sense that the councillors were sworn not to reveal its deliberations. While this privy council included selected magnates, its basic membership was naturally made up of those who were in fairly constant attendance upon the king, namely the dignitaries and officials of the royal household who composed a rudimentary civil service.

In England there already existed a large and complex civil service, well nourished on fees of office and expense accounts and imbued with *esprit de corps*. Although the English chancery and exchequer had originated in the royal household they were already departments of state established at Westminster rather than departments of the itinerant household. In Scotland, however, this development scarcely took place. Central government was established not in a fixed capital but in the royal household. As the king and his household toured the land so also did the machinery of central government. Catering for the king's household and his miscellaneous entourage in itself involved the delegation of authority, the keeping of accounts and the compilation of many administrative ordinances of the household.[83] There were senior clerks, lesser clerks, ushers and menials, as well as the three great officers of the household—the steward, the constable and the marshal [84]—whose offices had become hereditary and were vested in important baronial families. Those who had the right to be fed at table in the king's hall had duties which

[82] P. 181 below.
[83] Twenty-five rolls and memoranda of these existed among the royal muniments (*A.P.S.*, I. 114).
[84] For their duties and a description of the household as a whole see Mary Bateson, *op. cit.*, *S.H.S. Misc.* II. 1–43.

at the lowest level were purely domestic but which at higher levels merged into the functions of central government.

It was the chancellor and chamberlain who held the key posts in central government. Until 1335 the chancellor was always a cleric. He presided over the king's parliaments and councils and kept the king's great seal, the most solemn means of authenticating documents drawn up in chancery—the royal secretariat. Chancery was formally described as the king's chapel, for the clerics who served in the king's chapel made up the original staff who worked under the chancellor. Apart from an official salary of £100 the chancellor was paid a traditional fee for each brieve issued under the great seal. Besides the formalised legal brieves which set in motion many of the processes of justice, chancery issued charters conveying or confirming grants of land or office. It also issued brieves in the form of precepts or mandates, incorporating some administrative order in the name of the king. Already it was thought that no brieve of this type should be issued under the great seal unless it had first been warranted by a precept under the king's privy seal. The latter was to be entrusted to a wise and knowledgable man, for the office of the privy seal was 'the key and security of the great seal'.[85]

In contrast to the chancellor the chamberlain was usually a layman. The office—which corresponded to that of the English treasurer—was not beneath the notice of an earl and carried a salary of 100 marks. As chief financial officer of the crown the chamberlain was to receive feudal casualties and see to the administration of the king's burghs and the royal demesne lands.[86] The latter were leased out to fermours, and the royal muniments included nineteen rolls containing not only sheriffs' accounts but 'extents' of the demesne lands.[87] Although there existed an assessment of landed revenue, the *Antiqua Taxatio*, on which a land tax could be levied, such taxation was extraordinary and could be resorted to only in accordance with feudal custom for such occasions as the knighting of the king's eldest son. For his various financial activities the chamberlain had to render an account in exchequer. In Scotland the exchequer was not a permanent department of state,[88] though it was not necessarily less efficient than its imposing and unwieldy counterpart in England. Far from being a permanent institution the Scottish exchequer met for only a brief time at intervals that might be anything from six months

---

[85] *Ibid.*, 32.   [86] *Ibid.*   [87] *A.P.S.*, I. 118.
[88] Its characteristics are outlined by Athol Murray in 'The Procedure of the Scottish Exchequer in the early Sixteenth Century', *S.H.R.*, XL. 89–117.

to several years. The accounts presented by the chamberlain, the sheriffs, custumars, and bailies of burghs, were audited by an *ad hoc* commission that usually comprised the chamberlain, some lay and ecclesiastical magnates and senior clerks. The accounts themselves were drawn up in a simple form : first came the *oneracio*, a list of the revenues collected ; then came the *expense*, a list of what had been spent on behalf of the king. For the royal revenues were not merely collected locally but were used locally : sheriffs, custumars and bailies received precepts ordering them to make miscellaneous payments—for salaries, the upkeep of a royal castle, or pensions or donations to some religious house. In exchequer the surplus or deficit would be reckoned by an abacus and the moving of counters on the painted squares of the exchequer board. Financial reckoning was awkward : Roman numerals were used, so also were the denominations of pounds, shillings and pence, besides the mark (13s. 4d. or two-thirds of a pound), but the pound, the mark, and even the shilling, were merely units of account ; the only coins minted in Scotland were silver pennies equal in value to those of England. And much of the royal income was paid not in cash but in produce, which was stored in the royal castles and manors for the use of the king's itinerant household. It was assumed that the king should 'live of his own', financing his household and government from the traditional crown revenues. No distinction was drawn between the revenues of government and the revenues of the king : it was the king who governed.

By 1286 the Scottish kingdom was a fairly large political unit on the fragmented map of medieval Europe ; but the striking unification that had hitherto taken place was outward rather than inward. Diversity was more obvious than uniformity, local self-sufficiency more obvious than national interdependence. The concept of one race, one law, one tongue, did not apply in medieval Scotland—like Switzerland it became a nation despite its diversity.

In the field of law the diversity was marked. There was a 'confusion and intermingling of customary, Roman, feudal and canon law'.[89] It was acknowledged that all laws either 'ar manis law or Godis law',[90] and God's law was represented by the comprehensive code of canon law administered in the consistory court of a diocese,

[89] A. I. Dunlop, *St Andrews Acta*, I. cliii, n. 6. See also Peter Stein, 'The source of the Romano-canonical part of Regiam Maiestatem', *S.H.R.*, XLVIII. 107–23, and 'Roman Law in Scotland', *Ius Romanum Medii Aevi*, v. 13b, 1–51.
[90] *A.P.S.*, I. 739.

the 'court of Christianity' over which a bishop's 'official' presided. In addition, feudal law, soon to be exemplified in a treatise styled *Regiam Majestatem*,[91] was applicable throughout much of Scotland. There were also the beginnings of a statutory law: in the royal muniments there were rolls of statutes, laws and assizes of the land[92] —among them, no doubt, some obsolescent compilations such as the 'laws of Malcolm Makkenneth'[93] and the 'laws between the Brets and Scots'.[94] Yet law and custom varied from district to district according to the degree to which Celtic or Anglo-Norman tradition prevailed or co-existed. There was still room for Brehon law,[95] for the laws of Galloway,[96] the laws of the forests,[97] the laws of the four burghs, and even the law of Clan MacDuff.[98]

To some extent the diversity of law was mitigated: the king's brieves had the effect of imposing some uniformity; and baron court, sheriff court, justiciar's court and parliament made up a four-tiered structure combining feudal justice and feudal law with royal justice and whatever synthesis currently passed for 'common law'. But this system of inter-relating courts applied only to the 'royalty' of a sheriffdom. In a number of sheriffdoms some barons or religious corporations had been granted the right to hold lands in 'regality'.[99] The regalities were comparable to the English palatinates and were outwith the ordinary judicial system.[100] A grant of land *in regalitatem* was said to take as much out of the crown as the crown was capable of giving. No royal official, not even a justiciar, could exercise his office within a regality; there the king's brieves were of no force.

While the king's officers were excluded from the regalities, there were vast areas, comprising much of the Highlands, where they simply failed to appear, and where military force, the ultimate (and sometimes necessary) political sanction, could scarcely be brought to bear. The Highlands, with their distinctive characteristics, could still almost be equated with the high lands throughout all Scotland save the south-east. Although there were racial affinities between Highlanders and Lowlanders they were separated by an almost insuperable

[91] A. A. M. Duncan, 'Regiam Majestatem: a reconsideration', *Juridical Review*, N.S., VI. 199–217.
[92] *A.P.S.*, I. 114, 116–7.   [93] *Ibid.*, 709–12.   [94] *Ibid.*, 663–5.
[95] See John Cameron, *Celtic Law*, and James Mackinnon, *The Constitutional History of Scotland*, pp. 13–32.
[96] *A.P.S.*, I. 187.   [97] *Ibid.*, 687–92.   [98] *Ibid.*, 187.
[99] It has been calculated that prior to 1560 there were fifty-four regalities in Scotland (*Kirkintilloch Burgh Court Book* [S.H.S.], p. xlii, n. 2).
[100] See 'The Franchise Courts and Regalities', *Scot. Legal Hist.*, pp. 374–83.

barrier of language : as late as 1521 John Major was to remark that 'one half of Scotland speaks Irish [Gaelic]'.[101] But to think of a two-fold division of Scotland into Highlands and Lowlands would be something of an over-simplification. Some areas, still Gaelic, were in contact with Anglo-Scoto-Norman society and institutions. Others were far from the influence of any burgh, feudal lordship, or any other novel institution. In effect Scotland, like Gaul, was divided into three parts.

This tripartite division was reflected in the pattern of territorial lordship. In the south-eastern region, approximating to the diocese of St Andrews, government and administration were at their most intensive; the area was relatively fertile and, although it included the earldoms of March and Fife, a typical lordship was one such as the small but rich barony of Dirleton held by the family of De Vaux. Between the completely English-speaking south-east and the completely Gaelic-speaking north-west there stretched a band of earldoms and great lordships that began in Galloway and ended in Caithness. These incorporated lands that were Highland, lands that were Lowland, populations part English-speaking, part Gaelic-speaking. Here were to be found ten of the earldoms, headed by earls at least partly of Gaelic descent; and they, like the royal house itself, formed a link between the Gaelic past and the Anglo-Scoto-Norman present. To the west of this border zone, in the greater part of the West Highlands and Isles, there were four lordships held of the crown. William, Earl of Ross, grandson of Ferquhard MacIntsagairt, held not only Ross but Skye and Lewis. Three descendants of Somerled, onetime 'king' of the Isles, also had lordships : Alexander of Argyll—a MacDougal—held much of mainland Argyll; Angus MacDonald 'of the Isles'[102] was established in Kintyre, Islay and the neighbouring islands; and Alan MacRuaridh held Uist and Garmoran. All four attended the council at Scone in February 1284 where the last three figured among the barons of the realm.[103] But the reality was less baronial than Gaelic : chiefship and an emerging clan spirit were of more importance than homage, fealty, the niceties of feudal land law or royal justice.

Thus most of the region to the west of a line running from Dumbarton to Dornoch was virtually unaffected by the forces that had transformed eastern Scotland. Sheriff courts and justice ayres touched the fringes of this area but did not penetrate it. No burgh was to be found within it. Among the fairly numerous stone castles that

[101] Major, *History*, p. 49.   [102] *A.P.S.*, I. 447.   [103] *Ibid.*, 424.

E.H.S.—2*

guarded the entrances to glens and sea lochs there was as yet scarcely one that belonged to the king. Even the kirk was ill-represented with one small cathedral at Lismore, one abbey at Iona, another at Saddell, a few struggling priories, no friaries and no hospitals. This area, a third of Scotland, had many chapels but not many more than a hundred parish kirks while the remaining two-thirds had almost a thousand. It was a region that looked southward to Gaelic Ireland rather than eastward to the anglicised Lowlands.

Nonetheless, despite all the factors that made for division, the kingdom of Scotland formed a totality. Its modern equivalent would be a federal rather than a unitary state: the two main cultural groups, Gaelic and English-speaking, were loosely associated under an aristocracy of mixed origins, whose members, more often than not, spoke a neutral language, French, and, in varying degrees, ruled their lands with some autonomy. Unity was at least symbolised (as in England) by the phrase 'community of the realm', which recurs after 1286 in the official documents of the time. It would be unwise to read too much into this phrase or to idealise it; yet it may be admitted that 'Scotland had evolved during the peaceful thirteenth century a political identity or nationhood' and that this was 'a cause, not a result, of the war for independence'.[104] The sense of political identity was to survive even during the critical years between 1286 and 1292 when the chief agent of unity, the kingship, was in abeyance.

[104] A. A. M. Duncan, 'The Community of the realm of Scotland and Robert Bruce: a review', *S.H.R.*, XLV. 184–201, at 184.

2

A LAND WITHOUT A KING

In 1249, in a discussion that preceded the enthronement of the boy-king Alexander III, Walter Comyn, Earl of Menteith, is said to have remarked that a land without a king lay in as much perplexity as a vessel in the midst of the waves of the ocean without oarsmen or helmsman.[1] The truth of this remark was to be borne out many years later by the events that followed the fateful night of 19 March 1286 when Alexander III was thrown from his horse near Kinghorn. His accidental death was the culmination of a number of family misfortunes: one of his two sons had died in 1281, the other early in 1284; neither left issue; his daughter, Margaret, who had married Eric II of Norway, had died in 1283, leaving the babe-in-arms known as Margaret, the Maid of Norway. The stormy night that saw the death of King Alexander left the infant Maid as the sole surviving descendant in the direct line of the ancient royal dynasty.

Two years before, on 5 February 1284, a council had drawn up a tailzie (entail) to regulate the royal succession. It was then enacted that if King Alexander should die leaving no legitimate son or daughter the magnates would receive the Maid of Norway as 'our lady and rightful heir of our said lord the king of Scotland, of all the kingdom and of the Isle of Man [etc.]'.[2] Elsewhere in Western Europe the claim of a female to inherit a kingdom would almost certainly have been contested. The ill-advised tailzie of 1284 stored up trouble for the future. Its recognition of the Maid as heir presumptive may have been intended by Alexander to facilitate a dynastic union of Scotland and England,[3] or to preserve the existing friendship by a marriage alliance. More probably it was intended to

---

[1] *Chron. Fordun*, I. 293.   [2] *A.P.S.*, I. 424.   [3] P. 30 below.

27

prevent immediate dispute over the succession among magnates distantly related to the royal house and was a stop-gap measure. For after the death of his three children King Alexander still hoped to produce offspring of his own. In 1285 he married for the second time. On his death his widowed queen, Yolande, daughter of the Count of Dreux, claimed to be with child. If Queen Yolande were to bear a posthumous son to King Alexander, that son would have clear right to succeed; if she were to bear a daughter, that daughter would have a better right than the Maid.

Because of Queen Yolande's reported pregnancy there could be no immediate recognition of the Maid, or of anyone else, as the rightful successor to King Alexander. This uncertainty encouraged the ambitions of other possible claimants. When parliament met at Scone on 2 April 1286, Robert Bruce, the aged Lord of Annandale, seems to have denied the right of any female to inherit the kingdom and advanced his own claim as a descendant of David I. After a short adjournment of parliament John Balliol, another descendant of David I, arrived to contest the Bruce claim. There was 'bitter pleading' between Bruce and Balliol but nothing could be determined until the outcome of the queen's pregnancy was known. Parliament sensibly decided that all magnates should swear to keep the peace and take a non-committal oath of fealty to 'the nearest by blood who by right must inherit'. It still remained to be decided who was 'nearest by blood' to the late king. Meanwhile six guardians—William Fraser, Bishop of St Andrews, Robert Wishart, Bishop of Glasgow, Duncan, Earl of Fife, Alexander Comyn, Earl of Buchan, James the Steward and John Comyn, Lord of Badenoch—were chosen to carry on government in the name of the community of the realm and to supervise arrangements for the eventual determination of the succession.[4] Excluded from the regency the Bruces made ready to defy it. Robert Bruce the eldest, Lord of Annandale, and his son, Robert Bruce, Earl of Carrick, met at the latter's castle of Turnberry on 20 September 1286. The earl's son, Robert Bruce the youngest (future King of Scotland), seems to have been absent from the reunion. But other nobles of the Bruce connection were present. They concluded a bond of alliance in which they reserved their allegiance to the King of England—of whom most of them held lands—and their allegiance to the (unspecified) person who would obtain the kingdom of Scot-

[4] For this summary see the masterly reconstruction of events by A. A. M. Duncan, *op. cit.*, *S.H.R.*, XLV. 184–201, at 184–6.

land 'by reason of the blood of the Lord Alexander, . . . King of Scotland who last died, . . . and in accordance with the ancient customs hitherto approved and used in the realm of Scotland'.[5] The Bruces thus adhered to the oath of fealty exacted in the Scone parliament, probably hoping that they themselves might turn out to be the beneficiaries.

Although the Turnberry bond was ostensibly devised to give support to Richard de Burgh, Earl of Ulster, it was certainly the prelude to a show of force as soon as it became clear at the end of the year that Queen Yolande's pregnancy was either feigned or had resulted in a still-birth.[6] John Balliol was afterwards to claim that the Lord of Annandale and the Earl of Carrick attacked and seized the royal castles of Dumfries and Wigtown and made some sort of proclamation in the courtyard of the Balliol castle of Buittle in Galloway.[7] In the winter of 1286-7 there was civil war. The guardians called out the host—the able-bodied men obliged to serve in the defence of the land—and were successful in preserving their authority. By overhasty action the Bruces had compromised their chances of the throne. The guardians 'teetered through two further years on the brink of civil war'.[8] One guardian, Duncan, Earl of Fife, was ambushed and slain in the late summer of 1289. Shortly before, another guardian, the Earl of Buchan, had died a natural death. No one was chosen to fill the two vacancies, probably because agreement was impossible. The question of the succession was left unresolved—stalemate had been reached.

In the immediate aftermath of Alexander III's death the Scottish magnates had thought of Edward I of England as a person who might help them to resolve their difficulties. Scottish embassies followed in Edward's wake as he left for France on 13 May 1286. His response was probably to offer his good services only on condition that the Scots acknowledged him to be lord superior of Scotland.[9] This claim was of ancient origin : Scottish kings were solemnly enthroned on a ceremonial stone in the abbey of Scone;[10] but although they possessed a crown, and wore it, they were not formally crowned ; nor

[5] Stevenson, *Documents*, 1. No. xxi.
[6] A. A. M. Duncan, *op. cit.*, *S.H.R.*, XLV. 184-201, at 187-8.
[7] Palgrave, *Documents*, 1. 42.
[8] A. A. M. Duncan, *op. cit.*, *S.H.R.*, XLV. 184-201, at 188-9.
[9] *Ibid.*, pp. 187, 189.
[10] See M. Dominica Legge, 'La Piere D'Escosse', *S.H.R.*, XXXVIII. 109-13.

were they anointed;[11] it might therefore be questioned whether they were independent kings. The question of coronation and unction was linked to that of the homage that Scottish kings owed to those of England. In 1278 Alexander III had affirmed that he owed such homage only for the lands he held in England (Tynedale and Penrith); Edward had claimed it was due not only for these but for the kingdom of Scotland as well, and had then reserved the right to open the question at a later date.[12] Even in the troubles that followed Alexander III's death the Scots were unwilling to acknowledge the claim to overlordship, and Edward allowed them to simmer for three years in their own juice. In 1284 Alexander III had written to him hinting that the 'indissoluble bond created between you and us' might be strengthened and that 'much good may yet come to pass through your kinswoman, the daughter of your niece . . . the late Queen of Norway'. Alexander had not only hinted at the desirability of a royal marriage between the Maid of Norway and a member of Edward's family but had stressed that the Maid was his heir.[13] It required no great foresight to see that a marriage between the Maid and Edward's own heir, the young Edward of Caernarvon, might result in a union of Scotland and England. To Eric of Norway, moreover, it must have seemed that the chances of his daughter's succeeding to the Scottish kingdom were shadowy unless outside help were forthcoming. On 1 April 1289 an embassy was appointed at Bergen to approach Edward and treat of the marriage of the Maid.[14] On 3 October, at the request of Edward, who had lately returned from France, the guardians appointed the Bishops of St Andrews and Glasgow, John Comyn of Badenoch and the eldest Robert Bruce to treat with the Norwegian envoys in his presence.[15] Apart from the question of the Maid, there were other matters in dispute between the Scots and Norwegians.[16] It seemed that Edward, who had won a reputation for his mediation in continental disputes, was not un-

[11] The Information that Edward I supplied to the Paris lawyers whom he consulted during the 'Great Cause' (p. 39 below) began with the statement: 'The king of a certain kingdom [Scotland] was neither anointed nor crowned, but placed in a customary royal seat by the earls, magnates and prelates of the kingdom' (G. J. Hand, 'The Opinions of the Paris Lawyers upon the Scottish Succession c. 1292', Irish Jurist [New Series], v. 141–55, at 144).

[12] Dunfermline Registrum, No. 321; Foedera, I. pt. ii, 169, 176.

[13] Stones, Documents, No. 13.

[14] Diplomatarium Norvegicum, XIX. 230–1.

[15] Stevenson, Documents, I. No. lix; Foedera, I. pt. iii, 50.

[16] See Ranald Nicholson, 'The Franco-Scottish and Franco-Norwegian Treaties of 1295', S.H.R., XXXVIII. 114–32.

fitted to act as honest broker in the negotiations. Even so, the Scots were anxious as to the topics that might be raised at the forthcoming conference: their envoys were empowered to negotiate only on a basis that would preserve 'the liberty and honour of the realm of Scotland'.[17]

In a meeting at Salisbury there were 'many negotiations and great debates'. The Norwegians had asked Edward's aid and counsel so that his grand-niece should be accorded obedience as 'lady, queen and heiress' by her people of Scotland.[18] By the treaty of Salisbury of 6 November 1289 they won their objective. The Maid was to arrive in Scotland or England before 1 November 1290. She would then come under the custody of her great-uncle, Edward, who would send her into Scotland free of any matrimonial engagement as soon as that country was well secured and in peace. The Scots also conceded that if any of the Scottish guardians or officials should seem 'suspect' to the Norwegian envoys they should be replaced by other Scots. If Scots and Norwegians could not come to agreement English representatives would have the final say. Reports on the state of affairs in Scotland would be made to the Kings of England and Norway.[19]

What the Scottish envoys had conceded was vital. In the treaty of Salisbury they had recognised the right of Edward to intervene in Scotland; and the basis on which that right rested, whether good neighbourhood, kinship to the Maid, or feudal superiority, had not been clarified. Little had been saved of the honour and liberty of Scotland. Much had been compromised.

On 14 March 1290 an impressive number of Scottish nobles and prelates gathered in a council or parliament at Birgham near Roxburgh to ratify the treaty of Salisbury. Already there were rumours that the pope had granted a dispensation for a marriage between the Maid and Edward's heir. On 17 March the Scots sent a letter to Edward which alluded to his 'good neighbourhood', recounted their joy at the rumour of the dispensation and, in advance, gave consent to the intended match, providing that Edward would meet some reasonable requirements.[20]

The prospect of a marriage between the heir of England and the heiress of Scotland must have caused some heart-searching among responsible Scots. The Scottish clergy had long looked with suspicion on attempts to extend English influence over their kirk. Archbishops of Canterbury and of York had each formerly claimed to be metro-

[17] *Foedera*, I. pt. iii, 50. [18] Stevenson, *Documents*, I. No. lxxv.
[19] *Ibid*. [20] *A.P.S.*, I. 85–6.

politan of Scotland; and in the treaty of Falaise of 1174 the issue of
the feudal vassalage of the Scottish king had been linked to the issue
of the subjection of the Scottish kirk to its English counterpart. The
independence granted to the Scottish kirk as a 'special daughter' of
Rome in 1192 was something that a future papal bull might conceivably take away. Meanwhile, within the institutions that made up the
kirk there were attempts to preserve and assert independence and
to reduce outside influence, especially influence from England.[21] It
was symptomatic of this attitude that on 1 April 1289 Pope Nicholas
IV furiously denounced the 'detestable' custom of admitting only
native Scots to serve in the Scottish religious houses.[22] This xenophobic
attitude was possibly merely professional in its origins, but it might
amount to something like nationalism.

If the attitude of the Scottish prelates towards England was
guarded and apprehensive that of the Scottish nobles was perhaps
less so. The processes of marriage and heredity that had brought
unity to scattered lands within Scotland did not stop short at the
Tweed. Although no Scot seems to have held land in the coastal shires
stretching from Sussex to Cornwall, reports made to the English exchequer in 1295 show that there were at least twelve Scots who held
land in Yorkshire, sixteen in Cumberland, and twenty-four in Northumberland,[23] while John Balliol had manors in seventeen English
shires bringing in rents amounting to the large sum of almost £500
a year.[24] Nevertheless the importance of the English lands held by a
few of the Scottish nobility should not be exaggerated. Only in the
case of the Balliols, Bruces, Comyns and Umfravilles were the holdings of great value. Whether or not these English holdings were of
greater value than the Scottish lands of these families it was obvious
that even a Bruce or Balliol could play no dominant role in England
whilst he might well do so in Scotland. It was Scotland that the
Bruces, Balliols and Comyns thought of as the orbit of their ambitions; to that extent at least they were Scots.

Whatever the consensus of their accumulated traditions and
vested interests, the Scottish nobles and prelates must also have been
influenced in 1290 by the way in which Edward or his agents had
dealt with Scottish matters in recent months. Some years previously
Pope Gregory X had levied a tax of an annual tenth of clerical in-

---

[21] See Easson, *Religious Houses*, pp. 10–1, 53. The attitude of Scottish Franciscans is shown by W. M. Mackenzie in 'A Prelude to the War of Independence',
S.H.R., XXVII. 105–13.

[22] *Foedera*, I. pt. iii, 45.

[23] *Cal. Docs. Scot.*, II. No. 736.   [24] *Ibid.*

come throughout Christendom to finance a new crusade. Edward coveted the proceeds from Scotland and a bull of 18 March 1291 was finally to order the Scots clergy to pay the tax and its arrears to him.[25] Moreover Scottish merchants and other Scots with goods or property in England were affected by the 'sinister prosecution' set afoot in English courts by Jean Le Mazun, a Gascon merchant who was a creditor of the late Alexander III.[26] This and other cases led to a clash of Scottish and English jurisdiction.[27] In addition Edward's increasing involvement in Scottish affairs seemed to threaten the kingdom's territorial integrity. By 4 June 1290 he had assumed control of the Isle of Man[28]—part of the Scottish kingdom. A few weeks later he empowered the Bishop of Durham to receive the men of the Isles into his peace and take whatever other measures might be prudently desirable.[29] The Melrose chronicler was not blind to the fate that had befallen the Welsh, restive under 'the yoke of the English'.[30] It was, however, unthinkable that Edward could look on Scotland as another Wales. There had been peace between Scots and English for at least seventy years. Half of the Scots spoke English. Most of the Scottish barons were not outlandish figures in cosmopolitan society. Alexander II had married Edward's aunt. Alexander III had married Edward's sister. Whatever the technicalities of the relationship between the two realms the spirit of the relationship was one that left the Scots unaware of subordination. If they had misgivings about the future they were all the more determined that the status of their kingdom should be preserved.

In July 1290 the Scottish magnates once more gathered at Birgham to negotiate with English envoys a marriage treaty that would unite the heir of England and the heiress of Scotland and, so it was expected, lead to a state of affairs in which both realms would share a common ruler. In this marriage treaty the concern of the Scots was to keep intact their own rights, customs, laws, liberties and independence. No Scot was to be held to answer outwith the realm for any legal case that fell within it. No parliament was to be held outwith the

[25] *Foedera*, I. pt. iii, 84; F. M. Powicke, *The Thirteenth Century, 1216–1307* (1953), 264–7, 500; W. E. Lunt, *Financial Relations of the Papacy with England to 1327* (1939), I. 292, 296, 334, 338; D. E. Easson, 'Scottish Abbeys and the War of Independence', *Scot. Church Hist. Soc. Recs.*, XI. 63–81, at 68–70.

[26] Stevenson, *Documents*, I. Nos. li, civ, cix.

[27] *Ibid.*, Nos. li, lvi, lxxix, lxxvii, lxxxix, xc, cxx.

[28] *Ibid.*, No. ciii; *Foedera*, I. pt. iii, 74.

[29] Stevenson, *Documents*, I. No. cvii.

[30] *Chronicle of Melrose* (Facsimile Edition, ed. A. O. Anderson, M. O. Anderson and W. Croft Dickinson, 1936), p. 156.

realm on any matter concerning the status of the realm or its Marches (bounds). Even if Scotland and England were to share the same ruler, the Scottish realm was to remain 'separate and divided from England according to its rightful boundaries, free in itself and without subjection.'[31] This last clause summed up the attitude of the Scots, just as the English attitude was summed up in the words that the English representatives appended to the same clause : 'saving the right of our said lord [Edward I] and of any other, which may pertain to him or to any other, upon matters concerning the Marches or elsewhere before the time of the present concession, or in rightful manner might pertain in time to come'.[32] The treaty ended with a statement that its contents should be so understood that the rights of neither kingdom and neither king should be increased or diminished. This clause was far less a guarantee of Scottish independence than a retention by Edward of the right to deny it. The reservations expressed by the English negotiators nullified the safeguards devised by the Scots and reflected adversely on Edward's goodwill. His aim was not a settlement by which both kingdoms would share a common ruler yet preserve their identity. His ideal was an incorporating union under the English crown, a union in which the kingdom of Scotland would disappear; and he refused to recognise that this was unacceptable to most Scots. Stubborn adherence to an impracticable project was the reverse of statesmanship.

Edward's ratification of the marriage treaty was accompanied by new attempts to extend English influence in Scotland : he appointed the Bishop of Durham to act there as lieutenant on behalf of the Maid of Norway and Edward of Caernarvon and required the Scottish guardians to obey the bishop.[33] The bishop and other English emissaries also demanded custody of the Scottish castles 'on account of certain dangers and suspicions'. All that the guardians could do was obtain a delay of the delivery of castles until the arrival of the Maid.[34]

On 20 May 1290 Edward had despatched a ship from Yarmouth laden with extraordinary delicacies such as rice, sturgeon, ginger and whalemeat. The vessel came back a month later without the Maid. Eleven sailors were sick or dead, probably through food contamination.[35] Eric seems to have insisted that his daughter be sent in one of his own ships to Orkney; and there, on Norwegian territory, the final arrangements would be made for her transfer to Edward's custody.

[31] Stevenson, *Documents*, I. No. cviii, p. 167.   [32] *Ibid.*
[33] *Foedera*, I. pt. iii, 72.   [34] *Ibid.*
[35] Stevenson, *Documents*, I. Nos. xcvi, cxvii.

By 4 October English representatives had arrived in Wick, well equipped with cash for a final diplomatic tussle with the Norwegians.[36] Further travel was unnecessary. The Maid had set sail at the end of September and died after her vessel reached the Orkneys.[37] Scottish affairs were once more in turmoil, and dormant ambitions were stirred to more heedless confusion than ever.

By 7 October 1290 William Fraser, Bishop of St Andrews, one of the four remaining guardians, had heard rumours of the death of the Maid and wrote to Edward announcing that the eldest Robert Bruce had come to Perth with a great following; his adherents, the Earls of Mar and Atholl, were collecting forces; war and slaughter might result unless Edward intervened to allow the Scots to remain true to the oath they had taken on King Alexander's death. The letter ended with a piece of advice :

> If Sir John Balliol comes to your presence we advise you to take care so to treat with him that in any event your honour and advantage be preserved. . . . Let your excellency deign, if you please, to approach toward the Marches for the consolation of the Scottish people and to save the shedding of blood, and set over them for king him who of right ought to have the succession, if so be that he will follow your counsel.[38]

John Balliol's mother, the virtuous Lady Devorgilla, had died early in 1290 and the Balliol claim was strengthened by the fact that it was now indisputably vested in her son. At Gateshead, on 16 November 1290, Balliol issued a charter styling himself 'heir of the kingdom of Scotland' and in that capacity granted to the influential Bishop of Durham the lands in Northumberland and Cumberland that belonged to the Scottish crown.[39]

The eldest Bruce was no more scrupulous than Balliol, though possibly more ingenious. Apart from his threatening moves he instigated a formal protest against two of the guardians, Bishop Fraser and John Comyn of Badenoch, inhibiting them from setting up anyone as king. This protest ran in the name of 'the seven earls of Scotland', presumably holders of the more ancient earldoms who, in association with the 'community', had allegedly the right of 'making a king' and installing him on the royal seat. Bruce's theory, which may have been

36 *Ibid.*, Nos. cxi, cxiv, cxv, cxvi.
37 Letter of Bishop Audfinn in *Proc. Soc. Antiq. Scot.*, x. 417–9.
38 *Nat. MSS. Scot.*, I. No. lxx.
39 Stevenson, *Documents*, I. No. cxxv.

based upon the German imperial practice, was open to question; but it provided a basis on which to challenge any attempt of the surviving guardians to decide the succession. Bruce, the 'legitimate and true heir', was nowise willing to receive justice at the hands of Fraser and Comyn, the partisans of Balliol. Already, in the Turnberry bond of 1286, Bruce and his adherents had reserved their allegiance to the English king; now they placed themselves under the protection of Edward and appealed to the crown of England.[40]

Edward might conclude that those magnates who were enrolled in the rival factions of Bruce and Balliol would welcome his intervention to judge the Scottish succession. He might also conclude that there would be little opposition from those factions, or from the other less vociferous claimants, if he took the opportunity to insist on recognition as lord superior of Scotland. In the opening months of 1291 he gathered extracts from the registers and chronicles of English religious houses as evidence of his overlordship.[41] More significantly, he arranged that English ships would be ready, if need be, to blockade Scotland;[42] he sent to Newcastle 10,000 marks [43] to finance either warfare or diplomacy; he summoned the feudal magnates and the shire levies of northern England to muster at Norham Castle on the English side of Tweed on 2 June 1291.[44] Early in May he himself arrived at Norham and 'declared the reason for his coming as overlord of the land of Scotland before the magnates of Scotland, who, at his request, came to Norham to negotiate certain business touching the land of Scotland, which was then destitute of a king'. The Scots were informed that Edward 'by virtue of the overlordship that belongs to him' had come 'to do justice to everyone as sovereign'. He therefore asked for their 'kind agreement, and for acknowledgment of his overlordship'.[45]

Despite his suave words Edward had come prepared for a tussle; and at first it seemed that there would be one. The Scottish representatives at Norham asked leave to deliberate upon Edward's request for acknowledgment as lord superior. Edward allowed them three weeks, by which time the English levies were expected at Norham. A reply was forthcoming on behalf of those Scots who 'came to Norham the other day at your request, and the others whom they have

---

[40] Stones, *Documents*, No. 14.
[41] Palgrave, *Documents*, I. 56–138; E. L. G. Stones, 'The Appeal to History in Anglo-Scottish Relations between 1291 and 1401: Part I', *Archives*, IX. No. 41, 11–21.
[42] Stevenson, *Documents*, I. No. cxxvi.
[43] *Ibid.*, No. cxxiv.
[44] *Foedera*, I. pt. iii, 86–7.
[45] Stones, *Documents*, No. 15.

been able to consult in so short a time'. This Scottish reply outlined Edward's request for acknowledgment as lord superior and declared that

> the good people who have sent us here make answer that they do not in the least believe that you would ask so great a thing if you were not convinced of your sound right to it. But they have no knowledge of your right, nor did they ever see it claimed and used by you or your ancestors; therefore they answer you . . . that they have no power to reply to your statement, lacking a lord [king] to whom the demand ought to be addressed . . . for he, and no other, will have power to reply and to act in the matter.[46]

Edward took this reply at its face value. The 'good people' of Scotland, who, despite their homely description, were the substantially aristocratic community of the realm,[47] had admitted that they had no authority to answer his request. But an answer might be forthcoming from the claimants to the vacant throne : for someone among the competitors was presumably the rightful king; if all of them acknowledged Edward to be overlord of Scotland the community of the realm must follow suit. This was the flaw in the reply of the community.

Early in June the various competitors were asked if they acknowledged Edward to be lord superior of Scotland, and whether they would accept his judgment of the succession. The would-be kings, who now included another seven persons besides Bruce and Balliol, announced that Edward had convinced them that he was rightfully lord superior and they would abide by his decision of the succession;[48] sasine of the land and custody of the royal castles should be delivered to Edward so that he could restore them to the person adjudged to be the rightful king as soon as that person did homage to Edward as lord superior.[49]

At this point Edward encountered obstacles. Fourteen Scottish barons to whom the 'community' had once entrusted custody of the royal castles had scruples about delivering them to Edward. But nothing came of this last-ditch stand on behalf of the community : fortified by the acknowledgment of the competitors, Edward persuaded not only the latter, but the guardians as well, to assent to the

[46] *Ibid.*, No. 16.
[47] A. A. M. Duncan, *op. cit.*, *S.H.R.*, XLV. 184–201, at 190.
[48] Stones, *Documents*, No. 17.
[49] *Nat. MSS. Scot.*, I. No. lxxi.

transfer of the castles. The honour of the scrupulous barons was thus preserved and the castles were handed over to English constables.[50]

The submission of the competitors had weakened the chances of opposition from the Scottish magnates. Nor had there been warfare or even the presence of alien officials to arouse among the common folk any intense resentment at what must have seemed a political transaction involving a mere feudal technicality that could have no effect upon their lives. Thus Edward established his position not only as lord superior but as 'direct lord' of Scotland during the interregnum. He assumed thorough control of the kingdom and its revenues and administration, and ordered the arrest of those who refused to take an oath of fealty.[51] After a fealty-gathering tour as far as Perth he made his way to Berwick on 2 August 1291 to open the first session of the lawsuit known as the 'Great Cause' of the Scottish succession.

In deference to the spirit of thirteenth-century *legalitas* Edward prepared to determine the Great Cause with conspicuous formality. He himself, in theory, was to act only as president of the court and as the mouthpiece of its judgment. The court itself was composed according to a precedent of Roman law, the *judicium centumvirale*,[52] and numbered 104 auditors. Edward himself nominated 24 of the auditors—twelve English barons and twelve English ecclesiastics. Two of the competitors, John Balliol and his brother-in-law John Comyn, the guardian, were allowed to nominate jointly another forty auditors not only on their own behalf but on behalf of those other competitors who would abide by their nomination. Similarly Robert Bruce was allowed to nominate forty auditors on his own behalf and on behalf of those competitors who would abide by his nomination.[53] In practice, however, the choice of auditors reflected the twofold party division within Scotland. From the lists of auditors it is clear that the nobility of Scotland was fairly evenly divided in support of Bruce or Balliol; but the high ecclesiastical backing for Balliol outweighed that given to Bruce.

It is impossible in a brief summary to do justice to the complex issues raised by the proceedings of the court of auditors.[54] These pro-

---

[50] A. A. M. Duncan, *op. cit.*, *S.H.R.*, XLV. 184–201, at 191–2.
[51] *Cal. Docs. Scot.*, II. No. 508.
[52] G. Neilson, 'Bruce versus Balliol, 1291–2', *S.H.R.*, XVI. 1–14.
[53] Palgrave, *Documents*, I. Illustrations, ii, v–vi.
[54] The most recent survey is by G. W. S. Barrow in *Bruce*, pp. 52–68; see also E. L. G. Stones, 'The Records of the Great Cause of 1291–92', *S.H.R.*, XXXV. 89–109.

ceedings touched upon the nature of the state [55] as well as upon questions of feudal law, Roman civil law, and 'natural law'; Edward canvassed the opinions of doctors of law of the university of Paris [56] to help him through the maze. Some of the competitors (by this time twelve in number) had no hope of immediate success but were merely taking the chance to record their claims for possible future use. More serious claims were presented by Bruce, Balliol, John Hastings, Lord of Abergavenny, and Floris, Count of Holland.

The first three claimed as descendants of David, Earl of Huntingdon, grandson of David I. Earl David had left three daughters, Margaret, Isabella and Ada. John Balliol was the grandson of the eldest daughter, Robert Bruce was son of the second daughter, and John Hastings was grandson of the third daughter. [57] The object of Hastings's claim was not to gain the Scottish crown but to argue that the Scottish kingdom was like a barony which had descended to three co-heiresses : the lands and revenues should therefore be equally divided among the descendants of the co-heiresses. Bruce, for the time being, refuted the claim that the kingdom was partible. The laws observed by subjects, he asserted, were not applicable to the kings who ruled over them or to the kingdom as a legal entity : the law applicable to the Great Cause was that same law which held that a kingdom could not be divided, namely 'the law by which kings reign', which he equated with 'natural law'. [58]

Having thus countered Hastings's claim, Bruce went on to clarify his own. Again and again he stressed that he was one degree nearer the royal line than Balliol. If Balliol's mother had not recently died Bruce's claim would (he affirmed) be self-evident : for although Devorgilla was as near in degree to the royal line as he, and came of a senior branch, nonetheless it was Bruce who would have been preferred because (presumably by natural law) 'male blood is worthier and purer to claim and govern a kingdom than female blood.' [59] Balliol's claim came to him solely from Devorgilla, and since *her* claim was inferior to that of Bruce so also was her son's. Besides, claimed Bruce, Alexander II had once publicly recognised *him* as his heir, as some who were still alive well knew. [60]

[55] B. C. Keeney, 'The Medieval Idea of the State : the Great Cause, 1291-2', *Toronto Law Journal*, VII. 48-71.
[56] G. J. Hand, *op. cit., Irish Jurist* (New Series), v. 141-55.
[57] See Appendix 2, Genealogical Table A.
[58] Palgrave, *Documents*, I. 23, 25.
[59] *Ibid.*, p. 24.
[60] *Ibid.*, pp. 29-30; see also pp. 19-20.

To the minds of many of the auditors Bruce's arguments must have seemed strained. The auditors were familiar with the feudal laws of succession to a barony or an earldom and were unlikely to be eager to follow a wild goose chase after natural law. In this lay the strength of Balliol's case and he exploited it well. He asserted that the case should be tried according to the laws and usages of England and Scotland.[61] After the kingship itself the highest tenures were those of the earldoms. Like a kingdom an earldom could not be divided; and it descended by seniority of line, not by nearness of degree.[62] Thus should it be with a kingdom : Balliol, grandson of the first daughter of Earl David, had a better claim than Bruce, son of the second daughter.

But Floris, Count of Holland, presented an ingenious case that might dispose of all descendants of David, Earl of Huntingdon : Earl David, he claimed, had resigned his possible right of succession to the kingdom, and King William had then declared that if his own line should fail the succession should pass to his sister Ada, whose descendant was Count Floris. The count asserted that there existed in the Scottish treasury written evidence that would prove his case.[63] This gave the opportunity for a breathing-space. On 12 August Edward adjourned the court; it was to meet again at Berwick on 2 June 1292. Meanwhile the Scottish treasury, monasteries, and other likely places, were to be searched (fruitlessly, as it turned out) for documents relevant to Count Floris' case or that of other competitors.[64]

The breathing-space also allowed Edward time to try out the ground for a case of his own. Although recognised as lord superior of Scotland, even as 'direct lord', he was not wholly satisfied. At Norham in June 1291 he had informed the competitors (who did not demur) that he reserved his own hereditary right 'as one among others claiming right to the kingdom',[65] for Edward was a descendant of Malcolm III and Queen Margaret. Moreover as feudal superior he may have contemplated the tantalising possibility that Scotland might be declared a male fief, succession to which could not lie through a female; or alternatively that competitors might be excluded through the remoteness of their relationship to the royal stock; on one of these grounds, if not both, they might then be swept aside

[61] *Ibid.*, p. 28.
[62] *Ibid.*, p. 27.
[63] G. G. Simpson, 'The Claim of Florence, Count of Holland, to the Scottish Throne, 1291-2', *S.H.R.*, XXXVI. 111-24.
[64] Palgrave, *Documents*, I. 35-6.
[65] *Foedera*, I. pt. iii, 96.

after they had served their purpose;[66] the kingdom would then escheat to its lord superior, Edward. In August 1291 £10,000 were to be forwarded to him, ostensibly for the expenses of his household,[67] possibly for other uses: James the Steward and another five Scottish magnates were offered lands worth £100 or 100 marks a year 'if it happens that the realm of Scotland shall remain in the possession of the king and his heirs',[68] and the king in question was Edward. These offers were afterwards cancelled, presumably because no support was forthcoming for his candidature. But before the court of auditors re-assembled at Berwick Edward had tightened his hold on Scotland and had sought to win the good opinion of barons, prelates and burgesses by gracious concessions. After a year of his personal rule it would be difficult for any succeeding king to assert the independent tradition of Scottish monarchy.

When the Great Cause re-opened at Berwick on 2 June 1292 it seemed no nearer determination. Yet another competitor, Eric of Norway, sent procurators who presented a claim that depended not upon descent but upon ascent: if the Maid of Norway was rightful Queen of Scotland then Eric as her father was her rightful heir. But Eric's procurators advanced this dubious claim half-heartedly, possibly only as a bargaining point to give them greater chance of winning other claims upon Scottish revenues that they simultaneously brought before Edward.[69] In any case the court decided on 2 June, without prejudice to the claims of Eric and other competitors, to determine first of all whether Balliol or Bruce had the better claim.

As the aged Bruce sensed that his own claim would founder he clutched at the claim of the Count of Holland, which still drifted like flotsam on the stormy waters. From the first, Bruce and the count had been on good terms.[70] Now, on 14 June, their mutual friends persuaded the two to conclude an indenture: if Floris should become King of Scotland he would convey to Bruce one-third of Scotland; similarly, if Bruce became king he would convey one-third to Floris, partly redeemable, however, by a transfer of the Bruce lands in England to the count.[71] This interesting stipulation suggests that Bruce's interests were centred in Scotland.

---

[66] See G. J. Hand, op. cit., Irish Jurist (New Series), v. 141–55, at 144–5, 147–8, 151–2, 154.
[67] Stevenson, Documents, I. No. cxxiv.
[68] Rot. Scot., I. 3.
[69] Ranald Nicholson, op. cit., S.H.R., xxxviii. 114–32, at 123.
[70] They were associated in the Appeals of the Seven Earls (Palgrave, Documents, pp. 20–1). [71] Stevenson, Documents, I. No. cclv.

The indenture of 14 June 1292 represented the Lord of Annandale's last-ditch defence against Balliol : if Balliol's claim triumphed over that of Bruce it might yet fail before that of Count Floris, in which event Bruce would at least gain a third of Scotland. By 6 November the court had decided that Balliol had a better claim than Bruce. On the following day the disappointed eldest Bruce transmitted his rejected claim to his posterity—his son, the Earl of Carrick, and *his* heirs. Carrick and his heirs were accorded 'full and free power to sue for the realm, and to prosecute . . . the right which pertains to him in this matter, in the way that seems best to him.' [72] Though the eldest Bruce had failed he impressed upon his family his own burning conviction of the justice of his claim. This conviction was perhaps not shared by the Earl of Carrick, but it certainly was by the latter's son, the youngest Robert Bruce, who now came to the fore by reason of a further shift within the three generations of the Bruce family : on 9 November the Earl of Carrick resigned his earldom to the youngest Bruce,[73] who within fourteen years would seize the kingdom.

The Great Cause was not yet over. On 10 November the lawyers of the eldest Bruce modified his previous argument that the kingdom was indivisible and pleaded that, like Hastings, Bruce should receive a third of the royal demesne. This plea failed when the court decided that neither the kingdom nor its revenues could be divided.[74] Next came the turn of Count Floris to press his claim; Balliol's lawyers had merely to point out that he had produced no evidence to support it and Count Floris withdrew his claim. Another six competitors followed his example ; the claims of Eric of Norway, Roger Mandeville and John Comyn of Badenoch were rejected because of their 'failure to sue'.[75] One significant feature of the Great Cause was, in fact, the failure of John Comyn, guardian of Scotland and member of the most powerful Scottish baronial family, to press his own claim, based on direct descent from Donald Bane, who had endured a disputed reign in Scotland between 1093 and 1097. Just as, latterly, Count Floris was in collusion with Bruce, so also John Comyn was in collusion with Balliol, whose sister he had married. If Balliol be-

---

[72] Stones, *Documents*, No. 18. See the question of 'estoppel' in G. J. Hand, *op. cit., Irish Jurist* (New Series), v. 141–55, at 150.
[73] *A.P.S.*, I. 449.
[74] This was assumed by Edward in the *quaestio* he submitted to the Paris lawyers (G. J. Hand, *op. cit., Irish Jurist* [New Series], v. 141–55, at 144).
[75] Stones, *Documents*, No. 19.

came king the Comyns would undoubtedly be the power behind the throne.

On 17 November 1292 Edward gave judgment in favour of Balliol,[76] who was duly enthroned at Scone on St Andrew's Day. The new king joined Edward at Newcastle for the Christmas festivities and on 26 December did homage to him.[77] When Edward had ordered that Balliol should receive sasine of the kingdom he had qualified the award with a typical Edwardian reservation: 'saving our right and that of our heirs when we shall wish to speak thereupon.'[78] Edward had not given up hope of controlling Scotland directly rather than merely as the lord superior of a vassal king. It was ominous that Balliol was warned to govern justly so that no one should have cause to complain, lest the lord superior of Scotland should be obliged to apply a guiding hand.[79]

[76] *Ibid.*
[77] *Ibid.*, No. 20; Stevenson, *Documents*, I. 372.
[78] *Rot. Scot.*, I. 11; similarly Stones, *Documents*, No. 19.
[79] *Foedera*, I. pt. iii, 111.

3

KING JOHN, THE FRENCH ALLIANCE AND THE GUARDIANS OF SCOTLAND

It is understandable, though misleading, that the history of Scotland has usually been written from the point of view of the Bruces (who were ultimately successful) rather than from that of the Balliols (who were ultimately unsuccessful). It is even more misleading that John Balliol has gone down in history as Toom Tabard rather than as King John. Balliol set out to be no less a king than his predecessors : his family had had links with Scotland since the twelfth century; there was nothing to hinder the acclimatisation of the new dynasty, particularly since it was backed by the Comyns, not only the most powerful baronial family but one with the best claim to be regarded as 'patriotic'.[1] Almost certainly it was for King John's edification that a treatise was compiled in French outlining the traditional organisation of the Scottish royal household[2] and touching upon Scottish government in general. Between February 1293 and May 1294 at least four parliaments were held.[3] On one occasion parliament was to be the seat of 'the dispensing of justice upon a scale which may have been unprecedented in Scotland', for there was to be public summons before king and council of 'everyone with a complaint . . . to show the injuries and trespasses done to them by whatsoever ill-doers'. In general there is 'remarkable evidence that King John and his council were determined to secure the possessions and authority of the crown'.[4] Not only did King John try to restore royal authority through parliament but he tried to renew the policy of

---

[1] P. 47 below.
[2] P. 20 above.
[3] A. A. M. Duncan, *op. cit.*, *S.H.R.*, xlv. 36–58, at 40–3.
[4] *Ibid.*, 46.

assimilation that earlier kings had applied to the West Highlands and Isles. In his first parliament in February 1293 he ordained the erection of three new sheriffdoms in Skye, Lorne and Kintyre.[5] What might have proved the culminating stage in the extension of integrating institutions to the West Highlands and Isles achieved nothing: separatism came into its own in the welter of the wars of independence.

The origin of these wars can be traced to the very outset of King John's reign : shortly before he had arrived in Newcastle to perform his homage, judgment had been given there by Edward in a case involving an appeal from a Scottish court. This assumption of appellate jurisdiction followed from Edward's recognised position as lord superior; but the Scots had hoped that he would deal with appeals only on Scottish soil. On behalf of King John a number of Scottish magnates petitioned Edward that he should adhere to the provisions in the marriage treaty of Birgham which would forbid the hearing of such appeals outwith Scotland. On 2 January 1293, however, King John was forced to acknowledge in writing that Edward was released from any restrictions imposed by the treaty of Birgham or by his promises during the interregnum.[6]

Although there followed no flood of appeals from Scotland to England the few that were forthcoming, notably from MacDuff, brother of the late Earl of Fife, brought a crisis. Partly the fault was that of King John, who sought to evade the consequences of his admission of 2 January 1293. Had he sent attorneys to answer in his name to the appeals that were presented he might have avoided the humiliation of appearing in person to defend the judgments given in his own court. Because of John's evasion Edward's council drew up onerous rules to regulate the procedure of appeals from Scotland : the Scottish king must always attend in person to answer such appeals. In November 1293 King John did attend. In vain he affirmed 'that he is king of the realm of Scotland and dare not make answer at the suit of Macduff, nor in anything touching his kingdom without the advice of his people'. He was offered an adjournment to seek such advice but rejected it since that would have been an admission of the competence of the English court. King John was therefore adjudged guilty of contempt of court, and was sentenced to lose his three chief castles and towns. Had he held firm the result would have been war or the bitterest humiliation. He chose the lesser humiliation and

---

[5] *A.P.S.*, I. 447–8.
[6] Barrow, *Bruce*, pp. 70–3.

sought the adjournment that he had previously rejected. The Mac-Duff case dragged on with further adjournments.[7]

Edward himself, in his capacity as Duke of Aquitaine, had occasionally suffered humiliation at the hands of his overlord, the French king. Edward was inclined to treat King John no more gently than Philip IV treated *him*. But the Scottish kingdom, unlike the duchy of Aquitaine, had long possessed at least *de facto* independence and had as much right to be considered a distinct state as England. Edward paid no heed to the fact that the Scots had only reluctantly accepted him as lord superior. And both sides were poles apart in their interpretation of what was implied by Edward's position as lord superior: John was willing to behave as a vassal king; what Edward wanted was not a vassal king but a mere agent whose every action he might review. John's position was an impossible one: his own subjects regarded him as a king; Edward regarded him as a subject.

The situation was further complicated by the fact that Edward had been ruling Scotland directly between June 1291 and November 1292. There still remained unsettled matters of finance and justice that he had dealt with during this period; he assumed that he had a right to see that they were settled. Among the outstanding matters were the respective claims of the Count of Flanders and Eric of Norway to large arrears of dower or dowry that should have been paid from the Scottish revenues. In addition Eric was to claim that the Western Isles, ceded to the Scottish crown in 1266 in return for annual payment of a hundred marks in perpetuity, should revert to Norway since payment was in arrears.[8] To attain his ends in Scotland Eric was working not only through Edward but through the Bruces: in 1293 the widowed Eric married Isabella, sister of the youngest Bruce. This match took place at a time when there was a Bruce-Balliol dispute over the vacant bishopric of Galloway.[9] To King John it must have seemed that Edward, Eric, and the Bruces had banded together to undermine his authority and prestige, perhaps even to dismember his kingdom.

The trend of events can hardly have been hidden from the Scottish magnates. John Comyn, Earl of Buchan, had been among those who from the very first had sensed that the question of appeals

[7] *Ibid.*, pp. 74–83; Stones, *Documents*, No. 21.

[8] Ranald Nicholson, *op. cit.*, S.H.R., XXXVIII. 114–32 at 122–3, 129; A.P.S., I. 448.

[9] A. A. M. Duncan, *op. cit.*, S.H.R., XLV. 36–58, at 45; Robert J. Brentano, 'The Whithorn Vacancy of 1293–94', *Innes Review*, IV. 71–83; Barrow, *Bruce*, pp. 92–3.

menaced what remained of Scottish independence. During the minority of Alexander III, when Henry III of England was trying to control Scotland, the Comyns had acquired intimate experience of Anglo-Scottish relations and in 1258 had made an abortive alliance with the English king's foe, Llewelyn, Prince of Wales.[10] Between September 1294 and March 1295 the Welsh, lately subdued by Edward I, were once more striving for independence under Madog ap Llewelyn. Madog's rising had partly been in response to Edward's order that the Welsh should fight for him against the French.[11] The same demand was presented to the Scots. Their response was less spontaneous than that of the Welsh but it was all the more deliberate and prepared.

The outbreak of war between Edward and Philip IV of France had arisen from a naval incident off the coast of Brittany. As a result Philip eventually denounced his great vassal as contumacious and forfeited Edward's duchy of Aquitaine. Edward sent his defiance and made ready to defend the duchy. In the summer of 1294 King John was present in England at the great council that prepared for war with France and was induced to promise Scottish help.[12] The war had not only made Edward increase his demands upon the Scots but had created a situation in which the Scots were tempted to resist all Edward's demands, both present and past. On 5 July 1295 Scottish envoys were sent to conclude a treaty with the French king.

It was not the first time that the Scots had looked to France for help against the English; but the treaty that was drafted at Paris on 23 October 1295 was to have far more lasting effects than any previous Franco-Scottish pact. It was a defensive and offensive alliance directed against England; neither ally would make a separate peace; the alliance was to be given the more permanence by a projected marriage between the niece of the French king and Edward Balliol, son and heir of King John. The French asked that the treaty should be ratified not only by King John but by the Scottish prelates, barons, knights, and 'communities of the towns'. The Scottish burgesses made their entry into high affairs of state when the seals of six burghs were attached to the Scottish ratification at Dunfermline on 23 February 1296.[13] From the other seals attached to the ratification it is clear that the new alliance had powerful support within Scotland. King John, however, had misgivings. Although his own great seal

[10] D. E. R. Watt, 'The Minority of Alexander III of Scotland', *T.R.H.S.* (5th series), XXI. 1–23, at 17.

[11] Barrow, *Bruce*, p. 88.   [12] *Ibid.*, pp. 87–8.   [13] *A.P.S.*, I. 451–3.

was appended he himself seems to have been unwilling to accept responsibility : at the assembly in July 1295 that had decided to send envoys to France the implementation of the new policy was entrusted to a council of twelve—four bishops, four earls and four barons—which represented the main elements in the political community.[14]

The Franco-Scottish alliance was only one among the many alliances that were being made in Western Europe as Edward aimed at the encirclement of France and Philip built up counter-alliances that threatened England itself. Philip even swept Edward's Norwegian associates into his schemes : on the day before the conclusion of the Franco-Scottish alliance a Franco-Norwegian alliance was also concluded at Paris. The French persuaded both Scots and Norwegians to forget their own disputes for the time being : the aim of French policy was that the Norwegians would provide shipping for a seaborne invasion of England ;[15] the Scots would invade by land.

The Scottish host was summoned to muster at Caddonlea near Selkirk on 11 March 1296.[16] It would be made up, as most Scottish armies were to be made up during the wars of independence, of both 'feudal' and 'national' elements. Feudal military service provided a small number of well-armed and mounted knights, esquires and men-at-arms, but the bulk of the host, the ordinary rank and file, was drawn from the lower classes of society who furnished the *servitium Scoticanum* that dated back to pre-feudal times.[17] This 'Scottish service', known also as *communis exercitus*, 'common army', was the old military service, comparable to the Anglo-Saxon fyrd. It meant that every able-bodied man between the ages of sixteen and sixty could be summoned to join the levies of the sheriffdoms when the king's host was mustered for the defence of the country. There was thus a system of national conscription.

Similar developments had taken place in England ; yet there were vital differences between Scottish and English armies. The manpower of England, with a population five times larger than that of Scotland, was large enough to allow selection by commissioners of array of the best men levied in the shires ; and the commissioners soon learned to recruit men who were proficient in the use of the deadly long-bow. By contrast the Scottish levies turned up with a motley

---

[14] Barrow, *Bruce*, p. 89.

[15] Ranald Nicholson, *op. cit., S.H.R.*, XXXVIII. 114–32, at 116–9. Although the Norwegians never appeared the French made a few naval raids and forced the English to organise coastal defences (A. Z. Freeman, 'A Moat Defensive : the Coast Defence Scheme of 1295', *Speculum*, XLII. 442–62).

[16] Barrow, *Bruce*, p. 93.   [17] *Highland Papers*, II. 233–5.

assembly of weapons—spears, Lochaber axes, short-bow and sword. The manpower and wealth of the English feudal classes was great enough to allow a large proportion of the English host to be made up of well-armed cavalry; by contrast Scotland was weak in cavalry. In England, as in Scotland, the traditional period of military service was forty days in the year; but the English king was wealthy enough to pay daily wages of war to all his troops, from the haughtiest earl to the humblest groom; those who took the king's wages were more amenable to royal discipline and could be induced to serve longer than forty days. If Scottish troops were paid they were paid by those who sent them, not by the Scottish king. Often Scottish armies could be held together only through the prospect of a share in booty and plunder. Besides the lasting differences that were obvious even in 1296, the Scots had no recent experience of warfare; the English had perfected their military machine in the bitter campaigns that crushed the Welsh.

As the ill-trained Scottish host mustered at Caddonlea there were gaps in the ranks: the eldest Robert Bruce had died in the previous year at the age of eighty-four;[18] neither his son nor his grandson, the new Earl of Carrick, was prepared to fight for Balliol—they joined the Earls of March and Angus who fought for Edward.[19] From the Bruce lordship of Annandale, now held for King John by John Comyn, Earl of Buchan, a force set out on Easter Monday (26 March) to launch an unsuccessful assault on Carlisle,[20] where Bruce senior commanded the garrison. From the very outset of the war Edward could take advantage of Scottish rivalries and use one faction against another.

Before engaging in warfare, Edward had gone through the motions of holding a parliament at Newcastle to which he summoned King John; Edward had also summoned his army to Newcastle; King John understandably failed to appear. Immediately after the Scottish assault on Carlisle the English crossed the Tweed. Berwick, the most important Scottish burgh, refused to open its gates, although the burgesses were assured of good treatment if they capitulated. They had once written flattering letters to Edward; now they insulted him from behind their flimsy palisades. On 30 March 1296 the town was taken by storm and the inhabitants were indiscriminately butchered. In revenge, the Earls of Ross, Menteith and Atholl ravaged Tynedale and Redesdale.[21] Soon the Scots were to be taught for the

[18] *Cal. Docs. Scot.*, II. No. 689.   [19] Stones, *Documents*, No. 22.
[20] Barrow, *Bruce*, pp. 97–9.   [21] *Chron. Lanercost*, pp. 171–5.

E.H.S.—3

first time, but not for the last, the danger of waging pitched battle with
the English: at Dunbar on 27 April 1296 the Scottish host was overwhelmed by the Earl of Surrey.[22] This ended the bellicosity of the
Scots for the time being. The castles of Dunbar, Roxburgh, Jedburgh
and Dumbarton were surrendered by their garrisons. Edinburgh
Castle held out against siege machines for only a week. When
Edward arrived at Stirling it was to find that the garrison had fled,
leaving the gate-keeper to surrender the castle.[23] When he reached
Perth the local gentry hastened to submit and swear fealty.[24]

Soon after the fall of Berwick, King John had sent two Franciscan friars to the town to present a final and dignified remonstrance to
Edward: the latter had 'caused harm beyond measure to the liberties
of ourselves and our kingdom . . . for instance by summoning us outside our realm at the mere beck and call of anybody, as your own
whim dictated, and by harassing us unjustifiably'. The friars had renounced the homage and fealty 'which, be it said, were extorted by
extreme coercion on your part'.[25] Now came the time for John to eat
his brave words. Deserted by all save a few of his Comyn supporters
he had fled to the glens of Angus and Mearns and had little alternative save abject surrender. At the royal castle of Kincardine on 2
July 1296 he was obliged to seal a document in which he confessed his
wrongdoing and folly in allying himself with the foes of his overlord
and surrendered to Edward the land and people of Scotland.[26] Once,
King John had been ceremonially made king; now he was to be
ceremonially unmade. He was attired in royal splendour for the last
time, then the crown was taken from his head, the sceptre and sword
from his hands, the ring from his finger, the costly fur from his tabard
or surcoat. His tabard was 'toom'—bare or empty—and Balliol, the
unmade king, became 'Toom Tabard'.[27] Having 'stamped on
Balliol's name an image of perpetual disgrace', Edward marched as
far north as Elgin, meeting with no resistance. He returned to Berwick on 26 August 1296. According to a diarist of the expedition, he
had 'conquered and serched the kyngdom of Scotteland . . . in xxj

[22] *Ibid.*, pp. 175–7.
[23] 'Diary of the Expedition of Edward I into Scotland', *Bannatyne Misc. I.*
264–82, at 276.
[24] *Cal. Docs. Scot.*, II. 178–9.
[25] Stones, *Documents*, No. 23.
[26] *Ibid.*, No. 24.
[27] G. G. Simpson, 'Why was John Balliol called "Toom Tabard"?', *S.H.R.*,
XLVII. 196–9.

wekis'.[28] Those weeks had seen the end of decades of peace between Scotland and England. They were to be followed by two and a half centuries of enmity and warfare.

In the course of Edward's progress through Scotland many magnates had hastened to swear fealty to him and to renounce the Franco-Scottish alliance. When he held parliament at Berwick at the end of August 1296 further submissions were received and others were forwarded by the sheriffs he appointed. The names of hundreds of Scots, nobles, prelates and even men of lesser standing, filled the thirty-five membranes of parchment that came to be known as the Ragman Roll.[29] Less concern for such a legalistic recording of Scottish fealties, more concern to secure the real loyalty of the Scots, might have brought Edward better results. As it was, before he left for England in September he had already committed a blunder that alienated many who in course of time might have loyally accepted him. By feudal custom the escheat of a fief to its overlord left unaltered the rights and privileges inherent in the fief; and the escheated fief of Scotland was a kingdom. One course open to Edward was to appoint a new vassal king. Bruce senior was willing enough to step into the position that Balliol had vacated: at the very outset of Edward's Scottish campaign he and his son had joined Edward at Wark, affirming that 'we are, and always have been, faithful'.[30] The chronicler Bower narrates that after the English victory at Dunbar the elder Bruce asked Edward to install him as King of Scotland, only to be snubbed when Edward answered in French: 'Have we nothing to do but win realms for you?'[31] The two Bruces were sent with their tails between their legs to bring their own tenants of Annandale and Carrick to Edward's obedience.[32] There was to be no new vassal King of Scotland. Another course open to Edward after the deposition of Balliol was for him to assume the title of King of Scots himself. Instead, he ruled Scotland in his capacity as King of England. He let it be seen that, at best, the kingdom of Scotland was in abeyance, at worst, it had come to an end: the Scottish regalia and the Scottish muniments were sent to London, the enthronement stone was removed from Scone[33] and installed as a trophy of war in Westminster;

[28] 'Diary of the Expedition of Edward I into Scotland, *Bannatyne Misc. I.* 264–82, at 281.
[29] *Cal. Docs. Scot.*, II. No. 823.   [30] Stones, *Documents*, No. 22.
[31] *Chron. Bower*, II. 166.   [32] Stones, *Documents*, No. 25.
[33] For the history of the 'Stone of Destiny' see W. Douglas Simpson, *Dunstaffnage Castle and the Stone of Destiny* (1958).

Edward referred to Scotland not as a kingdom but as 'the land of Scotland'. The change of status was one that should not have befallen a mere barony, but it embodied Edward's consistent attitude towards Scotland. In his view the British Isles could hold only a single kingdom, that of England. Scotland, after 1296, would be administered separately from England, but no more separately, no more independently, than the lordship of Ireland or the principality of Wales. Although local civil government was left in Scottish hands central government was in English hands. For the first time the full scope of Edward's policy was clear to all Scots. They had once pitied the Welsh. Now they themselves were reduced to the same status. The only alternative to a future of humiliation was to fight for a restoration of the Scottish kingdom.

But who was to lead the fight? Not only John Balliol but many of the Scottish nobles taken prisoner at Dunbar were captive in England. The names of most of the remaining nobles swelled the Ragman Roll; and the English administration can hardly have worried over the absence of the name of William Wallace, esquire, second son of a simple knight, Sir Malcolm Wallace of Elderslie, vassal of James the Steward.

William Wallace was probably among those who had been driven to guerrilla resistance when Edward's justiciar, William Ormsby, was 'following steadfastly the command of the king' and 'outlawed without distinction of person all who were unwilling to take the oath of fealty to the King of England'.[34] After a brawl with the English garrison of Lanark Wallace escaped with the help of his wife (or mistress), who was put to death by his pursuers. In revenge Wallace came back to Lanark, slew the English sheriff, Sir William Hazelrigg,[35] and became the foremost leader of the 'outlaws'.

Wallace's personal grievances against the English occupying forces, and his personal reactions, were probably not unique. Nor was he the only Scot who was keenly aware of the issues raised by Edward's attempt to reduce Scotland to subordinate status. If the Scottish kingdom disappeared the Scottish kirk might well be the next victim. On 1 October 1296 Edward ordered that only English priests should be presented to vacant benefices in Galloway. Less than a year later the same order was applied to all Scotland.[36] By the intru-

---

[34] *The Chronicle of Walter of Guisborough*, ed. H. Rothwell (1957), p. 294.
[35] The traditional account given in Blind Harry's *Wallace* (S.T.S.), pp. 113–8, is supported by English sources.
[36] *Rot. Scot.*, I. 35, 47.

sion of English ecclesiastics the Scottish kirk could gradually be sub-
verted from within, and the last distinctive Scottish institution would
be converted into an agency of the English occupation. Although
numerous Scottish ecclesiastics had hastened to make their peace with
Edward [37] many others held aloof : 'out of a possible total of twelve
bishops of Scotland only three are known to have done homage to
Edward'.[38] One of the three was Robert Wishart, Bishop of Glasgow,
who, according to the Lanercost chronicler, 'conspired with the
Steward . . . for a new piece of insolence. . . . Not daring openly to
break their pledge to the king, they caused a certain bloody man,
William Wallace, who had formerly been chief of brigands in Scotland, to revolt against the king, and assemble the people in his support'.[39] It was probably through the underhand efforts of Wishart
and the Steward that Wallace was no longer the mere leader of a band
of outlaws but by May 1297 was a joint leader with Sir William
Douglas in an attack upon Ormsby the justiciar, who was holding
his court at Scone. When Ormsby was put to flight the smouldering
resistance that had lasted throughout the winter of 1296–7 flared
into a wholesale rising.[40]

Already there were suspicions of the younger Bruce's intentions.
Though obliged to take a solemn oath at Carlisle that he would remain loyal to Edward, he assembled his father's vassals, the knights
of Annandale, told them that the Carlisle oath had been given under
duress, and affirmed : 'No man holds his flesh and blood in hatred,
and I am no exception. I must join my own people and the nation
in which I was born.'[41] The patriotism thus expressed was doubtless
sincere ; but it was coupled with another motive. The younger Bruce,
a man of more mettle than his father, saw in the Scottish rising a
chance to pursue his grandfather's legacy of the quest for the crown.
In 1297 he joined the insurgents, 'aspiring to the kingdom, as was
commonly said'.[42]

The Earl of Carrick was with Wishart, Wallace and the Steward
in June 1297, when they encountered an English force at Irvine.
Wallace and the majority were fighting for the captive Balliol and
were at odds with their new ally, who was striving for his own
claims. One Scottish knight said that it was folly to fight for men who

[37] *Ibid.*, 1. 24–6.
[38] Barrow, *Bruce*, p. 111.
[39] *Chron. Lanercost*, p. 190.
[40] Barron, *War of Independence*, pp. 27–30; Barrow, *Bruce*, pp. 117–8.
[41] Barrow, *Bruce*, pp. 118–19.
[42] A. A. M. Duncan, *op. cit.*, *S.H.R.*, xlv. 184–201, at 194.

were divided against themselves and joined the English. He was followed by Bishop Wishart, the Steward, Bruce, and most of the other
Scottish leaders who claimed to act as spokesmen of 'the whole community of the realm'. A document of capitulation was drafted at
Irvine on 7 July 1297 [43] outlining the lenient terms on which they
were to be pardoned by Edward. The result was to discredit the
Scottish magnates politically almost as much as the battle of Dunbar
had done militarily.[44] Under the belief that Scotland had been pacified, Edward set sail for Flanders at the end of August, taking with
him some of the Dunbar prisoners, who were to have a chance of
winning their freedom by good service against the French.[45]

But if William Wallace had been previously a mere agent of
Bishop Wishart and the Steward, the capitulation of Irvine released
him from tutelage. He had established himself in Selkirk forest, then,
and afterwards, a sure retreat for the forces of resistance south of the
Forth; and with him he had a force that one of Edward's officials
described as 'a large company'.[46] For, so claimed an English chronicler, 'the common folk of the land followed him as their leader and
ruler; the retainers of the great lords adhered to him; and even
though the lords themselves were present with the [English] king in
body, at heart they were on the opposite side'.[47] By August 1297
Wallace had crossed the Tay to besiege the English-held castle of
Dundee [48] and to link up with staunch allies in the north, where the
rising had gone from strength to strength.

The chief leader of the northern rising was Andrew Moray. Like
Wallace he had personal grievances: his father and uncle were
Edward's captives; he himself had been imprisoned in Chester
Castle until he escaped. Also, like Wallace, Moray was a mere
esquire. Yet despite their equal military rank there was a vast
difference between the two young men. Wallace was no great landholder. Andrew Moray was heir to his father's large estates in Moray
and Cromarty, heir also to his uncle's lordship of Bothwell in Lanarkshire, centred upon Bothwell Castle, one of the new stonebuilt castles
in Scotland, and perhaps the most impressive. In the other family
castle of Avoch in the Black Isle Andrew Moray assembled his retainers in May 1297 and with Alexander Pilche, a burgess of Inver-

[43] Stevenson, *Documents*, II. No. ccccxlvii.
[44] *Ibid.*, No. ccccliv.
[45] *Rot. Scot.*, I. 44–5.
[46] Stevenson, *Documents*, II. No. cccccliii.
[47] *The Chronicle of Walter of Guisborough*, ed. Harry Rothwell (1957),
p. 299.   [48] *Chron. Bower*, II. 171.

ness, planned an attack upon the garrison of Urquhart Castle[49] on the shores of Loch Ness. By the end of July Edward's lukewarm Scottish supporters in Moray were on the defensive;[50] Andrew Moray took advantage of the rugged terrain to wage successful guerrilla warfare. Well might Edward's treasurer of Scotland write on 5 August that the outcome of the Irvine pacification was obscure in the regions north of the Forth.[51]

No details survive of the campaign that Andrew Moray must have waged in the following five weeks to obtain mastery of the whole region north of Tay; and nothing is known of the circumstances in which Moray's troops linked up with those of Wallace. An English force belatedly set out under the Earl of Surrey and Treasurer Cressingham, reached Stirling early in September, and found the troops of both Moray and Wallace massed on the Abbey Craig on the northern bank of the Forth. In July Treasurer Cressingham had had as many as 300 heavy cavalry and 10,000 footmen in his pay,[52] and it is unlikely that he and the Earl of Surrey had brought a smaller force to Stirling. On 11 September 1297 the English host, after two previous false starts, began for the third time to cross the narrow wooden bridge on which only two horsemen could ride abreast.[53]

The vanguard reached the northern bank only to be overwhelmed. Cressingham was slain, and the Scots made souvenirs of his skin.[54] Surrey rode post-haste to Berwick in humiliating flight. English losses were immense. The outcome was the utter overthrow of all that Edward had so far achieved in Scotland. An unknown contemporary writer composed Latin verses to celebrate the Scottish victory that had been attained through Wallace's inspiration: once more King John would be able to reign in his own kingdom.[55]

The same mood of optimism appeared in a letter of 11 October 1297 which Wallace wrote from Haddington to the merchants of Lübeck and Hamburg thanking them for their support and informing them that it was again safe to trade with Scotland, which was now 'recovered by war from the power of the English'. The letter ran

[49] Cal. Docs. Scot., ii. No. 922.
[50] Barron, War of Independence, pp. 37–67.
[51] Stevenson, Documents, ii. No. ccclxvii.
[52] Ibid., No. cccliii.
[53] Barrow, Bruce, pp. 123–4.
[54] For his career in Scotland see A. Z. Freeman, 'The King's Penny: the Headquarters Paymasters under Edward I, 1295–1307', Journal of British Studies, vi. 1–22, at 7–11.
[55] Chron. Bower, ii. 171.

in the names of Andrew Moray and William Wallace, 'leaders of the army of the kingdom of Scotland, and the community of the same kingdom'.[56] The army of the kingdom was thus accorded precedence over the community; the name of Moray was accorded precedence over that of Wallace. But Moray had been mortally wounded at Stirling bridge.[57] He died leaving a posthumous son and namesake who was to earn even greater fame than his father.

The death of Andrew Moray left Wallace supreme in Scotland. Within a few months one of the Scottish earls dubbed him knight. More than that, he was appointed sole guardian of Scotland and in one of his few known charters styled himself 'William Wallace, knight, guardian of the kingdom of Scotland and commander of its armies in the name of the famous prince the Lord John, by God's grace illustrious King of Scotland, by consent of the community of that realm'.[58] In the last resort, however, Wallace's power rested upon his position as commander of the Scottish army, not upon his position within the aristocratic 'community'.[59] He was 'the leader of a popular movement with a measure of social discontent in its makeup'.[60] And the army that Wallace formed was hardly the kind in which chivalric magnates would feel at home : the stress was laid upon the 'common army'. Lists of those liable to conscription were drawn up in every community from the sheriffdom to the merest rural township. Gallows were erected (and used) to hang those who disobeyed the call to arms; the recruits were formed into military units of five, ten, a hundred or a thousand men, and rigid discipline was demanded.[61] This was a 'New Model Army' comparable to that of Cromwell save in one respect—Wallace was fighting for a king. No one could challenge Wallace's position so long as he was successful in warfare; and at first he was. In November 1297 he led his new army into the north of England : at a time of famine in Scotland the army would be supported upon English booty and provisions.[62]

It was while Edward was absent in Flanders that Wallace had proved himself 'the hammer and scourge of the English'.[63] In March 1298 the king returned to England and immediately began prepara-

[56] *Documents Illustrative of Sir William Wallace, his Life and Times* (Maitland Club), No. xv.
[57] *Chron. Bower*, II. 171.
[58] Barrow, *Bruce*, p. 129
[59] See *Chron. Bower*, II. 174.
[60] A. A. M. Duncan, *Nation of Scots*, p. 16.
[61] *Chron. Bower*, II. 170–1, 172.
[62] *Ibid.*, 172.   [63] *Ibid.*, 169.

tions for a new campaign in Scotland.[64] By the beginning of July he had reached Roxburgh at the head of a powerful army and set out for Edinburgh to meet the supply ships that were expected in the Forth. Contrary winds prevented all but a few of the ships from reaching Leith; and they brought wine rather than victuals. Some of Edward's Welsh troops were drunk or dying; they had no love for their English conquerors and it was suspected they might defect to the Scots. Having advanced some ten miles west of Edinburgh, Edward was faced with the prospect of having to retreat. Then his loyal supporters the Earls of March and Angus arrived in camp with the news that Wallace lay in the wood of Callendar near Falkirk. On 22 July 1298 the two armies confronted one another.[65]

Since the campaign had begun, Wallace's strategy had been the one that was to bring success in future years: he had laid waste the country and burned the towns south of Forth so that they could not be used by the invaders;[66] he had harassed their stragglers, and almost starved the whole army into retreat. Yet this was not the way to win chivalric esteem; and Wallace, the newly dubbed knight, may have been taunted into action to preserve his military laurels. Somewhere near Falkirk he drew up his men in a defensive position protected by a palisade of stakes bound together with ropes. In front lay marsh and loch; on the flanks there was probably broken ground; behind these defences the spearmen were grouped in four great 'schiltrons'. These circular formations, from which spears projected like the spines of a hedgehog, may have been invented by Wallace in his reorganisation of the Scottish army. Between each schiltron were placed the archers of Ettrick forest. In the rear was the cavalry.[67]

Despite Wallace's careful preparations the Scots at Falkirk were far less favourably placed than they had been the year before at the Abbey Craig. It has been rightly said that Falkirk was a battle the Scots should never have fought.[68] They trusted most of all in their infantry spearmen,[69] who had to contend with the overwhelming superiority of the English both in archers and cavalry. Moreover, the small force of Scottish cavalry was contributed by nobles who were

[64] The preparations are detailed in *Scotland in 1298: Documents relating to the Campaign of King Edward the First in that Year, and especially to the Battle of Falkirk* (ed. Henry Gough, London, 1888), afterwards cited as *Scotland in 1298*.
[65] Barrow, *Bruce*, pp. 140–2.
[66] *Chron. Lanercost*, p. 191.
[67] *Scotland in 1298*, pp. xviii, xx, xxv, xxix.
[68] Barron, *War of Independence*, p. 77. [69] *Chron. Lanercost*, p. 191.

restive under Wallace's command. Few of them stayed to fight.[70] Deprived of cavalry support the spearmen in the schiltrons kept up a dour resistance. They were easy targets for the bowmen and were at last overwhelmed by repeated cavalry charges. English chroniclers narrated that thousands of 'the poor common folk'—and even some priests—were slain at Falkirk;[71] they could not grace their accounts of the English triumph—as they had done in writing of Dunbar and were to do in recounting future English victories—with long lists of Scottish nobles who were slain or captured.

From the slaughter of Falkirk Wallace had escaped with his life; but his power was shattered. On the banks of the Forth he resigned his post as guardian.[72] His meteoric rise had hardly been that of a proletarian hero: folk tradition took pains to stress his gentle birth. Yet Wallace was a member of a social class that had not hitherto shown initiative in affairs of state. His personal dominance, regarded as extreme presumption by his enemies, had briefly been enough to break down traditional feudal ties. As a Scottish Cromwell he might have fashioned Scotland anew. Though he failed to do this, his achievement was nonetheless a fundamental one. He had inspired a patriotic resistance among the common folk that outlasted defeat; and it was this resistance that was to frustrate the ambitions of Plantagenet imperialism.

With Wallace's fall from power the way was open for more traditional leaders to reassert themselves. Within a few months Robert Bruce, Earl of Carrick, grandson of the competitor in the Great Cause, was uneasily associated with John Comyn of Badenoch, the 'Red Comyn', son of the Comyn who had been guardian in 1286. They acted as 'guardians of the kingdom of Scotland in the name of the famous prince the illustrious King John, together with the bishops, abbots, priors, earls, barons and other magnates and the whole community of the realm'.[73] Once more the aristocratic community was to the fore; there was no longer mention of 'the army of the kingdom'— the nation in arms. But for the next five years only south-east Scotland, dominated by the castles of Edinburgh, Berwick and Roxburgh, was under firm English control; elsewhere the guardians re-established a Scottish administration.[74] They were aided by two new bishops: in

---

[70] *Chron. Bower*, II. 170, 175.
[71] *Scotland in 1298*, pp. xv, xvi, xxi, xxiii, xxv.
[72] *Chron. Bower*, II. 176.
[73] Barrow, *Bruce*, p. 148.   [74] *Ibid.*, pp. 148–9.

1297 Wallace had induced the chapter of St Andrews to elect William Lamberton as successor to Bishop William Fraser, who had died in France, and in 1299 David Moray, kinsman of the late Andrew Moray, had been elected to the bishopric of Moray; both Lamberton and Moray received consecration at the papal court and were to urge Boniface VIII to support the Scots.[75]

Lamberton returned to Scotland in time to join the Scottish leaders in a lively conference in the forest of Selkirk on 19 August 1299. According to an English spy who witnessed the proceedings, Sir David Graham 'demanded the lands and goods of Sir William Wallace because he was leaving the kingdom without the leave or approval of the guardians'[76]—Wallace, it seems, was preparing to set out on a self-appointed mission to France or Norway.[77] Sir Malcolm Wallace, who was present in the council, defended his brother. Graham gave him the lie and both drew their daggers. The fracas was enlivened when the Red Comyn 'leapt upon the Earl of Carrick [his fellow-guardian] and seized him by the throat', while the Earl of Buchan grappled with Bishop Lamberton 'until the Steward and others went between and stopped this scuffle'.

The upshot was a new organisation of the guardianship: Bishop Lamberton was to be chief guardian with control of the Scottish castles; Bruce and the Red Comyn were to be associated with him as guardians.[78] On 13 November 1299 the three were in the Tor Wood,[79] evidently besieging Stirling Castle (which fell by the end of the year). By May 1300, however, the Earl of Carrick was ousted from the triumvirate. When a parliament was held at Rutherglen on 10 May 1300 there were further alterations. Finally Comyn and Lamberton were both confirmed in office, and the place vacated by Bruce was given to Sir Ingeram Umfraville, who was associated with Balliol and the Comyns.[80]

When Edward invaded Galloway in the summer of 1300 he was met by the Earl of Buchan and the Red Comyn of Badenoch. The two Comyns proposed peace on condition that John Balliol be restored and that Scotsmen be permitted to buy back their forfeited English estates. Edward angrily rejected these terms. He had just besieged and captured Caerlaverock Castle—an exploit recorded in a chivalric

[75] Dowden, *Bishops*, pp. 21-2, 151-2; T. S. R. Boase, *Boniface VIII* (1933), p. 209; Palgrave, *Documents*, I. No. cxlix.
[76] *Nat. MSS. Scot.*, II. No. viii.　　[77] Barrow, *Bruce*, p. 164.
[78] *Nat. MSS. Scot.*, II. No. viii.　　[79] *Cal. Docs. Scot.*, II. No. 1109.
[80] G. O. Sayles, 'The Guardians of Scotland and a Parliament at Rutherglen in 1300', *S.H.R.*, xxiv. 245-50.

French poem by a war-correspondent who accompanied the expedition.[81] Edward continued his march through Galloway to the river Cree, where he put to flight an opposing Scottish force.[82] This encounter, more humiliating than disastrous for the ruling Comyn party, marked the end of the campaign. By 24 August 1300 the king had retired to Sweetheart Abbey. There he received the travel-weary Archbishop Winchelsea of Canterbury who had come to the wilds of Galloway to present the papal bull *Scimus fili* drawn up by Boniface VIII on 28 June 1299—the day of David Moray's consecration in the papal court—and now belatedly released.[83] When Winchelsea burst into the royal presence with the obnoxious bull Edward cut short his sermonising and interjected : 'By God's blood ! For Zion's sake I will not be silent, and for Jerusalem's sake I will not be at rest, but with all my strength I will defend my right that is known to all the world'.[84]

What was known to all the world was less clear to Pope Boniface. In the bull *Scimus fili* he informed Edward of a new issue : 'We in no wise doubt it to be contained in the book of your memory how from ancient times the kingdom of Scotland pertained by full right ... to the foresaid Roman Church, and that, as we have understood, it was not feudally subject to your ancestors ... nor is it so to you.'[85] Feudal subjection had been imposed by force and 'the fear which may befall even the steadfast'. If Edward did indeed claim a right to the kingdom of Scotland he should send envoys to the papal court furnished with proof.[86]

The pope's challenge placed Edward in a procedural dilemma.[87] It was decided that there should be a twofold response : in a counterblast to *Scimus fili* the English barons professed themselves wonderstruck by the pope's allegations ;[88] seven weeks later the result of much intellectual effort [89] was compressed into Edward's own more courteous reply to Boniface. The latter was informed that English claims upon Scotland dated from 'the days of Eli and Samuel the prophet', when fugitives from Troy had extirpated the giants in Albion. From this mythological history (much more acceptable then than it would be now) Edward drew important conclusions, which were reinforced

[81] See *The Siege of Caerlaverock*, ed. Nicholas Harris Nicolas (London, 1828).
[82] Barrow, *Bruce*, pp. 158–60.
[83] T. S. R. Boase, *Boniface VIII*, p. 210 and n.
[84] F. M. Powicke, *The Thirteenth Century*, p. 229.
[85] Stones, *Documents*, No. 28.
[86] *Ibid.*   [87] *Ibid.*, No. 29.
[88] F. M. Powicke, *The Thirteenth Century*, pp. 701–2, 705.
[89] *Ibid.*, pp. 701–2, 705.

by an account of more recent history concluding with Balliol's resignation of the realm into Edward's hands.[90]

While preparing the reply to Boniface Edward had graciously granted a French request that a truce be conceded to the Scots to last until May 1301.[91] In the summer of 1299 Edward had patched up his quarrel with the French and at their insistence had even released King John on condition that he be kept in papal custody.[92] The French set much store upon Balliol's recent release, and yet another alteration in the guardianship reflected the change: by May 1301 there was a sole guardian, Sir John Soulis, who seems to have been nominated by Balliol.[93] A new seal of government was used: on the obverse was the name and title of King John, on the reverse the name and arms of Sir John Soulis. No longer were documents issued in the name of guardians: now they ran in the name of King John himself; the new guardian figured modestly only as witness.[94]

In giving way to French and papal demands for the release of Balliol into papal custody, Edward had intended to exact a threefold price—Balliol's disappearance from politics, an undertaking that the pope would not meddle in Scottish affairs, and a tacit understanding that the French would also drop their interest in Scotland. On each point Edward was to be disappointed. A report made to him affirmed that Bishop Lamberton was displaying a letter under King Philip's seal, 'asserting that there will be no peace between him and the King of England unless the Scots are included. The people are putting their faith in this and in the success which they hope will be obtained by Master Baldred, their spokesman at the court of Rome.'[95]

Master Baldred Bisset, graduate of Bologna, was the most outstanding of the educated clerics—archdeacons, 'officials', deans, and the like—whose talents were employed not only in Scottish ecclesiastical affairs but in administration and diplomacy.[96] Together with two other graduates, Master William of Eaglesham and Master William Frere, archdeacon of Lothian, he was accredited to the papal court by Sir John Soulis to present a *Processus*, or legal argument, combating the English claims. Bisset affirmed that Edward 'refers to

[90] Stones, *Documents*, No. 30.
[91] Palgrave, *Documents*, I. pp. 247–9.
[92] Stevenson, *Documents*, II. Nos. dlxxi, dlxxiv, dlxxix, dlxxx, dlxxxvi.
[93] '*Johannes rex noster per suum custodem ibidem deputatum possidet plenarie totum regnum*' (Bisset's *Processus, Chron. Bower*, II. 218).
[94] Barrow, *Bruce*, pp. 168–9.
[95] Cited *ibid.*, pp. 167–8. [96] *Ibid.*, pp. 166–7, 376–7.

many things but proves few things'.[97] The English historical myths
were countered by equally exotic Scottish ones : Edward, a descendant of 'William the Bastard and his accomplices', had no connection
with the ancient Britons or Trojans; the origins of Scotland were to
be traced to Scota, daughter of Pharaoh, and 'the Egyptians may
claim more right in the kingdom of Scotland than the English'. Bisset
went on to give his own interpretation of recent times. Edward, he
claimed, had craftily taken advantage of Scottish dissensions through
'the fear which may befall even the steadfast'. He had extorted fealty
and homage from 'our king, John Balliol' and afterwards declared
that 'our king willingly confessed that he had committed treasons
and conspiracies against the King of England and . . . had thus rightfully lost his kingdom'. But, affirmed Bisset, 'surely it is not true nor
likely that such a person [Balliol] in so arduous a matter would willingly have uttered such serious and detestable confessions'. On the
contrary, Edward had forcibly taken the seal of the kingdom from
the chancellor and fabricated the letters of confession after sending
Balliol and his son to prison in England. These letters 'our king has
never ratified and never will'.[98] Bisset also appealed to wider issues
than those raised by the various precedents to which king and pope,
and society in general, then attached weight. What had happened in
the past represented no fixed and invariable pattern for subsequent
times : 'in the course of nature, which in itself cannot remain motion-
less, many changes have occurred'. Although this line of thought was
not pursued it was one that cut at the roots of all Edward's arguments,
based as they were on precedent, real or supposed. Moreover Bisset
asserted that by universal law (*de jure communi*) one kingdom ought
not to be subject to another, nor one king to another. In this approach
the *Processus* pointed the way to the Declaration of Arbroath.

The war of words, which was inconclusive, was followed by warfare in Scotland that was equally indecisive. In May 1301 the Anglo-
Scottish truce expired. In July Edward set out on a new campaign
in south-western and central Scotland with his son and heir, the
Prince of Wales.[99] The Scots made disconcerting moves that menaced
the English forces and harassed their attempts to set up an administration in occupied territories. Sir John Soulis was an unquestioned

---

[97] For the text of the *Processus* see *Chron. Bower*, II. 210–8; *Chron. Pluscarden*, I. 205–18.

[98] It is interesting that Sir Thomas Gray, an English knight, gives an account
of Edward's alleged forgery of a letter in the name of the aldermen of Ghent
(*Scalacronica*, pp. 128–9).

[99] Barrow, *Bruce*, pp. 170–71.

patriot and had the support of the Comyns. He showed himself an active leader, had the good sense to avoid a major engagement, and nonetheless kept up a constant pressure on the invaders. To add to Edward's difficulties, an English officer wrote from Edinburgh on 1 October 1301 reporting that 'the King of France's people have taken Sir John Balliol from the place where he was sent to reside by the pope to his castle of Bailleul in Picardy, and some people believe that the King of France will send him with a great force to Scotland as soon as possible.'[100] Edward hastily negotiated with the French and an Anglo-French truce, in which the Scots were to be included, was drawn up at Asnières-sur-Oise.[101] Edward had to agree that the lands, towns and castles he had lately captured in Scotland would be delivered into French custody pending negotiations for a general peace. This showed the price he was willing to pay to avert an immediate Balliol restoration.

Such a prospect was equally disquieting to at least one notable Scot. It is only by doubtful inference that Robert Bruce, Earl of Carrick, can be assumed to have taken an active part in warfare after being dropped from the guardianship in 1300: 'the silence of the sources suggests that he was sulking'.[102] For two years he had probably contented himself with defending his earldom against all outsiders, whether English or Scots. Yet neutrality would no longer suit his purposes when it seemed that a Balliol restoration was at hand; by February 1302 Bruce admitted that it was through evil counsel that he had risen in war against Edward and 'yielded himself to the peace and will of the king in hope of receiving his mercy'.[103]

The terms of the memorandum recording this submission are curious and have inspired controversy.[104] The word 'right' (le droit) is used with a tantalising and needless ambiguity that may have suited both Bruce and Edward. The latter held out some prospect that Bruce would be assisted to obtain, or retain, his 'right'. It has been shrewdly remarked that this 'right' was a 'rainbow of many colours', at the end

---

[100] E. L. G. Stones, 'The Submission of Robert Bruce to Edward I, c. 1301–1302', S.H.R., xxxiv. 122–34, at 132–4.

[101] Text in Palgrave, Documents, i. No. cxxii.

[102] A. A. M. Duncan, op. cit., S.H.R., xlv. 184–201, at 195.

[103] Stones, Documents, No. 32.

[104] For the text of the submission see ibid. Varying explanations of the terms and their background have been given by E. M. Barron, War of Independence, pp. 139–48; E. L. G. Stones, op. cit., S.H.R., xxxiv. 122–34; Barrow, Bruce, pp. 172–5. The best interpretation is that of A. A. M. Duncan, op. cit., S.H.R., xlv. 184–201, at 194–8.

of which Bruce hoped to find a pot of gold.[105] What is clear is that in submitting to Edward, Bruce consulted his own self-interest first and foremost. If, as has been claimed, Bruce was 'one of a number of the country's natural leaders to be inspired by the idea of the community of the realm' [106] he did not at that stage find the idea particularly inspiring.

Although the truce of Asnières brought a halt to warfare in Scotland it did not prevent Edward from consolidating what he had won south of the Forth in the campaign of 1301. The five hundred troops who served in his garrisons [107] were the basis of the military and civil administration of occupied Scotland and they obtained essential co-operation from some Scottish magnates. Had their local influence been hostile, had castles like Dunbar or Turnberry been in nationalist hands, the occupation regime could hardly have held its own. Yet collaboration was forthcoming: Alexander Balliol, a kinsman of King John, engaged to 'keep' the forest of Selkirk for King Edward with 30 men-at-arms, to be supplemented on four days warning with a further 600 footmen, and on eight days warning with 1,000;[108] if the occupation regime worked through Scots who possessed local influence, and if traditional forms were observed, traditional services would be forthcoming. Edward was well aware of this. If those who were 'in his peace' suffered from the exactions of his officials that was not his intention.[109] It is striking that in negotiating the truce of Asnières his envoys showed some concern lest such Scots as were 'the lowly folk of the land' (le menu pueple du pais) [110] should be troubled when (according to the treaty) a French occupation force arrived to take over the lands and castles that Edward had lately won.

No such force ever appeared. On 25 July 1302 King Philip gave feeble excuses to Edward,[111] who must have accepted them with some relief. On 11 July 1302 French military prestige—and the prestige of chivalry in general—had suffered a blow: at Courtrai French nobles had been disastrously defeated by the bourgeois Flemings who had for some time co-operated with Edward. Within a week the news was brought to a jubilant Pope Boniface, already intractably engaged in open quarrel with the French king.[112] Philip had his hands

[105] A. A. M. Duncan, *op. cit.*, *S.H.R.*, XLV. 184–201, at 198.
[106] Barrow, *Bruce*, p. xxi.
[107] *Cal. Docs. Scot.*, II. Nos 1324, 1337.
[108] *Ibid.*, No. 1287.
[109] See *ibid.*, No. 1321.
[110] Palgrave, *Documents*, I. No. cxxi, p. 244.
[111] *Ibid.*, No. cxxiv.   [112] T. S. R. Boase, *Boniface VIII*, pp. 311–12.

full. Boniface began to look on Edward with a kindly eye : 'the end of the elaborate memorials, the historical arguments, was a letter to the Scottish bishops blaming them for being the chief cause of war ; the Bishop of Glasgow in especial was "a stone of offence" who had broken his oath of fealty to the well-beloved King of England'.[113] The Scots had lost the support of the pope and it looked as if they would also lose that of the French king.

To avert this, Sir John Soulis headed a strong delegation to France, leaving John Comyn of Badenoch to act as guardian.[114] Philip wanted to include his Scottish allies in a final peace with England but Edward insisted on their exclusion. Philip's dilemma was solved when King John made a last disastrous decision : in a letter written from Bailleul on 23 November 1302[115] he consented that Philip should have a completely free hand in his negotiations with the English.[116] With this letter in his hand Philip could face the Scottish ambassadors.

On 25 May 1303 Lamberton and his fellow-ambassadors reported the result in a letter from Paris to John Comyn and the community :[117]

> A final peace was made and sworn between the Kings of France and England ... and on the same day it was ordained by the King of France and his council that solemn envoys ... be sent forthwith to the foresaid King of England to draw him back from the war of Scotland, ... if, however, the said King of England be so obdurate, in the manner of Pharaoh, that he will not consent to the truce ... manfully and as one man defend yourselves ... and if you knew how much honour has come to you throughout many regions of the globe from your last fight against the English you would greatly rejoice.

In this last remark the ambassadors were alluding to an engagement fought at Roslin on 24 February 1303. In Scotland the end of the Asnières truce on 30 November 1302 had brought fresh hostilities in which the Scots seized the offensive.[118] Their success had culminated at Roslin, where Simon Fraser and John Comyn defeated the English occupation forces under Sir John Segrave.[119]

---

[113] *Ibid.*, pp. 327–8.   [114] Barrow, *Bruce*, p. 177.
[115] For the date see E. L. G. Stones, *op. cit., S.H.R.*, xxxiv. 122–34, at 130, n. 8.   [116] Stevenson, *Documents*, ii. No. dcxxiv.
[117] *A.P.S.*, i. 454–5. This letter seems to have been intercepted by the English, but a duplicate may have eluded the naval blockade (E. L. G. Stones, 'An Undelivered Letter from Paris to Scotland [1303]?', *E.H.R.*, lxxx, 86–8).
[118] *Cal. Docs. Scot.*, ii. Nos. 1341, 1349; iv. p. 455.
[119] *Chron. Fordun*, i. 333–5.

Hope of an armistice disappeared. Before returning home from France, Bishop Lamberton wrote to Wallace 'and besought him for love of him [the bishop] and with his blessing, that he should with all his power give aid and counsel to the community of the said land of Scotland as he had done formerly'; Lamberton's servants were instructed to back Wallace with supplies.[120] Although Wallace was to serve only as a subordinate, the fact that he was once more in the fray was striking enough to make one English chronicler believe that in 1303, as in 1297, he was the chief instigator of Scottish resistance and had been chosen by the Scots as 'their commander and captain'.[121]

The testing time was at hand. The virtual end of the Franco-Scottish alliance was the signal for Edward to begin the campaign he had long prepared. For the first time since 1294 he could tackle Scotland without having to look backwards at the French king or the pope. He had realised that campaigns south of the Forth and Clyde could bring only limited success. The north, in which no English soldier had set foot since 1298, was a sure retreat for the forces of resistance, a base from which these forces might spring back as soon as an English field army had left the occupying administration uneasily cooped up in the southern castles. To conquer Scotland it was necessary to conquer the north. Yet a crossing of the Forth was perilous, particularly so when Stirling Castle was still in Scottish hands. Lowly carpenters, busy at King's Lynn since February, held the answer to the dilemma. While Edward mustered his army at Roxburgh a fleet of thirty ships set sail conveying three prefabricated pontoon bridges from Lynn to the upper reaches of the Forth.[122] Edward's timing was perfect: he set out from Roxburgh on 30 May 1303; no sooner were the bridges in place than he was across them with some 7,000 troops.[123] By 10 June he had occupied Perth. By September he had reached Kinloss on the Moray Firth. After the north had been subdued he moved south; Dunfermline was to be his headquarters until the spring of 1304.[124]

Time-servers, as always, hastened to make their peace. Edward astutely played on the fears of those who wavered, offering lenient terms to all who would submit before 2 February 1304.[125] On 9 February 1304 English envoys held a parley with John Comyn and his council at Strathord near Perth.[126] Long and detailed personal

[120] Palgrave, *Documents*, I. 333.
[121] Rishanger's Chronicle, cited in Barrow, *Bruce*, pp. 177–8.
[122] *Cal. Docs. Scot.*, II. No. 1375.
[123] *Ibid.*, No. 1599.   [124] Itinerary in *Rot. Scot.*, I. 53.
[125] Palgrave, *Documents*, I. No. cxxviii.   [126] *Ibid.*, No. cxxxi.

terms were drawn up for Comyn and for 'those who are of his accord', who seem to have been equated with the community :[127] the most they would suffer would be exile for a year or two and some pecuniary loss. Comyn was hardly in a position to dictate conditions: all that was saved from the political wreck of Scotland was a stipulation that laws, customs and privileges be observed as in the days of Alexander III; if any law were to be amended it was to be with the assent and advice of the responsible men of the land.[128]

Most Scottish leaders accepted these terms and the lenient personal penalties that went with them; but Sir John Soulis preferred permanent exile in France;[129] and Sir William Oliphant, to whom Soulis had once entrusted custody of Stirling Castle, continued to hold out. The shadowy kingship of King John, together with its practical expression in Scottish guardianship, had come to an end. To fight for an abstraction was alien to the age. Yet something impelled the garrison of Stirling to continue the fight: they were defending the castle, so they claimed, on behalf of the Lion.[130] The Scottish nation could not be seen, and King John had been lost from view, but on the royal standard above the walls of Stirling the lion rampant, symbol of Scottish kingship, could be seen by all. Not until 20 July 1304, after three months of bombardment by thirteen war engines, was the standard lowered. Even unconditional surrender was refused until Edward had bombarded the castle and its inmates for a further day with his fourteenth war engine, the newly constructed 'Warwolf'.[131] The surviving defenders were forced to beg mercy before being sent to English prisons.

In this instance, as in others, Edward showed himself gracious towards time-servers, vindictive towards staunch opponents. Early in March 1304 he had been asked whether terms should be offered to William Wallace (who may have made overtures of submission) [132] and had replied: 'Know that it is not our will that you hold out any word of peace either to him or to any of his company unless they place themselves absolutely in all things at our will, without any reservation whatsoever.' [133] In September Wallace was put to flight

[127] *Ibid.*, No. cxxxiii; Barrow, *Bruce*, p. 182.
[128] Palgrave, *Documents*, I. Nos. cxxxiii, cxxxiv.
[129] Barrow, *Bruce*, p. 182.
[130] *Scalacronica*, p. 127.
[131] *Cal. Docs. Scot.*, II. Nos. 1560, 1599.
[132] See J. G. Bellamy, *The Law of Treason in England in the Later Middle Ages* (afterwards cited as *Law of Treason*), 1970, p. 33.
[133] Stevenson, *Documents*, II. No. dcxxxiii.

in a last skirmish on the banks of the Earn.[134] Thenceforward he was a hunted outlaw with no alternative save unconditional surrender. It was a tribute to the loyalty which he still inspired that he remained at large until 3 August 1305, when he was taken near Glasgow and handed over to the English by Sir John Stewart of Menteith.[135] On 23 August he was brought to Westminster Hall, crowned in mockery with laurel leaves. The five judges followed the procedure that Edward had introduced in treason cases: 'there was no indictment by jury; no appeal by an individual, no accusation by the king's prosecutor but merely a statement of the crimes which the crown held Wallace to have committed, terminating with the judgement'.[136] Dragged on a hurdle to Smithfield he was hanged, cut down while still alive, and butchered; his head was set above London bridge and parts of his dismembered body were sent north for display.

The tragic conclusion of Wallace's career left a far deeper impression than that of any of the other Scots who within the following years would suffer a similar fate. This in itself is a testimony to the unique place that Wallace had held in the hearts and minds of the Scots. Blind Harry the Minstrel was merely echoing a long-established tradition when he declaimed: 'Rycht suth it is, a martyr was Wallace.'[137]

[134] *Cal. Docs. Scot.*, IV. 477.
[135] Barrow, *Bruce*, pp. 191, 193.
[136] J. G. Bellamy, *Law of Treason*, p. 35.
[137] Blind Harry, *Wallace (S.T.S.)* pp. 370-2, at 372; *Chron. Bower*, II. 230. See also Maurice Keen, *The Outlaws of Medieval Legend* (1961), pp. 64-77.

4

KING ROBERT, CIVIL WAR
AND PATRIOTIC WAR

Although Edward had crushed the Scots he was well aware that it was beyond his resources to control Scotland forever through sheer force. It was necessary through fear or favour to obtain the collaboration of Scottish leaders and to allow them a part in some scheme of government and administration. He had begun in March 1304 by summoning them to a parliament at St Andrews,[1] and when an English parliament met at Westminster in March 1305 it was arranged that the community of 'the land'[2] of Scotland should choose ten representatives who would join twenty-one Englishmen nominated by Edward. On 15 September 1305 they met at Westminster and drafted an ordinance for the establishment of a Scottish administration.[3] Many Scottish magnates had their lands restored to them; many Scots were appointed as sheriffs and keepers of castles.[4] Yet there were indications that this latest pacification might not be trouble-free, particularly in the province of Moray :[5] the ordinance of 1305 made mention of 'removing from Scotland those by whom the peace might be disturbed'; those who served Edward were to swear to disclose information about 'disturbances and hindrances . . . to the peace and quiet of the land'; and it was announced enigmatically that 'the Earl of Carrick be ordered to put the castle of Kil-

[1] A. A. M. Duncan, *op. cit.*, *S.H.R.*, xlv. 36–58, at 48–9; H. G. Richardson and G. O. Sayles, 'Scottish Parliaments of Edward I', *ibid.*, xxv. 300–17.
[2] Stones (*Documents*, No. 33) incomprehensibly translates the word *terre* as 'realm'.
[3] Text in *ibid.*, No. 33.
[4] *Cal. Docs. Scot.*, ii. No. 1646.
[5] Barron, *War of Independence*, pp. 196–208.

drummy in the keeping of a man for whom he himself is willing to answer'.[6]

Since 1302, when he had made his peace with Edward, Robert Bruce, Earl of Carrick, had served the English king in warfare,[7] unobtrusively, but well, and seemed to have purged himself of any excessive Scottishness. After the death of his first wife, Isabella, daughter of Earl Donald of Mar, Bruce married Elizabeth, daughter of Richard de Burgh, Earl of Ulster, the most prominent of Edward's Anglo-Irish supporters. Bruce was to pay a hasty visit to England in the spring of 1304 to secure his succession to the family estates which he inherited on the death of his father, the Lord of Annandale.[8] In March 1305, when he was again in England, it was natural that he should be entrusted by Edward with an important part in the preliminary stages of the Scottish pacification. Soon he was nominated to serve on the consultative council of Edward's lieutenant of Scotland,[9] but so were a score of other Scotsmen; it became clear that Edward would not allow Bruce any special position in Scotland. It has been convincingly shown that he had fallen from Edward's favour by the autumn of 1305, and less convincingly that the change was connected with Wallace's execution.[10] A more likely reason is that Edward may have received evidence, still inconclusive, to suggest that Bruce was plotting to obtain the Scottish crown.

Whether or not Edward had learned of it, such evidence did exist: on 11 June 1304, as Stirling Castle was being bombarded, two of the bystanders, Robert Bruce and Bishop Lamberton, concluded a bond of alliance in the nearby abbey of Cambuskenneth.[11] This indenture bound each to aid the other 'against any persons whatsoever'; neither Bruce nor Lamberton would attempt any 'arduous business' without consulting the other. Subsequent events make it clear that the 'arduous business' they had in mind was an attempt to place Bruce on the Scottish throne. Since 1302 he had expected his royal pretensions, of one kind or another, to be promoted by Edward, but nothing of the sort had happened—Edward disappointed the youngest Bruce just as he had disappointed his father and grandfather. By Edward's very success, however, the pathway that might lead the Earl of Carrick to the throne had been cleared of obstacles: although John Balliol was

---

[6] Stones, *Documents*, No. 33.
[7] *Cal. Docs. Scot.*, II. No. 1465; Stevenson, *Documents*, II. No. dcxli.
[8] Barrow, *Bruce*, pp. 199–200, 201–3.
[9] Palgrave, *Documents*, I. No. cxxxv.
[10] See Barron, *War of Independence*, pp. 159–74.
[11] Text in Palgrave, *Documents*, I. No. cxlvi.

to survive until 1313 as an exile in France, his cause had disintegrated; Bruce's rivals, the Comyns, 'had played their game and lost';[12] the institution of guardianship, never very inspiring, had come to an end; if Scottish resistance were to revive, a new leader and a new cause would be required; and Bruce could supply both. Now thirty years old, he was no longer restrained by a conformist father: he himself was head of his family and direct representative of the Bruce claim to the throne.

The Cambuskenneth bond of 1304 had brought Bruce the alliance of the most important figure in the Scottish kirk. There can be little doubt that Bruce sought other allies and, among them, the Red Comyn. In the latter were conjoined the original Comyn claim to the throne—bypassed in 1292—and a Balliol claim: for the Red Comyn was son of King John's sister. It is possible, as tradition has it, that Bruce offered to support the Comyn claim in return for a grant of the Comyn lands, or offered to grant Comyn the Bruce lands in return for support of the Bruce claim; such a transaction would merely have been a repetition of the deal that Bruce's grandfather had made with Count Floris in 1292. But Comyn was not won over. The two had a last interview in the Greyfriars kirk of Dumfries on 10 February 1306; as they stood near the high altar Bruce lost his temper and stabbed the Red Comyn; one or more of Bruce's companions decided to 'mak siccar'.[13] In hot blood Bruce had murdered a rival, committed sacrilege, confirmed suspicions of treason. There was no escape from the consequences save by immediately putting into action whatever plans had been laid for a revolution in Scotland.

The eventual success of Bruce's bid for the throne cannot disguise the fact that it was, at the time, rash, self-willed and premature, and occurred in dismal circumstances. Automatic excommunication was a consequence of the sacrilegious murder of the Red Comyn, which was all too reminiscent of that of Henry of Almain, Edward I's cousin, thirty-five years before. Bruce seems to have petitioned the *curia* for absolution, and on 23 July 1308 the grand penitentiary issued a mandate to the Abbot of Paisley to investigate the case.[14] Whatever the outcome, excommunication was fulminated in England by the summer of 1309,[15] and frequently thereafter. More serious was

[12] Barron, *War of Independence*, p. 152.

[13] Although the picturesque accounts that grew up concerning the events leading to the murder, and the murder itself, must be held in some suspicion (Barrow, *Bruce*, pp. 197–9, 206–8), someone *did* 'mak siccar'.

[14] Text in *Chron. Bower*, II. 231–2.

[15] *Chron. Lanercost*, p. 213.

the inescapable blood feud with the Comyns, their kinsmen and allies, who together composed the most powerful faction in Scotland, with lands and connections scattered from Galloway to Badenoch, Buchan to Argyll. A civil war would have to be waged as well as a patriotic war; and the event that must have been thought necessary for a successful rising—the death of the sick and ageing Edward I—had not yet occurred.

But it was Bruce's opponents, not he himself, who showed confusion and uncertainty. He was resolved to 'take castles, towns and people as fast as he could'; when he crossed the Forth with sixty men-at-arms it was Scone, the traditional site of Scottish enthronements, that was his goal. It was almost incredulously reported : 'he is attempting to seize the realm of Scotland'.[16] On 25 March 1306 he was installed on some substitute ceremonial stone by Countess Isabel of Buchan, sister of the late Earl of Fife, who had arrived to claim the traditional MacDuff privilege of setting a new king on the throne.[17] Two days later Bishop Lamberton, who had 'left the council of the king of England secretly and by night', was induced to celebrate a solemn mass.[18] More enthusiastic than Lamberton, who claimed to have been bullied into support of Bruce, was Bishop Wishart of Glasgow, who was reported to have absolved him from his sins and 'made him swear that he would abide under the direction of the clergy of Scotland'.[19] Edward had good cause for the complaints that he soon addressed to the pope : the abbey of Scone was 'placed in the midst of a perverse nation' and should be removed to a 'safer' place;[20] the perjured Bishop Wishart, who had been granted timber for the steeple of Glasgow Cathedral, had used it to make engines of war that were employed against the English garrison in Kirkintilloch; Wishart had also seized the castle of Cupar and held it 'as a man of war'; David Moray, Bishop of Moray, was announcing in his sermons that it was no less meritorious to fight for Bruce against the English than to set out against the pagans and Saracens in the Holy Land.[21] The latest Scottish rising had ended Edward's policy of pacification. Behind a new policy of ruthless repression [22] was his justified belief that he had been tricked and betrayed. He watched balefully but impo-

---

[16] Stones, *Documents*, No. 34.

[17] This account of Bruce's installation has profited from the helpful advice of Professor A. A. M. Duncan.

[18] Stones, *Documents*, No. 35.

[19] *Ibid.*, Nos. 34, 35.   [20] *Foedera*, I. pt. iv, 65.

[21] Palgrave, *Documents*, I. Nos. cxlviii, cl.

[22] Barrow, *Bruce*, pp. 215–6.

tently from his sickbed in the priory of Lanercost while his subordinates dealt with Bruce.

It is remarkable that despite the handicaps that faced the new Scottish king he soon gathered considerable support. Over a hundred landholders, great and small, from virtually every part of Scotland are recorded as having rallied to his side in 1306.[23] A good number came from Annandale and Carrick where the Bruce family interest was strong; but most came from the region between the Forth and the Moray Firth, perhaps the heartland of Scottish resistance. Recruits from Lothian and the remote regions of the north and west were as yet few, though this is not necessarily to be taken as proof of a lack of patriotism in either the wholly English-speaking south-east or the wholly Gaelic-speaking north-west. Bruce was strong enough in June 1306 to approach Perth, which Aymer de Valence had occupied, but on 19 June Valence overwhelmed the unwary Scots in the wood of Methven. Many of Bruce's leading supporters were taken prisoner; the common folk lost trust in him as a leader and deserted.[24] With the Earl of Atholl and James Douglas—one of the earliest and best of his recruits—the new king sought refuge in the central Highlands. There the hardships and high courage of the fugitives in the summer months of 1306 provided romantic material for John Barbour, who, seventy years later, composed his epic poem, *The Bruce*. As Barbour takes up his tale Bruce and his companions emerge from documentary impersonality and assume flesh and blood.

It is Barbour who incidentally mentions that Bruce had a foster-brother whose death he lamented.[25] Fosterage was then, and for centuries afterwards, a feature in the upbringing of a Gaelic chief, and was associated with instruction in Gaelic language and tradition.[26] Moreover 'the society of Carrick at the end of the thirteenth century remained emphatically Celtic';[27] and, it might be added, so was the language of Carrick until long afterwards.[28] Some aspects of Bruce's future career cannot be convincingly explained unless it is constantly borne in mind that he was at home in a Gaelic setting, and unless it is likewise borne in mind that about half of the population of Scotland still spoke Gaelic. This does not mean that throughout his career

[23] Barron, *War of Independence*, pp. 224–35. Barron's deductions are criticised, perhaps too strongly, by Barrow (*Bruce*, pp. 216–26).

[24] Barbour, *The Bruce*, I. 46.

[25] *Ibid.*, I. 157, 160, 169–71.

[26] *Highland Papers*, I. 206; II. 35, 38; *The Black Book of Taymouth* (Bannatyne Club), pp. xvi–xxii.

[27] Barrow, *Bruce*, p. 36.   [28] See Dunlop, *Bishop Kennedy*, p. 372.

Bruce could count on mass support from the Gaelic Scots, who were then, and thereafter, divided among themselves. They were particularly divided by Bruce himself, for the Comyn blood feud had far greater repercussions in the Gaelic regions, where the Comyn interest was strongest, than in the English-speaking Lowlands. In favourable circumstances Bruce could turn his acquaintance with Gaeldom to good account, but it was a different story in the summer of 1306 when he encountered John of Lorne, son of Alexander MacDougal of Argyll and kinsman of the murdered Comyn. At Dalry, on the borders of Argyll and Perth, the new king was defeated and his remaining military force was dispersed; he had no alternative save to escape from Scotland. Yet the very fact that the MacDougals were Bruce's foes helped to make other Gaelic families his friends: Neil Campbell and the Earl of Lennox aided his escape towards Kintyre, where Angus Og, a leading figure among the MacDonalds, aided his escape by sea from Dunaverty Castle to the nearby island of Rathlin.[29]

Where Bruce spent the remaining months of 1306 is uncertain. The Dowager Queen of Norway, Isabella Bruce, was his sister, and it has been convincingly argued that he took refuge in the Norwegian islands of Orkney.[30] Another view favours his sojourning in the Hebrides and visiting Ulster.[31] The truth is probably that Bruce visited all of these places: the whole western seaboard from Ulster to Orkney was linked by rapid sea communication, and, for various reasons, he had cause to traverse the whole of it. His brothers, Thomas and Alexander, were probably sent to recruit support in Ireland. He himself obtained help from Christina, heiress of the MacRuaridh descendants of Somerled, and 'lady of many lands and islands of the west'.[32] By the end of January 1307 Edward had heard at Lanercost that Bruce and his supporters were in the southern Hebrides, and despatched ships to intercept them.[33] It was too late. By way of Rathlin and Arran Bruce slipped unseen to his own earldom of Carrick and successfully attacked the English garrison at Turnberry.[34]

Bruce's descent on Carrick had been timed to coincide with a landing by his brothers at Loch Ryan on 10 February. Thomas and Alexander Bruce had with them a certain Irish kinglet, and, no doubt, other Irishmen, as well as a chieftain of Kintyre. They were at once

[29] Barrow, *Bruce*, pp. 231–3.
[30] Barron, *War of Independence*, pp. 248–59.
[31] Barrow, *Bruce*, pp. 237–42.   [32] *Ibid.*, pp. 241–2.
[33] *Cal. Docs. Scot.*, II. Nos. 1888, 1889, 1893, 1895, 1896.
[34] Barrow, *Bruce*, pp. 240–1.

attacked and captured by Dungal MacDowell, member of a foremost Galwegian family attached to the Comyns. The two Bruce brothers were sent to Edward at Carlisle. Although Alexander was dean of Glasgow his holy orders did not save him from being hanged and beheaded alongside his brother.[35]

The execution of the two Bruce brothers was only the latest in a series of afflictions that had lately befallen the family and its adherents. After the encounter at Dalry in the summer of 1306 King Robert's queen, his daughter Marjory and other ladies, had been escorted by the Earl of Atholl and Neil Bruce, another of the king's brothers, to the supposed safety of Kildrummy Castle. In September 1306 Aymer de Valence and the Prince of Wales besieged the castle, which had to surrender when a traitor fired the grain stored in the great hall. Neil Bruce was taken prisoner. Already, however, Atholl and the royal ladies had escaped to the north, pursued by Earl William of Ross, who seized the party in the sanctuary of St Duthac at Tain. Atholl was the first earl to be executed in England for over two hundred years.[36] Neil Bruce and Christopher Seton, Bruce's brother-in-law, were also executed. In August 1306 sixteen of Bruce's supporters were summarily tried at Newcastle. On Edward's orders they were not allowed to speak in their own defence and were hanged.[37] With less cause Edward meted out punishment even to his female prisoners. Bruce's queen was to be kept in a manor house, attended by two elderly pages and two servantwomen who were 'elderly and not at all gay'. Christian Bruce was sent to a nunnery; but Mary, another sister of King Robert, was to be securely guarded in a specially-constructed 'cage'—a prison of lattice work—in Roxburgh Castle. It was at first intended that Bruce's young daughter, Marjory, would be kept in a similar construction in the Tower of London. The Countess of Buchan, who had had the effrontery to assist at Bruce's enthronement, was certainly placed in a 'cage' in one of the towers of Berwick Castle. No Scotsman or Scotswoman was to be allowed to speak to her. Four years passed before she was less rigorously confined.[38]

It was probably only on his return to Carrick that Bruce learnt the full measure of the disasters that had been inflicted upon his family and friends. If hitherto he had been merely self-seeking and

[35] *Ibid.*, pp. 240–2.   [36] *Ibid.*, pp. 227–9.
[37] *Cal. Docs., Scot.*, II. No. 1811; J. G. Bellamy, *Law of Treason*, pp. 40–2.
[38] Palgrave, *Documents*, I. No. clv; Barrow, *Bruce*, p. 230.

ambitious he was no longer so. His crown had been too dearly bought by the sacrifices of others. Ambition and chivalric adventure had ended in a tragedy that he was to redeem by identifying himself completely with the highest traditions of kingship and devotion to the cause of independence.

Hard fighting lay ahead, not only against the English but against many a Scot who had reason to hate or reject the new king. From his sickbed in Lanercost Edward mustered forces to surround him as he lurked in the wild country on the borders of Carrick and Galloway.[39] Yet against overwhelming odds Bruce was amazingly successful and inspired confidence by his personal prowess in various feats of arms. The Lanercost chronicler ruefully remarked that 'notwithstanding the heavy vengeance inflicted on the Scots who took part with Robert Bruce, the multitude of those wishing to confirm him in his kingship was increased day by day'.[40] When Aymer de Valence sent a force into the fastnesses of Glen Trool he had the worse of the encounter. In May 1307 there followed a more important engagement at Loudoun Hill in Ayrshire. After heavy losses Aymer de Valence fled.[41] Methven had been avenged. On 15 May, a few days after this episode, one of Edward's adherents wrote from Forfar with the news that Bruce

> never had the good will of . . . the people . . . so much with him as now; and it now first appears that God is openly for him. . . . And they firmly believe, by the encouragement of the false preachers who come from the host, that Sir Robert Bruce will now have his will. . . . For these preachers have told them that they have found a prophecy of Merlin, how after the death of 'le Roi Coveytous' the Scottish people and the Britons [Welsh] shall league together, and have the sovereign hand . . . and live together in accord till the end of the world.[42]

Few people then doubted the relevance of the prophecies of Merlin to contemporary politics; and Edward I could, not unreasonably, be identified as 'the covetous king' to whom the prophet had alluded. He had summoned the English host to muster at Carlisle for a summer campaign. On 7 July 1307, as he reached Burgh-on-Sands on the shores of the Solway, he breathed his last.[43] The tale spread among the Scots that an English knight saw in a vision the demons of hell tormenting the late king.[44]

on the way to fight dies

---

[39] *Cal. Docs. Scot.*, II. Nos. 1895–913, *passim.*
[40] *Chron. Lanercost*, p. 207.   [41] Barbour, *The Bruce*, I. 181–201.
[42] *Cal. Docs. Scot.*, II. No. 1926.   [43] *Chron. Lanercost*, p. 207.
[44] *Chron. Bower*, II. 236.

The removal of the formidable figure of Edward I was an event from which King Robert's cause could draw immeasurable encouragement. The Prince of Wales, now Edward II, inherited all of his father's problems, but little of the forcefulness that alone could master them. Having led the English host as far as Cumnock in Ayrshire he withdrew to England leaving warfare to subordinates.[45] The initiative passed to Bruce; and for some years his chief opponents were scarcely the English but rather the Comyn-Balliol partisans in Galloway, Argyll and the north-east. In September 1307 some Galwegians fled to England with their flocks and herds, while the leading men of Galloway appealed in vain to Edward II for help and were forced to pay ransom to Bruce in order to obtain a short truce.[46] This left him free to move north. In November 1307 he obtained the surrender of Inverlochy Castle and advanced up the Great Glen to confront the Earl of Ross.[47] In a letter to Edward II [48] the earl claimed to have retained three thousand men in his pay for a fortnight. Despite this force, so he claimed, Ross, Sutherland and Caithness would have been overwhelmed if he had not agreed to accept a truce until 2 June 1308. With the three northernmost earldoms neutralised, Bruce destroyed the castle of Inverness, burned the castle of Nairn and won the castle of Urquhart. He next attacked Elgin Castle but made a truce with the defenders. On his way towards the castle of Banff he fell ill and thereafter had to conduct the campaign from a litter.[49] At Slioch, near Huntly, he and his force, which the poet Barbour realistically numbers at seven hundred men,[50] were encountered on Christmas Day 1307 by the troops of John Mowbray and John Comyn, Earl of Buchan, who apparently went off to seek infantry reinforcements. On their return, a week later, Bruce made off. When he left Slioch to cross the mountains towards Mar his foes affected to believe that he was in flight;[51] but they cautiously reinforced the castle of Coull, and some of them were already so demoralised that they moved to safer parts with their cattle; even John Mowbray accepted inclusion

[45] *Chron. Lanercost*, p. 209.
[46] *Ibid.*, p. 210; *Cal. Docs. Scot.*, III. Nos. 14, 15.
[47] See Patricia M. Barnes and G. W. S. Barrow, 'The movements of Robert Bruce between September 1307 and May 1308', *S.H.R.*, XLIX. 46–59, at 56.
[48] The letter is undated but must have been written in November or December 1307 (Barron, *War of Independence*, pp. 283–90).
[49] Barbour, *The Bruce*, I. 212, 214.   [50] *Ibid.*, 217.
[51] Although Patricia M. Barnes and G. W. S. Barrow state that it was John Mowbray who made a 'flight across the mountains' (*op. cit.*, *S.H.R.*, XLIX. 46–59, at 52), I agree with Professor A. A. M. Duncan that the word *fugiendo* in the relevant text (*ibid.*, 58, line 13) refers to Bruce.

in a truce at the end of February 1308. Bruce, or his supporters, then attacked the castles of Mortlach (Balvenie), Tarradale and Skelbo, and renewed the siege of Elgin on 7 April. Nonetheless Mowbray, writing to Edward II on 1 May, claimed to have raised the siege and driven Bruce into retreat.[52] It is clear that up to this time no really decisive engagement had occurred.[53] At Inverurie, however, probably on the date given by the chronicler Bower (23 May 1308)[54] there was a final confrontation. The Earl of Buchan and his supporters seem to have believed that Bruce was helpless as a result of his illness. When the ailing king rose from his sickbed and appeared on horseback, supported by a man on each side, his foes lost heart and were chased all the way to Fyvie. For the Comyns the consequences of the ignominious rout of Inverurie were disastrous : Bruce advertised their ruin by the 'herschip' (ravaging) of Buchan, the centre of the Comyn power. The whole earldom was laid waste, its inhabitants slaughtered. For fifty years afterwards the herschip of Buchan was a tragedy vivid in men's minds.[55] It was clear that Bruce had the will and the power to make his foes pay dearly for their opposition.

While the king continued operations north of Tay, winning Aberdeen in June or July 1308,[56] James Douglas was active in the south-west. On Palm Sunday (7 April) 1308 he had caught off-guard the English troops who occupied his own castle of Douglas and left their slaughtered bodies to burn with the castle and its stores.[57] After this episode of 'the Douglas larder' King Robert's remaining brother, Edward Bruce, was sent with a force of Islesmen to reinforce Douglas for an attack upon Galloway, where the local truce had expired. On 29 June 1308 the leading Galwegians were defeated in a battle on the banks of the Dee (or Cree), the MacDowell stronghold on the Isle of Hestan was burnt, and more fugitives sought safety in Eng-

[52] *Ibid.*, 52-3, 58-9.

[53] The documents published by Patricia M. Barnes and G. W. S. Barrow (*ibid.*, 57-9) do not bear out their suggestion (*ibid.*, 56) that the battle of Inverurie took place in January 1308.

[54] The chronicler Fordun simply assigns the rout of Inverurie to the year 1308 (*Chron. Fordun*, I. 344) which, by modern reckoning, signifies a date after 24 March. Bower's date, which is accepted by A. A. M. Duncan (*Nation of Scots*, p. 19), is indicated by a line of verse :

Anno milleno trecenteno dabis octo,
In festo Domini, quo scandit sidera coeli ...

(*Chron. Bower*, II. 241). In 1308 Ascension Day fell on 23 May.

[55] Barbour, *The Bruce*, I. 219.

[56] Barrow, *Bruce*, p. 259.

[57] Professor A. A. M. Duncan, who has investigated the chronology of this event, has kindly allowed me to make use of his findings.

land.[58] After a herschip of Galloway much of the province was
brought sullenly under King Robert's control. Although the strong
castles in the region remained in the hands of the English for some
time longer,[59] the latter feared in September 1308 that Bruce's partisans were about to raid England itself.[60]

Instead, King Robert confronted the MacDougals of Argyll and,
after an initial campaign in August 1308, obtained the submission of
their chief, Alexander of Argyll.[61] Earl William of Ross, who had
delivered Bruce's queen to the English in 1306, could no longer sit
on the fence after the king had proved his power by daunting Buchan,
Galloway and, apparently, Argyll : on 31 October 1308 he made his
peace with Bruce,[62] promised loyal service, and kept his word. The
submission of Alexander of Argyll proved less trustworthy. His son,
John of Lorne, was playing for time, and early in 1309 wrote to Edward II professing his loyalty.[63] Alluding to the campaign of August
1308 Lorne reported that Bruce had approached Argyll by land and
sea with ten or fifteen thousand men. Against such numbers (which
can hardly have existed outside the writer's imagination) Lorne could
oppose only eight hundred men, of whom five hundred were continually retained in his own pay to secure his borders. He had also
three castles to garrison and had to guard a loch twenty-four miles
long (Loch Awe) on which he was busy building and manning
galleys; the barons of Argyll would give him no aid and he was un-
sure of his neighbours on all sides. He had therefore concluded a truce
with Bruce but was awaiting help from England.

The help never came. Some time between August and October
1309, when the truce with Lorne had either expired or been broken,
King Robert, reinforced by James Douglas, conducted a second
campaign in Argyll. John of Lorne lay with a flotilla of galleys on
Loch Awe and had stationed men on Ben Cruachan to roll boulders
on Bruce's troops as they filed through the pass of Brander that ran
between the mountain and the loch. This stratagem was foiled when

[58] *Chron. Lanercost*, p. 212; *Chron. Fordun*, I. 345; Barbour, *The Bruce*, I.
228.
[59] *Rot. Scot.*, I. 80.   [60] *Ibid.*, 57.
[61] Professor Duncan has pointed out that there were two distinct campaigns
in Argyll. The chronology of the following account of these campaigns is based
upon his investigations, of which he has kindly allowed me to make use.
[62] *A.P.S.*, I. 477.
[63] The undated letter (*Cal. Docs. Scot.*, III. No. 80), which has been assigned
by Professor Duncan to early 1309, refers to events six months earlier, since when,
so Lorne claimed, he had been confined to a sick bed—perhaps by a diplomatic
illness.

Douglas led a force of archers to gain the heights of Ben Cruachan and take Lorne's men in the rear.[64] The battle of the pass of Brander broke the power of the MacDougals just as Inverurie had broken that of the Comyns: within a few months John of Lorne, his father, and Bishop Andrew of Argyll, had joined the Comyns as refugees at the English court.

The chronicler Fordun saw in Bruce's victory at Inverurie the turning point in the king's career.[65] Yet it was not that sole battle but rather his extraordinary mobility and his strategy of neutralising his foes and crushing them one by one that wrought the incredible change in Bruce's fortunes. In February 1307 he had been a hunted man in the wilds of Carrick and Galloway; by the end of 1309 he was master of more than two-thirds of Scotland. In Perth, Dundee and Banff, which could be reinforced and victualled by sea, English garrisons still held out; but so long as they were not supported by an English field army they were helpless. Bruce had won back the north, the loss of which had broken the back of Scottish resistance in 1303. The fortunes of war might fluctuate south of Forth, but the north, with its reserves of manpower and its defences of river, loch and mountain, was the hinterland that had to be secured before war against the English could be successfully waged.

Bruce's strategy and tactics, however brilliant, could hardly have won him success had he been faced by an overwhelmingly hostile population in the north. It is remarkable that a letter written from Forfar on 15 May 1307[66] had warned the English king that the men of those parts, encouraged by 'false preachers', were ready to rise with Bruce; and if the latter moved 'towards the parts of Ross' he would find people 'all ready at his will more entirely than ever'. The sequel bore out the truth of this warning: while the northern magnates were more or less hostile to Bruce, lesser landholders, perhaps particularly those of Moray,[67] were ready to accept him as king. It has been suggested that 'the most revealing point in the new evidence about 1307–8 is the statement that the Earl of Buchan [rectius John Mowbray] ... during a truce before the battle of Inverurie, had punished ... freeholders for supporting the king', and that 'the foundation of this war was a capacity to by-pass the reluctant traditional leaders of the "community" and to appeal to and command the opinion of other social ranks in the "nation" '.[68] Their adherence must have

[64] Barbour, The Bruce, I. 238–42.   [65] Chron. Fordun, I. 344–5.
[66] Cal. Docs. Scot., II. No. 1926.
[67] Barron, War of Independence, passim.
[68] Duncan, Nation of Scots, pp. 20, 21.

been increasingly forthcoming as Bruce revived the traditional functions and authority of the Scottish monarchy. It was perhaps typical
that when a parliament was held at Inchture in the Carse of Gowrie
in April 1312 an undertaking was given that he would follow the
traditional practice of dealing with the burghs through his chamberlain.[69] But if Bruce cultivated popular support he did not neglect to
win the adherence of those aristocrats who were aloof, uncommitted,
or hostile. One striking example was that of Sir John Stewart of
Menteith who had delivered Wallace into the hands of Edward I.
Although it was rumoured that Sir John plotted to double his
notoriety by betraying Bruce,[70] the plot, if any, came to nothing:
little by little, Sir John proved his loyalty and took high place among
the king's adherents.[71] More important was the adherence (reluctant
at first) of Thomas Randolph, nephew of Bruce but once a knight of
Balliol.[72] By 1312 Randolph had so proved his worth that the king
rewarded him with a specially created earldom of Moray.[73]

No less skilled in politics than in warfare, Bruce used his first
parliament (held at St Andrews in March 1309) to mount a publicity campaign to advertise his kingship. The necessary propaganda
was probably devised by Bernard of Linton, who was to hold the
office of chancellor from 1308 to 1328, together with the dignity of
Abbot of Arbroath to which he was appointed in 1311. On 17 March
1309 a carefully prepared declaration was issued from St Andrews in
the name of the Scottish prelates and clergy.[74] This document let it be
inferred that John Balliol had been only *de facto* king, wrongfully
installed by the English in place of the rightful Bruce claimant. After
many afflictions the Scottish people

> agreed upon the said Lord Robert, the king who now is, in whom the
> rights of his father and grandfather to the foresaid kingdom . . . still
> exist and flourish entire; and with the concurrence and consent of the
> said people he was chosen to be king, . . . and with him the faithful
> people of the kingdom will live and die, as with one who, possessing the
> right of blood, and endowed with the other cardinal virtues, is fitted to
> rule . . . since . . . he has by the sword restored the realm.

[69] Barrow, *Bruce*, p. 421.
[70] *Chron. Bower*, II. 243, n.
[71] Barrow, *Bruce*, pp. 401–2.
[72] *Foedera*, I. pt. iii, 95; Barbour, *The Bruce*, I. 236–7.
[73] Barron, *War of Independence*, pp. 397–8.
[74] Text in *A.P.S.*, I. 460. G. W. S. Barrow has shown (*Bruce*, p. 262, n. 4), that
the document was initially issued at the St Andrews parliament, not (as previously
thought) at a general council of the clergy held at Dundee.

A similar declaration was issued in the name of the nobles.[75] In addition to the acclamation of Bruce's kingship—ingeniously balanced on the four pillars of inheritance, virtue, election and conquest—another floridly-composed document, dated at St Andrews on 16 March,[76] answered a flattering letter which had been sent by the French king. There was to be no formal renewal of the Franco-Scottish alliance for another seventeen years; but Philip's friendly overture gave the impression that the alliance might readily be renewed in the event of future hostilities between France and England.

Nor was the French king alone in taking stock of the re-emergence of the Scottish kingdom. In vain Edward II wrote to Count Robert of Flanders in October 1309 protesting that Scottish traders and their German associates were carrying arms and victuals from the Flemish towns to Scotland:[77] the profits of warfare[78] and the seizure of some £7,000 of crusading tenths[79] gave King Robert the cash to pay the seamen and traders—Scots, German and Flemish—who from their bases in Flanders ran the English blockade to carry vital imports to Scotland, and who simultaneously waged a naval war of their own against English shipping in the North Sea.[80]

The war at sea, used by all participants as an excuse for piratical lawlessness, also extended to northern waters, where Scottish raiders captured and held to ransom the Norwegian seneschal of Orkney.[81] By this time Eric II, who had shown too ambitious an interest in Scottish affairs, had been succeeded by his brother, Haakon V. King Robert's own sister, Isabella Bruce, long outlived Eric, and, as Queen Dowager of Norway, no doubt used her influence to settle Scoto-Norwegian differences. The outcome was the conclusion of a treaty at Inverness on 29 October 1312.[82] This confirmed the annual payment of a hundred marks promised in the treaty of Perth of 1266 in return for the cession of the Western Isles.

The increasing recognition that Bruce won in Scotland and abroad reflected his success in winning the civil war and transforming it into a patriotic war. Circumstances played into his hands by giving him a powerful (though unwitting) ally in the person of Piers Gaveston. Edward II's passion for this Gascon favourite was the chief factor in the discord that existed between the English king and his magnates. The lack of co-operation between them, coupled with Edward's own

---

[75] Barrow, *Bruce*, p. 264.   [76] *A.P.S.*, I. 459.   [77] *Rot. Scot.*, I. 78.
[78] P. 96 below.
[79] D. E. Easson, *op. cit.*, *Scot. Church Hist. Soc. Recs.*, XI. 63–81, at 72.
[80] *Foedera*, I. pt. iv, 177.   [81] *A.P.S.*, I. 101.   [82] *Ibid.*

inadequacy as a ruler, meant that during the crucial period of civil war in Scotland Bruce had little to fear from England. It was not until the late summer of 1310 that Edward set out from Berwick to show the flag in regions that had lately submitted to Bruce and to entice the latter into battle.[83] All the marching and counter-marching of Edward's troops was in vain: according to the Lanercost chronicler, Bruce 'in his customary manner fled and did not dare to encounter them'.[84] It would be incorrect to think that Bruce always avoided battle: the engagements at Loudoun Hill, Inverurie, and the pass of Brander, as well as others still to be fought, all prove the contrary. On the other hand he did not wage battle indiscriminately: other less chivalric methods of warfare were less risky and might be just as effective. Avoiding confrontation with the main English army, he was nonetheless active in guerrilla warfare, sending detachments of his men to harass English foragers.[85] In 1310 his strategy proved its efficacy. By December Edward was back in Berwick. Although inept he was also stubborn and was to remain there until the summer of 1311,[86] when he and his favourite returned to England to face the truculent opposition of the lords ordainers and a state of virtual civil war that lingered on even after Gaveston had been murdered on 19 June 1312.[87] Edward's departure and his domestic troubles gave King Robert the chance to carry warfare into the north of England, which had been left unharmed since Wallace's invasion in 1297. On 12 August 1311 he crossed the Solway, raided Tynedale, and returned with a great booty in the shape of cattle.[88] This cattle raid was followed on 8 September by a longer raid into Northumberland. As a result its inhabitants paid £2,000 for a truce up to 2 February 1312.[89] Thus the mere demonstration of Scottish power extracted an income almost comparable to the peacetime revenues of the Scottish crown. Nor were the extortionate truces that neutralised northern England accompanied by the disbandment of Bruce's forces: a truce in one region was merely the signal for an attack upon another; and, despite his far-reaching activities elsewhere, Bruce did not ignore the chief object of his strategy—the expulsion of the English from the strongholds they still occupied in Scotland itself.

By 1312 in the whole region north of Forth only the garrisons of Perth and Dundee remained as a symbol of English power. The fall

---

[83] *Cal. Docs. Scot.*, III. Nos. 166, 171; *Chron. Lanercost*, p. 214.
[84] *Chron. Lanercost*, p. 214.   [85] *Vita Edwardi*, p. 12.
[86] *Rot. Scot.*, I. 103.
[87] May McKisack, *The Fourteenth Century*, pp. 11–31.
[88] *Chron. Lanercost*, p. 216.   [89] *Ibid.*, pp. 216–7.

of Dundee in the spring of 1312 [90] gave the Scots control of the estuary of the Tay and cut off Perth from the sea. To win the town Bruce resorted to the strategem of a feigned withdrawal. For a week he and his men were not to be seen and the defenders relaxed their vigilance. Then the besiegers stole back under cover of darkness. On the night of 7–8 January 1313 the king was the first to plunge up to his neck in the icy waters of the moat and set his scaling ladder against the ramparts. These and the other fortifications were deliberately destroyed after the capture of the town.[91] The fall of Perth was followed by the last phase in the Scottish recovery of the south-west : on 7 February 1313 Sir Dungal MacDowell, the king's hardened foe, surrendered Dumfries Castle,[92] by which time the other castles of the area—Loch Doon, Lochmaben, Caerlaverock, Dalswinton, Tibbers and Buittle— seem to have fallen to the Scots.[93] King Robert could leave a thoroughly subdued Galloway when he left for his conquest of the Isle of Man in May 1313.[94] On his route from Perth to Dumfries the king seems to have detailed part of his army under Edward Bruce to lay siege to Stirling Castle.[95] The tedium of a siege that began in Lent and lasted into the summer [96] probably weighed heavily upon the king's brother, who is represented as more chivalric [97] than sagacious. Sir Philip Mowbray, the Scottish knight to whom Edward II had entrusted the custody of Stirling, offered to surrender if an English army failed to appear within three miles of the castle by Midsummer Day 1314. Although a similar pact (deeply resented by Edward II) seems to have put Dundee in Scottish hands,[98] Edward Bruce has been criticised for accepting Mowbray's terms and is reported by Barbour to have been rebuked by King Robert.[99] Since 1311 no English army had taken the field in Scotland. The year-long respite granted to the defenders of Stirling was a call to arms that even the lethargic Edward II and his discordant barons might not ignore.

While an uneasy truce settled upon Stirling, the Scottish leaders took the offensive against other English garrisons, by this time virtually restricted to Lothian, the area between Forth and Tweed. In the

[90] Barron, *War of Independence*, pp. 388–9.
[91] Barbour, *The Bruce*, I. 221–6.   [92] *Cal. Docs. Scot.*, III. No. 304.
[93] *Chron. Fordun*, I. 346.
[94] A. W. Moore, 'The Connexion between Scotland and Man', *S.H.R.*, III. 393–409, at 404–6.
[95] Barron, *War of Independence*, p. 420.
[96] Barbour, *The Bruce*, I. 269–70.
[97] 'Of [his] hye vorshipe and manheid men mycht mony romanys [romances] mak' (Barbour, *The Bruce*, I. 227).
[98] *Rot. Scot.*, I. 108.   [99] Barbour, *The Bruce*, I. 272–3.

summer of 1313, the English, or their Scottish allies, still held Linlithgow, Livingston, Edinburgh, Luffness, Dirleton, Dunbar, Yester,
Berwick, Roxburgh, Jedburgh, Cavers, and perhaps Selkirk.[100] At
first sight this impressive combination of mutually-supporting major
and minor fortresses might well seem a unique obstacle, more formidable than any that Bruce had hitherto encountered. But the
castles of Lothian straggled in a crescent-shaped formation following
the coastline of the Forth and the North Sea and the valley of the
Tweed; they had the advantage of easy accessibility to the sea, but
the land routes that connected them were vulnerable to attack from
an opposing force operating from the Lammermuirs, the uplands that
projected into the concavity of the fortified crescent. Berwick, the
strategic link between the maritime fortresses and those of the Tweed
valley, was singled out for attack as early as 6 December 1312; the
barking of a dog alarmed the sleeping town and the projected assault
was abandoned.[101] The failure at Berwick was more than compensated by success at Linlithgow, Roxburgh and Edinburgh. Credit for
the capture of the peel of Linlithgow in September 1313 went to
William Binnock, a 'stout carle' or husbandman, who concealed
armed men in his hay waggon and brought it to a halt in the entry to
the peel so that the gate could not be shut nor the portcullis lowered.[102]
On the night of Shrove Tuesday (19 February) 1314 James Douglas
led his men, mantled in black so that they might be mistaken for
cattle, up to the walls of Roxburgh. The capture of this castle by
Douglas stirred Thomas Randolph to make an attempt on Edinburgh. On the night of 14 March 1314 some of the attackers diverted
the garrison's attention to the gateway while Randolph and others,
guided by a local man named William Francis, climbed the precipit-
ous northern face of the castle rock. Edinburgh Castle, like Linlithgow and Roxburgh, was dismantled on Bruce's orders 'lest the English
ever afterwards might lord it over the land by holding the castles'.[103]
    It was not only Englishmen who had held the castles of Lothian:
in contrast to the small number of Lothian gentlefolk who are known
to have joined Bruce by 1312 [104] there was a much larger number who
drew English pay to serve in the garrisons of Linlithgow, Roxburgh
and Edinburgh. At Linlithgow it was a local landholder, Sir Archi-

[100] Barron, *War of Independence*, p. 414.
[101] *Chron. Lanercost*, p. 220.   [102] Barbour, *The Bruce*, I. 244–7.
[103] *Chron. Lanercost*, p. 223; *Scalacronica*, p. 140; Barbour, *The Bruce*, I. 252–67; *Chron. Fordun*, I. 346.
[104] G. W. S. Barrow (*Bruce*, p. 269) seems to lay undue emphasis on this group.

bald Livingston, who had commanded the garrison.[105] Such instances give some point to the argument that the area between Forth and Tweed, the most intensively anglicised district of Scotland, was a region apart, with little sympathy for the cause that Bruce represented.[106] Part of the explanation lies in the attitude of the chief magnate of Lothian. Patrick, Earl of March and holder of the strategically-placed castle of Dunbar, had consistently adhered to the English between 1296 and his death in 1308; his successor, another Patrick, followed his father's policy. Another influential landholder, Sir Adam Gordon, served as justiciar of Lothian on behalf of Edward II.[107] Nominally, at least, Lothian was loyal to Edward, and many of its inhabitants were therefore regarded as disloyal by King Robert. Surviving petitions [108] sent from Lothian to the English king show that the inhabitants were forced to pay blackmail to Bruce in the same fashion as those of Northumberland or Durham. By 1313, however, some men of Lothian had evidently defected to Bruce, with the result that the remainder were held in suspicion by the garrisons of the English-held castles. The garrison of Berwick raided the earldom of March and carried off thirty persons for ransom besides four thousand sheep and other livestock; finally Sir Adam Gordon was arrested and released only on giving pledges for his appearance before the English king.[109]

When Sir Adam appeared at Westminster he brought with him a petition asking Edward to provide redress for the miscellaneous grievances of 'the people of Scotland'.[110] Edward's answer on 28 November 1313 was to urge his adherents in Scotland to persevere in their loyalty towards him : by midsummer 1314 he would muster an army at Berwick for their relief.[111] The appeal from Lothian, coupled with the situation at Stirling, had persuaded Edward once more to face the insurgent Scots. By 27 May 1314 he had learned that the latter were gathering a multitude of footmen 'in strong and marshy places (where access for horses will be difficult) between us and our castle of Stirling'.[112]

Edward's military and naval preparations, which had begun in

---

[105] *Cal. Docs. Scot.*, III. 406–11.
[106] Barron, *War of Independence*, pp. 188–9, 366–8.
[107] *Cal. Docs. Scot.*, III. Nos. 211, 299, p. 403.
[108] *Ibid.*, Nos. 186, 337. G. W. S. Barrow (*Bruce*, p. 269) assigns the first of these to 1312.
[109] *Cal. Docs. Scot.*, III. No. 337.
[110] *Ibid.*, Nos. 337, 344·   [111] *Rot. Scot.*, I. 114.   [112] *Ibid.*, 126–7.

March 1314 [113] had been preceded by a superficial reconciliation with his intransigent baronial opponents.[114] An imposing army of between fifteen and seventeen thousand footmen and between two and three thousand heavy cavalry [115] set out from Berwick and Wark on 17 and 18 June, and by way of Lauderdale reached Edinburgh a day or two later.[116] Further hard marching to meet the deadline of 24 June brought the English king to within three miles of Stirling Castle with one day to spare. He was met by its commander, Sir Philip Mowbray, who affirmed that the castle was thus technically 'rescued' in accordance with the bargain made with Edward Bruce.[117] But between the castle and the rescuing army lay the army of King Robert, probably between five and ten thousand in number. The 'rescue' could be turned into a triumph if the Scots were put to flight or defeated.

Bruce had by no means committed himself to waging battle. After mustering at the Tor Wood he had fallen back to the high ground of the New Park, two miles south of Stirling Castle, and there he kept his troops in a formation that hinted at withdrawal: the vanguard under Thomas Randolph, Earl of Moray, lay beside St Ninian's kirk, nearest Stirling; it was the rearguard under the king that faced the oncoming English; between the vanguard and rearguard lay the two other Scottish battalions, one under Edward Bruce, the other nominally under the youthful Walter the Steward but actually under the command of Douglas; at some distance to the west lay the 'small folk and poverale'—ill-armed footmen and camp followers whom Bruce kept apart from his fighting troops.[118] The high and wooded ground of the New Park screened the disposition of the Scottish troops and gave them some security from the attack of cavalry and archers. As a further precaution pits were dug and calthorps (three-pronged iron spikes) were scattered [119] where the road from Falkirk crossed the Bannock burn to enter the New Park on its way to Stirling.

It was here that an engagement took place in the afternoon of 23 June 1314. An English advance party was already in sight as King

[113] Ibid., 115–28; W. M. Mackenzie, The Battle of Bannockburn (1913), pp. 21–2.
[114] Vita Edwardi, p. 43.
[115] The numbers of the opposing forces are a matter of estimate. See Barrow, Bruce, pp. 293–8; J. E. Morris, Bannockburn (1914), p. 41; W. M. Mackenzie, The Battle of Bannockburn, pp. 21–32.
[116] Mackenzie, The Battle of Bannockburn, pp. 39–41.
[117] Scalacronica, p. 141.
[118] Barbour, The Bruce, I. 284–5, 288.
[119] Ibid, 286–7.

Robert rode out to supervise his frontal positions. Sir Henry de Bohun, nephew of the Earl of Hereford, spurred his charger forward hoping to win incomparable chivalric fame by killing or capturing the Scottish king. Though mounted on a palfrey and armed with only a battle-axe Bruce was too much of a knight to evade the encounter. As Bohun charged ponderously with his lance at the ready, the king sidestepped and with his axe cleft Bohun's skull. This was the signal for Bruce's battalion to drive back the dismayed English troops.[120] Though it momentarily cast the fate of Scotland into jeopardy the king's personal feat of arms enhanced the chivalric prestige that was essential to his success. Shortly before Bruce had displayed his personal prowess the morale of his followers had already been raised when Randolph snatched victory from what might have been a reverse. Sir Robert Clifford and Sir Henry Beaumont, at the head of some three hundred horsemen, had outflanked the higher Scottish positions by riding along the Carse in the direction of Stirling. Moray was reproved by Bruce for neglecting to check this manoeuvre. It was not too late: the earl led his infantry battalion downhill to the open country. By itself, unsupported by archers, the cavalry proved helpless before the compact hedgehog formation of the Scottish schiltron. Clifford withdrew ignominiously and Moray returned in triumph to his former position.[121] The incident demonstrated that in certain circumstances footmen might attack and rout cavalry. Nonetheless, when Sir Alexander Seton, a Lothian landholder, defected to the Scottish camp that night, he found its leaders disposed to withdraw to the Lennox. They changed their minds when Seton reported the poor morale of the English and the comfortless position in which they now found themselves.[122]

During the evening and night of 23–24 June the English army had abandoned the highway and 'come out on a plain fronting the water of Forth, beyond Bannock burn, a bad, deep, marshy stream, where the said host of the English settled down'.[123] Barbour confirms this account when he represents the English as making their bivouacks on a 'hard feld' somewhere 'doune in the Kers [Carse]'.[124] It is thus clear that they spent the night on a field that lay in the triangle of low-lying ground hemmed in on one side by the loops of the wide

---

[120] *Ibid.*, 298–300; *Vita Edwardi*, p. 51.
[121] Barbour, *The Bruce*, I. 292–7, 302; *Chron. Lanercost*, p. 225; *Scalacronica*, p. 141.
[122] *Scalacronica*, p. 142.
[123] *Ibid.*, 141–2.
[124] Barbour, *The Bruce*, I. 313, 314.

Forth and on the other by the Bannock burn, besides being further restricted by 'sykes' (marshes) and 'pollis' (pows or streams) of which the Bannock burn (an obstacle that the English had crossed only with some difficulty) was the most notable.[125] Whatever Edward's plans in selecting such a camp site they can hardly have envisaged the possibility of a full-scale Scottish attack. From the encounter between Moray's spearmen and Clifford's cavalry Edward had learned nothing and Bruce had learned much. The confined English position—'the gret stratnes of the plass'[126]—gave the Scots the opportunity of a narrow battlefront to deploy their inferior numbers in a repetition of Moray's tactics.

At daybreak on 24 June the three battalions commanded by Edward Bruce, Moray, Douglas and the Steward (the last two both newly knighted)[127] bore down on the cramped English position. The Earl of Gloucester lost his life leading the English vanguard in a fruitless cavalry charge against the leading Scottish schiltron,[128] that of Edward Bruce. When some of the English archers were at last put in an effective position they were taken in the flank by Sir Robert Keith's small force of light cavalry.[129] At this point King Robert threw in his own battalion. It numbered in its ranks Angus Og, all the men of Carrick, Argyll, Kintyre and the Isles, as well as a 'mekill rout' of armed men from the 'playne land' or Lowlands.[130] Doggedly the four Scottish schiltrons pushed forward like huge hedgehogs, pressing the ten English battalions into one helpless horde of horses and men. Eventually the rear ranks began to flee across the Bannock burn. In the contagious panic men fell and were trodden underfoot until the banks were bridged from side to side by the corpses. The inconspicuous stream 'that sa cummyrsum was of slyk [mud] and depnes for

[125] *Ibid.*, 283, 313, 314. There has been much controversy over the nature of the surface of the Carse and the site of the English encampment, since these factors more or less determined the site of the battle. See Sir Herbert Maxwell, 'The Battle of Bannockburn', *S.H.R.*, XI. 233–51; Thomas Miller, 'The Site of the New Park in relation to the Battle of Bannockburn', *ibid.*, XII. 60–75; J. D. Mackie, 'The Battle of Bannockburn', *ibid.*, XXIX. 207–10. The battlefield suggested by G. W. S. Barrow (*Bruce*, map 11) seems unacceptable: it includes steeply sloping ground—a circumstance not mentioned by the early writers—and is certainly not 'doune' in the Carse, however the Carse is defined. The sites favoured by W. M. Mackenzie (*The Battle of Bannockburn*, p. 74) and by General Sir Philip Christison ('Bannockburn—23rd and 24th June 1314. A Study in Military History', *Proc. Soc. Antiq. Scot.*, XC. 170–79) seem more likely.
[126] Barbour, *The Bruce*, I. 315.
[127] *Ibid.*, 314.
[128] *Ibid.*, 318; *Chron. Lanercost*, p. 226; *Vita Edwardi*, pp. 53–4.
[129] Barbour, *The Bruce*, I. 324.   [130] *Ibid.*, 285.

till pas', eventually gave its name to the battle for the simple reason that its existence turned the English defeat into a disaster.[131] The Scottish campfollowers added to the confusion of the stricken army by arriving on the scene to massacre and despoil the fugitives.[132] King Edward and some of the cavalry avoided the perils of the Bannock burn by escaping along the banks of the Forth to Stirling Castle. A cold welcome awaited them : Sir Philip Mowbray announced his intention of surrendering to Bruce. Edward and his entourage had to make a wide detour before fleeing eastward, pursued by Sir James Douglas. The king was chased to Dunbar where he boarded a small boat and sailed ignominiously south.[133]

[131] *Ibid.*, 335; *Scalacronica*, p. 142; *Chron. Lanercost*, p. 226; *Vita Edwardi*, pp. 53–4; G. W. S. Barrow's arguments (*Bruce*, pp. 304–9 that the battle was initially named not after the *burn* but after a *locality* 'Bannok or Bannockburn' do not provide conclusive evidence of the site of the battle.

[132] Barbour, *The Bruce*, I. 335.

[133] *Ibid.*, 336, 343–6; *Scalacronica*, p. 142; *Chron. Lanercost*, p. 227; *Vita Edwardi*, p. 54.

5

THE AFTERMATH OF BANNOCKBURN

So striking was the Scottish triumph at Bannockburn that its significance has been understandably exaggerated. The Scots can look back over a dismal vista of defeats to an unique occasion when they won the field in a full-scale pitched battle that amounted to a long-prepared duel between two incipient nations and their respective kings. Bannockburn was decisive in so far as the English, despite a supreme effort, had failed to win victory. It was indecisive in so far as they did not give up hope of subduing the Scots. Far from ending the war, Bannockburn scarcely marked the midway point. Yet the positive results of the battle were not negligible: it gave a boost to Scottish morale that survived later defeats and still influences the Scottish outlook; it gave a temporary military ascendancy that Bruce was to prolong and exploit as long as he lived.

At first the exploitation of the victory was easy enough. Save for the town and castle of Berwick all Scotland was recovered from the English. In the summer of 1314 James Douglas and Edward Bruce raided as far south as Richmond. Though Sir Thomas Gray and Sir Andrew Harclay staunchly held Norham and Carlisle, the north of England suffered from a Bannockburn complex. For a time there was talk of peace. But nothing resulted save an exchange of the captive Earl of Hereford in return for Bishop Wishart, King Robert's wife, his sister Christian, his daughter Marjory, and his nephew Donald of Mar.[1] Donald set out for Scotland but was fond of Edward II and turned back at Newcastle.

As the chances of immediate peace receded, a Scottish parliament met in Cambuskenneth Abbey, almost on the field of Bannockburn. There, on 6 November 1314, it was

---

[1] *Cal. Docs. Scot.*, III. Nos. 371, 372, 373, 393, 402, 403.

agreed, finally adjudged and ... made statute ... that all who have died
in the field ... against the faith and peace of the said lord king [Robert
Bruce] or who on the said day have not come to his faith and peace ... .
are to be disinherited forever of lands and tenements and all other
status within the realm of Scotland. And they are to be held in future as
foes of the king and kingdom, debarred forever from all claim of heritable right or of any other right whatsoever on behalf of themselves and
their heirs.[2]

Despite its ostensibly immutable character this act of disinheritance
was in practice an enabling statute that was not allowed to stand in
the way of reconciliation. King Robert was to show himself ready to
welcome back any disinherited Scot willing to serve him and him
alone. He was not ready to accept those who wished to regain their
Scottish lands, keep their lands in England, and serve two kings.

Now that Bruce's position within Scotland was uncontested it remained to secure the permanence of his dynasty. As yet, the king had
no legitimate son. His heir presumptive was his daughter Marjory,
just returned from captivity in England and still unmarried. The
probability of her accession was unwelcome. In April 1315 a parliament or council met in the parish kirk of Ayr where, with the consent
both of the king and his daughter, a tailzie (entail) was drawn up: if
King Robert should die leaving no legitimate son the crown was to
pass not to Marjory but to the king's only surviving brother, Edward
Bruce, a 'vigorous man ... highly skilled in warlike deeds'.[3]

The change in the succession was also the prelude to a change in
military and political strategy. Although the spring of 1315 had
brought a renewal of raids in which the Scots penetrated to the gates
of York, Edward II neither continued the war nor tried to end it. An
answer to the military stalemate was the opening of a second front
that might force the English to accept peace. The assembly at Ayr
that had just recognised Edward Bruce as heir presumptive to the
Scottish crown must also have sanctioned preparations for an expedition to install him as High King of Ireland. For although the English
administration at Dublin had furnished men and provisions for Edward I and Edward II in their Scottish campaigns[4] the native Irish
resented English rule and might be persuaded to co-operate with the
Scots. If Edward Bruce were successful there might even follow a
dynastic union between Scotland and Ireland. Thus from the outset

---

[2] *A.P.S.*, i. 464.   [3] *Ibid.*
[4] J. F. Lydon, 'The Bruce Invasion of Ireland', *Historical Studies*, iv. 111–25,
at 122. I am indebted to Dr. Lydon for helpful comments on this subject.

the Irish venture presented far-reaching opportunities, and these were related to the existence of two cultures, one of them Gaelic, within Scotland itself. The significance of the Gaelic regions in Bruce's career helps to explain his prolonged interest in Ireland. At some stage he addressed letters to the Irish 'kings' and clergy, asserting that Scots and Irish shared a common origin, a common language and common customs; the 'kings', prelates and inhabitants of all Ireland were asked to co-operate with Scottish envoys so that 'our people' (*nostra nacio*)—and by that Bruce seems to have meant a joint people of Scots and Irish—should be restored to its former freedom.[5]

When Edward Bruce landed in Ulster his prospects seemed bright. Having won an engagement at the Moiry Pass he sacked Dundalk on 29 June 1315 and slaughtered the burgesses.[6] Though outnumbered, the Scots profited from the dissensions among the Anglo-Irish. Richard de Burgh, the Red Earl of Ulster, spurned the help of Edmund Butler, the justiciar of Ireland. When the Red Earl was routed at Connor (or Conagher)[7] on 10 September 1315 he began to be suspected of collusion with the Scots (he was, after all, father-in-law to King Robert). On 1 February 1316 it was the turn of the justiciar to be routed at the battle of the Skerries in Kildare. The way to Dublin lay open but the Scots did not take it. Instead Edward Bruce marched back to press the siege of Carrickfergus Castle on Belfast Lough and to be invested on 2 May 1316 as High King of Ireland on the hill of Maeldon near Dundalk. Early in September 1316 Carrickfergus surrendered.[8] The stout resistance it had put up for almost a year was one reason for Edward Bruce's ultimate failure.

For the moment, however, his successes encouraged risings all over Ireland. These showed both the strength and the weakness of his position : his presence had persuaded the native Irish to rise; but they did so not in a concerted movement, nor even in a spirit of patriotism, but rather to work off old scores now that English and Anglo-Irish authority had been weakened. To complete his conquest Edward Bruce had to make his kingship respected among the native

[5] Ranald Nicholson, 'A sequel to Edward Bruce's Invasion of Ireland', *S.H.R.*, XLII. 30–40, at 38.

[6] Barbour, *The Bruce*, II. 4–11.

[7] See R. Dunlop, 'Some Notes on Barbour's Bruce', *Essays . . . presented to Thomas Frederick Tout*, ed. A. G. Little and F. M. Powicke (1925), pp. 277–90, at 281.

[8] G. O. Sayles, 'The Siege of Carrickfergus Castle, 1315–16', *Irish Historical Studies*, x. pp. 98–9; O. Armstrong, *Edward Bruce's Invasion of Ireland* (afterwards cited as *Bruce Invasion*), pp. 92–5.

Irish. And to do this, ancient custom demanded that the High King should make a circuit of the provinces of Ulster, Meath, Leinster, Munster and Connaught.

Such a project required reinforcements from Scotland. By February 1317 King Robert had joined his brother at Carrickfergus to march 'throu all Irland fra end to othir',[9] devastating a land already suffering from famine. In Meath the Red Earl set a trap for his royal son-in-law.[10] There was bitter fighting before King Robert extricated the Scottish rearguard and forced his father-in-law to flee to Dublin. There the mayor arrested the Red Earl and warded him in the castle. This was the prelude to a night of frenzied activity in the city. On 21 February 1317 the Scots were only eight miles away and an attack was expected. In the course of chaotic attempts to fortify the city the Dubliners caused damage estimated at £10,000.[11] Had the Scots attacked, it is difficult to see how the distraught citizens could have repelled them. Yet once more, as in 1316, the Scots by-passed Dublin. Having marched through Munster to the Shannon the Bruces made no assault on the city of Limerick. Nor did they cross into Connaught. The circuit of Ireland was a failure. In May 1317 King Robert and Thomas Randolph left Edward Bruce in Carrickfergus and sailed back to Galloway with many wounded.[12]

They had returned just in time. The Scots had never held the undisputed control of the sea passage that was vital to success in Ireland. By February 1315 John of Lorne, King Robert's inveterate foe, had expelled a Scottish occupation force from the Isle of Man [13] and prevented its being used as a naval base by the Scots. For a time it looked as if they would use Anglesey: on 12 September 1315 Thomas Dun, the Scottish naval commander, sailed into Holyhead with four Flemish sea captains and captured an English ship.[14] The local population was co-operative. Indeed the Welsh were so impressed by Edward Bruce's initial successes that they asked him to be their leader:[15] old prophecies foretold that by an alliance with the Scots the Welsh would regain their freedom.[16] By July 1317, however, Sir John of Athy, the Irish admiral, had captured Dun and learnt from him of Thomas Randolph's preparations against the Isle of Man

[9] Barbour, *The Bruce*, II. 50.   [10] *Ibid.*, 50–8.
[11] O. Armstrong, *Bruce Invasion*, pp. 103–6.
[12] Barbour, *The Bruce*, II. 76; *Cal. Docs. Scot.*, III. No. 543.
[13] *Cal. Docs. Scot.*, III. Nos. 420, 421, 450, 479, 521.
[14] *Ibid.*, No. 451.
[15] *Vita Edwardi*, p. 61; *Cal. Papal Letters*, II. 138.
[16] *Chron. Bower*, II. 457–8.

and Anglesey.[17] English control of the Irish Sea made it difficult to send aid to Ireland, let alone Wales.

In Ireland there was a lull in military operations, partly on account of the efforts of the new pope, John XXII, to bring about an Anglo-Scottish truce or peace. To the Scots and the native Irish it seemed that his intervention was biased in favour of Edward II. At the end of 1317 or beginning of 1318 an Irish 'Remonstrance' was drafted and sent to the pope.[18] This document ran in the name of Donal O'Neil, the chief Ulster ally of Edward Bruce. Donal styled himself 'king of Ulster and true heir by heritable right to all Ireland'. He was willing, however, to renounce his right in favour of Edward Bruce. The Remonstrance—which may have been the work of King Robert's propaganda department[19]—alluded to Greater Scotia (Ireland) and Lesser Scotia (Scotland) and it described the kings of Lesser Scotia as having all derived their original blood from Greater Scotia, 'keeping our language and way of life to a certain extent'. Edward Bruce, according to O'Neil, was a pious, prudent and modest man of ancient Irish descent, powerful enough to redeem the Irish from the house of bondage. But on 14 October 1318 Edward Bruce fought his last battle at Faughart,[20] near Dundalk, and was slain almost on the spot where he had been invested as High King. So great was the defeat of the Scots that the escaping remnant did not even attempt to hold Carrickfergus.

A map showing the easterly routes followed by Edward Bruce in his Irish campaigns[21] bears out the claim that he had 'wasted the whole of the land occupied by the English'.[22] It has been suggested that the Scots had accomplished their main objective by depriving the English of Irish troops and provisions: 'Ireland was ruined as a source of supply, the Anglo-Irish were diverted from Scotland, and Edward II had to divide his forces and switch his attention from

---

[17] *Cal. Docs. Scot.*, III. No. 562.

[18] For the text of the Remonstrance see *Chron. Bower*, II. 259–67; *Chron. Pluscarden*, I. 243–50. The Irish background of the Remonstrance is discussed by J. Watt, in 'Negotiations between Edward II and John XXII concerning Ireland', *Irish Historical Studies*, X. 1–20; G. J. Hand, *English Law in Ireland, 1290–1324*, pp. 198–20; and J. F. Lydon, *op. cit.*, *Historical Studies*, IV. 111–25, at 115.

[19] Ranald Nicholson, 'Magna Carta and the Declaration of Arbroath', *Edinburgh University Journal*, XXII. 140–44, at 143.

[20] J. F. Lydon, *op. cit.*, *Historical Studies*, IV. 111–25, at 115–21; O. Armstrong, *Bruce Invasion*, pp. 116–8.

[21] See the map in O. Armstrong, *Bruce Invasion*.

[22] *Chron. Pluscarden*, I. 240.

Scotland.'[23] All this is true. Yet it is difficult to believe that it was only
for ends such as these that Edward Bruce and his companions fought.
A far greater issue was at stake and in this the Scots failed. They were
unable to draw lasting profit from the 'special friendship' that King
Robert had alluded to in his letters to the Irish. The battle of Faugh-
hart removed Ireland from King Robert's strategy for almost a decade. It was the end of any hope of replacing English authority
in Ireland with a régime allied to Scotland; it was also the end of any
hope of a comparable development in Wales.

The opening of a second front in Ireland had not diverted the
attention of the Scots from warfare on the Marches and in the north
of England. While raids into England had a political motive in so far
as they might force Edward II to make peace, the more significant
motive was economic : King Robert 'went oft on this maneir in Yngland for till riche his men' ;[24] it was typical that in May 1318 the men
of Ripon offered a thousand marks to save their town from destruction.[25] The possibility of taking an English prisoner was a further inducement to serve on the Borders; when Sir Ralph Neville was
captured in 1316 his ransom was set at two thousand marks.[26] Foremost in the Border warfare that followed Bannockburn was Sir James
Douglas, whose exploits[27] were to be rewarded by large grants of
land in the Marches.

Meanwhile the town of Berwick was under blockade by land and
sea. In February 1316 the men-at-arms were eating the flesh of dying
horses[28] while Flemish privateers, notably John Crabb and his
nephew Crabbekyn, intercepted English supply ships.[29] And in
December 1317 King Robert, newly returned from Ireland, was busy
at Aldcambus, some twelve miles from Berwick, constructing siege
machines.[30] They were not needed. In June 1317 Edward II had
entrusted control of the town defences to the burgesses; disputes soon
arose between them and the garrison,[31] and the warden of the town
offended Piers of Spalding, an English burgess. At daybreak on 28

[23] J. F. Lydon, op. cit., Historical Studies, IV. 111–25, at 112–13.
[24] Barbour, The Bruce, I. 351.
[25] Chron. Lanercost, pp. 235–6; Cal. Docs. Scot., III. Nos. 707, 858.
[26] Cal. Docs. Scot., III. No. 527. See also Denys Hay, 'Booty in Border Warfare', Dumfriesshire Trans., XXXI. 145–66.
[27] Barbour, The Bruce, II. 37–47; Scalacronica, p. 143.
[28] Cal. Docs. Scot., III. Nos. 452, 470, 477.
[29] Ibid., Nos. 417, 455, 486, 511, 537.
[30] Foedera, II. pt. i, 141–2.   [31] Cal. Docs. Scot., III. Nos. 554, 555, 558.

March 1318 he betrayed the town to the Scots[32] and was rewarded by Bruce with an estate in Angus.[33] In contrast to his former policy of dismantling fortifications, the king not only preserved but strengthened those of Berwick and limited his strategy by committing himself to the defence of his new-won prize.[34]

When parliament met at Scone in December 1318 some of its enactments showed an awareness of the risk that had been taken. One statute sought to improve the arms and equipment of the common folk who did not owe feudal military service but were summoned to the king's host under the obligations of *communis exercitus* or *servitium Scoticanum*. Like their counterparts in England, who had to meet the requirements of an 'assize of arms', they were to have arms and equipment commensurate with their worldly goods : a man with goods to the value of one cow was to have a good spear or a good bow with a sheaf of two dozen arrows. After Easter each year the sheriff and the local lords were to hold 'wappinschaws' to see that the statute was observed.[35]

The military and disciplinary measures of the Scone parliament were soon put to the test for the loss of Berwick had stirred the lethargic Edward II once more to rally his disunited land in lengthy preparations for a major effort against the Scots. He achieved a reconciliation with his baronial opponents headed by Earl Thomas of Lancaster, and he tried (unsuccessfully) to persuade the authorities in Flanders to prevent Flemish traders and privateers from aiding the Scots by blockade-running.[36] Early in September 1319 he laid siege to Berwick with over eight thousand troops.[37]

The all too obvious means of countering the English threat was to march to the relief of Berwick and wage a pitched battle. But Bruce was too competent a strategist to run unnecessary risk : an attack on the entrenched English camp 'mycht weill turn to foly'.[38] Instead, King Robert sent Thomas Randolph and James Douglas on an invasion of England. One of their aims was to capture Queen Isabella, who had taken up quarters in York. She discreetly moved to Nottingham. Archbishop Melton of York tried to stop the Scottish depredations but was not destined to go down in history as a second

---

[32] *Ibid.*, No. 589; Barbour, *The Bruce*, II. 77–83.
[33] Barrow, *Bruce*, p. 395.   [34] Barbour, *The Bruce*, II. 84–7.
[35] *A.P.S.*, I. 465–6.
[36] *Cal. Docs. Scot.*, III. Nos. 639, 673, 683. For the background see W. Stanford Reid, 'The Scots and the Staple Ordinance of 1313', *Speculum*, XXXIV. 598–610, at 606–7.
[37] *Cal. Docs. Scot.*, III. No. 668.   [38] Barbour, *The Bruce*, II. 96.

Thurstan: at Myton-on-Swale near Boroughbridge his motley crew was routed on 20 September 1319 in a travesty of a battle that the Scots with grim humour styled 'the Chaptour of Mytoune'.[39] Meanwhile things had not gone well for King Edward at Berwick. He had constructed a 'sow' to undermine the walls; the Scots, under the direction of John Crabb, an engineer 'of gret subtilite', constructed a 'crane' to oppose the 'sow'. On 13 September the sow set forth for its combat with the crane and was reduced to ashes.[40] When news of the Scottish depredations in England reached the besiegers, the southerners, unaffected by the Scottish raid, pressed for continuation of the siege. The northerners were not so disinterested. King Edward's council 'fast discordit'. By 24 September most of his host had disbanded.[41] This humiliation, fresh Scottish raids into England, and renewed difficulties with his own barons, induced Edward to negotiate with the Scots. On 22 December King Robert ratified the conditions of a two-year truce.[42]

While the truce of 1319 brought a short pause to warfare it brought no slackening to a contest in which spiritual weapons were wielded. It was typical of Edward II's ambitions in this field that within a few years he petitioned the pope (in vain) that no Scot should be made a bishop within the Scottish kirk, 'for it is the prelates of Scotland who encourage all classes in their evil acts'.[43] Foremost among the bishops who from time to time opposed the English were Wishart of Glasgow, David of Moray, Lamberton of St Andrews, Sinclair of Dunkeld and Mark of the Isles. Master Baldred Bisset, Master Nicholas Balmyle and Master Walter Twynholm were representative of the important class of lesser dignitaries who supported the patriotic cause.[44] Similar support came from the friars, whose preaching 'could easily take the form of propaganda'.[45] Among monks and canons regular there was perhaps less commitment to the patriotic cause: before Bannockburn the regular clergy seem to have had 'far more frequent dealings with the English authorities in the interests of protection and privilege than the secular clergy'.[46] At the best of times the Scottish kirk was by no means a united body speak-

---

[39] *Ibid.*, 99–100; *Scalacronica*, p. 148; *Chron. Lanercost*, p. 239.
[40] Barbour, *The Bruce*, II. 100–4.
[41] *Ibid.*, 110; *Cal. Docs. Scot.*, III. No. 668.
[42] *Cal. Docs. Scot.*, III. No. 681.
[43] *Foedera*, II. pt. ii, 90.   [44] Barrow, *Bruce*, pp. 377–8.
[45] W. M. Mackenzie, *op. cit.*, S.H.R., XXVII. 105–13, at 112–3.
[46] D. E. Easson, *op. cit.*, Scot. Church Hist. Soc. Recs., XI. 63–81, at 66.

ing with a single voice, but rather a haphazard conglomeration of men and institutions, often at variance with one another over questions of money, privilege and prestige. Thus it has recently been questioned whether the Scottish kirk could have 'a clear policy, an opinion, an attitude distinctively its own'. It has been suggested that 'Scotsmen in clerical orders were not markedly different from Scotsmen out of them, that they were neither more nor less heroic and patriotic than their fellow-countrymen'.[47] But if the political outlook of ecclesiastics often corresponded with that of other members of the community of the realm it was not necessarily for exactly the same reasons. While ecclesiastics were part and parcel of Scottish society and were bound to be affected by the ideas current in that society they were formers of opinion rather than followers of it. And as formers of opinion they had motives which were peculiar to themselves and professional in origin, not least fears of the intrusion of English ecclesiastics into Scottish benefices.

On the whole, Clement V and John XXII aided the English policy of intrusion. Moreover, so long as the papacy withheld recognition of his title Bruce would choose to remain ignorant of its pacific initiatives.[48] The continuing Scottish raids convinced John XXII of Bruce's intransigence: in June 1318 sentence of excommunication was passed against him and his accomplices and Scotland was placed under interdict.[49] Although Bruce could prevent the promulgation of this sentence in Scotland it could hardly be hidden that it was published in England and that he, Randolph and Douglas were cursed thrice daily in every English church. The Scottish clergy were faced with the choice of obeying the king or the pope, and an English chronicle affirms that 'meny a gode preste and holy man . . . were slayn throuz al the reme of Scotland' because they 'wolde singe no masse azeynes [against] the Popes commaundement'.[50] In July 1319 Edward hopefully (but in vain) presented his own nominees to no less than seventy-nine Scottish benefices;[51] and papal letters of November 1319 cited the Bishops of St Andrews, Dunkeld, Aberdeen and Moray to appear before the pope by 1 May 1320 to give account of the state of affairs in Scotland.[52]

[47] G. W. S. Barrow, 'The Scottish Clergy in the War of Independence', *S.H.R.*, XLI. 1–22, at 3.　　　[48] Duncan, *Nation of Scots*, pp. 23–4.
[49] *Foedera*, II. pt. i, 151, 152.
[50] *The Brut*, or *The Chronicles of England*, ed. Friedrich W. D. Brie (1906), p. 211.
[51] *Cal. Docs. Scot.*, III. No. 653; see Nos. 655, 657, 658, 659.
[52] *Cal. Papal Letters*, II. 191.

As it turned out, the four Scottish bishops ignored the summons. The Scots hoped to avert papal wrath by sending the *apologia* that has become famous as the Declaration of Arbroath. This was a letter addressed to John XXII by the Scottish barons and dated at the monastery of Arbroath on 6 April 1320.[53] The Declaration began with allusions to the long and legendary history of the Scots ever since they had emerged from Greater Scythia. In their realm had reigned a hundred and thirteen kings of their own royal stock, no alien intervening. Although dwelling at the ends of the earth they had been singled out by God to be among the first to be brought to His holy faith—and by none other than the Apostle Andrew, brother of St Peter. They had received many favours from past popes; under such protection they had lived free and undisturbed until Edward I had taken advantage of them at a time when they themselves were guiltless of evil intent, unaccustomed to wars, and without a head. From the innumerable enormities perpetrated by him they had been delivered by King Robert, who, like a second Maccabaeus or Joshua, had cheerfully endured toil and weariness, fasting and peril. He had been made king in accordance with law and custom, rightful succession and the dutiful consent and assent of all the people. Were he to give up what he had begun, choosing to subject his people and realm to the King of the English and the English people, the Scots would strive to thrust him out and make another king, 'for so long as a hundred men remain alive we will never in any way be bowed beneath the yoke of English domination; for it is not for glory, riches or honours that we fight, but for freedom alone, that which no man of worth yields up, save with his life'.

By any standards the Declaration of Arbroath is an impressive and eloquent manifesto with a universal relevance. It is the solemn protest of a small country against the aggression of a more powerful neighbour, an appeal not only on behalf of national freedom but on behalf of a kind of personal freedom which is coupled with it. It may therefore seem cynical to question whether such language and sentiments arose spontaneously in the mouths and breasts of the eight earls and thirty-one barons in whose name it ran, or to question whether they ever met at Arbroath on 6 April 1320. Most probably

[53] See Sir James Fergusson, *The Declaration of Arbroath* (1970); Lord Cooper, 'The Declaration of Arbroath Revisited' in his *Selected Papers, 1922–1954* and in his *Supra Crepidam* (1951), pp. 48–59; A. A. M. Duncan, 'The Making of the Declaration of Arbroath' in *The Study of Medieval Records: Essays presented to Kathleen Major*; Duncan, *Nation of Scots*, pp. 25–37.

they merely complied with a royal request to bring, or send, their seals for authentication of the document.[54(a)] That the letter was an essay in propaganda can hardly be doubted. Its Latin eloquence is not of the artless and simple kind but betrays the penmanship of Bernard of Linton, Abbot of Arbroath and Chancellor of Scotland.[54(b)]

He, and the chancery clerks who no doubt helped him, set to work in an eclectic fashion, drawing ideas from the document issued by the Scottish clergy in 1309, from Sallust's *Catiline*,[55] and, most directly of all, from the Irish Remonstrance, on which it is conceivable that Abbot Bernard had previously tried his hand.[56] Unlike the Remonstrance, however, the Declaration avoids detailed representations of a juridical or legalistic nature that might weaken the impact of the rhetoric. To read into the Declaration 'a clear statement of the constitutional relationship between the king and the community' or to conclude from it that the community of Scotland was 'reaching full maturity'[57] is to mistake an emotive appeal abounding in hyperbole for a workaday constitutional treatise. The Declaration presents instead a few important ideas in cogent and sonorous phrases; and the field from which these ideas are drawn is not *legalitas* but *humanitas*. Simply because it is based on an assumption of certain universal human qualities the Declaration of Arbroath is the most impressive manifesto of nationalism that medieval Europe produced.

It is a measure of the author's skill that what he wrote has been, more often than not, taken at its face value rather than as an idealised picture of a transcendent nationalism that might beat in the breasts of some Scots, hardly in those of all. It was typical of the baronial tergiversations of the wars of independence that Sir William Oliphant, who gallantly defended Stirling Castle against Edward I in 1304, also defended the town of Perth for Edward II in 1313;[58] that Sir Lawrence Abernethy, who had come to Bannockburn to fight for Edward II, arrived late, saw the Scottish victory, and joined Douglas in chasing Edward II to Dunbar;[59] that Sir Adam Gordon, who had served for three years as Edward II's justiciar of Lothian,[60] was one of the two knights whom King Robert entrusted with the mission of

---

[54(a)] Barrow, *Bruce*, pp. 425–6.
[54(b)] Lord Cooper, *Supra Crepidam*, pp. 53–5.
[55] J. R. Philip, 'Sallust and the Declaration of Arbroath', *S.H.R.*, xxvi. 75–8.
[56] Ranald Nicholson, *op. cit.*, *University of Edinburgh Journal*, xxii. 140–4, at 143.   [57] Barrow, *Bruce*, p. 428.
[58] *Cal. Docs. Scot.*, iii. 425–7; *Rot. Scot.*, i. 105.
[59] Barbour, *The Bruce*, i. 343–4.
[60] *Cal. Docs. Scot.*, iii. Nos. 181, 135, 211, 299, 403.

delivering the Declaration of Arbroath to the papal *curia*.[61] Had the wars of independence ended (as was not impossible) with a Balliol restoration in 1302, shortly after Robert Bruce had made his peace with Edward I, Bruce, the exponent of nationalism, would have figured in history as an unpatriotic Earl of Carrick, rightfully disinherited, of no more significance than the contemporary Earl of Angus who loyally served the English king. It is even more striking that within four months of the issue of the Arbroath Declaration five of the barons who sealed it—William Soulis, Roger Mowbray, David Brechin, Patrick Graham and Eustace Maxwell—were accused with others of taking part in a treasonable conspiracy against King Robert's life.

The object of the conspiracy was to kill King Robert and to put Sir William Soulis on the throne. Sir William was grand-nephew of Sir John Soulis the onetime guardian of Scotland; his father, Nicholas Soulis, had been one of the unsuccessful claimants in the Great Cause; his mother, Margaret Comyn, was the daughter of Alexander Comyn, one-time Earl of Buchan; and another daughter of Alexander, Agnes Comyn, Countess of Strathearn, was also involved in the plot.[62] One indication of the strength of a medieval king was his ability to exact the full penalty for treason. In the summer of 1320 the conspirators were rounded up and brought before a 'full parliament' that met at Scone on 4 August. An assize acquitted Sir Eustace Maxwell and four others for lack of evidence. Sir William Soulis made a confession, and with his aunt, the Countess of Strathearn, was sentenced to life imprisonment. Sir Roger Mowbray had died before his trial: his corpse was placed on a litter and brought before parliament, probably in accordance with practice under the law of arms,[63] so that his trial could proceed; it was sentenced to be drawn, hanged and beheaded; only King Robert's clemency saved it from such vilification. Sir Gilbert Malherbe, Sir John Logie, Sir David Brechin and Richard Brown were condemned to be drawn at the tail of horses through the streets of Perth and then to be hanged and beheaded.[64] Although Bruce had not gone so far as to copy the English

[61] G. Donaldson, 'The Pope's Reply to the Scottish Barons in 1320', *S.H.R.*, XXIX. 119–20.

[62] *Scalacronica*, p. 144. For the background see *Scots Peerage*, VI. 135–7, VIII. 241–50.

[63] See W. C. Dickinson, ' "His body shall be brought to the lists" ', *S.H.R.*, XLII. 84–6.

[64] Barbour, *The Bruce*, II. 140–2. For other accounts of the conspiracy and its suppression see *Scalacronica*, p. 144; *Chron. Fordun*, I. 348–9.

practices of summary procedure followed by the disembowelling and quartering of the victims, the penalty he had exacted from the conspirators was, by Scottish standards, a severe one. He had demonstrated that there was no room for baronial intransigence in a kingdom that had bought unity and independence at a dear price. But contemporaries were less shocked by the treason of the Soulis conspiracy than by the severity of the 'Black Parliament' in crushing the treason.

While the Soulis conspiracy was being crushed in Scotland the Declaration of Arbroath was delivered in the *curia*, which since 1309 had been established in Avignon.[65] In a written reply dated there on 28 August 1320 [66] the pope dealt both with the Declaration and with letters that had been sent to him by King Robert. Pope John agreed to exhort the English to make peace,[67] and he also exhorted the Scots to make peace. Although he still called King Robert merely 'that illustrious man Robert, who assumes the title and position of King of Scotland' his reply can hardly be described as a 'remarkable feat of evasion'.[68]

In compliance with the pope's admonitions, negotiations for peace or truce took place between January and April 1321 at Newcastle, Berwick and Bamburgh,[69] in the presence of three envoys of the French king and two envoys of the pope. John of Brittany, Earl of Richmond, was to take with him exemplars of the record of the Great Cause so that the English delegation might 'refer to it as far as possible'.[70] If Edward thought that the Scots would take heed of documents that Baldred Bisset had rejected twenty years previously he was ludicrously mistaken. Early in January 1322, soon after the expiry of the two-year truce, the Scots were once more over the border under Randolph, Douglas and the Steward.

This Scottish attack coincided with deepening dissensions between Edward and his baronial opponents headed by the Earls of Lancaster and Hereford. The Scots concluded that they might obtain from the English baronial opposition the terms that Edward II had refused to concede. In the winter of 1321–22 there were negotiations

[65] G. Mollat, *The Popes at Avignon* (1949), p. xix.
[66] G. Donaldson, *op. cit.*, *S.H.R.*, xxix. 119–20.
[67] For the letters he sent to England see A. Theiner, *Vetera Monumenta* (Rome, 1864), No. ccccxxx; *Cal. Papal Registers*, ii. 428.
[68] Barrow, *Bruce*, p. 426.
[69] *Cal. Docs. Scot.*, iii. Nos. 718, 720, 722, 726, 743; Stones, *Documents*, No. 38.   [70] Stones, *Documents*, No. 38.

involving Douglas, Randolph, and Thomas of Lancaster, who in conspiratorial fashion adopted the pseudonym of 'King Arthur'. When open civil war broke out in England the Earls of Lancaster and Hereford retreated northwards to link up with the Scots. Before the Scots arrived, however, the two earls were intercepted by Sir Andrew Harclay. On 16 March 1322 Hereford was slain while trying to force a crossing over the Trent at Boroughbridge; Lancaster surrendered and was beheaded a few days later. Harclay received from his grateful king the new title of Earl of Carlisle.[71]

Having at long last crushed 'King Arthur', Edward II was in a mood to avenge himself on the Scots and in May 1322 began preparations for a new invasion.[72] By the time that his host crossed the Tweed in August 1322 the country in its path was stripped bare of livestock, victuals and fodder. Bruce's cautious scorched-earth strategy was justified by its results. Having reached Edinburgh without meeting opposition the English lingered for three days vainly awaiting their supply ships which were held back by contrary winds. On its withdrawal the starving army looted Holyrood and Melrose and set fire to Dryburgh.[73] The north of England was more demoralised than ever as Edward withdrew southward.[74]

As Edward found himself almost deserted Bruce was busy mustering 'all the power of Scotland, of the Isles, and of the rest of the Highlands'.[75] He crossed the Solway on 30 September and struck rapidly southward. On the evening of 13 October Edward, then at Rievaulx Abbey, was under the impression that the Scots were no nearer than Northallerton;[76] at dawn on the following day the Earl of Richmond reached the top of the escarpment between the abbeys of Byland and Rievaulx to discover that they had marched through the night and were fast approaching. In the engagement that followed, the earl was captured and Edward was chased to York,[77] where he was joined by Andrew Harclay, who found him 'confused' and returned to Carlisle ready to take an initiative of his own. On 3 January 1323 he made a private visit to King Robert at Lochmaben.[78]

---

[71] *Chron. Lanercost*, pp. 241–5; *Cal. Docs. Scot.*, III. Nos. 746, 749.
[72] *Cal. Docs. Scot.*, III. Nos. 751, 752, 754.
[73] *Chron. Bower*, II. 278; Barbour, *The Bruce*, II. 124–6.
[74] *Cal. Docs. Scot.*, III. Nos. 778, 790; *Scalacronica*, p. 149.
[75] *Scalacronica*, p. 149; *Chron. Lanercost*, p. 247.
[76] *Chron. Lanercost*, p. 247; *Cal. Docs. Scot.*, III. No. 790.
[77] Barbour, *The Bruce*, II, 129–35; *Chron. Lanercost*, pp. 247–8.
[78] *Chron. Lanercost*, pp. 247–8.

There Harclay negotiated 'on behalf of all those in England who wish to be spared and saved from war by Robert Bruce and all his men'. The preamble to the resulting indenture [79] affirmed that in the past the realms of England and Scotland had prospered so long as each had a king from its own nation and was maintained separately with its own laws and customs. It was to the common profit of both realms that Bruce might hold Scotland freely, entirely, and in liberty. To uphold the common profit there were to be twelve sworn commissioners, six to be chosen from King Robert's people and six to be chosen by Harclay. Within a year Edward was to consent that King Robert 'shall have his realm, free and quit, for himself and his heirs'. In return, Bruce was to make some concessions. He would pay the English forty thousand marks at the rate of four thousand a year. He would found an abbey in Scotland for the souls of those slain in the war and would endow it with five hundred marks a year. Edward would have the gratifying right to arrange the marriage of Bruce's male heir to one of Edward's own kinswomen. The final point of the proposed peace was that neither king 'shall be bound to receive in his realm a man who has been opposed to him, nor to render him the lands that he or his ancestors had in his realm if he does not wish to do it of his special grace'. Thenceforth there would be two national kingdoms, equal in status and distinct; Scots would be Scots, English would be English, and the Anglo-Scots would disappear.

It was a solution that was pragmatic, nationalist, and statesmanlike. But it held no appeal for Edward II: Harclay was 'a private person to whom it in no wise pertained to ordain such things'. On 25 February 1323 he was treacherously seized in Carlisle Castle. After a summary 'trial', he was degraded from his earldom and knighthood, drawn, hanged, beheaded, disembowelled and quartered.[80]

In ridding himself of Andrew Harclay Edward had deprived England of its staunchest defender. Almost immediately he himself had to open negotiations with the Scots, first at Newcastle,[81] then at Bishopthorpe near York. One reason why the victorious Scots were willing to accept a truce was a change of affairs in Flanders, whence they had lately obtained valuable aid: in the summer of 1322 Edward feared Flemish naval attacks on the English coast and alluded

---

[79] Text in Stones, *Documents*, pp. 155–7.
[80] *Chron. Lanercost*, pp. 249–51; J. G. Bellamy, *Law of Treason*, p. 52.
[81] *Cal. Docs. Scot.*, III. Nos. 796, 807; *A.P.S.*, I. 479–80.

to 'these evil Flemings'.[82] His difficulties were suddenly eased with the death of the troublesome Count of Flanders in September 1322. The count's successor was a child and the regents of Flanders were prepared to co-operate with Edward: on 18 April 1323 all Scots were ordered to leave Flanders.[83] On 30 May 1323 the terms of a long truce were at last settled at Bishopthorpe.[84]

The truce was to last for thirteen years, beginning on 12 June 1323. Apart from reciprocal clauses that were intended to restore peaceful relations there was one English concession: Edward bound himself not to oppose a Scottish approach to the papacy for the release of the Scots from excommunication and interdict. Basic problems, however, were left unsettled: nothing was said of those Scots or Anglo-Scots who had been disinherited on account of their adherence to Edward; nor did the English recognise Bruce as king.[85] He was little nearer his ultimate goal.

Nonetheless the truce of Bishopthorpe brought what was at least expected to be a long cessation of hostilities. In Scotland it was possible to repair the damages of war and to undertake more intensively the social, political and economic reconstruction that had hitherto been piecemeal and intermittent. Although there are signs of conscious attempts at reconstruction somewhat earlier, notably in the Scone parliament of December 1318, which had enacted over twenty statutes in a major review of law and legal procedure,[86] it was mainly between the years 1323 and 1327 that King Robert was free to concentrate upon domestic problems.

The background to these was the effect of prolonged warfare upon the economy. There were many areas of Scotland that saw no warfare at all, or experienced it for only a short time, but the areas that suffered most from warfare were those that had hitherto been the most developed: in 1317 an English writer reported that Annandale was so utterly wasted that there was neither man nor beast left between the border and Lochmaben.[87] In many areas the productivity

[82] *Cal. Docs. Scot.*, III. No. 778. The background of Flemish, German and other overseas aid to the Scots is given by W. Stanford Reid in 'Trade, Traders, and Scottish Independence', *Speculum*, XXIX. 210–22, and in 'Sea-power in the Anglo-Scottish War, 1296–1328', *The Mariner's Mirror*, XLVI. 7–23.

[83] W. Stanford Reid, *op. cit.*, *Speculum*, XXXIV. 598–610, at 608.

[84] Text in *Foedera*, II. pt. ii, 73–4; *A.P.S.*, I. 479–81.

[85] Compare the Scottish ratification issued at Berwick (*A.P.S.*, I. 479–81) and the Bishopthorpe text (*Foedera*, II. pt. ii, 73–4).

[86] *A.P.S.*, I. 466. For discussion of these see *Scot. Legal Hist.*, pp. 18–24; Barrow, *Bruce*, pp. 416–8.   [87] *Cal. Docs. Scot.*, III. No. 543.

of land probably fell by as much as a half [88] and there was bound to be a disruption of the rural routine that was the basis of Scottish livelihood: only the most optimistic could persevere in the laborious agricultural cycle when their crops were destroyed year after year either by the enemy or by the Scots themselves. While growing crops could not be lifted on the approach of an English army, it was possible to drive sheep and cattle to fastnesses in the hills: a disincentive to till the soil was probably accompanied by a greater emphasis on pastoral farming and the export of wool, woolfells (fleeces) and hides. By 1327 wool exports approached five thousand sacks a year [89] (roughly one-fifth of the English figure) and this volume was scarcely ever to be surpassed throughout the Middle Ages. Hence King Robert's anxiety to keep open the vulnerable trade route to the weaving towns of the Low Countries, his attempts to encourage Netherlanders and Germans to trade with Scotland,[90] his willingness to foster the interests of the Scottish merchant burgesses by resuscitating the merchant gild of Dundee and granting a merchant gild to the burgesses of Ayr.[91] Scottish wool paid for foreign manufactures—especially munitions of war. More than that, it brought revenue to the king.

Although export duties were being levied in the reign of Alexander III [92] it is only towards the end of King Robert's reign that information about them becomes available. They were then being levied at the rate of half a mark (6s. 8d.) on the sack of wool, 3s. 4d. on each hundred woolfells, and a mark on each hundred hides.[93] Wool, woolfells, and hides could be legally shipped only on the production of an export licence sealed with the coket seal of a custumar to certify that the king's 'great new custom' had been paid.[94] While the number of baronial or ecclesiastical burghs was increased during the reign,[95] few, new or old, were granted the use of a coket.[96] Without that they could not thrive. By contrast there was no question of withholding a coket from the king's own burghs:[97] when the new

---

[88] Ibid., No. 245. [89] E.R., I. 74–83.
[90] W. Stanford Reid, op. cit., Speculum, XXIX. 210–22, at 219–20; James W. Dilley, 'Scottish–German Diplomacy, 1297–1327', S.H.R., XXXVI. 80–7.
[91] R.M.S., I. 459; II. No. 3717.
[92] P. 15 above.
[93] E.R., I. xcviii–xcix.
[94] Ibid., c–ci; Dunfermline Registrum, pp. 232–3, 246, 247, 252–3; R.M.S., I. 438.
[95] Pryde, Burghs, pp. 43–6.
[96] Lochmaben and Dunfermline were exceptions (E.R., I. 99, 174, 175).
[97] For allusions to such cokets see ibid., 78, 101, 175, 322.

royal burgh of Tarbert was founded a coket seal was at once made for it.[98] In an exchequer audit of 1328 the custumars of ten leading royal burghs accounted for £1,851 14s. 4¾d. About a third of this came from the great customs of Berwick; next in importance came Edinburgh, Aberdeen, Dundee and Perth.[99] The prosperity that the export trade brought to the inhabitants of the royal burghs was one from which the king might also draw additional profit in the shape of increasing burghal revenues: in 1328 the ferms of twenty-six royal burghs came to £1,133 3s. 4d.[100] In relation to the total crown revenues the burgh ferms had probably reached the peak of their importance.

This owed much to a development that immediately benefited King Robert but prevented his successors from increasing the yield of the burgh ferms. In 1319 the king granted the burgh of Aberdeen and its endowments to the community of burgesses to be held in feu-ferm. When applied to a burgh this tenure meant that all the king's revenues in the burgh (except the great customs) were transferred to the community of burgesses in perpetuity. The community held their burgh and its endowments as a collective tenant-in-chief of the crown, paying a fixed annual ferm in perpetuity. In the case of Aberdeen this was set at £213 6s. 8d.[101] In the following year Berwick, which seems to have enjoyed feu-ferm status under Alexander III, was granted a feu-ferm charter for five hundred marks (£333 6s. 8d.) a year.[102] When the turn of Edinburgh came in 1329 it was let off lightly with a mere £34 13s. 4d. a year.[103] As yet, only one or two leading royal burghs were granted the privilege of feu-ferm status. And by 1327 Berwick could not afford its high ferm; the burgh was then leased to two barons.[104] Throughout the fourteenth century, however, most of the leading royal burghs were to acquire feu-ferm status.[105]

There were important consequences within the royal burghs themselves. The earliest surviving record of the proceedings of a burgh court, that of Aberdeen in 1317,[106] shows the community of burgesses acting in a judicial capacity. After the conferment of feu-ferm status the community could also act in a fiscal capacity. It had

[98] Ibid., 118, 175.   [99] Ibid., c.   [100] Ibid., lxxxviii.
[101] A.P.S., I. 478.   [102] Barrow, Bruce, pp. 423–4.
[103] E.R., I. lxxxvii.   [104] Ibid., 63.
[105] By 1400 it was enjoyed by at least Dumfries, Haddington, Rutherglen, Lanark, Dundee, Perth, Linlithgow, Forfar, Stirling and Montrose (E.R., III. 501–7), in addition to Aberdeen and Edinburgh.
[106] Aberdeen Burgh Recs., pp. 1–17.

taken the final step to self-government within the burgh; for already it was recognised that the bailies and the alderman (the later provost) should be chosen 'thruch the consaile of the gud men of the toune'.[107] Whether this amounted to a 'democratic' election is uncertain: the ultimate say must have rested with the merchant burgesses. But such craftsmen as became burgesses were certainly beginning to play a part in burgh administration; and warfare and its consequences probably made the merchant burgesses not unwilling to admit to burgess-ship those social inferiors who could share their burdens both military and financial. Royal policy was, however, conservative: as the king's chamberlain began once more to hold his ayre in Berwick and other royal burghs he was to see to it that the social niceties were observed; for he was to enquire whether any fleshers who had become burgesses continued to soil their hands with the offal of animals, and whether any of the king's *nativi* were lurking in the burgh.[108]

King Robert's conservatism in such matters was at variance with the provision made in the Scone parliament of 1318 for the holding of 'wappinschaws' to ensure that each man with goods to the value of one cow should be armed with a spear or bow:[109] a husbandman who was expected to wield a sixteen-foot spear in the schiltron could no longer be expected to be content to be tied to the soil. In a society shaken up by prolonged warfare old habits and customs might be discarded. Seven entries in the register of Dunfermline Abbey, one of them as late in date as 1332, give the genealogies of men who were serfs of the monastery.[110] But even among the serfs of Dunfermline there was a new self-confidence.[111] The last recorded legal suit for the recovery of a runaway serf was to be instituted by the Bishop of Moray in 1364,[112] and a few years later David II was to issue one of the last charters setting free a serf and his descendants.[113]

The obscure, though important, changes that were taking place at the lower levels of society were accompanied by more obvious changes at the upper levels. Thanks to the wars, the Scottish baronage was less open to English influences and more likely to develop

[107] *Leges Quatuor Burgorum (A.P.S.*, I. 347).
[108] *De Articulis Inquirendis . . . in Itinere Camerarii (ibid.*, 681, 682). See also *R.M.S.*, I. 460.
[109] *A.P.S.*, I. 466.
[110] *Dunfermline Registrum*, Nos. 325–31.
[111] *Ibid.*, No. 354.
[112] *Moray Registrum*, No. 143.   [113] *R.M.S.*, I. No. 345.

characteristics of its own. Although the position of the baronage within the community of the realm had not changed, it had come to depend upon military prestige as well as upon landed wealth. Moreover, the civil war had left a legacy of feud and faction—which the king had attempted to mitigate in one of the statutes of the Scone parliament of 1318.[114] The holding of land, always a vital question, had become mixed up in politics, and any political settlement, such as the establishment of Bruce's authority, implied a settlement of contesting claims to land. King Robert's attitude to this problem has been rightly described as one of 'patient conservation and restoration . . . reluctance to overthrow ancient rights or to offend feudal susceptibilities'.[115] While vast territories fell into the king's hands as forfeitures most of these were forfeited from a small group of irreconcilables, notably Balliol and the Comyns;[116] and the land forfeited from a small group was granted out to a group almost as small. It would be wrong to suppose that Bruce's forfeitures resulted in a 'new nobility', still less in the rise of 'new men' of relatively humble origin. The transfer of land—from the crown as well as from forfeited landholders—took place within the baronial class; and the greatest prizes went to a few men who were connected to Bruce by blood or marriage or by a long period of good service.[117] Notable among these were Thomas Randolph, the king's nephew, and Sir James Douglas, the king's foremost knight, who by 1325 held Douglasdale, Jedburgh and its forest, the wardenship of the king's forest of Selkirk, and at least five baronies in southern Scotland.[118]

If the king's attitude to the quantitative distribution of land can be characterised as conservative,[119] his attitude to the qualitative distribution—the manner in which land was held—was equally so. Although in England, and Western Europe generally, there was a marked tendency away from traditional feudal military service towards contract armies made up of paid troops, King Robert was still granting land in return for the service of a knight or an archer. This in itself is perhaps unimportant: from what is known of the charters he issued he could hardly have obtained much more than the services of an additional forty knights and forty archers. But while most of King Robert's charters granted lands on terms as vague and haphazard as those of his predecessors, more than thirty of his surviving

[114] A.P.S., i. 466.
[116] Ibid.
[118] R.M.S., i. 448–50.
[115] Barrow, Bruce, pp. 391–2.
[117] Ibid., pp. 381–96.
[119] Barrow, Bruce, p. 381.

charters use a novel phase : lands are granted *in liberam baroniam,* or, more fully, *in unam integram et liberam baroniam.*[120] It has been affirmed that 'the adoption of this novel standard formula was not accidental and can hardly have been a trivial matter of chancery procedure', that it was 'part of a deliberate policy of defining and stereotyping feudal rights as well as obligations'.[121] But the formula must be placed in its context : Bruce's chancery was also making grants *in liberam regalitatem, in liberam elemosinam, in liberum burgum, in liberam forestam, in liberam warennam* and *in liberum maritagium.* In these applications the word *liber,* so profusely used, means, if it means anything, 'privileged'; and there is nothing to show that a grant *in liberam baroniam* conveyed any specific privilege, or, for that matter, implied any specific obligation. It is difficult to find any lowest common denominator save the old word 'barony' that applies to these grants: some, but not all, conveyed forfeited lands; some, but not all, stipulated military service; some, but not all, stipulated suit to the court of the sheriffdom ; some, but not all, conferred a new unity upon lands that had previously been unattached to one another. Only in this does there seem to be novelty : scattered lands might become a unit with one *caput* and one payment of relief to the king; and for such increased convenience and baronial authority the holder might be expected to pay a higher relief. The significance of the grants *in liberam baroniam* (which were still being made centuries later) is not that they set up some new type of barony but that they set up more baronies of the old type and that King Robert was deliberately using the barony as an integral and important part of local government. To that extent he was re-vitalising a feudal institution that was decaying elsewhere and confirming it as a basis of local government rather than trying to supplant it by 'royal' government under the sheriffs, or, as as was the case in England, by commissions of *oyer* and *terminer* or the later justices of the peace. Thus the system of interlocking feudal and royal government that Bruce had inherited was preserved and all that was attempted was the tidying up of the feudal structure and the strengthening of the baronial basis on which local government rested.

This development was accompanied by grants that reduced royal control over local government. Malcolm, Earl of Lennox, was given heritably the sheriffships of Lennox and Clackmannan and Hugh, Earl of Ross, the sheriffship of Cromarty.[122] On 8 November 1325 the

---

[120] E.g. *R.M.S.,* I. No. 31.
[121] Barrow, *Bruce,* p. 410.   [122] *Ibid.,* p. 389; *Scots Peerage,* VII. 235.

king placed an emerald ring on the finger of Sir James Douglas as a token that the latter was infeft with the right to indict all robbers within his lands and that the jurisdiction of the king's justiciar was thereby diminished.[123] More extensive privileges went to those who were granted regalities. Those existing hitherto were mostly insignificant [124] and provided a precedent best forgotten; for the lord of a regality could exclude the royal officials and, to that extent, the regalities were bastions of feudal autonomy. Yet, just as he had re-vitalised the concept of barony Bruce also re-vitalised that of regality and thereby 'gave a fillip to the process by which the crown lost power through excessive delegation'.[125] For the time being, however, only a few grants of regality were made. Randolph was by far the most important beneficiary. By charters of 20 December 1324 his earldom of Moray and his lordship of the Isle of Man were erected into regalities and it was doubtless about the same time that his lordship of Annandale was similarly favoured.[126]

The new regality of Moray completed Bruce's settlement of the north, for Randolph now held complete civil and military control of the vast area between the river Spey and the Sound of Sleat. On the western seaboard also he was given responsibility as lord of the new regality of the Isle of Man. Elsewhere in the west the landed settlement had to take account of the three branches of the descendants of Somerled—the MacDougals, the MacDonalds and the MacRuaridhs. The first, as inveterate foes of Bruce, were forfeited and lived in exile as dependants of the English king. The MacDonald and MacRuaridh supporters of Bruce were duly rewarded: Angus Og of Islay obtained lands in the former Comyn lordship of Lochaber and was granted a charter of Morvern and Ardnamurchan.[127] On the mainland of Argyll it was the Campbells, hitherto not a particularly notable family, who received the lion's share of the spoil of the MacDougals,[128] while Sir Neil Campbell was given Bruce's sister Mary in marriage.

The landed settlement in the West Highlands and Isles had resulted in a delicate balance of power which it was probably Bruce's intention to maintain through personal supervision.[129] In 1326, with all Scotland to choose from, he went to some trouble to acquire land

---

[123] *R.M.S:*, I. 449.
[124] Barrow, *Bruce*, pp. 397–8.
[125] *Ibid.*, p. 398.
[126] *R.M.S.*, I. 444–7.
[127] *Ibid.*, 512.
[128] *Ibid.*, 534, 535, 554, 556.
[129] For the background see G. W. S. Barrow, 'The Highlands of Scotland in the lifetime of Robert the Bruce', *The Stewarts*, XII. 26–46.

at Cardross, near Dumbarton. There, in the Lennox, 'a strongly Gaelic district',[130] he built himself a manor-house [131] which became his home. While the king's strategy had generally led him to dismantle royal castles, and some baronial castles as well, his policy in the western approaches was different. The royal castle of Dumbarton was preserved intact and the castle of Skipness in Kintyre was repaired and victualled.[132] More strikingly, in 1325 he spent at least £450 on the construction of a large new royal castle on East Loch Tarbert where Kintyre and Knapdale met;[133] at West Loch Tarbert he constructed a smaller fortification styled a 'peel' and over the isthmus between the two—only a mile wide—he cut out a track,[134] designed probably not so much for ordinary traffic as to facilitate the haulage of galleys between the sheltered waters of the Clyde estuary and the sounds among the Western Isles. For Bruce was trying to revive the naval organisation that had existed along the western seaboard in Norse times [135] and had vessels of his own, including a 'great ship'.[136] His interest in Tarbert was not only strategic : beside the new castle rose a new royal burgh. He put the finishing touch to his western projects by enlisting the help of his most gifted cleric : Bernard of Linton gave up the abbacy of Arbroath and the chancellorship to appear in 1328 as Bishop of the Isles.[137] The king had given him £100 towards his election expenses and arranged that the abbey of Arbroath should grant him a seven-year pension.[138] He was not 'unaccountably promoted' : [139] the king's interest in the transfer suggests that Bernard's services in the Isles would be more than merely spiritual.

From the Scottish kirk as a whole, particularly from the episcopate, Bruce expected to receive political support; but though it was natural that he should bestow his benevolence upon his ecclesiastical supporters and their institutions, his benevolence was inspired less by political consideration than by spiritual remorse and a pious veneration, remarkable even by the standards of the time, for the saints, their relics and shrines. Possibly in expiation of his sacrilege in the friary kirk of Dumfries, he granted an annual rent of forty marks to

[130] Barrow, *Bruce*, p. 441. [131] *E.R.*, I. cxix–cxxi. [132] *Ibid.*, 56, 57.
[133] See Royal Commission on the Ancient and Historical Monuments of Scotland, *Argyll I: Kintyre* (1971), No. 316, and John G. Dunbar and A. A. M. Duncan, 'Tarbert Castle, a contribution to the history of Argyll', *S.H.R.*, L. 1–17.
[134] *E.R.*, I. 52–6. [135] *R.M.S.*, I. 446, 479.
[136] *E.R.*, I. 123, 126, 127, 133, 134. [137] *Ibid.*, 114.
[138] *Arbroath Liber*, I. No. 358. [139] Barrow, *Bruce*, p. 378.

the Franciscans of Dumfries and another twenty marks to each of the other Franciscan houses in Scotland.[140] On 5 July 1318 he attended the consecration of the newly-completed cathedral of St Andrews and bestowed a parish kirk to be appropriated to the cathedral; the Earl of Fife added another; and the Bishop of St Andrews donated two others.[141] Much more important were the grants lavished by Bruce on the monastic houses. At a time when the prayers of monks were coming to be generally regarded as less spiritually efficacious than the masses celebrated by secular priests Bruce showed himself, somewhat conservatively, to be 'the last munificent royal benefactor of the religious houses of Scotland'; they were thereby enabled to assume 'a new lease of life ere the decadence of the fourteenth century overtook them'.[142] Melrose was a notable beneficiary: in January 1326 Bruce granted the abbey an annual rent of £100 to be used to provide each monk with a daily helping of a rare delicacy—rice made with milk of almonds—the residue of the income was to be used by the monks to clothe and feed fifteen poor men at Martinmas.[143] In March 1326 the king went further and granted the abbey, in aid of its reconstruction, £2,000 to be levied under the supervision of Sir James Douglas from the feudal casualties of Roxburghshire. Perhaps because the grant was so large an encroachment upon the royal revenues, it was expressly stated to have been made 'at the instance of our full royal power in our full parliament last held at Scone'.[144]

Generosity to the religious houses must undoubtedly have contributed to the crisis in royal finances which King Robert reported to parliament when it met in Cambuskenneth Abbey on 15 July 1326: 'the lands and rents which of old used to pertain to his crown had been so diminished by divers gifts and transfers occasioned by the war that he did not have means of maintenance befitting his station'.[145] Parliament was asked to discuss the provision of sufficient financial maintenance for the king in grateful recognition of the hardships that he and his family had borne for the recovery of the liberty of all. For some reason or other the prelates and the rest of the clergy seem to have been excused from discussing the king's request, or at least from taking direct part in the arrangement that resulted. It was the earls, barons, burgesses and 'all the rest of the freeholders of the realm' who took the remarkable step of concluding an inden-

140 W. Moir Bryce, *The Scottish Greyfriars*, I. 204.
141 *Chron. Bower*, II. 271–2.
142 D. E. Easson, *op. cit.*, *Scot. Church Hist. Soc. Recs.*, XI. 63–81, at 77, 78.
143 *Melrose Liber*, II. No. 362.
144 *R.M.S.*, I. No. 331 and p. 430.   145 *A.P.S.*, I. 475.

ture with the king. In this they admitted that the king's request was 'reasonable' and agreed to pay to the king during his lifetime a 'tenth penny'—one tenth of all their ferms and revenues.[146] In return for this grant the king gratefully made a concession. He had hinted that he might maintain himself by imposing an 'intolerable burden'[147] upon his people: vast quantities of victuals were being despatched by royal officials to the king's household;[148] some of these victuals were almost certainly requisitioned as 'prises' for which little or nothing might be paid. In Scotland as in England the taking of 'prises' was an ancient and unpopular royal prerogative. King Robert conceded that he would exercise this prerogative more moderately, following the customs used in the time of Alexander III.

In England parliament made its consent to taxation conditional upon redress of grievance and thereby eventually obtained a dominant position in politics. At Cambuskenneth it looked as if the Scottish parliament, or a body drawn from it, had taken the first step on the same road. But development along English lines was not, in this important respect, to continue; it was, and remained, the chief point of Scottish constitutional theory that the king should 'live of his own', and that direct taxation should be used not to finance ordinary and recurrent expenditure but only for some occasional extraordinary purpose. The grant made at Cambuskenneth, which was in any case to end on Bruce's death, was seen as an innovation that was not to be taken as a precedent.

The Cambuskenneth indenture, to which both freeholders and burgesses were parties, makes it plain that the community of the realm had by then widened to comprise social classes that had scarcely before figured in politics. Yet there is no sign of any new theory to account for a change. King Robert evidently did not regard feudal or tenurial obligation as something that defined the membership of parliament: 'in parliament the king sought to do his business, and to it he summoned those appropriate for his business'.[149] From 1318 onwards they included not only such freeholders as were tenants-in-chief but those who were not crown tenants and who approximated to the class of lesser landholders, 'lairds', rather than 'lords'. In 1326 these freeholders must have attended in sufficient numbers for their concurrence in the Cambuskenneth indenture to be regarded as binding upon all members of their class.[150] The same was true of the burgess commissioners who at Cambuskenneth made their

[146] Ibid., 476.   [147] Ibid., 475.   [148] E.R., I. 196–202.
[149] A. A. M. Duncan, op. cit., S.H.R., XLV. 36–58, at 55.   [150] Ibid.

appearance in parliament, possibly for the first time : for 'the political significance of the burghs arose in Scotland as elsewhere from their taxable capacity'.[151] The widening composition of parliament was demonstrated in the summons to the parliament that was to meet at Edinburgh in February 1328 to ratify once more the Cambuskenneth indenture : the summons was a general one issued through the sheriffs, and its terms were 'social and not tenurial' ;[152] the sheriffs were to summon 'bishops, abbots, earls, barons, freeholders, and six competent persons from each burghal community'.[153] Burgess representation had come to stay.

In yet another respect the Cambuskenneth parliament of 1326 witnessed a significant transaction. Although the king had two surviving legitimate daughters and at least two bastard sons, his long marriage to Elizabeth de Burgh had seemed unlikely to result in a male heir. There was universal rejoicing when the queen gave birth to a son at Dunfermline on 5 March 1324. At the age of two David Bruce was brought before parliament at Cambuskenneth ; oaths of fealty were sworn firstly to him and secondly to the king's ten-year-old grandson, Robert Stewart,[154] son of Marjory Bruce and Walter the Steward. In the Scone parliament of December 1318, after the death of Edward Bruce at Faughart, Robert Stewart had been recognised as the king's heir presumptive.[155] With the birth of David Bruce he lost this position, and in a new parliamentary tailzie of 15 July 1326 was recognised as successor to David only if the latter should die without an heir of his own ;[156] it seemed that the Bruce dynasty was assured of continuation. Few could have supposed that the Cambuskenneth tailzie would be a live issue in politics some decades later.

Bernard of Linton had celebrated the birth of King Robert's son with Latin verses which foretold that David 'will hold warlike revels amid English gardens; or God will bring to pass a firm peace betwixt the kingdoms'.[157] In the winter of 1324 peace talks were in fact held at York, but Edward refused to contemplate 'the manifest disinheritance of our royal crown'—recognition of Bruce as independent king of an independent Scotland.[158] Thus the Scots had failed to achieve the main object that had been envisaged as following from the truce

---

[151] *Ibid.*, 51.   [152] *Ibid.*, 53.   [153] *Ibid.*, 52.
[154] *Chron. Fordun*, I. 351.   [155] *A.P.S.*, I. 465-6.
[156] The text of the tailzie, which survived till the mid-seventeenth century (*ibid.*, VI. pt. 2, 628, 664), has been lost, but the terms may be readily inferred.
[157] *Chron. Bower*, II. 279-80.   [158] Barrow, *Bruce*, p. 353.

of Bishopthorpe. And while Edward professed strict adherence to the truce he could not prevent English privateers from preying upon the vulnerable Scottish shipping route to Flanders. Piracy culminated in the seizure of the *Pelarym*, a Flemish vessel with a cargo worth £2,000. The Scots on board, including women and pilgrims, were massacred.[159] For this and other outrages Bruce demanded redress in vain.[160] Moreover although Edward had bound himself not to oppose moves for a Scottish reconciliation with the papacy he maintained his opposition.

As the prospect of peace receded, King Robert issued letters empowering Randolph and other envoys to negotiate an alliance with France. A year later, on 26 April 1326, a new Franco-Scottish alliance was concluded at Corbeil.[161] Both in peace and war French kings would aid and counsel the Scots against the English 'to the best of their power as loyal allies', while the Scots were bound 'to make war on the king of England to the utmost of their power' in the event of war between the English and the French. The renewed Franco-Scottish alliance imposed heavier commitments on the Scots than on the French, but henceforward Scotland would no longer be isolated : it had as its ally the richest and most powerful country in Europe ; if English kings attacked Scotland they would have to keep an eye on France. Bruce had set in place what was to be the keystone of Scottish diplomacy for the rest of the Middle Ages. And new cultural ties with France replaced those with England severed by long years of warfare. As early as 1313 Bishop David of Moray had projected a scheme for sending four poor scholars from his diocese to the university of Paris, and in 1325 he provided some endowment to make the scheme permanent.[162] Moreover, by 1336 Scots at the university of Orleans, the greatest law school north of the Alps, were numerous enough to comprise a distinct 'nation' (student association).[163]

Meanwhile England was racked by the dissensions that culminated in the deposition of Edward II at the hands of his wife and her paramour, Roger Mortimer, whose cruelty shocked the Scots.[164] Edward was imprisoned while Isabella and Mortimer misruled the land

[159] *Cal. Docs. Scot.*, III. Nos. 888, 889.
[160] Barbour, *The Bruce*, II. 145–6.
[161] Text in *A.P.S.*, XII. 5–6.
[162] It was not, however, until the late sixteenth century that the Scots College in Paris became a significant institution. See Violette M. Montagu, 'The Scottish College in Paris', *S.H.R.*, IV. 399–416, at 399.
[163] John Kirkpatrick, 'The Scottish "Nation" in the University of Orleans', *S.H.S. Misc. II.* 47–102, at 51.
[164] *Chron. Wyntoun*, II. 372.

in the name of the fourteen-year-old Edward III. Faithful to the last to the imprisoned ex-king was King Robert's nephew, Donald of Mar, who had been brought up at the English court. On the fall of Edward II he returned to Scotland to be welcomed back and restored to his earldom of Mar. It suited King Robert to give Donald a free hand in his plots to raise English, Scots and Welsh for the release of the captive Edward. When the latter's son was crowned as Edward III on 1 February 1327 the Scots marked the event by a surprise assault on Norham Castle.[165] Nothing would now content Bruce but a final peace and his recognition as independent king of an independent Scotland. Even before negotiations once more broke down over this issue Mortimer and Isabella had begun mobilisation to meet a new Scottish invasion.[166]

The brilliant strategy that Bruce had devised for the warfare that was renewed in 1327 was in three phases; and the first of these opened not in England but in Ireland. It was not for nothing that King Robert had lately paid so much attention to the western approaches. After Easter 1327 he landed in Antrim, hoping to take advantage of the disorders in Ulster that followed upon the recent death of his father-in-law, the Red Earl.[167] The second phase of his strategy came in July when the north of England was invaded by three Scottish battalions under Randolph, Douglas, and Donald of Mar. Hurriedly the English host arrived in Durham on 15 July to spend some days of rain-sodden hardship in search of the Scots, who were strongly stationed on the southern bank of the Wear near Stanhope. Heralds were sent in vain to invite the Scots to abandon their position. When they did cross the river it was in a night attack led by Sir James Douglas, who swept through the English encampment and cut the guy-ropes of the royal tent. The young Edward was 'wonder sore afraiede' but escaped capture. Thereafter the Scots had no difficulty in retiring from Weardale. On 7 August Edward was told of their 'escape' and 'ful hertly wepte with his yonge eyne'. The English host marched dejectedly back to Durham and then to York, where it disbanded.[168] This was the signal for the third phase of King Robert's strategy. On 12 July 1327 he had forced the Ulster seneschal to conclude a humiliating truce to last a full year from 1 August 1327.[169] As on previous occasions, the conclusion of a truce in one

[165] Nicholson, *Edward III*, pp. 13–36.   [166] *Ibid.*, pp. 15–21.
[167] Nicholson, *op. cit.*, *S.H.R.*, XLII. 30–40.
[168] Nicholson, *Edward III*, pp. 20–36.
[169] Nicholson, *op. cit.*, *S.H.R.*, XLII. 30–40.

locality was merely the prelude to Bruce's appearance in another. After the forces of Randolph, Douglas and Donald of Mar had safely returned to Scotland King Robert crossed the Tweed with a fresh Scottish army. Engines of war were erected before Norham by John Crabb and Bruce ostentatiously let it be known that his intention was to annex Northumberland and parcel it out among his followers— some charters were in fact issued.[170] While the English government could remain indifferent to raids upon the north it could not afford to ignore either the siege of Norham or the threatened annexation of Northumberland. The Weardale expedition had cost the English about £70,000.[171] It was impossible at short notice to raise a new force large enough to repel the Scots. Mortimer and Isabella had no alternative but to make peace.

In a letter dated at Berwick on 18 October 1327 King Robert dictated his terms. He was to have the realm of Scotland 'free, quit, and entire, without any kind of feudal subjection, for himself and his heirs forever'. There was to be a marriage between his son and the sister of the English king. No claim was to be presented for the restoration of those disinherited by either side. There was to be an alliance between both kings for mutual support in so far as this did not infringe the Franco-Scottish alliance. Edward was to use his good offices to persuade the pope to revoke the sentences of excommunication and interdict. The Scots would pay Edward £20,000 within three years after the confirmation of peace.[172] In some respects the six points of the Berwick letter differed from the terms of Bruce's indenture with Harclay in 1323 and showed the strengthening of the Scottish position. In other respects the characteristics of both sets of proposals remained the same : they were pragmatic and nationalist and showed Bruce's antipathy towards the disinherited Anglo-Scots.

By 1328 negotiations on the six points had gone so far that an English parliament was summoned to York to sanction the disagreeable concessions that would have to be made to the Scots. As a foretaste of what was to come, letters patent were issued on 1 March 1328 in the name of Edward III admitting that he and previous English kings had brought affliction to both realms by asserting rights of dominion, rule, or superiority over the realm of Scotland. Any such rights were now renounced. The realm of Scotland was now conceded to the 'magnificent prince, the Lord Robert, by the grace of God, King of Scots, our ally and dear friend'. Its boundaries were to be

[170] Nicholson, *Edward III*, pp. 42–5.
[171] *Ibid.*, pp. 38–40.   [172] Stones, *Documents*, pp. 158–60.

those of the time of Alexander III. It was to be 'separate in all things from the kingdom of England, assured forever of its territorial integrity, to remain forever free and quit of any subjection, servitude, claim or demand.' [173] Since Bruce was thus at long last recognised by the English as king, envoys were sent north to treat with him and his parliament at Edinburgh, a parliament to which there were summoned not only the lay and ecclesiastical magnates but freeholders and burgesses. After a week's discussion of the final texts the peace treaty was concluded on 17 March 1328 in the chamber in Holyrood where King Robert lay ill. On 4 May 1328 the terms of the 'final peace' were ratified by the English parliament at Northampton.[174] The papacy lost no time in making its own peace with Scotland : on 15 October 1328 it was decided to lift the interdict and release Bruce from excommunication.[175]

The treaty of Edinburgh-Northampton,[176] the culmination of King Robert's career, was destined to have no more lasting significance than the truce of Bishopthorpe : the 'final peace' and the thirteen-year truce each brought a cessation of hostilities for only four years. Given the character of Edward III it is unlikely that any settlement achieved in 1328 would have proved enduring. It is significant, however, that the treaty of 1328 excluded only one of the six points of 1327 and that it was this excluded item that eventually led to renewed war; for the terms of the treaty said nothing of the disinherited.

The most promising clause in Bruce's letter of 1327 and in the treaty was the proposed marriage, which held out the prospect of a return to the family relationship, close, but not too close, that had existed in the thirteenth century between the Scottish and English royal houses. Edward's sister, Joan, was to be assigned an income of £2,000 in Scotland as her dower (nothing was said of a dowry). She was to be conveyed to Berwick by 15 July 1328 and a marriage was to take place 'as soon as properly can be' between her and King Robert's son and heir.[177] On 16 July 1328 David and Joan were married at Berwick; the bride was seven years old and the bridegroom four. King Robert spent almost £1,000 on the wedding celebrations.[178]

[173] *Ibid.*, pp. 161–2.
[174] E. L. G. Stones, 'The English Mission to Edinburgh in 1328', *S.H.R.*, XXVIII. 121–32.   [175] *Cal. Papal Letters*, II. 289.
[176] Text in Stones, *Documents*, pp. 161–70.
[177] *Ibid.*, p. 165.   [178] *E.R.*, I. 118, 119, 185.

Mortimer and Isabella had conducted Joan to Berwick, and Isabella had more on her mind than her daughter's wedding. Just as the treaty of 1328 had said nothing of the disinherited so it had said nothing of the Scottish enthronement stone or of the Black Rood of Holyrood which Edward I had seized in 1296. Isabella was entrusted with a mission to persuade the Scots to restore some of the disinherited as the price of a restoration of these relics. She had intended to take the stone northwards as a tempting bait but was forced to negotiate without it: the Londoners prevented its removal from Westminster Abbey.[179] Even so, Isabella's diplomacy had some effect: on 28 July 1328 King Robert issued a charter allowing Henry Percy to sue in Scottish courts for recovery of the Scottish lands which had pertained to his father 'by hereditary right or in any just and legitimate manner whatsoever'. Similar charters were almost certainly issued at the same time in favour of Thomas Wake, William la Zouche and Henry Beaumont. By 1330 Percy had had his Scottish claims satisfied and, in return, Sir James Douglas and Sir Henry Prendergast had recovered ancestral lands in Northumberland. Wake, Zouche and Beaumont were left disappointed.[180]

It was an ill omen that Edward III had absented himself from the marriage festivities at Berwick. Although King Robert must have looked on the wedding as the ultimate symbol of his own triumph, he too failed to attend: a point of honour made him counter Edward's disparaging absence by his own. It was given out that King Robert lay sick at Cardross.[181] But the king's infirmity did not prevent him from sailing to Ulster within a few weeks. One of the wedding guests had been William de Burgh, grandson and heir of the deceased Red Earl and full cousin of the bridegroom. There were tortuous but obscure transactions involving King Robert, Queen Isabella, William de Burgh, and Carrickfergus Castle. When Bruce landed in Ulster it was to escort William de Burgh to his heritage, perhaps also to tidy up the situation in Ulster when the local truce of 1327 expired on 1 August 1328.[182]

A year before, a hostile observer had sent news to England that Bruce would not outlive the Ulster truce: 'Sir Robert de Brus is so weak and wasted that, God willing, he will not last that time; for he could scarce move anything save his tongue.'[183] In England men

[179] E. L. G. Stones, 'An Addition to the "Rotuli Scotiae"', S.H.R., xxix. 23–51, at 33, 51.
[180] Nicholson, Edward III, pp. 57–9.
[181] Barbour, The Bruce, ii. 174.
[182] Nicholson, op. cit., S.H.R., xlii. 30–40, at 34–8.   [183] Ibid., 34.
E.H.S.—5*

styled his illness leprosy.[184] The king's last expedition to Ulster in the summer of 1328 was also to be the last notable enterprise of his life; in the spring of 1329 he made a slow and wearisome pilgrimage to the shrine of St Ninian at Whithorn and spent some days seeking the intercession of the saint before being carried home to die.[185] In the restrained language of Froissart,[186] or the more poignant recital of the Scottish poet Barbour, the deathbed scene at Cardross recalls the *Morte d'Arthur*. Bruce had summoned all his lords and told them of his longing to go on crusade. His body could no longer go; but he bade them choose a noble knight to bear his heart against the foes of God. With the choice of Douglas he was well content. On 7 June 1329 the king died. As the tidings spread through the land, so it was said, even knights wept bitterly, drove their fists together, and tore their clothes like madmen.[187]

[184] *Chron. Lanercost*, pp. 259, 264; *Scalacronica*, p. 159. Barbour does not describe the illness but attributes its origins to a 'fundying' or severe chill brought on by the king's early hardships (*The Bruce*, II. 174).

[185] Barrow, *Bruce*, pp. 438–9.

[186] *Chron. Froissart*, I. 67–9.

[187] Barbour, *The Bruce*, II. 177–81.

6

THE SON OF KING ROBERT AND THE SON OF KING JOHN

When the body of King Robert had been laid to rest at Dunfermline Douglas set sail from Montrose with the king's embalmed heart. Alfonso XI of Castile and León welcomed his aid in the war against the 'Saracens' of Granada. On 25 March 1330 Douglas fought his last battle. His bones were brought back for burial in Douglas Kirk, and Bruce's heart, as he had desired, was interred in Melrose.[1]

Ever since the settlement of the succession at Ayr in 1315 Thomas Randolph, Earl of Moray, had been designated to act as guardian of Scotland in the event of a royal minority. His firm rule was based on a strict enforcement of justice even in the remotest areas. Fifty criminal heads set on spikes on the ramparts of Eilean Donan Castle demonstrated his rigour in pursuing 'mysdoaris' and led the chronicler Wyntoun to exclaim :

> Wes nevyr nane in justice lyk
> Till this Erle in oure kynryk.[2]

Meanwhile the treaty of 1328 had brought peace with England, though not cordiality. So long as Mortimer and Isabella stayed in power—and they did not hesitate to murder the captive Edward II in order to do so—the Scots had nothing to fear. The situation altered on 19 October 1330 when the adolescent Edward III carried out a *coup d'état* at Nottingham, arrested and executed Mortimer, and sent Isabella into well-deserved seclusion.

---

[1] Barbour, *The Bruce*, II. 183–96; *Chron. Froissart*, I. 69–70.
[2] *Chron. Wyntoun*, II. 377–80; for the Highland background see W. Matheson, 'Traditions of the Mackenzies', *Trans. Gaelic Soc. Inverness*, XXXIX. 1–36.

While the keynote of Edward I's reign had been *legalitas*, that of
Edward III's was to be *militia* or chivalry. Just as an outward respect
for legal principles had partly concealed the egotistic ruthlessness of
Edward I, so also the panache of chivalry partly concealed the aggressive ambitions of Edward III. Urbane and courteous, he nonetheless
kept an eye on the main chance; more opportunist and versatile than
his grandfather, he was always willing to abandon one road to his goal
as soon as he encountered a tedious obstacle. He had not concealed
his dislike of 'the shameful peace' of 1328 and put diplomatic pressure on the Scots to restore the disinherited Henry Beaumont and
Thomas Wake. The Scots took little heed.[3] Before long Edward was
to assert that he was not bound by the treaty of Edinburgh-Northampton since he had sealed it when he was under age. But he was
unlikely to press matters too far until the Scots had fully paid the
£20,000 promised under the treaty of 1328.

This sum was officially styled in Scotland 'the contribution for
peace'. No official explanation was ever given as to why the Scots
should make such a contribution, but it was popularly supposed to be
reparation for the damage inflicted on the English.[4] The assessment
already carried out for the raising of the 'tenth penny' granted at
Cambuskenneth was also used for the levying of the peace contribution. The burgesses, however, preferred to compound for their share
by paying a total of 1,500 marks in three equal instalments.[5]

By the time the last instalment of the peace contribution had been
paid to the English at midsummer 1331 it had become clear that
Edward's diplomacy was unlikely to secure the restoration of Wake
and Beaumont. Henceforward the Scots would have to deal not with
a mere segment of the disinherited but with all of them,[6] for the influential and talented Beaumont was organising an expedition in
which all those with claims on Scottish lands might unite to recover
those lands by force. To lend some dignity to the enterprise Beaumont
conducted to England Edward Balliol, son and heir of the late King
John.

For some time Edward Balliol had been living on the family
estates in Picardy to which his father had retired to die in obscurity.
His character was more forceful than that of his father, and by 1331
he was in the prime of life while the Bruce occupant of the throne

---

[3] Nicholson, *Edward III*, pp. 54–5, 64–5, 67–9.
[4] *Chron. Fordun*, I. 352.
[5] Nicholson, *Edward III*, pp. 59–60, 70.
[6] For the various classes of the disinherited see *ibid.*, pp. 65–7.

was a mere child. With Beaumont's help and the benevolent neutrality of Edward III Balliol was ready to make a bid for the throne that his father had too meekly vacated. Soon after the Scots had paid the last instalment of the peace contribution he returned to England and secretly did homage to Edward III for his prospective kingdom of Scotland. The English king was unwilling to allow so open a breach of the peace as an armed invasion across the border. He had no objection to a filibustering expedition by sea.[7]

Probably because of the unexpected revival of the Balliol cause Randolph hastened the first Scottish coronation. For King Robert had applied to the pope not only for the revoking of excommunication and interdict but also for the privileges of coronation and unction, which were conferred by a papal bull issued on 13 June 1329, six days after the king's death.[8] On 24 November 1331 King Robert's son was crowned and anointed in Scone Abbey by James Bennet, Bishop of St Andrews.[9] David II had succeeded not only to an independent kingdom but to a kingship from which the last hint of inferiority had been removed.

The festivities at Scone were symptomatic of a dangerous euphoria and over-confidence on the part of those who took for granted the victory that King Robert and his generation had wrested from defeat. The disinherited would face a Scotland outwardly united and secure, inwardly weakened by the recent deaths of King Robert, Sir James Douglas, Walter the Steward, Bernard of Linton, Bishop David of Moray and Bishop Lamberton of St Andrews; and Thomas Randolph was nearing his end.

The guardian was not blind to the menacing moves of the disinherited and was in the midst of military preparations south of the Forth when he died at Musselburgh on 20 July 1332. The disinherited were quick off the mark: they set sail from the Humber on 31 July and landed at Kinghorn on 6 August.[10] Their leaders included Edward Balliol, Henry Beaumont (claimant through his wife, Alice Comyn, to the earldom of Buchan), his son-in-law David of Strathbogie (claimant to the earldom of Atholl), Gilbert Umfraville (claimant to the earldom of Angus), Richard Talbot, Ralph Stafford, Henry Ferrers, Alexander and John Mowbray.[11] With them they had something like five hundred men-at-arms and a thousand footmen and archers. The Lanercost chronicler remarked: 'Oh how small a

---

[7] *Ibid.*, pp. 71-3, 75-8.　　　　[8] *Nat. MSS. Scot.*, II. No. xxx.
[9] *Chron. Bower*, II. 302-3.　　　　[10] Nicholson, *Edward III*, pp. 77-9.
[11] *Ibid.*, pp. 79-80. For their claims see *ibid.*, pp. 65-7.

number of warriors was this to invade a kingdom then all too confident of its strength !' [12]

But the moment was opportune. There was some acrimony when the Scottish magnates assembled at Perth on 2 August to choose a new guardian. They chose Donald of Mar, who, although a nephew of King Robert, had nevertheless been associated with some of the disinherited and had possibly pledged support to Edward Balliol. Once elected, however, Mar made ready to resist the invaders. The latter marched by way of Dunfermline towards Perth and reached the low southern bank of the river Earn to find the high bank on the other side—Dupplin Moor—already occupied by the forces of the guardian.[13]

From their superior position the Scottish troops could see that they greatly outnumbered the disinherited and spent the night in carefree carousal. During the night the disinherited stealthily picked their way across a ford and attacked part of the Scottish encampment. As dawn broke on the morning of 11 August 1332 they took up a strong defensive position : the knights and men-at-arms dismounted and formed a thin armoured line to strengthen the footmen, and archers were posted on either flank. Mar's great host, who had looked forward to an easy victory, were faced with a determined and well-prepared foe. At this critical time King Robert's bastard son, Sir Robert Bruce, accused the guardian of treachery. Mar gave him the lie and affirmed that he would be the first to come to blows with the enemy. There followed a confused and disorderly Scottish attack made even more disorderly as English arrows took their toll. The second Scottish battalion trod the first underfoot; more Scots died by suffocation than by the edge of the sword. The mass of dying men composed a little hill a spear's length in height. The guardian and many another Scottish noble lay among the fallen.[14]

If God fought for the righteous cause, He had shown at Dupplin that the righteous cause was that of Edward Balliol. After he had occupied Perth and successfully withstood a half-hearted siege, notable Scots from the neighbouring regions hastened to assure him of their loyalty. On 24 September 1332 Balliol was set on the throne at Scone by the Earl of Fife and crowned by Bishop William Sinclair of Dunkeld, whom Bruce had once styled 'my own bishop'.[15]

Soon after his coronation Balliol marched south to Galloway,

---

[12] *Ibid.*, pp. 80-1.   [13] *Ibid.*, pp. 81-5.   [14] *Ibid.*, pp. 85-93.
[15] *Ibid.*, pp. 84-94; *Chron. Bower*, ii. 259.

where Sir Eustace Maxwell of Caerlaverock had already put himself at the head of those Galwegians who had traditional loyalties to the Balliols and Comyns. After a brief stay to rally his Galwegian supporters Balliol established himself at Roxburgh. Meanwhile Sir Andrew Moray, son of Wallace's colleague and husband of Christian Bruce, King Robert's sister, had been chosen as guardian in succession to the late Donald of Mar. Not only was Sir Andrew uncle (by marriage) to the young David II but he was lord of Avoch in Ross and of Bothwell in Lanarkshire; his wide lands earned him the appellation 'le Riche'; and he was head of a family noted for its consistent patriotism.[16] When Balliol made his way to Roxburgh he was followed by Sir Andrew Moray and Sir Archibald Douglas. An attempt to capture Balliol misfired: it was Sir Andrew who was captured. With him was taken John Crabb, the Flemish military engineer and naval captain.[17] Until Sir Andrew was ransomed a year or two later the Scots were commanded by less competent military leaders.

Occasionally, however, they had their moments of success. On the capture of Sir Andrew it was Sir Archibald Douglas, youngest brother of the late Sir James, who was chosen to succeed as guardian. He seems to have concluded a truce with the unsuspecting Balliol. At Moffat Sir Archibald forgathered with Robert the Steward and John Randolph, the new Earl of Moray—both of them teenagers— and planned to take Balliol unawares. At dawn on 17 December 1332 they attacked at Annan while he and his entourage were still abed. The scantily-clad Balliol mounted an unbridled horse and rode pell-mell to Carlisle,[18] whence he sent envoys to plead with Edward III.

Already, on 23 November 1332, Balliol had issued letters patent at Roxburgh which set forth the relationship that he envisaged between himself and the English king. If King John had been a vassal king his son could not expect to be independent, thus the Roxburgh letters recognised that the English king was lord superior of Scotland. It was stated that Edward Balliol had already done homage and sworn fealty to Edward III in respect of the kingdom of Scotland. Balliol bound himself and his successors to renew this bond of homage and fealty. In return, the English king would maintain Balliol and his heirs in Scotland. In recompense for aid already received Balliol granted to Edward two thousand librates—lands worth £2,000 a year—to be selected from parts of Scotland adjacent to England and definitely to include the castle, town and sheriffdom of Berwick. The

16 Nicholson, *Edward III*, p. 92.
17 *Ibid.*, pp. 96–7.   18 *Ibid.*, 103–4.

two thousand librates would be separated from the kingdom of Scotland and annexed for ever to the kingdom of England.[19]

Despite this tempting bribe Edward toyed with the idea of ignoring both David Bruce and Edward Balliol and of striving to gain for himself the direct lordship of Scotland that his grandfather had once claimed. One obstacle to this inordinately ambitious policy was the obstructiveness of the English parliament. Another was Balliol's arrival as a helpless fugitive in Carlisle: the Bruce party was not, after all, so weak as Edward III had supposed; it would be necessary to follow only a moderately ambitious policy and to work with Balliol as an ally. Although the English parliament refused to accept responsibility for a renewal of the Scottish war Edward ignored it and began military preparations. In March 1333 Balliol rode over the border with a strong company of English magnates and men-at-arms and laid siege to Berwick. In May Edward arrived to direct the siege in person.[20]

In the great siege of 1319 the defenders had been notably helped by the technical skill of John Crabb. The siege of 1333 found him using his talents on behalf of the besiegers: after his capture at Roxburgh he had been forced to change sides in order to save his life and was to serve Edward III faithfully for the rest of his days.[21] So hard-pressed were the defenders that they handed over hostages to obtain a truce; if not relieved by the morning of 20 July 1333 they would capitulate to the English king.

All too belatedly the Scottish guardian had begun to ravage Northumberland and to threaten Edward's queen in Bamburgh Castle, but time was now on the side of Edward III and he refused to be drawn from the siege. Sir Archibald Douglas was forced to re-cross the Tweed and march rapidly to the relief of Berwick. The Scots were now in exactly the same situation as the English on the eve of Bannockburn. By the time the Scottish host neared Berwick the English had taken up a strong defensive position on Halidon Hill, which dominated all approaches to the town, leaving the guardian, on the afternoon of 19 July 1333, with no alternative but to attack or to see Berwick surrender. The Scottish host dismounted and clambered through a bog before climbing the hill. On top, Edward had also dismounted his troops and had formed them in three battalions, each flanked by a wing of archers. As the Scots advanced they were swept by a hail of arrows. Those who came to grips with the enemy

[19] *Ibid.*, pp. 97-9. [20] *Ibid.*, pp. 99-103, 105-18.
[21] *Ibid.*, pp. 120-1, 175, 188.

were forced to give way. The guardian and five Scottish earls were among the slain, and the stricken fugitives were slaughtered until night fell. Next morning the defenders of Berwick at last opened their gates to Edward.[22]

He at once took possession of Berwick and its sheriffdom as first instalment of the promised two thousand librates. Berwick was to be a useful base for English armies and fleets; with its varying hinterland it was to be the headquarters of English-occupied Scotland for more than a hundred years and symbolised the claims of successive English kings to the lordship of Scotland. Having seen to the administration of Berwick Edward III disbanded his troops and went rapidly southward. Among the Scots there remained scarcely anyone, so the English thought, who had the capacity, knowledge or desire to assemble a fighting force or to command it had it been assembled.[23]

This view seemed to be confirmed by the quiescence of the Scots in the aftermath of Halidon. Balliol was able to establish himself at Perth and to behave as if he were unquestioned King of Scotland. The disinherited were reinherited and their heritages were augmented: Henry Beaumont was to become Earl of Moray as well as of Buchan; Richard Talbot was to be Lord of Mar; David of Strathbogie, Earl of Atholl, was to be Steward of Scotland. As Strathbogie installed an English sheriff in Rothesay Castle, Robert the Steward escaped in a rowing-boat with his family charters and was welcomed in Dumbarton Castle, where David Bruce and his queen had already been sent for safety. Besides Dumbarton only the scattered strongholds of Kildrummy, Urquhart, Lochleven and Loch Doon kept alive the Bruce cause.[24] In February 1334 Balliol was able to hold a parliament at Holyrood.

The attendance at this parliament showed the strength and the weakness of Balliol's position. The Bishops of Glasgow, Aberdeen, Dunkeld, Galloway, Ross, Dunblane and Brechin had been induced to attend. The party of the disinherited was well represented. Patrick, Earl of March, temporarily in the pay of Edward III, had also come, but few other Scottish magnates made their appearance. Many must have been forfeited as traitors to Balliol; many must have been unwilling to take part in a parliament that was to receive English envoys who had come to press Balliol for a cession of the two thousand librates.

There was some delay before even this unrepresentative assembly could be induced on 12 February 1334 to issue documents ratifying

[22] *Ibid.*, pp. 123-36.   [23] *Ibid.*, pp. 137-8.   [24] *Ibid.*, pp. 138-51.

the Roxburgh letters patent. Thereafter Balliol had an interview with Edward III at Newcastle and on 12 June 1334 granted the full quota of the two thousand librates—the sheriffdoms of Berwick, Roxburgh, Selkirk, Peebles, Edinburgh and Dumfries, the constabularies of Linlithgow and Haddington, the forests of Ettrick and Jedburgh— to be annexed to the crown of England for all time to come. For what remained of his kingdom Balliol did homage to Edward a week later.[25]

Before this, however, the lull in Scottish resistance was coming to an end, and encouraging news arrived from France. Under the terms of the treaty of Corbeil the French king was not explicitly bound to make war upon the English in the event of an Anglo-Scottish war, but the French were bound to act as loyal allies of the Scots, and John Randolph, Earl of Moray, had gone to France to seek the aid of Philip VI. In the spring of 1334 Randolph returned to Dumbarton with a message inviting David II and his queen to take refuge in France. In May 1334 they landed safely in Normandy; Philip received them graciously and installed them in Château Gaillard on the Seine.[26] Edward III was to find Philip's diplomacy increasingly menacing as the war continued.

The return of Randolph with news of prospective French aid encouraged the Bruce party to take the offensive. In the summer of 1334 Randolph and the Steward, acting as joint guardians, overran most of south-west Scotland. Only in Galloway did they meet opposition : the Galwegians were divided in their allegiance, and, as the Lanercost chronicler complacently remarked, they mutually destroyed one another.[27] Next, Randolph and the Steward invaded the territories that Balliol had recently ceded to England for ever. The newly arrived English officials had to take refuge behind the walls of Berwick.[28]

They were soon joined by Edward Balliol, who was lucky to reach safety. In the face of a general Scottish uprising the disinherited had chosen to quarrel with Balliol and with one another over some Mowbray lands. Alexander and Geoffrey Mowbray joined the Bruce party. Richard Talbot and six of his knights were captured by the insurgents and held to ransom. David of Strathbogie was chased to Lochaber by John Randolph and on 27 September 1334 was forced to change sides and swear fealty to David II. Most important

[25] *Ibid.*, pp. 151–62.   [26] *E.R.*, I. 464.
[27] *Chron. Lanercost*, p. 278.
[28] Nicholson, *Edward III*, pp. 163–4, 167.

of all, Edward III had made the mistake of ransoming Sir Andrew Moray, the onetime guardian, in time to allow him a part in the Scottish rising. Sir Andrew and the turncoat Alexander Mowbray besieged Henry Beaumont in Dundarg Castle, an ancient Comyn stronghold on the Aberdeenshire coast that Beaumont had repaired. By the end of the year Dundarg had capitulated and Beaumont returned to England to find money for his ransom.[29]

Most of Scotland was lost to Edward III and to Balliol by the time the slow process of mobilising an English army was complete. Not until 14 November 1334 did Edward set out from Newcastle—winter campaigning was unpopular and he had mustered scarcely more than four thousand troops. He spent some months at Roxburgh rebuilding the castle and vainly demanding reinforcements. When the army disbanded in mid-February he had nothing to show for his efforts save a new stronghold in Roxburgh. Indiscriminate English raids in the lands between the Tweed and the Forth had alienated his chief Scottish adherent, Patrick, Earl of March, who now rejoined the Bruce party.[30] When Edward returned to England it was to face a French diplomatic offensive which resulted in an Anglo-Scottish truce to last from Easter to Midsummer 1335.

The truce suited Edward well: it allowed him time to organise English seapower for the blockade of Scotland, for the supply of his troops in the forthcoming summer campaign, and for defence of the English coast against possible French raids. In mid-July 1335 he set out from Carlisle at the head of over thirteen thousand troops; simultaneously a force under Edward Balliol set out from Berwick.[31] Although the Scottish leaders avoided the engagement that Edward was trying to provoke they did not remain inactive. The Count of Namur, cousin of Edward's queen, belatedly set out to catch up with the English army and was cornered in the ruins of Edinburgh Castle on 30 July 1335; he was forced to surrender and offer a ransom of £4,000. As John Randolph chivalrously escorted the count towards England the party was waylaid and Randolph was led off to several years of captivity in an English prison.[32]

Early in August 1335 Edward III and Balliol had reached Perth and made it their headquarters. The size of the English forces, unsurpassed in Edward's reign until the Crécy-Calais campaign of 1346, was intended to convince the Scots of the futility of resistance. David of Strathbogie hastened to make his peace with Edward and negoti-

[29] Ibid., pp. 168–72, 185–6.   [30] Ibid., pp. 174–91.
[31] Ibid., pp. 192–202.   [32] Ibid., pp. 212–4.

ated not only on his own account but on that of Robert the Steward and others. A pacification was concluded at Perth on 18 August 1335. Those who accepted its terms would be assured safety of life and limb and possession of their lands and offices; they would even be pardoned all trespasses they had committed from the creation of the world up to 18 August 1335. In addition, it was promised that the liberties of the Scottish kirk would be maintained; in the parts of Scotland directly ruled by Edward Balliol the laws of Alexander III's time would be observed. These terms amounted to little more than a face-saving formula under which David of Strathbogie could disguise the fact that he had changed allegiance for a second time.[33]

At first, Edward had high hopes of the pacification of Perth: on 22 August he rejected proposed French and papal arbitration and affirmed that by immense labours he had now established peace with the Scots. In September a fleet of fifty ships brought some 1,500 men from Ireland to attack the Steward's lands of Bute and Arran; Robert the Steward soon made his peace.[34] By mid-October both Edward and Balliol were back in Berwick. Although their vast forces had already disbanded they were confident that a short truce and some negotiation would soon bring the submission of Sir Andrew Moray and others who had not yet laid down arms. Talks were held with Sir Andrew at Bathgate but were broken off when news arrived of the activities of David of Strathbogie, whom Balliol had appointed his lieutenant in the north. Strathbogie was said to be rooting out every freeholder; he was also besieging Kildrummy Castle, which was defended by Sir Andrew's wife, Christian Bruce, sister of the late king.[35]

The threat to his wife brought Sir Andrew rapidly northward. With him he had the Earl of March and William Douglas—a Lothian landholder who was later to win notoriety as 'the Knight of Liddesdale'—and some eight hundred picked fighting men from the region south of Forth. They forded the Dee, entered the forest of Culblean which lay between them and Kildrummy, and during the night of 29 November 1335 followed a circuitous route to take Strathbogie unawares. At dawn they found him forewarned. Nonetheless a trick on the part of the crafty William Douglas provoked the enemy to break ranks in a wild onrush. As Strathbogie's men lost impetus on reaching a burn, Douglas gave a signal for his men to dash downhill with levelled spears. Strathbogie refused to yield and died fighting with his back to an oak tree.[36]

[33] *Ibid.*, pp. 207, 214–6.   [34] *Ibid.*, pp. 216, 219–22, 227.
[35] *Ibid.*, pp. 217–8, 224, 227–31.   [36] *Ibid.*, pp. 231–5.

His defeat and death in the forest of Culblean on St Andrew's Day, 1335, undid most of what Edward III had achieved in his great summer offensive. From the time of Culblean onward, claimed the chronicler Fordun, the fortune of war began to favour the Scots.[37] In vain Edward successively extended a truce up to May 1336 and received envoys from Château Gaillard at his March parliament in Westminster. It was too late to solve the Scottish question by some judicious dynastic juggling between Edward Balliol and David Bruce.[38] By February 1336 some Scots were disregarding the truce and asserting—as the defenders of Stirling had done in 1304— that they adhered to the Lion, the heraldic symbol of Scottish kingship.[39]

The victory at Culblean had confirmed the position of Sir Andrew Moray as chief leader of Scottish resistance. In the spring of 1336 a council held at Dunfermline re-appointed him as guardian of Scotland.[40] With the failure of peace talks Edward III was faced with the necessity of new campaigns in Scotland and dashed north with a small company to assume command at Perth.[41] On 12 July 1336 he rode out on an expedition that happily combined both a serious military objective and a flamboyant deed of chivalry—the rescue of Katherine Beaumont, Countess of Atholl, the widow of David of Strathbogie.

She had taken refuge in the island castle of Lochindorb and had been blockaded by Sir Andrew Moray. On 15 July Edward and his men rode twenty miles in hope of taking Sir Andrew by surprise. As the English drew near he was hearing mass in the wood of Stronkalter[42] and no one dared interrupt him. He showed remarkable coolness before withdrawing his troops at the last moment. Foiled in his hopes of bringing Sir Andrew to bay Edward pressed on to Lochindorb and had the satisfaction of rescuing Countess Katherine and 'othir ladys that ware luvely'.[43] He spent some time burning Forres and Kinloss and the neighbouring countryside, then turned southeast from Elgin (where he spared the cathedral) to take vengeance on Aberdeen, where Sir Thomas Roscelyn, a celebrated English

---

[37] Ibid., pp. 235–6.
[38] Rot. Scot., I. 384–91; Foedera, II. pt. iii, 142, 144; Chron. Lanercost, pp. 284–5.
[39] Rot. Scot., I. 401.   [40] Chron. Fordun, I. 360.
[41] Scalacronica, p. 166; B.M. MS. Nero C. VIII. Wardrobe Book, ff. 242, 242v.
[42] For its location see G. W. S. Barrow, 'The Wood of Stronkalter', S.H.R., XLVI. 77–9.
[43] Chron. Wyntoun, II. 428–30; Original Letters, ed. Sir H. Ellis, 3rd series, I. 35

knight, had lately met his death. On Edward's approach ten foreign vessels wisely put to sea without waiting to pay customs duties. The buildings in Aberdeen, which were among the most substantial in Scotland, were levelled to the ground.[44]

The campaign of 1336 had shown that Edward's chance of easy victory by one decisive battle had disappeared. Sir Andrew Moray had reverted to the tactics and strategy that King Robert had used so successfully. Increasingly, the English would have to rely on garrisons and fortifications to hold the Scottish territories that they hoped to control. Belatedly Edward set his military architects to work to erect in other parts of Scotland fortifications similar to those that safeguarded his control of the Borders. There, in the winter of 1334, he had repaired Roxburgh Castle. About the same time the Percies and the Bohuns, on whom he had respectively conferred Jedburgh forest and Annandale, had repaired and garrisoned the castles of Jedburgh and Lochmaben; and Eustace Maxwell, one of Edward's remaining Scottish supporters, had repaired and garrisoned his castle of Caerlaverock. Not until September 1335, however, did Edward take in hand the repair of Edinburgh Castle;[45] the summer of 1336 saw the repair and garrisoning of Dunnottar, Lauriston and Kinneff, new works in progress at St Andrews and Leuchars, and the fortification of Perth with walls and towers financed by levies on the neighbouring monasteries.[46] Balliol was to garrison Perth throughout the winter of 1336–7 while Edward retired southward. As he passed through Stirling he gave orders for the construction of a new 'peel' on the ruins of the former castle. As he passed by Bothwell he gave directions for the rebuilding of that castle.[47] After a brief visit to England to hold a parliament he came back to Bothwell and was to remain there until Christmas 1336.

The new fortifications that Edward was erecting were to serve not only as military strongpoints but as centres for his administration. In occupied Scotland his sheriffs were able to draw some revenue for the years between 1335 and 1337. But if Edward's administration was partly effective it was also intolerable. Much of the revenue was obtained from wholesale forfeitures; and from forfeited lands it was often impossible to obtain revenue since the lands were

[44] *Original Letters*, I. 35; *Chron. Fordun*, I. 360; *Chron. Wyntoun*, II. 422–3; *E.R.*, I. 449.

[45] Nicholson, *Edward III*, pp. 189, 224–6.

[46] *Chron. Bower*, II. 323.

[47] *Chron. Lanercost*, pp. 286–7; *Scalacronica*, pp. 166–7; *Cal. Docs. Scot.*, III. lvii.

waste and there was nothing left to distrain. The south of Scotland had been reduced to a desert.[48] Occupied Scotland had nothing more to lose by opposing Edward : he 'soon lost all the castles and towns that he had caused to be fortified in Scotland through default of good governance in the pursuit of his conquest'.[49]

Certainly in the months between October 1336 and May 1337 English power in Scotland suffered an overwhelming reverse. The prestige that Sir Andrew Moray had already won was increased by his remorseless attacks on the English-held strongholds. In the closing months of 1336 he captured and destroyed the fortresses of Dunnottar, Kinneff, Lauriston and Kinclaven. In February 1337, with the Earls of Fife and March and William Douglas, he was active in Fife. Only the castle of Cupar, held by Balliol's chamberlain, William Bullock, resisted the onslaught. St Andrews Castle held out for three weeks before it succumbed to a redoubtable siege machine aptly termed 'Boustour'. Each captured stronghold was destroyed. Edward looked on, apparently helplessly, from Bothwell, before leaving Scotland to spend Christmas in Newcastle. In March 1337 Sir Andrew and the 'Boustour' arrived at Bothwell and battered down the castle [50] while Edward was holding the fateful Westminster parliament that sanctioned a war more grandiose than that of Scotland.

Through his mother, sole survivor of the offspring of Philip IV, Edward could put forward a claim to the French crown. But his motive for war with Philip VI was scarcely a sudden recollection of a dynastic claim that had long remained dormant. From the dynastic issue Edward was willing to draw what profit he might— just as he had done in Scotland—but in addition warfare in itself held a lure for him and his magnates.[51] By 1337 it was clear that warfare in Scotland would bring little military glory and that expenditure upon it (£16,000 in 1336 alone)[52] far outweighed any possible return in revenue, ransom or booty. France, however, offered greater opportunities. In any case Edward had probably concluded that he could never crush Scotland until he had first disabled Scotland's ally. His efforts had been constantly hampered by fear of French naval preparations, and in 1336 the French galleys which had been assembled at Marseilles for a proposed crusade were transferred

[48] *Cal. Docs. Scot.*, III. 317–47, 368–93.
[49] *Scalacronica*, pp. 166–7.   [50] *Chron. Bower*, II. 323–4.
[51] May McKisack, *The Fourteenth Century*, p. 126.
[52] B.M. MS. Nero C. VIII. Wardrobe Book, ff. 244, 260, 280.

to the Channel ports. By continental warfare Edward hoped to
forestall Philip's designs against England. From 1337 onwards 'both
kings were engaged in feverish preparations, raising troops, ships, and
supplies, cementing alliances, devising schemes of invasion.'[53]

The waning of Edward's interest in Scotland was shown in March
1337 when Thomas Beauchamp, Earl of Warwick, was appointed
'captain and leader' of the army of Scotland to 'represent the person
of the lord king.'[54] Thus the organisation set up for Warwick's force
'inaugurated something in the nature of a standing Scottish command.'[55] It was not a success. In the summer months of 1337 the
forces under Warwick fluctuated wildly in number but probably
never exceeded 3,500 men.[56] From mid-June to mid-August the
shire levies were absent. On 7 August Sir Andrew Moray seized the
opportunity to raid Cumberland. At the end of September he was
raiding Northumberland. In mid-October, when Warwick had
only some three hundred men-at-arms, the Scots circled Carlisle and
burned the nearby manor of the bishop, who had unwisely accompanied Warwick in the field. By the raids over the border Sir Andrew
Moray 'enriched his army'.[57] Nonetheless much of the south of Scotland was still in English hands. At the end of the year Sir Andrew
failed in an attempt on Edinburgh Castle; and an engagement at
Crichton in which William Douglas distinguished himself was indecisive. There followed the 'wholesale destruction of Lothian'—apparently by both sides.[58] Meanwhile the unsuccessful Warwick was replaced by Richard Fitzalan, Earl of Arundel, and William Montagu,
Earl of Salisbury, who were to be joint captains of the English forces
in Scotland.[59] In contrast to the aimlessness of recent English strategy
the Arundel-Salisbury expedition had a definite objective—the castle
of Dunbar, rebuilt in 1333 at the expense of Edward III.[60] An attack
on Dunbar, which was a thorn in the flesh of the English administration in south-east Scotland, was a sensible way of using a small field
army to support the threatened English garrisons. If successful it
would give the impression of a resumed English offensive.

Delayed in Northumberland by the Christmas festivities, Arundel

[53] May McKisack, The Fourteenth Century, p. 127.
[54] Rot. Scot., I. 488; Chron. Lanercost, p. 289.
[55] N. B. Lewis, 'The recruitment and organisation of a contract army, May
to November 1337', B.I.H.R., xxxvii. 1–19, at 4–5.
[56] Ibid., 16–9.
[57] Chron. Lanercost, pp. 291–3; Chron. Bower, II. 324.
[58] Chron. Fordun, I. 362; Chron. Lanercost, p. 293.
[59] Rot. Scot., I. 503–10.   [60] Nicholson, Edward III, pp. 143-4.

and Salisbury did not begin the siege of Dunbar until 13 January 1338,[61] by which time some shire levies had already disbanded. Two Genoese galleys manned with crossbowmen had been hired to take part in a naval blockade, and engines of war had been shipped from Berwick and the Tower of London to bombard the castle. A remarkable number of sappers and military engineers—among them the talented John Crabb—set to work in the vicinity. The Earl of March had cautiously absented himself from Dunbar and left the defence in the hands of his wife, Agnes Randolph, sister of John Randolph, Earl of Moray, who had lain a prisoner in England since his capture in 1335. Countess Agnes, popularly known as Black Agnes 'be ressone scho was blak skynnit',[62] conducted the defence womanfully and with a certain flamboyance, mocking the attackers with word and gesture. When Edward III heard of her stout resistance he paid a flying visit to interview Montagu and the other magnates at Whitekirk,[63] probably in the old kirk which has survived the attacks of both English pirates and suffragettes. The king's long-postponed 'passage overseas' provided a smokescreen behind which the besiegers gracefully retired. The Dunbar expedition, which had cost almost £6,000,[64] ended with the granting of a truce to the Scots up to Michaelmas 1339.[65] An English chronicler might well remark that the outcome was 'wasteful, and neither honourable nor secure, but useful and advantageous to the Scots'.[66]

Edward III was at last ready for his 'passage overseas'. On 16 July 1338 he set sail from Orwell with 115 ships and landed at Antwerp, and with him went, sooner or later, many who had hitherto been foremost in the Scottish war, including Beaumont, who died in the Low Countries in 1340. The chronicler Wyntoun rightly affirmed that it was lucky for Scotland that Edward had embarked on the French war : if the English had concentrated on Scotland alone they would have 'skaithit it to gretly'.[67]

Good fortune was tempered with misfortune : at a time when the English threat was waning the Scots were to lose the sound leadership of Sir Andrew Moray. He had retired to his castle of Avoch in Ross, 'his own country', where he died in the spring of 1338.[68] Despite the miseries of the scorched-earth tactics he had been forced to em-

---

[61] *Chron. Fordun*, I. 363; P.R.O. Various Accounts, E. 101, 20/25.
[62] Pitscottie, *Historie*, I. 63.   [63] *Scalacronica*, p. 168.
[64] P.R.O. Various Accounts, E. 101, 20/25.
[65] *Chron. Lanercost*, p. 297; *Rot. Scot.*, I. 540.
[66] *Chron. Walsingham*, I. 200.   [67] *Chron. Wyntoun*, II. 435.
[68] *Ibid.*, 437–9; *Chron. Lanercost*, p. 296.

ploy he was remembered for his personal virtues and for the success of a strategy that had exactly copied that of King Robert: 'all the castellis he kest down'.[69] At his death the English held only two strongholds north of Forth—Cupar and Perth.

As Sir Andrew's career came to a close it was William Douglas and Alexander Ramsay of Dalhousie whose military reputations stood highest among the Scots. Each had proved himself a successful tactician. Whether either of them possessed a grasp of strategy comparable to that of Sir Andrew Moray is doubtful. In any case, neither of them had the landed authority to qualify for the post of guardian that became vacant on Sir Andrew's death. Almost inevitably the post went to Robert the Steward, now twenty-two years old and at last qualified by age to take full advantage of his position as heir presumptive to the crown. At this time, affirms the chronicler Bower, the Steward was young in years, but old in deeds, especially against the English.[70] What these deeds were it would be hard to say: although the Steward's submission to Edward III in 1335 had not lasted long there is no sign of any activity on his part for the next few years. Under the newly appointed guardian the Scottish offensive slackened. William Douglas went off to the court of Château Gaillard where the fourteen-year-old David II was beginning to be a figure to be reckoned with. It was from that quarter that a new initiative came: on 5 October 1338 French galleys burned Southampton;[71] in the following year there were similar raids along the south coast; and it was suspected that David II's court had a hand in these exploits.[72] Certainly it was with money from Château Gaillard that William Douglas hired the services of a French pirate whose five galleys blockaded the Tay [73] and cut off the English garrison in Perth from sea-borne victuals and reinforcements. Douglas also bribed William Bullock, the Scottish priest who held Cupar Castle for Balliol, to surrender the castle and join him at Perth, which was being besieged by the Earls of March and Ross and Robert the Steward.[74] Too late a relief army mustered under Balliol at the end of August:[75] Perth had capitulated on 17 August and its walls were cast down. The surrounding country had been so wasted in recent war-

[69] Chron. Wyntoun, II. 439.   [70] Chron. Bower, II. 328.
[71] Cal. Close 1339–41, pp. 550–1.   [72] Ibid., p. 6.
[73] E.R., I. 507; Chron. Bower, II. 330–1; Chron. Wyntoun, II. 451.
[74] Chron. Lanercost, p. 318; Chron. Bower, II. 330; Chron. Wyntoun, II. 451–4.
[75] P.R.O. Ancient Correspondence, S.C. I, vol. 42. No. 94a; Cal. Close 1339–41, p. 208.

fare that men died of hunger. A certain Crystyne Klek practised cannibalism.[76]

On 24 October 1339 a parliament met in Perth [77] and no doubt approved of arrangements for a siege of Stirling. Here there was no immediate success.[78] There were to be only desultory hostilities for almost two years. In the Low Countries too there was no decisive warfare; Edward established himself at Antwerp 'jousting and leading a jolly life'.[79] In diplomacy, however, he was active: Count Louis of Flanders was pro-French and, as Edward thought, had given aid and favour to the Scots as far as he could;[80] it was natural that Edward should ally himself with the bourgeois uprising against the count led by Jacques van Artevelde. The new Anglo-Flemish alliance affected the interests of Scotland as well as those of France. In 1340 David II emerged from Château Gaillard to take the field in Flanders alongside the Kings of France, Bohemia and Navarre.[81] At Lille the Earls of Salisbury and Suffolk were captured; Philip arranged that they should be exchanged for the captive Earl of Moray, and by the autumn of 1340 John Randolph was back in Scotland.[82]

He soon made up for his forced inactivity by inspiring a new Scottish offensive. He himself made a descent upon his lordship of Annandale [83] which Edward III had conferred upon the Bohuns. Meanwhile William Douglas and William Bullock devised a daring plan for the capture of Edinburgh Castle. Bullock and his men disguised themselves as English merchants and arranged to call at the castle on the morning of 16 April 1341. When the gate was opened they jammed the portcullis. A blast of a horn brought Douglas and his men from their hiding-place nearby and the townsfolk of Edinburgh rallied to their aid.[84] After winning Edinburgh the Scots could concentrate on the Borders. Randolph acted as warden of the West March, William Douglas held the Middle March, and Alexander Ramsay the East March. In the interior of the kingdom 'the land had rest' and good harvests brought an abundance of victuals.[85] The time had come to invite the king to end his seven-year exile in France.

[76] *Chron. Wyntoun*, II. 454–5.   [77] *A.P.S.*, I. 512.
[78] *Chron. Wyntoun*, II. 455–6; *Rot. Scot.*, I. 600.
[79] *Scalacronica*, p. 168.
[80] *Cal. Close 1337–39*, p. 327.   [81] *Chron. Froissart*, I. 119.
[82] *Chron. Wyntoun*, II. 462; *Cal. Close 1339–41*, p. 540.
[83] *Chron. Wyntoun*, II. 463.
[84] *Ibid.*, 457–60; *Chron. Fordun*, I. 365.
[85] *Chron. Wyntoun*, II. 463–4.

On 2 June 1341 David II and Queen Joan landed at Inverber-
vie from the two hired ships in which they had sailed secretly from
France. The seventeen-year-old king was 'ressavyd with blythnes' by
his people. He was unbridled in love; he liked jousting, dancing and
gaming, and, amusing himself with such pastimes, 'rade offt blythly
throw his land' [86]—which was what was expected of a young king.

David had come back to govern a land that had suffered the destruction of life and property, the clash of rival loyalties, the anarchy
caused by widespread invasion. Between 1332 and 1341 the Bruce
party had maintained an administration of sorts, especially in the
region between the Tay and the Moray Firth. There had been occasional parliaments, justice ayres, even exchequer audits, but the surviving financial records of the period show that the difficulties of
wartime administration were increased by baronial feuds and professional jealousies.[87] Not surprisingly, the chamberlain's account
covering the period 1334–1340 showed an accumulated deficit of
£2,881 19s. 2¼d. The only hope of recovery lay in a reconstruction
of strong royal government. With the king's return the guardianship
of Robert the Steward came to an end. For the next five years the
king's 'dearest nephew' was to be little more than the chief lay
witness to the royal charters.

Under David's personal rule there was progress toward more
settled conditions of government: a chamberlain ayre was held at
Inverness and the king was present when a justice ayre was held at
Cupar. In September 1341 parliament assembled at Scone and
sanctioned the levying of a 'contribution' from the kirk, from the
communities of the sheriffdoms, and from the burghs. This was a
'second contribution', for a 'first contribution' had already been
granted by a parliament held in Dundee sometime in 1340.[88] At the
exchequer audit of 1342 the chamberlain's receipts from these two
contributions came to about £1,205 in addition to some three hundred 'marts'. Thanks to this taxation the deficit on the chamberlain's account was a mere £1 19s. 4¼d.[89] This achievement no doubt
owed something to a new rigour in royal finance and to the abilities
of the new chamberlain—none other than Balliol's former chamberlain, the versatile William Bullock. Success in finance could hardly be
achieved without offending vested interests; a few months after he
had presented his accounts in 1342 Bullock was accused of treason,

[86] *Ibid.*, 466; *Chron. Fordun*, I. 365; *E.R.*, I. 506.
[87] *E.R.*, I. 435–68, *passim.*
[88] *Ibid.*, 511, 521, 501.   [89] *Ibid.*, clxvi, 512.

arrested by the king's command, and put in a prison where he shortly died.[90]

The contributions granted by the Dundee and Scone parliaments of 1340 and 1341 had a significance that was not only financial but constitutional: 'by September 1341 the burgesses had for the second time in about a year had their corporate part in payment of a contribution granted in parliament'.[91] Their share of the contribution was hardly a large one: of the total amount raised, about 70% came from the freeholders of the sheriffdoms, about 20% from the kirk, and less than 9%—or £100—from the burghs.[92] Yet, small though the share was, it can hardly have been made without the attendance of burgesses in the Dundee and Scone parliaments. In these two parliaments is to be found the missing link in the development of burgh representation between the end of the reign of Robert I and the later years of the reign of his son.

Burgh representation had survived a critical period, for there can be no doubt that the war had brought a severe setback to burgh life in Scotland. Aberdeen had been levelled to the ground in 1336. According to the 1342 exchequer accounts, Linlithgow and Haddington had been burnt, and Edinburgh was 'totally waste'. Perth and Inverness were 'in the hands of the king', presumably because of the dislocation of burghal administration. Yet recovery was swift: by 1341 Aberdeen had paid off its arrears to the chamberlain and was able to keep up payment of the £213 6s. 8d. that it owed each year in terms of its charter of 1319, and by 1343 Edinburgh was able to resume payment of its much smaller ferm and its export trade once more outstripped that of Aberdeen.[93]

To the Scottish kirk also, the war had brought setbacks. Some of these were a result of destruction which could be made good by renewed royal patronage—Kelso Abbey, which had probably suffered most, had its lands erected into a regality and was to have wood from the forests of Selkirk and Jedburgh for the repair of its burnt buildings.[94] But there were also setbacks in prestige and political power. There was a contrast between the part played by the Scottish kirk in the first war of independence and the part that it played in the second war of independence. In the former it had provided notable leaders and patriotic manifestoes. In the latter it provided neither:

---

[90] *Chron. Fordun*, I. 364–5.
[91] E. W. M. Balfour-Melville, 'Burgh Representation in Early Scottish Parliaments', *E.H.R.*, LIX. 79–87, at 86.   [92] *E.R.*, I. 501–3.
[93] *Ibid.*, 470, 471, 490, 521, 529, 533.   [94] *R.M.S.*, I. 483, 563, 569.

James Bennet, Bishop of St Andrews, had fled from Scotland after the disaster at Dupplin and soon died in exile in Flanders;[95] other Scottish prelates chose to leave Scotland and associate themselves, perhaps all too helplessly, with the court of Château Gaillard;[96] William Sinclair, Bishop of Dunkeld, had crowned Balliol and was present with another six bishops at Balliol's parliament in 1334; in 1335 the post of chancellor, hitherto invariably held by an ecclesiastic, went to a layman, Sir Thomas Charteris.[97]

For a time Edward III had hoped to obtain the collaboration of the Scottish kirk. He generously gave gifts of cash, wine and victuals to some religious houses,[98] but he could not resist the temptation to try to intrude Englishmen into Scottish benefices: in 1332 he had unsuccessfully informed the pope that the animosities between Scots and English would be assuaged if the treasurer of England, or, failing him, the keeper of the wardrobe, were provided to the vacant bishopric of St Andrews.[99] The policy of intrusion, coupled with the destruction of warfare, soon persuaded most of the Scottish prelates to abandon the primrose path of neutralism.

It was probably the lack of an acknowledged leader, rather than any other factor, that accounted for the merely passive resistance of the kirk to Edward III : during the nine-year vacancy in St Andrews 'the kyrk . . . ay stud in dowte and in peryle'.[100] Not until 1342 did Benedict XII come to the conclusion that the English had failed to make themselves masters of Scotland and that he might safely provide a bishop acceptable to the Scots. At the petition of David II and the King of France, William Landallis obtained the see, and was to hold it for more than forty years.[101] The Scottish kirk was on the way to recovery.

While long years of warfare had left their mark upon the burghs and the kirk they had had an even more pervasive influence upon the Scottish baronage. With some notable exceptions, such as Sir Andrew Moray, John Randolph, Earl of Moray, William Douglas and Alexander Ramsay, the Scottish barons had shown a fickle loyalty. Many had fought part of the time for Edward III and Balliol; few had fought all of the time for David Bruce; and some had fought not at all.

Among the last category was John of the Isles, son of Angus Og

---

[95] *Chron. Bower*, II. 307.   [96] *E.R.*, I. 450, 452, 466.
[97] *Ibid.*, 462, 468.   [98] E.g. *Cal. Close 1337–39*, pp. 223–4.
[99] Nicholson, *Edward III*, pp. 95, 110.
[100] *Chron. Wyntoun*, II. 393, 465.   [101] Dowden, *Bishops*, pp. 25–6.

and chief of the MacDonalds. In 1335 the Earl of Moray had negotiated with him at Tarbert but had failed to secure his adherence to
the nationalist cause.[102] On 12 September 1336 an indenture was concluded at Perth whereby Balliol augmented John's ancestral lands
with a grant of Kintyre and Knapdale and the Isle of Skye.[103] This
grant at least gave him a bargaining position which he could use
when the time came to make his peace with David II. On 12 June
1343 a 'final concord' was made at Ayr between the king and 'John of
Islay, our dearest kinsman'. John was confirmed in his possession of
many island and mainland territories, but Kintyre, Knapdale and
Skye were conspicuously missing.[104] A 'final concord' was simultaneously made with Ranald MacRuaridh and, probably about the same
time, charters were issued in favour of Alexander MacNaughton and
Malcolm and Torquil MacLeod.[105]

Just as the political settlement of the West Highlands and Isles
culminated in a series of land grants, similar grants were made elsewhere in Scotland to induce men to renew their allegiance to the
crown. Moreover David rewarded those who had fought for him : on
9 November 1341 a charter was issued creating the new earldom of
Wigtown to be held in regality by Malcolm Fleming, warden of
Dumbarton, who 'bore himself faithfully and laudably towards us in
both good times and bad';[106] and in the Scone parliament of 1341
David commanded the chamberlain to pay £100 as a reward to two
men who had taken part in the recent capture of Edinburgh Castle.[107]

The fall of Edinburgh Castle in April 1341, followed by the return of David II, challenged the waning English power in Scotland.
In November 1341 Edward III set out to spend Christmas at Melrose. During his stay he raided the forest of Ettrick 'in a very ill season', granted a short truce to the Scots and left for England 'half in a
melancholy with them that movid hym to that jornay'.[108] To represent English power on the Borders, Henry of Lancaster was left
behind at Berwick where he arranged a spectacular tournament with
the Scots in which Alexander Ramsay of Dalhousie distinguished
himself.[109] As Lancaster's troops disbanded at Candlemas (2 February
1342) King David went on a devastating raid through Northumberland as far as the Tyne.[110] This was followed by two notable successes

[102] *Chron. Wyntoun*, II. 419; Nicholson, *Edward III*, p. 221.
[103] *Cal. Docs. Scot.*, III. No. 1182 (wrongly dated 1335).
[104] *A.P.S.*, XII. 6.   [107] *E.R.*, I. 507.
[105] *Ibid.*, 6–8.   [108] *Scalacronica*, p. 299.
[106] *R.M.S.*, I. 484–5.   [109] *Chron. Wyntoun*, II. 440–4.
[110] *Scalacronica*, p. 299.

for the Scots: at dawn on 30 March 1342 Alexander Ramsay surprised and captured Roxburgh Castle; on 10 April, after a six months' siege, the garrison of Stirling capitulated.[111] It was symptomatic of a new confidence among the Scots that they no longer destroyed the castles that fell into their hands.

Yet much of what had been achieved was jeopardised by the ambition of William Douglas. On 18 July 1341 he had been rewarded for his services with a grant of the earldom of Atholl, but Douglas's interests lay in the Borders, where he held the wardship of Liddesdale on behalf of his godson and namesake, the future Earl of Douglas. Douglas was willing to abandon his northern earldom if he could secure Liddesdale for himself. In a general council at Aberdeen in February 1342 there were tortuous manoeuvres; as a result, Robert the Steward obtained the lands of the earldom of Atholl, Douglas obtained the lordship of Liddesdale, and his godson lost his heritage.[112] Thereafter William Douglas was known not only as 'the flower of chivalry' but as 'the Knight of Liddesdale'.

One obstacle to his schemes in the Borders was Alexander Ramsay, also styled a 'flower of chivalry'.[113] The king had rewarded Ramsay with the custody of Roxburgh and the sheriffship of Teviotdale (Roxburghshire) to which Douglas conceived that he had a prior claim. When Ramsay was holding his sheriff court in the parish kirk of Hawick on 20 June 1342 he was attacked by Douglas and carried off to Hermitage Castle. He did not live long. On the intercession of Robert the Steward the king granted a remission for the murder,[114] but though the king might 'remit his rancour'—and seems to have done so sincerely—this did not end the matter. Feud persisted. The chronicler Fordun saw in Ramsay's death the end of a good fortune that the Scots had enjoyed since the engagement at Culblean; thereafter 'all things which were attempted for the good of the kingdom straightway had ill result'.[115]

A truce lingered uneasily on the Marches. At the Westminster parliament of June 1344 it was announced that 'the Scots say openly that whenever the said Adversary [the King of France] lets them know that he does not wish to keep the truces they will not keep them either, but will raid upon England and accomplish as much damage

[111] *Chron. Fordun*, I. 365; *Cal. Docs. Scot.*, III. No. 1383.
[112] *Morton Registrum*, II. Nos. 53, 61, 62, 63; *R.M.S.*, I. 588.
[113] *Chron. Pluscarden*, I. 277.
[114] *Chron. Wyntoun*, II. 466–70; *Chron. Fordun*, I. 365–6.
[115] *Chron. Fordun*, I. 366.

as they can'.[116] Thus Edward Balliol was once more put in charge of the defence of the north,[117] as he had been from time to time in previous years. In the autumn of 1344 an Anglo-French peace conference held under papal mediation at Avignon brought no result.[118] Hostilities were renewed in 1345 when the English revenged themselves upon the turncoat Sir Dougal MacDowell, who, together with the 'captains' of the clans of Galloway, had been reconciled with King David.[119] This retribution was swift : an expeditionary force set sail from Cumberland, took the 'peel' of Hestan by surprise and burned it ; Sir Dougal and his household were carried off to England and sent to the Tower.[120]

Hostilities on the Borders were given a new perspective by Edward III's preparations for another campaign in France. On 12 July 1346 he disembarked in Normandy. About the same time a large Scottish force raided Cumberland and Westmorland. The banner of John Randolph waved over the expedition, but David II had also taken part.[121] In the course of this incognito visitation he probably made his own assessment of the defences of northern England which, in the circumstances of a successful and unopposed expedition, was unlikely to be a high one. There was a short lull on the Borders while both sides awaited news from France. This, when it came, was decisive enough. Edward had sacked Caen and had then won a resounding victory at Crécy on 26 August 1346. On 4 September he began his long siege of Calais.[122]

The Franco-Scottish alliance, like most alliances, was drawn up for the benefit of both parties and could not continue if the Scots did not on occasion give help to the French ; and in the autumn of 1346 the French stood in need of such help. But Scottish interests also called for military intervention. It was not a question of breaking a peace or even a truce : there already was war with England ; and the absence of Edward at Calais with the greatest army he ever raised undoubtedly weakened English military power at home and provided a tempting opportunity for a full-scale Scottish onslaught. King Robert's power had been based on success in war against the English ; similar success might bring similar power to his son.

[116] *Rot. Parl.*, II. 147.　　　　　　[117] *Ibid.*
[118] Eugène Déprez, 'La Conférence D'Avignon (1344)' in *Essays . . . presented to Thomas Frederick Tout*, ed. A. G. Little and F. M. Powicke (1925), pp. 301–20.　　　　　　[119] *R.M.S.*, I. 574, 578, 580, 590.
[120] *Chron. Anonimalle*, p. 19; *Cal. Docs. Scot.*, III. No. 1462.
[121] *Chron. Lanercost*, p. 341.
[122] May McKisack, *The Fourteenth Century*, pp. 133–5.

On 6 October 1346 the Scottish host mustered at Perth. Only two notable magnates seem to have been absent—Earl Malise of Caithness and Orkney, and John of the Isles. Yet there was a contingent under Ranald MacRuaridh, 'leader of the people of the Outer Isles'. Certain lands in Kintail had given rise to enmity between him and Earl William of Ross. When MacRuaridh took up quarters in the nunnery of Elcho he was murdered at the instigation of the earl. At this ill omen men deserted 'in gret rowtis'.[123]

The king, however, held to his plans and marched south with his remaining forces. Among the English there ran wild rumours of David's intentions: he had supposedly announced that he would soon see London [124] (which he certainly did). The small Border peel of Liddell was no fit object for the attention of the Scottish host, yet at least three days were wasted in besieging it.[125] Next, the Scots exacted blackmail from Cumberland and Westmorland and quartered themselves high-handedly in the priory of Lanercost before they descended on the priory of Hexham and 'stripped it of everything'. On 16 October they encamped in Bear Park, on the outskirts of the city of Durham.[126]

At dawn on 17 October 1346, when rain and fog swept over the countryside, the Knight of Liddesdale at the head of a foraging party ran into the three battalions of an army mustered under William La Zouche, Archbishop of York, and with difficulty escaped to spread dismay through the drowsy Scottish camp. The Scots hastily advanced to Neville's Cross, dismounted, and arrayed themselves, like the enemy, in three battalions. The chronicler Wyntoun asserts that the Scots numbered only two thousand armed men, and, like any chronicler worth his salt, exaggerates the numbers of the opposing side—allegedly twenty thousand archers and abundance of men-at-arms.[127] Certainly the English had not been taken by surprise and had had ample time to make plans for mobilisation : at the constant urging of Edward III defence preparations had been going on for months.[128] The initial successes of the Scots are perhaps more surprising than the eventual outcome.

Having learnt some lessons from the battles of Dupplin, Halidon and Crécy, both sides probably wished to remain on the defensive. A hail of arrows eventually forced the Scots to advance and abandon

[123] *Chron. Lanercost*, pp. 344–5; *Chron. Wyntoun*, II. 472; *Chron. Anonimalle*, p. 23.
[124] *Chron. Lanercost*, p. 347.   [125] *Ibid.*, p. 345.
[126] *Ibid.*, pp. 346–7; Raine, *Letters*, pp. 387–91.
[127] *Chron. Wyntoun*, II. 473–4.   [128] *Rot. Scot.*, I. 668–73.

their defensive position. The first Scottish battalion under John Randolph came upon a number of 'hey dykis'. These walls broke up its battle order and left it open to English attack. The survivors joined up with the second battalion under the king. But this too found itself in 'a full anoyous plas'. The discomfited troops after hard fighting fell back on the third battalion, under Robert the Steward and the Earl of March, stationed in a more favourable position; but the third battalion, the largest of the three, had no stomach for fighting. The Scottish chronicler Fordun admits that the Earl of March and the Steward fled. The English chroniclers poke fun at the pair: 'if the one was worth little, the other was good for nothing . . . these two, turning tail, fought with success, for with their battalion, without any hurt, they returned to Scotland and thus led off the dance, leaving David to caper as he wished.' [129] The king had been gravely wounded with an arrow in the face; on leaving the battlefield when all was lost he was overtaken by John Coupland but refused to yield. There was a hand-to-hand struggle in which David knocked out two of Coupland's teeth before he was overpowered.[130]

In the battle of Neville's Cross and the subsequent pursuit the losses of the Scots had been heavy. The chronicler Fordun tersely mentions the death of John Randolph, Earl of Moray, of Maurice Moray, Earl of Strathearn, of the constable, marshal and chamberlain of Scotland, 'with other innumerable barons, knights, esquires, and persons of worth.' [131] Apart from the king, the Earls of Fife, Menteith, Sutherland and Wigtown had been taken prisoner, as well as the Knight of Liddesdale whom the monks of Durham described as 'not so much valiant as malevolent.' [132] Two of the prisoners, Fife and Menteith, were tried for treason by Edward III; the former was spared by reason of his kinship with Edward, but the head of John Graham, Earl of Menteith, graced London bridge and his quarters were hoisted on high at York, Carlisle, Newcastle and Berwick.[133] Like Halidon, the battle of Neville's Cross had the appearance of the elusive final victory that the English had long sought, and it might have proved so had not the siege of Calais continued to divert the attention of Edward III and the resources of England. Not until 13

[129] *Chron. Wyntoun,* II. 475–7; *Chron. Melsa,* III. 62; *Chron. Fordun,* I. 367; *Chron. Lanercost,* p. 350.
[130] *Chron. Melsa,* III. 62; Raine, *Letters,* p. 389; *Chron. Knighton,* II. 44.
[131] *Chron. Fordun,* I. 367.
[132] Raine, *Letters,* p. 389; *Chron. Wyntoun,* II. 476–7.
[133] *Rot. Scot.,* I. 687–90.

May 1347 did Edward Balliol march out of Carlisle to 'recover the realm of Scotland'. His force, no more than 3,360 in number,[134] made a foray as far as Falkirk. There was a talk of a further advance to Perth, but the Scots seem to have bought a truce until 8 September, reportedly at the enormous price of £9,000. The expedition turned homeward, commended Balliol to God, and left him on the Isle of Hestan,[135] to hold disconsolate sway in Galloway where the Balliol name still counted for something.

Belated though it was, the campaign of 1347 had wrested back from the Scots most of what they had recovered in the four years prior to Neville's Cross : only the castles of Edinburgh, Stirling and Dunbar, still in Scottish hands, had prevented an English re-occupation of the land up to the Forth and Clyde. The sheriffdoms of Berwick, Roxburgh, Peebles and Dumfries, with the forests of Jedburgh, Selkirk and Ettrick, were once more subjected to an English administration. For more than a century the Scots would have to fight to win back what had been lost in 1347.

For the time being, however, there was a lull in hostilities, not only by reason of mutual exhaustion but on account of the Black Death, an outbreak of plague, in pneumonic as well as bubonic form, that swept all Europe and appeared in England in August 1348.[136] Since there was a time-lag before it reached Scotland, the Scots assumed that they had been spared the divine wrath that had smitten more sinful nations. They called the plague 'the foul death of the English', and are represented by an English chronicler as gathering in Ettrick forest for an attack on stricken England when the plague suddenly appeared in their own midst.[137] It came to be known as 'the first pestilence' to distinguish it from the second pestilence of 1362, the third of 1379, and the fourth of 1417,[138] after which numbering was abandoned. The plague was to range through Scotland in 1349 and 1350, striking chiefly the middle and lower classes and rarely affecting the magnates.[139]

[134] *Rot. Scot.*, I. 691-2.
[135] *Chron. Anonimalle*, p. 29; *Chron. Knighton*, II. 47; *Chron. Wyntoun*, II. 478; *Chron. Lanercost*, p. 352.
[136] May McKisack, *The Fourteenth Century*, pp. 331-4. Recent works on this subject include Charles Creighton, *A History of Epidemics in Britain*, Vol. I (1965), Philip Ziegler, *The Black Death* (1969), Geoffrey Marks, *The Medieval Plague: the Black Death of the Middle Ages* (1971), and J. F. D. Shrewsbury, *A History of Bubonic Plague in the British Isles* (1970). In a review of the last work (*S.H.R.*, L. 75-8), Rosalind Mitchison stresses the importance of the pneumonic form of the disease.   [137] *Chron. Knighton*, II. 62.
[138] *Extracta*, pp. 249-50.   [139] *Chron. Bower*, II. 347.

In contrast to their English and Irish counterparts the Scottish chroniclers paid comparatively little heed to the Black Death and devoted little more space to it than an outbreak of fowl pest that had lately afflicted Scottish poultry.[140] The chronicler Bower gives a solitary statistic when he affirms that twenty-four of the canons of the priory of St Andrews—about two-thirds of the total—had perished.[141] The lack of detailed comment makes it difficult to guess the effects of the plague upon Scotland but perhaps suggests that these effects were less severe than in other lands.

The effects of military disaster were more obvious. The contemporary chronicler John of Fordun affirms that the magnates had appointed the Steward as guardian, 'deeming that as he was the most powerful of all, the general interests would be the more strongly safeguarded by him. But how as guardian he governed the realm entrusted to him his deeds make known unto all times.'[142] Nothing is said of the Steward's deeds. As heir presumptive he was well placed to advance whatever ambitions he entertained but did not enjoy unlimited authority. He was formally styled 'the king's lieutenant' rather than guardian; and it is probable that the designation of lieutenant meant that his actions were subject to review by the captive king.[143] One surviving document perhaps epitomises the Steward's position: in 1348 he wrote to the sheriff of Dumbarton instructing him to stop unwarranted exactions upon Paisley Abbey —'for our own part we beseech you, and on the part of our lord the king we firmly command and direct you, that . . . you desist from exactions of this sort'.[144]

Yet the absent king had no machinery to enforce his will. After Neville's Cross it was the Steward who appointed sheriffs and other officials [145] and it was he who ought to have supervised their behaviour. In Aberdeenshire, at any rate, where the sheriff was one of those appointed by the Steward, there was administrative chaos: the sheriff did not account for any issues of his own court and asserted that there were none; he had obtained practically nothing from various lands set to ferm; his total receipts for the year 1347–8 came to only £19 7s. 8d.—and this sum was assigned to him for his fee.[146]

Another indication of the weakness of the Steward's administration was his appointment of sub-lieutenants or sub-guardians to take

[140] *Chron. Fordun*, I. 366–7; *Chron. Wyntoun*, II. 479–80.
[141] *Chron. Bower*, II. 347.   [142] *Chron. Fordun*, I. 368.
[143] Bruce Webster, *Acts of David II, 1329–71* (duplicated handlist, 1960), pp. 21–6.   [144] *Paisley Registrum*, pp. 208–9.
[145] *Chron. Wyntoun*, II. 478.   [146] *E.R.*, I. 542–4.

charge of areas in which their landed power predominated. Thus Thomas Stewart, Earl of Angus, became his lieutenant in Angus and the Mearns. From such a decentralisation of government it was the magnates who were most likely to benefit. But the death or captivity of some fifty barons as a result of Neville's Cross left the way open for others, often simple knights, to take their place. Most striking of all was the rise of Sir Robert Erskine, who became chamberlain and was to play a leading part in politics for more than thirty years.[147]

The temporary eclipse of the baronage also led to a closer association of the clergy with government and politics. The first lay chancellor had been killed at Neville's Cross and was to be replaced by a succession of ecclesiastics, while William Landallis, Bishop of St Andrews, began his long diplomatic career as a leader of the missions to England for the release of the king. Under the influence of Landallis the Scottish kirk was to show a bold face to Edward III when he renewed the policy of ecclesiastical intrusion.[148]

Intrusion less easy to resist was forthcoming from another quarter : by the middle of the fourteenth century the pope was providing his own nominees not only to the bishoprics, but to lesser benefices as well; by the end of the following century the practice was to be extended to insignificant benefices worth less than twenty-four florins a year. Already, too, the popes of Avignon were issuing 'expectative graces', which conferred prospective provision to benefices that were not yet vacant, and were 'reserving' the right to make a future provision to a benefice that was not yet vacant.[149] It was the benefices held by the secular clergy, rather than those held by the regular clergy, that were first affected by the various devices that emanated from the pope's plenitude of spiritual power : it caused some stir when Clement VI in 1351 made a provision to the abbey of Dunfermline.[150] Thenceforward the monasteries, as well as the institutions of the secular clergy, were to be increasingly subject to papal provision, though it is remarkable that some of the most important abbeys—Cambuskenneth, Melrose, Dryburgh and Jedburgh—do not seem to have been provided in papal consistory until the late fifteenth century.[151]

[147] *Scots Peerage*, v. 592–3.   [148] *Cal. Docs. Scot.*, III. No. 1558.
[149] Cameron, *Apostolic Camera*, pp. lxix, xciv; G. Mollat, *The Popes at Avignon*, p. 336.
[150] *Chron. Bower*, II. 349; *Cal. Papal Letters*, III. 423; Coulton, *Scottish Abbeys*, p. 253.
[151] Cameron, *Apostolic Camera*, p. xxxix.

The system of reservations and provisions, resulting in direct papal appointments to benefices, rather than capitular elections or presentations by a patron, was the main feature in the centralisation of the church achieved during the residence of the papacy at Avignon (1309–1377) and 'could, from certain points of view, be of benefit to the Church'.[152] But even if the system had affected only ecclesiastics, it held ample opportunities for acrimony, litigation and downright abuse : the career of almost every prominent Scottish ecclesiastic was spattered by contests over benefices,[153] and the main motivation of the contestants, as of the papacy itself, was undoubtedly financial.[154] In the case of the greater benefices, assessed at more than a hundred florins a year,[155] provision was made in consistory, and the beneficiary paid 'common services' (usually one-third of the yearly assessment of his benefice) as well as the five customary 'little services', which were proportionate to the common services. Half of the income from consistorial provisions went to the pope and the remainder was shared among the cardinals who attended him when the provision was made. In the case of lesser benefices, assessed at between twenty-four and a hundred florins yearly, provision was not made in consistory and the 'annates' that were paid (usually half of the first year's income of the benefice) went to the pope's own revenues after they had been paid locally to a papal collector. Between 1353 and 1373 this post was held in Scotland by William Greenlaw, a noted pluralist. To enforce payment he and his successors were granted ecclesiastical powers sufficient to bring to heel any recalcitrant bishop who refused to co-operate.[156] Equally stringent methods were used to extract the common services, which had to be paid directly into the *curia*. Those who had been provided in consistory had to enter into formal obligations for payment, usually within a year in two instalments. Increasingly they had recourse to the services of the bankers who served the *curia* ; and, although usury was condemned by the church, interest

[152] G. Mollat, *The Popes at Avignon*, p. 337.
[153] See, for example, the outline careers of sixty-one clerics in Burns, *Basle*.
[154] The following account is based (except where otherwise noted) upon Geoffrey Barraclough, *Papal Provisions* (1935), G. Mollat, *The Popes at Avignon*, pp. 310–44, Cameron, *Apostolic Camera*, pp. xiii–xciv, and J. Hutchison Cockburn's important article on 'Papal Collections and Collectors in Scotland in the Middle Ages', *Scot. Church Hist. Soc. Recs.*, I. 173–99. For the sake of clarity I have drawn a distinction between common services and annates (and have made other generalisations) that would be more applicable to the fifteenth century than to the fourteenth.
[155] The florin varied in value from 2s. 8d. to 3s. 7d. between 1329 and 1428 (J. Hutchison Cockburn, *op. cit., Scot. Church Hist. Soc. Recs.*, I. 173–99, at 188).
[156] A. R. MacEwen, *History of the Church in Scotland*, I. 286–7.

was paid by subterfuge : 'for practical purposes canonical precepts gave way to economic necessities'.[157] By the device of 'regress' the bulls of provision were delivered to the bankers as security for the sums they advanced on behalf of their clients, and the latter obtained the bulls only after their obligations had been discharged; if the clients defaulted, the bankers could return the bulls to the *curia* (hence 'regress') and claim from it the repayment of the sums they had advanced. This intricate system (which did not, however, save the papacy from financial stringency) throve upon the supplications for benefices presented by a growing multitude of petitioners who were not slow to realise that the surest pathway to ecclesiastical preferment lay through the *curia*.[158]

The increasing traffic in benefices imposed a corresponding financial burden upon the Scottish kirk at a time when it was impoverished as a result of Anglo-Scottish warfare [159] and the lawlessness prevalent during the Steward's lieutenancy.[160] There was, however, one panacea by which the greater ecclesiastical institutions could remedy their economic ills—appropriation. And if the parsonages (*rectorie*) of the parish kirks had already been appropriated (as most had), the revenues of the vicarages might also be appropriated, and the pastoral function entrusted not to a vicar who enjoyed a 'perpetual vicarage' with rights to a share in the teinds of the parish, but to a vicar-pensioner with insecure tenure, who had only the use of the manse and its croft and was paid a usually inadequate salary by the appropriator. Ultimately more than half of the vicarages were appropriated,[161] and ultimately 'those who served the altar could not live of the altar'.[162]

The financial stringency from which the kirk as a whole seems to have suffered made the clergy cling jealously to their economic privileges, to seek new privileges, and even to assume privileges in defiance of the exclusive trading rights of the burghs. In November 1351 David II granted to the monks of Arbroath the custom to be paid on items of trade within the burgh, port and regality of Arbroath; the abbey was to have its own coket seal, which was to be as valid as the cokets of the king's own burghs. The reaction of the Dundee bur-

---

[157] Cameron, *Apostolic Camera*, p. xxxiv.
[158] See the opening entries in *Cal. Scot. Supp., 1418–1424*, pp. 1–4.
[159] *Arbroath Liber*, II. No. 23; *Cambuskenneth Registrum*, No. 58; *Cal. Papal Petitions*, I. 250.
[160] *Paisley Registrum*, pp. 208–9; *Cal. Papal Petitions*, I. 200; Bruce Webster, *Handlist of the Acts of David II*, pp. 23, 25; *Arbroath Liber*, II. No. 27.
[161] Ian B. Cowan, *op. cit., Scot. Church Hist. Soc. Recs.*, XIII. 203–22, at 205.
[162] Ian B. Cowan, 'Vicarages and the Cure of Souls in Medieval Scotland', *ibid.*, XVI. 111–27, at 127.

gesses may be guessed from a royal mandate of March 1352 ordering the royal officials to see that no one hindered the monks in the enjoyment of their new trading privileges.[163]

The conflict of interests between the kirk and the royal burghs did not always go in favour of the kirk. By March 1352 the burgesses of Montrose and Dundee, and possibly those of other royal burghs, seem to have banded in defence of their privileges and obtained royal mandates against the Bishop of Brechin and the monks of Coupar Angus.[164] Whenever the burgesses of Dundee so desired, the justiciar and other royal officials were to go in person to the abbey of Coupar Angus, to the kirk of Alyth, to the townships of Kettins and Kirriemuir, publicly forbid trading in these places and seize the goods of the offenders.[165]

The official support thus given to burgess communities, even against great ecclesiastical institutions, was perhaps a sign of the increasing influence of the merchant burgesses. John Wigmer, burgess of Edinburgh, was numbered in 1348 among the envoys who were to go to England to treat of the king's liberation.[166] An even more notable burgess, John Mercer of Perth, had already risen in the world by 1352 when he married into the baronial family of Murray of Tullibardine.[167] A long spectacular career as merchant prince lay ahead of him. Not only were individual merchant burgesses increasingly important in their own right but they were members of a class capable of taking a collective initiative. There can be little doubt that something of the sort lay behind the decisions of a council held at Dundee on 12 November 1347,[168] where the council, acting in the name of the king, ordered reprisals against the hostile Flemings and ratified in advance a contract that had yet to be reached between the merchant burgesses of Scotland and those of Middelburg in the county of Zealand. Although the terms of this prospective contract are unknown its substance was to be the recognition of Middelburg as the Scottish staple port on the continent. Scottish wares were now being carried overseas not by Germans and Flemings but by Scottish merchants. In Middelburg they were to have their own resident mayor [169]—later known as the conservator of the staple—who would

---

[163] *Arbroath Liber*, II. No. 26. For a similar case in Aberdeen in 1385 see *A.P.S.*, II. 565.
[164] *Brechin Registrum*, II. No. ccciii.
[165] *R.M.S.*, II. No. 614.   [166] *Rot. Scot.*, I. 718, 721.
[167] W. Fraser, *The Sutherland Book* (1892), p. 16.
[168] *A.P.S.*, I. 514-5.   [169] *Ibid.*, 514.

presumably look after their interests and act as their commercial agent.[170] Although the institution of a Scottish staple in the Low Countries was to outlast the Middle Ages it was by no means permanently fixed at Middelburg: in 1348 Adam Tore and William Feth, burgesses of Edinburgh and Dundee respectively, went to Bruges to restore good relations with Flanders on behalf of the *quatre grosses villes de Escosse*.[171] This phrase undoubtedly signifies the four burghs—Edinburgh, Stirling, Roxburgh and Berwick. Since the last two were in English hands their place had possibly already been taken by other burghs: in 1369 Lanark and Linlithgow were formally appointed to fill the two vacancies.

Whether Scottish trade was centred in Middelburg or in Bruges the trading route along the English coastline was still a perilous one, even in time of truce. It was typical that when two vessels freighted in Flanders by John Wigmer and other Scottish merchants were wrecked on the Northumberland coast the cargoes, supposedly worth £4,000, were plundered.[172] In cases of this sort Edward III sought to provide redress. To Scottish merchants he was indeed to show himself remarkably favourable, perhaps for political reasons; during the lieutenancy there was the beginning of a trade between Scotland and England that was to reach impressive proportions by the end of the reign of David II. Two Scottish magnates who figured in Edward's political projects were also allowed to share in the profits of renewed Anglo-Scottish trade: in 1353, at the petition of William Douglas of Liddesdale, Edward granted safe-conducts to a number of Scottish merchants;[173] in 1357 a similar petition from John of the Isles resulted in safe-conducts for certain merchants of the Isles, who might trade in England and Ireland and the rest of Edward's dominions.[174]

This successful petition on the part of John of the Isles followed attempts on the part of the English to draw him to their side.[175] Uncommitted to either side he went his own way, striving with remarkable success to keep on good terms with the governments both of England and Scotland and meanwhile consolidating his own power. As a result of the murder of Ranald MacRuaridh on the eve of the Neville's Cross campaign the MacRuaridh inheritance had fallen to Ranald's sister Amy, the wife of John of the Isles. He thus obtained

[170] For the general background see Davidson and Gray, *Staple*, pp. 115–20, and M. P. Rooseboom, *The Scottish Staple in the Netherlands*, pp. 5–7.

[171] Rooseboom, *op. cit.*, p. 5.   [172] *Cal. Docs. Scot.*, IV. No. 10.

[173] *Rot. Scot.*, I. 758.   [174] *Cal. Docs. Scot.*, III. No. 1639.

[175] *Rot. Scot.*, I. 677; *Cal. Docs. Scot.*, III. No. 1606.

the lands of Garmoran on the mainland and Uist and other islands; probably every Hebridean island save Skye was now under his sway. Thereupon John found some pretext for annulling his marriage with Amy MacRuaridh,[176] and on 14 June 1350 a papal dispensation was issued for his marriage to Margaret Stewart, eldest daughter of Robert the Steward.[177] Thanks to this marriage, John seems to have been granted the feudal superiority of Kintyre and Knapdale.[178] The marriage was also marked by a Latin interpretation of the bridegroom's title : by Gaelic usage he could be styled *rí* (king); the Scottish government presumably regarded him as a baron; and in the papal dispensation of 1350 he was described as 'John of the Isles, Lord of the Isles of Scotland'. This style was to be passed on to his successors, together with the vast mainland and island territories that could now be described as the lordship of the Isles. John had revived the Hebridean power that his ancestor Somerled had created two centuries previously.

One potential threat to the MacDonald hegemony was the revival of the MacDougals under John of Lorne. This descendant of the John of Lorne forfeited by Robert I had by 1338 returned to Scotland in Balliol's wake [179] and was to be no mere bird of passage. But there was to be harmony rather than discord between him and MacDonald. According to an indenture of 8 September 1354 [180] John of Lorne, 'Lord of Argyll', and John of Islay, 'Lord of the Isles', would behave as brothers of one flesh.

The re-entry of the MacDougals into the society of the Gaelic west was marked by other pacts similiar to the indenture of 1354.[181] While the foremost of the Gaelic magnates were now more united than they had ever been, they were also to be increasingly associated with Robert the Steward. He had secured the Lord of the Isles as a son-in-law, and this relationship was to be further developed when Robert the Steward married for the second time. A papal dispensation of 1355 allowed him to wed John Randolph's widow, Euphemia of Ross, sister of William, Earl of Ross, who had himself married Mary, sister of John of the Isles.[182] Through the Gaelic culture of the

---

[176] *Highland Papers*, I. 26–7. A dispensation for the marriage had been issued on 4 June 1337 (*ibid.*, 73–5).

[177] A. Theiner, *Vetera Monumenta*, No. dlxxxviii.

[178] Landholding in Kintyre and Knapdale was complicated and obscure. Some time after 1337 lands in Kintyre had been granted, or confirmed, to the Steward and his eldest son (*R.M.S.*, I. 584).

[179] W. Fraser, *The Stirlings of Keir* (1858), p. 198, No. 2.

[180] *Highland Papers*, I. 75–8

[181] *Ibid.*, II. 142.

[182] *Scots Peerage*, V. 236–7, 239.

lands they controlled, through the intermarriages and diplomatic pacts that linked them, Robert the Steward, John of the Isles, the Earl of Ross, John of Lorne, and Gillespic Campbell, formed a sort of 'Highland Party' that David II would find troublesome when he returned to Scotland.

The fortune of war had condemned David to spend the prime of his manhood as a prisoner in England. Although his basic comfort was not neglected he was closely guarded.[183] Edward certainly hoped that he would be only too willing to escape from a wretched and hopeless position at the cost of a hefty ransom and political concessions. From 1348 onwards harsh conditions were outlined to the Scottish embassies that almost annually visited England to try to negotiate the king's release. The situation held out opportunities for Edward; it also posed problems,[184] some of which arose in unexpected quarters. When the English parliament met in March 1348 it was made a condition of a grant of taxation 'that David Bruce, William Douglas, and the other chief men of Scotland, are in no manner to be set free, either for ransom or upon their word of honour'.[185] Edward paid little heed but engaged in secret and devious diplomacy. Its character may be guessed from a memorandum of 1349 [186] addressed to 'Monsieur Rauf'—almost certainly Sir Ralph Neville. He was informed that the English king's weighty affairs were greatly hindered 'because Sir E. de B. [Balliol] will not agree to good ways of establishing peace such as would seem reasonable to one side and the other'; 'Monsieur Rauf' was to acquaint Balliol with the new offers made by 'D. de B.' [David Bruce] and with the pact made between him and 'W. de D.' [Douglas of Liddesdale]. This memorandum shows that Balliol was no mere puppet of Edward, but a person determined to insist upon his own rights and thus an awkward obstacle in the way of David's ransom; it also makes it clear that David and Liddesdale were organising a party in Scotland to promote some concessions demanded by Edward as the price of their liberation.

Concessions also figure in a petition addressed by David to Pope

[183] See 'Papers relating to the Captivity and Release of David II', ed. E. W. M. Balfour-Melville, *S.H.S. Misc. IX*, 1–56, and the review by Ranald Nicholson, *S.H.R.*, xxxix., at p. 47, n. 5.

[184] J. Campbell, 'England, Scotland and the Hundred Years War', in *Europe in the Late Middle Ages*, ed. J. R. Hale, J. R. L. Highfield and B. Smalley (1965), pp. 196–7.

[185] *Rot. Parl.*, II. 200–1.

[186] C. Johnston, 'Negotiations for the Ransom of David Bruce in 1349', *E.H.R.*, xxxvi. 57–8.

Clement VI. This petition, which was dealt with at Avignon on 7 August 1350, began by recalling to the pope's notice the adverse fortune that had befallen David and his fellow-prisoners.[187] The pope was asked to afford help and counsel, and to write to the King of France urging that the release of David and his fellow captives should be made a condition of any peace or long truce between the French and English. Then, without any explanatory preamble, David volunteered information on the terms that Edward III was alleged to be demanding—homage, military service against the French, attendance at English parliaments, the restoration of the disinherited, recognition of the King of England as David's heir if the latter should die childless, custody of Scottish castles as surety for fulfilment of these terms. David gave no indication whatever that he was ready to accept any of these demands, nor did he commit himself to rejecting them. The real nature of the appeal of 1350 was an attempt to put pressure on the French king to take action for David's release. Clement duly ordered that 'opportune letters' should be directed to the King of France—but to no avail.

Thus David continued to play his part in Edward's plans. In December 1350 William Douglas of Liddesdale obtained a safe-conduct from Edward to return on parole to Scotland to undertake 'certain business concerning David Bruce', to whom he was to report back before 9 February 1351.[188] The Knight of Liddesdale was to inform the Scots that David might be set free for a ransom of £40,000. As soon as the first instalment had been paid, Edward would surrender the Scottish castles and territories that he controlled. But all this was conditional on the acceptance by the Scots of one of the points outlined in the petition to the pope: if David died childless he was to be succeeded on the Scottish throne by one of Edward's younger sons.[189]

Edward's demand for this particular concession, rather than any other, was astute. Though David might be unwilling to hand over Scotland to English domination, an alteration in the Scottish succession did not, by itself, in theory at least, infringe Scottish independ-

---

[187] The following details are taken from the original entry in the papal register. I am indebted to the administrators of the Ross Fund of the University of Glasgow for showing me a microfilm of this important document, hitherto available only in an imperfect summary (*Cal. Papal Petitions*, 1. 203) which misrepresented David's attitude. See E. W. M. Balfour-Melville, 'David II's Appeal to the Pope', *S.H.R.*, XLI. 86.

[188] *Rot. Scot.*, 1. 737–8.

[189] E. W. M. Balfour-Melville, *op. cit.*, *S.H.S. Misc. IX.* 1–56, at 37.

ence. The obvious loser would be Robert the Steward, and David had little liking for the ineffective mediocrity who had deserted him at Neville's Cross. Edward had devised terms that David would undoubtedly support to the best of his ability, fortified by the hope that he would be liberated for a moderate ransom, would recover occupied territory from the English, and that in the end he might thwart Edward's dynastic policy by producing offspring of his own. Both Edward and David, having considered the imponderables of the situation, were willing to stake much on the vagaries of fortune.

By February 1352 David was in Scotland, released temporarily on parole.[190] A parliament or council that discussed the English terms seems to have been held at Scone between 28 February and 6 March 1352, when various royal charters were issued.[191] The English chronicler Knighton asserts that the Scots 'with one consent, in one voice' said they were willing to ransom their king, but not to be subject to the King of England.[192] The latter still had hopes that a favourable outcome might be reached by force, if not by negotiation. On 28 March 1352 he issued secret instructions: if it appeared that progress might be made 'in another way', and if David and Douglas of Liddesdale had ascertained that their friends would 'be of their accord', then David might be allowed to remain at large in Newcastle or Berwick until Whitsuntide 'so that one may see in the meantime what exploit he may effect'.[193] Nothing resulted. David could not, or would not, start a civil war in Scotland to force Edward's terms upon his own people. By 22 June he was once more cooling his heels in the Tower.[194]

His unsuccessful mission gave rise to rumours that he had sworn allegiance to Edward;[195] and these rumours later received spurious support thanks to the work of the fifteenth-century English forger, John Hardyng.[196] Yet despite the ambiguities of David's position in 1352 and even in later years, there is no convincing evidence that he was ever willing to acknowledge the feudal superiority of the English king.[197] The utmost that David was ready to concede was an alteration in the succession that would take effect only if he himself died childless.

[190] *Rot. Scot.*, I. 743–4, 748; *Cal. Docs. Scot.*, III. No. 1557.
[191] A. B. Webster, *Handlist of the Acts of David II*, pp. 22–3.
[192] *Chron. Knighton*, II. 356.
[193] *Rot. Scot.*, I. 748, 749, 750; *Foedera*, III. pt. i, 78.
[194] *Rot. Scot.*, I. 750, 751.   [195] *Chron. Knighton*, II. 69.
[196] Ranald Nicholson, 'David II, the historians and the chroniclers', *S.H.R.*, XLV. 59–78, at 64–5.
[197] E. W. M. Balfour-Melville, *op. cit.*, *S.H.R.*, XLI. 86.

For a time Edward abandoned his greater ambitions in order to concentrate on more limited objectives that might be gained through Douglas of Liddesdale, with whom he concluded an indenture on 17 July 1352. Indentures of 1349 and 1350 made with other Scottish prisoners had been concluded in the presence of David II, but the indenture of 1352 was not.[198] It would seem that he and Liddesdale had parted company and that the latter's conduct was from this point onward not only dubious but treasonable. For Douglas was not only to be released, but was to be installed by Edward III in the castle of Hermitage, in the lands of Liddesdale, and in certain lands of Annandale and Moffatdale. At a month's notice Douglas would be ready to fight for Edward III and his heirs against all men. Although Douglas would not be expected to make war upon 'his own nation of Scotland'—unless it should be to his own liking to do so—he would allow English forces unmolested passage through Liddesdale and his other lands.[199]

The country to which Douglas returned was one torn by feuds and dissensions.[200] He himself, a notable instigator of feud,[201] was soon to be a victim at the hands of his own godson and namesake. This William Douglas, second son of Sir Archibald, the Scottish guardian killed at Halidon, had passed his youth in France and returned to Scotland after Neville's Cross to piece together an inheritance that included the lands of his uncle, the 'Good Sir James'.[202] William was therefore Lord of Douglas and would have been Lord of Liddesdale also but for the machinations of his godfather.[203] In August 1353 the Lord of Douglas waylaid his godfather in the forest of Ettrick. The corpse of the 'flower of chivalry' was laid to rest in Melrose.[204] Like previous assassinations, the murder of the Knight of Liddesdale brought no judicial retribution to the perpetrator, whose territorial claims were fully recognised in a Scottish royal charter of February 1354.[205] Henceforward the Lord of Douglas would control the Scottish Borders. He had laid the foundations of a power that might control the crown itself.

The murder of the Knight of Liddesdale upset Edward's latest

---

[198] Text in *Rot. Scot.*, I. 752–3.   [199] *Ibid.*, 753.
[200] *Scots Peerage*, v. 595; W. Fraser, *The Red Book of Menteith* (1880), II. 29; *Chron. Wyntoun*, II. 478–9; *Chron. Bower*, II. 337.
[201] *Chron. Fordun*, I. 396; *Chron. Bower*, II. 348.
[202] *Scots Peerage*, III. 147–8.   [203] P. 144 above.
[204] *Scots Peerage*, VI. 341.
[205] *R.M.S.*, I. 487–8; Fraser, *Douglas*, III. No. 292.

policy and obliged him to resurrect schemes centred upon David II.[206] In an indenture concluded at Berwick on 13 July 1354, a draft treaty for his release was at last achieved : David would be released in return for a ransom of 90,000 marks (£60,000), to be paid in nine instalments over the following nine years; during that period there would be an Anglo-Scottish truce; the Scots would deliver twenty noble hostages as surety for payment of the ransom. In October 1354, Edward ordered that all the barons and knights of Northumberland should gather at Newcastle to witness David's deliverance in return for the Scottish hostages.[207] But something went wrong. Once more David was to be bitterly disappointed.

There can be little doubt that it was the Scots who were responsible for the failure of the latest negotiations. While it is understandable that on previous occasions they had rejected a ransom treaty which included political concessions, this objection did not apply to the draft treaty of 1354, which was a straightforward ransom treaty. The explanation for the Scottish action—or inaction—lay in France. As the current Anglo-French truce drew to a close both sides were preparing for war.[208] On 5 March 1355 King John of France ordered the Sire de Garencières to lead fifty men-at-arms to Scotland and to carry 40,000 deniers d'or à l'escu[209]—which the writer of the Scalacronica equated with 10,000 marks.[210] This sum was 'to be given among the prelates and barons of Scotland upon condition that they should break their truce with the King of England and make war upon him'.[211] Early in November 1355 Thomas Stewart, Earl of Angus, and Patrick, Earl of March, joined with Garencières in capturing and looting the town of Berwick in a surprise nocturnal assault,[212] after which they besieged the castle. As Edward III stepped ashore on his return from a brief campaign in the hinterland of Calais this startling news was brought to him, whereupon he at once began preparations to relieve Berwick Castle.[213] When his host reached the Tweed the Scots within the town of Berwick were too few to hold out—Garencières had withdrawn to France and no help was forthcoming from Scotland 'by reason of the discord of the magnates'.[214]

---

[206] Rot. Scot., 1. 765–6.   [207] Ibid., 768–71.
[208] J. Campbell, op. cit., Europe in the Late Middle Ages, p. 199.
[209] Ibid.   [210] Scalacronica, p. 303.
[211] Ibid., similarly Chron. Fordun, I. 371.
[212] Chron. Fordun, I. 372; Chron. Bower, II. 351; Chron. Wyntoun, II. 482–4; Scalacronica, p. 304; Cal. Docs. Scot., IV. Nos. 3, 21.
[213] Chron. Walsingham, I. 280; Scalacronica, p. 304; Rot. Parl., II. 264–5.
[214] Chron. Fordun, I. 373.

By 20 January 1356 Edward had recovered Berwick and arrived in Roxburgh, where, according to the Scottish chroniclers, Edward Balliol made his appearance 'like a roaring lion'.[215] Balliol's fate had indeed been a hard one. He was by no means the incompetent puppet that some modern historians have taken him for;[216] he had been willing to fight for his rights but when supplies of men and money from England dried up he was left powerless. Latterly his pretensions were increasingly ludicrous. Despite a long rearguard action in Galloway his position had become increasingly isolated : in 1354 his ancestral castle and birthplace of Buittle seems to have fallen to his opponents.[217] Balliol had lost his last toehold in Scotland and the stage was set for the dramatic gesture at Roxburgh in which he took the crown from his head, lifted a handful of earth and stones from Scottish soil, and handed them to Edward III [218] as a symbol that he had thereby resigned his kingdom to Edward to make of it what he could.

This resignation was formally recorded in a number of documents sealed at Roxburgh on 20 January 1356 or the following days.[219] Balliol drove a hard bargain : if he was to relinquish the position of penniless king he was determined to be a wealthy pensioner; Edward III was to pay him an annuity of £2,000 for life and a gift of 5,000 marks to meet his outstanding debts.[220] Until his death in January 1364 Balliol would have a creditor's satisfaction in dunning Edward III for debts, while he paid off those of his father, the late King John, and poached in royal parks.[221]

After the transaction at Roxburgh Scotland had a new pretender in the person of the English king. Once Edward discovered that his latest diplomatic manoeuvre had failed to impress the Scots he set out on what was to be his last military expedition in Scotland. Having crossed the Lammermuirs he spent ten days at Haddington where the Franciscan friary and its kirk, 'the lamp of Lothian', were set ablaze.

[215] Ibid.; Chron. Wyntoun, II. 485; similarly Scalacronica, p. 304.
[216] E. W. M. Balfour-Melville, 'Edward III and David II', Hist. Assoc. Pamphlet No. G.27, p. 17.
[217] R. C. Reid, 'Edward de Balliol', Dumfriesshire Trans., xxxv. 38–63; Bruce Webster, 'The English Occupations of Dumfriesshire in the Fourteenth Century', ibid., xxxv. 64–80; C. A. Ralegh Radford, 'Balliol's Manor House on Hestan Island', ibid., xxxv. 33–7.
[218] Chron. Fordun, I. 373.
[219] Rot. Scot., I. 787–8; Cal. Docs. Scot., III. Nos. 1591–2, 1596, 1603.
[220] Cal. Docs. Scot., III. Nos. 1594–5, 1598–9, 1601.
[221] Ibid., IV. Nos. 8, 11, 72; E. W. M. Balfour-Melville, 'The Death of Edward Balliol', S.H.R., xxxv. 82–3.

His ships disembarked 'piratical sons of Belial' who pillaged the Virgin's shrine at Whitekirk. Thus (so the Scots believed) through the intercessions of the Virgin a wind came from the north, prevented the English fleet from entering the Forth, scattered its vessels and sank some of them.[222] Edward had perhaps hoped to march to Scone to have himself crowned, but his campaign of 1356 was to be a replica of his father's of 1322, though more devastating. The expedition, which had begun early in February, left such a trail of destruction that the Scots talked of 'The Burnt Candlemas'.[223] It did little to restrain their continuing offensive on the Borders.[224]

Although there is no sign that Edward's 1356 campaign had daunted the Scots it has been claimed that its political results place it 'amongst the most effective Edward ever launched'[225]—the supposed political results being the negotiations for the release of David II that culminated in a ransom treaty in October 1357. But the ransom treaty was hardly a result of the Burnt Candlemas: the clue to the end of Anglo-Scottish hostilities lay in France. At Poitiers on 19 September 1356 the French suffered a disaster even worse than that of Crécy:[226] King John joined David II as a prisoner of the English; under the Dauphin Charles, who acted as regent, France lapsed into chaos, and the hopes that the Scots had rested on France were dashed to the ground.

On 17 January 1357 Robert the Steward presided as lieutenant over a council at Perth, whence he issued a commission for a full-scale embassy under Bishop Landallis to treat for 'the deliverance of our lord the king and final concord between the kings and their realms'.[227] In May the ambassadors reached London and an indenture was concluded which amounted to a draft treaty for David's release in return for named hostages and a ransom.[228] Next, the Steward summoned another council which was in session at Edinburgh by 26 September 1357,[229] and no doubt discussed the draft treaty. In both this council and the preceding one the burgesses were represented along with the prelates and nobles, and no formality was neglected to ensure that responsibility for the terms of the king's release was shared by each of

---

[222] *Chron. Bower*, II. 354-6; *Chron. Knighton*, II. 85; *Chron. Anonimalle*, pp. 33-4.
[223] *Chron. Bower*, II. 354.
[224] *Cal. Docs. Scot.*, III. No. 1616; *Rot. Scot.*, I. 795-6.
[225] James Campbell, *op. cit.*, *Europe in the Late Middle Ages*, p. 201.
[226] May McKisack, *The Fourteenth Century*, pp. 138-40.
[227] *A.P.S.*, I. 515; *Cal. Docs. Scot.*, III. No. 1609.
[228] *Cal. Docs. Scot.*, III. No. 1629.   [229] *A.P.S.*, I. 515-8.

the three political classes of the community.[230] Six ambassadors were to carry out the final negotiations at Berwick,[231] where David arrived under escort on 28 September [232] in readiness for his release.

The resulting treaty indenture,[233] sealed on 3 October 1357, seems to have been basically the same as the draft treaty drawn up in London in May. The king was to be set free for 100,000 marks (£66,666 13s. 4d.) to be paid at the rate of 10,000 marks a year, beginning at Midsummer 1358. The full ransom was to be paid even if David died before the instalments were completed. If the instalments fell into arrears he was to return to captivity, and until the ransom was fully paid there was to be a truce, during which the territorial *status quo* was to be observed. The main guarantee for the payment of the king's ransom was the delivery of twenty noble hostages by the Scots. These were, however, regarded by the English as inadequate : David was to deliver three supplementary super-hostages to be chosen from a list comprising the Steward and other leading magnates. It was stipulated that all hostages (who might be exchanged for others from time to time) should be treated 'courteously' in England but were to live there at their own expense.[234] The good faith of the Scots was to be secured not only by hostages but by stringent conditions of a less tangible nature that included ecclesiastical sanctions. So far as ingenuity could express itself on parchment the treaty of Berwick was assured of fulfilment.

It has been claimed that Edward III might never have obtained any ransom at all from Scotland and that to that extent the treaty was something of a victory for English diplomacy.[235] But it was also, in a way, a victory for the Scots : 'David was freed on heavy terms which settled no issue but that of his release'.[236] The omission of other issues from the treaty was thus a setback to Edward's cherished ambitions; he had simply recognised that the mere possession of the person of David Bruce would no longer serve his ends. On 7 October 1357,[237] a week or so before the eleventh anniversary of his capture at Neville's Cross, King David returned to his realm as a free man.

[230] *Ibid.*; *Cal. Docs. Scot.*, III. Nos. 1642-8, 1650-4.
[231] *A.P.S.*, I. 518.
[232] E. W. M. Balfour-Melville, *op. cit.*, *S.H.S. Misc. IX.* 1-56, at 22.
[233] Text in *Rot. Scot.*, I. 811-4; *A.P.S.*, I. 518-21.
[234] *Rot. Scot.*, I. 810; *Chron. Wyntoun*, II. 497.
[235] J. Campbell, *op. cit.*, *Europe in the Late Middle Ages*, p. 201.
[236] *Ibid.*, p. 200.
[237] E. W. M. Balfour-Melville, *op. cit.*, *S.H.S. Misc. IX.* 1-56, at 24.

7

THE RANSOM, THE SUCCESSION AND INTENSIVE GOVERNMENT

On 6 November 1357, a month after King David's return from captivity, a council met at Scone. There the Berwick ransom treaty was read to the assembled clergy, nobles and burgesses, and formally ratified.[1] Well aware of the burdens it had thus undertaken, the council considered how to raise money for the ransom. One expedient was to grant the king the right to requisition wool at cost price and apply the profit to the ransom.[2] Another measure was the appointment of assessors to carry out a general financial assessment (*taxatio*). They were to report the 'true value' of rents, movable goods, crops and livestock (with certain exceptions); even the names of all craftsmen were to be listed. On 14 January 1358, in little more than two months time, the assessors were to present the statistics to the king at Perth[3]—obviously in order that contributions could be levied. While making provision for the ransom, the council held fast to the one basic constitutional principle of medieval Scotland—the king should live of his own. In order to do this, David was authorised to revoke into his own possession all grants he had previously made of lands, rents or customs revenues, and what was thus revoked was not to be regranted save upon 'mature counsel'.

Although the council felt sore pressed by the burden of the ransom it showed no antagonism towards the king. His very presence seems to have inspired the enacting of ordinances designed to reform the judicial administration and restore law and order after the lax rule of the Steward :[4] 'the implication throughout is that the years of

---

[1] *A.P.S.,* I. 518–21.   [2] *Ibid.,* 491.
[3] *Ibid.*   [4] *Ibid.,* 492.

David's captivity were not years "of good peace" ' [5]—and that only the king could instil good peace. It was ordained that a justice ayre be held throughout the realm ; the king was enjoined to preside personally over this ayre in order 'to strike terror into wrongdoers'.[6]

Just as serious as the collapse of law and order during the Steward's lieutenancy was the chaos in financial administration. The accounts of the sheriff of Fife had not been audited since 1343, and those of the sheriffs of Aberdeen and Clackmannan since 1348.[7] For some years after 1357 there was to be a laborious, and ultimately successful, attempt to catch up with arrears.[8] From 1359 almost continuously until 1376 the post of chamberlain was to be held not by a great noble but by a civil servant, Walter of Biggar, whose receipts rose year by year : at the 1362 exchequer audit they totalled £7,380 16s. 4½d. and there was a surplus of £4,544 11s. 11¾d.[9] Such figures do not give a complete picture of crown finance and their relationship to payment of the ransom is a confused one. What is clear, however, is that by Scottish standards large sums of money passed through the chamberlain's hands within a few years of the king's homecoming.

This success was partly, but not wholly, a result of the implementation of the financial measures taken by the council of November 1357. One measure, revocation, was insignificant : little was revoked. Another measure, the requisitioning of the wool crop, proved to have moderately successful results. So also did the chief measure envisaged in 1357—the levying of contributions based upon a new assessment. Although no copy survives of an assessment of 1357 the exchequer accounts show that the work of assessment was at least begun,[10] and that contributions were certainly levied[11]—the first in 1358, the second in 1359 and the third in 1360, after which they temporarily ceased. Meanwhile, in order to meet the ransom payments, one vital item of the king's ordinary revenue had to be diverted. Up to 1357 export duties had been at the rate of 6s. 8d. on a sack of wool, 6s. 8d. on each 200 woolfells and 13s. 4d. on each 'last' of hides (about 100).[12] In the spring of 1358 these duties were doubled. By Whitsuntide 1359 they were trebled.[13] Simultaneously, all the great customs were

---

[5] Bruce Webster, 'David II and the Government of Fourteenth Century Scotland', T.R.H.S. (5th series), XVI. 115–30, at 121.
[6] A.P.S., I. 492.   [7] E.R., I. 545–8, 559–60, 570.
[8] Bruce Webster, op. cit., T.R.H.S. (5th series), XVI. 115–30, at 121.
[9] E.R., II. 112, 118.   [10] Ibid., I. 565–81.
[11] E.g. ibid., II. 46–8, 73–5.   [12] Ibid., xl–xli.
[13] Ibid., xl–xli. In 1368 the duties were quadrupled (p. 176 below).

'ordained to the payment of the ransom of the lòrd king'.[14] While it is uncertain how the first ransom instalment of 10,000 marks was paid it is clear that the great customs paid for the second. John Mercer, burgess and custumar of Perth, had been sent to Flanders as the king's agent,[15] and received from Scotland a total of £7,340 5s. 8½d. ; about half came from the customs of the current year, and most of the rest came from the Scottish burgesses, who had combined to advance a loan of 5,000 marks to the king on the security of the customs.[16]

The part played by John Mercer and his fellow-burgesses demonstrates the economic basis on which the increasing political prominence of the merchant burgesses rested, and one by-product of the king's ransom was to establish the burgesses beyond doubt as one of the recognised political classes. They had been summoned to the three successive councils held in 1357—at Perth in January, at Edinburgh in September and at Scone in November—and they had been indisputably recognised as an entity whose approval had to be sought for any measure that relied upon a consensus of responsible opinion. The situation was recognised in the council of November 1357 when the phrase 'the three communities' (*tres communitates*) made its appearance.[17] This apparently new phrase, rendered in English as 'the three estates' (clergy, nobility and burgesses), was to have more reality than the vague 'community of the realm' that had hitherto been used as a catchword to convey an impression of political unanimity; the new concept gave an assured political standing as one of the 'estates' to the burgesses. The view that they were only grudgingly admitted to parliaments and councils, and that for a time they were second-rate members,[18] must be discarded.[19] Their co-operation with David II was one factor in the relative success of the reign after 1357. Burgesses such as John Mercer of Perth, Roger Hogg of Edinburgh and John Crabb of Aberdeen,[20] not only advanced short-term loans to the king,[21] they represented their estate in parliament and council and were those who profited most from the truce with England inaugurated by the ransom treaty of 1357.

The treaty had been followed by a renewal of peaceful communication with England on a scale not seen since 1296. Once more Scot-

[14] *E.R.*, II. 7.
[15] *Ibid.*, 9, 21.
[16] *Ibid.*, 10, 12, 54–6, 83.
[17] *A.P.S.*, I. 491.
[18] Rait, *Parliaments*, pp. 247–9.
[19] See A. A. M. Duncan, *op. cit.*, *S.H.R.*, XLV. 36–58, at 53, n. 1.
[20] The last must not be confused with the famous Flemish engineer of the same name : see E. W. M. Balfour-Melville, 'Two John Crabbs', *S.H.R.*, XXXIX. 31–4.
[21] *E.R.*, II. 2–3, 77, 116, 131, 167.

tish earls, barons, ecclesiastics and burgesses could go on pilgrimage to the shrine of St Thomas at Canterbury, or pass through England to the shrine of St James at Compostela.[22] Once more, Scottish scholars (among them the poet John Barbour) could safely study at the two English universities.[23] But of all the classes of Scotsmen who applied for English safe-conducts it was the merchant burgesses who were the foremost; and it was undoubtedly the new trading opportunities in England that accounted for their increasing prosperity.

There were also many interchanges of a political nature. As soon as her unfaithful husband returned to Scotland Queen Joan led the way south 'to speak with her brother the king [Edward III] and to start negotiations for a greater treaty'[24]—doubtless a final peace. In February 1359 David himself set out for London,[25] apparently in search of the elusive final peace.

When it became clear that this was not to be readily obtained David sent his trusted envoys, Sir Robert Erskine and Norman Leslie, on a mission to France. In 1359 they informed the Dauphin Charles (regent for the captured King John) that David, while a prisoner, 'was never minded to abandon the French alliance, even although, if he had done so, the king of England would have released him more easily from prison'.[26] The envoys proposed that the Scots would renew war on the English if the French would pay King David's ransom. The French were unenthusiastic: the most they could offer was 50,000 marks to be paid at Bruges on 5 April 1360 on condition that the Scots renewed the old alliance and sooner or later made war on the English.[27]

Edward III certainly feared a Scottish attack when he was on campaign in France between October 1359 and May 1360. This latest campaign made it impossible for the French to pay the 50,000 marks they had promised the Scots. On 7 May 1360, with the drafting of the treaty of Brétigny, Edward gained (on parchment at least) much of what he was fighting for in France; although the treaty also stipulated that 'the King of France will altogether abandon the alliance of those of Scotland'[28] nothing so definite resulted. The treaty of Brétigny, as modified by later negotiations at Calais, brought not an Anglo-French peace but a precarious truce that might erupt into war and tempt the Scots to intervene. Meanwhile in midsummer 1360 the

[22] *Rot. Scot.*, I. 859–60.   [23] *Ibid.*, 808–9, 815–6.
[24] *Scalacronica*, p. 176.
[25] *Cal. Docs. Scot.*, IV. No. 27; *Rot. Scot.*, I. 835.
[26] R. Delachenal, *Histoire de Charles V* (Paris, 1909–31), II. 103–5.
[27] *Ibid.*   [28] *Scalacronica*, p. 195.

Scots stopped further payment of the ransom after belated payment of the second instalment.[29] No further payment was to be made until after a new ransom treaty had been negotiated in 1365.[30]

Whatever the reasons for the lapse in payment it was to be followed by disturbances within Scotland. For a few years after 1357 David had given signs of 'a deliberate effort to rule with circumspection and a wide measure of consent'.[31] In 1357 the Steward was granted the earldom of Strathearn, which had lapsed to the crown; in 1358 William, Lord of Douglas, already supreme on the Borders, was given added prestige by promotion to a newly-created earldom of Douglas.[32] Yet it soon became clear that the great nobles were being excluded from the king's inner counsels. David's mistress, Katherine Mortimer, seemed a fit victim for their resentment. In the summer of 1360 she was treacherously stabbed to death on the road near Soutra.[33] After Katherine's murder a new decisiveness can be seen in the king's actions: Thomas Stewart, Earl of Angus, suspected as instigator of the crime, was warded in Dumbarton Castle,[34] where he shortly died of a fresh outbreak of plague, named 'the second mortality' to distinguish it from the first of 1349. The imprisonment of Angus was followed by the king's seizure of the Earl of Mar's castle of Kildrummy in September 1362,[35] partly on account of an indenture of 24 February 1359 by which Mar had become the liege man of Edward III.[36] Having taken Kildrummy the king went farther north to spend the Christmas of 1362 at Kinloss. The royal visit was cut short in January 1363 by news of disquieting activities on the part of Robert the Steward, his sons and his allies.

It was said that the Steward and the Earls of March and Douglas had complained that money raised for the ransom was wasted 'by evil counsel' and demanded government by 'better counsel'.[37] The mention of the ransom money was a pretext that covered the self-interest and family interests of the conspirators: Douglas was brother-in-law of the disgraced Earl of Mar. The root of complaint was that the king's trusted political advisers were lesser nobles, knights and kirk-

---

[29] *E.R.*, II. 54–6.

[30] All future ransom negotiations take it for granted that only the first two instalments—20,000 marks—had been paid.

[31] Bruce Webster, *op. cit.*, *T.R.H.S.* (5th series), XVI. 115–30, at 126.

[32] *Scots Peerage*, III. 150; VIII. 257–8.

[33] *Chron. Bower*, II. 365–6; *Scalacronica*, p. 196.

[34] *Chron. Bower*, II. 365; *E.R.*, II. 167–8.

[35] *Chron. Wyntoun*, II. 505; *Scalacronica*, p. 202.

[36] *Rot. Scot.*, I. 836.   [37] *Scalacronica*, pp. 202–3.

men, and that his economic advisers were burgesses. The resulting 'evil counsel' was to be displaced by the 'better counsel' that would naturally be forthcoming from the Steward, Douglas, and their like. The latter also feared the possible consequences of David's latest amorous liaison. For his relationship with Dame Margaret Logie, daughter of Sir Malcolm Drummond and widow of Sir John Logie, was potentially matrimonial.[38] Queen Joan had gone to England in 1357 and stayed there till her death in 1362. David was free to marry for the second time. Dame Margaret had borne a son to her late husband; if she were to prove a fruitful spouse to King David, the Steward's hopes of the crown would be dashed and the ambitions of his many offspring would be frustrated.

Such a prospect, coming as it did at a time when the great nobles were restive, was too much to stomach. In Fordun's words, 'a great sedition and conspiracy arose and was hatched . . . by the greater and more powerful men ; . . . for the magnates united against their lord the king and took counsel with one another that they might bend him to their opinion upon a petition that to everyone seemed unrighteous, or else send him to exile'.[39] The unrighteous petition was probably a demand for the dismissal of the king's counsellors and Margaret Logie. The king would not give way but instead 'gathered together his lieges from the four corners of his land, offering them much money for their wages of war'.[40] David had learned from the English the advantage in discipline to be gained through the payment of wages of war; the lapse in payment of the ransom had allowed him to salt away 5,000 marks in a 'deposit' in Stirling Castle ; he drew over £600 for the wages of the host that mustered at Edinburgh.[41] Moreover he could count on the steadfast loyalty of Sir Archibald Douglas, 'the Grim', Sir Robert Erskine and Sir John Danielston, lesser nobles, who had respectively been appointed as well-paid keepers of the key castles of Edinburgh, Stirling and Dumbarton.[42] The king could also take advantage of the irresolution of the opposition : there was an almost superstitious unwillingness to face the royal standard on any field of battle. Among the rebels only the Earl of Douglas showed any initiative. At length David rode rapidly from Edinburgh and caught the earl by surprise at Lanark. Although Douglas escaped, the episode marked the end of the rising : the Steward deserted his allies ; Douglas and March had to submit.[43]

[38] *R.M.S.*, I. No. 124. [39] *Chron. Fordun*, I. 381.
[40] *Ibid.* [41] *Chron. Wyntoun*, II. 505; E.R., II. 164.
[42] *E.R.*, II. 92, 114, 221. [43] *Scalacronica*, p. 203.

In April 1363 the king celebrated his victory by marrying Dame Margaret Logie at Inchmurdoch, a Fife manor of the bishops of St Andrews.[44] The scene of the wedding was also the scene of the humiliation of the late rebels: on 14 May 1363 the Steward was forced to seal a document [45] announcing: 'I will be faithful for all the term of my life to ... the Lord David, illustrious King of Scots. ... I will aid, defend, ... maintain and uphold my lord ... and his officials and all those faithful to him, whomsoever they be.' The latter were at hand to act as witnesses to the Steward's submission. They included Bishop Landallis, Master Walter Wardlaw, archdeacon of Lothian and secretary to the king, Sir Robert Erskine and Sir Archibald Douglas.

The pacification of the great conspiracy was easier than the achievement of a settlement with England. There is something of an enigma in the fact that although the Scots had deliberately defaulted on the ransom payments this brought no retribution from Edward. But the outbreak of the great conspiracy had coincided with a hardening of his attitude: the situation called for a summit meeting; in November 1363 there were talks at Westminster between the Scottish and English privy councils in the presence of both kings.

The outcome of these talks was the drafting of two memoranda,[46] each listing a number of items that David was to put before the three estates as a possible basis for 'good peace and concord'. In the longer memorandum, dated 27 November 1363, it was stated that David would sound the inclinations of the estates as to whether the King of England might succeed David if the latter died without legitimate offspring. If the estates would yield that vital point Edward would make important concessions: he would forgo the residue of the ransom, release the Scottish hostages, restore Berwick and other occupied territory, compensate the remainder of the disinherited for the annulling of their claims on Scotland, grant back to the Scottish king the lands held in England by his predecessors. Homage would be required only for these English lands, not for the kingdom of Scotland. There were all-embracing and tightly-defined clauses that would take effect if the English king, by succeeding a childless David, became ruler of the two kingdoms. There would be no union of the kingdoms; the name and territorial integrity of the kingdom of Scotland would be carefully preserved and the 'King of England and Scotland' would

---

[44] *Chron. Wyntoun*, II. 506.   [45] *Chron. Bower*, II. 369–70.
[46] Texts in *A.P.S.*, I. 493–5; *Cal. Docs. Scot.*, IV. Nos. 91, 92.

undergo a second coronation at Scone upon the enthronement stone, which would be restored. A second and shorter memorandum was also drafted by which the succession to a childless David would go not to the English king but to one of his sons who was not heir apparent of England. Since this represented an abatement of Edward's ambitions he would make fewer concessions than those proposed in the first memorandum.

Only the first memorandum, with its carefully-defined safeguards for the preservation of a distinct Scottish identity, deserves to be considered as a possibly statesmanlike attempt to solve the troubled relationship of the two realms; it certainly invites favourable comparison with the terms of the union of 1707. The first memorandum had conceded so much to the Scots that, given English good faith—of which some Scots rightly entertained doubts—the future 'King of England and Scotland' would in Scotland have been a constitutional ruler bouhd by the terms of a fundamental written constitution. On the other hand, the Scots were called upon to disinherit a native-born Scot whose right of succession had been formally recognised in parliament, and to put in his place an English king whose depredations had brought misery to land and people.

On 4 March 1364 the three estates met in parliament at Scone. The texts of the Westminster memoranda were read aloud[47] and debate followed on one of the most crucial issues ever brought before a Scottish parliament. Unofficial jottings have survived of two arguments that were then presented[48] in favour of the first and second Westminster memorandum respectively. As it happened, some other argument, which eventually carried the day, must have been pressed to uphold the rights of the Steward as heir presumptive. Certainly the brief official record of the parliament states that 'it was expressly answered by the three estates . . . that they in no wise wished to grant, nor in any wise assent to, those things which were sought by the King of England and his council'.[49] The Scottish chroniclers, followed by later historians, make parliament's rejection of the English terms peremptory; and most of them represent David II as being annoyed by the decision.[50] On the contrary it may be inferred that David made no attempt to force either of the Westminster memoranda upon the estates and that both king and parliament were prepared to co-

---

[47] *Chron. Bower*, II. 369–70; *A.P.S.*, I. 492–5.
[48] Texts edited by E. W. M. Balfour-Melville, *op. cit.*, *S.H.S. Misc. IX.* 1–56.
[49] *A.P.S.*, I. 493.
[50] See Ranald Nicholson, *op. cit.*, *S.H.R.*, XLV. 59–78, at 68.

operate to meet the diplomatic crisis that was expected to follow their rejection.

For the next few years there was no specific crisis but rather a prevailing sense that one was impending. Councils or parliaments met in rapid succession to hear the reports of each embassy sent to England and to draft terms to be offered to the English in the succeeding embassy.[51] Edward's demands remained exorbitant. He would not even bind himself to a long truce. All that the Scottish envoys could obtain was an indenture of 20 May 1365 [52] which settled the ransom at £100,000, one third as great again as it had been in 1357. Previous payment of 20,000 marks was to be ignored. The £100,000 were to be paid in yearly instalments of 6,000 marks (£4,000) beginning on 2 February 1366. The truce was to last only until 2 February 1370, when either side might renew the war by giving six months notice to the other. In that case the obligation to pay £100,000 would be cancelled, but the Scots would still be obliged to pay the 80,000 marks outstanding under the treaty of Berwick.

When a council met at Perth on 24 July 1365 the four-year truce was considered inadequate. Once more, large concessions were drafted to obtain a final peace.[53] The English reaction was still unfavourable : by May 1366 they had drawn up 'four points' concerning homage, the succession, territorial cessions, and a reciprocal arrangement for military aid, and insisted that these be regarded as the basis of a final peace.[54] For the next two years one or other of the 'four points' was debated by the three estates, their envoys, and the English. Finally, when parliament met at Scone in June 1368 there was a discussion that lasted at least four days. It was then decided that 'it is not yet needful or expedient to initiate or attempt negotiation upon granting any of the said points' which had been reputed in a previous parliament as 'things unmeet, intolerable and impossible to be observed, and leading to express servitude'.[55] When parliament next met (at Perth in March 1369) [56] a renewal of the Anglo-French war was imminent,[57] and French envoys soon appeared in Scotland.[58]

Well aware of the changed diplomatic scene David accompanied a Scottish embassy to England in June 1369. It was now the turn of Edward to offer concessions, some of which concerned the Borders.

[51] *A.P.S.*, I. 495-6.
[52] *Cal. Docs. Scot.*, IV. No. 108; *A.P.S.*, XII. 12-3; *Rot. Scot.*, I. 894-5.
[53] *A.P.S.*, I. 496-7.   [54] *Ibid.*, 497.
[55] *Ibid.*, 503.   [56] *Ibid.*, 506-7.
[57] May McKisack, *The Fourteenth Century*, p. 144.
[58] *E.R.*, II. 328, 348.

David had never reconciled himself to a permanent English occupation of the Scottish Marches. Ever since 1357 he had unobtrusively nibbled at the English sphere of influence; he had appointed his own sheriffs in all the Border sheriffdoms and by 1360 he even drew revenue from them all.[59] In 1360, moreover, he had personally concluded an indenture with a representative of the Earl of Hereford and Northampton by which all the revenues of Annandale were to be equally divided between the earl and the king, and disorder was to be repressed to the benefit of both parties.[60] In 1366 the Annandale settlement was again renewed.[61] One of the concessions that David extorted in June 1369 was the extension of the Annandale arrangement to the whole of the sheriffdom of Roxburgh.[62] This agreement was part and parcel of the greatest concession of all—a third ransom treaty of June 1369[63] which ended discussion of the 'four points' and gave the Scots terms that in the previous few years would have been beyond their wildest hopes. A truce would be observed up to 2 February 1370 and would last for the ensuing fourteen years. The residue of the ransom was now fixed at 56,000 marks—in other words there was a return to the original ransom of 100,000 marks and allowance was made for the 20,000 marks paid under the treaty as well as for the four instalments of 6,000 marks already paid under the 1365 treaty. Payment of the remaining 56,000 marks was to be at the rate of 4,000 marks a year for the next fourteen years. It is incongruous that at a time when David's revenues were more flourishing than they had ever been,[64] the ransom instalment was reduced to a lower figure than ever.

To secure a peaceful Scotland in his rear Edward had paid what was for him a heavy price, for the renewal of the Anglo-French war occurred in circumstances that favoured the French rather than the English.[65] David was quite ready to fish in troubled waters. By June 1370 he was once more in London and to outward appearances on the friendliest of terms with Edward,[66] but simultaneously he sent Archibald the Grim on a mission to the French court.[67] Thus the ultimate trend of David's diplomacy remains an enigma: although he was playing off one side against the other he had not definitely committed himself to either the French or the English by the time he died.

[59] Ibid., 34–43.   [60] Cal. Docs. Scot., IV. No. 47.
[61] Ibid., IV. Nos. 127, 128.   [62] Rot. Scot., I. 939.
[63] Ibid., 933, 934–5, 938–9.   [64] P. 177 below.
[65] May McKisack, The Fourteenth Century, pp. 143–5.
[66] Cal. Docs. Scot., IV. No. 173; Rot. Scot., I. 938.
[67] E.R., II. 356, 358.

The extent to which nationalism figured in David II's diplomacy is difficult to determine. One of the charges that has been brought against him is that he was 'a lover of the gaudy chivalrous diversions of his day'.[68] Certainly David's long reign coincided with an upsurge of chivalry in Europe [69] which sometimes diverted attention from incipient nationalism. In 1365 Jean Froissart, whose chivalric chronicles and poems found a ready market wherever a French-speaking aristocracy existed, was welcomed at the Scottish court.[70] Patronage for literary works of a chivalric nature,[71] suits of tournament armour, a reported interest in the crusade, all combine to give a picture of King David as a man to whom chivalry meant much— and the current father-figure of European chivalry was none other than Edward III. Chivalry was undoubtedly the link in the special relationship that brought David and Edward together.[72] Yet it would be wrong to assume that chivalry was in either case so dominant a motive as to exclude every other. If David attended flamboyant tournaments and banquets in London he also engaged in hard bargaining. While ostensibly observing the truce he had nonetheless made inroads on English influence in the Scottish Marches, had won new and lucrative opportunities for the Scottish merchant burgesses and brought prosperity both to them and to the royal finances. Despite his chequered career he was to leave Scotland just as free and independent as it had been at his accession.

Though it is misleading to think of the later years of the reign of David II wholly in terms of Anglo-Scottish relations, the important developments that took place within Scotland itself were all influenced, directly or indirectly, by one aspect of Anglo-Scottish relations—what has melodramatically been styled 'the incubus of the ransom money'.[73] In accordance with the second ransom treaty of 1365, which had taken the place of the first ransom treaty of 1357, the Scots had not only to pay ransom instalments of 6,000 marks (£4,000) a year but had to bear in mind the possibility that the truce might nonetheless end on 2 February 1370, whereupon they would be liable to all the penalties and sanctions of the 1357 treaty unless they

[68] A. Lang, *History of Scotland*, I. 267.

[69] For its characteristics see Arthur Bryant, *The Age of Chivalry* (1963) and E. K. Milliken, *Chivalry in the Middle Ages* (1968).

[70] See A. H. Diverres, 'Jean Froissart's Journey to Scotland', *Forum for Modern Language Studies*, I. 54–63.

[71] *The Buik of Alexander* (S.T.S.), I. cxcv–cc, cciii, ccviii–ccx.

[72] 'For thare wes rycht gret specialté/Betwen hym and the King Edward' (*Chron. Wyntoun*, II. 501–2).   [73] George Burnett, *E.R.*, II. xlv.

had meanwhile paid the total arrears under that original ransom treaty. Thus the council that met at Holyrood on 8 May 1366 [74] concerned itself not only with the matter of raising ransom instalments of 6,000 marks a year but with preparation for payment of 80,000 marks within less than four years. Just as the council of November 1357 had called for a new survey of the country's financial and economic resources so also did the Holyrood council of May 1366. There was to be a general assessment of all lands and rents within the realm, both ecclesiastical and lay. [75] When parliament met at Scone on 20 July 1366, [76] a mere seven weeks later, most of the results of the new assessment were already available. [77]

In most cases two figures were given : the first was the *Antiqua Taxatio*, an assessment of lands and rents dating from the time of Alexander III, [78] and the second was the *Verus Valor*, the 'true' or current value as determined in the recent assessment. A comparison of the *Antiqua Taxatio* and the *Verus Valor* indicates an apparent wholesale decline in landed wealth between the later years of Alexander III and those of David II. For in monetary terms landed income had been halved in a period of less than a century : according to the *Antiqua Taxatio* the assessment of the Scottish bishoprics (including all kirks) came to £15,002 16s. 0d.; by the *Verus Valor* it came to only £9,396 6s. 6d.; in the twenty-two sheriffdoms for which returns are given the *Antiqua Taxatio* amounted to £48,249 7s. 8d. and the *Verus Valor*, though not fully ascertained, came to about £23,250. It has thus been affirmed that 'evidence of the poverty of the country appears from the taxations [assessments] which the estates imposed to try to pay off the ransom'. [79] Yet although the decline was real enough in monetary terms, money is not a fixed measure. One of the causes of the general economic malaise in fourteenth-century Europe was deflation caused by the drain of gold and silver to the Orient to pay for luxury goods. The new assessment of 1366 need not necessarily be taken as proof of 'poverty' but may be taken as proof of falling prices and rents and general deflation. If there was an economic crisis it seems to have been a crisis that concerned the value of money rather than the production of real wealth in the form of goods and services. It was no easy task to adjust the coinage to deal with either inflation or deflation, especially since it was thought desirable to keep Scottish coins on a par with those of England. The parity

[74] *A.P.S.*, I. 497.
[75] *Ibid.* [76] *Ibid.*, 498. [77] *Ibid.*, 498–501.
[78] *Ibid.*, 499–501, 476. [79] J. D. Mackie, *History of Scotland*, p. 88.

which had been precariously maintained was lost when a royal precept of 7 October 1367 [80] ordered that thenceforth a further tenpence should be coined from each pound weight (Scots) of silver. In practice this meant that the Scots were minting 23.5d. from the ounce of silver while the English minted only 22.5d. The debasement of 1367 was thus 'far from considerable',[81] though it pointed the way to subsequent drastic devaluations of the Scottish coinage in relation to that of England.[82]

Whatever the significance of the figures of the new assessment of 1366, its importance for contemporaries was its use for the levying of contributions. These were granted at varying rates and for only a year at a time but came by the end of the reign to approximate to a regular income tax. Although the contributions had crept into government finance under the wing of the ransom it was parliament itself that allowed them to be used for other purposes : when the Scone parliament of July 1365 ordained a large contribution of 8,000 marks it stipulated that the money was to be used 'for the expenses of the king and to pay his debts within the realm, and for the payment of the envoys, and for nothing more, since the great custom is ordained for the said payment of £4,000 for the ransom'.[83] Lest the insufficiency of the customs became the excuse for direct taxation in the shape of contributions, the Scone parliament of 12 June 1368 re-affirmed that the great customs should pay for the ransom and quadrupled the export duties [84] so that they were four times the rate of 1357, 26s. 8d. thereafter being levied on each sack of wool.

The quadrupling of the customs duties did not stop further parliamentary grants of contributions. Even although these were appropriated by parliament to some specific item of royal expenditure, attempts to segregate them from ransom funds proved cumbersome and unworkable. By the end of the reign all the customs were paid to the king's chamberlain, along with contributions and other revenue, and were used indiscriminately both for ransom payments and for ordinary royal expenditure.[85] The king had thus won full control over all sources of revenue, whether or not they were supposed to be set aside for the ransom ; it was he (and succeeding kings) who benefited from the quadrupling of the great customs. In addition another measure increased the economic resources of the crown : the parlia-

---

[80] *A.P.S.*, I. 502-3.   [81] G. Burnett, *E.R.*, II. xcviii.
[82] By 1390 the ratio of Scottish coins to their English counterparts stood at about 2:1; by 1451 2½:1; by 1456 3:1; by 1467 3½:1; by 1475 4:1 (R. W. Cochran-Patrick, *Records of the Coinage of Scotland*, I. lxxvi).
[83] *A.P.S.*, I. 498.   [84] *Ibid.*, 502-4.   [85] *E.R.*, II. lxxii.

ment which met at Scone on 27 September 1367 elected a commission representative of the three estates to consider the king's livelihood, and issued a sweeping act of revocation designed to restore to the crown all lands and revenues granted from the royal demesne ever since the death of Robert I in 1329.[86]

The measures taken in the closing years of the reign thus show King David's adroit manipulation of the constant obligation to pay the ransom, so as to increase the financial resources of the crown. The ransom itself was not always neglected : although only two payments of 10,000 marks had been made under the first ransom treaty of 1357, four payments of 6,000 marks were made under the second ransom treaty of 1365 and one payment of 4,000 marks was made under the third ransom treaty of 1369. At the exchequer audit held at Perth on 15 February 1371, a week before the king's death, the chamberlain reported that he had already set aside 4,000 marks for the next ransom instalment due at midsummer 1371, and he remarked that after that forthcoming payment the total outstanding debt on the ransom would stand at 48,000 marks.[87] The extent of David's financial triumph can be seen in his last exchequer audit covering the year from 19 January 1370 to 15 February 1371 : the chamberlain's total receipts were £15,359 14s. 9¼d.[88] The vast bulk of these receipts was forthcoming from the swelling export duties and contributions engendered by the beneficent 'incubus' of the ransom. It is doubtful if any medieval Scottish king, either before or after King David, was in so strong a financial position.

While the king's success is obvious it is less easy to determine how it affected the economic wellbeing of his subjects. The ineffective revocation of 1357 and the more effective revocation of 1367 were measures that—however unjust—became almost standard practice in succeeding reigns. The repudiation of royal debts in 1370 was also unjust; but in this respect David II was a model of financial rectitude when compared with Edward III. More fundamental was the imposition of higher export duties which might well have crippled the export trade. Yet nothing of the sort took place : the revenue from the customs increased year by year to a total of £9,521 2s. 8½d. in 1371;[88(b)] and the volume of exports did not diminish until after the king's death. In the matter of trade the interests of the king and the merchant burgesses coincided. It was typical that a royal charter of 28 March 1364 [89] in favour of 'our beloved

---

[86] *A.P.S.*, I. 501–2.   [87] *E.R.*, II. 355.   [88] *Ibid.*
[88(b)] *Ibid.*, 351.   [89] *Burghs Convention Recs.*, I. 538–41.

E.H.S.—7

Scottish burgesses', assured them the right to buy and sell anywhere within the trade precinct of their own burgh, while foreign merchants were permitted to buy and sell only from and to the merchants of the burghs, who were thus guaranteed their position as middlemen with the attendant profits. The charter also forbade 'any bishop, prior or other kirkman, any earl, baron or other layman, whatsoever may be his rank, to buy or sell wool, skins, hides or other merchandise ... save only from [or to] the merchants of the burghs within whose liberties [trade precincts] they live'.

While the king's financial policies met with no ascertainable opposition from the burgesses they ran into undoubted opposition in an area scarcely used to any government control, let alone taxation. When the functions of central government were few, so also were the political differences between Highlands and Lowlands. When under David II these functions increased, so also did the differences between the Lowlands, amenable to government control, and the Highlands, which were not. The long career of John of the Isles as a virtually independent potentate illustrates the growing difficulties that faced the crown in trying to hold Highlands and Lowlands in some sort of unity. Although John seems to have dropped his lukewarm adherence to Edward III he certainly resented David's attempts to extend to the Isles the assessment of 1366 and the contributions that followed upon it. He was not alone in his opposition to the new measures : the members of the 'Highland Party' that had formed during the Steward's lieutenancy were frequently (with the exception of the canny Steward himself) described as 'contumaciously absent' from parliament.[90] When the act of revocation was passed by the Scone parliament of September 1367[91] it became clear that it might bear heavily upon Robert the Steward, the Earl of Ross, and especially upon John of the Isles.[92] In fact, the act of revocation was not invariably put into effect : it gave the king a bargaining position vis-à-vis the magnates. John of Lorne and Gillespic Campbell made their peace with the king and attended parliament at Perth on 6 March 1369, but John of the Isles remained obdurate. It was ordained that the king should force him and his sons to obedience so that they should stand to law and undergo services and burdens as did the king's 'inland' subjects.[93] These were no empty words. In the winter of 1369 the king led an expedition to Inverness, where John arrived to make his submission.

90 *A.P.S.*, I. 498-9.   91 *Ibid.*, 499-501.
92 *Ibid.*, 528-9.   93 *Ibid.*, 506.

On 15 November 1369 an indenture was sealed in which he acknowledged that 'my redoubtable lord, David, by the grace of God, illustrious King of Scots, has been moved against my person by reason of
certain negligences committed by me. . . .'[94] John humbly begged remission, which the king graciously conceded in return for hostages
and an undertaking to obey royal officials and pay contributions. This
transaction at Inverness was accompanied by another : a few months
after the death of King David, William, Earl of Ross, was to present
a *querimonia*[95] or complaint, on the subject of the king's conduct
towards him and his brother ; Earl William had been forced to ratify
a grant of lands to Sir Walter Leslie 'on account of the rigour of the
same lord king and by fear of his wrath'.[96] In the last parliament of
the reign, on 23 October 1370, the earl was forced to resign all his
lands and to receive them back under the conditions of a tailzie[97] in
favour of Sir Walter Leslie, who was eventually to succeed to the
earldom of Ross.

The king's treatment of the Highland magnates was typical of his
treatment of the magnates as a whole. While royal patronage went to
a nobility of service, the 'stowt', and almost all who held the rank of
earl, were cowed into submission. On one pretext or another, the
magnates were made the victims of insecure tenure and found their
way of life increasingly subject to royal surveillance : it was enacted
by the Scone parliament of June 1368 that all dissensions among the
magnates and nobles were to be settled by the king and by way of
common justice, 'which our lord the king is bound always to administer impartially, without favour to anyone'.[98] Latterly, no noble,
no matter how great, could offend the king—or the queen—with
impunity : in the winter of 1368, when Robert the Steward and some
of his sons did something to incur the wrath of Queen Margaret, she
prevailed upon David to arrest and imprison them.[99] Although the
Steward was soon released, his plumage was again ruffled in 1369
when he was deprived of his earldom of Strathearn for a few
months.[100] And in 1370 the troublesome Earl of Mar was under
arrest as a prisoner on the Bass Rock.[101] The traditional view that the
reign marked 'the beginning of the end of medieval Scottish govern-

<hr/>

[94] *Ibid.*, XII. 16–7.   [95] *Aberdeen-Banff Illustrations*, II. 387–9.
[96] *Ibid.*   [97] *A.P.S.*, I. 537–8.   [98] *Ibid.*, 503.
[99] *Chron. Bower*, II. 379–80; *E.R.*, II. 309, 347.
[100] *H.B.C.*, p. 489; *Morton Registrum*, II. Nos. 96, 101. By 18 February 1370
he was once more styled Earl of Strathearn (*A.P.S.*, I. 534).
[101] *E.R.*, II. 357.

ment' has been justifiably challenged by the affirmation that 'there was no collapse in David's reign . . . the king was not overwhelmed by the power of his barons. Any collapse, if collapse there was, came after 1371.'[102]

In his dealings with the Scottish kirk David could show the same firmness that he displayed towards the great nobles. But the firmness was tempered by a conventional piety demonstrated in pilgrimages to Canterbury, kirk-building in honour of St Monan (who miraculously extracted an arrow barb from the king's head),[103] and the grant of a specific privilege that the Scottish bishops had long sought—the right to make testaments bequeathing their goods.[104] For the Scottish episcopate included persons who were closely associated with the king : Bishop Landallis had served him year after year as a diplomatist, so also had Master Walter Wardlaw, who had been the king's secretary before he was rewarded with the bishopric of Glasgow in 1368.

The prospect of appointment to a bishopric was an inducement that must have fired the ambition of the ecclesiastics who largely staffed the king's household and administration. Ecclesiastical preferment was not, however, the only inducement; there was beginning to be a real civil service : 'from the 1360's we first hear of the king's secretary, apparently as keeper of the privy seal. . . . From 1359 comes the first surviving example of the king's signet. These are only slight signs, but they indicate a gradual development in administration.'[105] Simultaneously government and administration were becoming less haphazard, more regular. Towards the end of the reign exchequer audits, often attended by the king himself, were regularly held at Perth in January of each year. The comparatively large bulk of parliamentary, exchequer and chancery records of the period 1357–1371 indicates not only the increasing regularity of government but its increasing intensity; and these records disprove the old view that David led a life of ease and show instead that he 'was much concerned in the business of government'.[106] Indeed his handling of this business was sometimes thought *too* personal : the very intensity of government led to the growth of rules and customs of which David occasionally fell foul.[107(a)]

[102] Bruce Webster, *op. cit.*, *T.R.H.S.* (5th series), xvi. 115–30, at 130.
[103] *Chron. Pluscarden*, I. 294.
[104] *R.M.S.*, I. No. 372; *Chron. Bower*, II. 389–90; see G. Donaldson, 'The rights of the Scottish crown in episcopal vacancies', *S.H.R.*, xlv. 27–35.
[105] Bruce Webster, *op. cit.*, *T.R.H.S.* (5th series), xvi. 115–30, at 121.
[106] *Ibid.*, p. 118.   [107(a)] E.g. *E.R.*, II. 111, 361.

But there were compensations for such peccadilloes. It is striking that Wyntoun specifically commends the king for his administration of justice : [107(b)] his reference to the frequent holding of parliament, and the speedy justice to be obtained there, clearly shows that its function as a court was still looked upon as of foremost importance. Possibly for this reason councils of the three estates were upgraded soon after 1357 to the status of 'full' or 'general' councils.[108] Freed (save on rare occasions) from the burden of judicial business, they had the same composition as parliament and were equally competent to deal with all affairs of state. In parliament also there was an attempt to streamline business by making special arrangements for its judicial functions : in the Perth parliament of February 1370 the three estates elected six clerics to represent the clergy, ten knights and four esquires to represent the baronage, and seven burgesses to represent the burghs. This body was to deal with 'those matters which concern common justice, namely falsed dooms, *questiones* and other plaints which ought to be discussed, settled and determined by parliament'.[109]

The delegation of judicial powers by parliament can be traced back at least to 1341 ; delegation was a 'natural and obvious device' [110] and was not restricted to judicial matters. Committees were appointed which reported their findings or recommendations to parliament as a whole. Commissions were appointed which did not report back but were invested with the full authority of parliament to 'determine' the points referred to them. A further development took place in the Scone parliament of September 1367 when 'certain persons were elected to hold the parliament, and leave was given to others to go home on account of the harvest'.[111] Leave to go home—*licentia redeundi* or *licentia recedendi*—was to be accorded to members of parliament from time to time during the next three reigns. In such cases parliament met only to delegate its full power to a commission that was under no obligation to account for its decisions to any future parliament. In 1367, admittedly, the commission was a large one— fifteen ecclesiastics, thirteen nobles (few of them great) and thirteen burgesses. A similar procedure was adopted in the Perth parliaments of March 1369 and February 1370.[112] Lord Hailes, finding little to say in his *Annals* concerning the year 1367, had some suspicion that

107(b) *Chron. Wyntoun*, II. 498, 506–7.
108 E.g. *A.P.S.*, I. 503, 526. In discussing the circumstances that inspired this change of nomenclature R. K. Hannay ('On "Parliament" and "General Council" ', *S.H.R.*, XVIII. 157–70, at 161–4) makes darkness more obscure.
109 *A.P.S.*, I. 508.
110 Rait, *Parliaments*, p. 349.
111 *A.P.S.*, I. 501.
112 *Ibid.*, 506, 507–8.

the king was using this device for his own nefarious ends.[113] But it would be wrong to dismiss out of hand the reasons officially given for the grant of *licentia redeundi* : the harvest or a scarcity of provisions were matters of some consequence. Moreover the parliamentary committees and commissions fit into the broad pattern of a government that had expanded its functions, subjected them to routine and regularity, and ruled with an unexampled intensiveness.

None of this would have been possible without a forceful king. In the eleven years after Neville's Cross David had suffered, literally as well as figuratively, from the slings and arrows of outrageous fortune. He had come back to Scotland, toughened by adversity and years of painstaking political intrigue, to govern his land with 'radure' so that 'nane durst welle wythstand his will' ; all were forced to be obedient, for he would always chastise 'mysdoaris'.[114] Political offenders suffered a chastisement that was sometimes capricious; but in the last years of the reign it was never cruel or vindictive; political misdemeanours might bring the loss of lands but no political offence was punished by execution. It is thus all the more striking that David, with few assets save his own astuteness and forceful personality, made himself so completely the master of Scotland. Only in his second wife did he meet his match.

When David had married Dame Margaret Logie 'by force of love which conquers everything'[115] he had 'magnificently exalted her as queen'[116] and 'endowed her with many lands and possessions'.[117] The weakness of Queen Margaret's position was that she did not provide the king with an heir. That was hardly her fault : she had already proved her fruitfulness while David had not proved his. In an attempt to retain her influence she may have feigned pregnancy.[118] Whatever the reason—and it seems to have involved the temporary imprisonment of the Steward in the winter of 1368—Margaret fell from royal favour. By 1369 David had cast amorous eyes upon Agnes Dunbar.[119] It was assumed that 'Lady Margaret Logie, onetime queen' would content herself with a pension of £100 which the king had thoughtfully assigned to her 'after the celebration of divorce'.[120] Instead she secretly boarded a ship in the Forth and made her way to Avignon, where her no doubt considerable charms won her the kindly eye of Pope Gregory XI and his cardinals. When Dame Margaret instituted

113 Hailes, *Annals*, II. 316.
115 *Scalacronica*, p. 203.
117 *Chron. Fordun*, I. 382.
119 *E.R.*, II. 328, 345, 357.

114 *Chron. Wyntoun*, II. 498.
116 *Chron. Bower*, II. 379.
118 *Chron. Pluscarden*, I. 307.
120 *Ibid.*, 345.

an appeal in the *curia* against her divorce there was talk of placing Scotland under an interdict until her death removed the danger in 1375.[121]

It was ironic that David II should leave a troublesome legacy to the Steward in the shape of the pertinacious Margaret Logie. When Margaret had fallen into disgrace the Steward had been admitted to something approaching royal favour. Yet, even then, David was probably reluctant to admit the inevitability of a Stewart succession. He himself was scarcely forty-seven years old and despite previous disappointments contemplated a third marriage. Agnes Dunbar had first been granted a pension of sixty marks,[122] fit enough for a royal mistress but not for a royal bride. The prospect of honourable matrimony opened before her eyes in a royal charter[123] which granted her a life pension of a thousand marks for her trousseau and adornment. Eleven days later, on 22 February 1371, King David unexpectedly died in Edinburgh. The long-suffering Steward at last secured his royal heritage.

[121] *Chron. Bower*, II. 380.   [122] *R.M.S.*, I. App. 2, No. 1652.
[123] *Ibid.*, App. 2, No. 32; *Morton Registrum*, II. No. 108.

8

THE ACCESSION OF THE STEWARTS, THE BEGINNING OF THE GREAT SCHISM AND OTHER AFFLICTIONS

I f the achievements of David II are to be seen in perspective they
must be viewed not only with the triumphs of Robert I in the fore-
ground but with the failures of the first Stewart kings in the background. For almost fifty years, until the new dynasty showed some
mettle in the person of James I, Scotland was to be racked by a mis-
governance which proved beyond doubt that there was no substitute
for a masterful king. Henceforward the threats that had to be faced
were to be not external but internal : the problem of the Highlands
became increasingly acute; a comparable problem arose in the Borders, an area that until the wars of independence had been among the
most settled in the whole kingdom ; and connected with these changes
was the rise of overmighty subjects such as the Douglases and the
MacDonalds of the Isles.

Robert the Steward had reached what was then the advanced age
of fifty-five when he succeeded to the crown as Robert II. He was,
reports the chronicler Bower, impressive in appearance, humble,
mild, affable, cheerful and honourable.[1] It was the new king's
humility that was the most significant of his attributes. Despite the
opportunities that had presented themselves during his uncle's reign,
Robert had only feebly and fruitlessly tried to elevate himself above
the rest of the baronage ; only two years before his accession he had
been imprisoned in Lochleven.[2] Although the new king was a grandson of Robert I, the line he represented was baronial rather than
royal. The contemporary poet, Barbour, is known to have written

---

[1] *Chron. Bower*, II. 383.   [2] P. 179 above.

upon "The Stewartis Orygenale'[3] and to have tried to throw lustre on the new dynasty by a fabulous Trojan descent, but the errors in this timely essay in genealogy were detected by Abbot Bower;[4] and it was no secret that the Stewarts were a cadet branch of the English Fitzalans.

Robert II's origins would have mattered little if he had shown something of the courage and vigour of his grandfather. Instead, the absence of these qualities was at once revealed when the first Earl of Douglas ominously let it be seen that he thought himself as 'royal' as any Stewart and put himself forward as a contender for the succession on the death of David II. At Linlithgow Douglas made some show of force and claimed the throne by reason of a flimsy connection with the Balliols or Comyns. He was prevailed upon to give up his unrealistic pretensions only through the forceful intervention of his stepfather, Sir Robert Erskine, George Dunbar, Earl of March, and John Dunbar, the earl's brother.[5] Thereupon the grateful new king bestowed honoraria not only upon the Erskines and Dunbars[6] but upon Douglas, who was made justiciar south of Forth and warden of the East March.[7] His son and heir, Sir James Douglas, was given an annuity of a hundred marks, the hand of the king's fourth daughter, Isabella, and a gift of £500.[8] Opposition was bought off; loyalty was not taken for granted but was richly rewarded.

On 26 March 1371, after the 'royd harsk begynnyng'[9] of the Linlithgow incident, the king was crowned and anointed at Scone by Bishop Landallis.[10] A notarial instrument was drawn up to record not only the circumstances of Robert II's coronation but also to record at much greater length the recognition of his first-born son, John, Earl of Carrick, as heir apparent to the crown. The prolixity of the language affirming him to be the king's true heir, and the fact that his right to succeed was first expounded in the privy council,[11] suggest that questions were raised, or were expected to be raised in future. In contrast to the childless David II the new king is known to have had at least twenty-one offspring, of whom only four were indisputably born in lawful wedlock.[12] John, Earl of Carrick, was not among these

---

[3] *Chron. Wyntoun*, II. 320.   [4] *Chron. Bower*, II. 60, n.
[5] *Chron. Wyntoun*, III. 8; *Chron. Bower*, II. 382; *Chron. Pluscarden*, I. 310;
Godscroft, *Douglas and Angus*, I. 99; E.R., II. lxxvii; *Scots Peerage*, v. 594;
Balfour-Melville, *James I*, p. 3.
[6] E.R., II. 364, 366, 433, 435, 460, 672.   [7] *Ibid.*, 394, 433, 435, 462.
[8] *Ibid.*, 364, 393, 433, 434, 435, 460, 501.   [9] *Chron. Wyntoun*, III. 9.
[10] *Chron. Bower*, II. 386; E.R., II. 393; A.P.S., I. 545.   [11] A.P.S., I. 545-7.
[12] *Scots Peerage*, I. 15-7; E.R., IV. cliii-clxx.

four. He was eldest of the 'many children of both sexes ... fair to behold' alluded to in a papal dispensation of 22 November 1347 [13] that belatedly permitted marriage between Robert the Steward and his first wife, Elizabeth Mure (or More) and declared their offspring legitimate. John had been born some ten years before the dispensation.[14] By canon law the subsequent marriage of parents made their issue legitimate; but it was questionable whether this could apply to a child born of parents who were within the 'forbidden degrees' of consanguinity.[15] Was John Stewart, technically speaking, born in incest and incapable of legitimation; and, if so, could he succeed his father on the throne? The four children of the Steward's second marriage to Euphemia of Ross were undoubtedly legitimate; one of these was Walter Stewart, Earl of Atholl, who, in a quest for the crown, would be a party to the assassination of James I, Carrick's son, in 1437. Yet it was probably not dubiety over the dispensation of 1347 but rather fear of some Douglas or English claim that caused concern over the succession: when the Franco-Scottish alliance was renewed in 1371 the possibility of a future succession dispute was envisaged;[16] in a parliament at Scone in April 1373 Robert II expressed a wish to end 'the uncertainty of the succession', and, in particular, to avoid the evils that might arise through the accession of females to the throne. Thus a tailzie was drawn up with the approval of the three estates.[17] The succession was to pass from father to son, starting with the king's first-born son, John Stewart, Earl of Carrick. If his line of descent should fail, the succession would then pass successively on the same terms to the lines of descent respectively headed by his younger brothers, Robert, Earl of Fife and Menteith, Alexander, Lord of Badenoch, David, Earl of Strathearn, and Walter, Earl of Atholl. Although the succession had passed to Robert II through a female the Scots were now imitating the French example of requiring unbroken male descent. Only on the failure of legitimate father-to-son descent in respect of the five surviving sons of Robert II's two marriages would the succession pass to heirs general.

Meanwhile the establishment of the new king's sons and daughters, legitimate or otherwise, in a landed status befitting their dignity, amounted to a large territorial settlement throughout Scot-

---

[13] *Cal. Papal Petitions*, I. 124; Dowden, *Bishops*, p. 65.
[14] *Scots Peerage*, I. 17.
[15] *Scot. Legal Hist.*, pp. 71–2, 78; *E.R.*, IV. cliv–clv; Balfour-Melville, *James I*, p. 4.
[16] Text of the treaty in *E.R.*, III. cii–ciii.
[17] *A.P.S.*, I. 549.

land.[18] Some of these progeny had been well-provided before their blood baronial was transformed into blood royal. Any deficiencies in land or title were soon made up. Most notable was the elevation of David, elder son of the king's second marriage, to the dignity of 'Earl Palatine of Strathearn and Caithness'.[19] The grant of these two earldoms in regality may well have been compensation for the precedence given to the sons of the first marriage. By 1377 seven of the existing sixteen earldoms (Carrick, Menteith, Fife, Atholl, Strathearn, Caithness and Sutherland) were in the hands of the king himself or his sons,[20] and through the marriage of his sons and daughters the new king was closely connected with the foremost noble families : the Earls of Moray and Douglas, the Lord of the Isles, the constable and the marshal, were, or soon became, sons-in-law to the king.

But the network of marriage and kinship was spread too widely to withstand strain. Nearly all the nobility of Scotland had been stewartised. Not all Stewarts were 'sib to the king', but many undoubtedly *were*, and consequently thought themselves specially privileged, or even above the law. It was to prove difficult enough for Robert II to hold patriarchal sway over his extended family circle, let alone rule Scotland. The chronicler Bower, flattering enough in his remarks concerning the king, significantly continues : 'But what shall I say concerning his sons? Some were peaceable and benign, some insolent and malign.'[21] On the whole, however, a sort of tranquillity settled upon Scotland while the new royal family digested the territorial sweetmeats that Robert II provided. The years between 1371 and 1378 had few of the stirring events that attracted the attention of chroniclers. The keynote of this first phase of Stewart rule was continuity from the days of David II.

It was in the sphere of royal finance that a change from the governmental policies bequeathed by David was to become most significant. At first, in finance, as in other respects, continuity was obvious. The chamberlain's accounts, which can be regarded as rough guides to the state of royal finances, show that no marked deterioration set in for some time. In the financial year 1373–4 the total receipts came to £14,584 9s. 9¾d. (including about £10,000 from the

[18] Grant, *Social and Economic Development*, pp. 207–8.
[19] *R.M.S.*, I. Nos. 389, 526, 666; *Morton Registrum*, II. No. 121; Innes, *Sketches*, p. 213.
[20] *Scots Peerage, passim.*   [21] *Chron. Bower*, II. 383.

great customs) [22] and there was a surplus of £1,878 17s. 1¼d. [23] The figures for this year were therefore almost as impressive as for the last financial year of David's reign. Moreover the receipts included the proceeds of a contribution of a shilling in the pound : [24] the sheriff-doms contributed £1,681 18s. 1od., the burghs £739 8s. 1d., and the clergy £166 9s. 5d. [25] Since these figures are incomplete no precise deductions may be made from them. More significant is a separate list of the total contributions raised in each sheriffdom. [26] Gillespic Campbell as sheriff of Argyll raised £56 2s. 4½d. From Lorne came at least £60 ; and from the lands of John of the Isles came at least £133 6s. 8d. [27] For the moment the Gaelic magnates were ready to co-operate with the new dynasty ; and the successful levying of national taxation in their lands might have effectively integrated their do-mains with the rest of Scotland. But after the contribution of 1373 no other was to be levied until 1399. [28] The practice of direct taxation, painfully evolved from David II's ransom, was allowed to lapse.

Other lapses followed. Sheriffs, and even custumars, were lax in attending the exchequer audit. In the last chamberlain's account of the reign there was no income from feudal reliefs 'because the sheriffs did not compear'. [29] In 1370–71 the chamberlain had received more than £9,000 from the great customs; in 1389–90, when the rate of duty was still the same, the total customs collected came to less than £5,000, [30] of which the chamberlain received little more than half. [31] For the gross receipts from the customs 'came to be encroached on year by year by grants of annuity, remissions of duty and the expenses of the king's family and household'. [32] In compensation, the diplo-macy of Robert II was not as costly as that of David II had been. Thus until 1382 the chamberlain's account showed falling receipts but no deficit ; and in 1380 the surplus amounted almost to £3,000. [33] But 1382, when Robert Stewart, Earl of Fife and Menteith, took over as chamberlain, brought an abrupt change : there was an immediate and lasting drop in the chamberlain's total receipts and from then until the end of the reign they ranged from little more than £3,000 to little more than £1,000. And although expenditure also tended to diminish there were occasional heavy deficits, amounting in 1385–6 to over £1,000. [34]

[22] *E.R.*, II. 429.   [23] *Ibid.*, 428–38.   [24] *Ibid.*, 418, 430.
[25] *Ibid.*, 430–1. In the next financial year arrears of £180 16s. 8d. were received (*ibid.*, 457).
[26] *Ibid.*, 417–27.   [27] *Ibid.*, 431.   [28] P. 217 below.
[29] *E.R.*, III. 203, 697.   [30] *Ibid.*, 202–13.   [31] *Ibid.*, 697.
[32] *Ibid.*, lix.   [33] *Ibid.*, 28–32.   [34] *Ibid.*, 679–84.

The events that had preceded the appointment of Robert Stewart to the post of chamberlain were dramatic. The previous holder of the office was John Lyon. Once the secretary of David II, he had been kept in office by Robert II, who in 1372 granted him the thanage of Glamis [35] and in 1377 made him chamberlain. Lyon made a clandestine marriage with Jean, one of the king's daughters, and by 1379 was duly recognised as the king's son-in-law and knighted. His advancement, so it was said, owed much to the good offices of Sir James Lindsay of Crawford, who, considering that his services had been insufficiently esteemed, murdered the thane of Glamis on 4 November 1382. The murderer was at the time sheriff of Lanark, and had recently been justiciar north of Forth. He was also the king's nephew.[36] Failure to punish the crime perhaps set as bad an example as the crime itself. Nor was it an isolated occurrence during the reign—the Scone parliament of March 1372 had seen danger signals in the many homicides that had recently been committed. Emergency measures were passed [37] that were to remain in force for three years, but when the three estates met in general council in Holyrood Abbey in November 1384 they asserted that 'offences and outrageous crimes have been wont to be committed against the law for no short time'.[38] A king who was neither a military leader nor a forceful personality had little chance of keeping law and order.

Robert II was only too anxious to shelve his responsibility. The first act of the Holyrood general council of 1384 was to record his desire to administer the laws of his kingdom justly and by the advice of his council. He undertook 'promptly and willingly to reform and repair any of his actions which had been negligent or contrary to law' ; anyone might complain of him in his council and he would accept his council's judgment. Then it was recorded that 'because our lord the king, for certain causes, is not able to attend himself personally to the execution of justice and the law of his kingdom, he has willed . . . that his first-born son and heir, the Lord Earl of Carrick, is to administer the common law everywhere throughout the kingdom.' [39] The three estates wished no ill to Robert II : there was no attempt to displace him altogether from government; instead, by a natural measure that associated the heir apparent with his father's

[35] *R.M.S.*, I. Nos. 411, 549.
[36] *Chron. Bower*, II. 395; *R.M.S.*, I. No. 679; *E.R.*, III. lii, liii, 657; *Scots Peerage*, VIII. 266-9.
[37] *A.P.S.*, I. 547-8.   [38] *Ibid.*, 550.   [39] *Ibid.*, 550.

government, Carrick was to have special and direct responsibility for one aspect of that government—the administration of justice.

There followed the enactment of a number of statutes to speed the apprehension of criminals:[40] if a suspect should withdraw himself from one sheriffdom to another, the first sheriff was to write to the second sheriff, who was to cause the fugitive to be cited by his serjeant to thole an assize. If the fugitive did not appear before the assize he was to be put to the horn as an outlaw. It was unanimously agreed that these statutes should apply even to the regalities and to the ecclesiastical franchises. Two nobles made a special reservation of their own rights under ancient law : Robert Stewart, Earl of Fife, as 'chief of the law of Clan MacDuff',[41] was willing to observe the statutes 'gratis', providing that this should not in future prejudice either himself or the law of Clan MacDuff; similarly, Archibald the Grim reserved certain points of the laws of the Galwegians, 'protesting on behalf of the privilege of his right and of the said law'.[42] The statutes of 1384, like those of 1372, were to remain valid for only three years.[43] During this period Carrick, as a new broom, might try to sweep away the lawlessness that was already bringing reproach upon the new dynasty.

The changes within Scotland that followed upon the accession of the Stewart dynasty were contemporary with important external developments. Not least of these was the outbreak of the Great Schism. Since 1309 the papal court had been established at Avignon. In 1377 Gregory XI ended this 'Babylonish Captivity' by transferring the *curia* back to Rome, where he soon died. On 8 April 1378 the cardinals elected the Archbishop of Bari as Pope Urban VI, only to be dismayed by his tyranny. Most of the cardinals gathered at Anagni to depose him on 9 August ; and at Fondi on 20 September 1378 they elected Cardinal Robert of Geneva as Clement VII. Urban VI refused to consider himself deposed and held on to Rome while Clement VII set up court at Avignon.[44] Thus began the 'lang lestand scysm' ;[45] for both popes had successors. In the course of time the Avignonese popes (who did not always reside at Avignon) have come to be regarded as anti-popes and the Roman popes (who did not always re-

[40] *Ibid.*, 550–1.
[41] See G. Neilson, *Trial by Combat* (1890, 1909), p. 121.
[42] *A.P.S.*, I. 550.   [43] *Ibid.*
[44] Walter Ullmann, *The Origins of the Great Schism*, pp. 9–68; John Holland Smith, *The Great Schism*, pp. 116–45.
[45] *Chron. Wyntoun*, III. 61.

side at Rome) as the true popes, but while the schism lasted each side regarded its own pope as the true one, and the one pope excommunicated the other. There was 'indescribable mental confusion';[46] the seamless garment of the church was rent, and a handful of radicals denounced even the institution of the papacy. Some rulers, through caution, or for reasons of policy, were hesitant in professing obedience to either pope, or withdrew obedience after they had professed it.

It was mostly, but not entirely, international politics that at first decided the prevailing attitude in each country. By 5 November 1378 the English government had proclaimed its adherence to Urban, an Italian who could be trusted to purge French influence from the *curia*. On 16 November Charles V, with the support of the university of Paris, adhered to Clement—most of his cardinals were French, and some, like Clement himself, were kinsmen of the French king.[47] The Scots had a natural desire to follow the opposite course to that of England and believed that they were held in great affection by Clement since he was descended from the sainted wife of Malcolm Canmore. The chronicler Wyntoun was not acquainted with all the stages of this genealogy but concluded that 'Robert the Second in Scotland . . . to this Clement wes cusyne.'[48] More substantial political ties with the French monarchy and intellectual ties with the university of Paris, the greatest theological school of Western Europe, brought Scotland wholeheartedly into the fold of Clement.[49]

In the past the secular states of Europe had tried to woo the favours of the papacy; now it was the turn of popes who had lost universal acceptance to woo the secular states. When a nuncio of Avignon was appointed to depose the Scottish adherents of Urban and distribute their benefices among the adherents of Clement he was furnished with various means of winning friends and gaining influence: he was empowered to grant benefices to poor clerks; he might grant dispensations to as many as two hundred persons whose illegitimate birth made them canonically ineligible to hold benefices; he might issue twenty dispensations for marriages within certain forbidden degrees of affinity; he might grant licence to two hundred persons to have a portable altar and licences to three hundred persons to choose a confessor who might give them plenary remission on their deathbed. During the schism the Avignonese *curia* (like the Roman *curia*) was little more than a receiver and grantor of petitions.[50] Peti-

---

[46] Ullmann, *op. cit.*, p. 99.
[48] *Chron. Wyntoun*, III. 61.
[50] *Cal. Papal Letters*, IV. 240–2.

[47] *Ibid.*, pp. 54, 91, 104–6.
[49] See Ullmann, *op. cit.*, p. 96.

tions for benefices presented by a combination of academics, nepotists and pluralists induced the compliant papacy to exploit to the utmost the powers of appointment that it had already begun to acquire under the practices of provision and reservation,[51] and, in the process, to draw financial profit. Meanwhile it became usual to delegate some prominent local bishop to act as disciplinarian [52] and to crush schismatics.

It was Walter Wardlaw, Bishop of Glasgow, who was singled out for this role in Scotland : on 23 December 1383 he was created a cardinal by Clement VII ;[53] and on 24 November 1384 he was appointed legate *a latere* in both Scotland and Ireland.[54] There the Archbishop of Tuam supported Avignon, and so also did an ecclesiastical assembly held at Roscommon in 1383.[55] The death of Scotland's first cardinal in September 1387 [56] ended a shrewd move that might have promoted in Ireland both the ecclesiastical interests of the Avignonese papacy and the political interests of the Scottish monarchy.

Elsewhere this conjunction of interests had important consequences. The Norwegian islands of Orkney and Shetland, subject ecclesiastically to the Archbishop of Nidaros, might have been expected to follow the Norwegian policy of allegiance to the Roman pope. But the issue was not clear-cut. About the middle of the fourteenth century a succession dispute had followed upon the death of Malise of Strathearn, who had held simultaneously the earldoms of Strathearn, Caithness and Orkney. After dispute and adjudication, a Lothian landholder, Henry Sinclair of Roslin, husband of Malise's second daughter, was invested by the Norwegian king on 2 August 1379 as Earl of Orkney.[57] It cannot have been without the support of the new earl that Clement VII provided Robert Sinclair to the bishopric of Orkney in 1384.[58] From this time onwards the bishops of Orkney were all Scotsmen.[59] In another portion of the Norwegian province of Nidaros the result of the schism was an ecclesiastical partition that corresponded to the *de facto* political partition. John Donegan, Bishop of Sodor (the Isles) adhered to the Roman pope and

---

[51] For the nature of this traffic and the procedure of the *curia* in dealing with it see the introductions to *Cal. Scot. Supp. 1418–1422*, and *Cal. Scot. Supp. 1423–28*.
[52] A. R. MacEwen, *History of the Church in Scotland*, I. 307.
[53] Dowden, *Bishops*, p. 315.   [54] *Cal. Papal Letters*, IV. 250–1.
[55] W. A. Phillips, *History of the Church of Ireland* (1934), II. 118–20.
[56] Dowden, *Bishops*, p. 315.   [57] *Scots Peerage*, II. 319–20.
[58] *H.B.C.*, p. 297; Dowden, *Bishops*, pp. 269–70.
[59] Dowden, *Bishops*, pp. 269–70.

continued in possession of the cathedral on the Isle of Man—the only part of the diocese under English control—while Michael, the unsuccessful Avignonese Archbishop of Cashel, was accepted in the rest of the diocese controlled by the Scots.[60] This division of the diocese of the Isles was accompanied by a break in the tenuous link that bound the Bishops of Galloway to their metropolitan at York. In 1378 Urban VI had provided Oswald, Prior of Glenluce, to the bishopric of Galloway. In the following year Clement VII more effectively provided Thomas Rossy, a prominent Scottish Franciscan.[61] From the outset of the schism ecclesiastical animosities had merged with Anglo-Scottish animosities. Urban VI and his Roman successors did not endear themselves to the Scots by their attempts to provide loyal Englishmen to Scottish bishoprics.[62] Thomas Rossy made 'authentic Scottish contributions to the controversies of the fourteenth century' not only in his treatise on the immaculate conception but in another treatise against the schismatic English, in which he challenged the bellicose Bishop of Norwich to single combat.[63]

The militancy shown by Rossy (and by many other Scots) in the period that began with the outbreak of the schism and the almost simultaneous death of Edward III would have been out of place earlier. Only gradually did the blows inflicted by Edward III fade from Scottish memory and allow self-confidence to revive. By itself the accession of Robert II caused no revolution in Scotland's foreign relationships. Three days after his coronation, parliament sanctioned a mission to France,[64] as a result of which Charles V issued letters patent renewing the Franco-Scottish alliance. On 28 October 1371 Robert II ratified this treaty of Vincennes; neither party would make truce or peace with the English unless the other gave its consent.[65] Certain more aggressive secret articles drafted by the French do not seem to have been ratified by Robert II. There had been no fighting with England since 1356. So far as he was concerned there would be no fighting in future. The fourteen-year truce of 1369 would not expire until February 1384, and Robert II decided to adhere to this truce, even at the cost of keeping up regular payment of the yearly

[60] Ibid., pp. 287–8; H.B.C., p. 254; Dunlop, Bishop Kennedy, p. 191.
[61] W. Moir Bryce, Scottish Grey Friars, I. 29–31; Dowden, Bishops, p. 376.
[62] Dowden, Bishops, pp. 45–6, 67–9, 94–6, 375–6.
[63] Hugh McEwan, ' "A Theolog Solempne", Thomas de Rossy, Bishop of Galloway', Innes Review, VIII. 21–9, at 28–9.
[64] A.P.S., I. 559–60.   [65] Text in E.R., III. xcvii–civ.

instalment of 4,000 marks on David II's ransom.[66] At midsummer
1377, however, a few days after the death of Edward III, the Scots
made their last payment on the ransom of David II, leaving 24,000
marks unpaid.[67] For some years Edward had been no real threat to
Scotland; but the disappearance of his name brought home to the
Scots their deliverance from the threat of domination. His successor,
Richard II, was a boy of ten. To the troubles of England, now
occasionally raided by Franco-Castilian fleets, were added those of a
royal minority. Although English kings would never forget their
claims to lordship over Scotland these claims would never again be
pursued so determinedly as in the days of the first three Edwards. The
wars of independence were over. A war of chivalry on the Borders
was about to begin.[68]

While Robert II was not eager to break the truce he could not
hold back his nobles.[69] The first of a series of Border raids began with
an incident at the fair of Roxburgh in 1378. At the next Roxburgh
fair the Earl of March sacked and burned the town.[70] This gave rise to
other incidents. In the case of some Scottish nobles, particularly the
Earls of March and Douglas, one motive behind Border warfare was
the recovery of territory still occupied by the English. Their motive
was less national than personal: they saw no reason why they should
not recover lands that were theirs by heritage. Others had motives
that the current vogue of chivalry made fashionable and took part in
what have been described as 'the selfish and disjointed expeditions of
an aristocracy whose principal objects were plunder and military adventure'.[71]

Hostilities were not confined to land. In 1376 John Mercer, merchant burgess of Perth and financial agent of the late King David, was
returning home with one of his ships when it was wrecked on the
Northumberland coast. Despite the truce his merchandise was seized
and he was imprisoned in Scarborough Castle.[72] The English
chronicler Walsingham lamented Mercer's eventual release: it was
'to the great loss of the whole kingdom . . . for if he had been held to

Rot. Scot., I. 945, 953; *E.R.*, II. 363, 394.

[67] *Rot. Scot.*, II. 38–9. George Burnett wrongly thought that the whole ransom was eventually paid (*E.R.*, II. lxxxiii), but later realised his mistake: after
1377 no trace is to be found in the Scottish exchequer accounts of any payment
of ransom instalments (*ibid.*, III. lvii–lix).

[68] The remainder of this chapter has benefited from the expert advice of Mr.
Anthony Goodman of the university of Edinburgh.

[69] *Nat. MSS. Scot.*, II. No. xlvi.

[70] *Chron. Fordun*, I. 283; *Chron. Wyntoun*, III. 9–10.

[71] P. F. Tytler, *History*, I. pt. ii, 333.   [72] *Nat. MSS. Scot.*, II. No. xlv.

ransom as a prisoner of war he would have enriched the king and kingdom with his inestimable wealth'.[73] Instead, Mercer returned to Scotland to act as temporary chamberlain on the death of Walter Biggar. When Mercer arranged the last payment of the ransom instalment in midsummer 1377 he paid only half, deducting 2,000 marks as damages for his lost merchandise.[74] But this did not satisfy his son Andrew: in 1378, at the head of a squadron of French, Spanish and Scottish ships, he sacked Scarborough, where his father had been imprisoned, and swept the English seas. The prominence of merchants of both sides in warfare at sea was underlined when a London merchant named Philpott took up Andrew Mercer's challenge, raised a naval force, and captured both Andrew and his fleet.[75]

While the English generally had the better of the Scots at sea, the situation was reversed on land.[76] When John of Gaunt, Duke of Lancaster, was sent north to attend a March Day [77] on 1 October 1380 he brought a memorandum that outlined the encroachments made by the Scots since 1357 upon English-occupied lands in Berwickshire and Roxburghshire. Part of his mission was to try to persuade the Scots to respect the boundaries of 1357,[78] but despite his intimidating retinue of two thousand men [79] no general settlement was reached. Another March Day, held at Ebchester near Ayton on 18 June 1381,[80] was interrupted by news that England was in turmoil thanks to a widespread peasants' revolt. While Gaunt's palace of the Savoy went up in flames in London he himself took refuge in Holyrood Abbey as the honoured guest of the Scots nobility.[81]

Despite the duke's stay in Scotland there seems to have been little eagerness on either side for a further extension of the truce, which would expire at Candlemas (2 February) 1384. In Scotland the royal castles were made ready for war.[82] In Edinburgh Castle a certain Dietrich, presumably a German or a Netherlander, was busy constructing military machines and was paid £4 for *unum instru-*

---

[73] *Chron. Walsingham*, I. 369. The reality of his wealth is suggested by the frequent references to the wardship of his son, Andrew, which was evidently valuable (*E.R.*, III. 229, 256, 302, 329, etc.).
    [74] *Ibid.*, lvii–lviii.   [75] *Chron. Walsingham*, I. 369–70.   [76] *Ibid.*, 373.
    [77] This was similar to a 'Day of Trewe' (Truce Day) and amounted to a diplomatic confrontation on the Marches (Borders).
    [78] *Cal. Docs. Scot.*, IV. No. 295.
    [79] R. L. Storey, 'The Wardens of the Marches of England towards Scotland', *E.H.R.*, LXXII. 593–609, at 595.
    [80] *Cal. Docs. Scot.*, IV. No. 297; *Rot. Scot.*, II. 38–9.
    [81] *Chron. Wyntoun*, III. 16–18.
    [82] *E.R.*, III. 80, 82, 87, 98, 117, 118, 660, 665, 667, 671, 672, 676.

mentum dictum 'gun' [83]—the first clear indication that the Scots were making use of firearms. Two days after the truce expired, Archibald the Grim and George Dunbar, Earl of March, secured the surrender of Lochmaben Castle, destroyed it, and thus ended the last vestiges of the English occupation of Annandale,[84] which reverted to the Earl of March. Retribution was at hand. An expedition set out under the Duke of Lancaster and encamped outside Edinburgh in March 1384. Mindful of the hospitality he had received in the town in 1381 Gaunt did not destroy it but contented himself with holding it to ransom.[85]

On 20 August 1383 Robert II had ratified an agreement whereby, in the event of Anglo-Scottish war, the French king would send to Scotland troops, money, and arms.[86] In the spring or summer of 1384 an unofficial advance party of some thirty French knights and esquires landed at Montrose, after which they joined a gathering of Scottish Borderers and raided the north of England.[87] Fear of further Franco-Scottish enterprises inspired special arrangements for the garrisoning of Berwick, Roxburgh and Carlisle at a cost of almost £10,000 to the English exchequer for the year beginning 1 August 1384.[88] The raid also showed that so far as Border warfare was concerned Robert II's authority meant nothing: Archibald the Grim did not scruple to arrange a truce of his own on 15 March 1385.[89]

While the Lord of Galloway was now peacably inclined, a general council which met in Edinburgh in April 1385 showed more warlike inclinations.[90] The French private adventurers of 1384 were followed by an official expeditionary force under Jean de Vienne, admiral of France, which landed at Dunbar and Leith at the end of May 1385. There were, so John of Fordun claimed, twenty-six bannerets, fifty knights and one thousand and fifty men-at-arms. With them they brought eighty suits of armour and eighty lances as well as a sum of fifty thousand gold francs to jingle before the noses of the Scottish king, Cardinal Wardlaw, and the more militaristic of the nobles.[91] A council of war drew up regulations in French at the be-

---

[83] *Ibid.*, 672. Saltpetre and sulphur, constituents of gunpowder, were also sent to various castles.   [84] *Chron. Fordun*, I. 383.

[85] *Chron. Wyntoun*, III. 20; *Chron. Bower*, II. 398; *Chron. Walsingham*, II. 111.

[86] *A.P.S.*, XII. 19.   [87] *Chron. Froissart*, III. 472–6.

[88] R. L. Storey, *op. cit.*, *E.H.R.*, LXXII. 593–609, at 598.

[89] *Rot. Scot.*, II. 73; see also *Chron. Froissart*, III. 476–7.   [90] *A.P.S.*, I. 552.

[91] *Chron. Fordun*, I. 383; *Chron. Froissart*, III. 494–5; IV. 22–3. For the distribution of the subsidy see *Foedera*, III. pt. iii, 188.

ginning of July 1385 for the discipline of a joint Franco-Scottish force
that would set out for the Borders.[92] Wark and two smaller strongholds in Northumberland were stormed.[93] Then came tidings that an
English army headed by Richard II and the Duke of Lancaster was
approaching. The French looked forward to a pitched battle in which
they could win renown. To their dismay the Scots withdrew and laid
waste their own land.

Jean de Vienne soon admitted that this scorched-earth strategy
was the only one feasible.[94] It was the first real campaign of the young
Richard II and a large army had assembled to do him honour.[95] The
existence of the Great Schism removed some religious sanctions : the
Scottish religious houses could now be regarded as nests of schismatics.
Melrose, Dryburgh and Newbattle went up in flames. When the
English army arrived in Edinburgh, the same fate befell the town
and the kirk of St Giles; Holyrood was spared only through the intercession of John of Gaunt.[96] But thanks to the strategy of the Scots the
invaders were soon starving and forced to return home.[97] Unable to
defend the Scottish Lowlands, the Franco-Scottish troops had set out
to invade the West March of England. In mid-August they plundered
Cumberland on an unparalleled scale and even made a show of
attacking Carlisle; in the bishoprics of Durham and Carlisle they
had burned and plundered, so the French said, more than could be
found in all the towns of Scotland put together.[98] When they came
back to Edinburgh through lands wasted by the retreating English
host, they found the countryside alive with people and cattle returning from hiding places to the primitive homes they had left to be
burned by the English.[99]

In this type of warfare there was little room for French knights.
The growing antagonism between them and their allies is vividly
portrayed by Froissart, whose admiration for the valour of the Scots
was mingled with contempt for their poverty-stricken uncouthness.
When the French knights, as was their custom, sent out their pages
to forage for victuals, they were attacked and some of their number

[92] *A.P.S.*, I. 554–5.
[93] *Chron. Wyntoun*, III. 24; *Chron. Bower*, II. 400–1; *Chron. Froissart*, IV.
49–51.   [94] *Chron. Froissart*, IV. 56–7.
[95] For the composition of the force and the financial background see N. B.
Lewis, 'The Last Medieval Summons of the English Feudal Levy, 13 June 1385',
E.H.R., LXXIII. 1–26, and J. J. N. Palmer, 'The Last Summons of the Feudal
Army in England', *ibid.*, LXXXIII. 771–5.
[96] *Chron. Bower*, II. 401 and n.   [97] *Chron. Walsingham*, II. 131.
[98] *Chron. Froissart*, IV. 58–63; *Chron. Wyntoun*, III. 24; *Chron. Bower*, II. 401.
[99] *Chron. Froissart*, IV. 63; *Chron. Bower*, II. 401.

slain. The French were not to be allowed to depart from Scotland until they gave satisfaction for the damages they had allegedly inflicted. The admiral had to remain behind in pawn until money was sent from Paris for his release.[100] Had the efforts of the French expeditionary force been accompanied (as was intended) by a seaborne invasion of England [101] much might have been achieved, but although the French toyed with invasion plans until 1388 the Scots appear to have been daunted by Richard II's expedition of 1385 and to have accepted a number of short truces while awaiting a favourable opportunity to renew warfare.[102]

The last of these truces was due to expire on 19 June 1388. As this critical date drew near the 'Merciless Parliament' was in session at Westminster and Richard II's authority temporarily crumbled. The Scots were tempted to take advantage of English domestic difficulties, which included rivalries between Percies and Nevilles on the Borders,[103] and seized the initiative as the truce ran out. In the summer of 1388 Robert, Earl of Fife, James, Earl of Douglas, and Archibald the Grim took a strong force across the Solway sands and spent three days raiding Cockermouth.[104] When the next expedition was planned it was decided to disconcert the English by dividing the Scottish force into two and attacking simultaneously on the east and west.[105] The larger of the two forces carried out a successful plundering raid as far as Burgh-in-Stainmore,[106] but it was the smaller force under the Earls of Douglas, March, and Moray that was to win the greater fame.

Its task was mainly to cause a diversion on the East March. There were affrays at the barriers outside the walls of Newcastle, after which the Scots withdrew. Henry Hotspur, son and heir of the Earl of Northumberland, had meanwhile discovered that the force on the West March was too strong to be attacked. He doubled back and

[100] Chron. Froissart, IV. 23, 24–6, 63–6.

[101] Chron. Walsingham, II. 129.

[102] Cal. Docs. Scot., IV. No. 360; Rot. Scot., II. 93. For the English background see M. V. Clarke, Fourteenth Century Studies, ed. L. S. Sutherland and M. McKisack (1937), pp. 36–52.

[103] Anthony Steel, Richard II (1941), pp. 143–61; Anthony Goodman, The Loyal Conspiracy: the Lords Appellant under Richard II (1971), pp. 41–9.

[104] Chron. Wyntoun, III. 29–30; Chron. Bower, II. 402–3.

[105] This is the account of Froissart, who claimed to have the facts from participants (Chron. Froissart, V. 210–11, 231). Wyntoun and Bower give the impression that there was no conscious division of forces but that the Earl of Douglas for some reason failed to join the Earl of Fife on the West March (Chron. Wyntoun, III. 34; Chron. Bower, II. 410).

[106] Chron. Bower, II. 410; Chron. Wyntoun, III. 34.

came upon the smaller force at Otterburn in Redesdale. Fighting began in the light of the setting sun and continued by moonlight throughout the night of 5 August 1388. Hotspur was taken prisoner by Sir John Montgomery of Eaglesham and Eglinton, who profited from an enormous ransom.[107] In the morning the body of the dead Douglas was found; no one knew who had slain him, but the victory was his. Froissart did not hesitate to narrate his last words : 'Thanked be God there hath been but a fewe of myne auncytours that hathe dyed in ther beddes. ... I praye you rayse up agayne my baner, whiche lyeth on the grounde. ... But, sirs, shewe nother to frende nor foo in what case ye se me in, for if myne enemyes knew it they wolde rejoyse'—and thus it was that a dead man won the field.[108] Whether or not Douglas ever had the chance to make a dying speech the sentiments attributed to him were those that the age of chivalry esteemed.

Although tidings of the fight at Otterburn and the death of the second Earl of Douglas influenced the deliberations of a general council held at Linlithgow on 18 August 1388, it broke up with its business unfinished and was prorogued to Edinburgh 'by reason of the Lord Earl of Carrick' :[109] it was probably during the sitting of this council that he was kicked by a horse belonging to Sir James Douglas of Dalkeith.[110] This mishap, which left the heir apparent lame, led to a constitutional revolution in so far as it gave a plausible excuse for Carrick's removal from the post of authority that he had held since 1384. Moreover his removal was to be associated with a virtual demission of office on the part of the king his father. The background to these striking political changes was Carrick's failure to maintain law and order, a failure which is reflected in a number of legal cases that figure in the records of the period.[111] It hardly helped matters when the king remitted amercements imposed by parliament upon offenders, as in the case of Sir Robert Danielston, who had been fined £160.[112] Neither the king nor his eldest son had enforced the law, nor had they won popularity by taking part in the recent warfare, nor did they strive to retain power: in a general council at Edinburgh on 1 December 1388 Robert II took the unusual step of

---

[107] *Scots Peerage*, III. 427–8; *Cal. Docs. Scot.*, IV. No. 395.
[108] *Chron. Froissart*, v. 211–31; *Chron. Bower*, II. 411; *Chron. Wyntoun*, III. 35–9.
[109] *A.P.S.*, I. 555.   [110] *Chron. Bower*, II. 414.
[111] *Morton Registrum*, I. No. 10; *A.P.S.*, I. 553.
[112] *E.R.*, III. 164.

delivering a schedule under his signet which was read aloud.[113] Its purport was that he submitted himself fully to the ordinance of his general council in matters affecting the administration of justice and the defence of the realm against enemies. He wished also that his heir apparent should submit to the ordinance of the three estates. Faced with this abnegation of royal authority, the three estates issued an ordinance alluding to 'the great and many defects in the governance of the realm' which had existed for no short time by reason of the disposition of the king, as well as of his age and otherwise, and the infirmity of his first-born son (Carrick) and the tender years of the latter's son and heir. The estates agreed to choose Robert Stewart, Earl of Fife, the king's second son, as guardian of the realm. Thereupon the king commanded the chancellor that he should deliver whatsoever letters the new guardian and the council should unanimously require upon points touching the common weal and the governance and defence of the realm.[114]

The new guardian, or governor,[115] had already been notably successful in the race for landed power. He had won the earldom of Menteith in 1361 by a marriage with its heiress, and the earldom of Fife in 1371 by a bargain with the much-married and much-widowed Countess Isabella.[116] Apart from his landed influence Robert Stewart had long played a prominent part in government. And although he was to show himself more of a politician than a fighter, he had realised the importance of associating himself with the leading nobles in their warlike enterprises. Never outstanding as a military leader, he nonetheless gave the impression of sharing the fashionable chivalric outlook of the day.[117]

Despite the earl's apparent qualifications, his appointment to the new post was hedged by limitations. He was to act as guardian only so long as he behaved 'well and usefully in the aforesaid office according to the determination and declaration of the general council or parliament'. This determination and declaration was to be made each year in future in full parliament or in general council; and the king commanded that meetings of parliament or general council

---

[113] A.P.S., I. 555–6.
[114] Ibid., 556. For an example of a mandate issued under this arrangement in May 1389 see Nat. MSS. Scot., II. No. xlvii.
[115] The Latin of the record calls him custos. Bower affirms that it was decided to call him governor (Chron. Bower, II. 414)—a title certainly applied to him in the contemporary exchequer rolls (E.R., II. 698, 703); Wyntoun styles him 'wardayne'—the vernacular version of 'guardian' (Chron. Wyntoun, III. 40).
[116] Scots Peerage, IV. 14.   [117] Chron. Wyntoun, III. 30.

should take place before the end of each year.[118] Moreover, Fife's appointment was to hold good only until such time as the heir apparent should recover from his infirmity or 'should arrive at the ability of governing that office according to, and by, the determination of the council of the kingdom'.[119] There is some doubt as to whether this last phrase signifies the privy council or a general council of the estates. What is clear is that a conciliar authority, whether broadly or narrowly based, was to supervise the executive. Thus the general council of December 1388 had taken some steps in the same direction as the. 'Merciless Parliament' that had met in England some months previously. Though the Scots avoided the blood-letting by which the English advertised their political revolutions the constitutional changes in Scotland were nonetheless drastic.

In such circumstances it is striking that Robert Stewart, having come to power in 1388, was to keep his position almost continuously for another thirty-two years. Initially, however, he had to feel his way cautiously. When the question of the northern justiciarship was raised in a parliament at Holyrood in April 1389 he saw to it that his son and heir, Murdoch Stewart, obtained the post; but parliament guardedly made the appointment for only a year.[120] And although it decreed a salary of a thousand marks a year for the governor a condition was attached—he was not to use his office to interfere with the royal revenue.[121] This was an empty proviso, for Robert Stewart was not only governor but chamberlain. But even in this capacity he faced criticism : when his account as chamberlain was audited at Perth on 14 February 1390 the auditors mistrustfully alluded to the thousand marks 'which he claims to be due to him from the office of governor'.[122]

The rise of Robert Stewart was accompanied by that of another magnate—Archibald the Grim, protégé of the late David II. When the second Earl of Douglas died at Otterburn he left no legitimate offspring to succeed him, thus bringing into operation a tailzie of 26 May 1342 [123] of which Sir Archibald, illegitimate son of the Good Sir James Douglas and cousin of the dead Earl of Douglas, was now the sole surviving beneficiary. According to this tailzie, he would fall heir to the Douglas lands proper, including Douglasdale, Lauderdale, Eskdale, and the forest of Selkirk.[124] His succession to at least

[118] AP.S., I. 556. [119] Ibid. [120] Ibid., 557.
[121] Ibid. [122] E.R., II. 698, 703.
[123] Fraser, Douglas, III. 357, 359; A.P.S., I. 557-8. [124] A.P.S., I. 557-8.

one of these estates—the forest—was contested by Sir Malcolm
Drummond of Strathord, brother-in-law of the dead earl, and brother
of Annabella, wife of the Earl of Carrick. It was probably this royal
connection which enabled Sir Malcolm to obtain letters of sasine
from chancery for his infeftment in the lands of Selkirk forest. But
this procedure misfired : on 2 April 1389 parliament censured the
chancellor (John of Peebles, Bishop of Dunkeld) for his unjust negligence in issuing such letters.[125] Another claimant to the unentailed
estates was Sir James Sandilands of Calder, son-in-law of Robert
II.[126] Sir James, it seems, made common cause with Sir Malcolm
and with Sir John Haliburton, for all three placed the lands they
possessed, or claimed, under the protection of Richard II, who was
planning (though in vain) a new invasion of Scotland. The letters of
protection were dated 19 June 1389 and on the same day the three
Scottish knights obtained safe-conducts to come to England with a
retinue of forty men apiece.[127] Another complication centred around
Margaret Stewart, Countess of Angus. She had been residing at Tantallon as the mistress of the first Earl of Douglas, who was the husband
of her sister-in-law, the Countess of Mar. To the first Earl of Douglas
the Countess of Angus bore a son, George Douglas, who was thus not
only illegitimate but born in incest.[128] On 9 April 1389, during the
Holyrood parliament, his mother resigned in his favour her earldom
of Angus.[129] By 1397, moreover, James Sandilands of Calder, heir of
line to the unentailed Douglas estates, had been induced by favour or
fear to grant his rights to the new Earl of Angus,[130] and it was probably by reason of this grant that the Douglases of Angus became
possessed of the mighty castle of Tantallon. In 1400, moreover,
Angus received from his half-sister Isobel, Countess of Mar, and her
husband Sir Malcolm Drummond, the lordship of Liddesdale. In the
meantime Archibald the Grim had obtained possession of all the
entailed Douglas estates and became third Earl of Douglas.[131]

Thus the result of the death of the second Earl of Douglas at
Otterburn had been a bifurcation of the main Douglas power. Archibald the Grim, son of the Good Sir James whom the English styled
'the Black Douglas', is himself styled 'Archibald the Black' by one
Scottish chronicler ;[132] certainly his descendants came to be known as

---

[125] *Ibid.*, 557. [126] *Scots Peerage*, VIII. 379–80.
[127] *Cal. Docs. Scot.*, IV. No. 391 ; Anthony Goodman, *The Loyal Conspiracy:
the Lords Appellant under Richard II* (1971), pp. 50–2.
[128] *Scots Peerage*, I. 171. [129] *A.P.S.*, I. 565–6.
[130] *Scots Peerage*, VIII. 381. [131] *Ibid.*, III. 159–60.
[132] *Chron. Pluscarden*, I. 939.

the 'Black' Douglases, while the Douglases of Angus became known as the 'Red' Douglases. In the circumstances in which both these territorial families originated may be found the motive for the rivalry that became apparent between them in the following century.

For the time being, the 'Black' Douglases far excelled the 'Red' Douglases in landed power. Ever since September 1369, when David II bestowed on Archibald the Grim eastern Galloway betwixt the Nith and the Cree,[133] Archibald's landed power had been increasing. In February 1372, Thomas Fleming, grandson and heir of the first Earl of Wigtown, had resigned his lands and rights in the earldom of Wigtown to him in return for a large sum of money,[134] and in October of the same year Sir Archibald obtained a royal charter confirming his possession of all the lands of the earldom, though not the title of earl, which lapsed.[135] The result of Archibald the Grim's acquisition of Wigtown was a reunification of the whole of the distinctive province of Galloway that had been split up in 1235. It now became the real basis of the power of the Black Douglases. Through his wife, Joanna Moray, Archibald had already obtained possession of the lordship and castle of Bothwell.[136] When, in addition, he obtained the entailed Douglas lands and the title of Earl of Douglas he emerged as unquestionably the most powerful magnate south of Forth. In the construction of his new tower-house of Threave, built as the centre of the lordship of Galloway, he helped to establish a new fashion in baronial architecture. In his ecclesiastical benefactions, notably the foundation of collegiate kirks at Lincluden and Bothwell, he earned the good opinion of kirkmen and helped to establish a new fashion in ecclesiastical development.[137] In warfare his prowess was unrivalled. Not only was he dexterous in acquiring lands but he was strong and just in administering them.[138]

Such a combination of qualities stood out in contrast to the futile and aimless Stewart kingship. After Robert I and David II the power and prestige of the crown had notably declined. It was already clear that nothing much was to be hoped for in the heir apparent. His younger brother, the Earl of Fife, cautiously working in co-operation with the three estates, had not yet stretched the wings of his authority when Robert II died on 19 April 1390 at the age of seventy-four in his castle of Dundonald.[139] With some justification John Major re-

133 *Scots Peerage*, IV. 144.   134 *A.P.S.*, I. 560–1.
135 *Ibid.*; *R.M.S.*, I. No. 507.   136 *Scots Peerage*, III. 612–3.
137 P. 271 below.
138 *Chron. Bower*, II. 429; *Chron. Wyntoun*, III. 77.
139 *Chron. Bower*, II. 415.

jected the eulogies of the chroniclers Wyntoun and Bower, and remarked : 'Now, whatever our writers may contend, I cannot hold this aged king, I mean this second Robert, to have been a skilful warrior or wise in counsel.' [140]

Those who had come to attend the obsequies of Robert II at Scone on 13 August 1390 remained to see John, Earl of Carrick, crowned and anointed on the following day by Walter Trail, Bishop of St Andrews. On 15 August it was the turn of the queen, Annabella Drummond, daughter of Sir John Drummond of Stobhall and niece of Margaret Logie, to be crowned by the Bishop of Dunkeld.[141] Because the name John was reckoned ill-omened (by reason of John Balliol and John II of France), the new king changed his name to Robert [142] and earned the by-name 'John Faranyeir'—'John of yester year'.[143] The change of name did not alter the omens.

At his accession Robert III was some fifty-three years old. His son and heir, named David, had been born in 1378 and was created Earl of Carrick after his father's accession to the throne. In addition to two illegitimate sons, the king's offspring eventually comprised a second legitimate son who died in infancy, a third son named James, who was finally to succeed to the throne, and four daughters, of whom one died unmarried, one was married to Archibald, fourth Earl of Douglas, another to Sir James Douglas of Dalkeith, another to George Douglas, Earl of Angus, after whose death she temporarily linked the royal family to other noble houses by a further three successive marriages.[144] Thus the stewartisation of the Scottish nobility that had begun under the first Stewart king was carried a stage further under the second. As yet, none of Robert's III's offspring was old enough to play a part in politics, and Robert himself was either too old or too incapable. He was the very person whom the three estates had discounted in 1388 as unfit to rule by reason of his infirmity ; the king's younger brother, Robert Stewart, Earl of Fife and Menteith, continued for a year or two to draw his salary of a thousand marks 'for the office of guardian'.[145]

In the months that elapsed between the death of Robert II and the coronation of Robert III the perpetration of outrages unexampled in time of peace made it plain that the futility of the new king was

---

[140] Major, *History*, p. 329.
[142] *Ibid.*; Major, *History*, p. 331.
[144] Dunbar, *Scot. Kings*, p. 180.
[141] *Chron. Bower*, II. 418.
[143] *Highland Papers*, II. 93, 95, n. 1.
[145] *E.R.*, III. 276, 280, 312.

already recognised. At the end of May 1390 the burgh of Forres went up in flames. On 17 June so also did Elgin with its cathedral, the hospital of the Maison Dieu, the parish kirk of St Giles, and eighteen houses of the cathedral canons and chaplains.[146] According to the chronicler Wyntoun these crimes were committed by 'wyld wykkyd Heland-men'.[147] Wyntoun carefully suppressed the fact that the wild and wicked Highlanders had been led by none other than the new king's brother, Alexander Stewart, Earl of Buchan, who, until sacked by the three estates in 1388, had served as justiciar of the north and had earned the by-name of 'Wolf of Badenoch'.[148]

It was not so much Highland ferocity as feudal rapacity on the part of the Wolf that ended in the burning of Elgin. The events that led up to the outrage went back at least to August 1370, when Alexander Stewart had taken an oath that he would be the protector and defender of the lands and men of the Bishop of Moray.[149] In February 1390, however, an indenture was concluded whereby the bishop left the costly protection of Alexander Stewart, to whom he had been paying what amounted to blackmail, and instead agreed to pay a pension to Thomas Dunbar, sheriff of Inverness and son of the Earl of Moray.[150] The bishop was to be taught a salutary lesson by the burning of his cathedral. Since it was the king's brother who had planned this deed his position protected him from undue criticism,[151] which vented itself instead upon the underlings whom he had employed—the Highland caterans.

The word 'cateran' (Gaelic *cathairne*) properly signified a warrior who was lightly armed as distinct from the more substantial and heavily armed gallowglass (Gaelic *galloglaich*); to the Lowlander, however, the cateran was merely a Highland robber. The general council of April 1385 had entrusted the future Robert III (then Earl of Carrick) with the fruitless task of suppressing the caterans.[152] Their participation in the burning of Elgin drew attention to a problem that was increasingly grave—not merely the superficial problem of upholding law and order in the Highlands but the more fundamental problem of holding together in one nation the two parts of Scotland that were divergent in language and culture.

Although the poet Barbour several times alluded to the 'Erischry' of Scotland, it was the chronicler John of Fordun, writing between

[146] *Moray Registrum*, Nos. 172, 303; *Chron. Wyntoun*, III. 55; *Chron. Bower*, II. 416.
[147] *Chron. Wyntoun*, III. 55. [148] *Chron. Bower*, II. 416.
[149] *Moray Registrum*, No. 154. [150] *Ibid.*, No. 170.
[151] *E.R.*, III. lxxvi–lxxviii. [152] *A.P.S.*, I. 553.

1384 and 1387, who was the first to leave an impression of the Gaelic Scots, their environment, and their relationship with the English-speaking Lowlanders. 'The language and customs of the Scots,' so he affirmed, 'vary with the diversity of their speech; for they use two languages, namely Scottish [Gaelic] and Teutonic [English]; those of the latter tongue possess the coastal and low-lying regions, whilst those of the Scottish tongue inhabit the mountains and outlying islands.' [153] Fordun thus shrewdly saw a combination of geographical and linguistic factors as marking the limits of the two peoples. Besides stressing the difference of language, Fordun detected other differences. The people of the seaboard were 'domesticated and cultured, trustworthy, patient and urbane, decent in their attire, law-abiding and peaceful, devout in religious observance, though always ready to resist the wrong-doings of their foes'. The Highlanders and Islanders, on the other hand, were a 'wild and untamed people, rough and unbending, given to robbery, ease-loving, of artful and impressionable temperament, comely in form but unsightly in dress'.[154] Later writers, such as Major and Buchanan, would elaborate this remark when contrasting the 'domesticated', 'civilised', or 'tame' Lowlanders with the 'wild' Scots.

It is significant that in Fordun's analysis there is to be found no hint of a contrast between a 'clan system' in the Highlands and a 'feudal system' in the Lowlands. This does not mean that neither clans nor feudalism existed; but it does suggest that there was in Fordun's time no clear-cut demarcation between the two. It has been said of the clan that 'kinship lay at its root. The members of the clan, from its chief downwards, were supposed to be united by the common bond of blood-relationship'.[155] But the same words could be applied to the great baronial families of Lowland Scotland. Both in Highlands and Lowlands feudal conveyancing was general. Yet in neither region was feudalism by itself capable of providing the secure social grouping necessary for survival in the time of lawlessness over which the early Stewarts presided. From the second half of the fourteenth century onwards the clan was evolving in the Highlands as an increasingly important social, economic and military unit, and was one of the factors in an impressive Gaelic resurgence that took place in Scotland (and more notably in Ireland). The Gaelic word *clann*, signifying children or offspring, acquired an extended meaning and was applied to groups, some old, some new, that could hope to achieve

153 *Chron. Fordun*, I. 24.   154 *Ibid.*
155 Mackenzie, *Highlands and Isles*, p. 83.

social, economic and political security under a patriarchal chief whose ancestry they held in reverence. In the Lowlands, when the loyalties of feudalism decayed, there was an unsuccessful attempt to maintain them by the money payments characteristic of 'bastard feudalism'.[156] But there was also a retrogression to the more primitive bonds of real or supposed kinship.[157] The development of the Highland clan was accompanied by that of Lowland families or 'kins', such as Crichtons, Livingstons, Homes and Hepburns; and family pride was expressed in tailzies to heirs male who were obliged to bear not only the heraldic arms of the family but its name as well.[158] Both in Highlands and Lowlands those who recognised a chief were expected to follow his leadership. In each region, moreover, there rose simultaneously a family that might be regarded as a 'super-kin' or 'super-clan'; for both the Douglases and the MacDonalds comprised subordinate kins or clans.

What struck the Lowlander about the Highland clan was not its social structure but its function when arrayed as a military unit. If in that function it did not differ much from the retinue of a Lowland baron, it certainly differed in appearance. According to John Major, 'the common folk . . . go out to battle with the whole body clad in a linen garment, well daubed with wax or with pitch, and with an overcoat of deerskin'.[159] When such uncouth warriors as these took advantage of the tremulous rule of the early Stewarts to descend on the braes of Angus, the Lowlanders began to think they were witnessing a new phenomenon and they linked it with the word 'clan'. The first time the word is known to have been used by a Lowland writer (the chronicler Wyntoun) was in connection with displays of Highland courage and ferocity in 1392 and 1396. Thereafter the word 'clan' was a bad word in Lowland mouths: clans did wicked things.

For the burning of Elgin was the prelude to further disorder in the north-east Highlands: in 1391 'there broke out such a struggle among the savage Scots that they troubled the whole country with their struggles, for throughout the whole county of Angus they could have no peace because of their marauding'.[160] Early in the following year there was 'hey grete discorde' when the braes of Angus were

---

[156] P. 212 below.
[157] For an indication of the significance a Lowland magnate attached to kinship see p. 218 below.
[158] See *R.M.S.*, II. Nos. 1045, 1064, 1191, 1214, 1534, 1595.
[159] Major, *History*, p. 49.   [160] *Chron. Pluscarden*, I. 253.

invaded by 'the Heyland men'.[161] At Gasklune in Stormont they held their own against a force led by Sir David Lindsay of Glenesk,[162] who was in full blossom as the latest flower of chivalry. It seemed that the armoured knight could no longer protect the Lowlands against ferocious Highland caterans. The latter soon gave another exhibition of their reckless courage: to settle discord between the feuding Clans Chattan and Kay a mortal combat was held on 28 September 1396 on the North Inch of Perth in the presence of Robert III, many of the nobility, and French and English knights; the contestants numbered 'thre score wyld Scottis men', thirty of them under 'Cristy Johnesone', and the other thirty under 'Schir Ferqwharis sone'; when the king cast down his baton to end the bloodletting only a dozen survived.[163]

If this clan duel had been devised to call a halt to Highland disorder, it was not very effective. New contestants were about to appear; and they were not primitive caterans but had behind them the resources and comparatively sophisticated organisation of the lordship of the Isles. Feudalism provided some of the bonds that united it; but although the Lord of the Isles issued Latin charters in feudal form he also issued a charter in Gaelic on 6 May 1408 [164]— surely not a solitary example—and signed it with his Gaelic patronymic—'McDomhnaill'. A homogeneous Gaelic culture contributed much to the inward strength of the lordship and made it a unique political expression of the Gaelic way of life. This was notably demonstrated in the solemn 'ceremony of proclaiming the Lord of the Isles',[165] during which he stepped into a footprint carved in a slab of stone. The inauguration was held at his manor house on an island in Loch Finlaggan on Islay.[166] A smaller island in the loch, reached by a causeway, was known as the 'Isle of Counsel'. Here, according to Archdeacon Monro's report in 1549, 'thair conveinit 14 of the Iles best Barons', together with the Bishop of the Isles and the Abbot of Iona.[167] This body was both judicial and advisory, for the Lord of the Isles occasionally issued charters 'with the consent, assent, and mature deliberation of all our council'.[168]

[161] *Chron. Wyntoun*, III. 58.   [162] *Ibid.*, 58–60.
[163] *Ibid.*, III. 63–4; *Chron. Bower*, II. 420–1. See also *E.R.*, III. lxxix–lxxx; Dunbar, *Scot. Kings*, pp. 173–4; George Neilson, *Trial by Combat*, pp. 251–5.
[164] *Nat. MSS. of Scotland*, II. No. lix.
[165] *Highland Papers*, I. 23–4.
[166] For a description of the site see Monro, *Western Isles*, pp. 95–100.
[167] *Ibid.*, p. 57.
[168] *Highland Papers*, I. 97. The council's composition and functions are discussed in Monro, *Western Isles*, pp. 103–10.

Such phraseology hinted at the singular status of the Lord of the Isles. It was a status that the English, at least, readily recognised, for in their eyes the house of Islay had a twofold importance : not only might it be used against the Scottish kings but it might be used in Irish affairs, or at least might be persuaded not to obstruct English interests in Ireland. On 14 July 1388, soon after the death of John of the Isles, Richard II appointed a mission to treat with his successor, Donald, son of John of the Isles and Margaret Stewart, on the subject of alliance, friendship, mutual aid and trade.[169] Simultaneously there was a worsening of relations between the MacDonalds and the Stewart monarchy. On 29 March 1389 the future Robert III (then Earl of Carrick) presented a complaint in parliament alluding to the wrongs committed against his sister, Margaret Stewart, widow of the late Lord of the Isles, by her own sons and their adherents.[170] A new source of trouble had appeared by 1394, when Thomas Dunbar, Earl of Moray, had to pay protection money to Alastair (Alexander) Carrach, Lord of Lochaber and younger brother of Donald of the Isles.[171] The depredations committed by Alastair Carrach inspired the three estates with a sense of crisis : in April 1398 it was decided that either David, Earl of Carrick, or his uncle, Robert, Earl of Fife, should lead an army in some 'crossing', presumably to the Hebrides. The submission of the rebels was not to be accepted save on condition that Donald of the Isles, his brothers Alastair and Ian, their chief councillors and other notables, together with the robbers and marauders associated with them, should compear to undergo justice at the hands of the king and council, or give notable hostages.[172] Donald appears to have obtained respite cheaply by restraining his brother Alastair —but not for long : in a council that met at Linlithgow in November 1399 it was decided that the king should send letters ordering Donald to compear before parliament to answer for having released Alastair, who was reputed a common freebooter.[173]

Donald of the Isles and those whom he harboured were by no means alone in scorning the admonitions of a distracted government. Under the year 1398 an entry in the chronicle of Moray declaimed :

> In those days there was no law in Scotland, but he who was stronger oppressed him who was weaker and the whole realm was a den of

---

[169] *Rot. Scot.*, II. 94–5.
[171] *Moray Registrum*, No. 272.
[173] *Ibid.*, 575.
[170] *A.P.S.*, I. 557.
[172] *A.P.S.*, I. 570.

thieves; murders, herschips and fireraising and all other misdeeds remained unpunished; and justice, as if outlawed, lay in exile outwith the
bounds of the realm.[174]

The chronicler was merely drawing on his own experience to
confirm and elaborate the words of a statute passed in a general council held at Stirling some time in 1397. There the three estates alluded
to 'grete and horrible destruccions, heryschippis, brynyngs and
slachteris that ar sa commouly done throch al the kynrike'.[175] The
sheriffs were to be ordered to proclaim, firstly, that no one should
travel with a greater retinue than he was prepared to support at his
own cost, and secondly, that crimes of violence would be punished by
death. After making this proclamation the sheriff was to seek out
offenders, arrest them, and exact surety that they would compear at
the next justice ayre. If the offender failed to attend he was to be put
to the horn (outlawed) and those who had entered surety for him were
not only to pay the surety but pay assythment (damages) to the plaintiffs. Those offenders who could find no sureties were forthwith to be
brought before an assize; if found guilty they were to be 'condampnit
to the deid'.[176] Further provisions were modelled upon those originally enacted as temporary measures by the Holyrood general council
of November 1384. A council held at Perth in April 1398 re-affirmed
the statutes of 1397 and added other provisions. Among these was a
revolutionary ordinance : not only the sheriffs but also the bailies of
regality were to be challenged by the justiciar during his ayre to ascertain whether or not they had implemented the statutes passed at
Stirling in 1397 and at Perth in 1398.[177] All this depended upon the
holding of justice ayres. There appears to be no evidence in the
exchequer rolls of the holding of ayres between 1392 [178] and 1404,
when, or soon after, ayres were held in Cupar, Stirling and Dumbarton.[179] The absence of allusion to the ayres need not mean that they
were not held; but if they *were* held, those who presided evidently
kept the proceeds.

This was only one example of the ways in which the royal
revenues were diverted into the hands of the nobles. The remission of
customs duties, fairly frequent under Robert II, continued under
his successor.[180] Moreover, in Robert III's reign the accounts of the
expenses of the chamberlain, the custumars and the bailies of burghs

---

[174] *Moray Registrum*, p. 382.   [175] *A.P.S.*, I. 570.   [176] *Ibid.*
[177] *Ibid.*, 570–1.   [178] *E.R.*, III. 315.   [179] *Ibid.*, 643.
[180] See *ibid.*, index, under the heading 'Customs, remissions from'.

were interspersed on every page with payments of life-pensions, heritable pensions, and gifts of cash, to nobles great, middling or small. After 1397 there tended to be a deficit in the chamberlain's account. The fact that until then there was occasionally a sizable surplus is remarkable, and the explanation must be that the royal household was supported by undisclosed revenue from the crown lands, augmented as they were by the ancestral Stewart heritage. The crown had retrogressed to a primitive dependence on land, while the benefits of the more sophisticated fiscal system evolved under David II were squandered in pensions to the nobles.

Usually no reason is given in the exchequer accounts for the grant of pensions. They may be attributed to Robert III's desire to please all men, especially those of the name of Stewart. Yet one type of heritable pension stands out with sinister clarity: Robert II had begun the practice of granting heritable pensions as a retaining fee (*pro retinentia*). Thus George Dunbar, Earl of March, was to receive a heritable annual pension of £100 for his services, past and future, to Robert II, and, after his decease, to John, Earl of Carrick, his first-born son;[181] the latter, now Robert III, expanded the practice of granting pensions of retinue. By about 1394 the process was in full swing. The king's brother, Robert Stewart, Earl of Fife and Menteith, received each year two hundred marks from the great customs of Cupar and Linlithgow 'for his homage and service and for his being retained in the service of David, our first-born son'.[182] Others who were jointly retained in the service of Robert III and the heir apparent included Sir Murdoch Stewart (eldest son of the Earl of Fife), Sir Walter Stewart, Lord of Brechin (brother of the king), John Dunbar, Earl of Moray (brother-in-law of the king), Sir William Stewart of Jedburgh (a kinsman of the king), Sir David Lindsay (soon to be Earl of Crawford), Sir William Lindsay of the Byres, Sir John Montgomery of Eaglesham, Sir William Danielston and Sir John Ramorgny.[183] This list suggests the forging of a special bond of service out of the basic materials of kinship and cash. Yet all of the persons listed were probably tenants-in-chief of the crown and, on that account alone, owed homage and service to the king and his heir.

Scotland was not alone among European countries in finding that the original feudal bonds binding a vassal to his liege lord were growing insubstantial. More and more, those who held fiefs of the crown

---

[181] *Ibid.*, 203, 224. See also *ibid.*, 49, 294, 372.   [182] *Ibid.*, 348.
[183] See *ibid.*, index, under the heading of 'Retinue'.

regarded them as absolute private property rather than as property held on condition of service. A heritable grant of land might bind the recipient to the crown during his own lifetime; by the time the heir succeeded to the land he regarded it as his own by right; the gratitude that his predecessor may have felt was not always transmitted to the heir, and his services might have to be bought by the crown by yet another reward. Only in times of wholesale forfeiture could the crown find at its disposal anything like a sufficiency of estates with which to reward supporters. When land was a scarce commodity for such reward it was inevitable that money should take its place. There was much to be said for this development. The great customs had brought to the crown increased financial resources. Service could be, and was, rewarded with occasional gifts; it could be rewarded, and was, with annuities limited to the lifetime of the recipient. What was disastrous was the practice that began under Robert II and became common under Robert III, of granting heritable annuities. These thus took the place of a landed fief. Often lip-service was paid to the original feudal concept: the heritable annuity was to be paid until such time as the king should infeft the recipient or his heirs in lands of the same annual value.[184] But this was a proviso that was scarcely ever implemented, and was probably regarded at the time as a mere form of words. Thus in Scotland, as in contemporary France and England, there emerged the 'money-fief'.

At the basis of the money-fief was a contract (known in Scotland as a bond or band). It was remarked by a nineteenth-century historian that the conclusion of such bonds between king and subject was 'a new feature in the feudal constitution of the country'.[185] This 'new feature' has more recently been styled 'bastard feudalism'.[186] It has been pointed out that the function of both 'true' and 'bastard' feudalism was the same: 'they differed only in the form of the reward. . . . Land ceased to be the way *par excellence* of acquiring followers; payment and sometimes mere assumption of interest supplanted it; . . . the idea of homage palled; a variety of oaths and documents were more to the taste of those who swore and those who contracted.'[187]

Among the variety of documents that were to make their appearance in Scotland bonds of alliance and bonds of manrent[188] would

[184] *Ibid.*, 287.   [185] P. F. Tytler, *History*, I. pt. ii, 7.
[186] See K. B. McFarlane, 'Bastard Feudalism', *B.I.H.R.*, xx. 161–80 and B. D. Lyon, *From Fief to Indenture*.
[187] P. S. Lewis, 'Decayed and Non-Feudalism in Later Medieval France', *B.I.H.R.*, xxxvii. 157.   [188] Pp. 231, 286, 358–9, 410 below.

predominate in the fifteenth century. At the close of the fourteenth century it was the bond of retinue that was most characteristic. Not only the king and the heir apparent, David, Earl of Carrick, made use of it : in 1372 the first Earl of Douglas had retained Sir James Douglas of Dalkeith to serve him with eight men-at-arms and sixteen archers against all men living, save the king; in return Sir James was to be paid six hundred marks within three years.[189] Documents of this sort, which bear a close similarity to French exemplars,[190] have mostly perished. That they were commonplace is suggested by an ordinance of the general council that met at Perth on 27 January 1399 : all the king's lieges were to support the government notwithstanding 'ony condiciouns of retenewis'.[191]

The king's brother, Robert Stewart, Earl of Fife and Menteith, was well placed to take advantage of the financial opportunities available under bastard feudalism : thanks to remissions of customs most of the wool and hides of his earldoms of Fife and Menteith were exported free ;[192] he drew annual fees of £200 as chamberlain,[193] of 200 marks as keeper of Stirling Castle,[194] and occasionally of 1,000 marks as guardian ;[195] in addition he had heritable pensions of 200 marks from the Abthania of Dull and 200 marks from the great customs of Linlithgow and Cupar.[196]

This last annuity, granted in 1394, was a pension of retinue for service to his nephew, David, Earl of Carrick, the heir apparent,[197] who was beginning to stretch his wings : at the exchequer audit of 26 May 1397 it was discovered that one of the Edinburgh custumars had paid almost £80 to the Earl of Carrick without a royal precept. At first the auditors refused to pass this item and decided to advise the king 'to inform his first-born son . . . that in future he is to receive nothing of the royal revenues from the custumars . . . without the king's written mandate . . . because the custumars do not dare, and cannot, resist him'.[198] David was evidently headstrong, and as he approached his majority it was natural that he should begin to question both the ample revenues and the ample powers that had been bestowed upon his uncle.

The reaction of Robert III to the antagonism between his brother

---

[189] *Morton Registrum*, II. No. 129.
[190] P. S. Lewis, *op. cit.*, Appendices Nos. 1, 2 and 3.   [191] *A.P.S.*, I. 573.
[192] *E.R.*, III. lxxxv.   [193] *Ibid.*, 644, 668.   [194] *Ibid.*, 427.
[195] This was certainly paid between 1389 and 1392 and partly paid in 1404 (*ibid.*, 238, 276, 312, 589, 610, 645).
[196] *Ibid.*, 427.   [197] *Ibid.*, 348.   [198] *Ibid.*, 407-8.

and his son was a characteristic attempt to placate both parties. In England the title of duke had existed since 1337, and on 29 September 1397 no fewer than four new dukedoms had been created.[199] It was a sign of the existing chivalric links between the Scottish and English courts that Robert III imitated the example set by Richard II: in Scone Abbey on 28 April 1398 David, Earl of Carrick, was raised to the dignity of Duke of Rothesay, and Robert Stewart, Earl of Fife and Menteith, to that of Duke of Albany. A week earlier Sir David Lindsay of Glenesk had been created Earl of Crawford and had his lands erected into a regality.[200] It was perhaps significant that while the heir apparent styled himself after the ancestral Stewart home his uncle's title hinted at the ancient kingdom of Alba (still the Gaelic term for Scotland) and pointed to pretensions that were royal rather than baronial. Certainly the new and equal dignities of the heir apparent and his uncle did nothing to reconcile them. At the exchequer on 2 May, a few days after the ceremony in Scone Abbey, the auditors called upon Albany to produce a charter under which he claimed payment in connection with a mysterious marriage contract. Nor did the auditors see eye to eye with Albany in his capacity as chamberlain; the account closed with mention of the enormous sum of £930 19s. 7d. which was in dispute between the auditors and the duke. It was probably Rothesay who was the figure behind the auditors: the dispute was to be referred to consultation between the king, Albany, Rothesay, and the council that had been 'limited' (specially assigned) to Rothesay.[201]

If this was the opening of a struggle between Rothesay and Albany, it was continued when a general council met at Perth in January 1399[202] and resulted in a revolution that did not quite succeed. Without mincing words it was declared that 'the mysgovernance of the reaulme and the defaut of the kepyng of the common law sulde be imput to the kyng and his officeris'. Robert III had doubtless caused exasperation,[203] but it was probably not against him but against his advisers, Albany in particular, that attack was directed: the king was given the opportunity to 'excuse his defautes'; he might summon those officers whom he had appointed and 'accuse thaim in presence

199 May McKisack, *The Fourteenth Century*, pp. 483–4.
200 *Chron. Bower*, II. 422; *Moray Registrum*, p. 382.
201 *E.R.*, III. 461.   202 *A.P.S.*, I. 572.
203 In April 1398 the council had revoked a grant which the king had made 'without the consent of the council and to the prejudice of the common weal of the realm' (*ibid.*, 571).

of his counsail'; after they had been heard the council would be ready to judge their defaults.[204] Despite this almost open invitation to accuse Albany, Robert III seems to have preferred to bear the burden of 'mysgovernance' on his own penitent shoulders. Somewhat thwarted, the opposition had to couch its attack on the duke in the form of an attack upon the king. This, however, did not take the form of the more sophisticated and more ruthless attacks made in the English parliament upon Richard II. The three estates simply stated as a matter of common knowledge that it was obvious and well known that the lord king, by reason of personal infirmity, was unable to undertake the labour of governing the realm or restraining transgressors and rebels. Therefore it seemed to the council most 'expedient'—the very word suggests the difference between the pragmatism of the Scottish estates and the political theorising of the English parliament—that the Duke of Rothesay should be the king's lieutenant for a period of three years. Careful attention was paid to the powers that Rothesay would exercise. He was to have a commission from the king to govern the land with full royal authority, and Robert III was to oblige himself not to interfere with the lieutenant in the exercise of his functions. Finally Rothesay as lieutenant was to have the 'dispenses and costages' that had lately been granted to Albany as guardian.[205]

While it is difficult to ascertain the members of the party behind this palace revolution, it seems clear that one of its chief members, apart from Rothesay himself, was Queen Annabella. In the Scone parliament of March 1391 the three estates had settled upon her the huge annual pension of 2,500 marks for 'her adornment and other things necessary for her rank and livelihood'.[206] Now she formally complained that the chamberlain's deputies obstructed the levying of her pension. The estates decided that due payment should be made 'without ony objeccioun'; also the chamberlain (Albany) was to be ordered not to hinder such payment in any manner.[207] The queen's Drummond kinsmen were probably behind her. More potent influences may be seen in Bishop Trail of St Andrews and Archibald the Grim, who were at least associated with the queen in the mind of Abbot Bower as a trio of virtuous persons.[208]

The indirect attack upon Albany was not wholly successful: he seems to have used his influence to curb the power of the new lieutenant through a 'special' council of twenty-one persons named by the three estates.[209] With the exception of Adam Forrester of Corstor-phine—an active figure as auditor of exchequer, envoy, custumar and bailie of Edinburgh, financial agent of all and sundry [210]—no burgess figured on the special council. For what it was worth, six of the members—Albany, the Earls of Moray and Crawford, Walter Stewart, Lord of Brechin, Sir William Stewart of Jedburgh and Sir John Ramorgny—had been receiving annuities of retinue for their past and future service to Robert III and Rothesay;[211] and Ramorgny—almost as active a figure as Adam Forrester—was Rothesay's personal chamberlain.[212] It was with this group of twenty-one 'wyse men' that Rothesay was to consult when the three estates were not in session. Every administrative act on the part of the lieutenant was to be recorded with the date and place and the names of those who had counselled it so that the latter might answer to the three estates and be punished for what the lieutenant did amiss. Rothesay was authorised to reward deserving persons with the escheats and forfeitures that fell due during his three years of office; but those who counselled him on such matters would have to answer for such awards to the king and his general council. For the time being the general council seems to have been regarded as the ultimate political authority while parliament was left with its judicial authority : it was ordained that for the next three years the king should hold an annual parliament on 2 November so that his subjects might be 'servit of the law'.[213] All this was on parchment admirable, but in practice there were too many checks and balances. The Albany and Rothesay factions were probably too finely balanced for firm government; the one faction in the 'special' council could thwart administration by refusing to accept responsibility; the other, by reason of such obstruction, might be driven to rash measures.

The general council of January 1399 also considered the international situation. Although the Franco-Scottish alliance of 1371 had been renewed in 1391 [214] the spirit behind it was no longer aggressive. Scotland had become a party to the international truces arranged at Leulighem in June 1389 and a state of truce was to be prolonged until 1399.[215] Meanwhile the chivalry-smitten armigerous classes of both Scotland and England, deprived of more serious warfare,

[209] *A.P.S.*, I. 572.   [210] *E.R.*, III. index, *sub nomine.*
[211] P. 211 above.   [212] *E.R.*, III. 487; index, *sub nomine.*
[213] *A.P.S.*, I. 572-3.   [214] Text in *E.R.*, III. xcvii-civ.
[215] *Cal. Docs. Scot.*, IV. No. 416; *Foedera*, III. pt. iv, 39-42; *Rot. Scot.*, II. 142-3; *E.R.*, III. lxxvi.

vaunted their martial ardour in the lists. They were encouraged by
Richard II, who patronised a court of chivalry in which affairs of
honour could be settled in trials by combat. A similar court seems
occasionally to have been extemporised in Scotland.[216] The Anglo-
Scottish chivalric combats so frequent in the last decade of the fourteenth century[217] had inspired mutual interest rather than mutual
bitterness and led to more courtly interchanges in which Queen
Annabella took a significant part.[218] There were even honest attempts
to remedy the constant breaches of truce that kept alive old enmities.
'Days of Trewe' were held fairly regularly to afford redress. It was on
these Truce Days, held with considerable formality and expensive
ostentation[219] at recognised trysting places—Reddenburn, Carham,
Hawdenstank or Clochmabenstane[220]—that there took place Anglo-
Scottish confrontations at the highest level: Rothesay, Albany and
Crawford, shortly before their elevation in rank, had met the Duke of
Lancaster and other English dignitaries at Hawdenstank in March
1398 and had arranged a prolongation of the truce until Michaelmas
1399.[221] The question of its renewal was raised in the Perth general
council of January 1399 and a commission of fourteen persons, drawn
from Rothesay's special council and headed by the new lieutenant
and Albany, was appointed to hold discussions with English envoys
at Edinburgh.[222] As soon as this commission had reached a decision
envoys were to be sent to England and a 'grete message', or embassy,
was to be sent to France.[223]

To finance this important diplomatic activity a contribution of
£2,000[224] was to be levied—the first evidence of direct taxation since
1373. The effect of the intervening lapse in levying such taxation was
reflected in the protestations formally recorded on the part of the kirk
and the burgesses. What had become customary and almost habitual
towards the close of the reign of David II was now regarded as unaccustomed and exceptional: the three estates united to protest that
the contribution had been granted on condition that the law would
be enforced; they also stipulated that collection of the tax was not to

[216] George Neilson, *Trial by Combat*, pp. 272-5.
[217] *Chron. Bower*, II. 422-4; *Chron. Wyntoun*, III. 50; *Cal. Docs. Scot.*, IV.
Nos. 414-33, *passim*.
[218] *Nat. MSS. Scot.*, II. No. xlix.
[219] Rothesay was granted £800 by Robert III for his expenses on one of these
occasions in 1398 (*E.R.*, III. 473, 474).
[220] *Cal. Docs. Scot.*, IV. No. 492.
[221] *Rot. Scot.*, II. 142-3; *Cal. Docs. Scot.*, IV. No. 502.
[222] *A.P.S.*, I. 573.   [223] *Ibid.*
[224] Not £11,000 as stated by P. F. Tytler, *History*, I. pt. ii, 9.
E.H.S.—8*

be entrusted to the chamberlain (Albany) but to nine special receivers, three appointed by each of the estates.[225]

The outcome of the subsequent diplomacy may be seen in the commission that Richard II issued on 22 March 1399 authorising negotiation not only for a renewal of truce but for a final peace.[226] On 4 May the Scots issued a similar commission: Rothesay headed the Scottish commissioners; Albany was conspicuously absent.[227] A meeting at Hawdenstank on 14 May prolonged the truce until Michaelmas 1400.[228] Whatever chance there was of a more significant outcome was frustrated by the landing of Henry Bolingbroke in England in June 1399, the deposition of Richard II on 29 September [229] and his reported death in February 1400. The Scots, conservative in their outlook upon the political and social vicissitudes of other nations, were deeply shocked.[230] While the two countries hovered on the brink of renewing the truce the new Lancastrian king received from Scotland itself an unexpected appeal for forceful action.

It was the behaviour of the romantically fickle Duke of Rothesay that had inspired the appeal. By paying to Robert III a large sum of gold George Dunbar, Earl of March, had obtained Rothesay's betrothal to his daughter Elizabeth.[231] Archibald the Grim 'at the insinuation of the king's council' paid a larger sum than the Earl of March, whereupon the king allowed Rothesay to jilt Elizabeth Dunbar and marry Marjory Douglas. The Earl of March remonstrated with the king and requested at least the refund of the marriage payment. Robert III was evasive and March was 'more moved than he ought to have been'.[232] On 18 February 1400 he addressed to Henry IV a singular epistle [233] that wasted no time on courtly preambles but straightway announced: 'I am gretly wrangit be the Duc of Rothesay, the quhilk spousit my douchter and now . . . spouses ane other wif.' The earl reminded the king that he and Henry were within the fourth degree of kinship, 'the quhilk in alde tyme wes callit neire'. Henry, who had lately deposed his own full cousin, was now called upon as fourth cousin of the Earl of March to take part in a Scottish feud over a breach of promise.

---

[225] No record of this contribution appears in the exchequer rolls, presumably because the receivers kept their own accounts.

[226] *Cal. Docs. Scot.*, IV. No. 515.

[227] *Ibid.*, No. 519.   [228] *Ibid.*, No. 520.

[229] See E. F. Jacob, *The Fifteenth Century*, pp. 1–18.

[230] *Chron. Bower*, II. 428.   [231] *Ibid.*   [232] *Ibid.*, 421.

[233] *Nat. MSS. Scot.*, II. No. liii.

But however lightly Henry treated kinship he was not blind to political expediency; March was to be asked to swear allegiance to him and to say whether he would deliver any of his castles in return for an annuity, how many men he would require, and by what time.[234] While the Duke of Rothesay married the daughter of Archibald the Grim in the kirk of Bothwell[235] the Earl of March made his way to England and joined forces with the Percies of Northumberland in a raid upon the countryside near Haddington.[236] On 2 July 1400 an English safe-conduct was issued for Adam Forrester,[237] who came as an envoy of Robert III in a last bid to avert war. At York Henry rejected a proposal for peace based on the terms of the treaty of 1328.[238] From Newcastle on 6 August he sent off a letter to Robert III reminding him that since the days of Locrine, son of Brutus, the kings of England were lords superior of Scotland: Henry would be ready to receive Robert's homage and fealty at Edinburgh on 23 August.[239]

Henry's expedition to Edinburgh was uniquely undestructive : he was reputed to have spared the countryside out of reverence for Queen Annabella.[240] By 21 August he had arrived at Leith and announced that he had come to Scotland because he had been styled a prodigious traitor in letters, or rather libels, sent to the king of France by a certain Scottish magnate 'in the balance of whose hands the equilibrium of the kingdom has perforce to sway up and down'. Henry had appeared to see if that magnate dared to fight with him and give him the opportunity to prove his innocence.[241]

The 'certain magnate' was probably Rothesay, who shut himself up in Edinburgh Castle, which Henry assaulted in vain.[242] Once more he summoned Robert III to do homage. Robert refused to be enticed. Meanwhile Rothesay sent a defiance to Henry (whom he styled not as king but merely as his 'adversary of England') and offered combat with a few hundred nobles on either side.[243] This challenge was not quite to the liking of Henry, who by 3 September was back in Newcastle.

Peace negotiations took place in October 1401 at Kirk Yetholm, where the English recited the time-honoured rigmarole beginning

[234] Balfour-Melville, *James I*, p. 17.   [235] *Chron. Bower*, II.. 428.
[236] *Ibid.*, 428-9; *Chron. Wyntoun*, III. 78.
[237] *Cal. Docs. Scot.*, IV. No. 547.   [238] Balfour-Melville, *James I*, p. 18.
[239] *Chron. Bower*, II. 506-8; *Moray Registrum*, Nos. 305, 306; *Cal. Docs. Scot.*, IV. Nos. 553, 554.
[240] *Chron. Pluscarden*, I. 341; *Chron. Bower*, II. 430.
[241] *Chron. Bower*, II. 430; *Chron. Pluscarden*, I. 341.
[242] *Chron. Bower*, II. 430; *Chron. Wyntoun*, II. 77; *Cal. Docs. Scot.*, IV. No. 562.   [243] *Foedera*, III. pt. iv, 189.

with Brutus the Trojan, and the Scots uttered 'some very undiplomatic language'.[244] Then the English asked if the Scottish king would consent to arbitration over the homage question. The Bishop of Glasgow rejoined by asking whether the right of Henry IV to the English throne might also be put to arbitration. The conference broke up.

Henry IV's intervention in Scotland had interrupted the constitutional experiment that had begun in the Perth general council of January 1399 with the appointment of Rothesay as lieutenant for a period of three years. Robert III had remained as at least a figurehead and presided over a council at Linlithgow on 20 November 1399 to which the two dukes and most members of Rothesay's special council were summoned, together with some other magnates.[245] This council dealt with a complaint from Walter Lindsay, who alleged that he had been made captive by Sir John Wemyss and had been forced to enter into some obligation towards him.[246] Sir John Wemyss was a prominent knight who in 1392 had received a licence to construct on his land of Reres in Fife a castle with towers of whatever height or strength he pleased.[247] His handiwork was soon put to the test: the Duke of Rothesay besieged Reres Castle 'for the public weal', using a wooden engine especially constructed at St Andrews at a cost of £80.[248] The Reres incident certainly suggests that Rothesay did not lack forcefulness. When the three estates met in parliament at Scone on 21 February 1401 [249] they passed a statute that made it easier for the weak (ecclesiastics, widows, orphans and minors) to seek the lieutenant's good services. Such plaintiffs were no longer to be required to give pledges for prosecution of their suit.[250]

What might have brought a return to sound government came to a dramatic end. Rothesay's position was weakened with the death of the three persons who seem to have supported him. Archibald, third Earl of Douglas, died on Christmas Eve, 1400. He was, wrote Abbot Bower, 'called the grim or terrible, who in worldly prudence, courage and boldness, excelled the other Scots of his day'.[251] His soul, according to Wyntoun, sped to paradise,[252] where it was joined before

[244] Stones, *Documents*, pp. 173–82, at 180. See also E. L. G. Stones, 'The Appeal to History in Anglo-Scottish Relations between 1291 and 1401: Part II', *Archives*, IX. No. 42, 80–3.

[245] *A.P.S.*, I. 574–5.   [246] *Ibid.*, 574.
[247] *R.M.S.*, I. No. 53, p. 214.   [248] *E.R.*, III. 552, 559, 560.
[249] *A.P.S.*, I. 575–6.   [250] *Ibid.*, 576.
[251] *Chron. Bower*, II. 429; *Chron. Pluscarden*, I. 340.
[252] *Chron. Wyntoun*, III. 77.

1 July 1401 by that of Bishop Walter Trail. This 'solempne clerk' had lived 'Godlikly' and was 'the strongest pillar of the kirk, a vessel of eloquence, storehouse of knowledge, and defender of the Catholic faith'.[253] Then at harvest-time in 1401 died Queen Annabella,

> Faire, honorabil and plesand,
> Cunnand, curtas in hir efferis,
> Luvand, and large [generous] to strangeris.[254]

With the death of these three, queen, bishop and earl, it was said 'almost proverbially' that the glory of Scotland had departed, its honour had withdrawn and its decency had died.[255] From the walls of Edinburgh Castle the Duke of Rothesay watched a comet, a 'brycht stern and a clere', blaze across the skies, and took it as a baleful omen. Priestly science deemed it a sign of pestilence or the death of princes.[256]

Rothesay's three-year term of office as royal lieutenant expired in January 1402. He is reported to have spurned the advice of the special council which had been assigned to him, and it thereupon resigned.[258] He tried to draw revenue from the custumars, took £70 'violently' from a custumar of Dundee and held a custumar of Montrose captive until he disgorged £24.[259] His final act of state was an expedition to St Andrews to take over the bishop's castle and exercise the other rights that pertained to the crown during the vacancy of the see after the death of Bishop Trail.[260] The king, 'powerless and decrepit', wrote to Albany, perhaps already appointed as Rothesay's replacement, with orders to arrest the heir apparent and hold him in ward until he mended his ways. But, explains Bower, 'what the king proposed for the improvement of his son turned out to his harm'. As Rothesay was on his way to St Andrews he was arrested by his own retainer, Sir John Ramorgny, and Sir William Lindsay of Rossie (whose sister he had once jilted). Albany and the new Earl of Douglas, Archibald the Tyneman, arrived at St Andrews to convey the duke in sorry state to the manor of Falkland, where he died on 26 or 27 March 1402, of 'dysentery' or 'as others would have it, of hunger'.[261] The chronicler Wyntoun consigned him to paradise with a pleasing

---

[253] *Chron. Bower*, II. 430.
[254] *Chron. Wyntoun*, III. 81.
[255] *Chron. Bower*, II. 431.
[256] *Ibid.*, 432.
[258] *Chron. Bower*, II. 431.
[259] *E.R.*, III. 549–50, 552, 599; compare p. 546.
[260] *Chron. Wyntoun*, III. 80; *Chron. Bower*, II. 431.
[261] *Chron. Bower*, II. 431–2; *Chron. Pluscarden*, I. 342–3.

obituary.[262] Others were not so ready to shut their eyes and ears. When a general council met at Edinburgh on 16 May 1402 it remained in session for many days. Albany and Archibald the Tyneman were accused and interrogated; they explained that they had arrested and imprisoned Rothesay for the public weal. The reasons they gave were, by the king's instructions, omitted from the record. Rothesay was known 'to have departed this life by divine providence and not otherwise'. The king publicly declared that Albany and Douglas were innocent; he strictly commanded that no one should 'murmur against them'.[263]

The suspect circumstances in which Albany was restored to power were soon lost to sight in new Anglo-Scottish involvements. In the declining years of the fourteenth century the more or less simultaneous weakening of central government in both Scotland and England had prevented either kingdom from successfully pursuing far-reaching ambitions against the other. In 1402, however, Albany felt strong enough to ignore the blandishments by which Henry IV sought to entice him towards an extended truce or final peace.[264] Three factors inspired the Scots to a fresh and ambitious bellicosity.

One of these was the rising of Owen Glendower, who hoped to establish an independent Welsh principality.[265] Political realism inspired him to seek an alliance with the French. The prophecies of Merlin led him to believe that Wales would be freed only with the aid of the Scots and native Irish.[266] Another factor was the appearance in Scotland of a person thought to be none other than Richard II, escaped from prison.[267] By 1417 Albany claimed to have spent no less than £733 6s. 8d. on the maintenance of 'King Richard of England'.[268] Although Henry IV denounced Albany's protégé as an impostor or 'Mammet' [269] it was widely believed for many years that Richard was alive in Scotland; until the Mammet was buried with royal honours at Stirling in 1419 [270] he was a figurehead for plots and risings in England. A third factor that made for war was the feud be-

---

[262] *Chron. Wyntoun*, III. 82.   [263] *A.P.S.*, I. 582–3.
[264] *Rot. Scot.*, II. 154–5.
[265] E. F. Jacob, *The Fifteenth Century*, pp. 41–2, 54–8.
[266] *Chron. Bower*, II. 452–8; Glyn Roberts, *Aspects of Welsh History* (1969), p. 314.   [267] *Chron. Wyntoun*, III. 76; *Chron. Bower*, II. 402, 427.
[268] *E.R.*, IV. 289.
[269] *Foedera*, IV. pt. i, 29–30. In a painstaking essay entitled 'Historical Remarks on the Death of Richard II', P. F. Tytler (*History*, I. pt. ii, 96–119) argued plausibly that the mysterious personage was indeed Richard II.
[270] *Chron. Bower*, II. 459.

tween the Earl of March and Archibald the Tyneman, fourth Earl of
Douglas, who occupied the earldom of March and the Dunbar lordship of Annandale. When the dispossessed Earl of March raided the
eastern Borders he was aided by former tenants, still loyal to 'their
native lord'.[271] A retaliatory raid led by Sir Patrick Hepburn of
Hailes ended at Nesbit Muir on 22 June 1402 with the capture of
'the flower of the chivalry of a great part of Lothian'.[272]

The Earls of Douglas, Angus and Moray set out to avenge this
reverse and harried Northumberland to the gates of Newcastle. Returning with their booty the Scots were overtaken on 14 September
1402 by Hotspur and the Earl of March. Archibald the Tyneman
cautiously stationed his troops on the summit of Homildon Hill, waiting to repel the expected English attack. All that came was a hail
of English arrows. Eventually Sir John Stenton led a handful of
knights to perish in a charge downhill. Others took to flight and
the remainder were killed or taken prisoner. The list of captives included the Earl of Douglas, who had earned his by-name of 'the
Tyneman' ('the Loser'), as well as the Earls of Moray and Angus, and
Murdoch Stewart, Albany's son and heir. It was 'as if the flower of
chivalry of the whole realm of Scotland was captured and held to
ransom'.[273]

Homildon wiped out the English reverse at Otterburn. Hotspur
was able to cross the border and obtain the surrender of a few fortalices. At one small stronghold, the tower of Cocklaws in Teviotdale,
he met with staunch resistance. Instead of pressing the siege Hotspur
made a truce : the tower would surrender if it were not relieved by
either Robert III or Albany on 1 August 1403. Albany exclaimed, so
says Bower, 'I vow to God and St Fillan that on the appointed day,
if alive, I will be there, although no one bears me company save my
boy Patrick'.[274] Those present marvelled at the high spirit of the duke
and wept for joy. The Scottish host marched to Cocklaws to an encounter that was expected to be a second Bannockburn or a second
Halidon. The sequel was ludicrous. The enemy did not turn up.
Albany marched his host round the little tower while a herald explained that Hotspur had been slain at Shrewsbury.[275]

When Hotspur had besieged Cocklaws and then left it 'in sus-
pense' he had done so either to entice the Scots to the elusive final
battle or, more likely, he had used the Cocklaws affair as an excuse

[271] *Ibid.*, 432.   [272] *Ibid.*, 432–3.
[273] *Ibid.*, 433–5; *Chron. Wyntoun*, III. 85–6.
[274] *Chron. Bower*, II. 437.   [275] *Ibid.*, 437–8.

for gathering troops to be used against an unsuspecting Henry IV,[276] against whom the Percies had conceived grievances. One of these concerned the disposal of the ransomable prisoners captured at Homildon : the Earl of Northumberland duly delivered Albany's son, Murdoch Stewart, to Henry IV; Hotspur held on to the captured Earl of Douglas, who seems to have engaged to pay his ransom by serving him in a conspiracy against the English king. With the help of Owen Glendower the Percies would set on the throne the legitimist Mortimer claimant, descendant of Lionel, second son of Edward III.[277]

At Shrewsbury on 21 July 1403 Hotspur was slain and his rebellion crushed. Scotsmen fought on both sides : the Earl of March had abandoned the Percies when they were joined by his rival Douglas, and gave good service to Henry IV ; Archibald the Tyneman, on the losing side as usual, led a force of Scots in Hotspur's vanguard and fell into Henry's hands as a prisoner.[278] Shrewsbury showed that both in Scotland and England the concept of nationalism which seemed to have taken root in the first half of the fourteenth century had been largely displaced by baronial self-interest decked in the trappings of chivalry.

Despite his victory Henry IV still had too many troubles to allow him to make war on the Scots. Negotiations resulted in a truce which seems to have been successively extended until 1406.[279] In the summer of 1403 there were abortive negotiations for the ransom and release of Archibald the Tyneman and Albany's son Murdoch.[280] Albany betrayed his anxiety over the fate of his son and heir in an obsequious letter that he addressed to Henry IV, probably in 1404 :

> I was most willing that you should keep my son Murdoch Stewart (your kinsman if it please you) with you in your honourable court ... and have fully understood . . . how graciously you replied with regard to the release of my foresaid son. . . . And if there be any useful tasks I can conveniently undertake in these parts [Scotland] be pleased to inform me of the same ... and I shall willingly perform them to the best of my power ...
>   Your kinsman, if it please you,
>   Robert, Duke of Albany,
>   Full brother of the King of Scotland and his lieutenant-general.[281]

[276] Ibid., 436, 438.
[277] Foedera, iv. pt. i, 35-6; Balfour-Melville, James I, p. 25; E. F. Jacob, The Fifteenth Century, pp. 45-8.
[278] Chron. Bower, ii. 438; Chron. Walsingham, ii. 368-9.
[279] Rot. Scot., ii. 164, 168, 173-4, 177.
[280] Ibid., 167.   [281] Nat. MSS. Scot., ii. No. lv.

The stalemate in Anglo-Scottish relations was interrupted by a plot of the Earl of Northumberland and Archbishop Scrope of York, who intended to muster at York with a force of Scots; the French would send an expedition to Wales to aid Owen Glendower, who was also a party to the conspiracy. The plan miscarried when Archbishop Scrope was beheaded on the orders of Henry IV. By June 1405 Northumberland was a fugitive in Scotland with his young grandson and the Welsh Bishops of Bangor and St Asaph.[282]

It was about this time that Archibald the Tyneman's younger brother, James Douglas, warden of the March (later to earn ill fame as James the Gross, seventh Earl of Douglas), took advantage of the situation by burning the town of Berwick and seizing £23 5s. 2d. from the Edinburgh custumars to cover his expenses in arranging the conflagration.[283] On 26 July 1405 he impatiently replied to the English king's reproaches in a letter that showed none of the obsequiousness of Albany and minced no words.[284] If James Douglas was representative of the outlook of the Scottish barons their mood was undoubtedly bellicose. Anglo-Scottish relations were left in topsy-turvy turmoil: the Dunbars of March were honoured guests in England; the Percies of Northumberland were honoured guests in Scotland and were intriguing for French help; Albany and Henry IV, both men of the same stamp, politic, ruthless, dissimulating, seekers of cheap popularity, were plagued by domestic troubles. This was the background to an event that was soon to place the heir to the Scottish throne in the hands of Henry IV.

After the death of the Duke of Rothesay only two lives lay between Albany and the throne, those of the ailing Robert III and his surviving son, James, born at Dunfermline in 1394,[285] probably on 25 July, the feast day of the Apostle James. The existence of the heir apparent made it likely that Albany's tenure of power would not be unduly long, and some factions were perhaps already preparing themselves for the time when James would enter politics on his own account. Certainly Albany was appointed to the office of lieutenant-general not for any long or indeterminate period but for only a year or two at a time, after which the appointment was renewed (possibly after a review of his performance) by the three estates. Thus, when a

---

[282] *E.R.*, IV. xliii; *Chron. Bower*, II. 453; *Chron. Pluscarden*, I. 441.
[283] *E.R.*, IV. 44, 81; *Rot. Scot.*, II. 177.
[284] *Nat. MSS. Scot.*, II. No. liv.   [285] *Ibid.*, No. xlix.

general council met at Linlithgow on 28 April 1404,[286] Albany presided as the king's lieutenant, and the king, who was also present, ordained that the duke should be his lieutenant with full royal power for two years commencing on Whitsunday next. But while the lieutenant could, and did, summon general councils, it was assumed that only the king could hold parliaments—which he was to do each year, beginning on 3 November, primarily, no doubt, for judicial purposes, for the other enactments of this general council show a concern for the improvement of the administration of justice.[287] From the exchequer records it would appear not only that the three estates had assigned a special council to advise and perhaps control the lieutenant, but also that the auditors were capable of calling him to account. This is all the more remarkable in so far as the auditors were scarcely men of power.[288] Just as Robert III had striven to surround Rothesay with a band of pensioned retainers he now began to do the same for himself and his surviving son, carefully avoiding the selection of royal Stewarts.[289] Within a few years the young James could be expected to become more than a figurehead for opposition to Albany. On the arrival in Scotland of the fugitive Percies it had been arranged that James, together with Henry Percy, son of Hotspur, a boy of his own age, should be reared in St Andrews Castle under the learned tutelage of Bishop Wardlaw, 'a man of great expenses'.[290] Probably with some presentiment of danger the old king ended this arrangement: he would send his heir to France, ostensibly for his education, more probably for his safety.

If James was to reach France in safety much depended on the rapidity and secrecy of his crossing, for no English safe-conduct had been requested. At first all went well. The king's trusted councillor, Sir David Fleming of Biggar and Cumbernauld, escorted James swiftly to North Berwick, whence he was rowed out to the Bass Rock to wait for a ship. Then things went wrong; on his way homeward on 14 February 1406 Fleming was waylaid and slain at Langherdmanston by James Douglas, the Tyneman's brother.[291] Albany did nothing to punish the murderers. Meanwhile James had to linger for a month among the gannets of the Bass Rock, attended by Henry

[286] It was attended by five bishops, one prior, eight abbots, two earls, twenty-one lords, seven knights (some of whom were of higher status than some 'lords'), the commissioners of eight burghs, and other unspecified persons. The text of the proceedings is published by A. A. M. Duncan in ' "Councils General", 1404, 1423', S.H.R., xxxv. 132–43.   [287] Ibid., 135–6.
[288] E.R., III. 608; see also 589, 610.   [289] Ibid., 291, 597, 625, 627, 635.
[290] Chron. Bower, II. 439.   [291] Chron. Pluscarden, I. 347.

Sinclair, Earl of Orkney, and a Welsh bishop. Finally, after a delay long enough for news to reach England, the party embarked in the *Maryenknyght* of Danzig, bound out of Leith with a cargo of wool and hides.[292] The vessel was off Flamborough Head when it was boarded on 14 March 1406 [293] by Hugh-atte-Fen and other reputable merchants and pirates of Great Yarmouth. As a truce was still in force [294] the equitable Henry IV envisaged restitution of the captured cargo. Restitution of the Scottish heir apparent was out of the question; James was lodged in the Tower. Many years later he was to write in the *Kingis Quair* of his ill-fated voyage and his capture :

> ... out of my contree,
> By thaire avise that had of me the cure,
> Be see to pas, tuke I myn aventure ...
>
> Upon the wavis weltering to and fro,
> So infortunate was us that fremyt day,
> That maugre, playnly, quhethir we wold or no,
> With strong hand, as by forse, schortly to say,
> Off inymyis takin led away
> We weren all, and broght in thaire contree.

News of his son's capture was brought to Robert III as he sat at supper in Rothesay Castle : 'his spirit forthwith left him, the strength waned from his body, his countenance grew pale, and for grief thereafter he took not food'.[295] The king, then in his sixty-ninth year, died on Palm Sunday, 4 April 1406.[296]

'In the days of this king,' wrote Abbot Bower, 'there was in the realm great fertility of victuals but the greatest discord, wrangles and strife betwixt magnates and nobles, because the king, weak in body, nowhere exercised rigour.' [297] Robert III had long laboured under a sense of personal failure. Once when Queen Annabella had inquired of him whether he would follow the example of his royal predecessors by arranging for the erection of a seemly tombstone and epitaph,

---

[292] Balfour-Melville, *James I*, pp. 30–1.

[293] For an examination of the date see *ibid.*, p. 31; *E.R.*, iv. cxcvi; *Chron. Bower*, ii. 439. Two literary historians (Jean Robert Simon and Matthew P. McDiarmid) have independently concluded that stanzas 20 and 21 of *The Kingis Quair* 'fix the day of the fateful voyage as 14 March' (McDiarmid in review of *Le Livre du Roi*, *S.H.R.*, xlix. 195–7, at 197).

[294] See the detailed examination of this question by E. W. M. Balfour-Melville (*James I*, pp. 32–3).

[295] *Chron. Bower*, ii. 440.

[296] Balfour-Melville, *James I*, p. 34. [297] *Chron. Bower*, ii. 440.

he is said to have answered : 'I would prefer to be buried deep in a midden, providing that my soul be safe in the day of the Lord. Wherefore bury me, I pray, in a midden, and write for my epitaph—"Here lies the worst of kings and the most wretched of men in the whole realm." ' [298]

[298] *Ibid.*, 440–1.

9

THE ALBANY GOVERNORSHIP AND
THE END OF THE GREAT SCHISM

ROBERT III was laid to rest not in a midden but in the abbey of Paisley that his ancestors had helped to found. In June 1406 the three estates met in general council at Perth to face the dire mischance of the capture of an heir apparent who had almost immediately inherited the crown.[1] Since the new king, James I, was scarcely twelve years old, and was constrained to reside in England, he could not exercise even the most nominal of royal functions. Albany, now heir presumptive, was appointed as governor of the realm and assumed more of the trappings of royalty than guardians or lieutenants had formerly possessed. Once at least, in a letter of 1410 to Henry IV, the duke styled himself governor of Scotland *Dei gracia* and wrote of his 'subjects'.[2]

Meanwhile possession of the person of the Scottish king allowed Henry IV to display a certain assurance in his dealings with the Scots. English safe-conducts were issued to Scottish knights and esquires, to Scottish pilgrims, to Scotsmen who went south to seek redress for injuries committed in time of truce, to Scottish clerics on their way to or from the continent, and, above all, to Scottish merchants and skippers, who were granted licences to trade in England on a scale not seen since the time of David II.[3] Henry's readiness to show himself obliging to a wide variety of influential Scots was a sign of his willingness to reach a settlement with Scotland. Between 1406 and the end of his reign there seem to have been almost annual meetings of commissioners, usually at Hawdenstank, to negotiate renewals of

---

[1] *Chron. Wyntoun*, III. 99; *Chron. Bower*, II. 441. No official record of this general council survives.
[2] *E.R.*, IV. xlvii–xlix. [3] *Rot. Scot.*, II. 178–201, *passim*.

truce.[4] Occasionally, as in 1409 and 1410, the terms of reference
even included discussion of a final peace.[5]

Albany's response was one of latent hostility interspersed with
occasional obsequiousness. The duke entertained envoys from France
and Wales;[6] and the disinherited Earl of Northumberland was
allowed to use Scotland as a base from which he set out on missions
to Wales, Brittany and Flanders, until finally, in February 1408, he
crossed the border only to be slain in Yorkshire.[7] The unsteady relationship between Albany and Henry, who resembled one another in
their deviousness, can be seen in the words with which Henry from
time to time described Albany in official documents: in 1407 he was
'lately our adversary of Scotland' or 'the Duke of Albany, governor,
as he asserts, of the realm of Scotland'; in 1408 he was 'our kinsman';
in July 1409 he was 'our dearest kinsman'; in November 1409 he was
once more 'governor, as he asserts, of the realm of Scotland'; and in
May 1411 he was once more 'our dearest kinsman'.[8]

Against this uneasy background were set various negotiations for
the release of Henry's captives—Archibald the Tyneman, Albany's
son Murdoch, and James I.[9] For the temporary release of the Tyneman Henry obtained a dozen noble hostages [10] and a certain written
undertaking. In this document of 14 March 1407 the Earl of Douglas
bound himself to serve Henry and his four sons against all men save
the Scottish king.[11] Henry expected that the Tyneman, once released
on parole, would act as his partisan in Scotland. It came as a shock
that the earl failed to return to England when his parole expired at
Easter 1409.[12]

Douglas's breach of parole was probably connected with the
restoration of his rival, the disinherited Earl of March. While the
Tyneman had been a captive in England, March and his family had
been refugees upon whom Henry IV had heaped benefactions, including an annuity of five hundred marks.[13] Nonetheless the Dunbars
were not at home in England and by 1409 were ready to abandon
Henry.[14] In their return to Scotland can be traced the hand of Albany,

[4] *Ibid.*, 181–99, *passim*; *Cal. Docs. Scot.*, iv. Nos. 750, 793.
[5] *Rot. Scot.*, ii. 190, 193.   [6] *E.R.*, iv. 71.
[7] Balfour-Melville, *James I*, p. 26.
[8] *Rot. Scot.*, ii. 183, 190, 191, 192, 197.
[9] *E.R.*, iv. lxx–lxxi; *Rot. Scot.*, ii. 178, 187, 196, 197; *Cal. Docs. Scot.*, iv
No. 751.   [10] *Rot. Scot.*, ii. 181–4, 186.
[11] Fraser, *Douglas*, i. 376; iii. 46.   [12] Balfour-Melville, *James I*, pp. 40–1.
[13] *Cal. Docs. Scot.*, iv. Nos. 579–642, *passim*.
[14] Balfour-Melville, *James I*, p. 41.

who was probably responding to public opinion.[15] Moreover the restoration of the Earl of March would serve Albany as a check upon the power of the Earl of Douglas.

Probably in order to win the Tyneman's consent to the Dunbar restoration a bond of alliance was drawn up at Inverkeithing on 20 June 1409 [16] between the governor and Douglas, who swore to keep 'full friendschip and kindnes' the one to the other. A compromise followed : March returned, and on 2 October 1409, in the presence of a gathering of nobles at Haddington, the earl and his eldest son resigned the lordship of Annandale to Albany, who forthwith granted it to the Earl of Douglas with rights of regality.[17] This was the price of the Tyneman's consent to the restoration of March, who received back his earldom but 'not without some dismemberment of his possessions'.[18]

The restoration of the Dunbars coincided with a renewal of Anglo-Scottish warfare. In the winter of 1409 Alexander Stewart, Earl of Mar, captured the *Thomas* of London, freighted with goods belonging to the Richard Whittington of pantomime fame. Probably in retaliation Sir Robert Umfraville raided the Forth and took thirteen ships as prizes.[19] By land, however, the English were less successful : on 7 May 1409 [20] some undistinguished men of Teviotdale (*mediocres Thevidaliae*) set an example to their betters by seizing Jedburgh Castle, which was immediately destroyed on Albany's orders.[21] The renewal of warfare gave the Dunbars a chance to prove their loyalty : Patrick, son of the Earl of March, seized Fast Castle, and sometime in 1410 or 1411 Gavin, another son of the earl, co-operated with the Douglases in breaking the bridge of Roxburgh and burning the town.[22]

Henry IV could not be expected to submit tamely to the ungracious desertion of his Dunbar protégés, the absconding of the captive Douglas, and the provocative warfare that had left the English with only two Scottish strongholds—Roxburgh and Berwick. It was Douglas's conduct that irked Henry most of all. On 4 April 1410 English commissioners were instructed to secure the Tyneman's return 'by all ways possible',[23] and an envoy was sent to Albany to let drop the suggestion that fifty thousand marks would be a suitable

---

[15] See *Chron. Wyntoun*, III. 78–9; *Chron. Bower*, II. 444.
[16] *E.R.*, IV. ccix–ccxii.   [17] *R.M.S.*, I. No. 920.
[18] *Chron. Bower*, II. 444.
[19] Balfour-Melville, *James I*, pp. 43–4.
[20] *Glasgow Registrum*, II. 316.   [21] *Chron. Bower*, II. 444.
[22] *Ibid.*, 444, 447.   [23] *Rot. Scot.*, II. 194.

ransom for his son, Murdoch. On the other hand, if Douglas returned to England as a captive, Murdoch might be released 'for litel or right noght takying for his raunceon'. Douglas wisely made his peace with Henry, apparently by paying a large ransom,[24] but Murdoch was not released, and his father was soon pre-occupied by a crisis in the north.

The growth of the landed power of the multitudinous members of the royal family had occurred north of the Forth, rather than to the south, and in areas that were at least partially, if not predominantly, Gaelic-speaking. Even before the Stewart family became 'royal' its members had obtained the earldoms of Atholl in 1342, Strathearn in 1357 (though it went by marriage to a Graham before 1406) and Menteith c. 1361. Caithness followed c. 1375, Buchan c. 1382, and the MacDougal lordship of Lorne by 1390. Further Stewart expansion was to bring in Mar c. 1405 (not without scandal) and Ross c. 1415 [25] (at the cost of a national crisis).

There were four royal Stewarts who were capable of independent action in the north. One was Walter Stewart, who at the end of his life was to gain lasting notoriety. Meanwhile he made himself useful to those in power and gained the earldoms of Caithness and Atholl. Another was Alexander Stewart, Earl of Buchan and Wolf of Badenoch, who lasted until 1405 or 1406. His illegitimate son, another Alexander Stewart, was a third striking figure who was to win for himself the earldom of Mar in curious circumstances. The earldom had descended to Isabel Douglas who had married Sir Malcolm Drummond, brother of Queen Annabella.[26] In 1402 Sir Malcolm was treacherously captured and held in prison until he 'deit in hard penawns'.[27] Whoever was responsible it was Alexander Stewart who was the beneficiary. To silence malicious tongues a ceremony was carefully stage-managed at Kildrummy on 19 September 1404: Alexander Stewart stood at the gates of the castle and handed the keys and charters to the countess to do with them as she pleased; holding the keys in her hand she chose him for her husband and granted him all her lands.[28] Alexander Stewart, as Earl of Mar and the Garioch, was to be chief government agent in the Highlands until his death in 1435. Even more important, however, was a fourth figure, Albany, whose attention to Highland affairs can be seen in

[24] Balfour-Melville, *James I*, pp. 43, 44, 55; *Rot. Scot.*, II. 205.
[25] For these details see *Scots Peerage* and *H.B.C.*, *passim*.
[26] *Scots Peerage*, V. 586.   [27] *Chron. Wyntoun*, III. 87–8.
[28] *Aberdeen-Banff Illustrations*, IV. 165–73.

his construction of the new castle of Doune to guard the route into the Highlands that passed through his earldom of Menteith. It was he who headed the wholesale stewartisation of the Highlands, reduced the friction that might otherwise have divided the royal Stewarts, and gave coherence to their expansion.

At the opening of the fifteenth century only one Highland magnate remained who was powerful enough to voice discontent at the Stewart encroachments and all that they represented—Albany's nephew Donald, Lord of the Isles. The issue that led to a collision between uncle and nephew arose over the earldom of Ross. When Alexander Leslie, Earl of Ross, died in May 1402 his young daughter, Euphemia, was heiress to the earldom; she was also the granddaughter of Albany, who assumed her wardship. The fate of other Highland earldoms suggested what the outcome was likely to be. On the other hand Donald of the Isles had contingent claims upon the earldom through his wife Margaret, sister of the erstwhile Earl of Ross. It was she who, by the terms of a tailzie of 1370, came next in the succession to the earldom if her niece, Euphemia Leslie, died without heirs or was otherwise disposed of.[29]

Probably to promote his own claim to the wardship of Euphemia, Donald let loose his younger brother, Alastair Carrach, founder of the MacDonalds of Keppoch, whose freebooting activities had been denounced in a council held at Linlithgow in 1399.[30] On 3 July 1402, some two months after the death of Alexander Leslie had opened the question of the succession to Ross, Alastair Carrach led his followers into the cathedral close of Elgin and sacked the houses of the canons; part of the burgh of Elgin was also set on fire. On 6 October 1402 Alastair returned to Elgin 'with a great army' seeking humbly to be absolved.[31] But all this did not bring the Lord of the Isles the wardship of Euphemia and her earldom : by 11 July 1405 it was Albany who was styling himself 'Lord of the ward of Ross'.[32]

Albany had thus won an initial advantage in the Ross affair. The next step in his policy came in 1406 when he conferred the earldom of Buchan upon John Stewart, his second son. According to the traditional MacDonald account, Albany, having brought up the heiress Euphemia in his own household, 'persuaded her by flattery and threats to resign her rights of the earldom of Ross to John . . . Earl of Buchan . . . much against her will. But others were of opinion

[29] See Scots Peerage, VII. 242; A.P.S., I. 537–8.   [30] P. 209 above.
[31] Moray Registrum, pp. 382–3.   [32] Scots Peerage, VII. 242.

she did not resign her rights'.[33] Certainly there is no surviving evidence
that Euphemia made any resignation prior to 1415, nor is there any
evidence that before then Euphemia had become a nun and was
therefore 'civilly dead'.[34] What seems likely is that Donald received
information that some step was about to be taken that would rob his
wife of her qhance of inheriting Ross.

There were other complications in the affair—the relationship
between Donald of the Isles and the captive James I, and the role of
the MacDonalds in international politics. In August 1407 an English
safe-conduct was issued to allow 'Ector Makgillane' (MacLean),
nephew of the Lord of the Isles, to come to the English court 'to have
colloquy with his liege lord the King of Scotland';[35] and in May 1408
English envoys were sent to negotiate peace and friendship between
Henry IV and his subjects and Donald of the Isles, Iain Mor, and
their 'subjects'.[36] There may have been talk of a scheme whereby
Donald and James would obtain conditional English help to oust
Albany and install James in Scotland. It is even possible that James
sanctioned Donald's plans, of which the immediate objective was the
earldom of Ross.

Within the earldom Donald seems to have been welcomed as
true heir;[37] the only resistance came from the Mackays of Sutherland.[38] Having seized the royal burgh of Inverness Donald struck
eastward across the Spey, apparently to win the lands that pertained
to the earldom of Ross in the sheriffdoms of Banff, Aberdeen and
Kincardine. But this aim was not incompatible with wider ambitions;
and it was at least feared that Donald intended to loot the city of
Aberdeen.[39] By 24 July 1411 his host had reached the township of
Harlaw in the Garioch, near Inverurie, less than twenty miles from
Aberdeen. Further advance was contested by Donald's cousin, the
Earl of Mar, who had begun his career as a leader of caterans, but
had latterly reformed his ways. With him Mar had the armed strength
of Mar and the Garioch, Angus and the Mearns, and Buchan, as
well as a troop of burgesses from Aberdeen. By Scottish standards a
full-scale army had been mustered on each side.[40]

Apart from Bower's conventional picture of the one side hurling
itself with wild yells against the levelled spears of the other[41] the only

[33] *Highland Papers*, I. 28.   [34] P. F. Tytler, *History*, I. pt. ii, 39.
[35] *Cal. Patent 1405–8*, p. 363.   [36] *Foedera*, IV. pt. i, 131.
[37] Boece, *History*, p. 341 v.
[38] *History of the Earldom of Sutherland*, cited in *Scots Peerage*, VII. 159.
[39] *Chron. Bower*, II. 444–5.
[40] *Ibid.*, 444–5, 500.   [41] *Ibid.*, 445.

account of the course of the ensuing battle is the MacDonald one. According to this [42] the left wing of Mar's troops under Sir Alexander Ogilvy was routed by MacLean; the central battalion under Mar was forced to give ground and was 'quite defeated'; Mar's right wing was forced back until it took refuge in a great cattle-fold, from which its residue emerged after the battle was over to take what plunder it could while Donald's troops were pursuing Mar on the way to Aberdeen.[43]

Thus, according to MacDonald tradition, it was Donald who was the victor. Abbot Bower, on the other hand, representing Lowland tradition, had no doubt that it was Mar who was victorious. But even on Bower's own showing it is clear that if Mar was the victor his victory was a Pyrrhic one.[44] Both Boece and Buchanan, writing long after the battle, somewhat cynically asserted that each side thought it had been defeated by the other.[45] John Major, more of an historian than the others, judiciously remarked:

> Though it be more generally said amongst the common people that the Wild Scots were defeated, I find the very opposite of this in the chroniclers; only the Earl [sic] of the Isles was forced to retreat; and he counted amongst his men more of slain than did the civilised Scots. Yet these men did not put Donald to open rout, though they fiercely strove, and not without success, to put a check to the audaciousness of the man.[46]

The check that Donald had received was made all the sharper by the unusually vigorous intervention of Albany. While Donald withdrew to the Isles the governor recovered Dingwall Castle in the autumn of 1411 and installed a garrison.[47] In the summer of 1412, Albany raised three armies. Although there is no account of their activities the result seems to have been the submission of Donald. He met the governor at Polgylbe, the modern Lochgilphead, handed over hostages, and took an oath to keep the peace.[48]

Despite Donald's submission there were fresh hostilities,[49] perhaps as a result of another move concerning the succession to Ross: on 12 June 1415, Euphemia was persuaded to resign her earldom, after which she appears to have entered a nunnery. By 24 May 1417 Albany's son was styling himself Earl of Buchan and Ross.[50] Whether

[42] *Highland Papers*, I. 30.   [43] *Ibid.*
[44] *Chron. Bower*, II. 445.
[45] Boece, *History*, p. 341 v.; Buchanan, *History*, II. 79.
[46] Major, *History*, p. 348.   [47] *Chron. Bower*, II. 445.
[48] *Ibid.*; *E.R.*, IV. 213.   [49] *E.R.*, IV. 265.
[50] *Scots Peerage*, VII. 242–3; *Aberdeen-Banff Illustrations*, IV. 383.

he obtained possession of Ross is another matter : Donald showed no hesitation in publicising himself as 'Lord of the foresaid Isles and of the earldom of Ross'.[51] Thus so far as the earldom was concerned the battle of Harlaw seems to have led to no definite settlement. Nor did the battle change the independent international position of the Lord of the Isles : in an Anglo-French truce arranged in 1416 by Sigismund, King of the Romans, the Lord of the Isles achieved the distinction of being named as an ally both of the English and of the French.[52]

What, then, was the significance of Harlaw? One historian regards the episode as 'really a family squabble, all the parties being related by blood or marriage'.[53] The same might be said of the Hundred Years War. Any attempt to play down the importance of the battle or to account for it on somewhat trivial grounds runs completely counter to the views held in Scotland in the fifteenth and sixteenth centuries. Harlaw was momentous because it was seen as a battle between Highlands and Lowlands. There were doubtless Highlanders who fought for Mar ; and Sir Alexander Seton—the 'Huntly' of the MacDonald account—was apparently on good terms with Donald of the Isles. But despite some blurring of the lines of demarcation each side was taken to represent one of the two cultural halves of Scotland. It was this division that one historian had in mind when he maintained that 'the battle of Harlaw (1411) ranks with the battle of Carham (1018) in its determining influence on the development of the Scottish nation . . . never since that day has Teutonic Scotland been in real danger from the Celtic race to whom it owed its being'.[54] This statement certainly requires modification : the division in Scotland was cultural rather than racial; nor was there any real danger that a decisive victory for Donald at Harlaw would have resulted in a political and cultural transformation of the whole of Scotland. Even the fearful Bower did not contemplate any such drastic revolution and thought merely that Donald intended 'to bring under his subjection the land as far as the Tay'.[55]

This was certainly a possibility : in Ireland the Gaelic resurgence of the fourteenth and fifteenth centuries drastically reduced the area of English speech subject to the Dublin administration ;[56] a decisive

[51] *Highland Papers*, IV. 166, 169.
[52] *Foedera*, IV. pt. ii, 179; *Cal. Docs. Scot.*, IV. No. 876.
[53] Mackenzie, *Highlands and Islands*, p. 94.
[54] P. Hume Brown, *History*, I. 167.   [55] *Chron. Bower*, II. 444-5.
[56] See J. F. Lydon, 'The Problem of the Frontier in Medieval Ireland', *Topic: A Journal of the Liberal Arts*, No. 13, pp. 5-22.

victory for Donald might similarly have narrowed the cultural and political bounds of Lowland Scotland and might, in so doing, have brought other far-reaching consequences in its wake. As it was, the indecisive result at Harlaw brought no drastic change. The battle showed that the forces of the two sides were, for the time being, too finely balanced for the one to prevail against the other. But the battle also raised to a higher pitch the antagonism between Lowlander and Highlander. The time for tolerance or easy assimilation had disappeared, but the time for a wholesale attack upon Gaelic culture and upon the separatist political tendencies of Gaeldom had not yet arrived.

Harlaw was only one demonstration of the disorder that affected most aspects of Scottish life during the Albany era. The Scottish kirk was in a peculiarly vulnerable position, victim not only of Scotland's internal troubles but of the external troubles of a divided papacy. Urban VI, the Roman pope, had at least retrospectively earned his 'deposition' by his subsequent conduct : he had tortured and murdered five of his own cardinals. Nonetheless on his death in 1389 another Italian was elected to perpetuate the Roman succession. At Avignon Clement VII had revived the less respectable features of the 'Babylonish Captivity'. His successor, Pedro de Luna, an Aragonese who ruled as Benedict XIII,[57] might in happier times have done much for the church ; as it was, his pontificate was a perpetual struggle, and the irregularities that had arisen during the early years of the schism were condoned rather than reprimanded.[58]

A glimpse of current conditions is given by a number of statutes passed by the synod of St Andrews c. 1400.[59] These diocesan statutes included enactments that holders of benefices should put away their concubines ; priests were not to carry long knives or celebrate several masses a day for the sake of remuneration ; dances, wrestling matches and other sports were not to take place in kirk yards ; consistories were to be held each year in the two archdeaconries of the diocese to instruct priests in the administration of the sacraments and the cure of souls ; and spiritual sanctions were to be used wholesale against a wide range of miscreants. These measures are evidence not only of irregularities but of an attempt at remedy, probably led by Walter Trail, a man of distinguished academic and ecclesiastical background

[57] John Holland Smith, *The Great Schism*, pp. 151–4.
[58] See *Cal. Papal Petitions*, I. 598, 605, 609, 610, 617.
[59] Robertson, *Concilia*, II. 64–73 ; Patrick, *Statutes*, pp. 68–77.

who had been provided to the bishopric of St Andrews by Clement VII in 1385.[60] Soon afterwards there were at least three meetings of the provincial council of the Scottish kirk.[61]

At the provincial council of 1388 Trail presided as conservator and upheld an appeal against an appointment made by the Bishop of Moray. It was symptomatic of the growth of secular influence over the kirk, partly as a consequence of the schism, that the Scone parliament of March 1391 reversed Trail's decision, ostensibly at the request of the clergy represented in parliament.[62] The same parliament confirmed a mortmain act forbidding the granting of property to the kirk without royal licence.[63] And when the three estates, in an act of February 1401, upheld the authority of the ecclesiastical courts, they simultaneously restricted appeals from Scotland to the *curia* : appeals against excommunication could be made to the conservator and his council, and could be taken a further stage to the provincial council 'where such matters are to be discussed so long as the schism lasts'.[64] Pragmatic as always, the three estates formulated no theory to justify this tacit denial of appeal to the papal court, but their action was a sign of secular interference in ecclesiastical matters that was to become increasingly obvious in the fifteenth century.[65]

A few months later the death of Bishop Trail left the bishopric of St Andrews vacant and thereby gave occasion for an outbreak of the unruliness typical of the period. The protagonist in this case was Master Walter Danielston, parson of Kincardine O'Neil, licentiate in arts and former student of civil law at Avignon.[66] He had already shown his talents when Sir Robert Danielston, keeper of Dumbarton Castle, had died in 1397.[67] The custody of Dumbarton, long held by the Danielstons,[68] was doubtless coveted by one or other of the royal Stewarts. Master Walter had no intention that it should slip from the grip of his own family and seized the castle,[69] where he behaved as a robber baron. Meanwhile, Archdeacon Thomas Stewart, illegitimate son of Robert II and protégé of Albany, had been elected Bishop of St Andrews but languished unconfirmed by the papacy.[70] Danielston therefore offered to exchange his castle for the bishopric. Albany met his brother Thomas at Abernethy, persuaded him to

60 Robertson, *Concilia*, II. 64–73; Dowden, *Bishops*, p. 27.
61 Robertson, *Concilia*, I. lxxvii.   62 *Ibid.*, I. lii; *A.P.S.*, I. 578.
63 *A.P.S.*, I. 577.   64 *Ibid.*, 576.
65 See, e.g. *Nat. MSS. Scot.*, II. No. lxv.
66 Dowden, *Bishops*, p. 29.   67 *E.R.*, III. 425.
68 *Ibid.*, II. 79, 80, 82.   69 *Chron. Wyntoun*, III. 76.
70 Dowden, *Bishops*, p. 29.

relinquish his claim, and in the summer of 1402 persuaded the St Andrews chapter to elect Danielston, who forthwith began to exercise episcopal authority. Probably to everyone's relief he died at Christmas.[71] Benedict XIII then provided Henry Wardlaw, chantor of Glasgow, doctor of canon law and nephew of the late Cardinal Wardlaw. The new bishop was to bring some stability by guiding the affairs of his bishopric for a further thirty-seven years.[72]

One of the problems that faced him was heresy. From the schism those of a conservative cast of mind had drawn the conclusion that the papal authority was the essence of the unity of Christendom and that an attack upon that authority was an attack upon the unity of the faith. Those less committed to tradition regarded the existing papacy as an obstacle in the way of unity. Others, such as John Wyclif in England, went further and not only attacked the papacy but 'denied current beliefs and challenged church authorities without setting forth adequate substitutes'.[73] In England Wyclif's followers, opprobriously termed 'Lollards', had been driven underground but survived until the eve of Henry VIII's breach with Rome.[74] Enough Lollard influence was felt in Scotland to alarm the lay and ecclesiastical authorities : in 1399, when Rothesay was appointed lieutenant, his oath of office pledged him to restrain heretics.[75] His successor, Albany, was singled out for praise as a defender of orthodoxy :

> He wes a constant Catholike;
> All Lollard he hatyt and heretyke.[76]

One Lollard, an English priest named James Resby, won renown by preaching in Scotland to the simple folk, but 'interspersed most dangerous conclusions in his teaching of dogma'.[77] According to Abbot Bower, Resby denied the efficacy of confession and the sacrament of penance. Perhaps more important, he held that the pope was not actually vicar of Christ and that no one could be the real pope or vicar of Christ unless he were holy. And Resby—so Bower believed—maintained forty conclusions, similar or even worse, which he had extracted from the heresies of the arch-heretic Wyclif. Such heretics, claimed Bower, were like Gog and Magog, worship-

---

[71] *Chron. Wyntoun*, III. 83-4; Watt, *Fasti*, p. 294.
[72] *Chron. Wyntoun*, III. 84-5; Dowden, *Bishops*, pp. 30-31.
[73] A. R. MacEwen, *History of the Church in Scotland*, I. 330.
[74] ·J. A. F. Thomson, *The Later Lollards* (1965), *passim*.
[75] *A.P.S.*, I. 573.   [76] *Chron. Wyntoun*, II. 100.
[77] *Chron. Bower*, II. 442; T. M. A. Macnab, 'The Beginnings of Lollardy in Scotland', *Scot. Church Hist. Soc. Recs.*, XI. 254-60.

pers of Antichrist, or like dragons that could fly, crawl and swim, for 'What is more heretical than to say that the actual pope is not the vicar of Christ?'[78] In 1406 or 1407 Master Laurence of Lindores, inquisitor of heretical pravity, presided over a council of the clergy which condemned Resby as a heretic. In the first known example of religious persecution in Scotland both he and his writings were reduced to ashes at Perth.[79]

It is perhaps no mere coincidence that Resby was an Englishman and that the next known exponent of radical religious views in Scotland was a certain Quintin Folkhyrde, or Folkard (Flockhart), a Scottish esquire not unknown at the English court. In August 1407 he obtained an English safe-conduct for some trip to London, whence he was to report back to Henry IV; in September he obtained another safe-conduct for a brief visit to Scotland.[80] It may be inferred that for political reasons Henry IV, like Henry VIII, was not averse to exporting religious dissent to Scotland. Folkhyrde was probably also instrumental in attracting to Scotland the interest of the Hussites of Bohemia,[81] later to be shown in the mission of Paul Crawar,[82] for it was to Prague that Folkhyrde addressed his 'News from Scotland' in 1410.

His news was embodied in four letters.[83] In the first he addressed all Christendom; the second was addressed to the Bishop of Glasgow (William Lauder) and his accomplices, and all the clergy of Scotland; the third was addressed to the secular lords and commons; and the fourth was addressed to everybody. That Folkhyrde was a zealot is obvious. The features of his seal of office, which he painstakingly described, suggest that he was a self-appointed reformer: he explained that his own surname meant herdsman of the people (*pastor populi*) and that in fear of eternal damnation and for remission of his sins he had to obey the call to denounce the evils of the clergy by 'riding through the countryside and openly publicising in the mother tongue the contents of the following letters'.[84] This mission was necessary since the temporal lords (and in his capacity as esquire he reckoned himself among them) had failed to do their duty as one of

---

[78] *Chron. Bower*, II. 442–3.
[79] *Ibid.*, 441–2. Duncan Shaw, in 'Laurence of Lindores', *Scot. Church Hist. Soc. Recs.*, XII. 47–62, suggests (pp. 57–60) that it was Laurence who shaped inquisitorial procedure in Scotland.   [80] *Cal. Patent 1405–8*, p. 362.
[81] T. M. A. Macnab, 'Bohemia and the Scottish Lollards', *Scot. Church Hist. Soc. Recs.*, V. 10–22.   [82] P. 300 below.
[83] Texts in *St Andrews Copiale*, pp. 230–6.   [84] *Ibid.*, p. 230.

the three estates in the Christian commonwealth. The contents of the letters are in disappointingly general terms: the luxury and other shortcomings of the clergy are condemned; the teaching of the faith in the vernacular is urged; so also is the obligation of clerics to sustain the poor; questions of doctrine are left untouched. The overall tone is denunciatory rather than constructively reformative.

Although nothing more is heard of Folkhyrde the existence of a Wycliffite movement in Scotland attracted attention on the continent.[85] Heresy certainly provided one motive for Bishop Wardlaw's decision to found Scotland's first university: in a charter of 28 February 1411, addressed to the doctors, masters, bachelors and scholars of St Andrews, the bishop drew attention to the benefits of higher education 'by which the catholic faith, by an impregnable wall of doctors and masters . . . is enabled to withstand heresies and errors';[86] a graduation oath formulated at St Andrews in 1417 made the graduands swear to 'defend the kirk against the attack of Lollards'.[87]

The setting up of the university was more than a reaction against heresy. For more than two hundred years Scots had sought a university education, not least on account of the material rewards to which it led: towards the end of the fourteenth century Clement VII evidently found it necessary to lay down a tariff of maximum incomes (by no means stingy) for four categories of graduates; and 'at a time when ordained vicarages were still valued as low as £10 or less, the top Doctors of Theology or Law in Scotland nearly all accumulated benefices to valued totals of between £100 and £300, and the intermediate grades did for the most part attain to proportionate incomes'.[88] Nearly all the Scottish bishops were graduates, 'more than can be said of contemporary England, where the proportion was more like two-thirds'. Graduates were also common in the archdeaconries and canonries, though less so in the parishes,[89] and 'in some cases at least it appears that once a benefice was put into the hands of an ambitious university man, he would as soon as possible arrange for a curate and it would be all too likely that the parishioners (if there were any involved) would see very little of the incumbent, whose learning was not for them'.[90] Analysis of the careers of the 400 Scots who are known to have graduated in the period 1340–1410 shows that no less than half had obtained degrees in law. Hence 'it is

[85] J. A. F. Thomson, *The Later Lollards*, pp. 202–3; W. Stanford Reid, 'The Lollards in Pre-Reformation Scotland', *Church History*, XI. 3–17, at 6.
[86] *Nat. MSS. Scot.*, II. No. lxiii.   [87] *St Andrews Acta*, I. 11–12.
[88] D. E. R. Watt, *op. cit.*, *Scot. Church Hist. Soc. Recs.*, XV. 77–88, at 84.
[89] *Ibid.*, pp. 79–83.   [90] *Ibid.*, pp. 85–6.

reasonable to conclude that a very high proportion of the 400 were not primarily concerned with preparing themselves to be fit clergy to occupy benefices with cure of souls, but were rather men with careers to make, who sought professional qualifications and then looked for ecclesiastical preferment as a basis for professional advancement'.

Of the 400 there were 230 who studied at Paris, 55 at Orleans, 34 at Avignon; and 90 had been granted English safe-conducts to study at Oxford or Cambridge, but 'it is a strange mystery that only 11 of these can be shown to have done so'.[91] Bishop Wardlaw's own academic career was typical: he had graduated in arts at Paris, studied civil law at Orleans and had studied also at the papal university at Avignon; and the eight teachers who first began to give university lectures at St Andrews had all gone to French universities, as had the prior and archdeacon of St Andrews.[92] Paris was pre-eminent for its teaching and theology and philosophy; and in Orleans, 'the one great and famous law school of northern Europe',[93] the Scots had had a 'nation' (student association) of their own since 1336. In 1411 the records of the Scottish nation at Orleans alluded to the current instability[94]—possibly an indication of difficulties caused by the schism. From 1378 onwards Scottish students were liable to be treated as schismatics in England and other countries (ultimately including France) and ran the danger of having their degrees withheld.[95] The time was propitious for the foundation of a Scottish university, and it was natural, rather than exceptional, that Scotland should share in the remarkable expansion of university education that was about to take place throughout Europe.[96]

The first university lectures were delivered in St Andrews after Whitsunday 1410,[97] but as yet there was no properly constituted university. A university, or, in current phrase, a *studium generale*, could be founded only by pope or emperor; and only a *studium generale* could confer a master's licence—the *ius ubique docendi*.[98] But Bishop Wardlaw (perhaps relying on his position as papal legate) issued a charter of 28 February 1411 to the scholars of St Andrews and referred to 'your university, instituted and founded in fact by us,

[91] *Ibid.*, pp. 78–9.
[92] See J. Maitland Anderson, 'The Beginnings of St Andrews University, 1410–1418', *S.H.R.*, VIII. 225–48 and 333–60.
[93] John Kirkpatrick, *op. cit., S.H.S. Misc. II.* 47–102, at 51.
[94] *Ibid.*, 74.   [95] J. Maitland Anderson, *op. cit.*, 349.
[96] See Rashdall, *Universities*. The Scottish universities are dealt with in II. 301–24.
[97] *Chron. Bower*, II. 445.   [98] Rashdall, *Universities*, I. 8–11.

saving, however, the authority of the apostolic see'.[99] As superior of the city, and lord of the regality of St Andrews, Wardlaw conferred upon all members of the university various fiscal and judicial immunities.[100] His charter, drawn up in the form of a notarial instrument, was sent to Benedict XIII with a petition for its confirmation. The application was supported not only by the three estates but by the captive James I,[101] who probably welcomed any chance of keeping in touch with Scottish affairs. In a bull issued at Peñíscola on 28 August 1413 Benedict duly agreed 'to add the strength of apostolic confirmation' to Wardlaw's foundation.[102]

On 3 February 1414 Master Henry Ogilvy arrived in St Andrews with the papal bull, to be welcomed, so says Bower, by four hundred clerics and novices. The next day the document was publicly read. Then there was a solemn procession to the high altar of the cathedral and a chanting of the *Te Deum*. The Bishop of Ross preached a sermon. At night bonfires were kindled in the streets and there was much indulgence in wine. A few days later the celebrations began afresh. There was a procession through the city. The clergy chanted and the populace danced while bells and organs pealed out. And the bishop of Ross preached another sermon.[103]

The university that so acclaimed Benedict XIII's generosity was soon to bite the hand that fed it. The foundation of St Andrews had come just in time for it to play its part alongside the other European universities in the ending of the Great Schism and in debating the issues soon to be raised by the conciliar movement, for the universities were at the height of their influence in the ecclesiastical politics that had become international politics thanks to the schism. Paris, under its chancellor, Jean Gerson, was particularly influential and had persuaded the French in 1398 to withdraw their obedience from Benedict XIII in a vain attempt to force him to accept 'the way of cession'. The French example was not followed and in 1403 France once more acknowledged Benedict as true pope.[104] The university of Paris had also debated 'the way of council', and was behind a further move in 1409 when a general council of the church met at Pisa. This deposed both the Roman and Avignonese popes (who paid no heed) and elected a 'Pisan' pope. Then there were three popes. An advocate

99 *Nat. MSS. Scot.*, II. No. lxiii.
100 For university courts see *Scot. Legal Hist.*, pp. 405–7.
101 Balfour-Melville, *James I*, p. 54.
102 *Nat. MSS. Scot.*, II. No. lxiii.   103 *Chron. Bower*, II. 446.
104 John Holland Smith, *The Great Schism*, pp. 160–3.

of 'the way of council' ruefully remarked that 'the infamous duality had spawned an accused [accursed?] trinity'.[105] The council of Pisa also caused an international re-alignment: the Roman pope was recognised only by some Italian states; France, which in 1407 had finally withdrawn obedience from Benedict XIII, joined England and the Empire in recognising the Pisan pope; Scotland, together with the Spanish kingdoms, continued to recognise Benedict XIII, who by this time was established in the fortified town of Peñíscola on the coast of Aragon.[106] Scotland showed a touching loyalty to Benedict XIII, even at the cost of falling out of step with its ally, and Benedict was grateful. In 1414 he kindly granted, as a contribution to the prospective ransom of James I and Albany's son Murdoch, half the money due to the papacy from vacant Scottish benefices in the following five years. Benedict was moved to this gesture 'since that realm blessed by God [Scotland] has always persisted in obedience and devotion to us and the Roman church and at no time, as we believe, will depart from them'.[107] Benedict's benign attitude is typified in the preamble to a mandate that he sent from Perpignan on 5 September 1415: 'The pope is very favourable to the just desires of petitioners and treats them with due favours.'[108]

Undeterred by the fiasco at Pisa, the university of Paris co-operated with Sigismund, King of the Romans, in assembling another general council that opened at Konstanz (or Constance) on 1 November 1414 and 'continued felicitously for four years'.[109] Most of western Christendom sent official representatives, who followed university practice by acting and voting as 'nations'. In May 1415 the council deposed the Pisan pope; in July the Roman pope was persuaded to abdicate; eventually Castile, Navarre, Portugal, and even Aragon, adhered to the council.[110] In the past the drawback to the 'way of council' had been the accepted view that only a true pope could summon a general council of the church.[111] Moreover the rival colleges of cardinals, not unwilling to convert the authoritarian papal monarchy into an oligarchy under their own direction, had not been elated at the prospect of their supersession by a more representative body. Only the universal feeling that the schism had to be ended by

[105] Ibid., p. 179.
[106] Ibid., p. 171; A. Francis Steuart, 'Scotland and the Papacy during the Great Schism', S.H.R., IV. 144–58, at 148–51.
[107] St Andrews Copiale, pp. 241–2.
[108] Wigtown Charters, No. 4; see also No. 3.   [109] Chron. Bower, II. 448.
[110] John Holland Smith, The Great Schism, pp. 191, 202–5, 208, 210–1.
[111] Walter Ullmann, The Origins of the Great Schism, pp. 57–8 and passim.

fair means or foul overcame the objections, legal or otherwise, to a general council; and the pent-up agitation of the conciliarists was by this time bound to find vent not only in a quest for a united papacy but in efforts to re-model the organisation of the church.

Although Scotland stayed aloof from the council a number of Scots, particularly those studying at Paris, had become incorporated at Constance, and the council sent Finlay of Albany, warden of the Dominicans of Ayr, on a mission to secure the adherence of Scotland.[112] When the Duke of Albany's lukewarm excuses were reported at Constance on 4 January 1417, an English doctor seems to have contrasted his behaviour with that of James I. In 1414 the university of Paris had sent to the captive king an *Epistola Consolatoria*—a letter assuring him of the university's sympathy and seeking his aid in ending Scotland's allegiance to Benedict XIII. James rightly judged that the council would succeed : Thomas Morow, Abbot of Paisley, and Thomas Myrton, canon of Brechin, probably acted at Constance as his personal representatives;[113] in ecclesiastical politics, as in other fields, James was trying to win whatever influence would facilitate his return to Scotland. When the council of Constance deposed Benedict XIII on 26 July 1417 Albany's position was an awkward one.

The council was now ready to elect a pope assured of recognition throughout all western Christendom save Scotland, the county of Armagnac, and Peñíscola. At this point difficulties arose. The council had been summoned to deal not only with the *causa unionis* (the restoration of unity) but with the *causa reformationis* (the reform of abuses). While the more radical conciliarists urged that reforms should be passed before a new pope was elected, the more conservative took the opposite view. As a compromise some moderate reforms were passed. Then on 11 November 1417 Odo Colonna was elected and styled himself Martin V.[114] A number of Scots, including James I, Archibald the Tyneman, and James Haldenstone, Prior of St Andrews, lost no time in professing obedience to Martin and asking him for favours.[115]

While Scotland wavered, it was the faculty of arts of St Andrews that seized the initiative : on 9 August 1418 it resolved that obedience should be withdrawn from Pedro de Luna 'once called Benedict'. It

---

[112] Balfour-Melville, *James I*, pp. 69, 70–1, 121–2.
[113] J. Maitland Anderson, *op. cit., S.H.R.*, VIII. 333–60, at 349–51. The Abbot of Paisley became a staunch conciliarist (John Holland Smith, *The Great Schism*, p. 229).
[114] John Holland Smith, *The Great Schism*, pp. 212–6.
[115] Balfour-Melville, *James I*, pp. 72–4; *Cal. Scot. Supp. 1418–22*, pp. 3–14.

was agreed to announce this 'in the face of the council before the governor and the three estates of the realm . . . and in case the governor does not wish to withdraw, but wishes to persevere in the obedience of Pedro de Luna . . . then the faculty will solemnise withdrawal'.[116] Albany was not willing to give in without a struggle. He produced a spokesman—none other than an English Franciscan, Robert Harding, master of theology. After an exchange of invective 'the whole university of St Andrews rose up against him'.[117]

When the general council of the three estates met at Perth in October 1418, it was called upon to make its choice between the rival popes. Harding, upheld by the governor, presented his case *per naturas, figuras, scripturas, puncturas et alia exempla* 'which to narrate in order would engender tedium in the reader'. His illustrations included a parable involving one tree, fourteen large elephants and one small elephant. The first large elephant represented the universal church, which had fallen while leaning against the tree of papal jurisdiction. One huge elephant (Sigismund, King of the Romans) had in vain tried to uplift the fallen beast. Equally unsuccessful were another twelve large elephants (other Christian kings and princes). Then came a small elephant (the Scottish kirk) which placed itself underneath the fallen beast and so put it on its feet again. The object of this parable was to show that the council of Constance could not reunite Christendom and that only the Scottish kirk was entitled to do so.[118]

The members of St Andrews University, headed by their rector, had turned up in full force to refute Harding : his propositions contained 'scandalous and seditious conclusions, most suspect of heresy, nutritive of schisms and non-inducive of the unity of holy mother kirk'.[119] Albany resigned himself to the inevitable and sent procurators to Martin V to render him the obedience of Scotland.[120] The Great Schism was over.

The closing years of the Great Schism had coincided with new turmoils in the relationships linking England, France, Scotland and Burgundy. In these the captive Scottish king became involved and played a dubious role in the hope of purchasing his liberation. At first it had seemed to him that this could be achieved if only his uncle stirred himself. On 30 January 1412, at the age of seventeen, he wrote

[116] *St Andrews Acta*, I. 12–3.   [117] *Chron. Bower*, II. 449.
[118] *Ibid.*, 450.   [119] *Ibid.*
[120] Balfour-Melville, *James I*, p. 75.

to Albany complaining that the duke had done nothing and had even neglected to answer the letters that James had sent him in the previous year; James called upon him to work for his release 'so dowly that in yhour defaut we be nouch send to sek remede of our deliverans other qware in tyme to cum'.[121] Another four letters of the same date were addressed to a total of eighteen influential Scots in whom James reposed 'speciale traste'; he affirmed that 'the delay of our hamecome standis alanely in thaim that sowlde persue for us'[122] (presumably Albany and his faction). James's intention was to build up a party of his own to force his uncle's hand. On 3 November 1412, when Sir William Douglas of Drumlanrig visited James at Croydon, the king issued a charter in his favour 'wrate with our propre hande'; this display of James's fine penmanship[123] was to be 'selit with our grete sele in tyme to come'. On 1 December 1412 Henry issued safeconducts for 'ambassadors appointed by the general council of Scotland'.[124] Just as the release of James seemed close at hand, negotiations were broken by the death of Henry IV on 20 March 1413.[125]

The situation that faced Henry V when he succeeded his father was one of widespread discontent and lawlessness, much of it springing directly or indirectly from the deposition of Richard II.[126] In August 1414 disaffected Lollards posted bills in London affirming that Richard II was still alive in Edinburgh; and in the following year the Lollards were supposed to have offered money to the Scots if they would conduct the Mammet to England.[127] In one way or another Scotland could add to Henry's domestic difficulties. At his accession the captive Scottish king and Albany's son had been sent to the Tower to be kept securely.[128] It seemed that Henry V might ease his domestic troubles by reviving the Scottish claims of the first three Edwards. Instead he contented himself with showing coldness towards the Scots. His ambitions lay in France.

France was at this time in the midst of civil strife. Since 1392 Charles VI had been stricken with fits of insanity and became a pawn in the hands of rival princes of the blood royal,[129] in whose service

---

[121] *Ibid.*, p. 49.   [122] *Ibid.*
[123] Facsimile in *Nat. MSS. Scot.*, II. No. lxii.
[124] *Rot. Scot.*, II. 202.   [125] Balfour-Melville, *James I*, p. 52.
[126] E. F. Jacob, *The Fifteenth Century*, pp. 127–30.
[127] J. A. F. Thomson, *The Later Lollards*, pp. 10, 13, 16. A connection between English Lollards and Scottish nobles bent upon the release of James I is traced by W. Stanford Reid, *op. cit.*, *Church History*, XI. 3–17, at 6–8.
[128] *Cal. Docs. Scot.*, IV. Nos. 837, 838, 839.
[129] E. F. Jacob, *The Fifteenth Century*, pp. 111, 139.

some chivalrous Scots enlisted. In January 1402 David Lindsay, first Earl of Crawford and admiral of Scotland, entered the service of the Duke of Orleans,[130] who 'had specyall affectiowne all tyme to Scottis natyown'.[131] In 1408 Alexander Stewart, Earl of Mar, commanded the vanguard of the army of the Duke of Burgundy when it quelled a revolt of the citizens of Liége. As prophecy had predicted, Mar won the field and by 'gret renown thare honouryt all his natiown'.[132] In the previous year the Duke of Burgundy had confirmed the privileges that Scots traders already enjoyed in his dominions in the Low Countries and allowed them to have local commissioners to look after their interests.[133] Thus commerce, as well as a chivalric connection, was an inducement to the Scots to keep on good terms with Burgundy. In April 1413 Archibald the Tyneman made a treaty in his own name with the duke. Douglas and Henry Sinclair, Earl of Orkney, seem to have spent some months in Burgundian service.[134] By this time, however, the houses of Burgundy and Orleans were engaged in deadly feud : in 1407 the Duke of Orleans had been murdered by John the Fearless, Duke of Burgundy. The Count of Armagnac headed a faction bent upon avenging the assassination, and both parties were willing to pay a price for English aid. A new dimension was given to French troubles when Henry V claimed the crown of France as heir of Edward III.[135]

In an attempt to buy Scottish neutrality he allowed negotiations for a new truce and for the ransom of Albany's son.[136] Shortly before mid-summer 1415, as Murdoch was being conveyed northward to freedom, he was 'feloniously abducted' in Yorkshire by Lollard plotters. Although he was soon recaptured the arrangement for his ransom fell through.[137] In July 1415 the Scots broke a six-year truce concluded in 1412 and began raiding on the Borders.[138] Meanwhile, on 11 August Henry set sail from Southampton with some nine thousand troops and landed in Normandy.[139] On 25 October, he vanquished a vastly superior French army at what the Scottish chronicler Bower called 'the unhappy battle of Agincourt'.[140]

[130] *Scots Peerage*, III. 16. [131] *Chron. Wyntoun*, III. 55–7.
[132] *Ibid.*, 104–16, at 115.
[133] Grant, *Social and Economic Development*, p. 330.
[134] Balfour-Melville, *James I*, pp. 51, 57; *St Andrews Copiale*, p. 238.
[135] E. F. Jacob, *The Fifteenth Century*, pp. 111, 136–42.
[136] *Rot. Scot.*, II. 213, 214.
[137] Balfour-Melville, *James I*, pp. 61–3; E. F. Jacob, *The Fifteenth Century*, p. 146. [138] Balfour-Melville, *James I*, p. 63.
[139] E. F. Jacob, *The Fifteenth Century*, pp. 148–9.
[140] *Chron. Bower*, II. 447.

Henry's return to England was followed by fresh negotiations with the Scots. On 28 February 1416 Murdoch was released for a ransom of £10,000 and in exchange for Hotspur's son, who was restored to the earldom of Northumberland. By 1417 Murdoch had been appointed lieutenant under his father and in this capacity was brought into the work of government.[141] His release did nothing to improve Anglo-Scottish relations. In the eyes of the Scots Henry V was no hero king but 'ingenious in evil, as is clear in all his warlike deeds in France and Normandy'.[142] When Henry once more embarked for France on 23 July 1417 [143] the Scots were ready to cause another diversion on the Borders. Archibald the Tyneman unsuccessfully besieged Roxburgh; Albany equally unsuccessfully besieged Berwick and 'returned home with dishonour'—it was the Scots themselves who styled this fruitless intervention 'the Foul Raid',[144] and it led to retaliation and further Border skirmishes. In 1420 some refugees from this wholly indecisive warfare sought safety in the priory kirk of Coldingham; the prior, William Drax, a monk of Durham, showed his English leanings by bringing cartloads of broom and timber so that the kirk might be set alight.[145] There were also the usual incidents at sea : as late as 1421 the canons of Inchcolm were deserting their island monastery in the summer for fear of English raids and returned only for the winter when naval activity had ceased.[146]

Such warfare brought no gains to the Scots and did little to distract English attention or resources from the war in France, where Burgundians and Armagnacs were too divided by their own quarrels to organise effective resistance. In 1418 the Burgundians proclaimed Queen Isabeau as regent while the Dauphin Charles, only surviving son of Charles VI, was recognised as regent by the Armagnacs. The hard-pressed dauphin sent ambassadors to Scotland [147] to seek aid, whereupon the three estates decided to send an expeditionary force, apparently equipped at French expense.[148] The troops were to be commanded by Albany's second son, John Stewart, Earl of Buchan and chamberlain of Scotland. Associated with him was his brother-in-

---

[141] Balfour-Melville, *James I*, pp. 65–6.
[142] *Chron. Bower*, II. 452, 453.
[143] E. F. Jacob, *The Fifteenth Century*, p. 171.
[144] *Chron. Bower*, II. 449 (mistakenly dated in 1416); *Cal. Docs. Scot.*, IV. No. 879.
[145] *Chron. Bower*, II. 459–60; *Nat. MSS. Scot.*, II. No. lxv.
[146] *Chron. Bower*, II. 467.
[147] E. F. Jacob, *The Fifteenth Century*, pp. 176–7.
[148] *Chron. Bower*, II. 458–9; *Chron. Pluscarden*, I. 353.

E.H.S.—9*

law, Archibald Douglas, the Tyneman's son and heir, who was given, or simply assumed, the title of Earl of Wigtown.[149] Since the aim of the Scots was to reconcile the French factions they may have pressed for a united front against the English. On 11 July 1419 an alliance was made between the dauphin and the Duke of Burgundy.[150] Already the dauphinists had made arrangements for forty Castilian vessels to transport the Scottish expeditionary force. Its numbers can hardly have amounted to the seven thousand troops mentioned by Bower,[151] but it was large enough to alter the situation in France when it disembarked at La Rochelle before the end of October 1419.[152]

The Scots had probably set sail before they heard of the disaster that was to give the English an easy predominance in France: on 10 September 1419 the Duke of Burgundy met his supposed ally the dauphin for an interview on the bridge of Montereau, and was assassinated by one of the dauphin's Armagnac followers.[153] This crime re-opened the old feud and threw the Burgundians into the arms of the English: on Christmas Day 1419 the son and heir of the murdered duke made an alliance with Henry V. King Charles and Queen Isabeau concurred: at Troyes on 21 May 1420 they concluded a great and final peace with England. Queen Isabeau let it be understood that she was an adulteress, that her son the dauphin was illegitimate, and that her daughter Catherine was therefore true heiress. On 2 June 1420 Henry married Catherine in the cathedral of Troyes.[154] One of the wedding guests was James I of Scotland.

James had been too long swung between the heights of hope and the depths of despair to refuse 'the king's command to serve him in his wars in France'.[155] On 8 December 1416, Henry V had responded to 'the frequent instances of the magnificent man James Stewart, calling himself king of Scotland', and prepared to accept hostages for his release on parole.[156] In March 1417 James had been sent to Yorkshire to hasten the coming of the hostages; but they failed to come.[157] The latest attempt to release James (though he himself was probably ignorant of it) had been an abortive scheme of a Welsh Lollard to rescue him from Windsor Castle.[158] Meanwhile the captive king was

---

[149] *Scots Peerage*, II. 265; III. 168.
[150] E. F. Jacob, *The Fifteenth Century*, p. 181.   [151] *Chron. Bower*, II. 459.
[152] Balfour-Melville, *James I*, pp. 78–9; *Chron. Pluscarden*, I. 353.
[153] E. F. Jacob, *The Fifteenth Century*, p. 181.
[154] *Ibid.*, pp. 184–7.   [155] *Cal. Docs. Scot.*, IV. No. 898.
[156] *Rot. Scot.*, II. 219.   [157] Balfour-Melville, *James I*, p. 67.
[158] J. A. F. Thomson, *The Later Lollards*, p. 17.

in straitened circumstances and was dependent on the English government even for his personal expenses.[159]

The £150 James received on being summoned to France in 1420[160] could hardly have allowed him to cut a fine figure. Yet in one respect Henry won a useful ally: the Scots in French service might be faced with the banner of their own king: when the town of Melun capitulated to Henry on 17 November 1420 the Scottish members of the garrison were hanged as traitors to King James.[161] This did not prevent the Earls of Buchan and Wigtown from undertaking a recruiting drive in Scotland and returning to France with reinforcements[162] while Henry conducted his French bride to London for her coronation. James accompanied Henry and Catherine on a state progress which was interrupted by news of a Franco-Scottish victory at Baugé in Anjou.

In this small engagement on Easter Eve (22 March 1421) the Scots, under Buchan, Wigtown, and Sir John Stewart of Darnley, successfully used tactics reminiscent of those displayed at Stirling bridge in 1297; the Duke of Clarence, heir presumptive to the English crown, was among the slain. When Pope Martin V heard the news he reputedly remarked that the Scots acted as an antidote to the English.[163] The fight at Baugé certainly demonstrated that the English were not invincible. The jubilant dauphin was said to have remarked to the detractors of the Scots: 'What think ye now of the Scottish muttoneaters and wine-bibbers?' The Earl of Buchan was made Constable of France and John Stewart of Darnley was granted the lordship of Concressault.[164]

After Baugé, there was less chance of detaching the Scots from well-rewarded service under the dauphin.[165] The most that Henry could hope for was to entice individual Scots to enter his service rather than that of the dauphin. In this policy James I still had a part to play: on St George's Day, 23 April 1421, Henry dubbed him knight and invested him with the order of the garter. On 30 May the Earl of Douglas contracted to serve Henry after the ensuing Easter with two hundred knights and esquires and two hundred mounted archers. The Tyneman had undertaken this service (against all men save the Scottish king) at the command of James, who received his reward on

159 Balfour-Melville, *James I*, pp. 80–81.
160 *Cal. Docs. Scot.*, IV. No. 898.   161 *Chron. Bower*, II. 462.
162 Balfour-Melville, *James I*, p. 85.
163 *Chron. Pluscarden*, I. 268; *Chron. Bower*, II. 461–2.
164 *Chron. Bower*, II. 459; Francisque-Michel, *Les Écossais en France*, I. 120–1.   165 Balfour-Melville, *James I*, pp. 85–6.

the following day: 'through the mediation of the Lord Archibald, Earl of Douglas', he was promised release on parole soon after the forthcoming campaign in France.[166] In June 1421 James sailed to France with Henry, who received some recruits from Scotland.[167] During the siege of Meaux English troops foraged in lands dedicated to St Fiacre (or Fergus), traditionally believed to have been the son of a Scottish king, and Henry contracted a disease which his doctors reportedly described as 'the malady of St Fiacre'. Thereupon, so says Bower, the king 'with contorted countenance and wild voice responded, "Wheresoever I turn I am bearded with Scots, dead or alive" '.[168] On 31 August Henry V died at Vincennes. James accompanied the funeral *cortège* from Rouen to Westminster.[169]

The death of Henry V had been preceded by that of Albany. He had died in Stirling Castle, probably on 3 September 1420,[170] 'in a good old age, being eighty years old or more, in possession of his faculties'. In Bower's view Albany was an outstanding man, distinguished in bearing, patient, mild, communicative and affable, 'a man of great expenses and munificent to strangers'.[171] Prior Wyntoun was even more enthusiastic: if all the princes of the world were gathered together Albany would stand out as the one worthiest of renown.[172] What both Wyntoun and Bower seem to have detected as a conceivable flaw in their paragon was the fact that he did not punish powerful offenders. But even this deficiency was easily turned into a virtue: 'if any enormities perchance were committed in the realm by the powerful, he patiently temporised, knowing how to reform them prudently enough at an opportune time';[173] if Albany spared persons when he had good reason 'to greve thaim sare' it was only on account of his compassion.[174]

Compassion was a quality easily evoked as an excuse for avoiding controversial measures. When it was decided to destroy Jedburgh Castle after its capture in 1409, a general council held at Perth intended to finance the apparently costly operation by levying a tax of twopence on each hearth throughout the kingdom. Albany was too wary to allow the sort of unfair taxation that had led to the English

---

[166] *Foedera*, IV. pt. iv, 30–1.
[167] *Ibid.*, 31–2, 42, 44, 47, 50; *Rot. Scot.*, II. 230–1.
[168] *Chron. Bower*, II. 462.   [169] Balfour-Melville, *James I*, pp. 90–1.
[170] See *E.R.*, IV. lxxix. It was a year of epidemic 'greitar nor ony pestilence that ever was in Scotland' (*Extracta*, pp. 249–50).
[171] *Chron Bower*, II. 466.   [172] *Chron. Wyntoun*, III. 99–101.
[173] *Chron. Bower*, II. 466.   [174] *Chron. Wyntoun*, III. 99–101.

peasant rising of 1381. He sanctimoniously affirmed that during his governorship no tax had ever been levied, or ever would be levied, lest the poor folk should curse him for having introduced such an abuse. He directed that the Borderers should be paid from the great customs [175] for the destruction of the castle. Thereupon 'he acquired the innumerable blessings of the common folk'.[176]

The panegyrics of the contemporary chroniclers cannot be discounted. They show that in his day Albany was a popular ruler who displayed a flattering interest in the lower orders of society: in the second year of his governorship he was to be found with a concourse of nobles supervising the narrowing of a street in Ayr to prevent the encroachment of sand; with his own hands he fixed a stake in the ground to indicate the new width of the Sandgate.[177] Thus it is easy to see how there circulated stories that projected the image of Albany as a simple and honest man who had the interests of the people at heart. It was recounted how, during the raid of Cockermouth in 1388, a supposed charter of King Athelstan was found among the booty; Albany (then Earl of Fife) admired its simplicity and brevity; when as governor he had to listen to 'the tedious and wordy charters of our modern days' he would recall Athelstan's little charter and assert that 'there was more truth and good faith in those old times than now, when the new race of lawyers has introduced such frivolous exceptions and studied prolixity of forms'.[178]

But if Albany sanctimoniously avowed dislike of 'the new race of lawyers'—unpopular in any day or age—he was himself a master of chicanery. He could use pressure to obtain supposedly voluntary resignations, draw up tailzies that deprived others of their own well-established rights of inheritance and insert in charters nominally concerning only a landed transaction clauses that made the beneficiary his dependant or retainer; as governor he could preside over legal actions to which he himself was a party.[179] All this, it seems, was hidden from the chroniclers or was deliberately suppressed by them: Bower and the Pluscarden writer fixed their eyes on events in France; Wyntoun devoted page after page of his rhymed chronicle to the colourful exploits of Alexander Stewart, Earl of Mar, meanwhile ig-

---

[175] Two such payments were made (*E.R.*, IV. 115, 117).
[176] *Chron. Bower*, II. 444.
[177] *Ayr Burgh Charters*, Nos. 43, 44.
[178] *Chron. Bower*, II. 403; *Chron. Wyntoun*, III. 30.
[179] W. Fraser, *Memorials of the Family of Wemyss of Wemyss* (1888), II. No.

noring Albany's governorship, though he was an eye-witness of it from beginning to end.

It is unfortunate that the scanty evidence of the chroniclers is accompanied by a similar lack of evidence from parliamentary records. No record of a parliament survives between 1401 and 1424; general councils were certainly held, but have left little trace. Apart from charters, only one class of evidence survives to elucidate the character of the Albany governorship—the records of the exchequer audits.

Between 1406 and 1423 these were held at Perth each year, save during the Harlaw emergency of 1411 and in 1419 when the Earl of Buchan sailed to France.[180] Buchan, second son of Albany, had become chamberlain in place of his father in 1408. Sir John Forrester acted as Buchan's chamberlain depute and probably performed the donkey work. Nonetheless the amount of money that passed through Forrester's hands was always negligible; and Albany continued to have a say in finance.[181] From the chamberlain's accounts it would seem that the royal revenues were either decaying or were being increasingly expended at source in the localities. Certainly the sums forwarded to the chamberlain were small: the audit of 27 June 1414 showed a total of £1,632 16s. 11½d.; that of 11 June 1418 showed a drop to £1,158 2s. 11d.[182] At the audit of 27 March 1408 Albany had complained that he had entertained French and Welsh envoys at his own expense 'because there was not the wherewithal from the king's revenues to pay such expenses'.[183] Usually Albany was successful in obtaining his annual fee of £1,000 as governor; by 1418, however, even this had fallen into arrears[184] and the accumulated arrears on the chamberlain's accounts came to £2,771 8s. 5d.[185]

Although much of this sum was owing to Albany and Buchan it is unlikely that they were disinterested lenders of money for the maintenance of government: their contemporary, Henry Beaufort, Bishop of Winchester, made much profit on his large loans to the English exchequer.[186] Certainly Albany and his son had methods of recouping themselves for any possible loss: in the audit of 1412 Buchan protested that 'if it befalls him to have memory of any receipts of which he has not charged himself . . . it should not be imputed to him as concealment'.[187] Two years before, a memorandum

---

[180] *E.R.*, iv. xli.   [181] *Ibid.*, 208–14, 306–9.   [182] *Ibid.*
[183] *Ibid.*, 71.   [184] *Ibid.*, 132, 309.   [185] *Ibid.*, 309.
[186] E. F. Jacob, *The Fifteenth Century*, pp. 226–9.
[187] *E.R.*, iv. 80.

n the exchequer records had alluded to the seamier side of govern-
nent finance : 'neither the sheriffs nor the chamberlain nor his de-
)ute rendered anything from the issues of justice ayres held south of
Forth by the Earl of Douglas, and nonetheless ayres *were* held in the
year of this account'.[188]

The chief stamping ground for financial corruption and extortion was provided by the great customs, which by 1418 were virtually
the chamberlain's only source of avowed revenue—less than £50
came from other sources.[189] Meanwhile the gross receipts from the
customs had fallen to £2,911 8s. 3½d.[190] Thanks to remissions of
customs duties,[191] and the annuities or fees paid by the custumars, the
chamberlain received little more than one third of this sum, and even
this was jeopardised. During the reign of Robert III there had been
occasional raids upon the customs,[192] but after 1406 'we are brought
into continual contact with this description of lawlessness'.[193] The
audits held between May 1409 and July 1420 inclusive showed that
Douglas had forcefully abstracted about £5,000 from the Edinburgh
custumars.[194] Usually he was good enough to give the custumars a
receipt; occasionally he even volunteered an explanation.[195] Sheltered
under his wing were others who obtained good pickings.[196] On at least
one occasion the extortioners fell out among themselves : sometime
between 1416 and 1418 the Tyneman besieged Edinburgh Castle, of
which he held custody, in order to oust his deputy keeper, Sir William
Crawford.[197] Then Douglas installed William Borthwick, whose depredations went unhindered since Albany obligingly dismissed the
Edinburgh custumars from office. The custumars, showing obstinate
zeal, continued to take notes of exported goods, whereupon Borthwick seized their records lest they be produced at an exchequer
audit.[198]

The irregularities and unruliness evident in the raids on the customs were only one aspect of a more general lawlessness that occasionally burst out in spectacular crimes : at the outset of Albany's
governorship James Kennedy was killed by his illegitimate brother ;[199]
in 1413 Patrick Graham, Earl of Strathearn through his marriage to
the heiress, Euphemia Stewart, was murdered at the instigation of

---

[188] *Ibid.*, 133.   [189] *Ibid.*, 308.   [190] *Ibid.*, 290–302.
[191] See *ibid.*, index, under 'custom, great, remitted or allowed'.
[192] *Ibid.*, III. 546, 549, 552, 567.   [193] *Ibid.*, IV. lvii.
[194] *Ibid.*, 80, 177, 201, 224, 253, 300, 322.
[195] *Ibid.*, 253.   [196] *Ibid.*, lviii–lxiv.
[197] *Chron. Bower*, II. 449.   [198] *E.R.*, IV. 321–2.
[199] *Scots Peerage*, II. 449.

Sir John Drummond of Concraig, with whom he had lately sworn a bond of perpetual alliance.[200] After he had executed the murderers of Earl Patrick, Albany sought (though in vain) to marry the widowed Countess of Strathearn to one of his grandsons.[201] Similarly he sought to draw profit from the Kennedy murder : after the crime Sir Gilbert Kennedy, father of both the murderer and his victim, tried to draw up a tailzie defining the succession to his lands and made an indenture with Albany at Stirling on 8 November 1408 ;[202] Albany undertook never to revoke the tailzie or impede it ; in return for this 'consent and gude will' Sir Gilbert was, in certain circumstances, to enter into 'speciale retenew with oure saide lorde the gouvenour and with his lauchfull ayris, in pece and in were'.

Through such indentures and bonds of alliance with individual magnates Albany did what he could to maintain his personal authority. His experience of men and affairs, acquired in a lifetime mostly spent in trying to rule Scotland, gave him a political astuteness that allowed him to hold his own. The talents which Albany possessed, and which he exercised deviously, might have shone more brightly had he not been always merely the power behind the throne. If he had been king, or even if he had been an outstanding military leader, much might have been achieved, for the international situation, on the whole, favoured Scotland.

That Albany hoped to become king is clear. His royal ambitions can be detected in the indenture which he made with the Tyneman on 20 June 1409. This was a bond of 'evin falowschip' in which Albany showed himself not as ruler of Scotland but merely as one magnate negotiating on terms of equality with another. But the governor did not forget his chances of wearing a crown : the indenture was to expire (though his friendship was to continue) 'gif it happynnis the said lorde, the Duc Albany, to grow in tyme to cum to the estate of king'.[203]

Since Albany was heir presumptive from 1406 until his death it would be captious to denounce him for hoping to become king ; whether his hopes led him to take a hand in manipulating fate is another matter. Albany was, at the least, indirectly responsible for the removal of one obstacle—Rothesay. There is no clear evidence that Albany failed to work for the release of James I ; but James certainly thought that his uncle was deliberately obstructive. When the

[200] *Chron. Bower*, II. 447; *Chron. Pluscarden*, I. 349–50; *Scots Peerage*, VIII. 260.   [201] *Scots Peerage*, VIII. 260.
[202] *Nat. MSS. Scot.*, II. No. lxi.   [203] *E.R.*, IV. ccxi; cf. p. 231 above.

duke died in 1420 James was still a prisoner, and the crown that had eluded Albany might yet be gained by his heir : Murdoch succeeded not only to the dukedom of Albany but to the position of heir presumptive and to the governorship of Scotland.

So far as outward appearances went, Duke Murdoch inherited the powers and perquisites that his father had possessed as governor. But Murdoch did not inherit his father's popularity and as governor was thought to be 'too remiss'.[204] Following in his father's footsteps he concluded an indenture [205] on 16 November 1420 with Alexander Stewart, Earl of Mar. In gratitude for 'certane gude dedis done till him' by Duke Murdoch the earl was to become 'man of speciale feale and reteneu till the forsaid Duck of Albany'. And the governor would do more good deeds ; most of all he would help the earl in his schemes concerning the earldom of Mar. For Alexander Stewart held only a liferent in the earldom ;[206] on his death it might pass to the rightful heir, Sir Robert Erskine. The Erskine claim, recognised by Robert III in 1391,[207] was an inconvenience to Earl Alexander, who hoped to intrude his illegitimate son, Sir Thomas Stewart, into the earldom. On certain conditions Duke Murdoch would confirm Sir Thomas's infeftment in the lands of Mar and Garioch. The main obstacle to these arrangements was none other than Duke Murdoch's son and heir, Sir Walter Stewart, who on 26 April 1421 obtained a dispensation for a marriage to Janet Erskine,[208] daughter of the rightful heir.

Sir Walter carried his defiance of his father further : he had been given custody of Dumbarton Castle, where he detained the custumars of Linlithgow until they disgorged £15 0s. 10½d.[209] In 1423 he had the audacity to issue a document from Stirling undertaking to help the dauphinists in France, to prevent his 'subjects' from helping the English, to allow no truce with England, but rather to continue the war when he should come to the throne, or at least to the governorship of the realm.[210] Through Sir Walter's behaviour and that of his younger brothers Alexander and James (likewise criticised for their insolence and lawlessness),[211] the days of Duke Murdoch's governorship were numbered : Mar was probably alienated; Douglas was aloof and extortionate.[212]

The exchequer audit of 1422 [213] displayed the cumulative effect

[204] *Chron. Bower*, II. 467.
[205] Text in *Aberdeen-Banff Illustrations*, IV. 181–2.
[206] *Scots Peerage*, V. 587.   [207] *Ibid.*, 601–2; *A.P.S.*, I. 578–9.
[208] *Scots Peerage*, I. 150.   [209] *E.R.*, IV. 365.
[210] Balfour-Melville, *James I*, p. 107.   [211] *Chron. Bower*, II. 467.
[212] *E.R.*, IV. 368.   [213] *Ibid.*, 373–8.

of long years of fiscal mismanagement, corruption and extortion. Duke Murdoch was supposed to receive a total of £1,469 6s. 8d., comprising various annuities and his salary of £1,000 as governor; in fact he received £970 8s. o½d., which was assigned to meet arrears already due to him; the total arrears still owing to him came to £3,809 15s. 8d. This was the last exchequer audit held during the governorship; the finances of central government had collapsed. In this respect, as in others, Duke Murdoch had proved that he was un-equal to the task of governing Scotland. There was an increasing demand for the return of James I.

Since 1421 it was Archibald the Tyneman who had shown most interest in obtaining the king's release, probably because Douglas resented the 'simulacrum of an Albany dynasty' [214] that seemed on the way to establishment. Circumstances favoured a renewal of nego-tiations. In England the death of Henry V had brought decisive changes. The only offspring of his marriage to Catherine de Valois was a babe in arms who was to reign as Henry VI in England and, by the terms of the treaty of Troyes, was heir to Charles VI in France. In England Humphrey, Duke of Gloucester, acted as 'protector' of the realm, while his elder brother, John, Duke of Bedford, acted as regent in France.[215] There the English conquests were threatened by the dauphinist resistance that the Scots mercenaries had helped to kindle. English finances were burdened with many commitments, in-cluding the heavy cost of garrisoning the Scottish border.[216] To some English problems the release of the Scottish king might be made to provide an answer.

On 6 July 1423 the English council drew up secret instructions for its commissioners.[217] They were to ask for the 'expenses' of James's long residence in England and try to obtain at least £36,000. If there were no time to work out the terms of a final peace the commissioners were to press for as long a truce as possible, coupled with an assurance that the Scots would send no more help to France and would with-draw the troops already there. If the Scots raised the question of an English bride for James, discussions upon a marriage could proceed. If, however, the Scots did not raise this point, it would not be honour-able for the commissioners to allude to it, 'since Englishwomen, at

214 Balfour-Melville, *James I*, p. 85.
215 E. F. Jacob, *The Fifteenth Century*, pp. 211–7.
216 *Ibid.*, p. 221.
217 *Foedera*, IV. pt. iv, 96–7.

least noble ones, are not wont to offer themselves in marriage to men of other parts'.

James had already encountered a lady in whom he perceived 'beautee eneuch to mak a world to dote'.[218] Joan Beaufort was granddaughter of John of Gaunt and Catherine Swynford, his mistress. It rankled in the minds of the Beauforts that they were of royal, but dubious, descent. In 1407 a charter of Henry IV had declared them legitimate but barred them from the English succession.[219] They were anxious to cast lustre upon the Beaufort name by a royal marriage and used their powerful influence to hasten the release of the potential bridegroom.

The Scots were now ready to do what was necessary: on 19 August 1423 Duke Murdoch issued letters from Inverkeithing, 'with the deliberate counsel of the three estates', appointing an impressive embassy.[220] On 10 September 1423 a draft treaty was sealed at York.[221] On 4 December 1423 the final treaty for James's release was sealed at London.[222] James was to pay £40,000 (sixty thousand marks) in English coin at the rate of ten thousand marks a year to cover the 'costs and expenses' of his involuntary stay in England. But already it was assumed that ten thousand marks would be remitted as the dowry of Lady Joan Beaufort.[223] For payment of the remainder Scottish nobles were to provide surety in the shape of twenty-one hostages. Opposite the name of each noble was set down his estimated annual revenue, ranging from fifteen hundred marks in the case of Sir James Douglas of Dalkeith and Duncan Campbell, Lord of Argyll, to four hundred marks in the case of Sir Alexander Seton of Gordon.[224] The hostages were to stay in England at their own expense until James's obligations were fully met; if a hostage died he was to be replaced within three months.

On 2 February 1424 the marriage of James and Joan was solemnised at the church of St Mary Overy (now the cathedral of Southwark).[225] By March James and his queen were in the neighbourhood of Durham for the final formalities of his release. So far, nothing had been settled on the question of truce or final peace. Peace was in practice ruled out by Henry VI's minority, and the English commissioners were instructed to accept a truce only on condition that for its dura-

[218] *Kingis Quair* (S.T.S.), p. 14.
[219] E. F. Jacob, *The Fifteenth Century*, pp. 103–5.
[220] *A.P.S.*, I. 589–90.   [221] *Foedera*, IV. pt. iv, 98–9.
[222] *Rot. Scot.*, II. 241–3.   [223] *Ibid.*, 246.
[224] *Ibid.*, 242; *Cal. Docs. Scot.*, IV. No. 952.
[225] Balfour-Melville, *James I*, pp. 99–100.

tion the Scots would not help the French.[226] This, however, was not quite what the commissioners obtained, and the credit must go to James: on 28 March he sealed an indenture at Durham providing for a truce of seven years, but professed himself unable to recall those Scots who had already set out for France; they would not be bound to observe the truce until their return.

A concourse of Scottish nobles had come to Durham to escort James and his queen to Scotland.[227] The king was faced with the delicate task of inducing about a third of them to remain in England as his hostages. The final list of the hostages included only two earls, Moray and Crawford, but the total number was increased to twenty-seven.[228] While most of them were sent southward to the Tower the royal couple crossed the border; by 5 April 1424 James had arrived in Melrose,[229] a free man after eighteen years of captivity.

[226] *Ibid.*, pp. 101, 104.   [227] *Rot. Scot.*, II. 244–6.
[228] See Balfour-Melville, *James I*, Appendix D, p. 293.
[229] *Cal. Docs. Scot.*, IV. No. 956.

10

SOCIETY, ECONOMY AND CULTURE IN EARLY STEWART SCOTLAND

It has been remarked that in medieval Scotland there was 'a natural affinity between the national characteristics of the people and the form of government that made the feudal system in a strange sense a truly popular one'.[1] Within at least the limits of the extended baronial families and their particular spheres of interest this was true. The Scotland of the early Stewarts saw individual acts of crime, feuds between family and family, clan and clan, and, above all, a withering of central authority; yet seldom was the general anarchy matched by a particular anarchy within the baronial or clannish communities that bounded the horizons of most of the population.

Indeed if the body politic as a whole was anarchic there was all the more need for social cohesion in each of its many component parts : 'every noble and laird in the constant struggles that went on was dependent upon the support not only of the phalanx of cadets of his house but on that of the lesser folk who formed the rank and file of his train, and these in turn were dependent on his protection'.[2] This was still the case when John Major wrote in 1521 of the relationship between the tenant farmers and their landlord : 'They keep a horse and weapons of war, and are ready to take part in his quarrel, be it just or unjust . . . if they only have a liking for him, and with him, if need be, to fight to the death.'[3] The French knights who came to Scotland in 1385 found to their surprise that the countryfolk were not a submissive peasantry. It was this very fact that prevented the accumulation of the agrarian discontent which in other lands, to the horror of

[1] Grant, *Social and Economic Development*, p. 197.
[2] *Ibid.*, p. 198.
[3] Major, *History*, p. 47.

the Scots,[4] sometimes burst out into peasant risings that were invariably followed by aristocratic repression. It would be wrong, however, to romanticise the condition of the Scottish rural classes : the ordinary countryman was personally free but possessed no rights upon the land.[5]

In the earliest surviving rental of a lay landholder conditions of tenure were certainly insecure. This rental of 1376–8,[6] compiled for Sir James Douglas of Dalkeith, covered extensive lands in Lothian, Dumfriesshire, Kirkcudbright, Fife, Moffatdale and Liddesdale. In these scattered lands, brought somewhat accidentally under the estate-management of Sir James, a uniform policy was being applied. In each barony the various holdings, corresponding to modern farms, were assessed, presumably in the local baron court, and were leased to tenants, sometimes described as husbandmen,[7] on tacks that were nearly all for only a year at a time. While it was not unusual for one person to be granted a tack it was more common for a group of men to combine as joint tenants. In one case a township was leased to eight husbandmen for two years;[8] in other cases of communal cultivation the groups of joint tenants varied in number from four to ten,[9] and paid a joint rent that averaged about £1 for each person in the group. Each tenant, whether he shared a tack with others or undertook it alone, had to find a person as his pledge that the rent would be paid.[10] Although rents paid in cash were now typical, they might still be paid in the form of produce and labour. The rents that Sir James Douglas drew each Whitsunday and Martinmas from Aberdour included four chalders of oats, sixteen bolls of barley, four sheep and two dozen hens, in addition to £15 15s. od.[11] From each of nine cottar-holdings in the barony of Kilbucho in Peeblesshire he drew a rent of 6s. 8d. and four days' labour service. This service, however, was probably not rendered directly to Sir James but to the persons to whom he had granted tacks of his demesne in the barony—the East and West Mains of Kilbucho.[12] If landlords still continued to farm their demesnes on their own account they must have relied much less upon stipulated labour services than upon labour hired on a casual basis from among the cottars, or upon landless hired men, the *famuli*,

---

[4] *Chron. Wyntoun*, II. 499–50; III. 16–7; *Chron. Pluscarden*, I. 302; *Chron. Bower*, II. 360–1; Pitscottie, *Historie*, I. 69–71.

[5] Grant, *Social and Economic Development*, p. 252.

[6] *Morton Registrum*, I. xlvii–lxxvi.

[7] *Ibid.*, lxiv, lxv.   [8] *Ibid.*, li.   [9] *Ibid.*, lvi–lxi.

[10] *Ibid.*, lxii.   [11] *Ibid.*, lxv.   [12] *Ibid.*, xlvii–xlix.

who in the earldom of Strathearn seem to have been paid about 1d. a day in 1380.[13]

Although the agricultural classes comprised the basic categories of husbandmen, cottars and hired men, it is unlikely that these categories were closely defined or stereotyped. Within the rural community of the barony there were considerable opportunities for economic and social advancement: a man might rise above his fellows through his individual enterprise.

By contrast, burghal life showed a zest for social stratification and rigid apportionment of economic opportunities among the carefully differentiated categories of persons who lived in the burgh or used its facilities.[14] Towards the end of the fifteenth century the poet Robert Henryson, in his fable of the two mice, was to confer upon the town mouse the highest status within his community by making him 'gilt bruther and . . . ane fre burgess'.[15] The merchant burgesses, entrenched in the gild, dominated the burghal hierarchy and controlled the burgh. It was not beyond the competence of the gild court of Aberdeen to pass an ordinance in December 1401 to prevent 'Templars' (holders of former Temple tenements in the burgh) from buying flour to the detriment of the burgh market.[16] On 5 March 1406 a royal charter granted the magistrates and council of Perth the right to make burgh statutes (with the consent of the gild brethren) and to enforce them by penalties both in the court of the bailies of the burgh and in the gild court.[17]

These developments had been preceded by a concession that increased the autonomy of the burgh: on 10 April 1394 a royal charter allowed the burgesses of Perth to have their own sheriff and shrieval jurisdiction.[18] This unique privilege was a sign of the desire of the burgesses to escape from the attentions of royal officials and from the influence of the local aristocracy—in 1385 the burgesses of Ayr wished that neighbouring lands should be leased in tack to simple husbandmen and not to any 'potent lord', and in 1418 they daringly

---

[13] *E.R.*, III. 33–8. See M. M. Postan, 'The Famulus: the estate labourer in the twelfth and thirteenth centuries', *Economic History Review Supplements*, No. 2, 1–48.

[14] See the *Iter Camerarii*, a document found in the Bute MS. which has been attributed to the reign of Robert II or Robert III (*A.P.S.*, I. 695).

[15] MacQueen, *Robert Henryson*, p. 123.

[16] *Aberdeen Burgh Recs.*, pp. lxvi, cxliv.

[17] Confirmation in *R.M.S., 1593–1608*, No. 1098.

[18] Confirmation in *ibid.*, No. 1098 and *R.M.S.*, I. App. 2, No. 1720.

claimed that all the king's burgesses were exempt from distraint by a sheriff.[19]

To a greater or less extent the king's burghs were self-governing and had direct access to the king. They were the wealthiest burghs : the contribution levied in 1373 brought the chamberlain (probably after deductions) £157 16s. od. from Edinburgh, £114 4s. 5d. from Aberdeen, £74 11s. 5d. from Dundee, and only £2 0s. 11d. from the bishop's burgh of Glasgow.[20] And in 1424 the four burghs—currently Edinburgh, Perth, Dundee and Aberdeen—acted as sureties for payment of James I's 'expenses' of fifty thousand marks as a condition of his release.[21] Thus the king's burghs were able to demand recognition of their own special status, perhaps as a preliminary to attempts to curb the ecclesiastical and baronial burghs which were growing in number.[22] A move of this sort may underlie the new phraseology of a royal charter of 12 January 1401 that made Rothesay a 'royal' burgh (*burgus regius* or *regalis burgus*).[23] A few months later, on 29 April 1401, another royal charter granted to Sir James Douglas of Dalkeith the erection of his town of Dalkeith as a 'free burgh of barony', with the same privileges (unspecified) as 'the rest of the barons of our realm enjoy and use most freely in their barons' burghs'.[24] Here, it seems, a distinction has crept in between the 'barons' burghs' (later to be regarded as 'unfree') and the king's burghs or 'royal' burghs (later to be regarded as virtually the only 'free' burghs).[25]

Another move towards differentiation between the two types of burgh was made when the court of the four burghs met at Stirling on 12 October 1405.[26] One of its enactments declared that no 'Templar' should buy or sell goods reserved to the members of the gild. Since the Templars were dissolved in 1309 this apparently anachronistic enactment has given the impression that the record is either spurious or misdated.[27] On the contrary the supposed anachronism concerned a contemporary issue.[28] There is thus no reason to doubt the authenticity of the important first enactment which stipulated that two or three commissioners from each of the king's burghs south of Spey should attend the 'parliament' of the four burghs each year, wherever it might be held, to treat of all things concerning the common weal

[19] *Ayr Burgh Charters*, Nos. 41, 42.
[20] *E.R.*, II. 431.   [21] *Rot. Scot.*, II. 243.
[22] *Kirkintilloch Burgh Court Book* (S.H.S.), pp. xxiv–xxv.
[23] *Ibid.*, pp. xxxviii–xxxix.   [24] *Morton Registrum*, II. No. 209.
[25] *Kirkintilloch Burgh Court Book* (S.H.S.), p. xl.   [26] *A.P.S.*, I. 703–4.
[27] W. M. Mackenzie, *The Scottish Burghs*, p. 77, note 1; Theodora Pagan, *The Convention of the Royal Burghs*, p. 14.   [28] P. 263 above.

of all the king's burghs, their liberties and their court. In this context the word 'parliament' suggests that the court of the four burghs was extending its functions and that its business was now definitely deliberative as well as judicial. This 'parliament' was to be—initially at least—one that was to exclude representatives from the baronial and ecclesiastical burghs. It was a body that could formulate the common interests of the royal burghs, no doubt as a preliminary to the presentation of an agreed policy by their commissioners in the three estates; the first step had been taken towards the establishment of an institution that still survives—the convention of royal burghs.[29]

Despite such developments the importance of the burghs must not be over-emphasised : even Edinburgh, which Froissart described as the Paris of Scotland, had less than four hundred houses and could hardly be compared with provincial continental cities such as Tournai or Valenciennes;[30] yet, along with Haddington, Dunbar and North Berwick, it shared some of the export trade that had formerly passed through Berwick and accounted for between a quarter and a third of the total Scottish customs revenue. Aberdeen had temporarily fallen behind Dundee and was on much the same level as Perth and Linlithgow in exporting about one third as much as Edinburgh.[31] By contrast the few burghs situated on the west coast had scarcely any share in the export trade.

The chief Scottish exports continued to be wool and hides, but the bulk volume of wool exports was no higher in 1378 than it had been in 1327 and was to decline after 1378. There was some compensation in an increasing export of hides.[32] Even so, in 1390 the gross receipts from the great customs on wool, hides and woolfells came to less than £5,000,[33] in 1407 to £3,070 4s. 1½d.,[34] in 1416 they roce to £4,739 11s. 11d.,[35] in 1418 they slumped to £2,911 8s. 3½d.[36] In this depressing situation it was natural that miscellaneous commodities that had begun to figure among Scottish exports should be singled out for the imposition of new export duties to try to halt the drop in the most important source of royal revenue. A council held at Perth on 22 April 1398 imposed various duties, notably a charge of 2s. in the pound on the value of exported cloth.[37]

[29] See *Kirkintilloch Burgh Court Book* (S.H.S.), pp. xxxix–xl; Theodora Pagan, *The Convention of the Royal Burghs, passim.*
[30] *Chron. Froissart*, IV. 23, where, however, the number of houses in Edinburgh is wrongly given as approaching 4,000.
[31] See Appendix I, Map C; *E.R.*, II. lxxxix; III. 202–13; IV. 1–17, 240–54, 290–302.   [32] *E.R.*, II. xc–xci.   [33] *Ibid.*, III. 202–13.   [34] *Ibid.*, IV. 1–17.
[35] *Ibid.*, 240–54.   [36] *Ibid.*, 290–302.   [37] *A.P.S.*, I. 571.

This suggests a revival of the manufacture of cloth (probably of coarse quality). Simultaneously there was an attempt to protect this manufacture by a heavy import duty of 40d. in the pound on the value of imported English cloth 'to avoid damage thereupon ensuing to the realm'.[38] This was virtually the first import duty to be levied in Scotland[39] and was a sign of the growth of a mercantilist outlook.

While Scottish exports were still mainly raw materials, Scottish imports were still mainly manufactured articles and luxuries. The wide variety of these is demonstrated in the cargo lists of vessels captured or 'arrested' by the English on the route between Scotland and Flanders.[40] From another direction, however, the Scots were importing commodities to make up two deficiencies that were becoming apparent at home : in the more settled parts of Scotland timber was becoming scarce, and the prevalence of sheep and cattle farming was accompanied by shortages of grain. By the end of the fourteenth century there was a two-way traffic that brought Scots skippers and merchants to the furthermost Germanic ports of the Baltic in search of grain and timber.

It was chivalry that had plotted the track. The long-lasting 'crusade' led by the Teutonic Knights against the heathen Lithuanians had provided yet another field for Scottish knighthood to display its prowess,[41] and chivalric contacts soon became commercial as well. In the opening years of the fifteenth century the Teutonic Order kept resident factors in Edinburgh and Linlithgow; in 1404 it shipped to Edinburgh wheat, rye, malt and wainscoting valued at 2,800 marks.[42]

At the same period there was increasing contact between Scotland and a second, and even greater, Germanic organisation, the Hanseatic League, which included the important Baltic trading cities of Lübeck, Stralsund and Danzig. In 1423 Scottish merchants already resided in Danzig and wrote home to complain of the restrictions imposed upon their activities.[43] The restrictive policy of the Hansa was one source of friction. Another was Scottish piracy,[44] which led to retaliatory

---

[38] *Ibid.*   [39] See, however, *E.R.*, I. cxxxv and III. lxxxi–lxxxii.

[40] *Cal. Docs. Scot.*, IV. No. 462. For trade with the Low Countries see Davidson and Gray, *Staple*, pp. 120–6; J. Yair, *An Account of the Scotch Trade in The Netherlands* (London, 1776), pp. 26–62; M. P. Rooseboom, *The Scottish Staple in The Netherlands*, pp. 9–18.

[41] *Rot. Scot.*, I. 869; II. 4, 13; *Chron. Bower*, II. 416; T. A. Fischer, *The Scots in Germany*, pp. 72, 275, and *The Scots in Eastern and Western Prussia and Hinterland* (afterwards cited as *Scots in Prussia*), p. 123.

[42] T. A. Fischer, *The Scots in Germany*, p. 10. The place-name 'Lettecowe' (Linlithgow) which occurs in some records has been wrongly taken by Fischer to represent Glasgow.   [43] *Ibid.*, pp. 14–5.   [44] *Ibid.*, pp. 5–6.

seizures and trade embargoes. After an outrage committed by the Earl of Mar, a meeting of the Hanseatic diet at Luneburg prohibited importation of Scottish wool and cloth and a further diet at Elbing ·in 1415 imposed a total embargo. This brought protests from the Duke of Albany and a temporary settlement through Flemish mediation.[45]

The frequency of maritime disputes had already led to the appointment of a Scottish admiral, whose business was not so much naval as legal : his deputes in the more important Scottish seaports held admiralty courts to administer maritime law.[46] In 1403 David Lindsay, Earl of Crawford, was acting as admiral of Scotland,[47] and by 1423 the office was held by the pirate Earl of Mar.[48] There was nothing strange in the appointment of two earls, acknowledged leaders of Scottish chivalry, to the post of admiral. The chivalric noble, at a time when the respectable merchant believed implicitly in an economic policy of multifarious restrictions and regulations, could alone indulge with impunity in exuberant private enterprise. From the fourteenth century onwards, when Scotsmen of all classes were increasingly accustomed to travel throughout Western Europe on business that was ecclesiastical, commercial, academic or political,[49] it was the chivalric noble who led the way in revealing farther horizons to his countrymen.

Henry Sinclair, first of that family to become Earl of Orkney,[50] even disclosed a transoceanic horizon. In 1391 he had gone on a successful expedition to the Faroe Islands where he met Nicolo Zeno, a shipwrecked Venetian mariner whom he made captain of his fleet. After they had defeated and killed a rival claimant to the earldom of Orkney they listened to fishermen who told of a rich and populous land westward across the ocean. Thereupon the resourceful earl crossed the Atlantic with Antonio Zeno, brother of Nicolo, and touched at least the coast of Greenland, if not the American continent.[51] Whatever Sinclair found was evidently unrewarding. The Scots ignored the possibilities of western discovery that might have transformed their position in the world.

As it was, the resourcefulness of Scottish traders and nobles seems to have resulted in rising imports at a time when exports were falling.

[45] *Ibid.*, pp. 5–6, 13–4.   [46] *Scots Legal Hist.*, pp. 396–400.
[47] *Cal. Papal Petitions*, I. 630.
[48] *Aberdeen-Banff Illustrations*, IV. 183.
[49] See A. I. Dunlop, 'Scots Abroad in the Fifteenth Century', Historical Association Pamphlet, No. 124.
[50] P. 192 above.   [51] *Scots Peerage*, VI. 568–9.

The outflow of bullion, partly the result of an adverse balance of trade, partly the result of cash payments to the papal court, led to a scarcity of bullion within Scotland. One apparent remedy, applied from 1385 onwards, was to restrict its export.[52] Another, applied from 1367 onwards, was debasement of the coinage. This upset foreign exchange rates: complaints about a new Scottish coinage were made in the English parliament in November 1373; on 24 July 1374 Edward III denounced the craftiness of the Scots, who, he alleged, were passing their inferior coins in England at the face value and abstracting good English coins into Scotland; henceforth 4d. Scots was to be accepted as worth only 3d. English.[53]

This was not necessarily bad in itself: special circumstances made the English coinage the most stable in Western Europe while other areas more active in trade and manufacture, such as northern Italy, continually debased their coinage.[54] The Scottish debasement of 1373 was thus part of a general European trend; but the trend did not operate equally and simultaneously in all areas and therefore posed problems.[55] From 1373 onwards the three estates were to show their concern over the coinage and related questions. For inflation followed in the wake of debasement: in 1409 the Abbot of Dunfermline granted forty shillings a year to each of his monks to buy clothing, 'considering that all things are dearer than they were in times past', and in 1454 the Bishop of Moray would complain that 'three marks, present money, scarcely equal one mark of old money, so that formerly where six marks sufficed for the sustentation of a vicar of the choir, today ten marks scarcely suffice'.[56]

Monetary troubles did not prevent a building boom that was to last throughout the fifteenth century, stimulated partly by the shrinking of other opportunities for investment, partly by the desire to repair what had been destroyed in the wars of independence and the sporadic warfare that followed. For the bulk of the population the occasional destruction of their primitive homes in wartime was a

[52] A.P.S., I. 554, 572.

[53] Rot. Scot., I. 964; E.R., II. 430.

[54] Carlo Cipolla, 'Currency Depreciation in Medieval Europe', Change in Medieval Society, ed. Sylvia L. Thrupp (1964), pp. 227–36.

[55] See Alison Hanham, 'A medieval Scots merchant's handbook', S.H.R., L. 107–20. This ready-reckoner of c. 1400 shows the expertise required in dealing with the variety of weights and measures in a few leading commodities and with 'the confusion of monetary systems' in the Low Countries.

[56] Dunfermline Registrum, No. 399; Cameron, Apostolic Camera, p. lvi, n. 1.

matter soon remedied,[57] but this was hardly the case with buildings that were royal, baronial or ecclesiastical, where considerable investment was involved. At Edinburgh Castle, which became the chief royal residence towards the end of the reign of David II, repairs which had begun in 1360 [58] were succeeded by new construction: from 1367 to 1379 work was in progress on 'the new tower',[59] soon styled 'King David's Tower'.[60] This stood on the site of the present half-moon battery and was the most striking feature of the castle until its destruction in the siege of 1573. From 1360 to 1371 the total building costs at Edinburgh came to £736 13s. od.[61] The lead given by David II was followed by the first two Stewart kings, who spent a good deal on the royal castles, particularly Rothesay.[62]

The magnates were no less eager than the crown to repair the damage of war and build anew. While some of the pre-war stone castles, such as Bothwell, Kildrummy and Dirleton, were repaired, and even elaborated by the construction of new accommodation within their 'closes', they seldom served as a model for new fortifications. Instead, the most striking development in baronial architecture was the building of tower-houses. These had their counterparts in other countries and other ages but were to become distinctively Scottish. They provided a modicum of security and domesticity without the expense of constructing the thick curtain-walls of the earlier castles of *enceinte*. The lower stories of the tower usually displayed only sheer walls, a few arrow-slits, and an unobtrusive and unwelcoming doorway. This opened on to a turnpike stairway which was the sole, and easily defended, means of reaching the domestic accommodation on the upper floors.

Such was the type of residence, free-standing, rectangular in plan, massive and lofty in elevation, that was erected by Archibald the Grim at Threave[63] as the headquarters of the lordship of Galloway which he had acquired in 1369. Threave was to have its replicas, great and small, throughout Scotland. Even in the sixteenth century some tower-houses were being built which scarcely differed from it, although development had meanwhile given rise to elaborations and variations in design.

For the austere functionalism of Threave was not to the liking of

[57] *Chron. Froissart*, IV. 23, 63. See also Aeneas Sylvius (Brown, *Early Travellers*, p. 25).   [58] *E.R.*, II. 78, 79.   [59] *Ibid*. See 'Guppild' in index.
[60] 'The greatest tower is still called David's Tower' (Boece, *History*, pp. 327–327v).   [61] *E.R.*, II. cviii–cxi.
[62] *Ibid.*, III. lxxiii, 313, 324, 357, 390, 463, 551, 610.
[63] See W. M. Mackenzie, *The Medieval Castle in Scotland*, pp. 133–6.

all of Archibald the Grim's noble contemporaries. At Tantallon and St Andrews a curtain wall strengthened with towers guarded the landward approach to a peninsula that required little defence on the seaward sides. At Doune the castle built by the first Duke of Albany was remarkable for two features, firstly the combination of the gate-tower with the 'keep' or 'donjon' reserved for the accommodation of the lord and his personal suite, and secondly the provision of segregated living quarters for the lord's retainers, supposedly less trustworthy in the days of 'bastard feudalism' when they were mercenary troops.[64] Not every noble had the same reason to suspect treachery as had the builder of Doune, who even arranged that the castle portcullis could be raised and lowered only from a window-recess in his private hall in the gate-tower. This hall, as was usual in tower-houses, occupied almost the whole of the first floor of the tower and was a sumptuous apartment with an ornate fireplace and minstrels' gallery. Above the great hall was the 'solar' or living-room, and a small oratory. A turnpike stairway from the solar gave access to bedrooms on the third floor and to a parapet walk at the top of the tower. The pitched roof of the tower was slated and had crow-stepped gables from which tall chimneys projected. Although the gate-tower at Doune was only part of a whole complex of buildings its internal arrangements were similar to those that might be found in many tower-houses throughout Scotland.

So far as ecclesiastical buildings were concerned there was rebuilding rather than new construction; in a number of cases it was a series of fires, accidental or deliberate, that made rebuilding unavoidable, as at the cathedrals of St Andrews and Elgin and the abbeys of Arbroath, Sweetheart, Melrose, Newbattle and Dryburgh. In most cases rebuilding was accompanied by extension and elaboration and permitted the introduction of new styles of architecture. At Aberdeen Bishop Leighton followed a style that was perhaps influenced by the Teutonic architecture of the Baltic and gave his cathedral an austere and embattled appearance. There is some evidence of the presence of French masons in Scotland and the rebuilt abbey of Melrose shows some 'flamboyant' features. Although Scottish ecclesiastical architecture followed no one ideal, and individualism was so prevalent that no distinctively Scottish style emerged, the kirks of Scotland were nonetheless to 'become recognisable as belonging to nowhere else'.[65]

[64] See W. Douglas Simpson, *Doune Castle* (n.d.), p. 17.
[65] Ian Finlay, *Art in Scotland*, p. 34.

Meanwhile new ecclesiastical construction, as distinct from reconstruction, received a stimulus from a change in devotional fashion whereby votive masses were regarded as more spiritually efficacious than the prayers of monks.[66] Such masses could be conveniently arranged by payment for a stipulated number, by the hiring of a secular priest to act as chaplain, or by the endowment of a chaplainry so that a priest might perpetually celebrate mass for the soul's weal of the patron and his nominees.[67] Thus at least two chaplains served in the chapel of St Monance which David II constructed at a cost of over £600.[68] Such chapels, or even parish kirks in which a number of chaplains served, might acquire the more dignified status of collegiate kirks. These obtained their name not from any educational function (though some maintained small schools for their boy choristers)[69] but from the *collegium* (incorporation) of priests, headed by a provost or dean, whose main function was the celebration of votive masses. In other respects—the ornateness of their architecture and furnishings, the provision often made for choral music—the collegiate kirks might roughly be compared to small cathedrals. Between 1342 and 1424 about ten had been founded by wealthy landholders.[70]

One of the wealthiest of these was Sir James Douglas of Dalkeith, who in 1377–8 was receiving annual rents of about £1,000.[71] His will and testament, drawn up in 1390,[72] some thirty years before his death, gives ample evidence both of his worldly riches and his conventional piety, which manifested itself in miscellaneous benefactions throughout his career. The most obvious feature of these was his desire to obtain votive masses. In 1384 he endowed a chaplainry in the chapel of his castle of Dalkeith,[73] and in 1406 he endowed six chaplainries in the chapel of St Nicholas that he had built in his burgh of Dalkeith. The chaplains, who were all to be priests, were to contribute to the soul's weal of Sir James and his kin, of David II, Robert II, Robert III and their successors, and with Bishop Wardlaw's approval Sir James laid down further regulations 'as is the custom in similar collegiate kirks'.[74]

---

[66] See the remarkable encomium of the mass in *Chron. Bower*, II. 467–71.

[67] See K. L. Wood-Legh, *Perpetual Chantries in Britain* (1965).

[68] *E.R.*, II. 121, 133, 266, cvi–cviii.

[69] D. E. Easson, *op. cit.*, *Scot. Church Hist. Soc. Recs.*, VI. 13–26, at 16–7.

[70] Easson, *Religious Houses*, pp. 173–88. See also D. E. Easson, 'The Foundation-Charter of the Collegiate Church of Dunbar, 1342', S.H.S. *Misc. VI*, 81–109.

[71] *Morton Registrum*, I. xlvii–lxxvi.

[72] *Ibid.*, II. No. 193.   [73] *Ibid.*, No. 176.   [74] *Ibid.*, No. 278.

Another of the collegiate foundations of this period was that of
St John the Evangelist, established in 1419 by Robert of Montrose,
canon of the chapel royal at St Andrews. St John's, the first collegiate
foundation to be connected with the university of St Andrews, was
headed by Master Laurence of Lindores and was to be used to foster
the study of theology and arts; but it was on too small a scale to act
as an important university institution.[76]

The university itself was a 'somewhat inchoate body of scholars
and masters',[77] since Bishop Wardlaw's charter and Pope Benedict's
bull had conferred privileges but no endowment. The accredited
university teachers, or 'regent masters', thus depended on the income
they obtained from running private 'pedagogies' (halls of residence)
in which they offered to students both board and lodging and tuition.
By 1417 competition among the regent masters to obtain student
lodgers seems to have driven the charge down to 1s. 8d. a week.[78]
The students who arrived at St Andrews, at the age of fifteen, or
even earlier, were grammar students rather than university students.
Their first task was to improve their Latin so that they could understand university lectures and take part in academic disputations; only
after this had been achieved would they 'incorporate' or become
matriculated students of the university. In theory the student had to
complete eighteen months of study and to have reached the age of
sixteen before his regent presented him as a 'determinant' for the
bachelor's degree in arts. Having 'determined' he might study for
something like a further two years to obtain his master's licence.[79]
The examination for the licentiate took the form of public disputation,
after which the licentiand received the master's licence which gave
him, in theory, the right to teach anywhere (*ius ubique docendi*).[80]
In its early days the university exacted an oath from the new masters
or 'incipients' that they would teach in the university for a further
two years. Before long, however, teaching was left entirely to the
regents, who became a sort of professoriate that perpetuated itself
through co-option, eventually excluded both students and incipients
from the election of the rector, and monopolised control of the
faculties.[81]

The foundation bull of Pope Benedict had permitted the setting

[76] *St Andrews Acta*, I. xix; *St Andrews Univ. Recs.*, p. xxi.
[77] *St Andrews Acta*, I. cxxxviii.
[78] *Ibid.*, I. 9; *St Andrews Univ. Recs.*, p. xxxii.
[79] *St Andrews Univ. Recs.*, pp. xxvi, xxxii–xxxiii; *St Andrews Acta*, I. xc.
[80] *St Andrews Acta*, I. cxvi–cxvii.
[81] *Ibid.*, cxxi, cxxvii, cxxxvii–cxxxviii.

up of five faculties—theology, canon law, civil law, medicine, and the liberal arts.[82] These faculties had varying fortunes. Until the sixteenth century medicine was studied only spasmodically at St Andrews.[83] The same was probably true of civil law, though lectures on the subject may have been given by canon lawyers who also held a degree in civil law; for 'in practice there had never been a hard and fast differentiation between canonists and civilists'.[84] To obtain a degree in canon law it was neither necessary nor usual to take as a preliminary the full arts course and obtain a degree in arts. This, however, was the normal requisite for the student of theology, which was thus the 'higher faculty' : it had distinguished teachers and a small number of advanced students. In terms of numbers and influence it was, however, the faculty of arts which dominated the university.[85] From the graduation rolls of the faculty (the earliest extant in the British Isles) [86] it appears that slightly more than 4,500 arts graduates were produced between 1413 and 1579, of whom about one third obtained the master's degree.[87]

The arts curriculum comprised the three philosophies (natural, moral and metaphysical) and seven liberal arts. These were divided between the introductory *trivium* (grammar, rhetoric and logic) and the more advanced *quadrivium* (music, arithmetic, geometry and astronomy).[88] Academic controversy over the prescribed reading for the subjects of the arts curriculum was common. So also (as in most medieval universities) was controversy between 'nominalists' and 'realists'.[89] The realists held that 'universals' (concepts) have a genuine existence, being reflections of 'forms' in the mind of God; the nominalists (among them Laurence of Lindores) held that universals existed only in the human mind in so far as it 'named', and thus categorised, the data perceived through the senses.

It was mainly clerics, or prospective clerics, who sought higher education at St Andrews. But more elementary instruction in Latin was available to a wider range of students in some ecclesiastical institutions [90] and in the grammar schools that, by the fifteenth century, were to be found in most of the Scottish burghs and even in the

[82] *Ibid.*, clvii.   [83] *Ibid.*, clvii–clviii.   [84] *Ibid.*, clii–cliii.
[85] *Ibid.*, cxxxix, 2–3.   [86] *St Andrews Univ. Recs.*, pp. xli–xlii.
[87] *Ibid.*, p. xxv.   [88] Rashdall, *Universities*, I. 456–7.
[89] *St Andrews Acta*, I. xxi, 3, 39–41, 48.
[90] Thus Hugh Kennedy, soldier, diplomat and ecclesiastic, had been placed with the Dominican friars of Ayr to learn grammar (*Cal. Papal Letters*, VIII. 553–4). See also Innes, *Scot. Middle Ages*, pp. 169–70, 271.

coal-mining township of Tranent.[91] It is significant that Sir James Douglas of Dalkeith possessed books of grammar and logic, books of the civil law and of Scottish statutes, as well as books of 'romance'. He bequeathed these books to his sons and enjoined that the books he had lent to others should be returned to his heir, while those that he had borrowed should be restored to their owners.[92] Now, if not before, there existed, outwith the royal court and the kirk, men with the wealth, the leisure and the taste to form a reading public.

Meanwhile the English language, which for some two centuries had been little more than the common speech of the lower and middle classes in England and in Lowland Scotland, advanced rapidly up the social scale and in Scotland began to become standardised as a dialect distinct from that of northern England.[93] Even time-honoured Latin suffered somewhat through the advancement of this Lowland vernacular, while the clearest sign that French had dropped out of use in common speech, and had become a foreign language, is to be found in the famous letter that the Earl of March addressed to Henry IV on 18 February 1400 : the earl excused himself for writing in English, not because he was ignorant of French, but because 'the Englishe tongue is maire cleare to myne understanding'.[94]

Though French was in rapid decline as a spoken tongue this was not, as yet, the case with Gaelic, which persisted as the language of half of Scotland's population; no serious decline from that position was to occur until the sixteenth century. The cultural unity of Gaelic Scotland and Gaelic Ireland was also unimpaired. It was typical that the poet Muireadhach of Lissadill, when forced to exile himself from Ireland in the early thirteenth century, took refuge in the Lennox and became known as Muireadhach Albanach ('the Scot'). He was to found the MacMhuirich bardic family that held lands in return for keeping a record of the genealogy and history of the MacDonalds.[95] The MacMhuirichs, 'probably the longest-lived literary dynasty in Europe', were to function as pro-

91 J. Grant, *History of the Burgh and Parish Schools of Scotland*, pp. 1–75. See also D. E. Easson, *op. cit.*, *Scot. Church Hist. Soc. Recs.*, VI. 13–26, at 17–22, and John Durkan, 'Education in the Century of the Reformation', *Essays on the Scottish Reformation, 1513–1625*, ed. David McRoberts, where a list of some sixty schools is given.

92 *Morton Registrum*, II. No. 196, pp. 179, 181.

93 Wittig, *Scottish Tradition*, p. 11.

94 *Nat. MSS. Scot.*, II. No. liii.

95 D. S. Thomson, 'The MacMhuirich Bardic Family', *Transactions of the Gaelic Society of Inverness* (1963), 3–31, at 4–6, 10.

fessional poets from the thirteenth century until the eighteenth.[95] They were a striking but by no means unique example of the class of professional bards who held high status under the patronage of the Gaelic lords and who composed 'classical' poetry, or poetic prose, in accordance with elaborate rules passed on from father to son or learnt after years of study in the Irish bardic schools that were probably mature institutions even in the days of St Columba.[97] While the tradition of formal artistic composition in Gaelic was one of the earliest to develop in Europe, a literary tradition in the Lowland vernacular was one of the latest. It had its origins in the folk ballads, of which the earliest extant fragments are the poignant lines concerning the death of Alexander III :

> Quhen Alysandyr oure Kyng wes dede,
> That Scotland led in luve and le,
> Away wes sons off ale and brede,
> Off wyne and wax, off gamyn and gle;
> Oure gold wes changyd in to lede.
> Cryst, borne in to Vyrgynete,
> Succoure Scotland and remede,
> That stad is in perplexyte.[98]

When John Barbour composed *The Bruce* in 1375 the verse form that he chose was identical with that of this earliest ballad. Indeed after his prologue Barbour begins his narration by adapting the first two lines of the Alexander ballad :

> Quhen Alexander the king wes deid,
> That Scotland haid to steyr and leid . . .[99]

At a much later date the poet Robert Henryson would similarly allude to a line from the Alexander ballad in his *Taill of the Scheip and the Doig.*[100] Thus this ballad not only marked the beginning of a Lowland literary tradition but helped to shape it.

Rapid maturity was reached in Barbour's *Bruce*, a sustained work of over thirteen thousand lines.[101] Nothing is known of Barbour's career prior to 1357, when he already was archdeacon of Aberdeen.[102] By the time of his death in 1395 his literary productions

---

[96] *Ibid.*, p. 29.
[97] D. S. Thomson, 'Gaelic learned orders and literati in medieval Scotland', *Scottish Studies*, XII. 57–78.
[98] *Chron. Wyntoun*, II. 266.   [99] Barbour, *The Bruce*, I. 3.
[100] P. 581 below.   [101] *Buik of Alexander* (S.T.S.), I. civ, ccvi.
[102] For an account of his career see *ibid.*, I. clxix–ccii.

included not only imaginary romances such as the *Buik of Alexander*, a *Troy Book* or *Brut*, now lost, and the *Ballet of the Nine Nobles*, but two works that were calculated to win royal favour. One, the lost *Stewartis Orygenale*, seems to have been a romantic genealogy that flatteringly traced the new royal dynasty back to Troy.[103] The second was *The Bruce*, the work on which Barbour's reputation as a poet principally rests.

It is tempting to relate this work to the contemporary work of Chaucer and Froissart, men of much the same social standing as the archdeacon, and men whom he may have met if he made use of his various safe-conducts. Chaucer's poetic career had, however, scarcely begun before *The Bruce* was completed. Froissart, on the other hand, had composed his romance *Meliador* shortly after his Scottish trip of 1365; and this work recounted the mythical tale of rival contenders for the hand of the King of Scotland's only daughter.[104] Long before, the thirteenth-century *Roman de Fergus* had also shown how Scotland could be made the setting for a chivalric romance.[105] Such examples may have encouraged Barbour to make Scotland and Robert Bruce, its hero king, a 'matter' of romance similar to, but distinct from, the fabulous Britain over which King Arthur had once held sway. If the glorification of Bruce was calculated to win for the poet the patronage of that hero's grandson, Robert II, so also the glorification of Sir James Douglas was calculated to flatter that hero's illegitimate son, the influential Archibald the Grim.

In the prologue to the poem Barbour affirmed that stories (histories) are 'delitabill' to read, even if they are only fables; how much more pleasing they are if they are 'suthfast'. His intention was

To put in wryt a suthfast story,
That it lest ay furth in memory.[106]

On the whole, despite the liberties he took with some of his material, Barbour the historian triumphed at the expense of Barbour the poet. His pertinacity in recording detail makes his poem an essential historical source for the period it covers.[107] If, like his contemporaries,

[103] *Ibid.*, cxxxi, clviii, cxc, ccxiii, ccxvii, ccxx–ccxxi.
[104] See A. H. Diverres, 'Froissart's *Meliador* and Edward III's policy towards Scotland', *Mélanges offerts à Rita Lejeune*, II. 1399–1409.
[105] M. Dominica Legge, 'Sur la genèse du *Roman de Fergus*', *Mélanges de Linguistique Romane et de Philologie Médiévale offerts à M. Maurice Delbouille*, II. 399–408.   [106] Barbour, *The Bruce*, I. 1–2.
[107] A detailed examination which confirms Barbour's relative accuracy as an historian is given in *The Buik of Alexander* (S.T.S.), I. ccxxvi–ccxxviii.

Barbour regarded history as being made by great personalities, of whose success or failure warfare was the ultimate test, he at least showed personalities of flesh and blood, endowed with the moral qualities necessary for the inter-action in history of the human and the divine. Moreover, Barbour had been influenced by the patriotic propaganda of King Robert's time and his own work was to transmit its influence to posterity. The best-known lines in his poem are those in praise of freedom :

> A fredome is a noble thing!
> Fredome mayss man to haiff liking;
> Fredome all solace to man giffis :
> He levys at ess that frely levys!
> A noble hart may haiff nane ess,
> Na ellys nocht that may him pless,
> Gif fredome failyhe . . .[108]

Archdeacon Barbour's association with the cathedral of Aberdeen may have brought to his acquaintance someone lower in the ecclesiastical hierarchy, a certain John of Fordun, possibly a chantry priest who celebrated mass at one of the altars in the cathedral.[109] While Barbour represented the new developments in vernacular literature Fordun remained true to the older practice of composition in Latin. But his work was no ordinary chronicle. Displaying a wide knowledge of the Latin classics [110] he was 'a careful compiler drawing upon material not otherwise known to have been preserved'.[111] Behind his erudition lay an argumentative patriotism : the chronicle was an apologia for Scottish independence and continued the propagandist tradition that began with Baldred Bisset's *Processus* and matured in the Declaration of Arbroath and in Bernard of Linton's Latin poem that celebrated the victory at Bannockburn [112]—a poem that was to have its counterpart in the Latin verses upon the victory at Otterburn composed by Fordun's contemporary, Thomas Barry, canon of Glasgow.[113] The importance of political argument based on mythology led Fordun to devote most of his chronicle, or at least most of what he completed, to the fabulous and dark ages. Posterity

---

[108] Barbour, *The Bruce*, I. 10.
[109] See A. R. McEwen, *History of the Church in Scotland*, I. 298–9.
[110] For his use of Juvenal see Innes, *Sketches*, p. 47.
[111] W. W. Scott, 'Fordun's Description of the Inauguration of Alexander II', *S.H.R.*, L. 198–200, at 200.
[112] It is translated by W. M. Mackenzie in his edition of *The Bruce*, p. 497.
[113] *Chron. Bower*, II. 406–13.

might have dispensed with an account of the reign of King Constantine, son of Heth the Wing-footed,[114] if Fordun, who died *c*. 1387, had chosen to write more about the reigns of David II and Robert II. In this respect Fordun's deficiencies were partly remedied by Walter Bower, Abbot of Inchcolm, who some fifty years later continued the earlier writer's work up to the opening years of the reign of James II. Bower's scholarly *Scotichronicon*, less austere than the annals of Fordun on which it was based, is amusingly perfervid both in its nationalism and its moral sententiousness and provides valuable indications of the outlook of fifteenth-century Scotland.[115] It concludes with an appropriate asseveration : 'Christ! he is not a Scot to whom this book is displeasing.'[116]

A chronicler of more limited talent than Fordun or Bower was Andrew of Wyntoun, Prior of Lochleven, who composed his *Orygenale Cronykil* sometime between 1420 and 1424. In the 'Prolog' Wyntoun showed that he could write tolerable verse when not encumbered by the need to narrate historical facts. His rhyming couplets were, however, ill-suited to cope with such topics as the succession of the Pictish kings :

> 'Drwst-Gygnowre wes fywe yhere kyng.
> And aucht yhere syne Drust-Hoddrylyng.
> Syne the fyrst Drwst yheris foure.
> Sex yhere Garnat-Gygnowre'.[117]

Although Wyntoun was well-versed in the learning of the age,[118] his chronicle was neither good history nor good poetry and has been likened to a 'somewhat weary pilgrimage from the Garden of Eden to the Scotland of Robert II [*rectius* Robert III]'.[119] Few harsh realities are allowed to mar the sentimental picture of loyalty, patriotism and virtue as Wyntoun speeds his great contemporaries on the way to paradise.

The lack of depth in Wyntoun's work becomes immediately apparent when it is compared with James I's *Kingis Quair,* a work

---

[114] *Chron. Fordun*, I. 163–4.
[115] David McRoberts, 'The Scottish Church and nationalism in the Fifteenth Century', *Innes Review*, XIX. 3–14, at 5–6.
[116] *Chron. Bower*, II. 513 (*rectius* 517).
[117] *Chron. Wyntoun*, I. 402.
[118] See the 'List of Authors etc.' (*Chron. Wyntoun*, III. 179–87). This list, compiled by David Laing, also illustrates Wyntoun's knowledge of geography.
[119] *Buik of Alexander* (S.T.S.), I. cxxii.

that had the character of a spiritual odyssey based upon James's own prolonged experience of the mutability of human fortune. He had set sail in March 1406 ostensibly for the good of his education. He returned in April 1424 a better-educated man than any of his royal predecessors. For, as Abbot Bower remarked, although he had been borne into England just as Joseph had been carried away to Egypt, James had learnt much from his period of bondage.[120] It is unfortunate that Bower expatiated upon James's musical talents (of which no trace survives to posterity) and wrote only in the most general terms of James's literary talents. Bower's reticence has even contributed to the advancing of an argument that James was not the author of the *Kingis Quair*, though this argument [121] is not now generally accepted.

Apart from its literary interest the *Kingis Quair* has an historical significance : beneath the allegory and symbolism there are autobiographical allusions. Just as Robert I emerges from the pages of Barbour as a real person, so also does James I acquire a personality denied to other medieval Scottish kings whose characters can be glimpsed only fleetingly in the encomia of chroniclers or the impersonal details of contemporary records. The very language of the poem—English after the fashion of Chaucer, interspersed with a few Scotticisms [122]— reveals the effect of a Scottish childhood followed by a sojourn of eighteen years in England. For James's model was not the poetry of Barbour but that of the English poets Gower and Chaucer,

> Superlative as poetis laureate
> In moralitee and eloquence ornate.[123]

In writing the tale of his own 'aventure' James tells how in his youth fortune had been his foe and 'how I gat recure off my distresse'.[124] The poem was undoubtedly finished after James's return to Scotland, for only then did he escape from the distresses of his youth. These had once led him to question whether any underlying order existed in the universe; in recounting his personal experience James gives his mature philosophical reflections on the subject of man's earthly fate. The medieval subtlety of the poem, its symbolism, and its 'prolixitee off doubilnesse',[125] have scarcely been penetrated by some critics, who

[120] *Chron. Bower*, II. 504–6.
[121] J. T. T. Brown, *The Authorship of the Kingis Quair* (1896).
[122] *The Kingis Quair* (S.T.S.), pp. xxiv–xxvi.
[123] *Ibid.*, p. 45.   [124] *Ibid.*, p. 5.   [125] *Ibid.*, p. 7.

have wrongly regarded it as a simple tale of courtly love.[126] In his description of his first glimpse of the lady who was to become his bride James does, admittedly, show a love that was at once courtly, warm and real. But love is merely the agency that stirs the poet from despondency to strive to escape from his fate by self-mastery. A dream-vision which occupies half the length of the poem concludes in his encounter with Dame Fortune, who sets him upon her revolving wheel of fate, bidding him to hold fast as he rises upon it.[127] On waking from this dream the poet receives a sign that its promise will be fulfilled in liberty and love—as did in fact befall when James returned to Scotland in 1424 with his bride :

To my larges . . . I am cumin agayn,
To blisse with hir that is my sovirane.[128]

[126] See the illuminating article by John MacQueen, 'Tradition and the Interpretation of *The Kingis Quair*', *Review of English Studies* (New Series), XII. 117–31.

[127] *The Kingis Quair* (S.T.S.), p. 42.

[128] *Ibid.*, p. 44.

11

A KING UNLEASHED

While the eighteen-year captivity of James I was in some ways a misfortune for him and Scotland it was not un-mitigated. He had observed at close hand the government of the country then the most intensively governed in all Europe, and had drawn from it some ideas that he was to try to apply in Scotland, one of the least intensively governed countries of Europe. It was no moonstruck poet who undertook the reconstruction of royal govern-ment. James was approaching his thirtieth year, besides his artistic and intellectual qualities he was strong, athletic,[1] and decisive. In his young manhood he had existed on pittances doled out by the English king and had possessed a royal title but not royal power; he was covetous of both wealth and power; his idealism, which could be genuine and disinterested, sometimes concealed selfishness when he assumed that his own interests were automatically the best interests of his people.

From the first days of his return to Scotland in April 1424 James showed himself to be easily aroused to wrath when the weak were oppressed by the strong, and easily aroused against the strong, guilty or otherwise, when they represented even a possible threat to his own position. Bower tells the story that when the king heard of the theft, fraud and extortion that afflicted the land, he exclaimed: 'If God grant me life and aid, even the life of a dog, throughout all the realm I will make the key keep the castle and the bracken bush the cow'.[2] On 13 May 1424, even before his coronation, James arrested Walter Stewart, eldest of Duke Murdoch's three surviving sons, as well as Malcolm Fleming of Cumbernauld, the duke's brother-in-law, and Thomas Boyd of Kilmarnock.[3] These spectacular arrests conveyed

---

[1] *Chron. Bower*, II. 505.   [2] *Ibid.*, 511.

the first warning to the Albany Stewarts that they no longer stood above the law.

A few days after his coronation at Scone James's first parliament met at Perth on 26 May 1424. Parliament, as distinct from general council, had probably not met for about twenty years.[4] This break in continuity was emphasised when James reverted to a procedure used in 1367, 1369, 1370 and 1372, when a commission had been appointed to hold the parliament, and the remainder of the three estates had been given leave to go home (*licentia recedendi*).[5] The same procedure was used in 1424, apparently for the last time, when 'certain persons were chosen to determine the articles given in by the lord king, the rest being given leave to withdraw'.[6] Although a procedure based on 'articles' was established it had not yet taken its final form. By the sixteenth century a committee of parliament would discuss the 'articles', draft them in the form of legislation, and then submit them to a full meeting of parliament for enactment. In 1424 however this was not quite the case : the 'certain persons' did not compose a committee that had to report back to parliament but a commission to 'determine' the articles, that is to bring them to a conclusion as legislation having the full authority of parliament.

Some of the articles which were 'given in' by the king and enacted by the parliamentary commission of 1424 immediately showed the directions in which the king's mind was turning. From the first it was evident that James intended to take a strong stand against lawlessness. It was enacted that no one should 'opinly or notourly rebell aganis the kyngis persone under the payne of forfautour of lif, landis and gudis' and that 'thar be maide officiaris and ministeris of lawe throu all the realme that can and may halde the lawe to the kingis commonis'.[7] There was even a threat that those who possessed heritable jurisdictions should be responsible to the king for any defaults of justice. These admonitory measures were summed up in the optimistic announcement 'that ferme and sikkir pece be kepit and haldin throu all the realme and amangis all and sindry liegis and subjectis of our soveran lorde the kyng'. Henceforth there were to be no more private wars and warlike feuds.[8]

Another major topic dealt with in the articles of 1424 was the

---

[3] *Ibid.*, 481–2; *E.R.*, IV. 380, 386.

[4] The last known parliament pre-dates 1406. A list of councils held during the governorship of the dukes of Albany is given by A. A. M. Duncan, *op. cit.*, *S.H.R.*, XXXV. 132–43, at 143.

[5] *A.P.S.*, I. 501, 506, 534, 547.

[6] *Ibid.*, II. 3.

[7] *Ibid.*, 4.

[8] *Ibid.*, 3, c. 2.

question of the royal revenues, and, coupled with this, the payment of 'the fynance to be made in Inglande'. It was decided that it would be 'grevous and chargeande on the commonys to raiss the haill fynance at anyss'—in other words that the money should be raised over a period of years rather than by one crippling levy. Meanwhile an aid or tax of one shilling in the pound was to be imposed on income and movable goods throughout the whole realm, including the regalities. In many respects the arrangements were modelled upon those devised in 1357 for payment of David II's ransom; once more a Scottish Domesday Book was to be compiled in a few weeks (by 12 July 1424) and the yield of 1s. in the pound was to be forthcoming by then.[9]

Just as the ransom of David II had brought the burgesses into a new prominence and assured them a permanent place as one of the estates of the realm, James I's 'fynance' was to lead to a further advancement of the merchant burgesses, whose goodwill he henceforth cultivated. In the parliament of 1424 the burgess commissioners 'in the name of the haill merchandis of the realme' undertook to pay the whole of the first instalment of the 'fynance' amounting to 10,000 English marks (or 20,000 English 'nobles') to be repaid from the proceeds of the valuation of the whole realm. To raise the first payment the burgesses thought it would be necessary to obtain 'chevisance'—a loan—in Flanders and undertook to contribute 300 'nobles' towards the expenses of the necessary mission. For this generosity some recompense was expected : henceforth no foreign merchant was to buy any goods for export from Scotland save from a Scottish merchant.[10]

While the ransom of David II had been met in fact not through direct taxation but from the increasing proceeds of the great customs, James was determined to pay his 'fynance' from direct taxation and keep the great customs to himself.[11] Meanwhile the opportunity was taken to impose new export duties on herring, horses, sheep and certain skins.[12] There was also an announcement that those who claimed pensions from the customs were to show evidence to the king, who would answer such a claim with the advice of his council; this

---

[9] *Ibid.*, 4, c. 10.
[10] *Ibid.*, 6, c. 27. George Burnett (*E.R.*, iv. cxxx) wrongly thought that the burgesses undertook to pay two-fifths of the king's 'fynance', amounting to 20,000 marks. A sum approximating to this was banked with the burghs (p. 290 below), and the burghs undertook to make a *loan* of 10,000 marks, but their own contribution to the 'fynance' was to be derived from the levy of 1s. in the pound on the basis of the new valuation, and its amount cannot be ascertained.
[11] *A.P.S.*, II. 4, c. 8.   [12] *Ibid.*, 6, cc. 22, 23.

hinted at a revocation of annuities payable from the customs (which was accomplished).[13] More than that, the sheriffs were to hold inquests to ascertain what lands, possessions or annualrents had belonged to the crown in the times of David II, Robert II and Robert III, and in whose hands they now were; the king might summon his tenants to produce their charters so that 'he may persave quhat pertenys to thame'[14]—and no doubt perceive what might be recovered from them.

What resulted from the financial arrangements of the 1424 parliament is not clear. The new export duties seem to have been unproductive.[15] But the proceeds of the traditional great customs showed an immediate increase: at the audit of July 1422 the gross receipts had come to £2,779 8s. 2d.;[16] at the audit of May 1425 they totalled £4,400 4s. 9½d.[17] These receipts were to rise as high as £6,912 2s. 5¼d. in 1428, though the average annual yield up to the end of the reign was little more than £5,000,[18] showing a level of exports higher than during the Albany governorship but lower than in the later years of David II when the export duties were the same.

Most significant of all was the outcome of the contribution of a shilling in the pound that the 1424 parliament had granted towards the king's 'fynance'. Over a two-year period the total yield came to little less than 40,000 English 'nobles',[19] or two-fifths of the total payment due to the English. This sum was paid to the burghs, which acted as the king's bankers in this vast transaction.[20] Although a good deal had been collected, it proved impossible to continue the practice of direct taxation as in the time of David II. The long gap in direct taxation since 1373–4 had hardened the Scots in their view that it was virtually unconstitutional. According to Abbot Bower, himself one of the auditors of the contribution, James's subjects were soon complaining that they were being turned into paupers by taxation.[21] Collection of the contribution for the English 'fynance' was stopped after the second year because of the outcry against it.

Thus the financial measures of the 1424 parliament were, from the point of view of the king, only moderately successful. While he could partially restore some of the crown revenues, such as the great customs, others were unproductive, unforthcoming, or static—the fixed feu-ferms of the burghs brought in about £550 a year but half

13 *Ibid.*, 4, c. 8; *E.R.*, IV. xciii.
14 *A.P.S.*, II. 4, c. 9.
15 *E.R.*, IV. cxxxvi–cxxviii.
16 *Ibid.*, 358–68.
17 *Ibid.*, xciii.
18 *Ibid.*, cxxv.
19 *Ibid.*, cxxxi.
20 *Ibid.*, 639–71.
21 *Chron. Bower*, II. 482.

of this went in long-standing ecclesiastical pensions; by 1424 the income from the crown lands was only about £1,000 a year;[22] the
king's total annual revenue can scarcely have exceeded £7,000; and
from this he was expected to maintain his household, finance government, and perhaps to meet his obligations to the English. Well might
Abbot Bower remark that at the king's return 'there remained too
little to him of the royal revenues, lands or possessions, besides customs, wards and reliefs, to sustain his position'.[23]

By contrast some of the Scottish nobles, with far smaller obligations, had an annual revenue of as much as £1,000. This emerges
from the figures given for the revenues of the hostages demanded by
the English in 1423–1424: the thirty-five nobles listed had a total
annual income of 21,700 marks.[24] This list by no means included all
Scottish nobles, nor did it include the richest—the Albany Stewarts
and the Black Douglases. A group of only four or five nobles headed
by either Albany or Douglas might have economic resources superior
to those of the king. If James were to rule Scotland as effectively as
he wished, it was no doubt necessary either that the economic resources of the crown should be augmented—or that those of the
greater nobility be diminished. The first alternative was soon shown
to be difficult. James was to concentrate upon the second. There is no
sign that he carried out the revocation of former crown lands that had
been envisaged in the legislation of the 1424 parliament. Such a
measure would have caused universal antagonism among the nobility.
Instead of wholesale revocation James's policy was to be one of for-
feiting individual noble families. By the end of the reign the area of
the crown lands had been greatly expanded, and with the increase
the crown's annual income from this source rose threefold to some
£3,000.[25] James was to set a precedent that the next three kings
would follow successfully, though perilously.

While there was an economic motive that influenced James's
policy towards the leading nobles there were political and personal
motives as well. James seems to have borne a grudge towards the Albany Stewarts for allowing him to languish in England—a grudge
perhaps sharpened by the fear that an Albany Stewart might succeed
to the throne. For when Queen Joan gave birth at Christmas 1424
her child was a daughter, Margaret,[26] who would be debarred from

[22] Balfour-Melville, *James I*, p. 265.   [23] *Chron. Bower*, II. 482.
[24] See *Rot. Scot.*, II. 242 and *Cal. Docs. Scot.*, IV. No. 952.
[25] Balfour-Melville, *James I*, p. 265.   [26] Dunbar, *Scot. Kings*, p. 191.

the succession by the tailzie of 1373.[27] Duke Murdoch was not only the greatest of the Scottish nobles but was heir presumptive. Besides these grounds of suspicion and jealousy there were perhaps others that harked back to the circumstances of the death of James's elder brother, the Duke of Rothesay—a theme on which the Scottish chroniclers wrote with caution. An English account was less reticent, and represented Rothesay's death as the result of a wholesale conspiracy on the part of the Scottish nobles.[28] Certainly the Rothesay affair might provide a pretext for the arrest and interrogation of almost any noble; Duke Murdoch must have been uneasy so long as his eldest son, Walter, and his brother-in-law, Malcolm Fleming, lay in royal custody. Their arrest early in 1424 was followed towards the end of the year by that of Sir Robert Graham, younger son of Sir Patrick Graham of Kincardine.[29] No one can have suspected what the ultimate result of the king's attack on Sir Robert Graham would turn out to be. It was more striking that Duncan, Earl of Lennox, the aged father-in-law of Duke Murdoch, was also arrested.[30] As James's second parliament opened at Perth on 12 March 1425 the net was beginning to tighten around the Albany Stewarts who were still at large.

In this parliament various 'articles' were proposed for 'the quiete and gud governance of the realme'[31] and were passed as legislation. James showed that he understood the dangers inherent in 'bastard feudalism': one statute referred to the leagues and bonds[32] that allied one magnate to another in factions that promoted feud and might also promote opposition to the crown; henceforth the making of such leagues was forbidden and any already made were pronounced null and void. This significant measure was designed to break up the contemporary forms of political association among the members of the only class that could actively oppose the crown. Whatever the immediate effect it was not lasting. Some other of the statutes passed by the 1425 parliament related to the current political situation. One was a statute against 'leasing making'—the spreading of tales 'quhilk may ingener discorde betuix the king and his pepill'.[33] Another 'item' instituted an inquiry to see whether the statutes of 1424 were properly observed; if they had been broken in any point those responsible

---

[27] P. 186 above.
[28] See *James I, Life and Death*, pp. 48–9. This fifteenth-century narrative has much information relating to the reign of James I that is not found in any other source.   [29] *E.R.*, IV. lxxxix.
[30] *Chron. Bower*, II. 482.   [31] *A.P.S.*, II. 7–8.
[32] See *Scot. Legal Hist.*, pp. 285–6.   [33] *A.P.S.*, II. 8, c. 22.

were to be punished in the manner laid down by the 1424 parliament.[34] It was possibly this item that cleared the ground for the king's sensational move on the ninth day of the parliament, when he arrested Duke Murdoch, his wife Isabella, daughter of the Earl of Lennox, and their second surviving son, Alexander, besides Sir John Montgomery, a henchman of the duke, and Alan Otterburn, the duke's secretary.[35] The youngest of Murdoch's sons, James Stewart, still remained at large; on 3 May 1425 he burned the burgh of Dumbarton and slew the king's illegitimate uncle, John, the Red Stewart of Dundonald.[36]

The Dumbarton affair must have played into the king's hands by making more plausible whatever charges were brought against the Albany Stewarts when they were tried on 24 May 1425 before an assize of twenty-one nobles during a session of parliament held at Stirling. Duke Murdoch's eldest surviving son, Walter Stewart, was convicted of *roborea*—presumably extortion—and was beheaded in front of Stirling Castle. On the following day the same fate was meted out to Duke Murdoch, his son Alexander, and the octogenarian Earl of Lennox.[37] The people mourned the fall of the Albany Stewarts, 'saying that they suppoised and ymagynd that the kyng ded ... that vigorious execucion upon the lordes of his kyne for the covetise of thare possessions and goodes'.[38] Certainly the executions brought rewards to the king. The forfeited earldoms of Fife and Menteith were worth about £900 a year,[39] and the king also obtained the earldom of Lennox when Inchmurrin Castle surrendered on 8 June 1425.[40] James Stewart and his followers, including the Dominican friar Finlay of Albany, Bishop of Argyll, fled to Ireland to end their days in exile.[41]

By his sensational destruction of the house of Albany the king had accomplished and dramatised a royalist revolution. How he achieved this is not clear. He had presumably played upon the hopes and fears of some of the greater nobles and used them for his own ends. In addition his other allies included knights, prelates and officials of the

[34] *Ibid.*, 7, c. 4.
[35] E. W. M. Balfour-Melville has shown (*James I*, p. 120, n. 3) that the supposition that James simultaneously arrested a further score of nobles is based upon a misreading of a somewhat ambiguous passage in Bower (*Chron. Bower*, II. 482–3).
[36] *Chron. Bower*, II. 482–3.
[37] *Ibid.*, 483–4; for discussion of the procedure at the trial see Rait, *Parliaments*, p. 329.
[38] *James I, Life and Death*, p. 49.   [39] *E.R.*, VI. lxxiv *et seq.*
[40] *Chron. Bower*, II. 484.   [41] *Ibid.*, 483.

same stamp as those who had stood by David II. But James's greatest source of strength was his own powerful personality and the moral support he drew from a people that longed for firm rule; the king who showed that he could oppress the mighty could prevent the mighty from oppressing the weak.

Apart from the internal factors that had facilitated the royalist coup of 1424–25, there were also external factors that from 1424 onwards indirectly strengthened King James's position at the expense of the Scottish nobility. Unlike his predecessors, James was faced by no serious threat from England and was therefore able to devote his energies uninterruptedly to the task of governing Scotland. Moreover, James's arrival in Scotland in 1424 had coincided with the departure of nobles who might otherwise have held him in check—some went as hostages to England, others went to France, where there were dazzling prospects for Scots, particularly those—and they were many—who considered themselves well-born.

The Franco-Scottish victory at Baugé in 1421 had soon been followed by the death of Henry V and of Charles VI. While John, Duke of Bedford, governed English-occupied France in the name of the infant Henry VI, the *parlement* of Paris, which had taken refuge in Poitiers, recognised the dauphin as Charles VII. For a number of years his fortunes were precarious. On 31 July 1423 his forces had the worse of an engagement at Cravant in which the Scottish contingent suffered heavy loss.[42] To remedy this setback Archibald the Tyneman and John Stewart, Earl of Buchan, had recruited a fresh Scottish expeditionary force that landed in France at the beginning of Lent 1424; Charles VII once more showed his gratitude and rewarded the Tyneman with the duchy of Touraine and his son, the Earl of Wigtown, with the lands of Dun-le-Roi in Berry.[43] But at Verneuil on 17 August 1424 the French and their Scottish allies were vanquished. The Tyneman, who had clattered his way in history from one lost battle to another, had lost his last battle. With him fell his second son, Sir James Douglas, and his son-in-law, the Earl of Buchan.[44]

Although the heavy losses of the Scots prevented the survivors

---

[42] *Ibid.*, 501; A. H. Burne, *The Agincourt War* (1956), pp. 188, 193; E. F. Jacob, *The Fifteenth Century*, pp. 242–3; Balfour-Melville, *James I*, p. 104; Francisque-Michel, *Les Ecossais en France*, I. 136–42.

[43] *Scots Peerage*, III. 166; Balfour-Melville, *James I*, p. 115.

[44] Balfour-Melville, *James I*, p. 115; E. F. Jacob, *The Fifteenth Century*, p. 244; A. H. Burne, *The Agincourt War*, p. 213.

from playing a dominant part in the continuing warfare, they persevered in the service of Charles VII under Sir John Stewart of Darnley
and Hugh Kennedy.[45] And in 1428 Charles VII made another attempt to obtain reinforcements from Scotland, as well as a renewal of
the Franco-Scottish alliance, and a marriage between James's three-
year-old daughter Margaret and Charles's almost equally young son
and heir, the Dauphin Louis. In July 1428 James promised to observe
the Franco-Scottish alliance, and a marriage contract was sealed :
Margaret was to be sent to France in a French fleet which would also
take on board six thousand Scots to enlist in the French service.[46] In
November 1428 Charles VII acknowledged that the despatch of
these troops might bring war between Scotland and England and
endanger the Scottish hostages; he therefore granted to James and
his heirs the county of Saintonge, the castellany of Rochefort-sur-
Charente, and the dignity of peer of France.[47] Though French kings
never implemented the grant, Scottish kings never forgot it.

Meanwhile the English had besieged Orleans. Sir John Stewart
of Darnley brought short-lived encouragement to the defenders but
was slain near Rouvray on 12 February 1429.[48] After this, Orleans
was regarded as virtually lost and Charles VII was supposed to have
been advised by the *parlement* to seek refuge in Scotland. But France
was to save itself by its own exertions : 'in those days the Lord exalted
the spirit of a certain wondrous maid . . . in the duchy of Lorraine'.[49]
Joan of Arc brought what seemed to be supernatural intervention.
On 30 April 1429 she entered Orleans at the head of a relief force. It
was a Scotsman, John Carmichael or Kirkmichael, who as Bishop of
Orleans welcomed Joan into the city. He was among those Scots who
followed the Maid as she conducted Charles VII into Rheims on 18
July 1429 [50] for the traditional ceremony of coronation and unction
that made him truly King of France.

Although the position of Charles VII became much stronger
James I put obstacles in the way of sending his daughter to France
for marriage to the dauphin ;[51] nor were the six thousand Scots troops
stipulated in the marriage treaty forthcoming. It was not until March

[45] Balfour-Melville, *James I*, pp. 79–80, 159.
[46] *A.P.S.*, II. 26–8; *Chron. Bower*, II. 484.
[47] *Spalding Club Misc. II*, 181–6.
[48] *Chron. Bower*, II. 501; *Chron. Pluscarden*, I. 363–4.
[49] *Chron. Pluscarden*, I. 365–7.
[50] *Chron. Bower*, II. 465; John Kirkpatrick, *op. cit.*, *S.H.S. Misc. II*. 47–102,
at 55; E. F. Jacob, *The Fifteenth Century*, pp. 247–8.
[51] Balfour-Melville, *James I*, pp. 213–20.

1436 that James's daughter sailed from Dumbarton. On 25 June 1436 the eleven-year-old princess was married at Tours to the thirteen-year-old Dauphin Louis, who thereafter neglected her.[52] Through this *mariage de convenance* James had attached himself closely to France at a time when the security of the Valois dynasty was at last assured. In the summer of 1435 an international congress at Arras saw the end of the Anglo-Burgundian alliance that had been essential to English success.[53] Had Margaret Stewart given birth to a future king of France the historical significance of her marriage might have been much greater.

Despite the fact that James latterly committed himself to France it was not until the end of his reign that the possibility of an alternative policy of co-operation with England became remote. James himself took advantage of access to English markets and employed two English merchants as well as a Florentine and Genoese as his factors in London. Their purchases on his behalf came to over £3,500.[54] Between 1423 and 1441 over fifty English safe-conducts were issued to persons engaged in Anglo-Scottish trade.[55] While avoiding a rupture with England so long as it suited him to do so, James also avoided full payment of his financial obligation to the English. Although some 40,000 'nobles' had been raised by taxation to help to meet the king's 'fynance' much of what had been collected remained in the hands of the burgh authorities[56] as late as 1432.[57] The king drew upon these credits as he saw fit, in payments to himself, his officials, and his commercial agents in the Netherlands.[58] Thus the total 'fynance' that the English ever received was only 9,500 marks (or 19,000 'nobles') in English coin.[59] Though the English soon resented James's failure to pay his 'fynance' they were also aware that he could not easily be forced to pay by the threat of war, which would have cost much more than what might be obtained in the way of 'fynance'. It followed that they could make use only of moral pressure and of the hostages that had been delivered in 1424 as surety for payment. But to James the hostages meant little; it probably suited him to see a

---

[52] *Ibid.*, pp. 225–7; Dunlop, *Bishop Kennedy*, pp. 17, 373; *E.R.*, iv. cviii; Louis A. Barbé, *Margaret of Scotland and the Dauphin Louis* (1917); R. S. Rait, *Five Stuart Princesses* (1902), pp. 1–46.
[53] E. F. Jacob, *The Fifteenth Century*, pp. 260–3.
[54] *E.R.*, iv. cxlvii–cxlviii.
[55] Grant, *Social and Economic Development*, p. 336, n. 1.
[56] P. 283 above.   [57] *E.R.*, iv. 673.   [58] *Ibid.*, cxxxii, 672–85.
[59] Balfour-Melville, *James I*, pp. 110, 146; *E.R.*, iv. cxxxii–cxxxiv.

number of potential opponents kept in England. The very arrangements that had been made in 1424 for the·possible replacement of hostages probably also played into the king's hands. It was he who might arrange (or not arrange) the release of one hostage in return for the sending of a new hostage to take his place.[60] There were to be three exchanges of hostages, one in August 1425, another in October 1427, and the last in July 1432. But these exchanges were not wholesale : some of the original hostages of 1424 were left unexchanged, to die in England or to languish there for decades.[61]

In the last resort James had nothing to fear from England so long as he did not give military or political provocation, and even in these respects he might go far before his bluff was called. Thanks to James's conduct the personal reputation of Bishop Beaufort (now a cardinal) was at stake : he was held responsible for the marriage of his niece to James and the subsequent release of the Scottish king. The cardinal hoped to gain a favourable settlement in a personal interview with his nephew at Coldingham in the spring of 1429.[62] Although James avoided giving any guarantees to the cardinal the existing truce was renewed on 15 December 1430 for a further five years. This was a diplomatic triumph for James. He had evaded any commitment about the hostages or the 'fynance'. He had obtained not the general truce by land and sea that the English wanted but a general truce by sea and a limited one by land, comprising 'all the realm of Henry' north of St Michael's Mount in Cornwall and 'all the realm of James' south of the river Findhorn.[63] The 'realm of Henry' in France was still fair game for Scottish mercenaries, and James had preserved not only his alliance with France but the marriage contract that might strengthen it.

On this point the English remained touchy, and so long as his daughter remained in Scotland James was in a strong bargaining position : to forestall the French match the English were ready by the autumn of 1433 to surrender Roxburgh and Jedburgh.[64] This offer was debated in a general council at Perth in October 1433.[65] Each of the prelates welcomed the chance of a final peace on such favourable

---

[60] *Morton Registrum*, I. xlii.
[61] See the remarks of the Pluscarden writer (*Chron. Pluscarden*, I. 370). Full details of the hostages and the three exchanges are given in Balfour-Melville, *James I*, appendix D, pp. 293–5.
[62] Balfour-Melville, *James I*, pp. 166–9.
[63] *Cal. Docs. Scot.*, IV. No. 1043.
[64] Balfour-Melville, *James I*, p. 209.
[65] *Chron. Bower*, II. 498–9; *Chron. Pluscarden*, I. 378–9.

terms until it came to the turn of Abbot Bower of Inchcolm and the Abbot of Scone, who dissented : the king could not make peace with the English on account of the Franco-Scottish treaty which had been examined by the university of Paris and confirmed by the pope. John Fogo, master of theology and Abbot of Melrose, countered their views, and since Fogo was the king's confessor it may be assumed that he was acting as the king's mouthpiece. In the course of his specious arguments, which did no credit to himself or James, Fogo questioned the validity of the Franco-Scottish alliance, only to be menaced by the ever watchful inquisitor, Master Laurence of Lindores, who suspected error in the theological propositions on which Fogo had based his case. The English proposals were rejected, and subsequent negotiations for a marriage between one of James's daughters and Henry VI were inconclusive. By May 1434 the English were making defensive preparations.[66] French envoys who arrived in Scotland in January 1435 declined James's unfulfilled offer to send six thousand troops to France but informed him that Charles VII would be grateful for help in the way of warfare on the Borders.[67] It was at this very time that James chose to deprive George Dunbar of his ancestral earldom of March.[68] The earl, who had adhered to the English along with his father in 1400,[69] may have been thought unreliable; certainly the forfeiture of his earldom on 11 January 1435 was calculated to make him less reliable. In the summer of 1435 James complained that the earl's brother, Patrick of Dunbar, 'the kingis rebell', was being maintained by the keeper of Berwick Castle; the pair 'with grete hoste and fere of wer' made a foray in contravention of the truce, only to be routed at Piperden on 10 September 1435.[70] When James's daughter arrived in France the Anglo-Scottish truce expired.

By the beginning of August 1436 the English council had heard that James was already besieging Roxburgh.[71] After a fruitless fortnight before its walls the Scottish host broke up and withdrew 'with the greatest shame'.[72] All the costly siege artillery that the king had fashioned at home or imported from Flanders [73] was abandoned to the English.[74] Since the latter had no desire to keep up a war with Scotland some sort of truce seems to have been arrived at.[75] James showed

---

[66] Balfour-Melville, *James I*, pp. 208–13.
[67] *Ibid.*, p. 220.   [68] P. 319 below.   [69] Pp. 218–9, 230–1 above.
[70] Balfour-Melville, *James I*, p. 221.   [71] *Rot. Scot.*, II. 294.
[72] *Chron. Pluscarden*, I. 380.   [73] *E.R.*, IV. cxlviii–cxlix, 677.
[74] *Chron. Pluscarden*, I. 376, 380; *Chron. Bower*, II. 502.
[75] Balfour-Melville, *James I*, pp. 230–1.

his frustration in a general council that met at Edinburgh on 22 October 1436 by passing a number of anti-English statutes.[76]

While much of James I's diplomacy was concerned with the triangular relationship that involved Scotland, France and England, there was another relationship—between Scotland and the papacy—that posed new diplomatic problems. If James felt the need to reassert royal authority after the lackadaisical government of the Albany Stewarts, Pope Martin V felt the need to re-assert papal authority after the disastrous divisions of the Great Schism of 1378–1418, and the spread of conciliarist ideas. Although the council of Constance had shown its adherence to doctrinal orthodoxy by making a martyr of John Hus, a Bohemian deviationist, it had also in 1415 issued the decree *Sacrosancta*, proclaiming that 'this synod legally assembled in the Holy Spirit, constituting a General Council and representing the Catholic Church, holds its power directly from Christ; every person, whatsoever his degree or his dignity, even though this latter be pontifical, is bound to obey it in everything relating to the faith and the above mentioned schism'.[77] The council had also voiced dislike of papal provisions and reservations and might have insisted on their abolition had it not been overtaken by weariness : at the critical moment 'everything that could be postponed was postponed', and Martin V, even before his coronation, 'had already been at work undoing as much as he could of the council's work for reform'.[78] His continuation and invigoration of the system of provisions was to be resented by James I, not only because of conflicts of interest between crown and papacy over the political and administrative issues involved in ecclesiastical patronage, but also because of economic issues that seemed no less important : mercantilist theories were growing in influence; in inculcating a sort of economic nationalism they corresponded to the subtle changes that were transforming feudal monarchy into national monarchy; in the long run both political and economic nationalism were to weaken the papacy, the last great bastion of medieval cosmopolitanism. James I, who fully shared the mercantilist outlook, looked askance at any outflow of bullion from his kingdom, particularly one that brought in return not an import of goods but merely a re-allocation of Scottish benefices, sometimes to the disadvantage of

[76] *A.P.S.*, II. 23–4.
[77] John Holland Smith, *The Great Schism*, pp. 196–7.
[78] *Ibid.*, pp. 216–7.

the crown. Thus James wished to control the practice whereby any cleric might go to the papal court, or send a procurator there, to 'impetrate' (petition) the grant of a benefice or of a pension from a benefice.

Like so much else in the reign the king's new policy towards the papacy was sign-posted in the 'articles' or 'items' of his first parliament in May 1424. Thus one item forbade kirkmen to go overseas or send procurators overseas without leave of the king. Another put a tax of 3s. 4d. on each pound's worth of gold or silver exported from the realm. Another forbade kirkmen 'to purchess ony pensione out of ony benefice'. This ruling was forthwith applied by the parliamentary commission of 1424 to settle 'the complaynt that Maister Nicholl of Cummock maide apone Maister Ingrem Lindissay that he purchest in the court of Rome ane pensione out of the denry [deanery] of Abirdene in dismembring of his benefice'.[79] In another dispute parliament even decided who was rightful Prior of Coldingham.[80] Though James proceeded pragmatically, and enunciated no theory or principle, he had insidiously carried much further the extension of secular control over the kirk that had begun to manifest itself in Scotland during the Great Schism. The culmination of James's programme came in the parliament of March 1428 when an act was passed which ordained that any cleric who wished to leave the realm should first approach his bishop, or the chancellor, and 'schaw to thame gude and honest cause of his passage and mak faith to thame that he do no baratry'.[81] The new offence of barratry was not defined but undoubtedly signified the purchase of benefices, or pensions from benefices, at the *curia*. Regardless of this act the barrators appear to have remained as active as ever.[82]

The development of James's attack upon papal patronage had coincided with the rise of the man who was to implement it—John Cameron, a cleric who in 1424 became the king's secretary and, shortly afterwards, keeper of the privy seal.[83] When the see of Glasgow fell vacant in 1425 the chapter bowed to the royal wishes by electing Cameron. Since the see had been 'reserved', Martin V quashed the election; as a result of royal pressure he relented and on 22 April 1426 provided Cameron to the bishopric.[84] By May 1427

[79] *A.P.S.*, II. 5, cc. 14, 15, 16; 6, c. 26.
[80] *Nat. MSS. Scot.*, II. No. lxv.   [81] *A.P.S.*, II. 16, c. 9.
[82] This may be inferred from *Cal. Scot. Supp. 1428–32, passim.*
[83] Balfour-Melville, *James I*, pp. 138–9; R. K. Hannay, 'James I, Bishop Cameron and the Papacy', *S.H.R.*, xv. 190–200.
[84] Balfour-Melville, *James I*, pp. 139–40; Burns, *Basle*, pp. 16–7.

Cameron, who had previously had custody of the great seal, was formally styled chancellor.[85]

In the case of the bishopric of Glasgow the pope had given way to the king in practice, but in theory had kept rights of papal patronage intact. The tacit understanding behind this concession and others was that the king would be allowed to share papal patronage and its profits on condition that he respected the system and did not interfere with it. The understanding was jeopardised when William Croyser, archdeacon of Teviotdale, became involved in a jurisdictional dispute with Bishop Cameron.[86] By the spring of 1429 Croyser had drawn Martin V's attention to developments in Scotland, representing that it was Cameron as chancellor, rather than the king, who was the moving spirit behind the barratry legislation.[87] Croyser's tales found sympathetic ears. Two cardinals concluded that Cameron was responsible for the acts of the Scottish parliament 'against ecclesiastical liberty and the rights of the Roman church'; he was 'so guilty as to deserve deprivation'. It was none other than Croyser who was given the pleasing task of citing Cameron to the Roman court in the summer of 1429.[88]

The king did not stand idly by to see his chancellor disgraced: in the summer of 1430 an embassy reached Rome to defend Cameron and to retaliate upon Croyser by citing him to appear before the Scottish parliament. A sort of truce followed: up to the time when Martin V died in February 1431 a violent clash between king and pope had been averted.[89] Nonetheless, the papacy was under no illusion that a permanent settlement had been reached. Croyser, the self-appointed watchdog of papal interests in Scotland, was to be well rewarded to encourage his unremitting zeal: one of the last acts of Martin V was to provide him effectively—he had already been twice provided ineffectively—to the archdeaconry of Lothian, which he was to be allowed to hold in addition to his archdeaconry of Teviotdale and his other benefices. The new pope, Eugenius IV, made it even clearer that Croyser was an agent of the papacy.[90]

It was at this stage, however, that a new and uncertain factor complicated the situation. In the decree *Frequens* the council of Constance had laid down that general councils of the church should be held periodically. Shortly before his death Martin V had been in-

---

[85] *E.R.*, iv. 400, 428; *R.M.S.*, ii. No. 89 (witness No. 74).
[86] *Glasgow Registrum*, ii. 140 and No. 332.
[87] Balfour-Melville, *James I*, p. 174. [88] *Ibid.*, p. 177.
[89] *Ibid.*, pp. 178-9; Burns, *Basle*, p. 23. [90] Burns, *Basle*, pp. 11-2, 23.

duced to summon another council to meet at Basel (or Basle), where the first full formal session was held on 14 November 1431. A month later, however, Eugenius issued bulls dissolving the council and summoning a new one to meet in Bologna, where it would be more amenable to papal control.[91] The council of Basel refused to be dissolved and re-opened old disputes by giving fresh publicity to the decree *Sacrosancta* of 1415.[92]

One of the rulers of western Christendom to whom the council appealed for support during its initial conflict with the pope was the Scottish king. Although he did not send official representatives Scotland was at least unofficially represented at Basel, notably by Thomas Livingston, Abbot of Dundrennan, who soon became a foremost member of the council[93] and was to adhere to it to the end. Meanwhile the pope changed his mind and on 18 December 1433 revoked his dissolution of the council: 'the prolonged initial conflict was over, and a period of comparative harmony began'.[94] It was 'to a council for the time being at peace with the pope that James I gave his support'.[95] At last, without incurring the reproaches of Eugenius, James could send representatives to Basel to enlist the council's aid in settling his dispute with the pope. But on the very day (8 February 1434) that Bishop Cameron was incorporated in the council so was his old foe, Archdeacon Croyser, who with no small exaggeration denounced the Scottish king and called for justice against him and his officials.[96] Croyser's conduct at Basel led to his denunciation as a traitor and rebel before the Scottish parliament (presumably the parliament that met at Perth on 10 January 1435). Judgment was given against him in his absence and he was deprived of his benefices and revenues; thenceforth the pope insisted on the restoration of Croyser as well as a modification of James's policies.[97]

During this crisis, in the spring of 1435, Cameron left Basel for the papal court to persuade the pope that the dispute might best be resolved by sending to Scotland a legate who could reach a direct settlement with the king.[98] Eugenius, however, remained suspicious and for the time being refused to send a legate. By June 1435 Cameron had returned to Basel to engage in further controversy with Croyser. Simultaneously the council promulgated decrees that attacked the whole basis of papal finance and ended 'the brief period

[91] *Ibid.*, pp. 10–1.
[92] *Chron. Bower*, II. 479.
[93] Burns, *Basle*, pp. 11–14.
[94] *Ibid.*, pp. 11–2, 13, 14–6.
[95] *Ibid.*, p. 16.
[96] *Ibid.*, pp. 25, 27.
[97] *Ibid.*, pp. 37–8.
[98] *Ibid.*, pp. 38–9; Balfour-Melville, *James I*, p. 237.

during which relations between pope and council were correct if not cordial'. Thus 'to join the council or have dealings with it after this period meant some degree of association with the anti-papal party'.[99] Yet Cameron remained at Basel and was soon joined by other Scots clerics, including two royal secretaries.[100] Meanwhile the pope wrote to seek the intervention of Nicholas Albergati, Cardinal of Santa Croce, who was presiding at the congress of Arras. As a result the cardinal sent to Scotland his secretary, Aeneas Sylvius, to restore 'a certain prelate to the king's favour'—undoubtedly Croyser.[101] Aeneas, the future Pope Pius II, compiled an unflattering account of the uncouth land where people heated themselves by burning a black stone instead of wood, where houses in the countryside were roofed with turf and those in the unwalled towns constructed without lime, where the common people were poor and destitute of all refinement, and the women fair, but not distinguished for their chastity. He concluded, shrewdly enough, that 'nothing pleases the Scots more than abuse of the English'.[102] Having acquired chronic rheumatism in Scotland he went back with no good news for the pope and the archdeacon. On 8 March 1436 Eugenius issued a bull that annulled the deprivation of Croyser and stigmatised unhelpful Scottish bishops as 'Pilates rather than prelates'.[103] Shortly afterwards he wrote directly to James demanding the restoration of Croyser and the repeal of the barratry legislation, 'which the pope, so far as is needful, himself annuls'.[104] The king can hardly have been left in doubt that he was running the risk of excommunication and interdict.

In one respect the pope's twofold demand was to be circumvented : through the mediation of the council of Basel, Croyser removed himself from the battlefield of royal and papal acrimony ; he even proved helpful to James by urging the pope to send the legatine mission that the king desired. On 2 July 1436 Antonio Altani, Bishop of Urbino, was appointed as legate. While it was no doubt envisaged that he would negotiate a concordat, it was not for this purpose alone that his presence was needed: 'the policy of securing a papal legate for Scotland had never, in James's eyes, been one of capitulation to papal demands'.[105] The terms of the legate's appointment show that it was

[99] Burns, *Basle*, pp. 39-40. [100] *Ibid.*, pp. 43-50.
[101] Balfour-Melville, *James I*, pp. 234-5.
[102] Brown, *Early Travellers*, pp. 25-38.
[103] Balfour-Melville, *James I*, p. 237; Burns, *Basle*, p. 50.
[104] Balfour-Melville, *James I*, pp. 237-8.
[105] Burns, *Basle*, pp. 51, 52 and n., 56; see also R. K. Hannay, *op. cit.*, *S.H.R.*, xv. 190-200, at 198-9.

the reformation of the kirk that James sought; equipped with generous powers of dispensation and discipline Altani was 'to visit and
reform all churches, monasteries, etc.' and to give heed to 'the
ecclesiastical state of the realm'.[106]

To James the Scottish kirk was 'a department of national life
which he was called to reduce to order',[107] and all members of the
clergy, even those in Galloway who were still nominally dependent
on the Archbishop of York, were to enjoy 'one law and privilege and
general liberty'.[108] Despite his altercations with the papacy the king
could boast of 'the gret favouris, graciose zele and mantenaunce' that
he displayed towards the kirk and its ministers.[109] His insistence
that the ritual of public worship should incorporate prayers for the
royal family [110] sprang not only from genuine piety, but from a desire
to cast a spiritual aura around the monarchy and to publicise its
unity with the kirk, which was itself to be reformed according to
high and uniform standards. For these purposes the co-operation of
the bishops had to be forthcoming. Apart from their role in public
life, James's bishops seem to have shown in the administration of
their dioceses qualities that were diverse, but respectable.[111] Even
Cameron, despite his involvement in affairs of state, was an active
administrator of his diocese and a zealous benefactor of his cathedral.[112] But if the episcopate was, by contemporary standards, competent and well-educated, there were defects in other quarters.

It was the monasteries that chiefly aroused the king's concern.
On 17 March 1425, while the three estates were in session at Perth,
James used this public occasion to draft a letter to the abbots and
priors of the Benedictine and Augustinian orders in Scotland,[113]
warning them that 'the downhill condition and most threatening ruin
of holy religion, now declining from day to day from the original
establishment of its foundation, fill us with apprehension'. They were
to take heed 'how in our realm the decline of monastic religion, everywhere defamed and reduced to contempt, tends to destruction'. If
the abbots and priors remained negligent and idle, 'the munificence

---

[106] *Cal. Papal Letters*, VIII. 229, 288–90; Balfour-Melville, *James I*, pp. 239–
40; Burns, *Basle*, p. 52.
[107] A. R. MacEwen, *History of the Church in Scotland*, I. 336.
[108] *R.M.S.*, II. No. 164.   [109] *A.P.S.*, II. 10.   [110] *Ibid.*, 8, 10.
[111] Balfour-Melville, *James I*, pp. 274–7.
[112] *Glasgow Registrum*, pp. 323–61, *passim*; Innes, *Scot. Middle Ages*, p. 270
and appendix pp. 336–40.
[113] *A.P.S.*, II. 25. The letter is also cited, apparently with approval, by Abbot
Bower (*Chron. Bower*, II. 508–9) who as an Augustinian abbot was one of the
persons to whom it was addressed.

of kings, who formerly . . . notably endowed your monasteries . . . may repent of having erected walls of marble when it considers that you have so shamelessly abandoned your religious character'.

Yet despite James's misgivings, he led no attack on monastic endowment, rather the reverse.[114] His old-fashioned generosity towards the monasteries sprang from the conviction that all was not yet lost : the vast investment in these institutions might be redeemed if only the abbots and priors would undertake 'an ascent to the highest reaches of perfection'.[115] James was ready to point the way, even at the cost of further investment : although no sizable monastery had been founded since 1273 the king immediately followed his denunciation of the Benedictines and Augustinians with plans for the establishment of a Carthusian monastery at Perth, to be partly financed by the annexation of the parish kirk of Erroll.[116] This Charterhouse of Perth (which obtained its name not from any connection with charters but from its association with the Grande Chartreuse) seems to have preserved the unsullied reputation for which its strict order was noted, though it scarcely served James's purpose of shaming the other Scottish monastic houses into an amendment of their way of life. The Charterhouse was the last monastery to be founded in medieval Scotland and was the first to be destroyed in the reformation-rebellion of 1559.

Significantly enough, John Knox, whose sermon at Perth in May 1559 led to the attack on the Charterhouse, began his *History of the Reformation in Scotland* with an account of his forerunners who had suffered for their beliefs during the reign of James I.[117] From Abbot Bower's extraordinary list of the virtues of the mass it may be inferred that anti-sacramental heresy required confutation.[118] Its sources were England, where Lollardy still lingered, and Bohemia, which was a centre not only of Hussitism but of millenarian sects, such as the Taborites, whose excesses shocked Abbot Bower. Moreover Bower affirmed that in Scotland the views of Resby (the English Lollard burnt at Perth in 1406 or 1407) were still rife.[119] Here was a situation in which King James could display his zeal as patron and protector of the kirk by following the example of the Lollard-burning

---

[114] Balfour-Melville, *James I*, pp. 178, 270, 272.
[115] *A.P.S.*, II. 25.
[116] Balfour-Melville, *James I*, pp. 272-3; *Cal. Scot. Supp. 1428-32*, pp. 108, 113.   [117] Knox, *History*, I. 1-7.
[118] J. A. F. Thomson, *The Later Lollards*, p. 204.
[119] *Chron. Bower*, II. 498; W. Stanford Reid, *op. cit., Church History*, XI. 3-17, at 9-12.

Henry V. In 1425 the Scottish parliament was to pass an act against heresy that was reminiscent of the English statute of 1401 : each bishop was to hold an inquest to apprehend 'heretikis and Lollardis' and punish them as the law of holy kirk required; the civil authorities would lend their support.[120]

Already in 1422 some heretic, possibly Quintin Folkhyrde, had been burnt in the diocese of Glasgow,[121] presumably as a result of a trial held under the bishop's authority. But it was the university of St Andrews under the leadership of Laurence of Lindores,[122] rather than the episcopate, that was most active in detecting and combating heresy. Master Laurence, who 'nowhere within the realm gave rest to heretics or Lollards',[123] had brought Resby to the stake and was to have a further resounding success in dealing with a certain Paul Crawar, a man who had studied in the universities of Paris, Montpellier and Prague and had served as physician to the king of Poland.[124] According to Abbot Bower, Crawar was a German who had been sent by the heretics of Prague with papers which testified to his medical skill, though his mission was to imbue the Scots with the Bohemian heresies. Brought to trial at St Andrews on 23 July 1433 Crawar was confuted by Master Laurence and burnt at the stake.[125]

But while James could commend the part that the university played under Lindores's guidance in suppressing heresy, there were some influences at St Andrews that were less to the king's liking. Bishop Wardlaw, chancellor of the university, and Prior Haldenstone, head of the Augustinian priory in the city and dean of the faculty of theology, had not supported the king in his stand against the papacy. James seems to have retaliated by taking sides in university politics. For 'a state of tension or at least of uneasy equipoise' prevailed between Wardlaw and Lindores, and the latter, though a theologian, had 'obviously at an early date transferred his energies and organising ability to the faculty of arts'.[126] The king's intervention tended to increase the influence of Lindores and the faculty of arts at the expense of Bishop Wardlaw and his theologian associates. At

[120] A.P.S., II. 7, c. 3.
[121] Knox, History, I. 1; T. M. A. Macnab, op. cit., Scot. Church Hist. Soc. Recs., v. 10–22, at 16.
[122] The various aspects of his career are studied by Duncan Shaw, op. cit., ibid., XII. 47–62. [123] Chron. Bower, II. 495.
[124] T. M. A. Macnab, op. cit., Scot. Church Hist. Soc. Recs., v. 10–22, at 16–22. [125] Chron. Bower, II. 495; St Andrews Acta, I. xx.
[126] St Andrews Acta, I. xvii.

first, indeed, James had more far-reaching designs and petitioned
the pope that the university be transferred from St Andrews to
Perth. The specious grounds of the royal petition probably concealed James's real motive, which was to remove the university from
Bishop Wardlaw's influence. On the failure of this scheme the king
showed his dissatisfaction by further intervention in university poli- ·
tics [127] and withheld a royal charter until such time as he saw the
university remodelled more to his liking. James's influence may have
been behind a project to set up a single 'pedagogy' for the faculty
of arts : no new private pedagogies were to be established in future
since they had led to a breakdown in studies and discipline. The new
pedagogy seems to have been completed by 1435 and was to be put
under the control of Lindores.[128] In March 1432 the king had at last
conferred his favour on the university and a royal charter was issued
confirming its foundation.[129] Nonetheless James still meddled in university affairs. On 13 November 1432 the faculty of arts reluctantly
accepted his proposals in an *appunctuamentum* which tended to
strengthen the disciplinary powers of its dean (Lindores).[130] Fortified
by the *appunctuamentum* the latter kept a tight grip over the
faculty.[31] The death of this spiritual and academic drill master in the
summer of 1437, some months after that of his royal patron, brought
a new tolerance to the university but also saw the onset of rivalries,
disputes over discipline, and quarrels between the scholars and the
citizens.[132]

Even before Lindores's death it is likely that there was a party in
the university united in resentment of his dominance, of the king's
interference in academic politics, and of the king's dealings with the
papacy and the council of Basel. The dissidents no doubt saw in the
visit of the pope's legate a long-awaited opportunity to voice their
discontent. Shortly before Christmas 1436 the Bishop of Urbino
arrived in Scotland and accompanied the court to Perth to be received in a general council that began its proceedings on 4 February
1437.[133] Up to this time thirty-seven Scottish clerics had been incorporated in the council of Basel, which was beginning to set out on the
course that would shortly lead to a rupture with Eugenius. Of all the
dioceses of Scotland the foremost, St Andrews, shared with poor and ·
remote Argyll the distinction of having sent no direct representatives

[127] Balfour-Melville, *James I*, pp. 129, 181.
[128] *St Andrews Acta*, I. xix; 26–7, 28–9.
[129] *R.M.S.*, II. Nos. 199, 200.   [130] *St Andrews Acta*, I. 34–5.
[131] *Ibid.*, xx.   [132] Dunlop, *Bishop Kennedy*, pp. 269–72.
[133] *Chron. Bower*, II. 502; *Chron. Pluscarden*, I. 390.

to Basel.[134] At St Andrews, if anywhere in Scotland, Eugenius could count on support. On 21 January 1437 arrangements were being made to send a university delegation to Perth, ostensibly 'for the preservation of our privileges',[135] but it can hardly have been forgotten that it was a university delegation that had swayed opinion in a general council which met in comparable circumstances in 1418. What might have happened in a final confrontation of royal and papal authority can only be guessed : while public attention was centred on the expected settlement of ecclesiastical affairs, some of James's political enemies were planning an event that, within a few days, would throw Scotland into turmoil and make the decade-long blusterings between king and pope seem a mere storm in a tea-cup.

From James I's dealings with the papacy, as also from his activities in international politics, nothing decisive emerged. In domestic politics it was a different matter. The intensive government characteristic of David II's last years was brought back in even more intensive form. One of its characteristics was increased use of the three estates. During the Albany governorship they seem to have been convened only infrequently ; between 1424 and 1436, on the other hand, there were to be at least ten parliaments and three general councils.[136]

To suit James's purposes it was necessary that these assemblies should authoritatively represent the political community, hence his concern over the attendance of the prelates and lay landholders. An act of March 1426 said nothing about the position of the burgesses, but affirmed that all prelates, earls, barons, and freeholders who were tenants-in-chief, were bound to attend the king's parliament and general council ; thenceforth they were to attend in person ; procurators could be employed only for 'lauchfull cause' [137]—an allusion to the recognised essoins, such as sickness, that would serve as excuse for non-appearance in a court. In the Perth parliament of July 1427 some of the tenants-in-chief who were legitimately absent were excused ; the others who 'contumaciously absented themselves' were to pay an amercement of £10 each.[138] If this was an attempt to enforce the act of 1426 by pecuniary penalty it merely showed the unworkability of that act : it was feasible to expect all prelates and earls to attend ; it was impossible to expect all barons and freeholders to do so. A compromise was reached in an act of March 1428 : the king

---

[134] Burns, *Basle*, p. 55.   [135] *St Andrews Acta*, I. 44.
[136] Balfour-Melville, *James I*, p. 252.   [137] *A.P.S.*, II. 9, c. 8.
[138] *Ibid.*, 13.

was to issue special precepts summoning individually all the bishops, abbots, priors, dukes, earls, lords of parliament and banrents (bannerets) whom he wished to attend.[139] No longer was personal attendance to be required from 'the smal baronnis and fre tenandis'. Instead, like the burgesses, they were to be represented in parliaments and general councils by elected members: in the head court of each sheriffdom (the Michaelmas meeting of the sheriff court) 'wise men' were to be chosen as 'commissaris [commissioners] of the schire'. Moreover these commissioners were to elect 'a wise and ane expert mann callit the common spekar of the parliament', who was to act as spokesman for 'the commonis'.[140]

In these provisions there was much that was suggestive of English practice. But much was left in ambiguity: if a parliamentary peerage had been created by the act of 1428 the act said nothing about an upper house; nor was any definition given of 'the commonis'. In any case there is no sign that any shire commissioners were ever elected under the terms of the act of 1428 and there was never to be a speaker in the three estates.[141] It is probable that barons resented being faced with the question as to whether or not they were 'small'; and the idea of paying the expenses of commissioners can hardly have been welcome. Not until the late sixteenth century was James's scheme for shire representation successfully revived. But the immediate failure of the scheme in James's own lifetime did not mean (as one authority seems to imply)[142] the virtual disappearance from parliaments and general councils of the small barons and free tenants: during the next three reigns their attendance was significant enough to require some statutory definition.[143]

While the act of July 1428 had no ascertainable effect so far as it concerned the small barons and freeholders, it was otherwise with the prelates and greater nobles who were to be individually summoned by special precept. This provision of the act of 1428 certainly took effect. There is no indication that James intended his 'lords of parliament' to transmit to their heirs or successors a right to sit in parliaments and general councils, but gradually the amorphous Scottish nobility came to be categorised and divided.[144] Those nobles who were not 'lords'—the 'small barons' alluded to in the act of 1428—would come to be described as 'lairds'. Even so, the division between

[139] Ibid., 15, c. 2.   [140] Ibid.
[141] Rait, Parliaments, p. 195.   [142] Balfour-Melville, James I, pp. 156-7.
[143] Rait, Parliaments, pp. 196-7.
[144] This subject is investigated by R. S. Rait (ibid., pp. 178-83); see also Highland Papers, II. 154.

lords and lairds was not so sharp as the division of peerage and gentry in England; the small barons or lairds continued to be associated with the greater barons or lords and to sit together with them as one of the three estates. The ultimate effect of the act of 1428 was merely to increase the numbers of the greater nobles and to augment their dignity within the otherwise unchanged three estates.

The most detailed record of attendance at parliament during the reign, one compiled on 10 March 1430,[145] gives an impression of the miscellaneous turn-out even after James had made attempts at definition; in 1430 parliament comprised the chancellor (Bishop Cameron), six other bishops, six earls, the constable and the marshal, and eight 'lords' besides 'many other [unnamed] prelates, barons, nobles and commissioners of burghs'. All these personages were seated in order of precedence: on 10 March 1430, when a vote was taken, the chancellor (who evidently presided) put the question to those present 'one by one, and one after the other, as they sat in order in their seats'.[146] Their votes happened on this occasion to be unanimous, but the voting procedure certainly allowed for dissent, and James was not always able to obtain what he wanted. This was particularly the case in matters of finance: the grants of taxation made on the king's return to Scotland in 1424 were not renewed—in marked contrast to the generous grants that David II continually obtained in comparable circumstances. In 1431, when James did obtain from the three estates a contribution towards the suppression of a Highland rising, the estates not only appropriated the contribution to that particular purpose but showed their distrust of the king's conduct in financial matters by imposing stringent conditions.[147] Since the records of parliaments and general councils unfortunately continue to be records of decisions, not of debates, it is almost impossible to discover what was the process of decision-making that could occasionally result in reverses for the king. Only in regard to the English proposals of 1433 is the veil briefly lifted by the chronicler Bower, whose account of the argument between members of the clerical estate [148] is reminiscent of the account of the arguments held in the three estates in 1364, or of those held in 1418 before the renunciation of obedience to Benedict XIII. It must be concluded that, at least on great issues, there could be lively debate within the three estates before a consensus of opinion was reached, and that the consensus was not always the one desired by the king.

Nonetheless, so far as legislation was concerned, it was James who

145 *A.P.S.*, II. 28, c. 6.
147 *Ibid.*, 20, c. 1.
146 *Ibid.*
148 Pp. 291–2 above.

kept the initiative : the contemporary chronicler Bower styled James
'our lawmaking king' and remarked that in the parliament of 1426,
(as in that of 1424) he 'proposed many things advantageous to the
state'.[149] It may be assumed that it was James's own 'articles' that
resulted in an output of legislation that was unprecedented in Scotland.

For none of James's predecessors or successors was so committed
as he was, persistently, determinedly and emotionally, to pursuing the
common weal. It was an elusive butterfly that James tried to catch
in a network of ordinances. The *laissez-faire* of the Albany Stewarts
was replaced by a sort of medieval totalitarianism that sought to
regulate or re-shape many aspects of Scottish life. Nothing was too
momentous or too inconsequential to escape legislation. This was
demonstrated in the articles which James presented to the parliament
of 1424 that initiated the new order. Incongruously intermingled
with those that were to bring revolutionary political changes were
others that ordered the destruction of rooks' nests and of all fish weirs
in tidal waters, and prescribed a mesh of at least three inches for nets
used in fresh water.[150]

One characteristic of James's miscellaneous social and economic
legislation was its somewhat puritanical stress upon utility : detailed
statutes of 1430 declared that no burgesses, except aldermen, bailies
and councillors, might wear furs ; ordinary yeomen were not to wear
coloured clothes longer than knee-length ; all articles of clothing and
adornment that contravened this sartorial code were to be forfeited to
the king.[151] The object of such sumptuary laws (already shown to be
unavailing in England) was to restrain extravagance and reduce imports at a time when the costume of fashion-conscious men and
women was exuberantly rich and fantastic. In other respects also
James sought to prevent his subjects from straying profitlessly along
primrose paths : one statute threatened with imprisonment anyone
found drinking ale in taverns beyond the hour of nine; another ordained that idle men should be forced on pain of imprisonment to
find employment.[152] James not only revived wappinschaws[153] but
tried to purge sport and divert it into preparation for war. Thus it
was enacted that 'the king forbiddis that na man play at the fut ball' ;
footballers were to be fined fourpence for persisting in their unpro-

[149] *Chron. Bower*, II. 482. [150] *A.P.S.*, II. 6, cc. 12, 20.
[151] *Ibid.*, 18, cc. 8, 9, 10; see also *Scot. Legal Hist.*, p. 288.
[152] *A.P.S.*, II. 11, c. 20; 24, c. 8.
[153] *Ibid.*, 8, c. 23; 10-1, c. 17; 18, cc. 11-14.

ductive pastime. By contrast, butts were to set up near parish kirks so that on holy days men might 'haif usage of archary'.[154] Thus James, so far as legislation availed, sought to make the most of Scotland's human and material resources and to replace wasteful practices with others that were of utility to the common weal.

This policy was particularly evident in the attention paid to all matters that directly or indirectly affected the well-being of the country's economy. Measures were enacted for the standardisation of weights and measures, for the observance of a close season in the netting of wildfowl, for the extermination of wolves, for the suppression of deer-poaching, rabbit-poaching, and theft from orchards and dove-cots; and since the Lowlands were being denuded of timber it was made a crime to steal wood or peel the bark of growing trees.[155] Paternalistic concern for the rural economy was coupled with concern for the welfare of even those at the lowest levels of rural society; their lot was to be improved by better methods of husbandry, which, it was optimistically assumed, could be inculcated by legislation. Thus James's second parliament enacted that each 'man of sympil estate that of resoune suld be a labourar' should either have a half share in an ox and engage in communal tillage or else dig each day an area at least seven feet square;[156] husbandmen who had a plough-team of eight oxen were to sow minimum quantities of wheat, peas and beans, besides the staple crops of bere, oats and rye; and barons were to do likewise on their demesne lands on pain of a forty-shilling fine.[157] One of the greatest hindrances to good husbandry—insecurity of tenure [158]—was perhaps slightly mitigated by the king's intervention : in 1428 he won the consent of the prelates and barons to his request that for a trial period of one year they would not evict their husbandmen and cottars unless the lands that the latter rented were required for the lord's own use.[159] In an attempt to remedy another grievance of the countryfolk James tried to control the companies of men, ranging from the retinues of nobles to bands of 'thiggers' or sturdy beggars, who in their travels bullied husbandmen and clerics into providing free food and lodging.[160] For law-abiding wayfarers provision was made by another enactment which exhorted the establishment of inns within the burghs and along the main highways;[161]

---

154 *Ibid.*, 5, c. 18; 6, c. 19. 155 *Ibid.*, 7, 12, 15–6.
156 *Ibid.*, 8. 157 *Ibid.*, 13.
158 For the background see Grant, *Social and Economic Development*, p. 256.
159 *A.P.S.*, II. 17; compare *ibid.*, I. 213.
160 *Ibid.*, II. 3, 4, 8, 15. 161 *Ibid.*, 6, 10.

and finally in 1427 the provision of inns was made a general responsibility of all the burgesses of the realm.[162]

The burgesses, with their complex society and institutions, received a fair share of James's attention. Concerned over the problems of public health and good order in their crowded communities he passed statutes restricting the entry of beggars and lepers. He also saw the need for precautions against the accidental fires that from time to time devastated the burghs—Stirling had been accidentally burnt in 1408, Linlithgow and Cupar in 1411, Aberdeen in 1423, and Linlithgow once again in 1424.[163] There was thus good reason for the detailed legislation of 1426 designed to reduce fire risks and initiate a fire-fighting service : the handling of combustible materials was to be strictly controlled; brothels, which were assumed to be particularly incendiary, were to be sited only in the outskirts of towns.[164]

Apart from such general measures there were many others that directly or indirectly affected the interests of the burgesses. The merchant burgesses in particular were subjected to the regulations by which the king tried to enforce an economic policy that was both mercantilist and nationalist. Few aspects of overseas trade were immune from regulation : it was typical that in 1425 the export of tallow and of horses less than three years old was prohibited.[165] Most important of all, however, were the statutes controlling the export of bullion.[166] These affected the interests not only of clerics but of merchants. In 1436 an act not only totally forbade all export of gold, silver and jewels but laid the merchants under an obligation that was probably unworkable—for each sack of wool and equivalent quantities of hides and salted fish that they exported they were to bring back three ounces of bullion to be coined at the royal mint. To ensure the enforcement of this statute the custumars were ordered to compile detailed lists of all export shipments 'for the serching and knowlege hereof'.[167]

But while the king could try through the three estates to regulate the economic activities of the merchants, so also could the merchants, through their gilds and their control of the burgh councils, try to regulate the economic activities of the other inhabitants of the burghs. Like the king, the merchants claimed to be promoting the common weal. Yet when they invoked the universally-accepted ideal of 'the

[162] *Ibid.*, 14.
[163] *Chron. Bower*, II. 441, 447, 463, 482; *Glasgow Registrum*, II. 316; *Chron. Pluscarden*, I. 349. [164] *A.P.S.*, II. 12.
[165] *Ibid.*, 7. [166] P. 294 above. [167] *A.P.S.*, II. 23, 24.

just price' their motives were not always altruistic : in 1428 the gild court of Ayr chose five persons to buy for the use of the gild all merchandise entering by sea.[168] It is likely that the merchants, through the gild or the burgh council, sought to extend their price-fixing to the goods produced by the craftsmen who were their fellow-burgesses. The emergence of craft gilds may thus have been an attempt on the part of the craftsmen to control not only their own standards of workmanship but their own prices and wages. The first sign of craft organisation (and of the reaction of the merchants against it) may be seen towards the close of the fourteenth century, when the chamberlain was instructed to hold a secret inquest in the course of his ayre to discover whether there was any 'confederacy' among any inhabitants of the town whereby the 'neighbours' were injured.[169] In a court held by the bailies of Aberdeen in 1398 an injunction was issued warning the websters that 'they are not to conspire among themselves to the prejudice of the community of Aberdeen'.[170] James was not the man to ignore such issues, and characteristically he sought a solution in legislation. In March 1425 it was ordained that in every town there should be chosen a member of each craft to act as deacon of that craft ; he was to be chosen jointly by his fellow-craftsmen and by the town council, and was to supervise standards of workmanship to prevent fraud on the part of 'untrew men of craftis'.[171] This measure was probably intended as a compromise ; but it said nothing on the controversial topic of regulation of prices and wage-rates, and the merchants were not content. In 1426 James yielded to their pressure : a new statute enacted that the deacons of crafts were to remain in office until the next parliament, but the goods of the craftsmen were to be priced by the alderman and council in each burgh and the council was to fix the wage-rates of such craftsmen as wrights and masons.[172] In the following year parliament lost all sense of moderation by forbidding the election of deacons of crafts and dismissing those already in office : they were not to hold their accustomed meetings 'which are presumed to savour of conspiracies'.[173] The merchants had evidently succeeded in convincing king and parliament that craft organisation was a threat to the established social order. The passive resistance of the craftsmen was countered by further legislation in 1428, which ordained that the council in each burgh should appoint a 'warden' for

[168] David Murray, *Early Burgh Organization in Scotland* (1924, 1932), II. 544–5.

[169] *Iter Camerarii, A.P.S.*, I. 695.   [170] *Aberdeen Burgh Recs.*, p. 27.

[171] *A.P.S.*, II. 8.   [172] *Ibid.*, 13.   [173] *Ibid.*, 14.

each craft who was to examine and maintain standards of workmanship and fix prices under the threat of heavy fines; similar powers were granted to each baron to fix prices and wage-rates within his barony.[174] This repressive measure put the livelihood of the craftsmen at the mercy of burgh councils controlled by the merchant oligarchy; fortunately for the craftsmen, the act of 1428 was intended as an experiment and was to remain valid for only one year.[175]

If the social and economic legislation of James I was on an unprecedented scale, and presented some novel features, the king was less open to the charge of innovation in dealing with legal and judicial matters for which the crown had a traditional responsibility that had been discharged only fitfully since 1371. In James's legislative programme there was an attempt to make up for past deficiencies: statute after statute testified to his constant pre-occupation with law, justice, and the preservation of order.

The sense of national identity evident in some of James's enactments came out strongly in an act of 1426 which ordained that all the king's subjects were to be governed only by the king's laws and the statutes of 'this realme' : the laws of other countries and realms were to be invalid in Scotland; and none of the king's subjects were to live under 'particulare lawis na speciale prevalegis'.[176] This was an omnibus measure that stressed the jurisdictional independence of Scotland. It may have been visualised by James as a counterpart of the English statute of *praemunire* that could be used to check the encroachments of papal jurisdiction. More obviously, however, the ordinance was directed against distinctive local practices such as the 'laws of the Galwegians' and the 'law of Clan MacDuff', both of which had been specially safeguarded as recently as 1384.[177]

The announcement that only the king's laws and statutes of the realm were to be observed was accompanied by an ambitious attempt to revise the two legal codes chiefly used in Scotland : a parliamentary committee of eighteen, composed of six wise men of each of the three estates, was to 'examyn the bukis of law of this realme, that is to say *Regiam Majestatem* and *Quoniam Attachiamenta*, and mend the lawis that nedis mendment'.[178] There is no sign that much mending of these older laws was achieved;[179] and already it was evident that it was not enough merely to re-define the traditional law; new laws

---

[174] *Ibid.*, 15. [175] *Ibid.* [176] *Ibid.*, 9.
[177] P. 190 above. [178] *A.P.S.*, II. 10.
[179] For attempts to codify Scots law in 1426, 1469 and 1487 see *Scot. Legal Hist.*, p. 31.

were required, and James's large legislative output brought the beginnings of a real statutory law.[180] Symptomatic of its growing importance was an enactment that new laws were to be registered and
publicly proclaimed by sheriffs and bailies so that no one could plead
ignorance of them.[181] Often the new laws clarified the technicalities
of judicial procedure.[182] A whole series of such statutes was enacted
in the Perth parliament of 6 March 1430.[183]

Many other enactments demonstrated the king's desire to secure
for his subjects justice that was speedy, efficient and impartial. In an
important measure of 1425 that was to become a permanent feature
of Scottish justice he ordained that judges should assign a 'lele and a
wys advocate' to plead for 'ony pur creatur' who could not pursue his
case through lack of wealth or knowledge.[184] In practice this measure
meant the appointment of free legal counsel for the poor—a provision
that was some five hundred years in advance of English practice. The
same statute ordered that judges should do justice 'als wele to pur as
to rych' without fraud or favour; if any judges failed to observe this
statute the king would see that they were 'rygorusly punyst' as an
'ensampill til all utheris'.[185] It is clear that James's intention was to
purge the whole judicial system of corruption. Jurors who sat on
assizes were to swear that they had received neither financial rewards
nor solicitations from any litigant.[186] Another act legislated against
'maintenance' by forbidding anyone to come to court with 'multitude of folkys na with armys'.[187] The courts were not to be intimidated
and were repeatedly enjoined to act with fairness and impartiality.[188]

The fulfilment of these ideals depended on the character and
training of judges and lawyers. In Scotland there were no institutions
comparable to the English inns of court to produce a body of pro-
fessionally-trained lawyers who might hope for advancement to the
judiciary. The Scottish approach to legal training was more academic
than professional and was based upon the study of canon and civil
law at the universities, together, perhaps, with a notarial apprenticeship that taught the techniques of conveyancing. By the fifteenth
century men with such training could make their livelihood as lawyers. But, save in the ecclesiastical courts, there were no openings for
professional judges such as multiplied in England from the reign of
Henry II onwards. The Scottish judicial system as it existed in the

[180] *Ibid.*, p. 282.
[181] *A.P.S.*, II. 11; see also Rait, *Parliaments*, pp. 444-6.
[182] For procedure in civil cases see *Scot. Legal Hist.*, pp. 415-8.
[183] *A.P.S.*, II. 17-9.   [184] *Ibid.*, 8.   [185] *Ibid.*
[186] *Ibid.*, 23.   [187] *Ibid.*, 16.   [188] *Ibid.*, 9, 14, 16, 23.

reign of David I had remained virtually unaltered, and incorporated feudal elements that had long been discarded in England. Although James did not attempt to end this state of affairs, he did try to insist that the holders of heritable jurisdictions should appoint competent deputes for whose acts they would be held responsible;[189] and towards the end of the reign there were signs that the king was prepared to interfere more drastically to remedy the defects of franchisal justice.

It would be wrong to assume that the primitive Scottish judicial system was more riddled with abuses than the evolved and intricate English system (which, from fifteenth-century accounts, left much to be desired), but in Scotland the openings for bribery, intimidation, procrastination and general inefficiency were undoubtedly many. It was the king's duty as 'fountain of justice' to remedy any default of justice; and remedy could therefore be sought in any body in which the king took counsel. Hence it was that parliament and the privy council came to be burdened with 'billis of complayntis' or appeals for 'remeid of justice'.[190] The hearing of appeals, as well as miscellaneous cases of first instance, could take up much of the time of parliament or privy council at a time when both bodies were primarily concerned with state affairs rather than justice. Although judicial committees continued to be elected by parliament in James's reign,[191] and sometimes parliament as a whole dealt with lawsuits,[192] the reign saw the earliest attempt to divert elsewhere some of the mass of litigation that threatened to overwhelm king in council. First came an act of 1425 which gave parliament the option of remitting cases to the ordinary courts. A more important act of 1426 stated that the king should choose certain discreet persons of the three estates to hold 'sessiouns' thrice a year under the presidency of the chancellor. These sessions were to determine all causes and complaints that the king's council was competent to deal with. To those who served on the sessions there was offered somewhat vague hope of remuneration through the profits of justice.[193] It is clear that the sessions were not intended to displace the jurisdiction of parliament but were to exist alongside it with equal authority and competence. In this procedure can be seen the origin of the future court of session as supreme court in all civil causes.[194]

James's concern with the machinery of justice was accompanied by a campaign to make his subjects more law-abiding and to repress

[189] *Ibid.*, 3.   [190] *Ibid.*, 8.   [191] *Ibid.*, 14, 22–3, 26.
[192] *Ibid.*, 28; R.M.S., II. No. 146.
[193] A.P.S., II. 11.   [194] See Rait, *Parliaments*, pp. 460–7.

crime. But even if a criminal were arrested and brought before a court his lord might 'maintain' him by browbeating judge and assize; and if the crime fell within the competence of the lord's own court the criminal could be repledged to that court, where, perhaps, justice that was more lenient, or more mercenary, awaited him. There were thus obstacles in the way of an enactment of 1425 which announced that no lord or baron was to 'thole' thieves or reivers or to maintain them; if he was unable to deal with them he was to certify the king's officers.[195] The latter, however, were not always dependable. In May 1432 a semi-judicial committee of parliament issued a number of ordinances 'for stanching of the fellone slauchteres'.[196] These ordinances, which in substance merely copied those issued by the Stirling general council of 1397,[197] ended with an admonition to the sheriffs, who paid little heed. Two years later, in the parliament of March 1434, James gave vent to his wrath and threatened to take severe action against every sheriff in Scotland, whereupon the prelates besought him to mitigate his anger and obtained a pardon for the errant sheriffs, who were again warned to do justice and to enforce the acts of parliament; the lords of regality received a similar warning.[198] For James was increasingly assuming that it was his duty to see that justice was done in the regalities as well as in the 'royalty' of the sheriffdoms.[199] In the general council held at Edinburgh in October 1436 came the last and most drastic instalment of his plans for more efficient criminal justice: no lord of regality, sheriff, or baron, was to 'sell' (ransom) any thief, or agree upon a fine for the theft. The king was given certain discretionary power in enforcing this statute, which was to last during his pleasure.[200] What must have seemed even more ominous to those who enjoyed franchisal jurisdictions was an act which stated that for the next seven years the justiciars and sheriffs were not to pay too much heed to the obstructive franchises of the regalities or of the burghs: they were 'noucht to defer till regaliteis na til burghis'.[201]

Such masterfulness was to be seen also in the administrative side of government. It has been remarked that 'James, more than his immediate predecessors or successors, formulated and pursued his own policy with the aid of servants, who were little more than willing, if able, tools'.[202] Only one royal servant, Bishop Cameron, seems to have been allowed any pre-eminence. After the death of the Earl of

[195] A.P.S., II. 7–8.   [196] Ibid., 20–2.   [197] P. 210 above.
[198] A.P.S., II. 22.   [199] Ibid., 8, 21, 22, 23.   [200] Ibid., 23.
[201] Ibid., 24.   [202] Balfour-Melville, James I, p. 254.

Buchan at Verneuil his successor as chamberlain was not a great nobleman but Sir John Forrester of Corstorphine, a lesser noble of burgess origin who had acted as chamberlain depute since 1405.[203] And by 1428 the chamberlain, hitherto the chief financial officer of the crown, was receiving practically nothing from the royal revenues and 'had ceased to be a fiscal officer'.[204] While the chamberlain continued to supervise the burghs, his financial duties were entrusted to two new officials: influenced by English practice James introduced into Scotland the offices of treasurer and comptroller. Between the two there came to be recognised a division of duties, though perhaps not until the end of the century. The comptroller was to receive the rents of crown lands, the burgh ferms and the great customs; from these sources he was supposed to meet the expenses of the royal household. The treasurer, on the other hand, was to receive the crown's feudal services and casualties, the profits of justice, and any special contributions or taxes; from these sources he was to meet the expenditure of the crown in business that was not connected with the royal household.[205] The intention that underlay James's introduction of the two new financial officers was probably to exclude the great nobles from crown finance: the first appointments that he made to the posts of treasurer and comptroller were either of minor nobles or of ecclesiastics; and in this policy he set the pattern for more than a century.[206] Even so, James was not content with this re-shuffle of offices: in his reign revenues were not concentrated in the hands of either the comptroller or the treasurer; often large sums were paid directly to the clerk of the spices or to a variety of *ad hoc* financial agents, notably John Turyne, an Edinburgh merchant, John Winchester, canon of Glasgow, and Thomas Myrton, dean of Glasgow.[207] In matters of finance James evidently believed in keeping his left hand ignorant of what his right hand was doing; so far as the formulation of policy was concerned his attitude was probably similar. Lacking any personal involvement in government the faceless men who served him felt no commitment to his ideals, and some of them longed to display their own clashing individualities as soon as he was removed from the scene.

James's only apparent partner in government had been the three estates. In outward appearance at least, they had attained a higher

[203] *Ibid.*, p. 254.   [204] *Ibid.*, p. 255.
[205] See the notes on treasury administration by Athol L. Murray in *T.A.*, xii. xii–xlix.   [206] See *H.B.C.*, pp. 180–5.
[207] *E.R.*, iv. xcv; Balfour-Melville, *James I*, p. 255.
E.H.S.—11*

stature than ever before. Nonetheless, the impetus behind their pursuit of the 'common profit of the realm' came solely from the king. Even the admiring Abbot of Inchcolm was under no illusion about the practical results of James's programme: in the parliament of 1426 the king made divers statutes, some of them profitable enough to the realm 'if they were observed'. And Bower went on to cite Aristotle : 'to enact new laws with facility, and to change the old with facility, is marvellous damaging to good order'.[208] Despite Bower's qualms the precedents that James had set were not forgotten; and if, after his death, the three estates no longer hectically pursued the common weal, they did not altogether abandon the chase.

Throughout James's reign it was usually at Perth that the estates held their meetings, and it has been affirmed that 'the history of the reign suggests that James was trying to make Perth the capital of his kingdom'.[209] But James was at least as often at Edinburgh as at Perth, and his itinerary hardly ever deviated from the route connecting Edinburgh, Linlithgow, Stirling and Perth.[210] Perth was on the northernmost periphery of the king's regular peregrinations; it was not a centre from which his personal activity radiated equally to all parts of his realm, Highland as well as Lowland. More than any previous Scottish king James identified himself with the Lowlands. While the legislation of his first parliament had regarded the problem of disorder as a general one and had made no distinction between Highlands and Lowlands, the second, which opened at Perth in March 1425, thought it 'spedful' that 'consideracioun salbe had of the Hieland men, the quhilkis, befor the kingis hame cumyng, commonly reft [robbed] and slew ilk ane utheris'.[211] In the parliament of September 1426 it was further ordained that lords who had lands beyond the Mounth in which there had once existed a castle, fortalice or manor-house, were to repair it and maintain it as a residence 'for the gracioss governall of ther landis'.[212] They were to set an example of 'gude polising'—efficient and 'civilised' estate management—that would induce the natives to abandon their barbarous ways. This policy, which the Dublin administration adopted in vain in medieval Ireland, was to have some gradual success in Scotland. In Campbell-dominated Argyll, at least, there existed the 'gude

[208] *Chron. Bower*, II. 487–8.
[209] Balfour-Melville, *James I*, pp. 129–30, 258.
[210] See James's itinerary, *ibid.*, Appendix C, pp. 285–92.
[211] *A.P.S.*, II. 8.   [212] *Ibid.*, 13.

polising' that parliament desired, together with a shrieval and baronial administration through which the king's will could be implemented;[213] but in many Gaelic areas such administration can have been merely nominal; and in the Isles in particular it can hardly even have been that.

In 1423, Donald of the Isles, the protagonist at Harlaw, had died at his castle of Ardtornish, whereupon his eldest son, Alexander, 'was proclaimed Earl of Ross and Lord of the Isles after the accustomed manner'.[214] So far as Ross was concerned [215] the king seems to have let sleeping dogs lie.[216] A more serious issue concerned sovereignty over the Isles : it is likely that Alexander was intriguing with King Eric of Denmark, Norway and Sweden to bring about a re-assertion of Norwegian suzerainty.[217] In respect of the Isles the Scottish king was still bound to make annual payment of one hundred marks to the Norwegians; but payment was long in arrears. At Bergen on 29 July 1426 James's envoys negotiated a settlement whereby Eric cancelled outstanding claims and obtained a promise (apparently disregarded) of regular payment in future.[218] This settlement was followed in August 1428 by a striking demonstration of royal power. According to Abbot Bower and the Pluscarden writer, James had summoned a parliament to Inverness.[219] Although no record of such a parliament exists, some sort of summons must have been issued, possibly to a social gathering of the royal court; for the northern magnates flocked to Inverness. As they appeared they were craftily arrested, to the number of about fifty, while, so claims Bower, the king composed jubilant Latin verse. Most of those taken at Inverness were imprisoned in various castles until their subsequent release or their condemnation and death as criminals; a few were tried and executed forthwith.[220] Alexander of the Isles, who had also fallen into the king's trap, was brought prisoner to Perth.[221] There was a prospect that he might be allowed to enter into 'special retinue' with the king; but this gracious attempt to turn the Lord of the Isles into a court lap-dog failed : in a short while he absconded, burned the burgh of Inverness and besieged the castle.[222] On 23 June 1429 the

---

[213] See *Highland Papers*, II. 114–98. [214] *Ibid.*, I. 34.
[215] See pp. 235–6 above.
[216] *Scots Peerage*, I. 148, 264; II. 264. [217] See *Highland Papers*, I. 38.
[218] *Diplomatarium Norvegicum*, XX. 764–6; see also *Chron. Bower*, II. 509.
[219] *Chron. Bower*, II. 488; *Chron. Pluscarden*, I. 375. See also Balfour-Melville, *James I*, Appendix B, p. 284, 'The Inverness Parliament'.
[220] *Chron. Bower*, II. 489. [221] *Highland Papers*, II. 18.
[222] *Chron. Pluscarden*, I. 375; *Chron. Bower*, II. 489.

king and his host came upon the Lord of the Isles and his men beside a bog. in Lochaber. When the royal standard was displayed Clan Chattan and Clan Cameron deserted MacDonald.[223] On 27 August 1429 he appeared before the high altar of Holyrood in the humiliating garb of a penitent; on his knees he presented his sword, hilt foremost, to the king; the queen and the nobles pleaded with James to show mercy. After this stage-managed spectacle, Alexander was warded in Tantallon.[224]

His submission did not, however, mean the end of military operations. When parliament met at Perth on 6 March 1430 it was enacted that all those barons and lords whose lordships lay near the sea 'in the west and on the north partis and namely fornent the Ylis' were to have galleys for the king's service by May 1431.[225] As a preliminary to some new expedition James seems to have intended to seize the lands of Alexander's uncle, Alastair Carrach, to whom Donald of the Isles had granted much of Lochaber.[226] In the summer of 1431 Alexander Stewart, Earl of Mar, still acting as government watchdog in the north, levied an army to take possession of the country. Alastair Carrach had taken to the hills above Inverlochy with some two hundred archers. He was cheered by the appearance of the galleys of Donald Balloch, a cousin of the Lord of the Isles. This time the king was not present in person to daunt the opposition and it was in Mar's army that the waverers were to be found: attacked in front by Donald Balloch's men they were harassed in the flank by Alastair Carrach and his archers. The result was the rout of Mar's force with heavy loss. After some adventures and the composition of an appropriate Gaelic couplet the earl regained the safety of Kildrummy Castle.[227]

Following the defeat of the royal forces at Inverlochy in the summer of 1431 the king showed his resentment and his determination to equip another expedition 'for the resisting of the kingis rebellouris in the northe lande'.[228] To meet the cost parliament agreed to the levy of a contribution of a shilling in the pound. There is no surviving evidence that it was ever levied;[229] and there is conflicting evidence as to whether there was another Highland expedition. In any case James decided to come to terms with the captive Lord of the Isles.

[223] *Highland Papers*, II. 18; *Chron. Bower*, II. 489.
[224] *Chron. Bower*, II. 490; *Chron. Pluscarden*, I. 375–6; *Highland Papers*, II. 19.
[225] *A.P.S.*, II. 19.
[226] *Highland Papers*, I. 32, 39.
[227] *Ibid.*, 40–3.
[228] *A.P.S.*, II. 20.
[229] Balfour-Melville, *James I*, p. 196.

There was another stage-managed spectacle, probably late in 1431, when the queen and the prelates and nobles interceded on behalf of MacDonald and a fellow-prisoner, none other than the Earl of Douglas, who was simultaneously released.[230] Alexander seems to have regained the lordship of the Isles unimpaired and to have avoided falling out with the king during the remainder of the reign. According to the Pluscarden writer the king, as a result of the 'parliament' of Inverness, 'pacified the country for a long time, and it remained in peace'.[231] But this was too optimistic a view. James's all too facile trickery at Inverness had led to a strife that was wasteful and inconclusive. His Highland policy had turned out to be a complete failure : it had led to increased disorder and had widened the estrangement between Highlanders and Lowlanders.

The blatant flouting of convention shown in James I's arrest of the Highland chiefs at Inverness was not the only instance of headstrong waywardness on the part of the king.[232] The long dearth of government that had followed the death of David II had given way to an over-active government which concerned itself with every aspect of life. However good James's intentions, his rule was totalitarian and menaced vested interests that had come to be regarded as legitimate. He had established a royal autocracy that was sometimes cantankerous and vindictive, one that, lacking the resources necessary for its perpetuation, depended entirely upon the strong personality of the king and the awe in which he was held.

Apart from any dislike they felt for the general character of James's rule his subjects resented his exactions. When a contribution of 2d. in the pound was imposed in 1433 for the expenses of an embassy to France 'the people began to murmur, saying that their property was manifoldly reduced by "gelds" of this sort'. On this occasion the king saw the danger signal ahead and, according to Bower, himself one of the auditors of the tax, quickly ordered the return of all the money that had been collected.[233] On the whole, James's attempts to increase his revenue from direct or indirect taxation met with stout resistance and only limited success. He therefore resorted to other fiscal expedients, sometimes novel, sometimes archaic. Even in his first parliament he had enacted that any mines capable of producing silver worth 1½d. from each pound of lead were

[230] *Chron. Bower*, II. 490; *Chron. Pluscarden*, I. 377.
[231] *Chron. Pluscarden*, I. 375.
[232] See *Chron. Bower*, II. 510.   [233] *Ibid.*, 482.

to belong to the king 'as is usuale in uthir realmys'.[234] The 'recognition' of lands into the hands of the king by reason of some infringement of feudal practice became frequent.[235] Other expedients were applied in the burghs: two of them—Inverkeithing and Dundee—were heavily amerced for false judgments given in their burgh courts.[236] The chamberlain ayres were now being held in many burghs and had become a sizable source of revenue, bringing in as much as £360 13s. 4d. in 1435.[237] Heavy amercements were also levied for the old offence of forestalling—the buying and selling of goods before they had been publicly exposed for sale in a burgh market. This source of income, which brought in £342 9s. od. in 1435, affected not only the inhabitants of the burghs but their country neighbours: many landholders purchased remissions from the king for their offence.[238] While regulations that were out-of-date were strictly enforced for the king's profit 'certain poor people' of Irvine had to wait eight years for payment of victuals bought from them by the king.[239] The rich were also occasionally victimised: one of James's expedients was the collection of voluntary gifts, like the later English 'benevolences', from the most substantial persons of each of the three estates.[240] This practice 'may have been a factor in increasing the antagonism of the nobles, already uneasy at his numerous attacks upon their possessions and privileges'.[241]

The more serious of these attacks took the form of confiscation. The process began with James's questionable acquisition of the earldom of Buchan in 1424 [242] following the death of John Stewart at Verneuil. Then came a rich windfall—the earldoms of Fife, Menteith and Lennox—that fell into the royal lap in 1425 with the forfeiture of the Albany faction. In 1427 James turned his attention to the earldom of Strathearn, held by Malise Graham, son of the earl murdered in 1413.[243] On some pretext Malise was deprived of Strathearn [244] and its revenues—probably more than £300 a year;[245] by way of partial compensation he was granted the title of Earl of Menteith and some of the lands of that earldom, while other lands,

[234] A.P.S., II. 5; see also E.R., IV. cxxiii.
[235] Grant, Social and Economic Development, p. 200; Chron. Bower, II. 484.
[236] E.R., IV. 669.   [237] Ibid.   [238] Ibid., 669-71.
[239] Ibid., VI. 394.   [240] Chron. Bower, II. 485.
[241] Balfour-Melville, James I, p. 228.   [242] Scots Peerage, I. 148, 264; II. 264.
[243] Pp. 255-6 above.   [244] Scots Peerage, VI. 142-3.
[245] In 1381 the gross revenues of the earldom amounted to £406 9s. 11½d. (E.R., III. 33-8)

together with the castle of Doune, were kept in the hands of the king.[246]

By 1433 the income from royal lands—many of them recently acquired—was at least £2,000.[247] It had been shown that of all the methods of money-raising employed by James it was confiscation that was the most profitable. It continued. George Dunbar, Earl of March, held the earldom that had been forfeited from his father in 1400 and restored by Albany in 1409.[248] James maintained that the restoration was invalid. Although the earl was given the opportunity of defending his rights in the parliament held at Perth in January 1435, judgment went against him;[249] the family of Dunbar, which for three centuries had held the earldom of March, had lost it once and for all. A few months later the king was also to acquire the earldom of Mar and the Garioch, ostensibly *ratione bastardie*—as an escheat on the death of the bastard Alexander Stewart, Earl of Mar.[250] The king's proceedings, like others before them, disregarded the prior claims of Sir Robert Erskine.[251]

To many it must have seemed that James's whole reign was one of ruthless extortion. After the execution of the Albany faction in 1425 'the comoners of his land secretly clepid [called] hym nat rightwes [righteous] bot a tirannous prynce'.[252] Even Abbot Bower, a wholehearted admirer of the king, admits that James 'was given to the acquisition of things'.[253] Over £5,000 were spent on the rebuilding of Linlithgow Castle after it had been destroyed by an accidental fire.[254] It was to be replaced by an imposing royal residence, more palace that castle. In addition the items that the king imported from Flanders strikingly suggest the luxury of James's court : they included ostrich feathers, purple velvet, sable mantles, spices, wine, tapestry, and jewels; even stage-players or 'mimers' were hired in the Netherlands, outfitted at the king's expense, and brought to Scotland to entertain the court.[255] James's genuine concern for the poor and the oppressed had its blind spots, and the luxury of the court must have contrasted flagrantly with a chronic misery that was heightened by natural disasters : in February 1431 the plague broke out in Edin-

---

[246] *Scots Peerage*, VI. 142-3. For the king's expenditure on Doune in 1433 see E.R., IV. 593.
[247] Pp. 285, 287 above.   [248] Pp. 218-9, 230-1 above.   [249] A.P.S., II. 23.
[250] R.M.S., II. No. 488; *Scots Peerage*, V. 588-9; E.R., V. 55; VI. cxxi.
[251] See A.P.S., I. 578; *Aberdeen-Banff Illustrations*, IV. 165; *Scots Peerage*, v. 602.
[252] *James I, Life and Death*, p. 49.   [253] *Chron. Bower*, II. 486.
[254] Balfour-Melville, *James I*, p. 261.   [255] E.R., IV. 678, 680.

burgh; the winter of the same year was so bitterly cold that nearly all animals perished; in 1432 'the volatile pestilence' broke out at Haddington; in 1434 a bitter frost lasted more than three months so that the water-mills could not turn to grind corn; in 1435 there was great dearth in Teviotdale.[256]

In such circumstances James's apparent self-gratification, coupled with his heavy-handed acquisitiveness, was likely to make him unpopular. His various policies were strewn with victims who were bound to be resentful. The swing of the pendulum from the laissez-faire of the Albany governorship to the authoritarian totalitarianism of James's personal rule was too violent to go unchecked. But from the very outset of his personal rule James had been well aware of the risks he ran. There was an element of fatalism in his vow that began with the words: 'If God grant me life . . .'[257] He had even prepared for the worst by an act of 1428 that required oaths of fealty to be sworn to the queen, and by a similar act of 1435.[258] But while James was apprehensively aware of an undercurrent of general opposition it was only sporadically that it touched the political surface. And generally it was revealed not in the activities of the king's opponents but in the steps taken by the king to forestall them, as in 1431, when James arrested his nephews, Archibald, fifth Earl of Douglas, and Sir John Kennedy of Cassillis. Douglas, who was kept for a time in Lochleven, was released at the same time as Alexander of the Isles; Kennedy was imprisoned in Stirling till at least 1434 and finally escaped abroad.[259]

It has been surmised that the reason for Douglas's arrest sprang from his relationship with Malise Graham, erstwhile Earl of Strathearn. Shortly before the latter was deprived of Strathearn and fobbed off with a truncated earldom of Menteith Douglas had married Malise's sister, Euphemia Graham.[260] Not only did Malise lose Strathearn but he was immediately packed off to England when the second exchange of hostages took place in October 1427 and was to remain a hostage in England until 1453.[261] The king's arrest of Douglas may have been in retaliation for the earl's covert negotiations with the English, presumably intended to secure the release of Malise.[262] Another nobleman who doubtless resented the king's harsh treatment of Malise was the latter's paternal uncle, Sir Robert

[256] *Chron. Bower*, II. 490, 491, 495, 500, 502.
[257] P. 281 above.   [258] *A.P.S.*, II. 17, 23.
[259] *Chron. Pluscarden*, I. 377; *Chron. Bower*, II. 490; *E.R.*, IV. 591.
[260] *Scots Peerage*, III. 170.   [261] Balfour-Melville, *James I*, p. 294.
[262] See C. Macrae, 'The English Council and Scotland in 1430', *E.H.R.*, LIV. 415–26, at 419, 426.

Graham. In his youth he seems to have studied at Paris in the company of John Stewart, an illegitimate son of Robert II.[263] Possibly as a result of a university training Sir Robert was a man 'of grete wit and eloquence, wundir suttilye wittyd and expert yn the lawe'.[264] His opposition to the king was based not only on family grievances but on grounds of political theory, a common enough justification for rebellion in England but rare in Scotland. For some unrecorded offence Sir Robert was arrested in 1424 and imprisoned in Dunbar Castle,[265] from which he either escaped or was released. This experience did not daunt him. He is said to have shown no little indiscretion on one occasion—the date is not given—when he confronted the king in parliament : Graham

> rose upe with a grete corage, with a violent chere and countenance, sette handes upon the kyng, saying thos wordes 'I arrest you yn the name of all the Thre Astates of your reume . . .; for right as youre liege peple be bundun and sworne to obeye your majeste rialle, yn the same wise bene ye sworne and ensurid to kepe your peple . . . so that ye do hem no wronge, bot yn all right mantene and defend hem.[266]

Sir Robert rashly expected his action to be applauded, but the dumbfounded estates 'kapid silence'. Then the king, 'perceyvyng all this presumptuous rebellion', arrested Sir Robert, 'and commandid to put hym yn sure and hard prisone', after which he was banished 'and all his heritage and goodes deemed as forfaturs to the kyng'. Instead of going into exile abroad, so continues the story, Graham

> toke his way ynto the cuntreis of the Wild Scottis . . . and furthwith he renounced his legeance, and by wordes and by writyng he defied hem, seying that he had destruyd hym, his wif and his childerne, his hartages and all his other godes, by his cruell tyranny. Wherfor he said he wold slee hym with his owne handes as his mortall enmye.[267]

Whatever the truth of this tale the impression that it leaves is that Sir Robert Graham was a political idealist. Abbot Bower conveys the same impression of Graham, though the good abbot hardly shared the latter's views.

What made this ardent idealist dangerous was his eventual association with the Stewarts of Atholl. Possibly the hapless fate of the hostages helped to bring them together : David Stewart, son and heir of Walter, Earl of Atholl, had gone to England as a hostage in 1424

---

[263] *Scots Peerage*, VI. 214–15.
[264] *James I, Life and Death*, p. 50.
[265] *Chron. Bower*, II. 482.
[266] *James I, Life and Death*, p. 50.
[267] *Ibid.*, pp. 50–1.

and had died there some ten years later. Despite this the king does not seem to have suspected the Earl of Atholl (his uncle) of harbouring disaffection. Indeed it was Atholl who apparently profited from Malise's deprivation, for the king did not keep Strathearn in his own hands but on 22 July 1427 conferred it, with its palatine rights, upon Earl Walter.[269] This was, however, only a device to make James's seizure of Strathearn seem less blatant : he granted the earldom to his uncle of Atholl only in life tenure, and since the latter was then nearing his seventieth year it was not likely that James would have to wait long to secure Strathearn for himself. But this circumstance may have been of some significance to Atholl's grandson and heir, Sir Robert Stewart, son of the David Stewart who had been left to die as a hostage in England.

If the Atholl Stewarts had grounds for grievance and apprehension they also had grounds for ambitious hopes. In the eyes of the Pluscarden chronicler Earl Walter was 'that old serpent inveterate in evil days' who had craftily cleared the pathway for his own accession to the crown : acting the part of an innocent lamb he had helped to encompass the death of the Duke of Rothesay in 1402 ; he had been foremost in counselling the destruction of Duke Murdoch and his sons in 1425.[270] Whatever the truth behind these allegations it is true that the disappearance of rivals brought the Earl of Atholl closer to the throne : James's daughters were excluded by the tailzie of 1373 that barred female succession; with the last of Duke Murdoch's sons a desperate fugitive in Ireland, Earl Walter might be reckoned in terms of the tailzie of 1373 as heir presumptive to the crown until Queen Joan gave birth to twin sons at Holyrood on 16 October 1430. The publicity given to this event [271] reflected the king's joy that the problem of the succession had apparently been settled. Although the elder prince, Alexander, died in infancy, the younger, James, was established at Doune Castle, where he survived a diet of forty-eight pounds of almonds. By 1434 he had been dignified by the title of Duke of Rothesay and had his own household.[272] But the existence of an heir apparent did not end the hopes of the former heir presumptive and his grandson. Instead their hopes took more radical form : if the descendants of Robert II and Elizabeth Mure were of illegitimate descent,[273] King James was a usurper and the rightful king was

[269] Balfour-Melville, *James I*, p. 149.
[270] *Chron. Pluscarden*, I. 389; similarly *Chron. Bower*, II. 503.
[271] *Chron. Pluscarden*, I. 376; *Chron. Bower*, II. 490.
[272] *E.R.*, IV. 529, 603.   [273] See p. 186 above.

the Earl of Atholl, only surviving son of Robert II and Euphemia Ross. It was perhaps Earl Walter's heir, his grandson Sir Robert Stewart, rather than the earl himself, who coveted 'the throne usurped by the elder line',[274] but the aged earl was at least partly involved in the schemes of his grandson; and the latter had secured the adherence of Sir Robert Graham in a conspiracy based partly upon political ideals, partly upon dynastic ambitions.

Their enterprise was no doubt carefully timed to coincide with a rising tide of general disaffection. Even physically James was no longer the man who had once inspired respect: Aeneas Sylvius, who saw him in 1435, described him as 'thick-set and oppressed by much fat'.[275] The greed and ruthlessness so evident in his later years had begun to drive victims to desperation—the brother of the Earl of March had been so offended by the latter's dispossession in 1435 that he had rebelled against James and co-operated with the English.[276] James's commanding position in domestic politics had owed much to his abstinence from warfare. By taking the field at Roxburgh in August 1436 he broke the spell hitherto cast by his powerful personality: the expedition was militarily an inglorious failure. More than that, the concourse of nobles in the huge host gathered at Roxburgh bred political trouble: there was 'detestable schism and most wicked division sprung from envy'.[277] From these laconic phrases of the Pluscarden chronicler it may be deduced that in 1436, as in a better-known episode of 1482, the nobles, when arrayed for war, sensed their own power and were no longer daunted by the king. In these circumstances, when a general council met at Edinburgh in October 1436, James showed political tactlessness in passing measures that threatened the independence of baronial jurisdictions.[278]

With one opponent at least, the papacy, James was by this time ready to seek reconciliation. The Bishop of Urbino had arrived as papal legate[279] in time to join the king and his court at Perth for 'a solempne fest of the Cristynmes'.[280] At Perth, the king and queen resided in the Dominican friary while the rest of the court was dispersed in lodgings in the town. It was none other than Sir Robert Stewart, grandson of the Earl of Atholl, who was chamberlain of the royal household and in charge of its domestic arrangements. On

---

[274] Balfour-Melville, *James I*, pp. 4, 247.
[275] Brown, *Early Travellers*, p. 25.   [276] P. 292 above.
[277] *Chron. Pluscarden*, I. 380.   [278] P. 312 above.   [279] P. 301 above.
[280] *James I, Life and Death*, p. 52. James was certainly in Perth by 1 January 1437 (Balfour-Melville, *James I*, p. 292).

the night of 21 February 1437 he laid planks over the fosse of the
friary and the conspirators entered.

There were eight of them, including Sir Robert Stewart and Sir
Robert Graham. To James, who was alone with the queen and her
ladies, the noise of clanking armour gave warning of the approaching
danger. The door of the apartment could not be secured—Sir Robert
Stewart had 'left the kynges chamburs doore opyne, and had brussed
and blundird the lokes of hem yn such wise that no man myght shute
hem'.[281] Using a poker the king wrenched up the planking of the floor
and let himself down to the sewer that ran beneath. Its outlet had
been sealed a few days previously since the king had lost so many
tennis balls there. He remained hidden in this noisome tunnel while
the conspirators burst into the chamber above. One of them wounded
Queen Joan, who 'fledd yn hir kirtill, her mantell hongyng aboute
hir; the other ladyes yn a corner of the chambur crying and wepyng
all destraite.'[282] Disappointed in their quest the conspirators left the
chamber only to return when one of them remembered the sewer.
By the light of a torch they caught sight of the king in his hiding
place. Though unarmed he fought manfully before he died by the
strokes of the assassins. Too late the courtiers and townsfolk rushed
with torches to the scene of the murder. Only one, Sir David Dunbar,
brother of the dispossessed Earl of March,[283] managed to overtake
the assassins and was wounded by them as they fled to the fastnessess
of the 'Wilde Scottes'.[284]

[281] *James I, Life and Death*, pp. 52–5; *Chron. Pluscarden*, I. 389; *Chron.
Bower*, II. 503.
[282] *James I, Life and Death*, p. 57.
[283] *Scots Peerage*, III. 275.   [284] *James I, Life and Death*, p. 60.

12

THE MINORITY OF JAMES II AND THE LITTLE SCHISM

When the Bishop of Urbino inspected the corpse of the murdered king he kissed its many wounds and, with tearful sighs, announced to the bystanders that James had died as a martyr for the defence of the state and the execution of justice.[1] Just as the murder of Archbishop Thomas Becket won him an adulation after his death that he had never enjoyed in his lifetime, so the melodramatic demise of James I cast a retrospective aura of good fame over the whole of his reign and dazzled the judgments of most contemporary writers [2] and of their successors. James's posthumous reputation must also have been enhanced by the undoubted contrast between his one-time masterful rule and the anarchy that followed during his son's minority. Thus there is some exaggeration in the view that 'the tragedy of James I lies in the wreck of his high purpose upon the stubborn individualism of the Scottish nobles'.[3]

In any case only a few nobles had planned the king's death. If the remainder breathed a collective sigh of relief at James's removal they at least showed a sense of propriety in disowning the removers. Sir Robert Graham was brought to trial before the justiciar at Stirling and reputedly accepted his doom with a prophetic utterance :

> Ye shalle se the daye and the tyme that ye shalle pray for my saule for the grete good that I have done to you and to alle this reaume of Scottland, that I have thus slayne and delyveryed you of so cruelle a tirant.[4]

[1] *Chron. Pluscarden*, I. 390.
[2] See *ibid.*, 389; *Chron. Bower*, II. 512, 514.
[3] Balfour-Melville, *James I*, p. 280.
[4] *James I, Life and Death*, pp. 62–4; *E.R.*, v. xlii, xliii.

Sentence against the Earl of Atholl and his grandson, Sir Robert
Stewart, was probably passed in the parliament that met in Edinburgh on 25 March 1437.[5] The lack of sympathy for the regicides
can be seen in the fiendishness of the punishments inflicted upon
them, which on this unique occasion even surpassed English
practice.[6]

Meanwhile on 25 March 1437 the surviving son of the dead king,
a boy of six, was crowned and anointed as James II, not at Scone, near
the scene of his father's murder, but in the abbey of Holyrood, to
which he was conducted by the three estates 'with the greatest applause
and display'.[7] It seems likely that parliament then made arrangements for the government of the realm during the minority. Although
the three estates entrusted the queen mother with the custody of the
young king and his sisters, and appointed a council to assist her,
assigned Stirling Castle as a residence, and set her yearly allowance
at four thousand marks,[8] she emerged as something less than a regent.
It was the late king's nephew, Archibald Douglas, fulsomely styled
'Duke of Touraine, Earl of Douglas and Count of Longueville, Lord
of Galloway and Annandale', who was to head the government as
lieutenant-general.[9] The view that he had been influential during the
reign of James I 'rests largely on indirect evidence'.[10] Although Earl
Archibald had shunned the political limelight his self-effacement had
not prevented his being temporarily arrested by James I.[11] The new
lieutenant-general probably saw no reason why he should act as a
drudge on behalf of the house of Stewart. It was a time of misery: a
visitation of plague was followed in 1438 and 1439 by famine, 'and
werraly the derth was sa gret that thar deit [died] a passinge peple for
hunger'.[12] To these afflictions was added the lawlessness so vividly
portrayed by Abbot Bower:

> even I who am writing these things have seen and heard this very day
> the poor people of my own neighbourhood being stripped of their gar-
> ments and inhumanly despoiled of their utensils.[13]

[5] *A.P.S.*, II. 31.
[6] *James I, Life and Death*, pp. 61–2, 64–5; *Chron. Pluscarden*, I. 390–1.
[7] *A.P.S.*, II. 31; *Chron. Bower*, II. 514.
[8] These arrangements of 1437 may be inferred from the proceedings of the
general council at Stirling in September 1439 (*A.P.S.*, II. 54).
[9] *Ibid.*, 31.
[10] W. Stanford Reid, 'The Douglases at the Court of James I of Scotland',
Juridical Review, LVI. 77–88, at 88.   [11] P. 320 above.
[12] *Chron. Auchinleck*, pp. 12, 53; *Chron. Bower*, II. 514.
[13] *Chron. Bower*, II. 474.

It was in vain that the lieutenant-general and his council, meeting in Edinburgh on 24 December 1438, passed an ordinance dealing with 'spuilzie' (spoliation).[14] Another council, which met at Stirling in March 1439, found it necessary to pass an ordinance dealing with 'rebellys or unrewlfull menne within ony castellys or fortalicis'.[15]

Among the 'unrewlfull menne' was doubtless Sir Robert Erskine, who at the outset of the minority tested the strength of the government by attempting to obtain the earldom of Mar and the Garioch that had come into the hands of James I in 1435.[16] He began by seizing control of the royal castle of Dumbarton (or, if he already held it, refused to relinquish it). On 10 August 1440 an indenture was made at Stirling 'be way of amiable composicioun' between Erskine and a committee of thirty-one representatives of the three estates specially appointed by the general council; Erskine was to have custody of Kildrummy Castle in Mar until the king came of age; as soon as he was installed in Kildrummy Castle he was to hand back Dumbarton Castle.[17] Mar was not the only earldom that inspired trouble: Sir Alan Stewart of Darnley, who had lately headed the Scots mercenaries in France, sought to make good a claim (through his mother) to the earldom of Lennox.[18] He fell foul of Boyd of Kilmarnock by reason of an old feud between the two families and was treacherously killed by Sir Thomas Boyd.[19] On 7 July 1439 the Lennox Stewarts had their revenge : 'Schir Thomas Boyd was slane be Alexander Stewart "Buktuth" and his sonnis and Mathow Stewart with his brother, and uther syndry.'[20] The result of this 'plaine battell' was that 'the heill southvest of Scotland was devydit in twa pairtis'.[21] The Lennox affair also involved Alexander, Lord of the Isles, now officially recognised as Earl of Ross.[22] His goodwill was sought by the government.[23] By 22 February 1439 he had been appointed justiciar north of Forth,[24] and he was present in the general council held at Stirling on 4 September 1439.[25] On the following day some Islesmen, whom Pitscottie styles 'notabill thevis and murtheraris', took part in

[14] A.P.S., II. 32.   [15] Ibid.   [16] Pp. 257, 319 above.
[17] A.P.S., II. 55-6; see also Aberdeen-Banff Illustrations, IV. 189-90.
[18] Scots Peerage, V. 347-8; Dunlop, Bishop Kennedy, p. 24, n. 3.
[19] One source (Chron. Auchinleck, p. 3) places the murder a few miles from Falkirk; another (Pitscottie, Historie, I. 23-4) places it near Glasgow.
[20] Chron. Auchinleck, 3, 33. Alexander was the brother of the murdered Sir Alan (Pitscottie, Historie, I. 24).
[21] Pitscottie, Historie, I. 24.   [22] H.B.C., 487.
[23] E.R., V. 33-4, 73, 84, 86, 166.
[24] Col. Leslie, Historical Records of the Family of Leslie (1869), I. 87.
[25] A.P.S., II. 54-5; p. 329 below.

an affray on the banks of Loch Lomond near Inchmurrin and slew John Colquhoun of Luss. Whether the Islesmen had been called in by the government or came to settle scores of their own the result was probably the same : 'the Lennox was heill ovirthrowin'.[26]

The opening disorders of the minority were accompanied by squabbles among various factions for control of government. On this subject the surviving official records are usually silent, though one record, that of the 'Appoyntement' of 4 September 1439,[27] confirms the picture of suspicion, intrigue, plotting and violence, that the narrative sources depict. These sources include the scrappy (but contemporary) *Auchinleck Chronicle* and the melodramatic *Scotorum Historiae* of Hector Boece, first published in Paris in 1527. This work gives picturesque details and set speeches but omits to supply chronology and corroboration. The same is true of the *Historie* of Robert Lindsay of Pitscottie, which, up to 1460, is basically a translation of Boece,[28] but one that, being colourfully composed in the Lowland vernacular, conveys an effect of verisimilitude that may sometimes be misleading. It is particularly unfortunate that Bower ended his chronicle just as the factions were girding their loins for political battle. Thus the politics of the minority have the character of a jigsaw puzzle from which some of the pieces are missing and in which alien pieces may have been jumbled.

What seems indisputable is the sudden rise to power of Sir William Crichton and Sir Alexander Livingston of Callendar. The former had been a trusted servant of James I, who had appointed him to the new and honourable post of master of the household, granted him the custody of Edinburgh Castle with a salary of £100, and made him sheriff of Edinburgh.[29] The baronial family of Livingston was of much the same standing as that of Crichton ; and the prolific Livingstons had a wide connection, which included the prominent conciliarist, Thomas Livingston, Abbot of Dundrennan.[30]

Thanks to the fact that the coronation of James II took place in Holyrood, Sir William Crichton was able at the very start of the minority to use his posts as sheriff of Edinburgh and keeper of its castle as a means of acquiring further influence.[31] Pitscottie relates that soon after the coronation Crichton obtained control of the young king ; the queen mother pretended to set out on a pilgrimage to White-

---

[26] Pitscottie, *Historie*, I. 29; *Chron. Auchinleck*, 3, 34.
[27] P. 329 below.   [28] Pitscottie, *Historie*, I. 12, n. 1.
[29] *Scots Peerage*, III. 52–8; *E.R.*, IV. 607.
[30] Duncan Shaw, 'Thomas Livingston, a Conciliarist', *Scot. Church Hist. Soc. Recs.*, XII. 120–35, at 123.   [31] *E.R.*, V. xlv, 63.

kirk, smuggled her son out of the castle in one of the coffers of her baggage, and instead of sailing from Leith to Dunbar sailed up the Forth to Stirling Castle, to be welcomed by Sir Alexander Livingston, who proposed to besiege Crichton in Edinburgh Castle; thereupon Crichton pointed out the hostility of Douglas towards both himself and Livingston and sought a reconciliation with the latter.[32] Although the picturesque details of this tale are suspect, its substance might account for a political change that occurred in May 1439 when Bishop Cameron was replaced as chancellor by Sir William Crichton.[33]

In the following month the Earl of Douglas died of a fever.[34] No new lieutenant-general was appointed. The queen mother ambitiously tried to fill the gap and married a minor noble, Sir James Stewart, 'the Black Knight of Lorne', who 'thocht, seing the cuntre swa devydit . . . to have had sum reull in the realme alsweill as ony utheris, be ressoun he had mariet the kingis mother'.[35] On 3 August 1439, shortly after the nuptials, Sir Alexander Livingston showed his resentment by imprisoning the queen and her new husband.[36] Since the Livingstons now had control of the boy king they could hope to dominate Scotland. At first their scheme went well: a general council of the three estates met at Stirling, and on 4 September 1439 negotiated an 'Appoyntement' for the release of the captives.[37] Queen Joan affected to believe that the Livingstons had held her in durance only through motives of zeal and loyalty towards her and her son the king. She remitted her 'griefe and displeasance', and in token of the 'traiste and hartliness' with which she now regarded the Livingstons she confided her son to their keeping until he came of age. Meanwhile she 'lent' to her son her residence of Stirling and granted to Sir Alexander Livingston the annuity of four thousand marks once assigned to her by the three estates. All the parties to the 'Appoyntement' took oath on the gospels to observe it, and it was sealed by many notables, including Chancellor Crichton. But one morning when the young king rode out with a few attendants to hunt in Stirling Park he was waylaid by the chancellor and a band of a hundred armed men, thereupon 'the king began to smylle, quhairthrow thay undirstude the king to be content of thair coming and glaid to gang

---

[32] Pitscottie, *Historie*, I. 16–23.
[33] See Dunlop, *Bishop Kennedy*, pp. 26–7.
[34] Pitscottie, *Historie*, I. 24; *Chron. Auchinleck*, pp. 4, 34.
[35] Pitscottie, *Historie*, I. 26; *Scots Peerage*, v. 2.
[36] *Chron. Auchinleck*, pp. 3, 33–4; *E.R.*, v. liii, n. 1; *R.M.S.*, II. No. 324.
[37] Text in *A.P.S.*, II. 54–5; *Chron. Auchinleck*, pp. 3, 34.

with thame, and thairfor hynt his hors be the bryddill and convoyit him to Edinburghe'.[38] This exploit stole the thunder of the Livingstons. But Crichton was prepared to be accommodating : a new reconciliation between the two factions was arranged. Livingston, it seems, was once more to have custody of the king, while Crichton continued as chancellor and was to receive a salary of seven hundred marks until the king came of age.[39] Some thought was even given to the public weal. A general council held at Stirling in August 1440 ordained that the justiciars should hold their ayres twice a year, and that the king himself should attend, or at least be nearby 'quhar his consale thinkis it maist spedful'. It was also thought 'spedfull' that the king should hastily 'ride throu oute the realme . . . quhar ony rebellione, slauchter, byrning, refe, forfalt, or thift, happynis' [40]—a tall order.

There remained one real or potential source of trouble—the young Earl of Douglas—fear of whom had probably forced Crichton and Livingston to their reconciliation. When Archibald, fifth Earl of Douglas, had died in 1439 he had been succeeded by his son William, then some fourteen or fifteen years old.[41] He was a kinsman of the young king; his father had been lieutenant-general; and it was natural that Earl William should aspire to the same post. Whatever his ambitions they were soon removed. He accepted an invitation to Edinburgh Castle and turned a deaf ear to warnings that mischief was afoot. With his brother David, and his family counsellor, Sir Malcolm Fleming, he dined in the castle on 24 November 1440. At the close of the dinner Chancellor Crichton placed a bull's head on the table, 'quhilk was ane signe and taikin of condemnatour to the death'. The two Douglas brothers were seized and put through a rigmarole of a trial before being beheaded on the castle hill.[42]

This 'Black Dinner' might have been expected to arouse a hornets' nest of Douglases thirsting for blood. Nothing of the sort happened. If Crichton and Livingston, for their own motives, good, bad, or indifferent, were eager for the demise of the Douglas brothers, there was another person, himself a Douglas, who was even more eager. This was James Douglas of Balvenie and Abercorn, whose corpulence earned him the sobriquet of 'the Gross'.[43] In his early days he had

---

[38] Pitscottie, *Historie*, I. 31–2. [39] *Ibid.*, 34–9; *E.R.*, v. 125.
[40] *A.P.S.*, II. 32–3. [41] *Scots Peerage*, III. 170–1.
[42] Pitscottie, *Historie*, I. 40–6; *Chron. Bower*, II. 514 (additional notes of the reign of James II). [43] Pitscottie, *Historie*, I. 46.

shown a bold spirit.[44] He was, according to Pitscottie—though the same might have been said of most of his contemporaries—'gredie to conques great rentis to his posteritie'.[45] Although James the Gross had been created Earl of Avondale a few months after the death of James I, this elevation in rank had brought him no new lands. On the other hand, James was second son of Archibald the Grim, third Earl of Douglas, and, thanks to the Douglas tailzie of 1342, it was James who came next after his grand-nephew Earl William, and the latter's brother, David, in the succession to the bulk of the Black Douglas estates.[46] Circumstantial evidence leaves little doubt that James the Gross played the part of a wicked grand-uncle and encouraged Crichton in the view that 'this realme sould be at greattar tranquilitie gif the Earle of Douglas and his brother had bene cutted of sudenlie'.[47] Earl James, at any rate, was the person who most obviously profited, for although the Douglas brothers had been executed as traitors no sentence of forfeiture was passed against them; thus James succeeded to the earldom of Douglas. By contrast, Sir Malcolm Fleming of Biggar and Cumbernauld, who shared the fate of the Douglas brothers, was sentenced to forfeiture before his execution. On 7 January 1441 his son and heir, Sir Robert Fleming, went to the mercat cross of Linlithgow and asserted, in the traditional terms of such an appeal, that the sentence was evil, false and rotten.[48] Soon Sir Robert was allowed to succeed to the forfeited lands and was given in marriage a daughter of James the Gross,[49] who thus atoned both for the slaughter of Sir Robert's grandfather in 1406 and for the judicial murder of Sir Robert's father in 1440. With the powerful James the Gross anxious to hush matters up no one stirred himself on behalf of the two dead Douglases.

Meanwhile there was some re-allocation of the Black Douglas territories. It was only to the entailed estates that James the Gross succeeded. The duchy of Touraine with the other lands in France lapsed to the French crown in default of heirs male in the direct line. For the same reason the Scottish crown received as a titbit the lordship of Annandale. The lordships of Bothwell and of Galloway (east and west) went to the young sister of the sixth earl, Margaret Douglas, 'the Fair Maid of Galloway'.[50] What had been dismembered was partly replaced by the lands that James the Gross already

---

[44] Pp. 225, 226 above.   [45] Pitscottie, *Historie*, I. 47.
[46] *Scots Peerage*, III. 172–3.   [47] Pitscottie, *Historie*, I. 43, 46.
[48] *E.R.*, v. lvi; P. F. Tytler, *History*, I. ii, 382–3, Notes and Illustrations, Letter K.
[49] *Scots Peerage*, VIII. 529, 533.   [50] *Ibid.*, III. 171, 176; *E.R.*, v. lvii.

held as Earl of Avondale. From his castle of Abercorn on the shores of the Forth near Linlithgow, he dominated the valley of the Avon from which he took his earlier title; he also held lands in Banffshire, Inverness-shire, Buchan and Moray,[51] and was soon exercising his mind to secure further territories for his posterity. James Dunbar, Earl of Moray, had died in 1429 leaving as co-heiresses his daughters Janet and Elizabeth. Janet, the elder daughter, had married James Crichton, son and heir of the chancellor; James the Gross arranged the marriage of her younger sister to his third son, Archibald. A tailzie of 26 April 1442 was the first move in Earl James's manoeuvres to win the earldom of Moray for his third son at the expense of Janet Dunbar and James Crichton.[52] The ingenuity required for the Moray affair was scarcely needed for a more ambitious venture—the reunification of the Black Douglas lands. By the simple expedient of a marriage between the Fair Maid of Galloway and William, son and heir of Earl James, all would be regained with the sole exception of Annandale. During Lent in 1443 or 1444 William Douglas, a youth of some eighteen years, married his cousin Margaret in the kirk of Douglas; she had not yet reached the nubile age of twelve.[53]

The acquisitiveness of the seventh Earl of Douglas (and of others) had been stimulated not only by the turmoil of political faction but also by new ecclesiastical divisions. There was a short lull before the storm of dissension, and some old divisions were healed before the new made their appearance: the barratry laws stayed unrepealed but unenforced, and Eugenius IV even showed his magnanimity on 28 December 1439 by pardoning Bishop Cameron's misdemeanours.[54] But the bishop seems to have been too closely associated with the victims of the Black Dinner: on 3 March 1441 a petition in the name of James II informed the pope that Cameron had aided 'several other lords of the king's council' in rebellion, sedition and other enormities.[55] Although Cameron kept his bishopric he was discredited and almost finished as a political figure. Just as Bishop Cameron was no longer the spokesman of the Scottish government in ecclesiastical affairs, so his old antagonist, William Croyser, was no longer the spokesman of the pope: the archdeacon had made a *volte-face* and

[51] *Scots Peerage*, III. 173.
[52] Dunlop, *Bishop Kennedy*, pp. 35–6 and 36, n. 1; *Scots Peerage*, VI. 306–9.
[53] Pitscottie, *Historie*, I. 47–8; *Cal. Papal Letters*, x. 130–1.
[54] Dunlop, *Bishop Kennedy*, p. 27; *Cal. Papal Letters*, VIII. 294.
[55] *St Andrews Copiale*, pp. 308–9; Burns, *Basle*, p. 70.

adhered to the council of Basel,[56] with which the pope's relationship was once more strained.[57]

In 1437 Eugenius had issued a bull transferring the council to Ferrara, whence it afterwards moved to Florence. A majority of the council of Basel refused to be either transferred or dissolved, remained doggedly in session, and on 25 June 1439 deposed Eugenius (who ignored the deposition), styling him, among other things, an incorrigible schismatic, a deviate from the faith, and a pertinacious heretic; on 5 November 1439 Amadeus, Duke of Savoy, was elected at Basel as Felix V.[58] Once more there was a schism.

While Scottish contact with the former council of Constance had been 'limited and equivocal',[59] as many as eleven Scotsmen who were bishops between 1425 and 1475 were in some way associated with the long-lasting council of Basel.[60] The most distinguished of these was Thomas Livingston, Abbot of Dundrennan,[61] who addressed the imperial diet at Mainz on 10 August 1439 and posed the rhetorical question :

> What stability would there be in the Christian polity if it could be entirely overthrown by a single sinner [the Pope] who might not, even if he persevered in his violent course, be checked by any individual or by any council or assembly? [62]

The most significant part of Livingston's career was spent on the continent. In Scotland the conciliarist influence of two other graduates of St Andrews, John Athilmer and James Ogilvie, was more direct.[63] By 1439 the pair were teaching in St Andrews. Their advent shortly followed the death of Laurence of Lindores and shortly preceded that of Bishop Wardlaw. Old influences were removed and the way was open for new. The philosophic realism of Cologne (where both Ogilvie and Athilmer had studied) won toleration alongside the nominalism of Paris.[64] More importantly, the careers of these two men, who

---

[56] Dunlop, *Bishop Kennedy*, p. 37; Burns, *Basle*, p. 65.
[57] For the background see John Holland Smith, *The Great Schism*, pp. 240–45.
[58] Burns, *Basle*, pp. 56, 62, 64; Dunlop, *Bishop Kennedy*, p. 37; *Chron. Bower*, II. 481.
[59] J. H. Burns, 'The Conciliarist Tradition in Scotland', *S.H.R.*, XLII. 89–104, at 90.   [60] Burns, *Basle*, p. 86.
[61] His whole career is studied by Duncan Shaw, *op. cit., Scot. Church Hist. Soc. Recs.*, XII. 120–35.   [62] J. H. Burns, *op. cit., S.H.R.*, XLII. 89–104, at 96–7.
[63] See *St Andrews Copiale*, pp. 204–9.
[64] J. H. Burns, *op. cit., S.H.R.*, XLII. 89–104, at 91–2, 94; Burns, *Basle*, p. 77; *St Andrews Acta*, I. 48–9.

were still prominent at St Andrews a generation later, illustrate how 'something like a Scottish conciliarist tradition was created' and how conciliarist ideas were 'part of the mental equipment of educated Scots as the Reformation approached'.[65]

The controversies that drew new vigour from the contest between Eugenius and Basel were not merely intellectual and academic. Abbot Bower, who avoided taking sides, stressed the scandal caused by the schism and devoted five chapters of his *Scotichronicon* to an historical account of various schisms since 349 A.D. Despondently he remarked :

> What and how many damages accursed schisms of this sort caused in their time not only to human bodies but to souls it is not of our faculty to evaluate.

When Bower was writing, the contest between the Roman pope and the conciliar pope still continued and, so Bower says, 'still is as if *sub judice*'.[66] It was to continue until 1449. So far as Scotland was concerned the Little Schism of 1439–49 was not complicated by international rivalries ; but internal ones made it more disruptive than the Great Schism of 1378–1418 during which kirk and nation had been fairly united in their adherence to one pope. If some kirkmen stayed neutral (like Abbot Bower) others were staunch conciliarists or papalists. There was no strong figure in the government to impose a definite policy ; and in the kirk itself, after the eclipse of Cameron, there was no recognised leader on either side until Eugenius put his trust in James Kennedy.

One of the last acts of James I had been to thrust his nephew Kennedy into the bishopric of Dunkeld.[67] When Eugenius retrospectively sanctioned this Erastian appointment by a provision of 1 July 1437, he set Kennedy off on a career in which he was to show himself the most distinguished figure in the Scottish kirk of his time. In 1439 Kennedy headed those Scottish ecclesiastics who answered the pope's summons to the council of Ferrara-Florence. He must have witnessed the triumphant spectacle of the reunion of the Greek and Roman churches under Eugenius and, at what must have seemed to some contemporaries the apotheosis of the papacy, committed himself permanently as a loyal supporter of the Roman pope. Kennedy lingered at Florence and received special recognition on 23 September 1439 when Eugenius conferred upon him the abbey of Scone to be held *in*

[65] J. H. Burns, *op. cit.*, *S.H.R.*, XLII. 89–104, at 89; see also Burns, *Basle*, pp. 85–6.

[66] *Chron. Bower*, II. 475–81. [67] Dunlop, *Bishop Kennedy*, p. 19.

commendam.[68] This early application of a practice that was to become disastrously frequent meant that Kennedy as 'commendator' did not have to perform in person the duties of an abbot, but controlled the abbey's revenues and could use them to supplement those of his bishopric of Dunkeld. Papal favour continued : on the death of Bishop Wardlaw on 9 April 1440 Kennedy was translated from Dunkeld to St Andrews; since he was unable to raise the usual 'common services' of 3,300 gold florins he automatically incurred excommunication but was graciously granted absolution and remission of half the sum.[69].

In Kennedy the papalist party now had a strong leader, and in some meeting of the three estates, probably in May 1441, it was ordained 'that no Scot may go to Basel, adhere to the council, or obey it'.[70] But no sooner had the three estates repudiated Basel and the conciliar pope than there ensued a struggle over conflicting provisions to benefices. Eugenius provided Alexander Lauder to Dunkeld, Thomas Tulloch to Ross, Ingeram Lindsay to Aberdeen, and probably 'John Hectoris' to the Isles; Felix provided Thomas Livingston (who had been deprived of his abbey of Dundrennan by Eugenius) to Dunkeld, Andrew Munro to Ross, and the sixteen-year-old James Douglas, son of James the Gross, to Aberdeen.[71] When a provincial council of the Scottish kirk met in July 1442 the bishops who had been provided by Eugenius deprived and excommunicated those who had been provided by Felix. James the Gross attended this council, probably leading with him his son (the supposed Bishop of Aberdeen) and William Croyser; they proclaimed their adherence to Basel and began to issue counter-deprivations, whereupon 'certain prelates fled by night'.[72]

On 31 August 1442 Earl James wrote to Basel to report his achievements, and in October Croyser re-appeared at Basel and joined with Thomas Livingston in persuading the council to support Douglas. On the way home, however, the archdeacon was captured by bandits and for a time was held in prison in Strassburg.[73] Earl James was thus deprived of his most useful agent. Meanwhile Eu-

[68] Burns, *Basle*, pp. 62, 64.   [69] Dunlop, *Bishop Kennedy*, pp. 39–41.
[70] See R. K. Hannay, 'A Letter to Scotland from the Council of Basel', *S.H.R.*, xx. 49–57, at 54.
[71] Dunlop, *Bishop Kennedy*, pp. 40–2; Dowden, *Bishops*, p. 289; Burns, *Basle*, p. 73.
[72] *St Andrews Copiale*, pp. 322–3.
[73] Burns, *Basle*, p. 79; Dunlop, *Bishop Kennedy*, p. 45; R. K. Hannay, *op. cit.*, *S.H.R.*, xx. 49–57, at 54.

genius tried to dispossess Croyser of his two archdeaconries and to provide two of his own nominees. In so doing the pope fell out of step with Bishop Kennedy, who collated another two nominees. One of the resulting five contestants was Patrick Home, a 'ner kynnesman' of Sir Alexander Home of Dunglass. Patrick reported that he could not visit his archdeaconry save with a mighty band of armed men.[74]

The Homes were concerned not only with the archdeaconry of Teviotdale but with the perennial problem of the priory of Colding-ham. So many vested interests were involved that Coldingham was at the root of much of the trouble that occurred in south-east Scot-land throughout the fifteenth century. In 1442 there were difficulties not only over the appointment of a prior,[75] but concerning the bailiary or justiciarship of Coldingham. Such an office conferred administra-tive control and temporal jurisdiction over the lands of a religious house and was highly coveted. Moreover, in the power vacuum left in the region by the forfeiture of the Earls of March in 1435 there was a struggle between the local baronial families of the Hepburns and Homes. Even the Homes were divided: the bailiary was coveted both by Sir Alexander Home of Dunglass and his nephew, Sir David Home of Wedderburn (supported by Sir Adam Hepburn of Hailes, who was feudal superior of both). On 20 May 1442, after an inter-change of views between the Prior of Durham and the Scottish coun-cil, it was settled that Sir Alexander Home should have the bailiary for life. Then James the Gross stirred up the issue anew. As justiciar south of Forth he asserted that the decision of the king's 'partiale consale' was 'of na strenth na vertu'. With this encouragement Sir David Home seized Coldingham and drove out the prior. When the latter managed to return he confirmed Sir Alexander Home in the office of bailie, and allegedly allowed him to use the priory as a forta-lice garrisoned by Border reivers who stole more than two thousand sheep from Sir David Home and Sir Adam Hepburn. The Earl of Angus mediated: Sir David was compensated for his losses by a de-creet arbitral on 16 January 1444 and the two Homes were recon-ciled.[76]

The meddling of James the Gross in the Coldingham dispute was probably one of his last interventions in ecclesiastical politics: he is said to have died at Abercorn on 25 March 1443.[77] His son and heir,

---

[74] Dunlop, *Bishop Kennedy*, p. 47.   [75] *Ibid.*, pp. 49–50.
[76] *Ibid.*, pp. 51–4.
[77] *Scots Peerage*, III. 173. He 'deceissit in Abercorn the thrid zeir efter h' was maid earle' (Pitscottie, *Historie*, I. 47).

William, the new eighth Earl of Douglas, rapidly concluded that the council of Basel and its pope were doomed to failure : their main support came from the universities, still conciliarist in outlook; but the secular rulers stood aloof. After May 1443 the council even discontinued its solemn sessions at Basel.[78] In Scotland it became clear that the Black Douglases could no longer be relied upon to support the conciliarists. The result was probably seen in a general council at Stirling on 4 November 1443, when it was ordained that recognition should be given only to 'actis of generale and provinciall consalys publicit and notifiit of befor and proclamit be the kingis autorite'. It was also ordained that 'ferme and fast obedieince be kepit till our haly fadir the Pape Eugenne' and that 'na persone, spirituale na temporal, change the said obedience quhil the king and the realm ordane and decrete therapone'.[79] The kirk, unable to control itself, was being controlled by the state. If the proceedings of the general council of November 1443 represented 'an ecclesiastical victory for the Bishop of St Andrews'[80] it was perhaps a hollow one ; and the restoration of Eugenius's authority was scarcely complete when his death on 23 February 1447 once more raised the hopes of the adherents of Felix V. Although no time was lost in electing Nicholas V as Eugenius's successor Felix hoped to take advantage of the situation by seizing the initiative in Scotland, where Bishop Cameron had died on 24 December 1446. This reopened the possibility of manoeuvre within the Scottish episcopate. On 20 March 1447 Felix appointed the conciliarist Thomas Livingston as his legate to Scotland.[81] But the mission was in vain : Livingston speedily returned to the continent to witness the bargaining that took place as the end approached for Felix V and the council of Basel. In June 1448 the council was obliged to leave Basel and settle at Lausanne. There, on 7 April 1449, Felix V abdicated. On 18 April the council 'elected' Nicholas V and thus ended the schism.[82]

Both the council and Felix had made the most of their nuisance value and obtained generous terms from the victorious side. Livingston and the versatile William Croyser left the commends in Savoy and the Lyonnais formerly granted them by Felix, and made their way back to Scotland where 'a genuine spirit of reconciliation does seem to have prevailed'.[83] Other prominent Scottish conciliarists,

[78] John Holland Smith, *The Great Schism*, p. 246; Burns, *Basle*, p. 81.
[79] *A.P.S.*, II. 33.
[80] Dunlop, *Bishop Kennedy*, p. 307, n. 4.   [81] Burns, *Basle*, pp. 83–4.
[82] *Ibid.*, p. 84.   [83] *Ibid.*, pp. 83, 84, 85.

thanks to Bishop Kennedy, found academic openings in the university of St Andrews. With the ending of the ten-year schism the Scottish kirk was restored to as much harmony as could be expected.

The gradual restoration of order within the kirk was, however, accompanied, and sometimes interrupted, by flagrant political disorder. Through his marriage the new eighth Earl of Douglas had re-united the whole of the Black Douglas territories with the exception of Annandale and the elusive lands in France; and the earl and his kin had by no means lost hope of recovering these from the Scottish and French crown respectively.[84] Before long, Earl William was building up a party to take over the government, which was increasingly distracted by continuing lawlessness [85] and rivalry between the Crichtons and the Livingstons. Despite Pitscottie's rambling tale of repeated squabbles and reconciliations between these two factions, the members of both families had continued to figure side by side in the witness lists of royal charters until 8 February 1443, after which a gap in the records occurs.[86] Up to at least that date the two families kept up the appearance of joint participation in government. Thereafter, however, they became open foes, probably by the instigation of Earl William of Douglas, who wished to gain power by using the Livingstons against the Crichtons.

The way for a Douglas-Livingston alliance had been cleared on 16 August 1443 when Sir Alexander Livingston of Callendar purged himself by oath, in the presence of Bishop Kennedy and three other bishops, 'of having given any counsel, assistance or consent to the slaughter of Sir Malcolm Fleming' at the Black Dinner.[87] The Livingstons could now be respectably associated under Earl William in an alliance that also numbered the Flemings, the Hamiltons, and at first, the Kennedies, including the Bishop of St Andrews. Bishop Kennedy's interest in the fortunes of his family can be seen in a transaction concluded on 2 July 1444 'at Cascyllis, near the great garden thereof', when he witnessed letters of retinue by which Sir John Kennedy of Blaucharne and his son and heir 'became men for the term of ten years to Gilbert Kennedy, Lord of Dunure'; Gilbert was to pay twenty marks a year to Sir John, and a further ten marks for his homage and service; 'and because the said sum of ten marks seemed

[84] See a document of 29 October 1445 concerning Annandale cited in *Scots Peerage*, III. 172. For Touraine see Fraser, *Douglas*, I. 396–7, 462–3.
[85] *Chron. Auchinleck*, 4–5, 35; Pitscottie, *Historie*, I. 48–9; Dunlop, *Bishop Kennedy*, p. 56 and n. 3.   [86] *R.M.S.*, II. 49–62.
[87] Dunlop, *Bishop Kennedy*, p. 34, n. 3.

to be too small, the Bishop of St Andrews bound himself to pay to him two marks in addition'.[88] It can hardly be taken for granted that 'Kennedy's eyes were fixed on far horizons while the faction leaders were rending Scotland with their feuds'.[89] The advancement of Douglas, who by July 1444 seems to have been styled lieutenant-general,[90] was accompanied by the attempted demotion of Crichton. Claiming to be acting 'on behalf of the king' the two custumars of Edinburgh (one of them a Livingston) formally ordered Crichton to proceed no further with some 'process' which was being held about the lands of Castlelaw. They also cited him to answer before the king for some alleged default, and saw to it that three notarial instruments were drawn up as evidence that the inhibition and summons had been duly served.[91] Probably because Crichton did not obey this summons, the chamberlain, Sir John Forrester of Corstorphine, was instructed to proceed with distraint.[92] He required the help of Douglas, who was presumably acting as the king's lieutenant-general. On 20 August 1444[93] the earl came with an armed host 'on the king's behalf' to the tower-house of Barnton on the outskirts of Edinburgh and called for its surrender. Barnton was the residence of Sir George Crichton, admiral of Scotland, sheriff of Linlithgow, and cousin of the chancellor, and its inmates put up some defence before capitulating. Thereupon Douglas saw to it that this Crichton stronghold was 'cassin doun to the groun'. But despite Douglas's initial success Sir William Crichton remained secure in Edinburgh Castle and was even able to take the offensive : he and his adherents ravaged the Forrester lands of Corstorphine, while Sir George Crichton attacked Earl William's lands near Linlithgow.[94] The downfall of the Crichtons was not going to be easily accomplished, even by the Black Douglas and his allies.

Their next move was to arrange the holding of a general council at Stirling at the end of October 1444[95] to denounce the Crichtons as rebels. The intensity of political activity may be gauged from the

[88] *Cassillis Charters*, cited in Dunlop, *Bishop Kennedy*, p. 67.   [89] *Ibid.*
[90] Boece, *History*, p. 364. Douglas is probably the figure who appears in a joint petition of the king and lieutenant-general to the pope on 8 July 1444 (Dunlop, *Bishop Kennedy*, p. 409).
[91] *E.R.*, v. lxxxiv, 146, 147.   [92] Pitscottie, *Historie*, I. 52–3.
[93] The Auchinleck chronicler (*Chron. Auchinleck*, pp. 5, 36) gives the date as 20 August 1443. It is clear, however, that he is mistaken in the year.
[94] *Ibid.*, pp. 5–6, 36–7; Pitscottie, *Historie*, I. 53.
[95] No precise reference to this assembly is given in surviving records; and the Auchinleck chronicler has introduced a further complication by amalgamating this general council with the one that took place in Stirling exactly a year earlier (*Chron. Auchinleck*, pp. 5, 36).

number of royal charters (nearly all witnessed by the Livingstons) that
were issued at Stirling between 25 October and 4 November 1444 [96]
in an attempt to consolidate opposition against the Crichtons. The
formation of a grand coalition which included Sir Robert Erskine,
temporarily styled Earl of Mar,[97] had apparently royal sanction. For
on 16 October 1444 James II was fourteen years old and it could be
held that he was no longer under tutelage : a charter of 13 November
1444 even stated that alienations of crown rights had been revoked
by the king 'on his majority at the last general council at Stirling'.[98] If
Douglas had acted rashly in his unsuccessful attack on the Crichtons
in the summer of 1444 he had certainly learned to act more deliberately by the autumn, when the general council 'blewe out on Schir
William of Crechtoun'.[99]

But the blast of a horn and a sentence of outlawry against the
Crichtons did not bring easy victory to the Black Douglases and
Livingstons, who had meanwhile lost the support of the influential
Bishop Kennedy. Kennedy, who had hitherto been associated with
Douglas, is reputed to have been made chancellor in place of Crichton, presumably in May or June 1444, but to have resigned within a
few weeks, after which the post certainly went to James Bruce, Bishop
of Dunkeld.[100] The growing importance of James Bruce may have
been resented by Kennedy; and it was significant that even Bishop
Cameron had been brought from retirement to serve as an auditor of
exchequer in June 1444;[101] it was becoming evident that the Douglases and Livingstons were not disposed to put all their ecclesiastical
eggs in the basket of the Bishop of St Andrews. It was even arranged
that the king should write to the pope (and persuade the King of
France to do likewise) for a revocation of Kennedy's commend of
Scone. In this case, however, Eugenius upheld Kennedy.[102] Even
before the bishop became an open foe of the Black Douglases and the
Livingstons, he reputedly joined with James Douglas, Earl of Angus,
in giving underhand aid to the Crichtons during the skirmishing

[96] *R.M.S.*, ii. Nos. 274–82.   [97] *Ibid.*, No. 279.
[98] Dunlop, *Bishop Kennedy*, p. 308, n. 1.
[99] Despite the statement of the Auchinleck chronicler (*Chron. Auchinleck*,
pp. 5, 36), it was undoubtedly this general council of 1444, not the general council
of 1443, that outlawed the Crichtons.
[100] *H.B.C.*, p. 175.   [101] *E.R.*, v. 143.
[102] Dunlop, *Bishop Kennedy*, p. 71. Later the commend of Scone was replaced by that of the priory of Pittenweem. John Major sensibly remarked:
'Two points in this man's conduct I cannot bring myself to praise—to wit, that
along with such a bishopric he should have held a benefice *in commendam*; . . .
nor do I approve the costliness of his tomb' (*History*, pp. 388–9).

that took place before the general council met at Stirling in the late autumn of 1444.[103] The Red Douglas had grievances of his own against the ruling faction.[104] So also had the queen mother, whose husband, the Black Knight of Lorne, was banished 'because he spake sumtymes raschlie that the realme was evill gydit, quhilk redounded to the defamation of the Earle of Douglas'.[105] Meanwhile the Crichtons still held Edinburgh Castle despite the sentence of outlawry passed against them in the general council. In all this there were the makings of an opposition party for Bishop Kennedy to lead. On 17 November 1444, just after the disbandment of the general council at Stirling, Kennedy and the queen mother, together with their adherents, addressed letters of inhibition to the magistrates of Aberdeen (and probably to those of other burghs) forbidding any payment of revenue 'to tha persownis that nu has the kyng in governance'. The magistrates cautiously resolved to take no action but wait and see 'qwat ordenance war made thairapon be the thre estattis'.[106]

The Black Douglases and Livingstons, who had, for their own ends, just publicised the king's 'majority' in the general council, speedily responded to the challenge offered to their authority : by 29 November 1444 they had conducted James to take part in besieging and capturing Methven Castle,[107] which was held by some member of the opposition. Then came a direct attack upon Kennedy himself. There was 'ane richt gret herschipe [ravaging] maid in Fyff be thir personis, the Erll of Crawfurd, James of Livingstoun . . ., kepar to the king and capitane of Strivling, the Ogilveis all, Robert Reach [Robertson of Struan], the lord of Kadyoch [Sir James Hamilton of Cadzow] and uthir syndry'.[108] The raiders harried 'nocht onlie the bischopis landis bot also the haill landis adjacent thairto, and brocht great pryssis of goodis out of Fyfe unto Angus'. Douglas is said to have urged his accomplices to seize Kennedy and imprison him in irons, but the bishop discreetly 'committit himself in saifgaird'— probably in St Andrews Castle—'thinkand it become him nocht to be ane fichter'.[109]

Having daunted Bishop Kennedy the ruling faction summoned

103 Godscroft, *Douglas and Angus*, p. 167.
104 Dunlop, *Bishop Kennedy*, p. 62.   105 Pitscottie, *Historie*, I. 57.
106 *Aberdeen Council Register*, I. 399.
107 A royal charter was dated at Methven on 29 November 1444 (*R.M.S.*, II. No. 283). For allusions to the siege and the king's presence at it see *E.R.*, v. 186, 187, 230.
108 *Chron. Auchinleck*, pp. 7–8, 38–9; *E.R.*, v. lxiii.
109 Pitscottie, *Historie*, I. 53–4.

a parliament to Perth, where it met on 14 June 1445. By 28 June, however, it was transacting business in Edinburgh, whither it had been prorogued [110] 'becaus of the sege that was liand about the castell on the kingis behalf'.[111] Sir William Crichton yielded up the castle on terms that testified to the strength of his own position : far from being disgraced he at once appeared in the king's council alongside Douglas and the Livingstons.[112] The accounts presented when the exchequer audit opened at Edinburgh on 5 July 1445 show that Crichton had his former allowance of 700 marks increased to £700, of which he received £233 6s. 8d. (350 marks) as payment for part of the year. In the following audit Crichton was paid £700 towards the total due to him for that and the previous year, amounting in all to £933 6s. 8d.[113]

It was during the session of parliament at Edinburgh that Douglas's adherents were rewarded for their patriotic services. On 28 June 1445 Sir James Hamilton of Cadzow was confirmed in all his lands, which were created a 'true, free and united lordship'—the lordship of Hamilton—while Sir James was elevated to the heritable title of lord of parliament.[114] This grant provides the first clear proof that the word 'lord', previously used loosely of any baron, was now being used as a specific and heritable title of rank, the third in the hierarchy headed by duke and earl. Among the witnesses to the grant were five other persons—Campbell, Graham, Somerville, Maxwell and Montgomery—who had previously been elevated to this new rank and were also described as lords of parliament. Moreover two new earldoms seem to have been created by charter at this parliament : Sir Alexander Seton of Gordon and Huntly, who was soon to use Gordon, rather than Seton, as his family name, was styled Earl of Huntly; at the same time Hugh Douglas appeared as Earl of Ormond, a title that took its name from a hill in the lands of Ardmannoch in the Black Isle. Another Douglas brother, Archibald, emerged at the same time as Earl of Moray in respect of his wife's lands as co-heiress of the last Dunbar earl.[115] Others saw the waning of their hopes. James, Earl of Angus, failed to compear to answer for 'cryme committit til his majeste and rebellione'; on 1 July 1445 all the lands and goods of the Red Douglas were declared escheated unless he should come within a year and a day to 'undirgang the law'.[116] Simi-

---

[110] A.P.S., II. 33, 59.   [111] Chron. Auchinleck, pp. 6–7, 37.
[112] Pitscottie, Historie, I. 57; Dunlop, Bishop Kennedy, p. 63.
[113] E.R., v. 180, 221.   [114] A.P.S., II. 59.
[115] Ibid.; E.R., v. lix, lxi.   [116] A.P.S., II. 59–60.

lar sentence was passed against the queen mother's husband, Sir James Stewart of Lorne.[117]

Another striking feature of the 1445 parliament was that it was presented with a sort of ultimatum on behalf of 'the prelates and clergy of all Scotland'.[118] John Winchester, Bishop of Moray, acted as their procurator and approached John Cranach, Bishop of Brechin, conservator of the privileges of the Scottish kirk, asking for an official notarial transumpt to be made of two papal bulls. An official deputation of thirty-six representatives of the three estates apparently raised no objection. The first bull, once issued by Gregory XI, gave papal approval to the charters of David II and Robert II that renounced the right to seize the movables of bishops on their death, and, by implication, granted them the right of testament.[119] In return, however, the prelates and clergy were expected to co-operate with the ruling faction. The second bull that was publicised was one of Martin V that detailed the process of deprivation against Bishop Finlay of Argyll by reason of his rebellion against James I.[120] There was no point in raking up this old affair unless there was talk of depriving some present bishop—and the obvious candidate was Bishop Kennedy, who does not seem to have attended the Edinburgh parliament and was probably licking his wounds in St Andrews Castle. There seems no ground for the view that Kennedy influenced the parliament of 1445, even by 'indirect means'.[121] If the publicity given to Martin V's bull was intended as a threat to Kennedy there were evidently powerful forces ready to back it up : the transumpt of the two bulls on 28 June 1445 was witnessed by Chancellor Bruce, Bishop of Dunkeld, three other bishops, nine abbots, eleven barons and six commissioners of the burghs—thirty in all, probably representing a majority of the deputation of thirty-six delegated by the three estates.[122] Nor is there any sign that the deputation had been 'packed' : it included no Douglas and only one Livingston, a commissioner for Edinburgh.

Since the herschip of Fife by his enemies Bishop Kennedy had 'held himself verie quyit, awaitand upoun ane better fortoune'.[123] His former political allies had deserted or disappeared. Crichton had made his peace. Angus soon followed after his barony of North Ber-

---

[117] Pinkerton, *History*, I. 477, appendix xiv.
[118] *Brechin Registrum*, I. 98.
[119] *Ibid.*, pp. 99–100. For the bishops' rights of testament see G. Donaldson, *op. cit., S.H.R.*, XLV. 27–35.   [120] *Brechin Registrum*, I. 100–2.
[121] Dunlop, *Bishop Kennedy*, pp. 64, 609.
[122] *Brechin Registrum*, I. 103.   [123] Pitscottie, *Historie*, I. 66.

wick had been plundered.[124] The queen mother, who had taken refuge in Dunbar Castle, then in the custody of Sir Adam Hepburn of
Hailes,[125] died there on 15 July 1445 while the castle was under
siege.[126] Her second husband, the Black Knight of Lorne, soon applied
for an English safe-conduct [127] and went into exile, while Sir Adam
Hepburn surrendered Dunbar Castle. Kennedy's attempt at a *coup
d'état* had completely collapsed; and he himself was left in isolation.
Menaced with the same fate as the late Bishop Finlay, Kennedy escaped it by reason of a dramatic coincidence that enhanced the reputation of his spiritual powers. Some months earlier, when his lands in
Fife were being harried by his foes, the bishop had summoned the
Earl of Crawford before the spiritual court and there 'led upoun him
ane sentance of curssing for his contemptioun of the censouris of hallie
kirk'.[128] But excommunication was losing its terrors through familiarity. Thus although Kennedy 'cursit solempnitlie with myter and
staf, buke and candill, contynually a yer' [129] the Earl of Crawford paid
no heed. What seemed to be the obvious sequel came in the shape of a
deadly conflict between the Lindsays and the Ogilvies, two great
families that had hitherto been closely allied, and which, only a year
previously, had jointly taken part in the raid upon Kennedy's episcopal lands.

The origin of the quarrel between the Lindsays and Ogilvies was
much the same as that involving the Homes and Hepburns and the
priory of Coldingham : Sir Alexander Lindsay, Master of Crawford,
had been appointed bailie or justiciar of the regality of Arbroath but
had been displaced by Sir Alexander Ogilvy of Inverquharity.[130] The
Hamiltons supported the Lindsays; and the Earl of Huntly, a chance
guest of the Ogilvies, felt constrained to fight for them until such time
as the processes of digestion had rid him of obligations towards his
hosts. On 23 January 1446 the armed bands of both sides marched to
Arbroath. The Earl of Crawford, whose wife was an Ogilvy, heard
of the impending affray and rode from Dundee to try to make peace.
One of the Ogilvies mistook either the earl's identity or his inten-

[124] Fraser, *Douglas*, II. 39; III. 427; Godscroft, *Douglas and Angus*, p. 210;
E.R., v. 194.
[125] On the seizure of the earldom of March in 1434–35 James I had entrusted the castle to Hepburn's keeping (*E.R.*, IV. 620). In 1444 he was described
as steward of the earldom (Dunlop, *Bishop Kennedy*, p. 75, n. 2).
[126] *Chron. Auchinleck*, pp. 7, 38. In an exchequer account presented at Edinburgh on 17 July 1445 she is described as 'the late queen' (*E.R.*, v. 196).
[127] *Rot. Scot.*, II. 327, 331, 347.　　　[128] Pitscottie, *Historie*, I. 54.
[129] *Chron. Auchinleck*, pp. 8, 39.　　　[130] Pitscottie, *Historie*, I. 54.

tions and speared him. The slaying of the earl made battle inevitable. The Ogilvies, who had the worse of it, suffered heavy losses and had to flee as best they could. For four days the corpse of the excommunicated Earl of Crawford lay unburied until Kennedy sent the prior of St Andrews to remove the curse.[131] The violent and dramatic death of the third Earl of Crawford seemed to demonstrate that God was on the side of Bishop Kennedy—not that this unduly daunted Sir Alexander Lindsay, the new fourth Earl of Crawford, whose long beard earned him the name of 'Earl Beardie' and whose other qualities brought him the alternative name of 'the Tiger Earl'.[132] Under his leadership the Lindsays 'held the Ogilvyis at gret subjectioun, and tuke thair gudis and distroyit thair placis'.[133] Gradually, however, royal power was reasserted and the passions of the various factions began temporarily to cool. Even the Hepburns and Homes who had quarrelled over the spoils of Coldingham sought in 1449 to settle their differences by a double marriage alliance.[134]

The last years of the decade not only saw more settled conditions in kirk and state but brief return to normal conditions in Anglo-Scottish relations—open hostility. The mutual toleration that had resulted from truces concluded in 1438 and 1444 ended, even though the latter truce was valid until 1454.[135] The reasons for a brief eruption of hostilities are obscure, though obviously connected with the internal politics of England. There the mutual harassment of Cardinal Beaufort and Humphrey, Duke of Gloucester, had terminated with the death of both in 1447. Although Henry VI had come of age he had already shown himself incapable of ruling effectively in person. By 1448 ascendancy in the English council had passed to William de la Pole, newly created Duke of Suffolk. This stimulated the growth of an opposition, as yet latent, headed by Richard, Duke of York.[136] While the two parties, with their ramifications throughout all England, jockeyed for power, military prestige was a valuable commodity, and the Percies, who held the wardenship of the English East March, and were later to prove Lancastrian, were at loggerheads with the Nevilles, who held the wardenship of the West March and were later to prove Yorkist.[137] Provocation from the Scots was

---

131 *Ibid.*, 54–5; *Chron. Auchinleck*, pp. 7–8, 38–9.
132 *Scots Peerage*, III. 21.   133 *Chron. Auchinleck*, pp. 7, 38.
134 Dunlop, *Bishop Kennedy*, p. 77.
135 *Rot. Scot.*, II. 306; *Cal. Docs. Scot.*, IV. No. 1167.
136 E. F. Jacob, *The Fifteenth Century*, pp. 481, 487, 489.
137 R. L. Storey, *op. cit.*, *E.H.R.*, LXXII. 593–609, at 607.

not lacking. In reprisal an English force under the Earl of Northumberland forded the Solway, encamped by the water of Sark, and began to raid Annandale. On the following day, 23 October 1448, the invaders were routed by a Scottish force under Hugh Douglas, Earl of Ormond.[138]

In preparation for the English retaliation that was to be expected, the Earl of Douglas summoned the lords, freeholders, and 'eldest Bordouraris' to meet in a warden court at the collegiate kirk of Lincluden on 18 December 1448. There they were put on oath to testify what statutes, ordinances and customs had been used on the Marches in the days of 'Blak Archibald of Douglas' (Archibald the Grim) so that all might be recorded.[139] Among the points that Earl William approved as 'rycht speidful and proffitabil to the Bordouraris' were some which sought to maintain the cohesion and discipline of the Scottish forces, and others which arranged that ten beacon fires were to be set up on the hills of Annandale and another nine on those of Nithsdale; whenever the beacons were set ablaze all men were to assemble in a host for the defence of the countryside. These precautionary measures were soon put to the test: in the early summer of 1449 the English burned Dunbar and Dumfries and the Scots burned Alnwick and Warkworth,[140] after which a truce was concluded on 15 November.[141]

Meanwhile the Anglo-French truce had given way to renewed warfare in France. By the end of October 1449 Rouen had fallen to the French.[142] As Charles VII entered the city he was attended by the *garde écossaise*, an élite corps of Scots guardsmen which had been formed in 1445 as the senior company of the household troops of the French monarchy.[143] The days were past when huge contingents of Scotsmen fought alongside the French armies, but the Scottish guard continued to provide some openings for Scots of gentle blood who were attracted to the well-paid service of the French king. There were also individual adventurers: in the campaign of Normandy William Monypenny won his knighthood;[144] for many years thereafter he was to be employed on Franco-Scottish diplomatic missions. Apart from the many personal connections that drew France and

---

[138] *Chron. Auchinleck*, pp. 18, 40; Pitscottie, *Historie*, I. 73–6.
[139] 'The Statutis and Use of Merchis in Tym of Were' (*A.P.S.*, I. 714–6).
[140] *Chron. Auchinleck*, pp. 27, 39. Dr A. I. Dunlop points out (*Bishop Kennedy*, p. 104, n. 3) that 'the editor has assigned these events to the year 1448, but the original gives the year as 1449'. [141] *Rot. Scot.*, II. 334–6.
[142] E. F. Jacob, *The Fifteenth Century*, pp. 489, 491.
[143] W. Forbes Leith, *The Scots Men-at-Arms and Life-guards in France*, I. 58–9. [144] Francisque-Michel, *Les Ecossais en France*, I. 203.

Scotland together there remained strategic reasons for the continuance of the Auld Alliance: Charles VII desired (and achieved) the recovery of Normandy and Gascony; James II was to show himself eager to recover Berwick and Roxburgh. English troops deployed in Normandy (at a cost of £20,000 annually in time of war) [145] could not be deployed on the Borders; nor could the troops on the Borders (whose maintenance in the garrison of Berwick alone cost £5,200 in time of war) [146] be deployed in Normandy. To synchronise efforts in warfare and diplomacy against the distracted and financially embarrassed English the Franco-Scottish alliance was renewed at Tours on 31 December 1448. [147]

This was preceded and followed by intensive matrimonial diplomacy: James I had left six daughters, as well as his son and heir, all of whose marriages could be used to confirm the good will of various potentates towards Scotland and France. The process had started with the marriage of James II's sister Margaret to the dauphin in 1436. In 1442 Isabella (or Elizabeth) had married Francis, Duke of Brittany. In 1444 Mary had married Wolfaert van Borselen, son of the Lord of Campvere (or Veere) in Zealand. At the end of the same year Annabella was betrothed to Count Louis of Geneva. In 1445 the remaining two sisters, Eleanor and Joan, had been sent to France, only to find that the death of the dauphiness had coincided with their arrival. Escaping the prospect of a particularly dubious match with the dauphin, Eleanor married Sigismund, Duke of Austria, in 1449. Joan, 'the dumb lady', and Annabella, whose betrothal to the count of Geneva was eventually broken off, were to come home in 1458 to find husbands in Scotland. [148] Meanwhile, however, the marriages, or prospective marriages, of James II's sisters gave Scottish diplomacy a wider scope than it had ever before enjoyed: those who were, for the time being, friends of France, had at least a nodding acquaintance with France's poor but warlike ally.

Thus the question of the marriage of James II himself was one that aroused wide interest on the continent. The Scots, with a view to their commercial interests in the Low Countries, desired a match with a suitable princess of the house of Burgundy, Guelders or Cleves. On 6 September 1448 Philip the Good, Duke of Burgundy, was empowered by Duke Arnold of Guelders to treat of a marriage be-

[145] E. F. Jacob, *The Fifteenth Century*, p. 488.
[146] *Cal. Docs. Scot.*, IV. No. 1195.   [147] Dunlop, *Bishop Kennedy*, p. 94.
[148] *Ibid.*, pp. 61, 66, 84, 88–9; *E.R.*, v. lxii, lxix, lxx.

tween the latter's daughter (Philip's niece) and the Scottish king.[149] With the concurrence of Charles VII Scottish ambassadors made treaties with Burgundy and Guelders on 1 April 1449 :[150] Philip of Burgundy was to be responsible for his niece's dowry of sixty thousand crowns, to be paid in two years. The clause in the treaty that provided for perpetual friendship and alliance between Scotland and Burgundy[151] was one that allowed Scottish merchants a favourable status in all the Burgundian dominions. Duke Philip had also undertaken to send his niece to Scotland at his own expense. The expected demonstration of magnificence was forthcoming : Mary of Guelders was escorted to Scotland by Netherlandish potentates in a well-armed fleet of fourteen vessels.[152] On 3 July 1449 the marriage ceremony took place in Holyrood Abbey, and the new queen was crowned shortly afterwards.[153]

The marriage of the nineteen-year-old king signalised his entry into politics. James II had been better trained to play his part than most recent Scottish kings. Unlike Robert I, Robert II or Robert III, he had grown up not in expectation of the crown but in possession of it. Unlike David II and James I he had spent the whole of his youth in Scotland and was thoroughly familiar with the prevailing conditions. A surviving portrait, commissioned by an Austrian visitor to James's court, shows, in what is probably the earliest reasonably authentic likeness of a Scottish king, a slim young man fashionably dressed in pointed shoes, long hose, large hat, and tunic with padded shoulders.[154] Although the king's expression seems innocently self-assured the artist suggests darker aspects : James's hands are on the hilt of the dagger at his waist; and in the colouring of his face there is a hint of the sinister fiery birthmark described by François Villon in his poem listing the worthies who had departed this life like the snows of yesteryear. It can hardly be taken for granted that 'subtle callousness and sustained duplicity . . . were foreign to the nature' of James II.[155]

The first to feel the weight of revived royal power were the Liv-

---

[149] J. H. Baxter, 'The Marriage of James II', S.H.R., xxv. 69–72, at 71.
[150] Dunlop, Bishop Kennedy, p. 100.
[151] P. F. Tytler, History, I. pt. ii, 144.
[152] Pitscottie, Historie, I. 58–9; Chron. Auchinleck, pp. 24–5, 41.
[153] Chron. Auchinleck, pp. 25, 41; Extracta, p. 238 and n.; Chron Bower, II. 515; E.R., v. lxxvii–lxxviii.
[154] The likeness is reproduced in Dunlop, Bishop Kennedy, facing p. 112.
[155] Ibid., p. 106, n. 3.

ingstons. What made their faction all too vulnerable was its lack of a strong territorial base on which traditional loyalties might have been grounded : its strength was derived not from land but from crown offices. Sir Alexander Livingston of Callendar, head of the tribe, was justiciar. His eldest son and heir, James, was keeper of Stirling Castle, and, as late as May 1448, was 'keeper of the royal person'; in the summer of 1448 he also became chamberlain. A younger brother, Alexander, was captain of Methven Castle, while Robert of Callendar had custody of Dumbarton and Dunoon, and John Livingston was captain of Doune. The post of comptroller, held by Henry Livingston between 1442 and 1444, had by 1448 gone to Robert Livingston 'of Linlithgow', a cousin of Sir Alexander. Robert, who was 'probably the most considerable merchant in Linlithgow', had been a custumar of the burgh and master of works at Linlithgow Palace since the previous reign.[156] As comptroller he was intimately concerned with the very considerable finances of the royal household.[157] While it is not impossible that he engaged in peculation this can hardly be proved from surviving records; nor is it known to have been brought as a charge against him. Nonetheless the comptroller had evidently become wealthy enough to loan the king £930, which James was committed to repay on 1 April 1450 out of the instalment of the queen's dowry that was expected from the Duke of Burgundy. It must have been a tantalising consideration that forfeiture of the comptroller would save repayment of a large debt.[158]

For although there is insufficient material for an estimate of the financial position of the crown at this time, the indications are that more than the usual stringency prevailed. The customs accounts of fourteen burghs for the period July 1445–July 1446 showed gross receipts of about £4,360 but, after payments made by the custumars, there was a net deficit of about £700;[159] for the period September 1448–July 1449 there was a similar deficit of about £800.[160] And there remained the embarrassing problem of assigning the queen's dower lands for the maintenance of her own establishment : by the terms of the marriage contract James had bound himself to bestow on Mary of Guelders the enormous annual income of ten thousand French écus (evidently equivalent to £5,000 Scots [161]). It was probably financial desperation that led the king to attack the Livingstons,

[156] E.R., v. lxxx, n. 4. [157] See ibid., 312–3, 346.
[158] Dunlop, Bishop Kennedy, p. 109. [159] E.R., v. 215–35.
[160] Ibid., 336–48.
[161] Dunlop, Bishop Kennedy, p. 108, n. 4; A.P.S., ii. 60–1, 66–7.

knowing full well that in some quarters their downfall would not be unwelcome.

Possibly, however, a real political issue was involved—one that connected the house of Callendar with that of the Isles. Alexander, Earl of Ross and Lord of the Isles, had died early in May 1449, leaving as his successor his son John, who was scarcely fifteen years of age.[162] The Livingstons aimed high when they arranged that the young earl should be contracted to marry Elizabeth, daughter of James Livingston, the chamberlain. If the king hoped to forestall a Livingston-MacDonald match he was too late : just before the Livingstons were arrested on 23 September 1449 the chamberlain's daughter escaped from Dumbarton to Kintyre and afterwards married the Earl of Ross.[163]

Meanwhile those who had been arrested were brought for trial before a parliament that opened in the tolbooth of Edinburgh on 19 January 1450.[164] It appears that they were accused of 'crimes commitit agaynis the king or again [against] his derrest moder'.[165] The fact that James was harking back to the early days of the minority suggests that no more recent crime could reasonably be imputed to the disgraced faction. Lest impartial justice should prevail in parliament, a statute was passed which ordained that no man should rebel against the king's person or his authority; it was in this statute that mention was made of crimes committed against the king and the late queen, crimes for which those responsible were being brought to justice. The same statute gave due warning that '. . . gif it happynis ony man til assist, in rede[advice], confort, consal, or mayntenance, to thai that ar justifiit be the king in this present parliament, or sal happyn to be justifiit in tym cummyn . . . he sal be punyst in sic lik maner as the principale trespassouris'.[166] In other words, if anyone spoke in defence of the Livingstons he was to be reckoned a traitor. The opportunity was taken to pass another ordinance that extended the traditional definition of treason given in *Regiam Majestatem*.[167] On 21 January, the third day of parliament, Robert Livingston (the comptroller) and Alexander Livingston, a younger son of the Knight of Callendar, were suspended from the gallows and beheaded on the castle hill. Only two executions took place, although all the accused suffered the forfeiture of their lands and goods, and some of them, including Sir

---

[162] *E.R.*, v. xci, n. 1; xcii; *Highland Papers*, 1. 47.
[163] *Chron. Auchinleck*, pp. 24–6, 41–3.
[164] *A.P.S.*, II. 33.   [165] *Ibid.*, 35, c. 3.   [166] *Ibid.*
[167] *Ibid.*, 36, c. 12; *Scot. Legal Hist.*, p. 283.

Alexander Livingston and James, his eldest son, as well as James Dundas and Robert Bruce of Clackmannan, underwent temporary imprisonment.[168]

It was at least ironic that a charter assigning the queen's dower was issued on 22 January 1450, on the day after the execution of the two Livingstons, and recorded the consent of the three estates in order to make it 'firmer and more secure'.[169] This charter, in a valiant attempt to secure for Mary of Guelders an annual income of ten thousand French *écus*, bestowed on her the earldoms of Atholl and Strathearn and numerous lordships and miscellaneous revenues. A further transaction took place in parliament on 24 January when the bishops knelt before the king and took up a matter that had been left unfinished in the Edinburgh parliament of June 1445 : James was persuaded to renounce the 'abusive custom' whereby the crown claimed the movables of deceased bishops and he granted the bishops the power to bequeath them by testament ; it was also conceded that during an episcopal vacancy the crown would not meddle with the 'spiritual' revenues of the see, such as offerings and teinds ; on the other hand, during a vacancy, the crown would still assume possession of the temporality of the bishopric and would have rights of presentation to those benefices of which the bishop held the patronage.[170]

In other respects the parliament of January 1450 was an important one. Advice was sought on eight miscellaneous statutes passed in the previous reign.[171] Furthermore, a committee of four kirkmen, four barons, and four representatives of the burghs, was chosen to examine all acts of parliament and general council that had been issued in the king's reign and in that of his father ; the committee, whose findings have not survived, was to report to the next parliament or general council which of these acts 'ar gude and accordande for the tym'.[172] Apart from these indications that James II was preparing to follow in his father's footsteps, the legislation of the Edinburgh parliament is reminiscent of that of the former reign, showing a fourfold concern for justice, social order, economic stability, and royal authority. In all this there was something ominous for the remaining factions.

---

[168] *E.R.*, v. lxxx and n. 3; *Chron. Auchinleck*, pp. 26, 43.
[169] *A.P.S.*, II. 61; *R.M.S.*, II. No. 306.
[170] *A.P.S.*, II. 37–8; *R.M.S.*, II. No. 307; G. Donaldson, *op. cit.*, *S.H.R.*, XLV. 27–35.
[171] *A.P.S.*, II. 33–4; see also *ibid.*, Chronological Table, p. 7.
[172] *Ibid.*, 36, c. 10.

The Crichtons, if they had ever strayed from the narrow path of loyalty to the crown, had evidently read the omens successfully and were to continue to do so: Sir William Crichton was styled Lord Crichton in 1447 and by April 1448 was once more chancellor. While it is understandable that he and his kinsfolk encouraged the king to attack their old Livingston rivals it is something of an enigma that the latter were not protected by the Black Douglases. The explanation may be that an estrangement had followed upon the appointment of James Livingston to the post of chamberlain in the summer of 1448 [173] in place of Sir John Forrester of Corstorphine, whose patron was Earl William. This appointment was, moreover, only part of a new phenomenon that must have been disturbing to a faction like the Black Douglases whose view of politics was bound to be that of territorial magnates who equated land with power. For the Livingston faction was one of lairds rather than lords, indeed perhaps one of burgesses rather than lairds—even the heir of the Knight of Callendar was son-in-law of an Edinburgh burgess. It was men such as the Livingstons who would eventually break the power of the landed aristocracy in England. Well might the Black Douglases have smiled when James II wrecked a new kind of power complex instead of merely turning it to his own advantage. Politics were once more the preserve of the lay and ecclesiastical magnates, with the Crichtons—a combination of lesser lords and office-holders—being left as the faction that was least traditional in its composition. Nonetheless, if the young king had made a tactical blunder he had forcefully shown that in practice, if not in theory, his minority was effectively at an end and that, unlike his royal counterpart in England, he could wield personal authority.

[173] *H.B.C.*, p. 179.

13

THE FALL OF THE BLACK DOUGLASES
AND ITS CONSEQUENCES

After the attack on the Livingstons harmony temporarily prevailed. It was demonstrated in the loans made to the king
between September 1449 and August 1450: the Earl of
Douglas contributed £100, merchants of Edinburgh £131, Chancellor Crichton £500, and Bishop Kennedy £200.[1] Although the
bishop seems to have played no part in the overthrow of the Livingstons and did not 're-emerge from obscurity' until the parliament
of January 1450,[2] he and his kinsmen were nonetheless among those
who took the place of the Livingstons at court.

The apparent formation of a new triumvirate, acting under the
king and composed of Chancellor Crichton, Bishop Kennedy, and the
Earl of Douglas, was interrupted by the decision of the last two to set
out on pilgrimage for Rome. For Nicholas V had proclaimed 1450
a jubilee year and Rome was the centre of a celebration that marked
the end of schism and the inauguration of what was wrongly expected to be a resplendent new era in the history of the church.
Kennedy had reached the city by 12 January 1451, after which he
obtained some favours from the pope. But Bishop Turnbull of Glasgow, who stayed at home, fared almost as well as his pilgrim colleague,[3] perhaps because Nicholas V recognised the rising political
importance of this former keeper of the privy seal, who in Kennedy's
absence assumed his place in the royal counsels in close co-operation
with Chancellor Crichton and Admiral Crichton.[4] On the way back
from Rome Kennedy took part in the procession of the Holy Blood
at Bruges on 3 May 1451, after which 'a curtain falls upon his move-

---

[1] *E.R.*, v. 393.   [2] Dunlop, *Bishop Kennedy*, p. 106, n. 3.
[3] *Ibid.*, pp. 117-20   [4] Law's MS., cited in *E.R.*, v. lxxxv, n. 2.

ments for almost a twelve-month'.[5] His fellow-pilgrim, Earl William, had also set out from Scotland in October 1450. He had filled all Rome 'with the expectation of his coming',[6] and by reason of his display of magnificence 'was commended by the supreme pontiff above all pilgrims'.[7] Earl William had arrived in Rome at much the same time as Bishop Kennedy, and, apparently, by the same route. If their paths had hitherto crossed, or even coincided, they separated on the return journey when Kennedy made for Flanders and the earl for England. There his coming aroused almost as much interest as it had done in Rome: in February 1451 Garter king-of-arms was sent to the coast to await the earl's arrival and to conduct him to court.[8]

It was a time when the general instability in international relationships[9] was surpassed by the instability within England itself. In May 1450 the Duke of Suffolk was murdered at sea while on his way to exile abroad. In June rebellious peasants led by Jack Cade occupied London and murdered the treasurer. A few days later the Bishop of Salisbury was assassinated. In August, Richard, Duke of York, for whom the rebels professed a high regard, returned from Ireland, while his rival, Edmund Beaufort, Duke of Somerset, was brought back from France to counter the influence of York.[10] Meanwhile the two factions were almost equally balanced and each may have coveted the support of Douglas, while the earl may have sought English help to redress his grievances in Scotland, where his position had been jeopardised.

Before leaving Scotland Douglas had appointed one of his brothers—either the Earl of Ormond or, more probably, Lord Balvenie—as bailie of his estates.[11] The most trustworthy account of what ensued narrates that during Douglas's absence Bishop Turnbull, Chancellor Crichton and Admiral Crichton conspired against the earl, aiming at his death:

> For by their counsel King James II besieged all the castles of the earl and slew many free tenants of the said earl, received the rest to his peace upon oath.[12]

[5] Dunlop, *Bishop Kennedy*, p. 135.
[6] Godscroft, *Douglas and Angus*, p. 181.
[7] Law's MS., cited in *E.R.*, v. lxxxv, n. 2.
[8] *Cal. Docs. Scot.*, IV. No. 1231.
[9] See Dunlop, *Bishop Kennedy*, p. 126.
[10] E. F. Jacob, *The Fifteenth Century*, pp. 492, 496–7, 499, 502–3.
[11] Pitscottie, *Historie*, I. 80; Lesley, *History*, p. 22. For an example of letters of bailiary see *R.M.S.*, II. No. 369.
[12] Law's MS., cited in *E.R.*, v. lxxxv, n. 2.

This succinct but dramatic passage is 'the only account of these proceedings on which it is possible to place any reliance'.[13] It is unfortunate that the records give little information concerning what must be assumed to have been a major royal expedition against the lands of the absent earl.

One clue to the king's motives is to be found in his financial troubles. The audit of the comptroller's account on 27 August 1450 had revealed a deficit of £1,315 15s. 10½d.[14] By 1 May 1450 James had received 20,000 écus of his wife's dowry;[15] but of the remaining 40,000 the Duke of Burgundy still owed 35,000 as late as 3 January 1452 when partial payment was ordered;[16] it is therefore possible that the duke was delaying payment on the excuse that the question of the queen's dower lands had not been satisfactorily settled; and the high-sounding lordships in the central Highlands with which the queen had been fobbed off in January 1450 [17] must speedily have revealed their incapacity to contribute an annual income of £5,000. The king may have found some pretext to augment the resources of his spouse as a result of the death of his aunt,[18] Margaret Stewart, widow of the fourth Earl of Douglas and titular Duchess of Touraine, who as recently as 26 January 1450 had resigned her rights in Galloway to Earl William.[19] On 25 May 1451, despite this resignation, the king made a heritable grant of the sheriffship of Wigtown to 'his familiar esquire, Andrew Agnew'.[20] In another charter of 20 June 1451 James made a grant to the Prior and monastery of Whithorn, reserving to himself 'and his successors, the Lords of Galloway', the service of the prayers of the monks.[21] It is thus clear that by the early summer of 1451 James regarded himself as being in possession of the earldom of Wigtown and the lordship of western Galloway. It was doubtless his attempt to make good his incredible pretensions that had led to resistance on the part of Earl William's representatives during the latter's pilgrimage to Rome.

By April 1451 Douglas had arrived back in Scotland, whereupon 'the king forthwith gathered an army against the earl . . . and approached Craig Douglas [a small Douglas stronghold on the Yarrow] in warlike fashion, and having taken the castle, razed it to

[13] *Ibid.*, lxxxv. See also Fraser, *Douglas,* i. 467. [14] *E.R.*, v. 397.
[15] *R.M.S.*, ii. No. 345. [16] Dunlop, *Bishop Kennedy,* p. 135, n. 3.
[17] P. 351 above.
[18] Dunlop, *Bishop Kennedy,* p. 124. The exact date of her death is unknown but seems to have taken place during Douglas's absence from Scotland (*ibid.*, p. 131).
[19] *A.P.S.*, ii. 64. [20] *R.M.S.*, ii. No. 447. [21] *Ibid.*, No. 453.

its foundations'.[22] Something of a confrontation, resulting in a compromise between antagonistic interests, seems to have occurred after parliament opened in the tolbooth of Edinburgh on 28 June 1451. Firstly the king recounted his former promise to bestow upon the queen lands worth £5,000 yearly, and a new charter was issued on 1 July 1451 with the consent of the three estates.[23] This apparently did not rescind the grants made to the queen on 22 January 1450 but specifically confirmed some of them and added new grants of lands and revenue. Next the three estates gave their consent to other charters that concerned Earl William.[24] The earl had made a token submission by resigning his lands into the king's hands, whereupon the king restored them, 'notwithstanding any crimes committed by the said William, Earl of Douglas . . . or by occasion of forfeiture or of treason, treachery, or otherwise'.[25] Between 6 and 8 July no less than eighteen charters were issued,[26] restoring and confirming to Earl William his awesome collection of lands and offices and adding a few useful extra privileges. Neither in the charter issued in favour of the queen nor in the charters issued in favour of the earl, was there any mention of the earldom of Wigtown, which apparently remained in the hands of the king. Douglas's more or less complete restoration in the Edinburgh parliament is accurately represented by the Auchinleck chronicler:

> . . . the king resavit him till his grace at the request of the quene and the thre estatis, and grantit him all his lordschippis agane, outtane [except] the erldom of Wigtoun . . . and gaf him and all his a fre remissioun of all thingis bygane. And all gud Scottis men war rycht blyth of that accordance.[27]

But by the time another parliament assembled at Stirling in October 1451 Earl William had evidently rallied sufficient strength to force James to disgorge the ill-gotten earldom, as well as the lordship of Stewarton and Dunlop in Ayrshire, which had presumably been seized at the same time as Wigtown. The witnesses to the resulting charters of 26 October 1451 [28] seem to have been almost entirely made up of the king's supporters, who doubtless felt their humiliation keenly when Earl William now pointedly styled himself not only

---

[22] Law's MS., cited in *E.R.*, v. lxxxv, n. 2.
[23] *A.P.S.*, II. 66–7; *R.M.S.*, II. No. 462.
[24] *A.P.S.*, II. 67–71.   [25] *Ibid.*, 68.
[26] *R.M.S.*, II. Nos. 463–82, *passim*. Some of these are also printed in *A.P.S.*, II. 67–71.
[27] *Chron. Auchinleck*, pp. 9, 45.   [28] *A.P.S.*, II. 71–3.

Earl of Douglas and Avondale and Lord of Galloway but Earl of Wigtown,[29] a title which he had not previously used.

Thus the king's actions against Earl William in the winter of 1450–1 had brought no lasting material gain : James had led an offensive against the Black Douglas and had failed to prevail, with the result that Douglas was tempted to high-handed actions that would weaken his opponents' will to resist by proving the king's inability to protect his own adherents. The Auchinleck chronicler reports that on 21 August 1451 Sir John Sandilands of Calder, a kinsman of the king, was slain by Sir Patrick Thornton, a henchman of Douglas.[30]

A more gruesome (though less reliable) picture is painted by Boece and Pitscottie. One of their tales concerns John Herries of Terregles, 'a faithful subject to the kingis majestie at all tymes', whose lands had been harried by 'sum theiffis of Douglasdaill'. Failing to secure redress from Earl William, Herries tried to exact revenge. When his 'attempt succeidit unhappilie' he was captured in Annandale, brought before Earl William, and 'hangit schamefullie as [if] he had bene ane theif, nochtwithstanding the king commandit in the contrair'.[31] Another tale recounted by Pitscottie (though not by his predecessor Boece) concerns a certain tutor (guardian) of the laird of Bombie. This gentleman, named MacLellan, 'wald on na wayis . . . ryd with the erle of Douglas' and was imprisoned in Douglas Castle. His uncle, Patrick Gray, Lord Gray's son and heir, obtained letters under the signet asking Douglas to deliver MacLellan, and arrived at the castle, where he was courteously entertained at dinner, only to be told afterwards :

> Schir Patrick ze ar come a litill to leit; bot zondar is zour sistir sone lyand; bot he wantis [lacks] the heid; tak his bodie and do with it quhat ze will.[32]

It is likely that these stories had some factual basis, though they underwent picturesque embellishment and were invariably twisted in such a way as to cast discredit upon the Black Douglases.

---

[29] He styled himself in this way as witness to a royal charter of 13 January 1452 that confirmed some of the lands of Paisley Abbey (R.M.S., II. No. 523; cf. p. 160). Mistakes have sometimes occurred (as in *ibid.*, p. 160 and *Wigtown Charters*, No. 136) by a misreading of Avondale as Annandale.
[30] *Chron. Auchinleck*, p. 45; Pitscottie, *Historie*, I. 126; *Scots Peerage*, VIII. 383. [31] Pitscottie, *Historie*, I. 88; Boece, *History*, pp. 372–3.
[32] Pitscottie, *Historie*, I. 89–92.

It was the MacLellan incident, so Pitscottie thought, that induced the king and his privy council 'to dauntoun this wickit man' [33]—Earl William. But the clue to subsequent events is more likely to be found in another incident reported by Pitscottie—an unsuccessful attempt to waylay Chancellor Crichton. In retaliation the chancellor 'gadderit ane great companie of his freindis and assistaris, and come fordwart to Edinburgh, to be revengit upoun the Earle of Douglas . . . quho was remaning thair witht ane small number'. Thereupon Douglas was forced to flee 'to saif himself'. Well might Pitscottie remark that the 'mutuall injurieis and despytfull consaittis movit on everie syde exasperit baitht the parties . . . that the ane of thame appeirit suddenlie to bring the uther to destructioun and ruin'.[34]

The Edinburgh incident must have occurred shortly after 13 January 1452 when Earl William witnessed royal charters at Edinburgh.[35] This episode would explain why the earl, when next summoned to the royal presence at Stirling a month or so later, demanded, and obtained, a safe-conduct as a guarantee of his security.

On 21 February 1452, under the king's 'speciale assouerans and respit', Earl William arrived in Stirling Castle, then in the custody of Chancellor Crichton.[36] On the following day after supper the king broached the subject of what had come to be the outstanding issue that lay behind the current animosities—a bond that united the Black Douglases with the Earls of Crawford and Ross.[37] To these great nobles royal authority must have seemed irrelevant at the local level: it was not the business of the king to meddle in the localities which were their spheres of influence; still less was it tolerable that James should make attacks (as his father had done) upon the landed inheritance of his nobles; and to prevent such royal encroachments it might be necessary not only to band together for mutual defence but to take the offensive by encroaching upon the royal power and reducing the king to the position of ceremonial figurehead. To Douglas and his allies it must have seemed that their bond was the only security against a king who might otherwise victimise them one by one. It was James, however, who felt himself about to be victimised. Thus, (so Pitscottie reports) he told Earl William:

[33] *Ibid.*, 92.   [34] *Ibid.*, 85–7.   [35] *R.M.S.*, II. Nos. 522, 523.
[36] *Chron. Auchinleck,* pp. 9–10, 46–7; *E.R.*, v. 458, 478, 596.
[37] Pitscottie, *Historie,* I. 89; *Chron. Auchinleck,* pp. 9–10, 46–7; Boece, *History,* p. 373.

It is gevin me to understand that . . . thair is sum confideratioun maid betuix zow and ane part of the nobillis of this realme. I pray zow thairfoir to braike sic bandis . . . that is nocht wount to be within ane realme under ane prince.[38]

The Auchinleck chronicler reports the interchange more laconically and brusquely : when James charged Douglas to break his bond the earl answered that 'he mycht nocht, nor wald nocht'. Thereupon James rejoined :

'False traitor, sen yow will nocht, I sall!' and stert sodanly till him with ane knyf and strak him in the coller and doun in the bodie, and Patrick Gray strak him next efter the king with ane poleax·on the heid and strak out his brains.[39]

By the time that the courtiers had finished the gory work the corpse of the murdered earl bore twenty-six wounds.

In personally murdering Earl William on 22 February 1452 James II had perpetrated a crime comparable to Robert Bruce's killing of Red Comyn. If the one murder was an act of sacrilege, the other, committed in contravention of solemn obligations and the laws of hospitality, was probably more odious in the eyes of contemporaries. At first the Black Douglases were stunned ; but within a month they rose in rebellion. Thanks to a number of tailzies James, Master of Douglas, had succeeded to the title and estates of the childless eighth earl. James had previously been marked out for a clerical career : in 1441 he had hoped to become Bishop of Aberdeen under the auspices of Felix V ;[40] in 1443 he had matriculated as an arts student in Cologne University ;[41] in 1447, however, an indenture had been concluded by which he was recognised as having been born before his twin brother, Archibald Douglas, Earl of Moray ;[42] he was therefore heir presumptive to the eighth earl of Douglas and had soon demonstrated appropriate martial prowess by fighting a Burgundian champion in the lists at Stirling.[43] Now, in the great crisis that had

---

[38] Pitscottie, Historie, I. 93–4. Here the date is given as 20 February. The Auchinleck chronicler, whose authority is generally accepted, gives the date as 22 February (Chron. Auchinleck, pp. 10, 47).

[39] Chron. Auchinleck, pp. 9–10, 46–7.
[40] P. 335 above.   [41] Burns, Basle, p. 71.
[42] Text in a royal confirmation of 9 January 1450 (R.M.S., II. No. 301); see also Fraser, Douglas, I. 447.
[43] Brown, Early Travellers, pp. 32–8; Chron. Bower, II. 515; Chron. Auchinleck, p. 40.

befallen the Black Douglases, the new earl responded forcefully. With his brother Hugh, Earl of Ormond, and Lord Hamilton, he led some six hundred men to Stirling on 17 or 27 March 1452.[44] There, to the blast of twenty-four horns, the king and his council were denounced as forsworn and perjured. The safe-conduct issued to Earl William was put on show at the mercat cross, then, nailed to a board, it was dragged through the streets at the tail of a horse. Pitscottie reports that the Douglases and their adherents 'gaif the king uncomlie wordis, sayand they sould never obey him, nor acknowledge him againe as ane king . . . bot sould be revengit upoun his cruell tyrannie'.[45]

What seems to have taken place was a ceremony of *diffidatio*, whereby a vassal might renounce his fealty to his lord. This betrayed the conservative outlook of the king's opponents : remaining loyal to the traditions of strict feudalism they acted as injured vassals, and, at the outset of a deadly conflict that involved their lives and lands, failed to see that the struggle was one that could not be solved within a feudal context but only within a national one. Their best chance of success would have been to have declared James deposed as a perjured tyrant and to have set up an alternative government to legitimise their actions. Failing to take so decisive a step they demonstrated their antiquated attitude by sacking the burgh of Stirling and setting it on fire.[46] Such an act of aristocratic arrogance was politically inept and merely made it plain that the rebels had nothing to offer save a policy of thoughtless revenge.

The king was not slow in taking advantage of the situation : 'the great bombard'—possibly Mons Meg[47]—was used to reduce the castle of Hatton in Midlothian, which belonged to one of the rebels ;[48] and from March to June numerous charters were issued at Edinburgh to woo the lairds and lesser lords.[49] Conspicuously uncommitted to the royal cause were members of the higher nobility, with the exception of Alexander Gordon, Earl of Huntly, William Sinclair, Earl of Orkney, and George Douglas, Earl of Angus. Two bishops— those of Glasgow and St Andrews—also rallied to the king. By 14 April 1452 Bishop Turnbull had lent James eight hundred marks from the proceeds of the jubilee indulgence recently granted by the

---

[44] *Chron. Auchinleck*, pp. 10, 47. The chronicler gives the date both as 27 March and St. Patrick's day in Lent (17 March). He probably meant the latter.

[45] Pitscottie, *Historie*, I. 95.

[46] *Chron. Auchinleck*, pp. 10, 47; Pitscottie, *Historie*, I. 95.

[47] See W. H. Finlayson, 'Mons Meg', *S.H.R.*, xxvII. 124–6, and *T.A.*, I. ccxvii.   [48] *E.R.*, v. 604–8; *R.M.S.*, II. Nos. 536, 544.

[49] *R.M.S.*, II. Nos. 537–86, *passim*.

pope to Glasgow Cathedral.[50] In return for this timely loan the bishop was for ten years to levy the crown rents of Bute, Arran and Cowal, and the customs of Ayr, Irvine and Dumbarton.[51] Shortly afterwards James received a loan of £50 from Bishop Kennedy,[52] whose mysterious year-long absence from public notice ended on 18 April 1452 when he witnessed a royal charter.[53] There were no doubts about Kennedy's loyalty, for it was to his castle of St Andrews that the pregnant queen was sent for safety. There, towards the end of May 1452, she bore a son who would later reign as James III.[54] His birth gave promise of the unbroken continuity of the royal succession and encouragement to those who, for the sake of stability, were prepared to overlook the father's crime after the initial shock had inevitably lessened.

The royalists were further encouraged by the discomfiture of Douglas's ally, the Earl of Crawford. Between him and the Earl of Huntly, the only powerful royalist north of Tay, there were animosities that dated back to the engagement at Arbroath in 1446.[55] The two once more came into conflict : Crawford had 'assembillit the haill folkis of Angus witht ane great companie of his kin and freindis' and encamped beside Brechin to intercept Huntly, who was 'command fordward witht ane great airmie for the kingis suport'. At Brechin on 18 May 1452 Huntly won the day, though not without heavy losses. And 'albeit the Earle of Crawfurde was overcome . . . he remanit in the contrie of Angus as he did of befoir, and persewit all them that was nocht of his factioun witht great cruelltie, waistand all thair landis by fyre and suord'.[56] Huntly gave up his plan of pressing south to join forces with the king, perhaps because his own country was left defenceless against Douglas's brother, Archibald, Earl of Moray, who 'enterit in the landis of Strabogie and . . . hierieit the contrie witht all utheris landis pertening to the Earle of Huntlie'. In retaliation the latter 'invaidit the landis of Murray witht greater cruelltie . . . nor was done in his boundis'.[57] Thus the royalist Earl of Huntly and the rebellious Earls of Crawford and Moray were kept busy north of Tay and none of them was free to intervene in the contest in the south.

There remained, however, another northern magnate from whom

---

[50] P. 387 below. [51] *R.M.S.*, II. No. 542.
[52] *E.R.*, v. 604. [53] *R.M.S.*, II. Nos. 544, 553, 556, 566.
[54] Thomas Dickson's theory that James III was born on 10 July 1451 (*T.A.*, I. xxxvii) has been shown to be incorrect (A. I. Dunlop, 'The Date of the Birth of James III', *S.H.R.*, xxx. 202–4; *Bishop Kennedy*, p. 136, n. 1).
[55] P. 344 above. [56] Pitscottie, *Historie*, I. 96–9. [57] *Ibid.*, 99–100.

Douglas hoped much—John, Earl òf Ross and Lord of the Isles. In March 1452 he openly joined the rebellion by seizing the castles of Inverness, Urquhart and Ruthven, perhaps in revenge for the ruin of his Livingston kinsfolk in 1449; for his father-in-law, James Livingston, former chamberlain, escaped from royal surveillance in Holyrood arid assumed charge of Urquhart Castle under Mac-Donald's patronage.[58] While the Earl of Ross could cause trouble in the north he could also, in his capacity as Lord of the Isles, do the same in the west. On 12 May 1452 Douglas interviewed him in Knapdale [59] and seems to have enlisted the naval forces of the Isles under the command of Donald Balloch, who had acquired by marriage the barony of the Glens of Antrim and a powerful position in the north of Ireland.[60] On 10 July 1452 his fleet of birlings raided Inverkip in Renfrew, then harried Bute, the Cumbraes and Arran, and levied blackmail.[61] This incursion was perhaps particularly designed to embarrass the rent-collecting of the royalist bishop of Glasgow.[62] Another bishop who suffered from Donald's attentions was George Lauder, who had been provided to the see of Argyll in 1427.[63] This Lowland intruder was attacked and driven into sanctuary in fear of his life.[64]

Besides the aid forthcoming from his allies in Scotland, Douglas hoped to receive aid from England. On 3 June 1452 Henry VI appointed commissioners to negotiate with 'our dearest kinsman, James, Earl of Douglas' on 'certain articles signed by the hand of our kinsman'. They were also empowered to admit Douglas to the English king's liege homage or fealty.[65] There is no evidence that at this stage Douglas did render homage to Henry VI; and in any case Earl James's intrigues had been outstripped by events in Scotland.

There, despite the widespread activities of Douglas's allies, it was the king who was left with the initiative. He had been sending out summonses to parliament, general council and exchequer, as well as letters 'for the assembly of the king's lieges to his host'.[66] Parliament

---

[58] *Chron. Auchinleck*, pp. 16, 44. See also *E.R.*, v. xciii, n. 1.

[59] *Chron. Auchinleck*, pp. 13, 54. For the date see Fraser, *Douglas*, I. 486, n. 1. A. I. Dunlop's argument (*Bishop Kennedy*, p. 151, n. 2), in favour of a date in 1454 seems less convincing.   [60] *Highland Papers*, I. 43-4.

[61] *Chron. Auchinleck*, pp. 13-4, 54-5; *E.R.*, v. 571, 577, 578.

[62] Pp. 360-1 above.

[63] He is strangely ignored by Duncan Shaw in 'The Ecclesiastical Members of the Lauder Family in the Fifteenth Century', *Scot. Church Hist. Soc. Recs.*, XI. 160-75.

[64] *Chron. Auchinleck*, pp. 14-5, 50-1.

[65] *Rot. Scot.*, II. 358.   [66] *E.R.*, v. 607.

opened at Edinburgh on 12 June 1452 and was informed that it had come to the king's notice that certain of his rivals and rebels were trying to blacken and 'blaspheme' his reputation within the realm and abroad. James required the estates to investigate the circumstances of the death of Earl William and to record their findings in an official document. This duly affirmed that, if Earl William had been under any respites and other securities on the day of his death, he had expressly renounced these 'before a multitude of barons, lords, knights and nobles'. Moreover from many letters and documents, sealed with the earl's seal, and other clear deductions and proofs, it was obvious that he had made leagues and conspiracies with certain magnates 'in oppression and offence of the most serene royal majesty', as well as frequently perpetrating rebellions with his brothers and accomplices. Nor, after 'many sweet persuasions, as well by the king as by divers barons and nobles . . . on the day of his death', had Earl William been induced to aid the king against his rebels. The earl's 'stubborn obstinacy' thus 'seems to have procured, and given, grounds for his death'.[67]

The parliament that had cleared the king's good name was one made up of his own supporters. Some who had still to obtain a reward for their co-operation were not disappointed: the Auchinleck chronicler correctly writes that 'thar was syndry landis gevin to syndry men in this parliament be the kingis secret counsall'.[68] Among the beneficiaries was Bishop Kennedy: a lengthy royal charter was issued on 14 June confirming previous grants to the bishopric of St Andrews and annexing certain lands to its regality. The charter was a grateful recognition of Kennedy's services and of the birth of the future James III in his episcopal city—something which the king did not fail to publicise as securing 'the lineal succession of our royal majesty'.[69]

The witness list to this charter suggests that James had by this time strong support from the ecclesiastical hierarchy and from the middling nobility. But only one earl (Angus) was named. An answer to the hostility or aloofness of the higher nobility was to create new earls. By 8 July Admiral Crichton had been belted Earl of Caithness. About the same time William Hay, constable of Scotland, who had a few days earlier figured as 'Lord Hay', was 'beltit Erll of Erroll'. Another new earl was James Crichton, the chancellor's son and heir,

[67] *A.P.S.*, II. 73.
[68] *Chron. Auchinleck*, pp. 10-1, 48-9. See also *R.M.S.*, II. Nos. 568-87 *passim*.   [69] *A.P.S.*, II. 73-4.

husband of the elder Dunbar heiress, who was now recognised as Earl of Moray [70] in place of Archibald Douglas, husband of the younger heiress.

The king also turned to good account the new title of lord of parliament, realising that its award cost the crown nothing but was gratefully received by those who desired to rise in the world. Hence, according to the Auchinleck chronicler, 'thar was maid VI or VII lordis of the parliament and banrentis [bannerets]', whom he enumerates as the Lords Darnley, Hailes, Boyd of Kilmarnock, Fleming of Cumbernauld, Borthwick, Lyle of Duchall, and Cathcart.[71] From the remarkable distribution of lands, privileges and titles that had begun in March and had culminated during the Edinburgh parliament it is clear that James had made 'an effort to win the wavering and to build up a new party in the state'.[72]

Simultaneously there was an effort to ruin the king's opponents : Crawford was forfeited; and Douglas and others were summoned to compear in parliament on a certain day to underlie the law. The contempt in which the Black Douglases held these proceedings was shown by their behaviour : manifestoes were surreptitiously posted up in Edinburgh declaiming that 'the king was bot ane blodie murtherar . . . breaking of the law of hospitalietie; ane fallis ungodlie thrister of innocent bloode witht out just quarrell or occatioun witht money uther contumulus sayingis unworthie to rehearse'.[73]

James had rightly judged that it would take more than parliamentary action to bring his opponents to submission. Soon after 8 July, when the business of parliament was over, the host set out. Marching by way of Peebles, Selkirk and Dumfries it 'did na gud, bot distroyit the cuntre richt fellonly', cornfields and orchards were laid waste, and the army in its depredations did not discriminate overmuch between the lands of the king's foes and those of his friends.[74] The campaign was evidently over by 26 August 1452, when parliament once more met in Edinburgh. This was the parliament to which the Black Douglases had been summoned. But instead of proceeding with their forfeiture it concerned itself with economic matters and passed ordinances against hoarding of corn [75] during a dearth that was perhaps caused by the recent depredations. Negotiations for the submission of the Black Douglases were already in

---

[70] Chron. Auchinleck, pp. 10–1, 48–9; A.P.S., II. 75.
[71] Chron. Auchinleck, pp. 10–1, 48–9. For the holders of these new titles see Scots Peerage, passim.   [72] Dunlop, Bishop Kennedy, p. 139.
[73] Pitscottie, Historie, I. 100; similarly Chron. Auchinleck, pp. 10–1, 48–9.
[74] Chron. Auchinleck, pp. 11, 49.   [75] A.P.S., II. 41.

progress and resulted in an 'Appoyntement', dated at Douglas Castle on 28 August 1452,[76] which Earl James and Lord Hamilton subscribed and swore to observe. In this document Douglas and his adherents forgave those responsible for the death of Earl William. Douglas also guaranteed to revoke 'all leagues and bands, if any hes been made be me in any tyme bygane contrare to our said soverayne lord' ; nor would the earl make any such leagues and bands in future ; instead, being given reasonable surety for his own personal safety, he would show the king honour and worship and would defend the Borders and keep the truce.

It is striking that in the very first clause of the 'Appoyntement' Earl James bound himself not to try to obtain possession of the lands of the earldom of Wigtown until he received written permission from the queen. Similarly he undertook not to 'persew' the lands of the lordship of Stewarton until special licence had been obtained from the king. The prominence given to these provisions suggests that to king and earl the lands formerly held by the late Duchess of Touraine were still a savoury bone of contention. They figured again in a bond of manrent which Douglas concluded with the king at Lanark on 16 January 1453.[77] This document was more remarkable for the services promised by the king than for those promised by the earl. The latter bound himself to renounce all leagues against the king, swore to render him full manrent and service, and to make a declaration of this in parliament after James had fulfilled his promise of granting re-entry in the lands of Wigtown and Stewarton. Even more astonishingly James bound himself to aid the earl to consolidate his territorial power by furthering a marriage betwixt Earl James and the latter's sister-in-law, the widowed Fair Maid of Galloway, to whom, remarks Pitscottie, 'ane great part of the landis fell throw deceis of hir husband besyde the landis that apperteinit to hir in heritage quhilk he [Douglas] could be na maner of way obtein'.[78]

A papal dispensation was obviously required for such a marriage, and the king had already joined with Earl James and Countess Margaret in the petition to obtain it. It was issued on 27 February 1453 on the conventional grounds that it was intended 'to put an end to wars etc. between their respective families and friends'.[79] When Earl James 'without law or ony respect to God or goode

---

[76] Text in P. F. Tytler, *History of Scotland*, I. pt. ii, Notes and Illustrations, pp. 386–7.   [77] Fraser, *Douglas*, I. 483–4 and n. 1.
[78] Pitscottie, *Historie*, I. 101.   [79] *Cal. Papal Letters*, x. 130–1.

conscience . . . tuik and marieit his brotheris wyfe'[80] he was just as much master of the whole Black Douglas territories as his late brother had been. The murder of Earl William, and all the hostilities that followed upon it, had been of no more avail in weakening the Black Douglas power than had been the attack upon the Douglas lands in the winter of 1450–51. Nor did the king make any lasting gain by the forfeiture of the Earl of Crawford in the Edinburgh parliament of June 1452. Pitscottie devotes no few pages of his *Historie*[81] to describe the heart-rending scene as Crawford humbly sought (and obtained) pardon for his misdeeds, with 'teiris brustand out aboundantlie'. The rhetoric, one may suppose, is rather that of Pitscottie himself than that of the Tiger Earl, 'a rigorous man and ane felloun', who 'held all Angus in his bandoun, and was richt inobedient to the king'.[82]

Men had rightly foreseen that the settlement of lands and titles in the Edinburgh parliament of June–July 1452 was one that 'wald nocht stand': the forfeited Earl of Crawford had been restored; Archibald Douglas was still Earl of Moray, and the other menaced leaders of the Black Douglas faction had been reconciled with the king. By contrast, for one reason or another, it was royalist adherents who had been displaced. Indeed the Crichtons, who for more than a decade had been a political family of the first rank, were suddenly relegated to obscurity: not only had Admiral Crichton, Earl of Caithness, and James Crichton, sometime Earl of Moray, died in August 1454, but they had been predeceased shortly before by Chancellor Crichton, the head of the family,[83] 'ane mane of great forsight and singular manheid and ane faithfull subject and sicker tairge [sure shield] to the commone weill'.[84] These sudden and almost simultaneous deaths broke up a faction on which the king had often relied. In September 1454 death removed another stalwart royalist, Bishop Turnbull of Glasgow, whose successor, Andrew of Durisdeer, seems scarcely to have been a man of comparable political importance. In part recompense for the singular mortality among the royalists there emerged from the debris of the former Livingston faction none other than James Livingston, father-in-law of the Earl of Ross and onetime chamberlain. His re-admission to royal service after his escapade at Urquhart in 1452[85] was no doubt symptomatic of a reconciliation between the king and the Earl of Ross. By 1 July

---

[80] Pitscottie, *Historie*, I. 101.
[82] *Chron. Auchinleck*, pp. 17, 51.
[84] Pitscottie, *Historie*, I. 127.

[81] *Ibid.*, 104–12.
[83] *E.R.*, v. cvii, cviii.
[85] P. 362 above.

1454 Livingston had regained his old office as chamberlain, which he was to hold until 1467.[86]

In parliament intense factionalism had, for the time being, disappeared : on 16 July 1454 the three estates re-affirmed old statutes for 'the keping and execucione of justice'; they dealt with a continuing dearth by ordaining that 'strangearis that bringis in wittalis be favorabily tretyt'; and they showed a healthy spirit of independence by limiting the king's use of purveyance to the requisitioning of 'alsmekill as will serf his houshalde'.[87]

In this Indian summer of politics, in 1453 or 1454, Richard Holland composed *The Buke of the Howlat* for the entertainment of his patrons, Archibald Douglas, Earl of Moray, and the latter's wife, Elizabeth Dunbar. While this long poem deserves consideration for its literary interest and for the light it casts upon the general social background of the time it has also some relevance to contemporary politics. Indeed the anti-hero of the poem—the howlat or owl—has been thought, partly on the basis of a mistranscribed word, to represent none other than James II.[88] But the character of the howlat was doubtless suggested by an incident at a synod held in Rome in 1411 by Pope (or Anti-pope) John XXIII, when 'a large owl . . . flew out from behind the altar . . . and fixing its eyes on the pope, sat screeching at him, until the cardinals, flapping at it, drove it away'.[89] Hence it is likely that the lugubrious howlat represents an ecclesiastic—and Bishop Kennedy, foe of the Black Douglases, is the likeliest. Much of the poem is undoubtedly a panegyric of the Douglases, 'the wer wall [bulwark]' of Scotland, whose very name

> . . . is so wonder warme, and ever yit was,
> It synkis sone in all part
> Of a trewe Scottis hart,
> Rejosand us inwart
> To heir of Dowglas.[90]

Whether all this was guileless poetry or political propaganda on the eve of renewed conflict between the Black Douglases and the crown remains uncertain.

Equally uncertain are the causes of the renewed conflict. Alluding to the settlement reached in August 1452 one historian remarks :

---

[86] *H.B.C.*, p. 179.   [87] *A.P.S.*, I. 41.
[88] *The Buke of the Howlat* (Bannatyne Club, 1823), p. ii.
[89] John Holland Smith, *The Great Schism*, p. 179.
[90] *The Buke of the Howlat*, stanza xxx.

'If the reconciliation was sincere on the king's part, he was to find that he had been nourishing a viper.'[91] It requires, however, some niceness of judgment to determine which side was the more viperish or the more insincere. Each side, at any rate, watched events in England to see if they could be turned to its own advantage in Scotland, and Anglo-Scottish relations afforded unexampled opportunities for political permutations in which it is difficult to recognise precisely which interests, partisan or national, were involved. On 18 April 1453 Douglas was commissioned by James II to negotiate in England for the renewal of the truce.[92] Apart from this 'national' business Douglas joined with Lord Hamilton in petitioning for the release of Malise Graham, Earl of Menteith, who had remained in England for twenty-five years as a hostage for the 'fynance' of James I.[93] By a private arrangement Douglas achieved something that the Scottish crown had disgracefully omitted to do. According to one historian, however, the 'evident motive' was 'to involve James II in trouble by a revival of the old question regarding the respective rights of the two families of Robert II'.[94] Another historian surmises that Malise's liberators 'meant to use him as a tool', though 'nothing came of their designs'.[95] At any rate the release of Malise did not figure among the offences afterwards imputed to Douglas by James. Indeed Malise was one of the earls who was to pass sentence against Douglas in the parliament of June 1455.[96] It was perhaps more significant that on 22 May 1453 Douglas and his three brothers, together with Hamilton and their usual large entourage, had obtained English safe-conducts, valid for four years, ostensibly for a journey to Rome.[97] Another safe-conduct, issued on 16 June 1454,[98] and valid for two years, entitled Douglas's mother, Countess Beatrix, his wife, Countess Margaret, and his youngest brother, John, Lord Balvenie, to travel in the English king's dominions for the sake of pilgrimage. This safe-conduct was issued when the Duke of York was at the head of the English government, having been appointed protector of the realm on 27 March 1454, when it became indisputable that Henry VI had lapsed into temporary insanity. The Yorkist accession to power was accompanied by the imprisonment of Edmund Beaufort, Duke of

[91] Dunlop, *Bishop Kennedy*, p. 145.
[92] *Cal. Docs. Scot.*, IV. Nos. 1249, 1257, 1261.
[93] P. 320 above; *Rot. Scot.*, II. 368.   [94] G. Burnett in *E.R.*, VI. xxviii.
[95] Dunlop, *Bishop Kennedy*, p. 146, n. 2.
[96] *A.P.S.*, II. 77.   [97] *Rot. Scot.*, II. 362.
[98] *Foedera*, v. pt. ii, 56. A. I. Dunlop (*Bishop Kennedy*, p. 156, n. 1), points out that the year is wrongly given as 1455 in *Rot. Scot.*, II. 374.

Somerset,[99] uncle of the Scottish king. It was in vain that James sent his stepfather, Sir James Stewart, the Black Knight of Lorne, to intercede with the English council on behalf of Somerset.[100] While James II was thus associated with the Lancastrian faction the Black Douglases had perhaps aligned themselves with the Yorkists. The surviving records merely show that in 1453 and 1454 Douglas was in touch with the English court, sometimes as an official Scottish representative. If he took the chance to engage in intrigue its purpose (as suggested by the safe-conducts issued to himself and his family) was probably precautionary.

In any case it is unlikely that the earl's transactions in England furnished the motive for the Scottish king's third attack upon the Black Douglases, though it is highly likely that events in England gave the opportunity for an attack that had long been premeditated : the Yorkists fell from power in February 1455 when Henry VI recovered his senses; Somerset was released from prison; and Queen Margaret headed a Lancastrian administration while York moved north to muster forces for the first skirmish in the Wars of the Roses.[101] Neither Lancastrians nor Yorkists were likely to be in a position to intervene in Scotland in pursuit of either factional or national advantage.

Wasting no time James seized an opportunity that might not last : at the beginning of March 1455, he suddenly besieged and 'kest doune' Douglas's castle of Inveravon.[102] He then marched to Glasgow where he was joined by his adherents from the west country and the Highlands. Near Lanark there was some skirmish with Douglas's supporters; before returning to Edinburgh the king ravaged Douglasdale, Avondale and the Hamilton lands. At Edinburgh he collected a fresh force and raided the forest of Ettrick, 'and all that wald nocht cum till him furthwith, he tuke thair gudis and brynt thair placis, and tuke faith of all the gentillis [gentry]'.[103] By the beginning of April Douglas's castle of Abercorn was being besieged by the royal forces.[104] In a letter to the French king, James reported that its towers

[99] E. F. Jacob, *The Fifteenth Century*, p. 509.
[100] Dunlop, *Bishop Kennedy*, p. 154, n. 1.
[101] E. F. Jacob, *The Fifteenth Century*, pp. 509–11.
[102] The Auchinleck chronicler's statement is borne out by an entry in *E.R.*, VI. 12, recording the purchase of equipment for the siege and demolition of the tower of Inveravon.
[103] *Chron. Auchinleck*, pp. 12, 53; *E.R.*, VI. 161.
[104] In a letter of 8 July 1455 to Charles VII (printed in Pinkerton, *History*, I. 486–8), James II stated that he laid siege to Abercorn in Easter week. In 1455 Easter Day fell on 6 April.

collapsed through the continual blows of 'machines' (*machinarum*).[105]
If these were old-fashioned engines of war they were certainly supplemented by 'the gret gun the quhilk a Frenchman schot richt
wele'.[106] Eventually, after a month's siege, so James reported to
Charles VII, the castle was taken by storm, the chief defenders were
hanged, and the lesser folk were graciously admitted to the royal
mercy. Then the fortifications were razed to the ground.[107]

It was in vain that Douglas had marched to the relief of the
castle : in a confrontation near the river Carron he advanced, only
to retire when he saw the king's host steadfastly awaiting battle. Lord
Hamilton drew his own conclusions from this indecision and 'left the
Erll of Douglas all begylit, as men said'. On the morrow Douglas
found himself deserted and fled to England with a few attendants.[108]
He left behind him, as representatives of his cause, his three brothers,
Moray, Ormond and Balvenie. At Arkinholm on the Esk near Lang-
holm they were eventually encountered by the laird of Johnstone with
a band of some two hundred men, traditionally said to have been
composed of the leading Border families. On 1 May 1455, so James
reported to the French king, there was a 'lethal conflict' in which the
Douglases were totally defeated. Lord Balvenie managed to escape
to England. The Earl of Ormond was wounded, captured, and soon
executed. Archibald Douglas had fallen in the fight, and the king
gratefully received a present of his severed head.[109]

Shortly before the fight at Arkinholm James had taken the step
that should have preceded his attack on the Black Douglases : on 24
April James Livingston, specially appointed as sheriff of Lanark
for this sole purpose,[110] summoned Douglas to answer charges of
treason. This was tantamount to a declaration of war seven weeks
after the king had opened hostilities. The deliberate delay in summoning the Black Douglases for trial had given them enough opportunity to sharpen the axe that James hoped to apply to their necks :
by the time that parliament opened at Edinburgh on 9 June 1455
allegations of 'traitorous conspiracy' and 'traitorous rebellions'[111]

---

[105] Text in Pinkerton, *History*, I. 486–8, at p. 486.
[106] *Chron. Auchinleck*, pp. 12, 54.
[107] James II–Charles VII in Pinkerton, *History*, I. 487; *E.R.*, VI. 12.
[108] Pitscottie, *Historie*, I. 119–22; *Chron. Auchinleck*, pp. 12, 53; James II–
Charles VII in Pinkerton, *History*, I. 487.
[109] Law's *Chronicle* (excerpt printed in P. F. Tytler, *History*, I. pt. ii, Notes
and Illustrations, p. 387); Pitscottie, *Historie*, I. 122–3; James II–Charles VII
in Pinkerton, *History*, I. 487.
[110] He is described as sheriff of Lanark *in ea parte* (*A.P.S.*, II. 76).
[111] *Ibid.*

could be supplemented by some specific accusations relating to incidents that had probably taken place *after* the king had begun his onslaught on his victims and had forced them to defend themselves. This point has generally been missed by historians [112] who have taken official propaganda at its face value, assuming that it was not the king but his opponents who started civil war in 1455. On the basis of this assumption the same historians have concluded that the Black Douglases would not have taken so desperate an initiative unless they were ready to claim the crown. The possibility that it was not Douglas who conspired against the king but *vice versa* has hardly been considered; nor has the absence of any evidence of a 'claim' deterred speculation.[113] Yet although the indictment of the Black Douglases was an exercise in royalist propaganda [114] it is clear that even this biased compilation stopped short of specifically accusing Douglas of aiming at the crown either for himself or on behalf of anyone else.

Whatever the pros and cons of the accumulation of charges brought against the Black Douglases it was at least clear that according to a celebrated French definition they were blameworthy—they had defended themselves when attacked. Understandably the accused did not attend to plead their cause in a parliament composed of timeservers and royalist supporters. The failure of the Black Douglases to compear could comfortably be taken as additional evidence of their guilt; on account of their contumacious absence it remained only for the crown to present its case. After discussion among the members of parliament Earl James was found guilty of treason. Similar sentences were passed against Countess Beatrix, Archibald Douglas, 'pretended Earl of Moray', John Douglas of Balvenie and four obscure adherents of the family.[115] Hugh Douglas, Earl of Ormond, had presumably been forfeited before his execution.[116] After the three estates had been committed to the forfeiture of the Black Douglases parliament was prorogued until 4 August.[117] In the intervening time its members doubtless donned their armour again : on 8 July, when James wrote to the French king, he could boast that the castles of Douglas, Strathaven and other strongholds had surrendered and had been levelled to the ground; the only Douglas stronghold that still

[112] Even by A. I. Dunlop (*Bishop Kennedy*, pp. 151–2), whose detailed study of the period is the best available.
[113] See G. Burnett in *E.R.*, v. civ–cv.
[114] Text in *A.P.S.*, II. 75–7.
[115] *Ibid.*, 41–2, 76–7.
[116] *E.R.*, VI. xxxvii.
[117] *A.P.S.*, II. 42.

resisted was Threave, which was under siege. Thus, so James affirmed,

> under the disposition of divine clemency, after the prosperous turn of events, we preside felicitously over our realm without any rebellion on the part of our barons or subjects, the forementioned conspirators having been wholly extirpated and expelled.[118]

The same letter alluded to another matter that revealed James's capacity for swift decision and unscrupulous behaviour: when his campaigns against the Black Douglases were drawing to a successful conclusion he had not hesitated to use his forces in a less successful venture against the English. Lancastrians and Yorkists had come to blows at the first battle of St Albans on 22 May 1455, where the Duke of Somerset and other leading Lancastrians had been slain and Henry VI had fallen into the hands of the victorious Yorkists. James had been informed by men of the Marches acquainted with conditions in English-occupied Berwick 'that if we should approach thither with our army suddenly and unexpectedly we should be able to take that town without difficulty'. Unfortunately for James his scheme was 'betrayed' by an Englishman. Notwithstanding this reverse the king still hankered after the recovery of Berwick, 'our town, long wrong-fully detained by the English'.[119] Meanwhile the resentment aroused in England by James's treacherous breach of the truce was swiftly turned to advantage by the fugitive Earl of Douglas: on 15 July, in order to save Threave, he granted it to Henry VI. The latter, on the advice of his privy council (now Yorkist) paid the earl £100 'for succour, victualling, relief and rescue of the castle of Treve'.[120] On 4 August Douglas was also granted an annuity of £500 in return for services that he was expected to render to the English crown. The full amount would be paid 'till he is restored to his heritage . . . taken from him by him who calls himself King of Scots'.[121]

But Douglas's plans for a relief expedition had come too late to save Threave. Already at the sieges of Hatton and Abercorn the king's bombards had proved their worth; now at a cost of over £110 they were brought to Galloway. Among them was 'the great bombard', already mentioned in connection with the siege of Hatton. On its laborious progress towards Threave its escort was entrusted to no

---

[118] James II–Charles VII in Pinkerton, *History*, I. 487.
[119] *Ibid.*, 487–8.
[120] *Cal. Docs. Scot.*, IV. No. 1272.
[121] Dunlop, *Bishop Kennedy*, p. 157; *E.R.*, VI. xxxvii–xxxviii.

less a person than William Sinclair, Earl of Orkney.[122] The effect produced by the royal artillery was supplemented by a more ancient weapon—bribery : some of those who were in the castle at the time of its surrender received profitable rewards.[123]

The fall of Threave allowed the king to adhere to the timetable he had set in June, when he had prorogued parliament to 4 August 1455. On the appointed day the three estates duly assembled at Edinburgh to complete the ruin of the Black Douglases. An act, which was intended to remain in force forever, ordained that anyone who gave any aid or comfort to the survivors of the family would *ipso facto* incur the penalty of treason, and forfeiture of life, lands and goods. Not only did this act re-affirm the forfeiture of the Black Douglases that had been passed in the June session of parliament but it ordained that no descendant of those who had been forfeited would ever be permitted to succeed to, or lay claim to, any lands or possessions in Scotland.[124] This drastic measure was doubtless inspired by recent English examples :[125] the nearest Scottish precedent was probably the act of disinheritance passed at Cambuskenneth in 1314. From the other important measures passed in the parliament of August 1455 [126] it may be gathered that the civil war was regarded as ended; other issues had come to the forefront; and these were dealt with in a way which made it plain that a new era of royal supremacy had been inaugurated.

There were many factors that had contributed to the king's triumph in 1455. One of them was his grasp—unusual in that age—of the importance of heavy artillery.[127] In other respects James may reasonably be compared to Robert I. Like Bruce he had not been dispirited by early reverses but had learned from them : undeterred by failures in 1451 and 1452 he had continued to work with persistence and duplicity for the destruction of the Black Douglases. Like Bruce he was a talented military leader : he had a remarkable sense of timing and a swiftness of decision that verged upon impetuosity; he could hold his forces together and move with a rapidity that

---

[122] *E.R.*, vi. xxxiv, 200, 201–2, 204, 209; *T.A.*, i. ccxvii.
[123] *E.R.*, vi. xxxv, 199, 202, 204.
[124] The text of this act has been recorded in the vernacular and also (in fuller and more formal language) in Latin (*A.P.S.*, ii. 42, c. 2, and 43–4, c. 14).
[125] See J. G. Bellamy, *Law of Treason*, pp. 186–7.
[126] Pp. 377–9 below.
[127] See M. Toynbee, 'King James II of Scotland : artillery and fortifications', *The Stewarts*, xi. 157–62.

must have disconcerted his opponents; he had a clear view of his objectives—the enemy castles—and, like Bruce, did not hesitate to destroy them, not only, perhaps, for military reasons, but as a sign that their former holders had been uprooted for ever. Finally, like Bruce, James had learned to neutralise one opponent while dealing with another. His task was made easier by the death of the Tiger Earl in September 1453, which deprived the Black Douglases of the valuable alliance of the Lindsays. Another mainstay of the Douglases, John, Earl of Ross, played no part in the civil war of 1455, partly as a result of timely concessions: his seizure in 1452 of the royal lands and castle of Urquhart and Glen Moriston was regularised by a royal grant allowing him to hold them for life.[128] And if MacDonald was too aloof to attend in person the decisive parliament of June 1455, he at least had the good grace to appoint procurators who acquiesced in the forfeiture of the Black Douglases.[129] It was the neutrality of Ross that allowed James a free hand in the south. In this case, as in others, the king knew the price of most men, and he was willing (like Louis XI of France) to pay it.

Bribery alone was not likely to have diverted men from loyalty to Douglas. It was rather that they came to distrust the political and military capacity of Earl James. In contrast to the decisiveness and impetuosity shown by the king the earl had acted aimlessly, and sometimes sluggishly. He did not aspire to the crown and failed to find any other objective save what was suggested by personal and territorial grievances. Nor could he dispel from the minds of his men the superstitious dread that demoralised them at the sight of the royal standard. It was an age in which, for complex reasons, the peoples of Western Europe began to put trust in monarchy rather than in aristocracy. Once James II had not only survived the consequences of his murder of Earl William but had expelled the latter's successor it was clear that in Scotland the crown could do no wrong. Despite the interruption of a long and disordered minority James II had confirmed a political trend that had first become apparent in the days of his father.

This was a triumph for the Stewart dynasty, not necessarily for the people of Scotland as a whole. Nor was the triumph achieved without cost: between 1450 and 1455 James II had instigated three outbreaks of civil war, each of which had lasted for months. These spasms of strife were fewer and less spectacular than those of the long-drawn-out Wars of the Roses in England, but were possibly

---

[128] *E.R.*, vi. 68, 217.　　　　[129] *A.P.S.*, ii. 77.

more destructive and had harsher consequences for the generality
of the population. This is suggested not only by the verbose accounts
of the civil wars in the pages of Pitscottie but also by the shorter and
more telling passages of the Auchinleck chronicler, who remarks that
'subjects at this time war sa upprest [oppressed] with the weiris . . .
that few travelling in the waye durst tell quhidder he wes the kings
man or the Earle of Douglases'. The same writer gives another glimpse
of a time of suffering when he tells how the king 'brynt all Douglasdale and all Avendale, and all the Lord Hammiltonnis landis, and
heriit [despoiled] them clerlye'.[130] The accounts of the king's chamberlain of Galloway show that shortly after its conquest by the royal
forces the income from some fifteen holdings of land, including the
forest of Buchan, had been reduced *'propter vastitatem'*, a phrase
which in this case almost certainly indicates destruction. And, so the
chamberlain affirmed, certain tenants 'cannot be distrained on account of their poverty'.[131] When some of the rural population lived
on the margin of subsistence it was not surprising that devastation and
dislocation were followed by epidemics. Thus in 1455, so runs a
laconic entry in annals of the time, 'there was a great pestilence and
mortality of men through the whole kingdom of Scotland'.[132] In the
autumn of 1456 the three estates adopted methods of control proposed by the clergy : there was to be no reckless burning of infected
houses; those who had sufficient wealth could be quarantined in their
own dwellings; the poor who were infected could be 'put forth of the
town' but were not to be allowed to move freely and contaminate
the countryside. Meanwhile the prelates were to 'mak generale pro-
cessiounis throu out thair dyoceis twyss in the wolk for stanching of
the pestilence'.[133]

During the years of civil war the king had found support in the
three estates. They were evidently both serviceable and amenable;
and in the years of relative stability that followed the royalist triumph
of 1455 James II had no desire to ignore them. The records, which
may not be complete, show that after 1455 at least one general council was held (in 1456) while parliament met about once a year. Its
tenurial composition, which had always been blurred by practical
considerations, was further disregarded by an act of 1458 : no
tenant-in-chief who held lands of the crown less than £20 in annual
value was to be constrained to come to parliament or general council

[130] *Chron. Auchinleck*, pp. 12, 53.   [131] *E.R.*, VI. 196–9, *passim*, 207–8.
[132] *Extracta*, p. 243; *Chron. Bower*, II. 516.   [133] *A.P.S.*, II. 46.

unless he was a baron, or unless his attendance was specially commanded by the king.[134] There can hardly have been a sinister ulterior
motive :[135] it was the current political situation, rather than any constitutional change, that affected the relationship between the king and
the three estates and made the latter somewhat sycophantic. If
patriotism had conferred a sort of unity upon Scotland in the fourteenth century, devotion to monarchy subsumed other ideals after
1455 and became the main source of unity. God had so favoured
the king, so declared the parliament of March 1458, 'that all his
rebellys and brekaris of his justice ar removit out of his realme, and na
maisterfull party remanande that may causs ony breking in his
realme'.[136] MacDonald provided the only question-mark that could
be posed against this assertion, but James's tactful treatment of the
earl [137] prevented, for the time being, any large-scale eruption in the
Highlands. In the Lowlands there remained no 'kin' that could by
itself compete with the crown in prestige and power. Thenceforth if
baronial opposition were to be successful it had not only to take the
form of a coalition but had to acquire a 'royalist' character by securing a member of the royal family as a real or nominal leader.

Although the new 'lords' had supported the king against the
Black Douglases, who had almost personified the higher nobility, it
was not James II's intention to dispense with a higher nobility : as
death or forfeiture caused gaps in its ranks they were speedily filled;
above the new lords appeared new earls, and, indeed, new earldoms
were erected. The Gordon earldom of Huntly dated from 1445, the
Hay earldom of Erroll from 1452. In 1457 or 1458 Colin, Lord
Campbell, was created Earl of Argyll, George, Lord Leslie, was
created Earl of Rothes, James Douglas, Lord of Dalkeith (or Lord
Dalkeith) was created Earl of Morton, and William, Lord Keith, was
created Earl Marischal. Apart from the erection of these new earldoms there took place between 1455 and 1458 a re-distribution of old
ones. Caithness went to William Sinclair, already Earl of Orkney,
and scions of the royal house received the consideration that was to
be expected : Atholl went to the king's half-brother, Sir John
Stewart; March went to the king's second son, Alexander, for whom
the dukedom of Albany was also revived; Moray went briefly to the
king's third son, David, who died shortly afterwards; and Mar
(filched from the Erskines) went to John, the king's youngest son.[138]

[134] *Ibid.*, 50.
[135] A. I. Dunlop (*Bishop Kennedy*, p. 311) is nonetheless suspicious.
[136] *A.P.S.*, II. 52.   [137] Pitscottie, *Historie*, I. 128–9; *E.R.*, VI. li.
[138] *Scots Peerage, passim.*

The proliferation of new titles and the re-distribution of old titles has given rise to the view that James II was 'building up a new nobility to counteract the influence of the old'.[139] It was, however, within the ranks of the ecclesiastical hierarchy or those of commerce, administration, and law, not within those of the nobility, that 'new' men of humble origin were given advancement. But if the titled nobility remained unchanged in its social origins, it did nonetheless, for the time being, lack the assurance and independence that came from hereditary succession : it was not by that, but by recent royal favour, that many nobles, however impeccable their birth, had acquired titles and even lands. Though they formed a nobility of ancestry they were also a nobility of service.

Measures designed to prevent in future the rise of any noble to the position of independent authority lately held by Douglas were taken in the very parliament of 4 August 1455 that witnessed his final forfeiture. Here a frontal attack was made on one hoary abuse— heritable tenure of office : in future no office was ever to be given in fee and heritage; any such grant issued since the death of James I was revoked.[140] Another act ordained that rights of regality should be granted only with the approval of parliament.[141] The horse had bolted before the stable door was shut. Nonetheless it was possible to bring *some* regalities to an end; for it was also ordained that 'all regaliteis that ar now in the kingis handis be anext to the rialte',[142] in other words that they should lose their distinctive jurisdictions and be merged in the royalty[143] of the sheriffdom. This was a repetition of an act first passed in the parliament of January 1450 in a more expanded form[144] that elucidated the king's motives. He intended to re-invigorate the traditional curial system of royal government, which had been debilitated by so many exemptions : the diversity of juris-dictions would gradually be reduced to uniformity in proportion to the crown's acquisition of regalities. An initial impetus to the process was certainly forthcoming with the forfeiture of so many regalities formerly held by the Black Douglases. Thereby the royal courts must have benefited from an influx of new suitors and new business. A justice ayre held at Wigtown and Kirkcudbright in 1455 or 1456

---

[139] Dunlop, *Bishop Kennedy*, p. 188.

[140] *A.P.S.*, II. 43. Another act of 1458 (*ibid.*, 50) sought to make holders of heritable office accountable for their misdeeds by threatening them with fines and loss of office for a year and a day.

[141] *Ibid.*, 43.   [142] *Ibid.*

[143] For the meaning of this term see p. 24 above.

[144] *A.P.S.*, II. 36.

brought in no less than £600 6s. 8d.;[145] and three ayres held at Dumfries in the next few years imposed amercements of £1,105 (though these were compounded at about half the sum).[146] The yearly profits of justice from the newly acquired lands may even have approached in value the annual rents of the lands.

The rents themselves received immediate and high-powered attention from commissioners (including Bishop Kennedy) who were appointed to make assessments.[147] From these it appears that the gross rents from East Galloway amounted to £562 3s. 4d. in 1456, and those from West Galloway to £189, besides, in both cases, large quantities of victuals. These assessments were, however, either too optimistic or too harsh : by 1460 the rental of East Galloway had fallen to £356 4s. 5½d. and that of West Galloway to £115 4s. 5d.[148] The gross rents of Ettrick for the first three terms after the forest came into the king's hands amounted to £779 10s. 0d.; afterwards the rental was fixed at £519 13s. 4d. a year.[149] Besides payments in victuals the gross rents of the earldom of Moray came to £339 18s. 8d.[150] In all, the forfeited Black Douglas lands must have brought the king gross cash rents of at least £2,000, about one-third of the total for all the crown lands.[151]

James II was anxious to see that this spectacular addition to the landed wealth of the crown, won by himself at such risk, would not be frittered away by his successors. Thus the very parliament of 4 August 1455 that disinherited the Black Douglases passed an act of annexation to endow the monarchy with an inheritance partly composed of the lands that its foes had lost forever. This act[152] ordained that in each part of the realm certain lordships and castles should be annexed to the crown; they were not to be granted in fee or freehold without the decree of the whole parliament, which was to be given only for weighty reasons.

Although the preamble to the act mentioned only lordships and castles the list of annexations was headed by 'the haill custumes of Scotland' : the king was to revoke all grants from the customs that had been made since the death of James I. Next the act went on to

[145] E.R., vi. 195, 206.
[146] Ibid., 557–8. By contrast a justice ayre held in Aberdeen in the same period produced only £68 (ibid., 158).
[147] Ibid., 201, 203, 206, 226, 227.   [148] Ibid., cx.
[149] E.R., vi. 225, 443, 544.   [150] Ibid., cxxxix–cxl.
[151] See G. Burnett's detailed survey of the crown lands for the period 1455–60, ibid., lxxii–cxlvi.
[152] A.P.S., ii. 42–3. G. Burnett provides a more accurate text in E.R., vi. cxlvii–cxlviii.

enumerate the castles and lordships that had been annexed. It may be estimated that the annexed lands which were old crown property provided gross annual rents totalling some £1,600, besides additional payments in victuals;[153] those that had formerly been Black Douglas possessions contributed some £1,450, besides payments in victuals.[154] Altogether, the whole annexed lands, plus the customs (currently bringing in some £3,000 a year, gross)[155] should have given the crown a permanent endowment that in 1455 was worth some £6,050 a year in cash. A distinction thenceforth existed between crown lands that were annexed and those that were unannexed and of which the king might freely dispose without seeking parliament's approval. The annual rents of these unannexed crown lands exceeded £3,500.[156]

The act of annexation might be regarded as a tailzie, variable only with parliament's consent, that attached lands and castles to the crown, with which, it was hoped, they were 'perpetualy to remane'.[157] One express motive was that in each part of the realm there should be lordships and castles (including Edinburgh, Stirling and Dumbarton) set aside 'for the kingis residence'. Another motive, left unexpressed, was strategic and military : for control over lands gave control over their manpower; and castles, which were not an economic asset but an economic liability, were useful not only as residences but as strongholds—in the next reign the royal castles would rightly be described as 'the keys of the kingdom'.[158] Nonetheless the chief motive behind the act of 1455 was undoubtedly an economic one, and one which was made to seem particularly attractive. For, so affirmed the preamble to the act, 'the poverte of the crowne is oftymis the causs of the poverte of the realme and mony uther inconvenientis, the quhilkis war lang to expreyme'.[159] Among the inconveniences that parliament had in mind was taxation, the need for which would be (so it was hoped) removed. Thus the act was thoroughly in accord with the Scottish constitutional tradition that the king should live of his own. Whether the act would work was another matter. Within a year its efficacy was open to question.[160]

---

[153] *E.R.*, vi. lxxii–lxxxv, xc–ciii, cxl–cxliii.
[154] *Ibid.*, cix–cx, cxv–cxvii, cxl–cxlii.   [155] *Ibid.*, 113–32.
[156] This would follow from a comparison of the revenues of the annexed lands, as given above, with those of the totality of crown lands, including those held by the queen in dower (*ibid.*, lxxii–cxlvi). Some of the lands held in liferent by the queen, such as the earldom of Fife and the lordship of Brechin (*A.P.S.*, ii. 66–7), were among the annexed lands.
[157] *A.P.S.*, ii. 42.   [158] *Ibid.*, 113.   [159] *Ibid.*
[160] As in the case of Urquhart and Glenmoriston (*E.R.*, vi. 217, 221).

The patrimony of the crown was to be better preserved by acts of revocation : on 15 November 1455 James, having attained his perfect majority of twenty-five years, revoked all previous alienations of crown property with the exception of those made in favour of the queen and his second son.[161]

The acts of annexation and revocation showed the growing importance attached to the crown lands as the main source of royal revenue. This was also indicated after 1437 in the emergence and increasing prominence of a new class of accounts in the exchequer rolls—the accounts of the *ballivi ad extra* or managers of the crown lands.[162] It was these royal bailies or receivers—who might also hold posts as local stewards, chamberlains, serjeants, mairs or crowners— who now, rather than the sheriffs, accounted in exchequer for the ferms of the crown lands.[163] It is perhaps significant that in 1455-6 every sheriff seems to have been a noble,[164] whereas the bailies of crown lands, whose financial responsibilities were often greater, were of miscellaneous social status. Some, admittedly, were nobles, but others were obscure men (presumably of proven ability) such as James Patonson, who was in charge of the ferms and grain-rents of Fife, the most valuable of all the earldoms.[165]

The bailies had to collect (and disburse) the crown rents on the basis of rentals that were the subject of frequent assessment after 1455.[166] The rents were paid by *firmarii* (fermours) of varying social status, who leased landholdings by the year, or, as tacksmen, enjoyed longer leases, perhaps for five years, renewable on payment of a grassum.[167] The tacksmen, who could sub-let the land they leased, probably made up a rural middle class, having been given some security of tenure by an act of 1450.[168] Meanwhile, however, there remained a 'variety and confusion of tenure' which comprised 'every possible combination of lease and ward and blench-ferm holding',[169] and to these might be added holdings in wadset, whereby land could be held by a beneficiary until redeemed by payment of a stipulated

---

[161] Dunlop, *Bishop Kennedy*, p. 176.
[162] *E.R.*, v. xxxv; vi. xxvii.   [163] *Ibid.*, vi. lxv, lxx.
[164] See the sheriffs' accounts rendered in 1455 and 1456 (*ibid.*, 83–109, 140– 89). These two rolls of sheriffs' accounts are the only ones extant for the period 1437–60 (*ibid.*, v. xxxv; vi. xxvii).
[165] See *E.R.*, vi. 408–87.
[166] P. 378 above; Dunlop, *Bishop Kennedy*, p. 339, n. 5.
[167] *E.R.*, vi. lxx; Dunlop, *Bishop Kennedy*, p. 339.
[168] *A.P.S.*, ii. 35; p. 351 above; *Scot. Legal Hist.*, pp. 193–6.
[169] R. L. Jones, cited in Grant, *Social and Economic Development*, pp. 39–40.

capital sum.[170] Some standardisation was eventually to be produced by the development of holdings in feu-ferm.

The term was not new;[171] but it had undergone some definition which made it so attractive that over the course of centuries it was to become, and remain, the most prominent form of landholding in Scotland, and a form peculiar to Scotland alone. By the mid-fifteenth century the holder of a feu was not liable for certain of the customary feudal casualties; yet his tenure was heritable and secure so long as he and his heirs paid each year a fixed and unalterable feu-duty in cash. So advantageous were these terms that the feuholder was expected to pay a lump sum when he received his feu-charter; and the feu-duty might be set at a figure considerably higher than the former rent of the land. Since the early fourteenth century the crown had granted feu-ferm tenure to the communities of royal burghs, and in the mid-fifteenth century feuing sometimes retained burghal associations: in 1452 two feus of crown land were granted to the community of Cupar;[172] and on 13 July 1459 no less than twenty-three feu-charters were granted to various inhabitants of the so-called 'burgh' of Falkland [173] that had sprung up alongside the old castle that James II had begun to turn into a favourite royal residence.[174] From 1450 onwards, however, feuing was applied outside the royal burghs to the crown lands in general; and it was landholders of some standing, rather than burgesses, who were granted feu-charters.[175] The king's financial stringency doubtless prompted this new development, which was still on a small and experimental scale. In the Edinburgh parliament of March 1458 feu-ferm was included among the 'items' for discussion and enactment. It may be inferred that the king had recommended general adoption of the practice. The pointed response of 'the lordis' was that he should 'begyne and gif exempill' for others to follow, while assurance of royal approval and ratification was to be given to each 'prelate, barone or frehaldare that can accorde with his tenande apone setting of feu ferme of his awin lande'.[176]

This cautious attitude perhaps sprang from a conservative dislike of anything that savoured of a permanent alienation of land. For this reason the papacy had long tried to restrain the kirk from the experiments in feuing in which it had led the way in the fourteenth

[170] See *Wigtown Charters*, No. 146, p. 168.
[171] See p. 6 above.　　　　　　[172] *R.M.S.*, ii. Nos. 580, 581.
[173] *Ibid.*, Nos. 706–28.　　　　[174] *E.R.*, vi. lxxviii–lxxix.
[175] See *R.M.S.*, ii. Nos. 304, 305, 372, 373, 405, 406, 458, 473, 515, 528, 533, 553, 567, 572, 580, 581.　　　　[176] *A.P.S.*, ii. 49, c. 15.

century and which had notably contributed to the definition of the new tenure.[177] Apart from a conservative dislike of alienations there were (and are) economic objections to feuing : the feu-duties, however attractive in comparison to existing rents, were perpetually fixed. But contemporaries were painfully aware that the coins in which the feu-duties were paid were by no means fixed in value or in bullion content : in 1393 44 pennies had been coined from the ounce of silver; by 1440 the number had risen to 64, by 1451 to 96, and by 1483 to 140.[178] Throughout the whole reign the three estates were constantly pre-occupied with the problem of 'the money' :[179] in the parliament of March 1458 the decision was made to cease altogether the striking of further coins until a committee of the estates had examined the question.[180] It was thus understandable that the same parliament should give only a lukewarm welcome to the king's advocacy of feu-ferm tenure : the old system of adjustable rents made it possible to compensate for changes in the value of money, even although insecure tenure hindered agricultural improvement.

Not that the 1458 parliament was blind to the desirability of agricultural improvement : a number of measures that it enacted were concerned with rural husbandry.[181] To remedy the shortage of timber, landholders were ordered to let their lands each Whitsuntide on conditions that required their tenants to plant not only woods and hedges but broom, which was used both for fuel and winter fodder. Fences were forbidden since their place was to be taken by hedges of 'lyffand wode' which might 'grow and plenyss'. Another act ordered, on pain of a ten-shilling fine payable in the baron court, that each man who worked with a plough-team of eight oxen should sow at least a firlot of wheat, half a firlot of peas, and forty beans. The barons were to do likewise on their own demesne lands on pain of the same fine to the king, and they would also be fined forty shillings if they neglected to enforce the ordinance upon their tenants. It has been pointed out that 'the introduction of the sowing of peas and beans would have been a most important innovation had the idea been to use them as a substitute for fallow'.[182] They were, however, to be sown only in small quantities in the cottar's kailyard rather than in the rigs of the open fields.

The rural legislation of 1458, to which some landholders paid

---

[177] Grant, *Social and Economic Development*, pp. 40, 98, 265–6.

[178] R. W. Cochran-Patrick, *Records of the Coinage of Scotland*, I. lxxv. See also *E.R.*, IX. lxi–lxviii.

[179] E.g. *A.P.S.*, II. 41, 46, 48.   [180] *Ibid.*, 48.   [181] *Ibid.*, 51–2.

[182] Grant, *Social and Economic Development*, p. 291.

heed,[183] came at a time when 'the rural communities of Scotland were by no means in a stable condition'. The subdivision of holdings was a sign of an upward trend in the population, so also, perhaps, was 'a considerable change from pastoral to arable farming'. Simultaneously however, there was beginning to be 'considerable displacement of the lesser folk', firstly through the development of the tacksman system, and, somewhat later, by the development of feuing.[184] The existence of agrarian troubles is hinted at in an act of 1458 concerning those who 'occupy maisterfully lordis landis'; at any lord's request such 'maisterfull men' were to be evicted by the local sheriff.[185] Those who were evicted doubtless swelled the ranks of miscellaneous 'sorners' who roamed the countryside as vagrants extorting hospitality.[186]

The prosecution of sorners and other vagrants could take place in baron court, burgh court, sheriff court, or even in an inquest held in the king's presence on his arrival in the head burgh of a shire.[187] This was typical of the current use of miscellaneous agencies to enforce law and order and to promote justice. What was striking was 'the fragmentary dispersal of judicial power and its corrupt inefficacy'.[188] It was presumably because of lapses in the holding of justice ayres that the parliament of March 1458 thought it 'speidfull' that they be held yearly throughout the realm 'for gude of the communys'.[189] It was probably because of the irregular sittings of the justice ayre (which alone was competent to deal with cases of robbery) that the criminal jurisdiction of the sheriffs was extended through new laws dealing with spuilzie [190] (spoliation)—a happily ambiguous term which 'was used to cover almost any action in which goods were taken brevi manu'.[191] In civil cases the delay of proceedings in the justice ayre was sometimes avoided by the appointment of special justiciars in hac parte, who were instructed to determine a certain case.[192] Despite innovations in judicial machinery the old parliamentary committee of causes and complaints was still active.[193]

[183] Rental Book of the Cistercian Abbey of Cupar Angus (Grampian Club), I. 141–2; Dunlop, Bishop Kennedy, p. 345, n. 1.
[184] Grant, Social and Economic Development, pp. 98, 291.
[185] A.P.S., II. 51.
[186] Ibid., 36, 43, 45. An act of 1458 arranged for the licensing of disabled beggars (ibid., 49–50); Scot. Legal Hist., p. 285.
[187] A.P.S., II. 36, 43, 45, 49–50.
[188] Scot. Legal Hist., p. 20.
[189] A.P.S., II. 49.
[190] Ibid., 34, 36.
[191] Fife Court Bk., pp. 325–6.
[192] A.P.S., XII. T4.
[193] Ibid., II. 77–9; XII. 22–3.

Meanwhile there was further experiment with the 'sessions' that from time to time had been employed as one of the several possible types of supreme civil court, whether parliamentary or conciliar. In 1439 the work of the sessions was to be done by the lord lieutenant and the king's chosen council, who would hold two sessions a year.[194] In 1450 the king was to choose certain discreet persons of the three estates, who, together with the chancellor, would hold three sessions a year.[195] In 1456 three representatives of the clergy, three of the barons, and three of the burghs, were to hold sessions for one month, after which they would be relieved by another group of nine representatives plus the clerk of register, who after a month's service would in turn be relieved by another group of nine.[196] The parliament of March 1458 made similar arrangements for the sessions. Their jurisdiction was primarily to comprise actions of spuilzie and civil actions that did not concern fee and heritage, and from their decisions there could be no appeal to either king or parliament. This scheme was not intended to be merely a temporary expedient, but its obvious weakness was the lack of money to finance it: the three estates thought that the lords of session 'of thair awne benevolence sulde beir thair awne costis'.[197] Since there was unlikely to be much enthusiasm to undertake the unpaid work of the sessions the lords of council continued to act as an alternative supreme court.[198]

While litigants were faced with a bewildering variety of courts the operations of the courts, spiritual as well as temporal, were liable to be perverted by the practice of 'maintenance'. The parliament of March 1458 enacted that all those who attended any sort of court should come 'in sobyr and quiet maner' with no more followers than their daily household and 'familiaris'. As soon as they had taken up lodgings they were to lay aside their weapons and armour.[199] But little could be expected of this enactment when justiciars and other itinerant legal officers had themselves to be warned to reduce their retinues 'to eschew grevans and hurting of the pepill'.[200] When, despite the prevalence of maintenance, offenders were pronounced guilty, they often escaped the legal consequences by the purchase of remissions from the king. In accounts running from July 1457 to June 1458 the king's chamberlains north of Spey alluded to some two hundred remissions that had been granted.[201] There was good reason for the parliament of March 1458 to pass an act that curbed

---

[194] *Ibid.*, II. 32.   [195] *Ibid.*, 34.   [196] *Ibid.*, 46.
[197] *Ibid.*, 47–8.   [198] *Ayr Burgh Charters*, No. 49, decreet of 1460.
[199] *A.P.S.*, II. 51.   [200] *Ibid.*, 36.   [201] *E.R.*, VI. 485–6.

the judicial immunity hitherto conferred by remissions so that the rights of plaintiffs were at least partly safeguarded.[202]

At the close of this parliament, so notable for its attempts to improve justice, the three estates hinted that the king and his ministers should promote 'the quiet and commoune profett of the realme' and see that justice was 'kepit amangis his liegis'; and 'with all humilite' they exhorted the king 'to be inclynit with sik diligence to the execucioune of thir statutis . . . that God may be emplesit of him, and all his liegis . . . may pray for him to Gode, and gif thankynge to Hime that sende thame sik a prince to thair governour and defendour'.[203] It may be inferred that at least some of the judicial reforms of 1458 did not spring from royal initiative, and that they may have been unwelcome to the king. It has been affirmed that it was Bishop Kennedy who 'inspired parliament to do all that parliament could do in the way of judicial reform', and that it was he who 'tried to systematise the procedure of the lords of session as an independent court'.[204] Of this however, there is no evidence. It was perhaps the clergy in general, rather than Bishop Kennedy in particular, who inspired judicial reform; in the general council of 1456, at any rate, the clergy considered that an 'artikill belangande justice'—presumably drafted by a committee of the articles—was 'weill made', and besought the king to implement it.[205]

The obsequiousness generally shown by the clergy reflected the king's 'remarkable success in securing bishops after his own heart'.[206] Nor was the king's control of ecclesiastical appointments contested by the pope; no objection seems to have been made to an important extension of the crown's patronage *sede vacante*. In 1450 this had been limited to benefices in the bishop's gift.[207] In 1457, however, a provincial council of the clergy agreed that it extended also to major elective benefices within the diocese and even to benefices that had been reserved for papal provision, and, in 1459, in another provincial council held at Perth, the decision of 1457 was formally recorded. It was to be re-affirmed by parliament in 1462 since the king's rights allegedly sprang from a usage that was ancient, customary and laudable.[208]

Although Bishop Kennedy is not known to have actively resisted

[202] *A.P.S.*, II. 50.   [203] *Ibid.*, 52.
[204] Dunlop, *Bishop Kennedy*, pp. 324, 326.   [205] *A.P.S.*, II. 46.
[206] Dunlop, *Bishop Kennedy*, pp. 188-9.   [207] P. 351 above.
[208] *A.P.S.*, II. 83-4.

the crown's growing influence over ecclesiastical appointments it may be surmised that he had no sympathy for developments that tended towards royal domination over the kirk. It has been pointed out that 'Kennedy's absence from the royal councils during the last years of the king's reign is both marked and significant' though it 'was not unrelieved'. Certainly there 'was no fundamental breach between the two cousins' (James II and Kennedy) and it may well have been the case that 'Kennedy's seclusion from political life was largely self-imposed in order to devote his energies to the things of education and religion'.[209] As 'ordinary' of the diocese of St Andrews he was appointed by the parliament of March 1458 to sit with the chancellor (George Shoreswood, Bishop of Brechin) on a commission of inquiry that was to investigate and reform hospitals. The most obvious result of this visitation seems to have been the annexation of the revenues of the decayed hospital of Soutra to the new Trinity College Hospital that Mary of Guelders was to found in Edinburgh shortly afterwards.[210] Kennedy was also associated with the queen in patronising the Observant Franciscans. This branch of the Franciscans had been founded by St Bernardino of Siena (d. 1444), the great mission preacher of the age. The Observants, like the earlier 'Spiritual' Franciscans, differed from the established 'Conventuals' in their eagerness to observe the original ideals of St Francis. By 1458 they were settled in a friary in Edinburgh; about the same time Kennedy established another in St Andrews; and in 1460 a third was set up in Perth.[211] The Observants were more successful than the thirteenth-century Franciscans in maintaining an ascetic tradition and 'brought a wind of spiritual revival to Scotland'.[212]

While it was to Bishop Kennedy's credit that he favoured the new evangelical movement, his contribution to higher learning— still primarily a concern of the kirk—was more significant and more personal. As Bishop of St Andrews Kennedy was also chancellor of the university. His advent came at a time when there were clashes between town and gown, chiefly over questions of the university's jurisdiction. In May 1444 Kennedy held an enquiry in the tolbooth of St Andrews and as arbiter produced a 'contract of peace'.[213] His

---

209 Dunlop, *Bishop Kennedy*, pp. 192, 194.
210 *A.P.S.*, II. 49. For the background see Dunlop, *Bishop Kennedy*, pp. 406–10; Coulton, *Scottish Abbeys*, p. 228; Easson, *Religious Houses*, p. 143.
211 A. R. MacEwen, *History of the Church in Scotland*, I. 364–5; Easson, *Religious Houses*, pp. 109–13.
212 Durkan, *Bishop Turnbull*, p. 58.   213 Dunlop, *Bishop Kennedy*, p. 271.

efforts to bring the faculty of arts under the control of the university were less successful.[214] Another deep-seated problem was that of the rival pedagogies: in 1454, at Kennedy's suggestion, it was agreed that one united pedagogy should be established for a trial period of five years, later extended for a further two in the hope of repressing the quarrels of the masters and the 'dissoluteness of scholars'.[215]

Kennedy's generation was one that regarded higher education as a panacea for the ills of both kirk and kingdom. James II, who had confirmed the privileges of St Andrews University in 1445,[216] aided his staunch supporter, Bishop Turnbull, to set up a new university at Glasgow. On 7 January 1451, in response to the royal petition, Nicholas V issued a bull conferring upon the new university all the privileges and immunities enjoyed by the university of Bologna, with which he himself had been associated.[217] The Auchinleck chronicler tells how the bull 'was proclamit at the croce of Glasqu on the Trinite Sonday the XX day of June. And on the morne thar was cryit ane gret indulgence' [218]—the jubilee indulgence, from which the new university perhaps indirectly benefited. In April 1453, the king, who had erected the city and barony of Glasgow into a regality in 1450,[219] took the university under his protection, and in December the bishop, now a lord of regality, granted a charter of privileges.[220] Although Bologna had been intended as a model for the new university its first teachers, such as William Elphinstone, dean of the faculty of arts and father of the famous future Bishop of Aberdeen,[221] and Andrew of Durisdeer, who succeeded Turnbull as Bishop of Glasgow, were better acquainted with conditions in St Andrews, Louvain, Cologne and Paris. Durisdeer had been a member of the household of Cardinal d'Estouteville, who carried out a reform of the university of Paris in 1452, and this reform is reflected in the Glasgow statutes.[222]

While it may be inferred that instruction in theology and medicine was available in Glasgow it was probably the intention that the university would specialise (like Bologna) in legal studies, and that the western Scottish university would thus be 'complementary to that in the east', where theology was dominant among the higher

---

[214] *St Andrews Acta*, I. xxvi–xxix.
[215] Dunlop, *Bishop Kennedy*, pp. 289, 293–4.   [216] *Ibid.*, p. 272.
[217] *Glasgow Registrum*, II. No. 361; Dunlop, *Bishop Kennedy*, p. 276; Durkan, *Bishop Turnbull*, p. 36.
[218] *Chron. Auchinleck*, pp. 16–7, 45.   [219] Dunlop, *Bishop Kennedy*, p. 119.
[220] *Glasgow Registrum*, II. Nos. 353, 356.
[221] Dunlop, *Bishop Kennedy*, p. 278.
[222] Durkan, *Bishop Turnbull*, pp. 34–44. The cardinal appears to have been well known among Scottish ecclesiastics (Cameron, *Apostolic Camera*, p. xxii).

faculties. Probably through lack of sufficient post-graduate students such specialisation did not take place : 'both universities in the fifteenth century had a struggle to maintain their existence, and in both the faculty of arts was the preponderating element'.[223] At first it seemed that there would be rivalry between east and west; but initial fears in St Andrews must have been allayed when the death of Bishop Turnbull in 1454 deprived Glasgow of powerful patronage. Some encouragement was forthcoming in 1460 when Lord Hamilton granted a tenement adjacent to the Dominican friary, where the faculty of arts built a regular 'college of the faculty' or 'pedagogium'. The existence of this common hall of residence, which could practically be equated with the university, prevented the development of private pedagogies run by regent masters, so that there was 'more homogeneity in the Glasgow tradition than at St Andrews'.[224]

There, indeed, Bishop Kennedy had followed the opposite course by adding to the existing diversity, for on 27 August 1450, a few months before the foundation of Glasgow University, Kennedy had founded the college of St Salvator and endowed it from the income of four parsonages. The college was to have thirteen foundationers. Three, including the provost, were to be theologians; four were to be masters of arts in holy orders; and six were to be poor clerks studying in the university. Eventually there were also 'commoners' who were fee-paying students not on the establishment. The subordination of the new institution to the university was achieved by provision for a yearly visitation by university representatives.[225]

What made St Salvator's a 'college' in the usual fifteenth-century sense of the term was not its educational function but its corporate character and the fact that the duties of this corporation included the ministrations of the altar. For besides being an establishment for the higher education of clerics it was also one of a number of new collegiate kirks.[226] It is remarkable that none of these was instituted in the more settled years of James II's reign but that all can be dated to the troubled years of the minority and the conflicts with the Black Douglases, and it was often the leaders of faction who were the

---

[223] Dunlop, *Bishop Kennedy*, p. 277; Durkan, *Bishop Turnbull*, pp. 37, 53–6.
[224] Durkan, *Bishop Turnbull*, p. 58; Innes, *Sketches*, pp. 58–9.
[225] Dunlop, *Bishop Kennedy*, pp. 274–5, 279, 281; *St Andrews Acta*, I. xxii–xxv; R. G. Cant, *The College of St Salvator* (1950).
[226] Kilmun was founded in 1441, Dunglass in 1443, Dirleton in 1444, Roslin (initially and incompletely) in 1446, Crichton in 1449, Hamilton and St Salvator's in 1450, and Dumbarton in 1454 (Easson, *Religious Houses*, pp. 173–88). See also Easson's articles on 'The Collegiate Churches of Scotland' in *Scot. Church Hist. Soc. Recs.*, VI. 193–215; VII. 30–47.

founders, or would-be founders. At Roslin William Sinclair, Earl of
Orkney, was busy not only enlarging his castle but building nearby
what would become architecturally the most striking (though not
the most pleasing) of all Scottish collegiate kirks. Not far away, Chancellor Crichton, who was also enlarging his castle, obtained collegiate
status for the neighbouring parish kirk. While the foundation of
collegiate kirks was largely left to the nobility the burgesses were not
far behind in demonstrations of religious munificence, and the parish
kirks of Edinburgh, Peebles, Stirling and Aberdeen would sooner or
later receive collegiate status. Other burgh kirks were being extended
or built anew. Those of St Mary at Dundee and Haddington, and
St Michael at Linlithgow, scarcely differed from the collegiate foundations of the barons and even surpassed most of the latter in size,
architectural distinction, and the number of their chaplainries. Together with the song schools or grammar schools that were attached
to them the burgh kirks fell increasingly under the patronage of the
town councils.[227] They manifested civic pride and gave some hint of
relative prosperity.

This must have been derived more from domestic than from
foreign trade. Of the sixty-eight burghs of barony that were created
between 1450 and 1513 eleven dated from the last decade of James
II's reign [228] and were doubtless authorised in response to a growing
need for local markets. Confirmation of old burghal privileges, and
grants of new ones, were also forthcoming from the crown,[229] though
not lavishly—Aberdeen, which in 1445 hoped to obtain the right to
have its own sheriff within the burgh, was to be disappointed [230] and
its inhabitants felt some concern for their security. For the burghs
were not immune from the less favourable characteristics of the age :
Stirling and Dalkeith were sacked and burnt by the Black
Douglases;[231] and internal factionalism was revealed in an act of 1458
which declared that no bands or leagues were to be made within the
burghs; there was to be 'na commotioun nor rysing of commownys
in hindering of the common lawe'; no inhabitant of a burgh was to

[227] D. E. Easson, op. cit., Scot. Church Hist. Soc. Recs., VI. 17-9. See also
the agreement about the construction of the burgh kirk of Dundee in 1443
(Brechin Registrum, pp. 90-5). [228] Pryde, Burghs, pp. 51-7.
[229] Grant, Social and Economic Development, pp. 369-70; Dunlop, Bishop
Kennedy, p. 341; R.M.S., II. Nos. 337, 431, 507.
[230] Aberdeen Council Register, I. 14; Aberdeen Burgh Recs., p. cxl; Alexander
M. Munro, Memorials of the Aldermen, Provosts, and Lord Provosts of Aberdeen,
1272-1895 (1897), p. 44. [231] Chron. Auchinleck, pp. 10, 47; A.P.S., II. 77.

'be fundyn in manrent nor ride nor rowt in feir of weir witht na man bot witht the king or his officiaris or witht the lorde of the burghe'; nor was any inhabitant to 'purches ony lordschipe in oppressione of his nychtburis'.[232] Nevertheless even the greatest burghs could not ignore local lords : 'Aberdeen . . . looked to the Earl of Orkney as its defender in 1450 and to the Earl of Huntly in 1462–3, and Edinburgh came to an agreement with Logan of Restalrig in 1454–5.'[233] The king's fear of such tendencies, which threatened the crown's control of its own burghs, probably underlay the act of 1458.

In other respects the relationship between king and burghs was also uneasy. It is remarkable that in the general council of 1456 'The universale burowys of the realme' complained that the poor commons were greatly oppressed by the king's sheriffs and constables.[234] This complaint may have originated in 'the court of the parliament of the four burghs', which, according to a royal charter of 1454 that reaffirmed an ordinance of the previous reign, was to meet annually in Edinburgh.[235] The institution had presumably had a continuous existence from the time of the first known meeting of the 'parliament' of the four burghs in 1405.[236] But while the 1405 'parliament' was a representative assembly of commissioners from the burghs south of Spey, and was apparently free to discuss all matters of common concern, the act of 1454 emphasised the curial character of the assembly : the suitors of the court were to be simply the commissioners of the four burghs—Edinburgh, Stirling, Linlithgow and Lanark; and the phraseology hints at repression of discussion of matters of common concern. Thus the act of 1454, which was important enough to have a galaxy of notables as witnesses, seems to have been an attempt to prune the 'parliament' into the shape of the fourteenth-century court of the four burghs, useful to the king as a source of judicial profits. There are other signs of a self-interested antiquarianism in James II's dealings with the burghs : a chamberlain ayre held in Aberdeen on 14 February 1456 levied amercements of £25 4s. 4d. upon burgesses who offended against pristine burghal custom by dwelling outside the burgh; another chamberlain ayre in Lanark levied fifty-seven shillings for the same offence.[237] It is not surprising that in the parliament of March 1458 reference was made to chamberlain ayres 'be the quhilkis all the estatis, and specialy the pure commownis, ar

---

[232] A.P.S., II. 50.
[233] Dunlop, Bishop Kennedy, p. 382; Aberdeen Burgh Recs., pp. cxl–cxli.
[234] A.P.S., II. 46–7, cc. 9 and 10; similarly ibid., 50, c. 22.
[235] Ibid., XII. 23–4.   [236] P. 264 above.   [237] E.R., VI. 102, 158.

fairly grevyt'; the three estates exhorted the king to have pity on account of the many and great inconveniences caused by the ayres and to provide 'suddane remeide and reformacioune therof'.[238]

Not only did James II exploit the chamberlain ayres but in 1457 he even revived direct taxation : the burghs were stented, and, in addition, loans were exacted from merchants. There is no surviving evidence that on this occasion similar burdens were laid upon the kirk or the baronage. It was Andrew Crawford, a burgess of Edinburgh, who in 1457 accounted for 'the finance of the burghs and loans made, granted to the lord king by the burgesses and communities of burghs, as well in Flanders as in the realm'.[239] The total loans came to at least £92 16s. 8d. Flemish (almost £300 Scots) of which, according to the account, no less than £80 9s. 8d. Flemish was forthcoming from eighty-five Edinburgh merchants, who were repaid in the following year.[240]

The financial importance of the Edinburgh merchants was doubtless based on the burgh's control of virtually two-thirds of Scotland's export trade. The custumars' accounts for the period July 1455 to October 1456[241] show that the total export duties from fourteen burghs came to £3,029 1s. 7d.; Edinburgh answered for £1,908 2s. 6½d., which included the custom (£91 17s. od.) on 1,917 'dozens' of woollen cloth exported from Leith. But the total volume of Scottish exports was lower than it had been a generation earlier, and was only one-third as much as it had been in 1370–71.[242] Economic trends common to all Europe doubtless contributed to this situation, and as markets shrank there was a tendency for restrictions to increase, as, for example, in a statute of March 1458 'anent the estat of merchandice'. Its intent was to limit the 'multitude' of 'saylaris in merchandice'—not mariners but men who embarked with goods which they hoped to sell personally overseas—such men were to be restrained from sailing unless they were resident burgesses 'of gud fame'.[243]

The pattern of Scottish trade remained much the same as it had been at the opening of the century, though Kirkcudbright was now prospering modestly, presumably from the opening of La Rochelle and Bordeaux to Scottish trade after the expulsion of the English from France, which, with the exception of Calais, was completed by 1453. Another feature of James II's reign was the intermittent renewal of

---

[238] *A.P.S.*, II. 50.
[240] *Ibid.*, 306–7, 384.
[242] P. 177 above.

[239] *E.R.*, VI. xlv–xlvi; 305.
[241] *Ibid.*, 113–32.
[243] *A.P.S.*, II. 49.

trade with England, 'with the quhilk this realme has part of com-monyng'.[244] The 'commonyng' was mostly by sea, and there are indications that Scottish seapower was by no means negligible. It was 'commonly repute and haldin' that Bishop Kennedy had spent equal amounts of money upon his tomb, the college of St Salvator, and his 'barge', also called the *Salvator*, supposedly a 'ship the biggest that had been seen to sail upon the ocean'.[245] The English safe-conducts, which become more revealing in the mid-fifteenth century, evidently deal with humbler vessels, though some were of respectable size for their time as reckoned by the maximum tuns of wine they could carry. They included the *Andrewe* of Scotland of forty tuns, the *Renyan* (*Ninian*) of Galloway (sixty), the *George* of Leith (eighty), the *Mary* and the *Cuthbert*, also of Leith (a hundred), the *Nicholas* and *Marie* of Aberdeen (eighty and a hundred respectively).[246] A larger vessel, the *Marie* of St Andrews (one hundred and sixty tuns), is re-corded in more detail. In February 1453 a safe-conduct was issued for this vessel and its cargo, together with its master, up to thirty mariners, four merchants and their four servants.[247] Homeward bound 'with 125 tuns of wine and other lawful merchandise' the vessel was cap-tured by English pirates and taken to Devon. By February 1456 the *Marie* of St Andrews had become the *Antony* of Dartmouth and was being used to ferry pilgrims to Compostela. James II and Bishop Ken-nedy, who seem both to have had a financial interest in the vessel, had tried in vain to secure restitution, the first by diplomacy, the second more pertinaciously, but equally fruitlessly, by litigation in the English courts.[248]

Such incidents stirred the ground-swell of animosities that kept Anglo-Scottish relationships stormy.[249] Pope Pius II, idealistically organising a crusade to try to drive the Turks from Constantinople, which they had taken in 1453, was realist enough to know that the warlike kingdoms of Scotland and England would not take part by reason of their mutual antagonisms.[250] Meanwhile Scottish diplomacy was increasingly far-reaching, complex, and devious. Various factors

---

[244] *Ibid.*, 39.
[245] Lesley, *History*, p. 37; Boece, *History*, p. 383; Major, *History*, p. 389; Pitscottie, *Historie*, I. 154.
[246] *Cal. Docs. Scot.*, IV. Nos. 1244, 1264; *Rot. Scot.*, II. 328, 344, 346, 358, 360.   [247] *Rot. Scot.*, II. 360.   [248] Dunlop, *Bishop Kennedy*, p. 350.
[249] *Cal. Docs. Scot.*, IV. No. 1287; *E.R.*, VI. 498.
[250] See *Memoirs of a Renaissance Pope: The Commentaries of Pius II*, ed. Leona C. Gabel (1960).

combined to destroy the former simplicity of the triangular relationship involving France, England and Scotland. The divisions between France, Scotland's chief political ally, and Burgundy, which controlled Scotland's chief markets abroad, posed diplomatic problems, while the situation was further complicated by tentative French support for the Lancastrians and more positive Burgundian support for the Yorkists.[251] There were also issues arising in France itself that evoked James's personal interest : he claimed that his two nieces had been wrongfully excluded from the Breton succession, and hoped that Charles VII would recognise him as their guardian and let him dabble in the revenues of the duchy.[252] On 8 November 1458 he hopefully (but fruitlessly) instructed his envoys to obtain sasine of the county of Saintonge on the basis of the treaty concluded thirty years previously between his father and Charles VII.[253] Two days before, on 6 November 1458, James had also commissioned his envoys to treat, with the advice of the French king, 'about the renewal of a truce and perpetual peace' between Scotland and Denmark[254]—an initiative that would have an important sequel in the following reign. Another diplomatic initiative was also taken on 6 November 1458 when James issued a florid letter authorising his envoys to conclude an alliance with Castile.[255] In 1456 he had also tried to enlist the aid of Ludovico Sforza, Duke of Milan, perhaps also that of the King of Aragon and Naples. For, so James informed Charles VII in a letter of 28 June 1456, 'we hope confederate princes would concur with us against the English, who are the principal disturbers of the peace of all Christendom'.[256]

When parliament met at Stirling on 13 October 1455 it dealt almost exclusively with defence, and passed thirteen ordinances[257] similar to those formerly enacted in the warden courts that had been shorn of some of their powers in the previous parliament.[258] One enactment made detailed provision for defence of 'the est passage betuix Roxburghe and Berwik' : watch was to be kept at the fords, where the sentinels were to give warning of the enemy's approach by lighting beacons. Another enactment ordained that three garrisons should be maintained on the Borders : one of two hundred spearmen and two hundred archers was to be kept on the East March,

[251] Dunlop, *Bishop Kennedy*, p. 195 and n.   [252] *Ibid.*, pp. 179–81.
[253] P. 289 above; *R.M.S.*, II. No. 647; Dunlop, *Bishop Kennedy*, pp. 195–6; Balfour-Melville, *James I*, p. 163.
[254] *R.M.S.*, II. No. 642.   [255] *A.P.S.*, II. 79.
[256] Dunlop, *Bishop Kennedy*, p. 167 and n. 1.
[257] *A.P.S.*, II. 44–5.   [258] *Ibid.*, 43.

another of the same size on the Middle March, and a third, of one hundred spearmen and a hundred archers, on the West March.[259] The apprehensions evident in such measures were also voiced in instructions of 20 November 1455 that James gave to his envoys at the French court. They were to stress that the English forces which had once occupied Normandy and Aquitaine were now poised against Scotland; if Scotland were overwhelmed France would again be threatened; moreover the time was ripe for a simultaneous French attack upon Calais and a Scottish attack upon Berwick.[260]

Although Charles VII urged peace James renounced the Anglo-Scottish truce in May 1456. Early in July he invaded the Scottish lands subject to the English garrison of Roxburgh and encamped far to the south of the castle on the water of 'Calne'—the Kale, a tributary of the Teviot.[261] On 28 June 1456, a few days before this expedition, James, having dropped his former championship of Henry VI, had written to inform Charles VII that the Duke of York 'had a clear right to the throne of England'; in response to his appeals James had promised to help him to win the crown.[262] Thus it was on the basis of an understanding with the Yorkists that James appeared on the water of Kale. There, however, he was met by mysterious English envoys who induced him to abandon his enterprise.

If trickery was involved (as the Scottish writers state)[263] the king did not labour long under the deception : on 26 July 1456 a letter in the name of Henry VI was addressed to 'James, calling himself King of Scotland', rhetorically asking : '. . . have you lived so ignorant of what penalties await the rebel . . . who is so hardy as to deny his homage to his liege superior?'[264] On the basis of this ludicrous epistle the English factions appear to have achieved outward unity for a few weeks, and in response James set out on 16 August on his 'first voyage into England', reputedly passing twenty miles into Northumberland, winning and destroying seventeen towers and fortalices, and spending six days and nights on enemy soil before returning home 'with gret worschip' and no significant loss.[265] Subsequent special truces that were to last on the East and Middle Marches until 2 February 1457[266] were evidently not renewed; for in that month

[259] *Ibid.*, 44.   [260] Dunlop, *Bishop Kennedy*, p. 164.

[261] *Ibid.*, pp. 164, 166 and n. 1, 168; *E.R.*, vi. xlii, 258.

[262] Dunlop, *Bishop Kennedy*, p. 167.   [263] See *E.R.*, vi. xlii–xliii.

[264] Text in *Rot. Scot.*, ii. 375–6, where, however, the year is wrongly given as 1455 (Dunlop, *Bishop Kennedy*, p. 168).

[265] *Chron. Auchinleck*, pp. 20, 56, 57; *Chron. Bower* (continuation) ii. 516; *E.R.*, vi. xliii.   [266] *A.P.S.*, ii. 45.

THE FALL OF THE BLACK DOUGLASES 395

James launched another abortive attack on Berwick.[267] A new truce, concluded on 20 June 1457, was optimistically extended first to 1463, then to 1468.[268] Probably open diplomatic activity was less significant than the secret consultations that it covered:[269] 'James was plotting with Lancaster against York, while counterplotting with York against Lancaster.'[270] On 10 July 1460 the Lancastrians were defeated at Northampton and Henry VI fell into Yorkist hands. But his wife, Margaret of Anjou, a far more effective leader, was still in the field, and James rightly judged that the battle was the beginning of an English civil war rather than a final triumph for the Yorkists. England's troubles provided an opportunity, and with his characteristic rapidity of decision the king took advantage of it.

His decisiveness was not in this case an impetuous gamble: he had long waited for such a chance and had long tried to prepare his people to meet it by a revival of wappinschaws and encouragement of archery. Those over sixty years of age might meanwhile 'use uther honest gammys'—but presumably not football and golf, which were to be 'uttirly cryit doune and nocht usyt'.[271] From the proceeds of the burghal tax and loan of 1457 [272] Andrew Crawford had purchased in Flanders large quantities of war materials, including gunpowder and its ingredients and 8,800 pounds of iron, probably for the fabrication of guns in Scotland;[273] and in the general council of 1456 it was thought 'spedfull' that the king should request certain great barons to make 'cartis of weire', each of which would hold two guns of the two-chamber type, attended by 'ane cunnande man' to fire them.[274]

There was nothing that intrinsically distinguished James II's military preparations from those of his father, who had nonetheless failed dismally in his expedition of 1436.[275] There were, however, vital differences between father and son that affected their capacity in warfare: the former gave no proof of military skill while the latter, who 'gave himself with all zeal to the things of war', emerged creditably from his campaigns against the Black Douglases and the English. And though James II was 'politique in councell' he did not lack the common touch but was 'fellow to every private soldier'.[276] His passion for hunting [277]—a gregarious sport—no doubt won him popular

---

[267] Dunlop, *Bishop Kennedy*, p. 171.   [268] *Rot. Scot.*, II. 378–83, 393–8.
[269] *Ibid.*, pp. 390, 391; *Cal. Docs. Scot.*, IV. No. 1301; Lesley, *History*, pp. 29–30.   [270] Dunlop, *Bishop Kennedy*, p. 205.
[271] *A.P.S.*, II. 45, 48.   [272] P. 391 above.   [273] *E.R.*, VI. 309–10.
[274] *A.P.S.*, II. 49.   [275] Pp. 293, 323 above.
[276] Major, *History*, p. 386; Lesley, *History*, p. 32.   [277] *E.R.*, VII. xxxiii.

esteem, so also did his interest in tournaments.[278] Chivalry still counted for much, as is shown in the literary work of Sir Gilbert Hay, who, at the request of the chancellor, William Sinclair, Earl of Orkney, translated chivalric French treatises, which he rendered as *The Buke of the Law of Armys* and *The Buke of the Ordre of Knychthede*. These were compiled in Roslin Castle in 1456 and provide the earliest extant examples of sustained literary prose in the Lowland vernacular.[279] When enthusiastic adherence to the chivalric outlook was still a prerequisite in Scotland for effective military leadership, James II, 'un vaillant chevalier et homme de grant corage',[280] had valuable attributes that were lacking in his father, a man of deeper intellect and of severe and withdrawn temperament.

It was with a great host drawn from all Scotland that James laid siege to Roxburgh Castle towards the end of July 1460. The unity that he had achieved, by fair means or foul, was shown by the presence not only of staunch supporters such as the Earls of Angus and Huntly but onetime enemies such as the Earl of Ross.[281] In the same place, more than twenty years previously, James I had seen his force disintegrate; but in 1460 the host would remain united even after James II was no longer there to lead it. His objective was no easy one : its garrison had been maintained at the cost of £1,000 a year in time of truce and £2,000 in time of war.[282] It was a stronghold worthy of a full-scale national effort. On Sunday, 3 August 1460, Mary of Guelders arrived at Roxburgh to inspire enthusiasm, and 'on account of joy at the arrival of the queen' [283] the bombards were ordered to discharge a salvo. James, 'mair curieous nor becam him or the majestie of ane king',[284] stood nearby to watch his cherished artillery in action. When one of the guns exploded he was struck in the thigh by a fragment and achieved an unusual death, being 'unhappely . . . slane with ane gun, the quhilk brak in the fyring'.[285]

[278] *Extracta*, pp. 238, 243; *Chron. Auchinleck*, pp. 19, 55.
[279] *Gilbert of the Haye's Prose Manuscript* (S.T.S.), I. 2.
[280] Cited in Dunlop, *Bishop Kennedy*, p. 208, n. 3.
[281] *Chron. Auchinleck*, pp. 20, 57; Pitscottie, *Historie*, I. 142; *Extracta*, p. 244; Major, *History*, p. 386.
[282] Indenture of 12 February 1453, *Rot. Scot.*, II. 360–1.
[283] *Extracta*, pp. 243–4.
[284] Pitscottie, *Historie*, I. 143.
[285] *Chron. Auchinleck*, pp. 20, 57.

14

THE MINORITY OF JAMES III
AND THE ACQUISITION OF
ORKNEY AND SHETLAND

James II had died a few months before his thirtieth birthday. It was a testimony to the influence of his powerful personality that the great host which he had assembled remained united for a week or two longer. An old prophecy that a dead man would win Roxburgh Castle was fulfilled when it fell to the besieging army; the demolition of the castle—the burgh had already disappeared— marked the end of the English occupation of Teviotdale; hostilities temporarily ceased. Meanwhile there was 'gret dolour throu all Scotland',[1] not least on account of the political instability that was bound to follow upon the sudden and unexpected removal of a powerful adult king.

The surviving progeny of James II numbered five—two daughters, Mary and Margaret, and three sons, James, Alexander and John. The last, already styled Earl of Mar, was about a year old. Alexander, who had been created Duke of Albany, Earl of March, Lord of Annandale and Man, was some six years old and was absent with Bishop Kennedy in the Low Countries or France.[2] The eldest son, James, who was eight years old, was hastily crowned in Kelso Abbey on 10 August 1460, only a week after his father's death.[3] Well might the Pluscarden writer lament that 'our kings are often young'.[4] Another contemporary source laconically states : 'Death of James II.

---

[1] *Chron. Auchinleck*, pp. 21, 57–8; *Extracta*, p. 244; Pitscottie, *Historie*, I. 152–3.
[2] *H.B.C.*, pp. 57–8; Dunlop, *Bishop Kennedy*, pp. 194, 199.
[3] *Chron. Auchinleck*, pp. 21, 57–8.   [4] *Chron. Pluscarden*, I. 391.

Tumult in Edinburgh.'[5] And it has been remarked that 'the very fact that for some months there is a gap in all official records is itself evidence that chaos reigned'.[6]

When the first parliament of the new reign opened at Edinburgh on 23 February 1461 a number of nobles attended to answer complaints or to register complaints of their own. The contemporary Auchinleck chronicler asserts that 'thai did litill gud in the forsaid parliament'. What particularly annoyed him was that the magnates 'gaf the keping of the kinrik [kingdom] till a woman'[7]—Mary of Guelders, the queen dowager. Ten years later, James III, alluding to these proceedings, declared that parliament had confirmed an act of his father's reign which made it a crime of high treason to lay hands upon the sovereign without parliament's consent; parliament had also committed 'the tutory of our person to our sweetest mother . . . and to the lords of her council'.[8] These lords seem to have been Bishop Kennedy, Bishop Durisdeer of Glasgow, and the Earls of Angus, Huntly, Argyll and Orkney.[9]

While deciding that the young king 'suld ay remane with the quene', parliament had also declared that 'scho suld nocht intromit with his profettis bot allanerlie with his person'.[10] The records of the first exchequer audit of the reign, held in Edinburgh in March 1461, suggest that the king's revenues were controlled by the lords of the regency council and that the queen's revenues were delivered to her own officials.[11] Though Mary of Guelders was not allowed to dabble in the crown revenues she had ample of her own to allow her to play a leading part in politics. As a widow she had full control over her dower. When she held an exchequer audit of her own at Edinburgh in July 1463 her officials accounted for almost £4,000 forthcoming from her dower lands, besides large quantities of victuals.[12] Her total annual income may well have amounted to the enormous total of £5,000 formerly granted to her.[13] Certainly she was wealthy enough

[5] Brief Latin Chronicle, cited in Dunlop, Bishop Kennedy, p. 213.   [6] Ibid.

[7] Chron. Auchinleck, pp. 22, 59.

[8] C. A. J. Armstrong, 'A Letter of James III to the Duke of Burgundy', S.H.S. Misc. VIII. 19–32.   [9] Lesley, History, pp. 33–4.

[10] Chron. Auchinleck, pp. 23, 60. George Burnett (E.R., VII. xlvi–xlvii) without justification assigned this decision to July 1462. The entry in the chronicle is linked to the arrival of the 'lord of Curthous' (Louis de Bruges, Lord of Gruythuse) who came to Scotland as a Burgundian envoy at the close of 1460 (Dunlop, Bishop Kennedy, pp. 214–7, 222; p. 403 below).

[11] E.R., VII. 2, 4, 28, 29, 31, 35.

[12] Ibid., 161–200. The rents of the earldom of Strathearn were for three terms, those of the earldom of March, presumably administered on behalf of the Duke of Albany, were for one term.   [13] Ibid., xlix.

to improve the amenities in her dower-houses (Stirling Castle and the manor of Falkland) and to spend over £600 on the construction of a new castle, Ravenscraig, on the south coast of Fife,[14] 'probably the earliest structure in Scotland designed specifically for use with guns'.[15] She also spent some £1,100 on her foundation of Trinity College in Edinburgh, which comprised a collegiate kirk served by a provost, eight prebendaries and two choristers, and a hospital for the maintenance of thirteen poor persons.[16]

The widowed queen 'had apparently come to occupy a position similar to that enjoyed by Joan Beaufort after the death of James I, and in that time of faction the result was equally unsatisfactory'.[17] So at least believed Bishop Kennedy, who, on his return to Scotland, probably early in 1461, reported to Charles VII that the kingdom was menaced with perdition. He had 'found a great division in the said country caused by the queen, whom God pardon, from which there resulted a great dissension between the said queen and me, and great likelihood of slaughter between the kinsmen and friends of either party'.[18] One of the queen's partisans is noted by the Auchinleck chronicler, who remarks that after the death of James II she 'tuke Master James Lyndesay for principale counsallour, and gart him kepe the preve sele'.[19] Lindsay, who had formerly been keeper of the privy seal, was already provost of the collegiate kirk of Lincluden and was to acquire the chantorship of Moray and the deanery of Glasgow.[20] Soon the regency council was divided into two factions—the 'young lords', headed by the queen, and, perhaps, by Colin Campbell, Earl of Argyll, and the 'old lords', headed by Bishop Kennedy and George Douglas, Earl of Angus.[21] Foreign policy helped to define the two factions, for while Kennedy was at first consistently pro-Lancastrian, Mary of Guelders followed a more wayward course.

The vicissitudes of Scottish domestic politics were a storm in a tea cup when compared to those of England. As a result of the battle of Northampton on 10 July 1460 the Yorkists came to power; and in October 1460 the Duke of York was recognised as Henry VI's

[14] *Ibid.*, xlix–lii.
[15] E. M. Jope in review of Stewart Cruden's *The Scottish Castle, S.H.R.*, XLII. 148–54, at 153.
[16] *E.R.*, VII. lii–liv. 　　　　　[17] Dunlop, *Bishop Kennedy*, p. 219.
[18] Waurin, *Anchiennes Cronicques*, cited in Dunlop, *Bishop Kennedy*, pp. 211, 219. 　　　　　[19] *Chron. Auchinleck*, pp. 22, 59.
[20] *H.B.C.*, p. 181; *Cal. Docs. Scot.*, IV. Nos. 1310, 1366, 1382.
[21] Dunlop, *Bishop Kennedy*, p. 233; *E.R.*, VII. xlvii, where, however, Kennedy is wrongly regarded as one of the 'young' lords.

heir while the latter's young son, Edward, Prince of Wales, was disinherited. Margaret of Anjou was by no means content with this
settlement and came to Dumfries with her son to beg 'help and suple
aganis the Duke of Yorke'. In the nearby collegiate kirk of Lincluden,
where the provost, James Lindsay, doubtless acted as host, the English
queen was welcomed by the Scottish queen. According to the Auchinleck chronicler 'thai remanit thar togidder x or xii days. And thai
said thai war spekand of mariage betuix the forsaid prince [of Wales]
and King James the thridis sister [Mary] and sum said that thai war
accordit on baith the sydis'.[22] It was probably in December 1460 that
the Lincluden conference took place.[23] It was interrupted by cheer-
ing news of a great Lancastrian victory at Wakefield on 30 December
and of the death of Richard, Duke of York. Margaret of Anjou
thereupon hurried south with a 'great army of Scots, Welsh and other
strangers and Northmen'.[24] Despite a victory at the second battle of
St Albans on 17 February 1461 she was out-matched by Duke
Richard's son, Edward, who on 4 March proclaimed himself king as
Edward IV. When he defeated the Lancastrians at Towton on 29
March 1461 his authority was, for the time being, incontestable. By
April Queen Margaret was back in Scotland as a fugitive with the
deposed Henry VI, Prince Edward, the Dukes of Somerset and
Exeter, and other notable Lancastrians.[25]

In return for hospitality and the prospect of Scottish military
support the exiles paid a high price: on 25 April 1461 they surrendered Berwick.[26] The burgh, which had been in English hands
almost continuously since 1333, was sufficiently re-assimilated by
1465 to send its custumars to account at the Scottish exchequer; but
since the customs, great and small, amounted to only £31 5s. 1½d.[27]
it is clear that there had been a catastrophic decline from the prosperity that had existed before the English occupation. Strategically,
however, the recovery of Berwick was important for the Scots and
gave them hope of security on the East March. The exiled Lancastrians had not only restored Scotland to its traditional bounds
but had also promised to cede Carlisle, which they and the Scots
soon besieged, only to be repulsed in May 1461.[28]

[22] Chron. Auchinleck, pp. 21, 58; E.R., VII. 8.
[23] For this dating see Dunlop, Bishop Kennedy, p. 215, n. 6.
[24] Chron. Auchinleck, pp. 21, 58; Three Fifteenth-Century Chronicles, cited
in Dunlop, Bishop Kennedy, p. 220.
[25] Dunlop, Bishop Kennedy, pp. 220–1; E.R., VII. xxxvi–xxxvii.
[26] Rot. Parl., v. 478; E.R., VII. xxxvii–xxxviii.   [27] E.R., VII. 364.
[28] Rot. Parl., v. 478; Paston Letters, cited in E.R., VII. xxxviii.

It was now the turn of Edward IV to try to stir up trouble in Scotland. He found a ready agent in the disinherited Earl of Douglas, who on 22 June was appointed to head a mission to negotiate with the Earl of Ross and Donald Balloch.[29] Already disorders were rampant in the Highlands and Isles. After the death of James II 'the first slauchter' occurred on Kerrera, when Colin Campbell, Earl of Argyll, descended on the island and rescued his kinsman, John Stewart of Lorne, who was being kept in durance by Alan of Lorne, his brother or half-brother, described as sister's son of Donald Balloch,[30] the kinsman and close associate of the Earl of Ross. The latter was specially summoned by Marchmont herald to compear as a defendant at the first parliament of the new reign in February 1461.[31] When he arrived he was attended by 'all the lardis of the Ilis'[32] and apparently remained undaunted, for at the end of June 1461 Bishop Kennedy and Bishop Durisdeer of Glasgow interviewed him in Bute in an attempt to reach an understanding 'by treaty or otherwise'.[33]

But it was to Yorkist overtures that Ross paid heed. According to an indenture concluded at London on 13 February 1462[34] he, Donald Balloch, and the latter's son and heir, John, together with their 'subgettez', were at Whitsuntide 1463 to become the liegemen of King Edward, after which, to their 'uttermest myght and power' they would aid him in his wars in Scotland and Ireland. From Whitsuntide 1462 the earl was, during his lifetime, to receive from the English king a hundred marks yearly in time of peace and £200 in time of war; Donald Balloch would receive £20 in peacetime and £40 in wartime; and his son would receive £10 in peacetime and £20 in wartime. They were also entertained with the hope of sharing with the Earl of Douglas in certain territorial spoils. For

> if it so be that hereafter the said reaume of Scotlande or the more part thereof be conquered, subdued, and brough to the obeissaunce of the said most high and Christien prince [Edward IV] . . . the same erles [Ross and Douglas] and Donald shall have . . . all the possessions of the seide reaume beyonde Scottish See [the Forth].

These lands were to be divided equally among them as vassals of the English king, while Douglas was also to 'have, enjoie and inherite

[29] *Rot. Scot.*, ıı. 402; *Cal. Docs. Scot.*, ıv. No. 1317.
[30] *Chron. Auchinleck*, pp. 21–2, 58–9; *Scots Peerage*, v. 3.
[31] *E.R.*, vıı. xxxix–xl, 20.   [32] *Chron. Auchinleck*, pp. 22, 59.
[33] Dunlop, *Bishop Kennedy*, p. 223; *R.M.S.*, ıı. No. 1196.
[34] Text in *Rot. Scot.*, ıı. 405–7.

all his own possessions, landes and enheritaunce on this syde the seid Scotysshe See'.

The Earl of Ross now acted more boldly than ever : according to the Auchinleck chronicler he 'past till Inverness and tuke the kingis fermes and all vittalis of the kingis, and proclamit all the gudis and the landis of the kingis intill his handis and gaf remissionis and respittis'.[35] Although the government was long unaware of Ross's secret league with the Yorkists, it was soon aware of the earl's activities at Inverness, which James III afterwards styled a 'treasonable usurpation upon our royal authority and royal crown'.[36] Earl John was summoned 'under pane of forfalt' to answer charges in parliament. The earl, however, 'comperit nocht', whereupon the three estates adjourned the case until 24 June 1462 and 'continewit the forsaid parliament till that day, to be haldin in Aberdene'.[37] There was presumably no parliament since the king 'did not come'.[38] Soon after January 1463 MacDonald, having doubtless met opposition to his rent-collecting in some of the crown lands near Inverness, laid them waste by fire.[39]

Thus the treaty of London had results serious enough, but hardly comparable to those envisaged in its terms : before it was concluded Ross had already behaved in boisterous fashion, and afterwards he merely behaved in a more exaggerated fashion. His outlook may be compared to that of Charles the Bold : if the latter had no liking for the evolution of a unitary state under a new monarchy in France, the former had no liking for similar developments in Scotland; and the domains of the Earl of Ross had a cultural homogeneity that made them potentially better material for home-rule than the rich hotchpotch of French and Netherlandish territories conglomerated since 1433 under the house of Burgundy.[40] It has been affirmed that 'there can be no doubt that Ross was steeped in duplicity',[41] and that through him Edward IV could 'stab Scotland in the back with the Celtic dirk'.[42] But the Lowland Douglas was equally obliging with a Sassenach poniard, and in his duplicity MacDonald did not differ overmuch from many of his contemporaries. The Scottish government, despite its official welcome to the Lancastrians, seems to have

[35] *Chron. Auchinleck*, pp. 23, 60.   [36] *A.P.S.*, II. 108–9.
[37] *Chron. Auchinleck*, pp. 23, 60.   [38] *E.R.*, VII. 143.
[39] *propter vastitatem terrarum . . . per incendium comitis de Roos* (*E.R.*, VII. 347, 357).
[40] See M. P. Rooseboom, *The Scottish Staple in The Netherlands*, pp. 15–16.
[41] Dunlop, *Bishop Kennedy*, p. 223.
[42] A. Lang, *History of Scotland* (1900), I. 336.

sent Lord Hamilton on an exploratory mission to Edward IV in April 1461.[43] And a few months later Edward was not only initiating his scheme for a dismemberment of Scotland with the complicity of the Earl of Ross but was commissioning the Earl of Warwick, his chief general and diplomatist, to negotiate a truce with the ambassadors of his 'dearest kinsman', James, King of Scots. In September and November 1461 Edward issued safe-conducts for imposing Scottish embassies, whose members, after talks on the subject of a truce, seem to have been escorted home by Windsor herald.[44]

The ambassadors, who included Master James Lindsay, were probably despatched on the initiative of the 'young lords' attached to Mary of Guelders, who to Kennedy's annoyance toyed with the idea of reaching an accommodation with the Yorkists. Bishop Kennedy, at any rate, professed to have met with obstruction from Queen Mary, while 'all the great lords of the realm' allegedly complained that Scotland was threatened with perdition to please the King of France, whose 'exhortation and charge' Kennedy was avowedly trying to implement in fostering a Scottish-Lancastrian alliance.[45] On the other hand the French king's disaffected vassal, Duke Philip of Burgundy, whose niece was Mary of Guelders, hoped that the Scots would support the Yorkists, and at the close of 1460 had sent the Lord of Gruythuse as an envoy to Scotland to advocate their cause.[46] Moreover the queen's policy was perhaps not uninfluenced by personal factors. For it was rumoured that she had had a love affair with the refugee Lancastrian Duke of Somerset, that he had spread abroad the news of his amorous conquest, and that Mary, finding herself scorned, had in a fit of repugnance urged Patrick Hepburn, Lord Hailes, to try to slay the duke.[47] If he tried he failed, but his son, Adam Hepburn, was to replace the duke in the queen's affections.

Adam, the Master of Hailes, was seeking a divorce from his wife, and the queen's relationship with him 'caussit hir to be lichtlieit [scorned] witht the haill nobilietie of Scottland'.[48] After a brief and penitential reconciliation with Bishop Kennedy during Lent in 1462,[49] Mary ensconced herself in Dunbar Castle, of which her lover's father, Lord Hailes, was keeper,[50] and was doubtless the source of

[43] *Rot. Scot.*, II. 402.   [44] *Ibid.*, 402-4; *Cal. Docs. Scot.*, IV. No. 1326.
[45] Kennedy's despatch, cited in Dunlop, *Bishop Kennedy*, pp. 215, 216.
[46] *Ibid.*, pp. 214-7, 222.   [47] *Ibid.*, p. 227.
[48] Pitscottie, *Historie*, I. 158; Major, *History*, p. 388; *Scots Peerage*, II. 148.
[49] Dunlop, *Bishop Kennedy*, p. 227, n. 5; *E.R.*, VII. 78-80.
[50] *Chron. Auchinleck*, pp. 22, 59.

the 'evil and peril' and 'great division' of which Bishop Kennedy complained.[51]

The queen certainly continued to act independently. On 17 March 1462 she had advanced a total of £290 to Margaret of Anjou,[52] doubtless to finance the English queen's voyage from Kirkcudbright to Brittany, which she reached on 16 April 1462 on her way to plead her cause before the new French king, Louis XI.[53] Having bid farewell to her guest, Queen Mary immediately received the Earl of Warwick at Dumfries. There, in April 1462, they talked of 'a long truce, double alliances and friendship', to be cemented by royal marriages, including, so it was rumoured, a match between the queen herself and Edward IV. In May 1462 Warwick sent a report of 'good news from the Scots',. who, in a parliament held at Stirling, were to have appointed envoys to follow up the talks at Dumfries. Because of Kennedy's opposition, however, no envoys were appointed. Nonetheless, at the end of June 1462 Queen Mary and her 'young lords' went to Carlisle to negotiate with Warwick. Whatever 'appoyntements' were made at Carlisle, they were reported in England as having been made 'by the yong lords of Scotland, but not by the old'; the former were believed to have dealt fraudulently, 'as was afterwards plainly evident'.[54] Indeed despite Kennedy's fears of Queen Mary's supposed Yorkist proclivities, it is possible that she, no less devious than others, was merely driving time until the result was known of Queen Margaret's mission to France.

There in June 1462 Margaret made a treaty with Louis XI and in October sailed back to Scotland with Sir William Monypenny and Pierre de Brézé, seneschal of Normandy. Having collected Henry VI and Somerset they disembarked in Northumberland and installed garrisons in the castles of Alnwick, Bamburgh and Dunstanburgh.[55] In retaliation, Edward IV allowed the disinherited Earl of Douglas to harry the Borders[56] and sent Warwick to beleaguer the Lancastrian garrisons in Northumberland. Margaret of Anjou, Henry VI and De Brézé, most of whose ships were wrecked, made a stormy escape by sea to Berwick.[57] Soon the garrisons of Dunstanburgh and Bamburgh capitulated, and Somerset temporarily made his peace with Edward IV. The Scots had, however, engaged their honour to rescue

[51] Kennedy's despatch, cited in Dunlop, *Bishop Kennedy*, pp. 238, 256.
[52] E.R., vii. 80.   [53] Dunlop, *Bishop Kennedy*, p. 227.
[54] Ibid., pp. 227–30.   [55] Ibid., p. 231.
[56] Cal. Docs. Scot., iv. Nos. 1332, 1333; Rot. Scot., ii. 404.
[57] Dunlop, *Bishop Kennedy*, p. 231; Pitscottie, *Historie*, i. 156.

the garrison of Alnwick; and the Earl of Angus had further inducement since on 22 November 1462 Henry VI had promised him an
English dukedom if he would pass 'with hym into his reaume of
England ageyns his rebelles and traitours, for the recoverynge of
the saide reaume and the destruccioun of the same rebelles'.[58] On
5 January 1463 a relief expedition under Angus and De Brézé successfully brought the garrison of Alnwick to safety despite Warwick
and his men. No sooner had Warwick left Northumberland than
Margaret of Anjou once more placed garrisons in Bamburgh, Dunstanburgh and Alnwick. To follow up this success she bargained for
full-scale Scottish intervention. It was rumoured in England that she
had promised Kennedy the archbishopric of Canterbury, and had
tempted the Scottish king with the prospective cession of seven English 'sherifwicks' as well as a marriage between his sister Mary and
Prince Edward. Early in July 1463 Henry VI, Queen Margaret,
Queen Mary, and the young James III set out with a Scottish army
and 'great ordnance' to besiege Norham Castle. At the approach of
Warwick they ignominiously retreated; and it was reported that they
would regret their enterprise until the Judgment Day on account of
a devastating retaliatory invasion of the Scottish Borders.[59] In this
emergency[60] Bishop Kennedy had prepared to take the field in person
alongside the young king. Eventually, so reported Kennedy, 'the
enterprise of the said King Edward was broken, and the said traitor
[Douglas] repulsed, and justice taken on his brother'.[61] The latter,
Lord Balvenie, had been captured and was executed at Edinburgh,
while his captors shared prize money of 1,200 marks.[62] Queen Margaret realised that after the fiasco at Norham nothing was to be
gained by remaining in Scotland. She left Henry VI housed under
Kennedy's care at St Andrews while she herself sailed from Bamburgh
with her son and De Brézé to beg succour from none other than her
adversary the Duke of Burgundy.[63]

The departure of Queen Margaret reduced Bishop Kennedy's
obligations to the Lancastrians; and the death of George Douglas,

[58] Fraser, *Douglas*, III. 92–3. [59] Dunlop, *Bishop Kennedy*, pp. 232, 236–7.
[60] See the fragmentary undated record described as 'Minutes of Parliament'
(*A.P.S.*, XII. 30–1, at p. 31). This record has been assigned to the close of 1464
by A. I. Dunlop (*Bishop Kennedy*, pp. 322–3) but must surely be dated in the
opening months of that year, probably in mid-January 1464, when Lord Kilmaurs
presented a complaint in some otherwise unrecorded parliament (*A.P.S.*, XII.
29–30).
[61] Kennedy's despatch, cited in Dunlop, *Bishop Kennedy*, p. 237.
[62] W. Fraser, *The Scotts of Buccleuch* (1878), II. 63–4.
[63] Dunlop, *Bishop Kennedy*, p. 237.

Earl of Angus, in March 1463, followed by that of Queen Mary in December,[64] left him to dominate the political stage : in some meeting of the three estates, presumably early in 1464, he obtained custody of the young king.[65] The situation was critical : on 8 October 1463 the commissioners of Louis XI and Edward IV had agreed to an abstinence of war, and Louis had omitted to include Scotland. Not surprisingly, as Kennedy pointed out, 'the whole of the said realm was much dismayed'.[66] The bishop, hitherto committed to a Franco-Scottish alliance, soon demonstrated that he, like others, could change his mind, and that he did not regard the French as indispensable allies. Negotiations with the Yorkists culminated at York on 1 June 1464 with the conclusion of a truce to last for fifteen years.[67] Edward IV took the precaution of paying annual pensions, totalling £366, to Bishop Kennedy and Bishop Spens of Aberdeen,[68] whose behaviour in accepting such funds was not altogether irreproachable even by the standards of the time. Edward evidently suspected that Henry VI might again be allowed to use Scotland as a base. The capture of the deposed king in Lancashire on 13 July 1465 [69] removed a major source of friction, and an indenture concluded at Newcastle on 12 December 1465 even prolonged the existing fifteen-year truce until 1519.[70] This was carrying optimism too far; but for over a decade Anglo-Scottish relations were to subside into an abnormal state of relative tranquillity.

Bishop Kennedy, who may be credited with beginning the settlement of Scotland's external problems, was no less successful in dealing with the country's internal problems, of which the most pressing were those posed by the activities of the Earl of Ross. Trouble had again flared up on the western seaboard, where Alan McCoule had slain John Stewart, Lord Lorne and Innermeath, probably in pursuance of the earlier feud in which the Earl of Argyll had intervened.[71] A parliament that met early in 1464 ordained that the culprit be put to the horn and that 'nochtwithstanding the lettres written of befor to the Erle of Ross . . . new lettres be writtine baith be autorite of the king

[64] E.R., VII. liv–lv; Pitscottie, Historie, I. 157–8.
[65] Dunlop, Bishop Kennedy, p. 241 and n. 6.
[66] Kennedy's despatch, cited in Dunlop, Bishop Kennedy, p. 238.
[67] Rot. Scot., II. 410–2; Cal. Docs. Scot., IV. No. 1341.
[68] Cal. Docs. Scot., IV. No. 1360. On 13 July 1467 Bishop Spens was paid a further £133 6s. 8d. (ibid., No. 1371).
[69] Dunlop, Bishop Kennedy, p. 248 and n. 5.
[70] Cal. Docs. Scot., IV. Nos. 1362, 1363; Rot. Scot., II. 418–20.
[71] P. 401 above.

and of parliament chargeing hym that he nothir supple nor resett the saide Alane in the saide dedis'.[72] By August 1464 Kennedy had arrived in Inverness, where the Earl of Ross was confronted with the lords of council and, in the course of a reconciliation, had to confess his seizure of £74 12s. 3d. from the burgh customs.[73] Although Ross did not attend a 'congregation' of lords spiritual and temporal that assembled in Edinburgh on 11 October 1464, he at least took the trouble to appoint procurators, a formality that he was also to observe when parliament met in 1467 and 1471.[74]

The 'congregation' seems to have been an afforced privy council, composed of five bishops, three abbots, five earls, the procurators of another three earls, a score of lords, and, reportedly, many other un-named nobles, as well as a few officials.[75] It is remarkable that this assembly, which did not include burgesses,[76] dealt with business that ought more properly to have been brought before the three estates in parliament or general council. It has been supposed that after 1456 general councils were no longer held.[77] On the other hand it has been conjectured that 'a register of the proceedings of general councils in the reign of James IV and possibly in that of James III has been lost'; and there exist stray references to general councils that met in 1473, 1497, 1511 and 1512.[78] It therefore seems likely that there was con-tinuity between the general councils of the fifteenth century and the 'conventions' of the sixteenth century.[79] Nonetheless general councils may have altered in character : for 'a tendency to omit the summons of burgesses marked the development of general council into conven-tion until the active reign of Queen Mary'.[80] This tendency is certainly apparent in the composition of the 'congregation' that Bishop Ken-nedy had summoned.

Part of its business concerned the working of the act of August 1455 that had annexed certain lands to the crown :[81] it was agreed that the annexed crown lands alienated by James II should be re-sumed by the crown without legal process.[82] Although the surviving record tells only of the act of resumption the assembly had also been summoned 'for the peace and tranquillity of the realm and doing

---

[72] 'Minutes of Parliament', A.P.S., XII. 31.   [73] E.R., VII. 296–7.
[74] A.P.S., II. 84, 87, 98.   [75] Ibid., 84.
[76] R. K. Hannay (op. cit., S.H.R., XVIII. 157–70, at 167) wrongly writes of 'a considerable assembly of representatives of the estates'.
[77] Dunlop, Bishop Kennedy, p. 315.   [78] Rait, Parliaments, p. 139.
[79] R. K. Hannay (op. cit., S.H.R., XVIII. 157–70, at 167–8). For the nature of these conventions see A.P.S., II. 594, 598, 606.
[80] Rait, Parliaments, p. 139.   [81] Pp. 378–9 above.   [82] A.P.S., II. 84.

justice'.[83] A parliament that had met some months earlier had thought it 'speidfull' that three sessions be held each year, one in Edinburgh, another in Perth, and another in Aberdeen, to deal with civil cases which had arisen since 'the cessing of the last sessionis',[84] presumably those which, according to the Auchinleck chronicler, the first parliament of the reign had 'ordanit . . . to sit' at Aberdeen, Perth and Edinburgh.[85]

While Bishop Kennedy could wholeheartedly promote justice by trying to revive the sessions, and could likewise show zeal in securing the crown's landed patrimony by the act of resumption, his attitude towards the crown's control of ecclesiastical patronage was ambiguous. At the Edinburgh parliament of October 1462, which he must have attended,[86] he did not lend his name to a re-assertion of the extended rights of the crown during episcopal vacancies that had been won by James II towards the close of his reign.[87] Perhaps Kennedy saw a man after his own heart in his nephew, Patrick Graham, to whom he lent his support when the bishopric of Brechin became vacant : Graham, who had 'academic qualifications and a local family influence', but apparently no previous experience in royal service, was provided to Brechin on 28 March 1463.[88] When Kennedy died on 24 May 1465 it was Patrick Graham who was to succeed him as Bishop of St Andrews.

With the possible exception of the advancement of Patrick Graham, Bishop Kennedy's achievements in the last year and a half of his life, the only period when he was undisputed head of government, support the testimony of Pitscottie that he was 'maist abill of ony lord . . . to gif ane wyse consall or ane ansuer . . . and spetiallie in the tyme of parliament . . . [in dealing with] trubillis that appeirit [in] the realm, and spetiallie contrair the leisemajestie'.[89] Certainly the minority of James III, despite squabbles and disaffection, had not lapsed into the anarchy that had marked the minority of James II when Kennedy's influence was more circumscribed. At his death the crown was outwardly strong, not least, perhaps, on account of the recovery of the late queen's dower lands : in 1462 the bailies of the crown lands had accounted for money rents of slightly less than

[83] *Ibid.*   [84] 'Minutes of Parliament' (*ibid.*, XII. 31).
[85] *Chron. Auchinleck*, pp. 22, 59.
[86] Kennedy was in Edinburgh at the time (see his itinerary, Dunlop, *Bishop Kennedy*, p. 435).
[87] *A.P.S.*, II. 83–4. Nor had Kennedy witnessed the act of the provincial council of 1459 on which the 1462 act was based (p. 385 above).
[88] Dunlop, *Bishop Kennedy*, pp. 251–2.   [89] Pitscottie, *Historie*, I. 160.

£3,000 a year;[90] in 1465 the crown rents, exclusive of victuals, though inclusive of heavy arrears,[91] were yielding over £7,500 a year.[92]

There were tempting pickings for those who remained to share power when the successive deaths of Angus, Queen Mary, and Bishop Kennedy left the thirteen-year-old king at the mercy of lesser politicians. If outward respectability was maintained it was thanks to the continuity supplied by professional civil servants : Andrew Stewart, Lord Avondale, an illegitimate descendant of Duke Murdoch of Albany, served as chancellor from 1460 to 1482 ; Archibald Whitelaw, archdeacon of Lothian, was secretary from 1462 to 1493.[93] Other steadying influences were provided by the Abbot of Holyrood and Colin Campbell, Earl of Argyll, master of the royal household since 1464,[94] both of whom were fairly active in government and served as auditors of exchequer.[95] Lord Livingston, chamberlain from 1454 to 1467,[96] was a former leader of faction who had not altogether mended his ways; and more volatile politicians were to be found among the Kennedies and Boyds, who took advantage of the aloofness of the earls in order to emulate the example set by the Livingstons and Crichtons during the minority of the previous reign.

Robert, Lord Boyd, son of the Sir Thomas Boyd slain by Alexander Stewart in 1439, and himself probably the slayer of Sir James Stewart at Drumglass in 1445, held a territorial power centred on Kilmarnock.[97] In 1463 and 1464 he had been a member of Scottish embassies to England alongside his more prominent younger brother, Sir Alexander Boyd of Drumcoll,[98] who by June 1466 was evidently one of the lords of council and was serving for the second time as one of the auditors at exchequer.[99] In 1464, moreover, Sir Alexander had been appointed captain of Edinburgh Castle with an annual fee of two hundred marks.[100] He seems also to have been appointed to instruct the young king in chivalric exercises[101] and was certainly by March 1466 chamberlain of the royal household.[102] Thus he had

[90] The total was about £4,300; but all save one of the accounts ran for three terms, thus the yearly income was about £2,800 (*E.R.*, vii. 107-36).
[91] The arrears of Galloway alone were £729 8s. 6¼d. (*ibid.*, 308).
[92] *Ibid.*, 308-61. In this estimate allowance has been made for the fact that some of the accounts run for more than two terms.
[93] *H.B.C.*, pp. 175, 186.   [94] *Cal. Docs. Scot.*, iv. No. 1341.
[95] *E.R.*, vii. 107, 302, 308, 380, 520.   [96] *H.B.C.*, p. 179.
[97] *Scots Peerage*, vi. 141-2; p. 327 above.
[98] *Cal. Docs. Scot.*, iv. No. 1341; *Rot. Scot.*, ii. 409.
[99] *E.R.*, vii. 302, 380, 424.   [100] *Ibid.*, 284, 362, 422.
[101] *Ibid.*, lvii.   [102] *R.M.S.*, ii. No. 867; see p. 365, No. 40.

control of the chief stronghold in the kingdom and easy access to the king.

The implications of this potentially dangerous situation do not seem to have been realised by Bishop Kennedy, who throughout his career had by no means neglected to promote the interests of his own elder brother, Gilbert, Lord Kennedy, and the other members of his prolific kin. Lord Kennedy, who in 1463 had been granted the custody of Stirling Castle with an annual fee of £80,[103] began to figure in 1465 as a frequent witness to royal charters.[104] There was every reason to suppose that, reinforced by his numerous and well-placed kinsmen and by his royal descent, he would step into the shoes of his younger brother the late bishop. Nor were the Boyds expected to oppose such a move : Sir Alexander Boyd had married a certain Janet Kennedy; and Lord Boyd's son and heir, Thomas, was contracted on 20 January 1465 to marry the youngest daughter of Lord Kennedy.[105]

An indenture sealed at Stirling on 10 February 1466 [106] gives a revealing picture of contemporary politics and shows that the dominant Kennedies and Boyds had momentarily to share power with Lord Fleming. It made mention of other bonds that were to be respected by the various parties : Lord Fleming had made earlier 'bandis' with Lord Livingston and Lord Hamilton; Lord Kennedy and Sir Alexander Boyd had made bonds with the Earl of Crawford, Lord Montgomery, Lord Maxwell, Lord Boyd, Lord Livingston, Lord Hamilton and Lord Cathcart, as well as with Patrick Graham, the new Bishop of St Andrews. Other records show that the last-named, on 30 June 1466, used a marriage contract as a vehicle for an indenture of alliance between himself and the Earl of Morton,[107] who in turn would receive from Hugh Douglas of Borg in 1474 a bond of manrent promising service in peace and war against all persons save the king.[108] It is perhaps no mere accident of survival that from about 1460 onwards there is increasing evidence of the bonds of alliance and manrent by which men of rank sought in shifting times to achieve, at the least, security, and, at the most, political power and the prizes that went with it.

In the indenture of 10 February 1466 that bound Lord Kennedy and Sir Alexander Boyd in an alliance with Lord Fleming, it was agreed that these three nobles and their 'kyn, friendis and men' would

103 *E.R.*, vii. 346, 392.
104 *R.M.S.*, ii. Nos. 832–75, *passim*; see also p. 365, No. 20.
105 *Scots Peerage*, v. 142, 148.
106 Text in Tytler, *History*, i. pt. ii, 387–8, Notes and Illustrations, Letter O.
107 *Morton Registrum*, ii. No. 222.   108 *Ibid.*, No. 227; see also No. 236.

stand together during their respective lifetimes 'in all thair caussis and querell, leifull and honest . . . aganis al maner of persones . . . thair allegiance til our soveran lord alanerly outan [excepted]'.[109] The addition of the last phrase shows that this particular bond was not one that directly menaced the monarchy but one designed to turn the royal minority to good account by sharing the spoils of political power. It was agreed that Lord Fleming should be 'of special service and of cunsail to the kyng' as long as Lord Kennedy and Sir Alexander Boyd were in the king's council. Fleming undertook that he would not 'tak away the kyngis person fra the saidis Lord Kennedy and Sir Alexander', nor would he aid anyone else to do so but would warn them of any such plot. He would also advise the king 'to be hertly and kyndly to the foirsaidis Lord Kenedy and Sir Alexander, to thair barnis [children] and friendis'. In return, if some suitable royal office should happen to fall vacant, Fleming was to be 'furderit thairto for his reward', while in preference to anyone else he was to have wards, reliefs, marriages or offices for a reasonable composition. The parties to the indenture thereupon gave their oaths to observe its terms without fraud or guile, having sealed it and touched the gospels.[110]

The upshot came a few months later while the exchequer audit was being held at Linlithgow.[111] According to Buchanan, the earliest writer to describe the incident, the young king was taken from the exchequer on a hunting party; when Lord Kennedy suspected that all was not well he was felled by a blow struck by Sir Alexander Boyd, who rode off with the king and installed him in Edinburgh Castle, where Sir Alexander held sway.[112] Parliamentary records show that the abduction took place on 9 July 1466 and that those responsible were Lord Boyd, Sir Alexander Boyd, Lord Somerville, Adam Hepburn, son and heir of Patrick, Lord Hailes, and Andrew Kerr, son and heir of Andrew Kerr of Cessfurd.[113] All these, with the curious exception of Sir Alexander Boyd, were soon to receive a royal remission for their action. For on 13 October 1466, a few days after parliament had opened in the tolbooth of Edinburgh, Lord Boyd knelt before the throne in the presence of the three estates and asked whether his majesty had conceived any indignation against him and his companions for 'riding with him after the exchequer from his palace of Linlithgow to Edinburgh', whereupon the king, ripely advised, announced that Boyd had acted by royal command and that

[109] P. F. Tytler, *History*, i. pt ii, 388. [110] *Ibid.*
[111] *E.R.*, vii. 380. [112] Buchanan, *History*, cited in *E.R.*, vii. lix.
[113] *A.P.S.*, ii. 185-6.

no rancour was held against him and his companions—a declaration that Boyd cautiously asked should be recorded among the acts of parliament and issued under the great seal.[114]

In the same parliament the king announced that it was his pleasure that his kinsman, Lord Boyd, should have governance of the royal person, the king's brothers and the royal castles, as well as execution of the royal authority and justice, until he himself had reached the age of twenty-one.[115] Parliament also appointed 'certane lordis', presumably of the Boyd faction, to have the full power of parliament until 1 February 1467 to deal with a number of matters, notably the marriages of the king, his brother and sister. This commission was also 'to sit and juge the persouns that haldis [withholds] fra oure soverane lorde the king, or fra my lorde of Albany, thare castellis'.[116]

The intended victims of this last provision were Gilbert Kennedy of Kirkmichael, who held Dunbar Castle (the property of Albany by reason of his subsidiary title as Earl of March) and Lord Kennedy, who held the royal castle of Stirling. Before long, Archibald Boyd had replaced Gilbert Kennedy as captain of Dunbar,[117] and by 25 October 1466 the court was at Stirling, where letters under the great seal were issued re-affirming the remission granted to Lord Boyd and his appointment as keeper of the royal person and exerciser of the royal authority.[118] Lord Kennedy did not resist : he was held under arrest for a few months in Stirling Castle, custody of which was transferred from him to Chancellor Avondale.[119] It seems highly unlikely that Lord Kennedy had connived at the abduction of the king from Linlithgow, making merely 'a feint of opposition' and submitting to 'a brief imprisonment . . . for appearance sake'.[120] After the Linlithgow episode Kennedy ceased to be a frequent witness to royal charters. There can be no doubt that he and his kin, on the point of establishing a hegemony of their own, had been foiled by the Boyds, while Lord Fleming was by-passed as insignificant. The Kennedies were lucky to escape with relatively small loss while the Boyds battened on the spoils of their *coup d'état*. What is remarkable is that a further *coup* appears to have taken place within the Boyd faction: after the seizure of the king, Lord Boyd became a frequent witness to royal charters;[121] but his younger brother, Sir Alexander, appears as

[114] *Ibid.*, 185.   [115] *Ibid.*
[116] *Ibid.*   [117] *E.R.*, VII. 494.
[118] *A.P.S.*, II. 185; *R.M.S.*, II. Nos. 891, 892.
[119] *E.R.*, VII. 441, 443, 458, 522, 601.   [120] G. Burnett, *ibid.*, lix.
[121] See *R.M.S.*, II. Nos. 881–983, *passim*, and p. 365, No. 8.

a witness virtually for the last time in August 1466.[122] Soon afterwards he was supplanted by Lord Boyd in the well-paid custody of Edinburgh Castle [123] and retired into obscurity for a year or two until he was made to pay for the misdeeds of his more successful brother and nephew. The latter, Lord Boyd's son and heir, Thomas, had not hitherto figured on the political scene, but was intended by his father to be the real beneficiary of the family's daring bid for power. The king's sister, the Lady Mary, might have been a useful (though costly) asset in international diplomacy. James wept for shame when she was bestowed in marriage upon Thomas Boyd.[124] In prospective cash she brought a poor dowry of only a thousand marks to her husband;[125] but he was created Earl of Arran, and, with his wife, received a considerable territorial settlement based upon that new earldom.[126]

The marriage of Thomas Boyd to the king's sister had doubtless been arranged by the commission of lords appointed by parliament in October 1466, whose powers were to expire on 1 February 1467 :[127] Thomas Boyd had been created Earl of Arran at least as early as 22 February 1467,[128] which suggests that the marriage had by then taken place. No doubt it could be explained away—the report which the commission was to receive from 'certaine lordis now beande in Inglande' probably made it clear that the Yorkists were for the present, unable, or unwilling, to offer suitable matrimonial terms to the Scottish royal family. Hence, perhaps, a decision to marry off the Lady Mary cheaply within Scotland, to keep the king's brothers in reserve, and to seek a continental match for the king. One possible match was already contemplated : for the parliament of October 1466 had significantly empowered the commission of lords to deal not only with royal marriages but 'the annuale of Norway';[129] and this, together with other grounds for animosity between the crowns of Scotland and Denmark-Norway, had formerly led Charles VII of France to propose a marriage settlement on the eve of a meeting of Scottish and Danish envoys at Bourges in 1460. There, shortly after the death of James II,[130] the Scots had proposed incredible conditions for a marriage settlement : all arrears of the Norway annual, which

[122] He witnessed a royal charter at Lochmaben on 13 August 1466 (*ibid.*, No. 884 and p. 365 No. 15).   [123] *E.R.*, vii. 500, 591, 663.
[124] C. A. J. Armstrong, *op. cit.*, *S.H.S. Misc. VIII*. 19–32, at 30.
[125] *E.R.*, vii. 463.   [126] *R.M.S.*, ii. Nos. 912–5.
[127] *A.P.S.*, ii. 85.   [128] *Cal. Docs. Scot.*, iv. No. 1368.
[129] *A.P.S.*, ii. 85; pp. 46, 82, 315 above.
[130] K. Hørby, 'Christian I and the pawning of Orkney', *S.H.R.*, xlviii. 54–63, at p. 56.

the Scots had not paid since 1426 and only rarely before, were to be remitted; the bride was to bring a dowry of 100,000 écus for her 'adornments'; and the crown of Denmark-Norway was to surrender to that of Scotland its rights to Orkney and Shetland.[131] The first condition was statesmanlike but the remaining two were exorbitant. It is not surprising that Christian I, who in 1460 'was probably at the peak of his power',[132] far from negotiating on these terms, took a closer interest in the islands that the Scots openly coveted.

There the authority of the Danish crown had been weakened by a remarkable 'scotticisation', that had gone far in Orkney, though less so in Shetland. This had taken place through two agencies—the kirk and the house of Sinclair.[133] Although the bishopric of Orkney was still subject to the metropolitan authority of Nidaros, the Bishops of Orkney and many of the clergy had long been Scottish,[134] so that 'by 1450 it is thought that there was not a single Norse or native ecclesiastic in Orkney'.[135] Scottish ecclesiastical influence was supplemented by that of the Sinclair earls.[136] In 1434 Earl William of Orkney had done homage to an earlier Danish king but he had not renewed his homage to King Christian, whereas, by contrast, the earl's contacts with the Scottish monarchy had been close. On 8 December 1461 he was summoned to do homage to the Danish king, but although he had recently protested his loyalty he does not seem to have obeyed the summons: in the next few years prior to 1468 'there is evidence that the earl's attitude hardened into outright hostility'. By 1466 Christian was trying to use Bishop William Tulloch and the lawman of Orkney to maintain his authority, with the result that in 1467 the bishop was temporarily imprisoned by the earl's eldest son.[137] Christian (who was faced with rebellion in Sweden and opposition in Denmark)[138] may have realised that the maintenance of Danish authority in Orkney was, for the time, impracticable, and that a solution of some problems might be reached by way of a marriage alliance. Thus a commission of the three estates, which met at Stirling on 12 January 1468 with the full power of parliament, decided 'anent the mariage of our soverane lord' that 'thar be send ane ambassate in all gudely hast betuix this and the monethis of Marche or Aprile next

[131] Barbara Crawford, 'The pawning of Orkney and Shetland', *S.H.R.*, XLVIII. 35–53, at pp. 36, 39.
[132] K. Hørby, *op. cit.*, p. 57.   [133] Barbara Crawford, *op. cit.*, 40.
[134] P. 192 above.   [135] Barbara Crawford, *op cit.*, 40.
[136] For an outline of their history and genealogy see *E.R.*, VIII. xxxv–xxxix, lxxiv–lxxvii.   [137] Barbara Crawford, *op. cit.*, 41, 42, 44 and n. 3.
[138] K. Hørby, *op. cit.*, 61–2.

tocum in Denmark and uther placis'; and this embassy was also to receive from the king and his council instructions 'anent the mater of Noroway'. The embassy was to be financed by a levy of £3,000 granted by the commission 'throu vertu of the powere committit to thaim in the last parliament'. To make up this sum each of the estates was to contribute £1,000.[139] Possibly delays in raising the contribution hindered the appointment of the embassy : it was not in March or April but on 28 July 1468 that its members were named in letters issued at Edinburgh under the great seal. Most notable among the eight ambassadors were Chancellor Avondale, Thomas Boyd, Earl of Arran, Andrew Durisdeer, Bishop of Glasgow, and William Tulloch, Bishop of Orkney,[140] who although he had no official position in Scotland, and was a subject of the Danish king, was doubtless valuable as an interpreter and mediator—he was on good terms with King Christian both before and after the negotiations.[141]

The resulting treaty, ratified by Christian on 8 September 1468, settled that his only daughter, Margaret, would marry the Scottish king. The latter would bestow upon her in dower the palace of Linlithgow and the castle of Doune, together with one-third of the royal revenues—the maximum permitted under an ordinance passed by the Scottish parliament in October 1466.[142] It was also agreed that thenceforth each king and his successors would be obliged to render aid to the other against all parties save existing allies. If the Scottish alliance brought Christian little hope of effective help it at least removed one party from the list of his potential enemies. Moreover the main source of past animosities was neatly removed : for the dowry that Margaret of Denmark was to bring to her husband included the ending of the Norway annual and a quitclaim for all arrears and damages. The rest of the dowry was to consist of 60,000 Rhenish florins. Ten thousand were to be paid before the Scottish ambassadors left Denmark; until the remainder was fully paid, the Scottish king was to have all the lands, rights and revenues pertaining to the Norwegian crown in the Orkney Isles.

This impignoration, which in Scottish terms was neither more nor less than a wadset, was to prove by far the most significant feature of the treaty. There has been some discussion as to whether Christian

[139] *A.P.S.*, ii. 90–91.
[140] Their commission is recorded in the resulting marriage treaty, the text of which is printed in *E.R.*, viii. lxxvii–lxxxvii, and (with translation) in *Royal Charters and Records of the City of Kirkwall* (ed. John Mooney, 1950), pp. 96–109.
[141] Barbara Crawford, *op. cit.*, 43, 49.   [142] *A.P.S.*, ii. 85.

ever intended that he or his successors might redeem by payment what he had surrendered, or whether he merely intended to disguise a permanent cession of a troublesome liability. The latter view is, however, questionable : there was nothing unusual in the Orkney wadset since Denmark itself 'was largely pawned already' and 'mortgaging parts of the kingdom was . . . a common transaction both within and without Scandinavia'. Nor was there anything in the treaty to suggest that the arrangement was meant to be permanent.[143] Moreover in one contingency the treaty made specific provision for the ending of the wadset : if Margaret were to outlive her husband she would have the option, within three years of his death, of leaving Scotland, providing that she undertook not to marry the King of England or any of his subjects; on leaving Scotland she would lose her dower of the third part of the royal revenues, but would in compensation receive from the Scots the sum of 120,000 Rhenish florins, less 50,000 florins, which would be deducted as payment of the residue of her dowry; thereupon the rights of the Norwegian crown in Orkney would be redeemed and the lands would be restored. Since the previous two Scottish queens had outlived their husbands the possibility that Margaret might be able to take advantage of this complex provision was, to contemporaries, a very real one; and the provision (which has not been noted in recent studies) received additional Scottish ratification on 13 May 1471.[144]

There is thus no evidence that Christian intended to cut the link between Orkney and Norway; and his wadset of the islands must be regarded as primarily a financial expedient. Indeed his resources were so straitened that he could pay only two thousand of the ten thousand florins that were due before the departure of the Scottish ambassadors. The outcome was another financial expedient : on 28 May 1469 he issued letters granting to the Scottish king a wadset of the royal lands, rights and revenues in the Shetland Isles until such time as the deficit of eight thousand florins was paid.[145] In this case no mention was made of the contingency that Margaret might leave Scotland as a widow, and, indirectly, redeem the wadset.

After the twelve-year-old Margaret of Denmark had been wed to the eighteen-year-old James III in Holyrood Abbey on 10 July 1469 [146] the Scots were free to make the most of the concessions they had won from King Christian. They had gone remarkably far to-

---

[143] Barbara Crawford, *op. cit.*, 45–51.   [144] *A.P.S.*, II. 187–8.
[145] The text of this document is printed as an appendix in Barbara Crawford, *op. cit.*, 52–3.   [146] Lesley, *History*, pp. 37–8; *T.A.*, I. xliv.

wards attaining the terms they had proposed at Bourges in 1460; and James was soon to show some ingenuity in consolidating his newly acquired rights in the Northern Isles, thereby making the Danish concessions even more valuable than at first they appeared to be. Seven royal charters, issued on 17 September 1470,[147] show that William Sinclair, Earl of Orkney and Caithness, had resigned the first of those titles, and, as Earl of Caithness and Lord Sinclair, received compensation from the king in return for conveying to him the castle of Kirkwall and the earldom of Orkney, presumably with its dependency of Shetland.[148] The compensation included the castle of Ravenscraig (newly built by Queen Mary), certain adjacent lands in Fife, a life pension of fifty marks (soon increased to four hundred) from the great customs of Edinburgh,[149] and a variety of miscellaneous privileges.[150] On the whole James had paid a fair price for his new acquisitions and there is no need to suppose that Sinclair had been forced to resign his rights.[151]

The result of James's bargain was that the Scottish crown now possessed permanently all the comital rights in Orkney and Shetland. When parliament on 20 February 1472 annexed the earldom of Orkney and lordship of Shetland to the crown, 'nocht to be gevin away . . . except anerly to ane the kingis sonis of lauchfull bed',[152] it can have been only these comital rights that were annexed. Nonetheless the king, by reason of the treaties of 1468 and 1469, also held a wadset of the royal rights in the Northern Isles and was thus completely their master.

In August 1472 Bishop Tulloch, already appointed keeper of the privy seal,[153] was granted a tack of the Northern Isles, which apparently included custody of Kirkwall Castle and certain profitable rights,[154] in return for a yearly rent of £466 13s. 4d., of which £120 were to be paid in cash and the remainder in barley and salted marts which were sent to Leith.[155] By 1476, however, assessment in terms of

[147] *R.M.S.*, II. Nos. 996–1002.   [148] But see the following footnote.
[149] The question of this annual pension involves some difficulties: the grant of 17 September 1470 was of fifty marks (*R.M.S.*, II. No. 998); a confirmation of 11 May 1471 puts it at four hundred marks (*A.P.S.*, II. 101)—which the earl actually received annually during his lifetime (*E.R.*, VIII. 120, 190, 191, 253, 312, 390, 466, 546). Perhaps the pension was increased from fifty to four hundred marks as a result of some unknown transaction conveying the lordship of Shetland to the king.
[150] *R.M.S.*, II. Nos. 997, 999, 1001, 1002; *A.P.S.*, II. 101. See also *E.R.*, VIII. xlvii, n. 2.   [151] As stated by G. Burnett in *E.R.*, VII. lii, n. 1.
[152] *A.P.S.*, II. 102.   [153] *H.B.C.*, p. 296.
[154] See *R.M.S.*, II. No. 1376.   [155] *E.R.*, VIII. 224–5.

barley had been reduced, making the total annual rent worth only
£366 13s. 4d.[156] Two years later, by which time Tulloch had been
advantageously translated to the see of Moray, the tack was granted,
during the king's pleasure, to Andrew Painter, Tulloch's successor as
Bishop of Orkney.[157] By 1485, when Painter was still tacksman, the
arrears of rent stood at £374 8s. 6d.; part of this sum was remitted
and the bishop's previous factor was arrested.[158] Meanwhile disregard
for Norse custom was shown by a decision of the auditors of exchequer
in 1476 that the fee of the lawman of Orkney should no longer be paid
save by a special mandate from the king.[159] And if control by the
Scottish crown brought an end to depredations by the Hebrideans,
the inhabitants of Shetland were by 1484 being plundered 'by the
lords of Norway and their agents'.[160]

When the vessels that had brought James III's bride to Scotland
anchored in the Forth, the ship of the Earl of Arran had been boarded
by the Lady Mary, who bore her husband such tidings of her brother
the king that Arran hoisted sail and sped back to Denmark with his
wife.[161] His precaution was well justified : when parliament met in
Edinburgh in November 1469 its members not only witnessed the
queen's coronation but heard charges of treason against the Boyds.[162]
The usually garrulous Pitscottie surprisingly says nothing of the
attack on the Boyds. Nor does the evidence of royal charters, which
is remarkably sparse between February 1469 and April 1470,[163] give
any clue as to the formation of a faction antagonistic to the Boyds. By
May 1468 the latter had even strengthened their position by a marriage between Lord Boyd's daughter, Elizabeth, and Archibald, Earl
of Angus, head of the Red Douglases.[164] If an opposing faction had
arisen it may have included the king's uncles—John and James
Stewart, half-brothers of his father, who both rose to some prominence on the fall of the Boyds.[165] John Stewart was already Earl of
Atholl; his brother, James Stewart of Auchterhouse, was created Earl
of Buchan sometime between April and September 1470, and, in the
only significant change of office that accompanied the fall of the
Boyds, supplanted Lord Boyd as chamberlain.[166] Since the other offi-

[156] *Ibid.*, 363, 453, 483, 614.
[158] *E.R.*, ix. 306–7.
[160] *Ibid.*, xlix.
[162] *A.P.S.*, ii. 93–8, 186–7.
[164] *Ibid.*, No. 945; *Scots Peerage*, i. 182–3.
[165] Both are thereafter fairly frequent witnesses to royal charters (*ibid.*, *passim*).
[157] *R.M.S.*, ii. No. 1376.
[159] *Ibid.*, viii. 364.
[161] Lesley, *History*, pp. 37–8.
[163] *R.M.S.*, ii. 203–4.
[166] *H.B.C.*, pp. 179, 471.

cials remained in office they certainly acquiesced in the attack on the Boyds and may have co-operated in it. The leader of the attack was, however, undoubtedly the king himself; and the attendance of no less than ten earls in the parliament of November 1469,[167] as compared with the less imposing comital attendance at the parliaments of October 1467 and January 1468,[168] shows that the greater nobles were ready to associate themselves with James as soon as he had made his intentions clear by formally summoning the Boyds.

The summons, which must have been issued at least forty days before the opening of parliament, was duly executed at Kilmarnock and the mercat cross of Ayr : Lord Boyd and his eldest son, Thomas (no longer described as Earl of Arran) were called upon to compear on 22 November 1469 to answer for having traitorously abducted the king from Linlithgow on 9 July 1466, as well as for 'the traitorous vituperation and degradation of our royal authority and majesty, in treasonably taking upon themselves the rule and governance of our person and our brothers; and for many other treasonable actions, rebellions, crimes and transgressions'.[169] Lord Boyd realised that in the circumstances his royal remission [170] was worthless : just as his son had fled to Denmark so he fled to England.[171] It was therefore an easy task for David Guthrie, clerk of the rolls and register, who acted as royal 'proloquutor', to produce 'many reasons, allegations, laws, acts and statutes of parliament' to demonstrate the guilt of the two accused. Thereupon the clergy removed themselves, and the dempster of parliament delivered sentence of forfeiture of life, lands, rents, possessions, offices and goods.[172] Sir Alexander Boyd, lately spurned by his brother and nephew, was nonetheless involved in their fall. He too had been summoned, and, unlike his kinsmen, did not escape. On 22 November 1469, when he was brought before parliament, he vigorously denied his guilt and submitted himself to the verdict of an assize of fifteen barons, headed by the Earls of Crawford and Morton. Since Sir Alexander had obtained no specific royal remission for the abduction of 1466 he was particularly vulnerable; he was beheaded on the castle hill of Edinburgh and his property was forfeited.[173]

Meanwhile in Denmark the forfeited Earl of Arran and his wife seem to have received a cold welcome : by February 1470 the pair had arrived in Bruges, where they were lodged in the Hôtel de Jerusalem, the residence of Sir Anselm Adournes. It was probably under

[167] *A.P.S.*, II. 93.   [168] *Ibid.*, 87, 88, 89,   [169] *Ibid.*, 186.
[170] Pp. 411-2 above.   [171] Pp. 476, 479, 491 below.   [172] *A.P.S.*, II. 186.
[173] *Ibid.*, 186-7.

the auspices of the Boyds that this Flemish patrician had been knighted, for his connection with Scotland, which was to be a long one, had begun in 1468, when he had been sent there as an envoy of Bruges.[174] Soon after receiving Arran, who seems to have been joined by his father, Lord Boyd, Sir Anselm chivalrously set forth on a pilgrimage to the east. In his absence Arran sought the patronage of Charles the Bold, Duke of Burgundy, a kinsman of the earl's wife : the Duchess of Burgundy (Margaret of York) acted as godmother to Arran's son. Another temporary resident in Bruges was none other than the duchess's brother, Edward IV, who had been driven from England in October 1470 and was to return victoriously in March 1471. It is conceivable that Edward and his brother-in-law of Burgundy 'saw in the Boyds a means of weakening the Franco-Scottish alliance'.[175] When Sir Anselm returned from his eastern travels he set out from Calais on 4 October 1471 in the company of the Boyds. On their arrival in England, where Edward IV was now happily restored as king, Arran undertook a mission to the court on behalf of the Duke of Burgundy and remained safely in England with his father while the Lady Mary went on with Adournes to Scotland to try to soften the heart of her brother.[176] Their efforts were unavailing. Sir Anselm was to be consoled by a grant of the liferent of Cortachy, and in 1472 the king even granted him some of the lands forfeited from Lord Boyd.[177] Whether by compulsion or complaisance Mary married Lord Hamilton. On 12 July 1474 the king issued a charter in favour of his sister and her new husband.[178] It was not until 1476, by which time two children had been born of this match, that a papal dispensation was obtained to remove the impediment of blood relationship.[179] Mary had also borne two children, James and Margaret, to her first husband.[180] It is uncertain whether her marriage to him had been ended by divorce or by his death.[181] Arran was survived by his father, Lord Boyd, who joined the disinherited Douglas as a pensioner of Edward IV.[182]

Apart from any personal rancour that James III may have felt towards Arran, the disposal of the Boyd lands must have put an obstacle in the way of the restoration of the earl and his father. For the for-

---

[174] C. A. J. Armstrong, *op. cit.*, *S.H.S. Misc. VIII.* 19–32; W. H. Finlayson, 'The Boyds in Bruges', *S.H.R.*, xxviii. 195–6, at 195.

[175] W. H. Finlayson, *op. cit.*, p. 195.   [176] *Ibid.*, p. 196.

[177] *R.M.S.*, ii. Nos. 1060, 1123.   [178] *Ibid.*, No. 1177; see also No. 1178.

[179] *E.R.*, viii. lii–liii. Hamilton's first wife, Euphemia Graham, was divorced before his second marriage.   [180] *T.A.*, i. xlii; p. 512 below.

[181] *E.R.*, viii. l–lii.   [182] Pp. 476, 491 below.

feiture of the three leading Boyds had characteristically inspired a landed settlement in favour of the royal family. On 27 November 1469 some morsels of forfeited property were included among the annexed crown lands, but most of the forfeitures, including Arran, Stewarton and Kilmarnock, were added to Bute, Cowal and Renfrew to be annexed to the 'principality' of Scotland as a patrimony for the first-born son of each Scottish king, so that none of these annexed lands was to be alienated without the consent of parliament.[183] This did not prevent James from granting the queen a liferent of the barony of Kilmarnock. This grant of 25 June 1470 was to pay for her gowns and 'the ornaments of her head' and was a token of James's 'great affection and love'.[184] It was not part of the queen's dower, which seems to have been cautiously withheld until after she bore a child. On 17 March 1473 Margaret presented James with a son and heir, the future James IV, who within a few months was styled Duke of Rothesay, Earl of Carrick and Lord of Cunningham.[185] Probably in thanksgiving, Queen Margaret, whose piety was marked, went on pilgrimage to the shrine of St Ninian at Whithorn.[186] In March 1476 Margaret was to bear a second son, also named James, so that if his elder brother died without legitimate offspring there might yet be a King James. A third son, John, was born in December 1479.[187] Meanwhile on 11 October 1473 certain lands and revenues were at length assigned as the queen's dower with the consent of the three estates.[188] Queen Margaret's acquisitions were not to prove so troubling in politics as those of her predecessor. In practice her revenues were collected by the king's officials,[189] and her expenses were met by the king's treasurer, who in 1473–4 disbursed no less than £757 9s. 10d. for her clothes and a few miscellaneous items.[190]

[183] *R.M.S.*, II. No. 992.   [184] *Ibid.*, Nos. 992, 1340.
[185] *T.A.*, I. xlv; *R.M.S.*, II. No. 1127.   [186] *E.R.*, VIII. 215; *T.A.*, I. 44.
[187] *H.B.C.*, p. 58.   [188] *A.P.S.*, II. 188–9; *R.M.S.*, II. Nos. 1144, 1365.
[189] *E.R.*, VIII and IX, *passim*.   [190] *T.A.*, I. 29–39.

15

PARLIAMENT AND ITS BUSINESS,
1469-1488

The events of 1469 conformed to what was to be the cyclical pattern during the reigns of most of the Scottish monarchs of the fifteenth and sixteenth centuries—a royal minority, or its equivalent in the case of James 1, was followed by an attack led by the king upon those who had hitherto ruled in his name. Within this broad pattern there was a particular similarity between the events of 1449 and 1469 : just as the marriage of James II and Mary of Guelders had marked the king's entry into politics, being followed by the downfall of the Livingstons, so also the marriage of James III and Margaret of Denmark marked the virtual end of the royal minority and the king's personal political career was initiated by the downfall of the Boyds. Although James's subsequent career was clouded by a grave crisis in 1482 and ended tempestuously, it was also interspersed with what were, from the viewpoint of the crown, a number of bright successes of the type already won through the forcefulness of his father and grandfather. A study of parliament and its preoccupations is therefore not one that reveals an uninterrupted progress towards a sorry end; but it does reveal some of the mistakes and mischances that beset the king.

During the reign parliament met almost invariably once a year at Edinburgh;[1] and in some years, notably 1478, more than one session of parliament was held. General councils were also held, though their records have not survived.[2] Those of parliament, on the

---

[1] See *A.P.S.*, ii. Chronological Table, pp. 10-8.
[2] Rait, *Parliaments*, pp. 138-9; *A.D.C.P.*, p. v; p. 407 above.

other hand, are available after 1466 in the extant parliamentary register,[3] which relates proceedings in somewhat fuller form than in the earlier lawyers' collections. One apparently new feature was the recording, from 1468 onwards, of the names of those who attended parliament. Thus, virtually for the first time, it is possible to check the actual attendance against the theoretical attendance. The latter remained unaltered, and a general reference in 1471 to the compearance of 'all those who ought, and wished, appropriately to be present'[4] may have been intended to cover the inclusion of those whose right to attend was not particularly apparent. In the parliament of June 1478, for example, the king's secretary, the clerk register, and the 'officials' of Glasgow, Dunkeld· and Lothian attended, the first two being listed under the heading of 'abbots and prelates' and the three 'officials' forming a separate group by themselves, to which no description was attached.[5] In the parliament of March 1479 the exceptionally large attendance was made up of eight bishops, the Prior of St Andrews (who took precedence over the fifteen abbots with whom he was grouped) eleven earls, twenty-one lords of parliament (including Chancellor Avondale), twenty barons and the commissioners of twenty-eight burghs,[6] some burghs probably sending more than one commissioner. Generally, however, there seems to have been difficulty in securing adequate attendance. In October 1474 couriers were sent with letters 'to the lordis that come nocht to the parliament.'[7] On 24 February 1484 there was concern over 'the estatis and lordis that ar nocht cumin to this parliament to gif ther consale.' It was agreed that they 'suld be blamyt' by the king, for by this time absenteeism was a sign of political disaffection.[8]

The practice of continuing (proroguing) parliament, which was common in the later fifteenth century, was partly connected with the difficulty of obtaining adequate attendance, though other reasons also operated.[9] Continuations publicised a forthcoming session of parliament and elicited the attendance of those present at the original

[3] Rait, *Parliaments*, p. 138.   [4] *A.P.S.*, II. 98.
[5] *Ibid.*, 116.   [6] *Ibid.*, 120–1.
[7] *T.A.*, I. 53.   [8] *A.P.S.*, II. 165; pp. 520–3 below.
[9] An act of November 1469 (*A.P.S.*, II. 97 c. 14) which stated that the continuation of courts (including parliament) was not essential for judicial purposes, does not seem to have settled the question. See in general Rait, *Parliaments*, pp. 329–34. On one occasion in 1475 or 1476 parliament was continued to avoid an outbreak of plague (Lesley, *History*, p. 41). This continuation is not mentioned in extant records, though the exchequer rolls show that there was a plague during 1475–6 and that 70 marts were sent from Orkney to support the infected, who had been isolated on Inchkeith (*E.R.*, VIII. 364).

session. Often the existing parliament was continued to some future date and a commission representative of the three estates was appointed to have the full power of parliament and to meet as parliament on the specified day. Thus on 6 May 1471 parliament was continued to 2 August, when it was to be held by the Duke of Albany and a cómmission of eight clerics, six earls, ten lords, and nine burgh commissioners. This commission, which was given powers of co-option, was to conclude business unfinished in the May session of parliament and deal with other matters 'for the commone gud of the realme'.[10]

There must always have been a temptation to 'pack' commissions (and committees as well), and this was obviously suspected in 1488,[11] but the commissions seem to have been fairly large bodies, varying in number from twenty-four to over fifty, and always representing, more or less on equal numerical basis, each of the three estates; such bodies were scarcely more, or less, amenable to royal or factional pressure than was parliament itself. Since the aim of James III, particularly in the troubled conditions towards the end of his reign, was to secure a large attendance at parliament, there is no reason to doubt that the explanation of the use of commissions was simply that put forward by the three estates in June 1478 : 'for sparinge of lauboure and travale of thaim self'.[12]

The commissions differed only in their unlimited power from the committees that were also frequently appointed in parliament. The record of the session of June 1478 gives a picture of the organisation of parliament in its fullest form.[13] Not only was a commission of eight members of each estate appointed to meet in the coming October,[14] but to cope with the work of the existing session three committees were appointed : one committee *ad causas* to deal with causes and complaints, the miscellaneous suits brought before parliament as a court of first instance ; a second committee *ad decisionem judicii* to deal with falsed dooms; and a third committee *pro articulis advisandis* to discuss and draft 'articles' for enactment by the three estates. Each of these three committees was composed of nine members—three from each estate—the committee of the articles being composed, in the main, of the more consequential members of parliament. In addition the clerk register was to be *ex officio* a voting member of each committee ; with this exception no member of one committee was a member of another. Thus from a total attendance

[10] *A.P.S.*, II. 100-1.   [11] P. 525 below.   [12] *A.P.S.*, II. 119.
[13] *Ibid.*, 116-7.   [14] *Ibid.*, 119.

in parliament of perhaps sixty no fewer than twenty-eight were engaged in committee work. About half of these were also appointed to the commission of twenty-four that was to meet in October, the other half of the commission being mostly made up of members of parliament not appointed to one or other of the committees. Thus, in all, about two-thirds of the members of parliament were engaged on one or other of the four bodies it appointed. It was provided that no committee member should be allowed to absent himself save for reason of sickness, his personal involvement in a matter under discussion, or his exclusion at the request of a litigant. These arrangements (or some of them) were intended to serve as a model 'to be kepit . . . in all tymes tocum'.[15] While the records do not show that it was the invariable practice to appoint three committees in every parliament there is enough evidence to show that each type of committee was fairly frequently employed.

Least frequently employed was the committee to deal with falsed dooms, which seems to have been appointed on only five occasions between 1467 and 1485.[16] In a few instances the decisions of the committee were recorded along with the proceedings of parliament : in 1469 the auditors rejected an appeal against a judgment given in a sheriff court and justice ayre held at Dumfries and amerced the appellants ;[17] in 1478 an appeal against a judgment given in a justice ayre at Cupar was upheld and the suitors amerced. In this instance the judgment of the auditors, uttered by the mouth of the dempster of parliament, was also 'affirmed' by the king, 'sitting in the place of judgment in royal state'.[18]

A committee for causes and complaints was appointed on at least fourteen occasions during the reign, usually being made up of nine members, three from each estate.[19] From the cases recorded as being brought before the auditors in April 1481 it appears that it was not only persons of consequence, such as Patrick, Lord Hailes, but obscure persons as well, who sought its services—one case concerned the disputed ownership of a certain brown horse.[20]

The committee of the articles, the history of which may go back to the reign of James I,[21] was certainly prominent in the parliaments of James III. On one occasion the king seems to have presented articles of his own (as James I had done in 1424), for in July 1473 the estates furnished 'avisment' on 'the articlis opinnit be our

[15] Ibid., 117.   [16] Ibid., 88, 93, 114, 117, 169.
[17] Ibid., 93.   [18] Ibid., 117.   [19] E.g. ibid., 124.
[20] Ibid., 134. See also A.D.A., passim.   [21] Pp. 282, 286, 305 above.

soverane lorde in this instant parliament'.[22] Generally, however, it was left to a committee to draft and present articles for enactment. Such a committee was appointed on at least fourteen occasions between 1467 and 1485. Its membership varied between nine and sixteen, and, each estate was always represented, more or less equally.[23] No indication is given of the method of appointment or election to this committee (or to other committees or commissions). Usually the work of the committee was begun and finished during one session of parliament. Thus on 9 May 1485 parliament was opened in Edinburgh; on the following day the committee of the articles, fifteen in number (about one-quarter of the membership of this parliament), was appointed; on 26 May the report of the committee, comprising seventeen items, was approved by the king and the three estates.[24] It was exceptional that in the parliament of November 1469 a committee was appointed to advise upon certain specific matters, and, in general, 'uppone all uthir articulis that salbe thocht spedfull', and to refer their recommendations 'to the next parliament or generale consail'; since this committee of twelve was to remain in session for two months its members were to have their expenses paid by their respective estates.[25] It was probably the matter of expenses that prevented the repetition of this experiment.

The same reason inhibited the holding of judicial sessions: in a parliament of 1468 it was thought 'speidfull' that a session be held at Edinburgh for one month, and another at Perth for five weeks; three clerics, three barons and three burgh commissioners were named to hold these sessions. But a reference in the parliamentary record to 'the expensis of thaim' was deleted, and the nine lords of session were evidently to be financed unsatisfactorily from the 'unlaws' that they levied in their court.[26] For the rest of the reign there is no other reference to the holding of judicial sessions, nor was there any other move towards the creation of a salaried and professional judiciary.[27]

Instead, the place of the lords of session was taken by the lords of council: it was settled in October 1467 that all cases left undecided in parliament should be referred to their decision.[28] What they lacked in payment for their judicial services was doubtless partly compensated by their access to political power; they were the king's

---

[22] *A.P.S.*, II. 103.   [23] E.g. *ibid.*, 121.   [24] *Ibid.*, 168–73.
[25] *Ibid.*, 97.   [26] *Ibid.*, 92.
[27] Dunlop, *Bishop Kennedy*, p. 324.   [28] *A.P.S.*, II. 88.

nominees, and since they were not appointed in parliament there was no need to include representatives of the third estate.[29] It would seem that they dealt with the same types of litigation as the auditors of causes and complaints, with the exception of actions involving fee and heritage;[30] and the immediate popularity of their court may be seen not only in the hundreds of cases brought before it but in attempts to reduce the flood of litigants. An act of November 1469 (re-affirmed in November 1475)[31] stipulated that litigants in civil actions should first take their suits before the judges ordinary (justiciars, sheriffs, stewards, bailies, barons, provosts or bailies of burghs). Only if the judge ordinary refused justice, or administered partial justice, was complaint to be made to king and council, who would do justice and punish the culpable judge with suspension from office. In May 1474 the judges ordinary were exhorted to give justice so that plaintiffs 'vex nocht our soverane lorde nor his consale with no complayntis bot gif it be on officiaris that will nocht do justice'.[32] In October 1487 there was a further attempt to limit recourse to the lords of council: all civil cases were to go to the judges ordinary, save for certain categories—those pertaining to the king, complaints made by kirkmen, widows, orphans, minors and foreigners, and complaints made against officials. A few months later, in January 1488, this act was repealed on the grounds that 'it wer deferring of justice to mony partiis that couthe nocht get law ministerit to thame before ther ordinaris'.[33] It must be inferred that the ordinary courts were inefficient or corrupt. In November 1469 parliament took it for granted that there were judges ordinary 'quhilkis wil nocht execut thare office and ministir justice to the pure pepil';[34] an act of October 1487 arranged that on the last day of each justice ayre an assize should be held to inquire whether sheriffs and crowners had performed their duties properly; if not, they were to be punished.[35]

It was the justice ayres in particular that were concerned with the punishment of serious crime. An act of November 1475 ordained the holding of the ayres twice a year through all the realm to deal with criminal cases; and this was only one of seven acts passed between 1458 and 1488 that enjoined the holding of the ayres.[36] From this it would seem that against the general background of curial ineptitude the ayres stood out as being worthy of respect.

[29] This is evident from the sederunts (*A.D.C.*, I. 3–79).
[30] *Ibid.*, 4.   [31] *A.P.S.*, II. 94, c. 2; 111, c. 3.
[32] *Ibid.*, 107, c. 11.   [33] *Ibid.*, 177–8, c. 10; 183, c. 17.
[34] *Ibid.*, 94, c. 2.   [35] *Ibid.*, 177, c. 8.
[36] *Ibid.*, 111, c. 2; *Scot. Legal Hist.*, p. 19.

The trouble was that they were not frequent enough. An act of November 1475 complained that sheriffs, stewards, bailies and other officers, had been holding 'courtis of guerra'—a resort to judicial duel under the laws of arms. Possibly this was, at best, an expedient to counter the infrequency of the ayres; but it was held that 'justice aris . . . ar spylt [spoiled] be the said guerra courtis', which were believed to lead to 'grete hereschip and skathe' and were no longer to be held by anyone; whoever disregarded this prohibition would be considered guilty of manslaughter and usurpation of royal authority.[37] It may be assumed that the holding of justice ayres remained infrequent, for an act of May 1485 ordained that 'for the encres of justice and tranquilite' they should be held twice a year (in spring and autumn) 'unto the tyme that the realme were brocht to gude rewle'. In October 1487 there was again an admonition that justice ayres should be arranged 'in al gudely haist in al partis of the realme'.[38] Part of the difficulty in arranging ayres may have been finding suitable persons of 'wisedome' who were minded to execute justice and who had 'powere and strenthe of ther aune' and required only slight support from the crown. In 1487 and the following year it was evidently decided to acknowledge the accomplishments of such ideal justiciars by styling them 'justices general' or 'gret justices'.[39] In October 1487 the three estates had also undertaken that lords of regalities and other franchise holders would not exercise partial justice or make fines with transgressors.[40] This was the only enactment of the reign that directly dealt with the regality courts, hitherto a common target of legislative criticism. It may be suspected that they were no longer criticised not because they had improved but because the government had enough to do in trying to deal with defects in the royal courts.

The obvious weaknesses in the administration of justice during the reign derived not only from the lack of a professional judicial bench but from other causes—the attitude of the king, contempt for law and order in a society where 'maintenance' was taken for granted, and the confusion of the law itself. In November 1469 a parliamentary commission was instructed to consider 'the reductione of the kingis lawis, Regiam Majestatem, actis, statutis and uther bukes'; the intention was that these diverse legal sources 'be put in a volum and to be autorizat, and the laif [rest] to be distroyit'.[41] In

---

[37] A.P.S., II. 112, c. 11.   [38] Ibid., 170, c. 4; 176, c. 2.
[39] Ibid., 176. c. 2; 182, cc. 5, 6. See also p. 523 below.
[40] A.P.S., II. 176, c. 3.   [41] Ibid., 97, c. 20.

July 1473 parliament was again concerned with 'the mending of the lawis for the declaracioun of diverss obscure materis.' The barons besought the king to take two wise persons of each estate 'to fynd gude invenciouns . . . for to declare the daily materis that cumys befor the kingis hienes that as yit thare is na law for the decisioune of thame'. Their findings were to be shown to the next parliament for ratification so that 'at that tyme thare be a buke maid contenand al the lawis of this realme that sall remain at a place quhare the lafe may have copy and nane uther bukis be usit, for the gret diverssite now fundin in diverss bukis put in be diverss persouns that ar callit men of law'.[42] But James III was no latter-day Justinian. Nothing was done to produce a digest of Scottish law; and the only 'mending' of the law that took place was piecemeal and on a small scale.[43]

What vitiated the work of the courts was not so much the state of the law as the general disregard for the law. In May 1474 it was necessary to legislate against the 'gret derisione ande skorne of justice' shown by persons who preferred to pay 'ane litill unlaw of silver' rather than answer charges in the justice ayre.[44] Perjury was evidently common, leading to 'falss inquestis and assisses'[45] that must have disheartened the law-abiding. In October 1487 an act guarded against 'maintenance' by re-affirming a former statute which enjoined litigants to come to court unarmed 'in sobre and quiet wise'; if a sheriff heard that 'ony partiis makis convocacioun and gadering of armis to cum to the courtis' he was to order the illicit gathering to disperse; if it did not, he was to dissolve the court and inform the king, so that the disobedient might be warded for a year.[46] The list of feuds brought to the notice of a parliamentary commission in March 1479[47] shows the background whence 'maintenance' sprang.

Great as were the problems of lawlessness and disorder they might nonetheless have been partly overcome (as they were to be in the next reign) if the king had shown constant determination. At first it had seemed that he would apply himself to the task. The acts of the parliament of November 1469 suggested that a strong royal initiative would be forthcoming; and in May 1471 proclamation was ordered that those complaining of acts of slaughter since the previous parliament should present their complaints to the king, who would afford them impartial justice.[48] By July 1473, however,

---

[42] Ibid., 105, c. 14.
[43] E.g. ibid., 94–5, c. 3; 95, c. 4; 96, c. 12; 106–7, c. 6; 107, cc. 8–10; 112, c. 8.   [44] Ibid., 107, c. 14.
[45] Ibid., 97, c. 20; 100, c. 9; 111–2, c. 4.
[46] Ibid., 177, c. 9.   [47] Ibid., 122.   [48] Ibid., 99, c. 3.

it was evident that the king's interests lay elsewhere; the prelates exhorted him

> to tak part of labour apone his
> persone and travel throw his
> realme and put sic justice and
> polycy in his awne realme that the
> brute [renown] and the fame of
> him mycht pas in utheris contreis;

the realm would be easy to rule if James would

> mak bot esy travel in his
> awne persone in the execucioune
> of justice.[49]

In March 1479 it was affirmed that the king

> is of gud mynd and dispositioune
> to the putting furthe of justice . . .
> and sall, God willing, in tyme
> tocum, with the aviss of the lordis
> of his counesale, attend
> deligently tharto be setting and
> halding of his justice aieris in
> all partis, and utherwais as
> accordis and salbe thocht
> expedient and proffitable.[50]

Three years later it was announced that the king, being grateful for the 'hertfull lufe' of his lieges

> has now schewin and declarit
> his mynde opinly . . . [to] ger
> justice be evinly ministerit . . .
> and apply him to the puttin
> of gude reull in all partis
> of his realme.[51]

The inference to be drawn from these pronouncements is that James was, at best, only intermittently zealous in the execution of justice, though the situation was to change at the end of his reign, when treason was the most prominent of crimes.

It may also be gathered that by his undue grants of respite and

[49] *Ibid.*, 104, cc. 6, 7.   [50] *Ibid.*, 122.   [51] *Ibid.*, 139, c. 3.

remission the king himself set up one of the stumbling-blocks in the way of improvement. In July 1473 the three estates besought him 'that he walde closs his handis for al remissiounis and respettis for slauchter . . . for a certane tyme'.[52] In June 1478 the reason that slaughter, treason, robbery and theft were 'sa commoun throuout the hale realme' was imputed to grants of remission and respite, where-upon the king 'at the gret instant request of the lordis of the thre estatis' agreed to stop such grants for three years to come in respect of manslaughter committed since his twenty-fifth birthday, so that 'in the meyntyme the cuntre may be put in pece'.[53]

Parliament's preoccupation with the problem of law and order was matched by its preoccupation with the problems of the currency and the shortage of bullion : an act of May 1471 affirmed that 'the mater is gret and tuechis the hail body of the realme in gret nernes' ; one act of July 1473 described the king's lieges as being 'bare of money', and another deplored the 'skantnes of bullioune that is in the realme'.[54]

It is difficult to reconcile these statements with the evidence of the accounts of the moneyers : for in the thirteen years from 1437 to 1450, when no great outcry was raised, they coined 48 pounds of gold and 611 pounds of silver; in the nine years between 1460 and 1469 by which time concern was apparent, they coined 21 pounds of gold and 900 pounds of silver.[55] The two accounts that survive for the rest of the reign show an improvement : in one, covering the period March 1473 to July 1476, the amount of gold coined was given as 13 pounds 5 ounces, and the silver as 421 pounds 13 ounces;[56] the other apparently covering the period October 1486[57] to August 1487 shows the amount of gold coined as 8 pounds 1 ounce, and of silver as 181 pounds, from which the king's profits in seigniorage were £30 11s. 8d.[58] It must be admitted, however, that the coinage was not solely the result of the smelting of newly acquired bullion but of the re-coining of money of earlier date. Even so, it would seem that currency shortage was not occasioned so much by a reduction in the supply of bullion as by an increase in the demand for it. Possibly this arose from the import trade, for which there are no

---

[52] *Ibid.*, 104, c. 7.   [53] *Ibid.*, 118, c. 2.
[54] *Ibid.*, 100, c. 8; 105, cc. 12, 15.   [55] *E.R.*, ix. lxii, lxiv.
[56] *Ibid.*, viii. 392.
[57] Mistakenly given as 1487 in the record (*ibid.*, ix. 549).   [58] *Ibid.*, 548–9.

statistics of consequence;[59] but since the export of coin or bullion was restricted (by statute at least) this seems questionable. More probably the growing demand for currency arose through an expanding domestic market : an increasing volume of business transactions required an increased monetary circulation. To contemporaries, however, this was not apparent and the whole problem was seen as the result of a shortage of bullion. Certainly it was one that could have been solved had supplies of bullion been forthcoming to meet the demand for an increased volume of currency.

It is curious that measures were not devised to bring existing stocks of bullion into circulation : though parliament was aware that 'there is mekil bullioune put in diverss werkis' there was no attempt to restrict the conversion of bullion into plate; parliament's concern was rather to see that the work of goldsmiths (who were held in suspicion) should be supervised by a warden and deacon of the craft, who would examine and stamp the works produced.[60] In other respects, however, legislation showed an awareness of possible solutions to monetary difficulties : measures were adopted which were somewhat similar to those used by modern governments.

A number of statutes concerned the 'in halding' (conservation) of bullion. Early in 1464 it was decided that searchers should be appointed at all ports to see that no one carried out more bullion than would suffice for his expenses as far as the Low Countries.[61] In October 1466 the 'moderate expenss' allowed to those travelling overseas was set at one English 'noble' (then worth about 25s. Scots) and this regulation was to apply to clerics as well as laymen.[62] In July 1473 parliament advised the appointment of 'sercheouris and inquisitouris' to stop illicit export of bullion. It also intended to appoint a commission of three clerics, three barons and three burgesses 'ffor the serching of the money'.[63] By February 1484 attention was turned to the 'grete skaith and damage' caused through the export of money by prelates and clerks 'for promociouns and pleis in the court of Rome'. In an act reminiscent of the barratry legislation of James I it was ordained that whoever had business at the papal court should be permitted only the stipulated travelling expenses and should come to the auditors of exchequer to 'mak knawin his finance made in merchandiss of the realme to the avale of the some that he spendis in the court of Rome'.[64] The intention, which was sensible enough,

[59] Import duties (mostly on goods from England) remained negligible (*ibid.*, lxxv).   [60] *A.P.S.*, II. 105–6, c. 17; 172, c. 15.   [61] *Ibid.*, XII. 30–1.   [62] *Ibid.*, II. 86, c. 12.   [63] *Ibid.*, 105, cc. 11, 16.   [64] *Ibid.*, 166, c. 11.

was that trafficking at Rome should be financed by the export of Scottish products rather than cash or bullion. Conservation was also to be fostered by restriction of certain imports. In May 1471 it was on account of 'the gret poverte of the realme' that the wearing of silk (a luxury import) was limited to knights, minstrels, heralds, and those with landed rents of at least £100 a year.[65] In July 1473 parliament also re-affirmed a statute of James II which forbade the import of English cloth : it was not to be received in return for the export of salmon and other fish ; instead the exporters were to bring back gold and silver.[66]

For together with the policy of 'in halding' of bullion went one of 'in bringing' of bullion. Early in 1464, in an act that conflated previous measures, it was provided that both Scottish and foreign merchants were to bring in four ounces of silver for each serplar (half a sack) of staple wares that they exported. The intention was to secure a favourable balance of trade by ensuring that the proceeds of export were not entirely spent upon financing imports. The silver thus imported by the merchants was to be taken to the master of the mint, who would give coins to the value of 8s. 9d. for each ounce; and this procedure would be supervised by the exchequer.[67] Similar measures were approved by parliament in October 1466, May 1474, November 1475, February 1484 and May 1485; the amount of silver to be compulsorily imported varied from two ounces to four ounces for the export of each serplar of wool, last of hides, last of salmon, or four hundred pieces of cloth; the price paid by the mint for each ounce of silver rose from 8s. 9d. in 1464 to 9s. 2d. in October 1466, to 12s. od. in November 1475 and May 1485.[68] In addition, in 1468 and 1473 parliament re-affirmed in general terms all previous acts concerning the conservation and import of bullion, as a result of which it trusted that 'thare sulde sudanly cum bullioune in the realme in gret quantite'.[69]

Another means to the same goal was to alter rates of exchange. This was a more complex business than it would be today, for there were two distinct but inter-related rates of exchange—the domestic and the foreign. The domestic rate was that between Scottish coins and the pounds, marks, shillings and pennies, which were not coins but merely units of account. On this basis there were 12 nominal pennies in the nominal shilling, 160 in the nominal mark, and 240

[65] Ibid., 100, c. 7.   [66] Ibid., 105, c. 15.   [67] Ibid., XII. 30-1.
[68] Ibid., II. 86, c. 11; 106, c. 4; 112, c. 6; 166, c. 10; 172, c. 16.
[69] Ibid., 105, c. 11; 90, c. 8; 92, c. 1.

in the nominal pound. But in addition there were actual coins called pennies, which might be 'black' (composed mainly of copper) or 'white' (composed mainly of silver) and even pennies of gold.[70] Thus a rate had to be fixed between the actual black, white and gold pennies and the unit of reckoning known as a penny; similarly with other Scottish coins such as the groat, the demy and the lion. When the three estates complained in October 1467 that the whole realm was 'gretumly hurt and skathit' since the money of the realm had 'lawer courss than uther realmis about us has' they meant that actual Scottish coins were undervalued in terms of the nominal units of account and that this was the reason why 'the mone of this realme is borne out in gret quantite'.[71] Ostensibly in order to conform with rates in Flanders, the Scottish coins were therefore revalued upwards in terms of units of account—the demy and the lion, each formerly valued at 10s., were raised to 12s.[72] But at the same time foreign coins which circulated freely in Scotland were also revalued upwards, and proportionately more so than Scottish coins. Thus, for example, the English rose noble, which stood at 25s. in October 1466, was now raised to 32s.[73] In fact the Scottish revaluation of 1467 concealed a devaluation in terms of foreign exchange—a natural response to a situation in which it was desirable to attract foreign currency into Scotland.

Tampering with the domestic rate of exchange was bound to cause trouble. Nor was this unforeseen, for in the parliament of October 1467 it was recognised that the upward valuation of coins in terms of units of account would have serious repercussions, since it was in these units, not in actual coin, that all payments were expressed. Thus it was pointed out that 'ilk estate sulde be gretly hurt and skathyt in the changing and heing [raising] of the courss of the mone . . . bath in dettis paying and contractis, bigane annuellis, wedsettis and landis set for long termes, custumis and procurass of prelatis and all uther dettis'. It was therefore ordained that 'payment be maide in the samyn substance and valour'. Nonetheless Archibald Whitelaw, king's secretary and dean of Dunbar, and Richard of Kintore, burgess of Aberdeen, in the name of the clergy and the burghs respectively, requested with some foresight that the interests of their estates be safeguarded if the king 'proclamis his mone to lawer price'.[74] By 1468 there was 'grete romour . . . because of diversiteis

[70] *Ibid.*, 88–9, c. 1; 90, c. 5; 166, c. 10.
[71] *Ibid.*, 88, c. 1.
[72] Compare *ibid.*, 88, c. 1 and 92, c. 1.
[73] *Ibid.*, 86, c. 12; 88, c. 1.
[74] *Ibid.*, 89, cc. 2, 4.

of payment within the realme throu the takking in of the rentis be the auld payment and gevis it oute agane be a derrar price'. There had also been inflation, since 'the penny worthis ar rysin with the penny and mekle derrar than thai war wont to be'. Therefore 'to content the commons' it was ordained that 'the mone have fra hinefurth universaly a [one] cours throw out the realme'. And that 'cours', or rate, was to be the one that prevailed before the revaluation of October 1467. Thus the revaluation was rescinded : the lion and the demy, set at 12s. in October 1467, were to return to the previous rate of 10s.[75] But foreign currency was not quite reduced to the pre-1467 rates, for the intention was 'to draw it within the cuntre';[76] thus the English rose noble, which had been set at 32s. in October 1467, dropped only to 28s. instead of to the 25s. at which it stood in October 1466.[77] In November 1475, when there was 'gret scantnes and want of gold . . . throw having out the samyn becauss it stands here at lawere price than in uther cuntreis', foreign gold coins would again be revalued upwards in terms of units of account and the rose noble would be set at 35s. Simultaneously parliament made provision 'to remove discorde . . . betuix creditouris and thare dettouris' resulting from 'variacione of the courss of gold and silver'.[78]

Apart from the variations inspired by the hope of attracting an influx of foreign currency there were others caused by the unsettled state of the Scottish currency : as new coins were minted, with higher or lower bullion content than preceding coins of similar type, domestic rates of exchange had to be modified. In May 1474 it was recommended that the three estates should appoint a commission not only to fix rates of exchange but to devise new money.[79] In the following year the coiner was to be instructed to mint twelve groats from the ounce of silver, having the same fineness as the new English groat.[80] This coinage was to be minted not by smelting existing coins but from the quota of silver that merchants were obliged to import, for parliament believed that the practice of re-minting existing coins resulted in a loss of bullion through 'the translacione be the fire'. It was therefore ordained that thenceforth no currency, whether Scottish or foreign, should be smelted either by the king's coiners or by goldsmiths, unless by the king's special command.[81] This enactment was evidently ignored by the king, for in June 1478 parliament complained that the realm was 'wastit of money' since most of the old

[75] Ibid., 92, c. 1.   [76] Ibid.
[77] Ibid., 86, c. 12; 88, c. 1; 92, c. 1.   [78] Ibid., 112, cc. 9, 10.
[79] Ibid., 106, c. 4.   [80] Ibid., 112, c. 6.   [81] Ibid., 112, c. 7.

gold and silver coinages, both Scottish and foreign, had been 'trans-
latit and put to fyre'. Because of this complaint the king agreed to
cease further minting until the realm was 'stuffit of bulzeone that it
may be sene and knawin quhareof that new money may be strikin';
he was to take the minting irons from the coiners and put them in
sure keeping 'sua that ther cum na mare hurt to the realme throu the
stryking of moneye in tyme cumming'.[82]

If the minting of gold and silver coins led to criticism there was
even more discontent as a result of the minting of copper coins. In
October 1466 parliament had enacted that 'for the eiss and susten-
tatioune of the kingis liegis and almous deide to pure folk' there
should be issued £3,000 worth of copper coins, four to the penny, to
be used for the purchase of common necessities such as bread and
ale. Since there was some question whether 'white' pennies should
have 'hale courss',[83] in other words be acceptable in unlimited quantity as full legal tender, it is not surprising that the 'black' pennies
were to be only limited legal tender—in the purchase of 'grete merchiandice' they were to be accepted only to the extent of 12d. in the
pound. From the resulting coinage the king made a profit of £650
in seigniorage.[84]

For some unstated reason this experiment soon lost favour and
the moneyer responsible won notoriety as 'Wille Goldsmyth called
Halfpeny man'—for the black money had been issued as halfpennies,
not farthings as parliament had directed.[85] In October 1467 parliament announced that the coining of 'the blak pennyis' was to be
stopped, so that 'thar be nane strikyn in tyme to cum under the payne
of dede'.[86] Nonetheless there were evidently further issues of pennies
and 'plakkis' which contained some silver but aroused suspicion: in
July 1473, it was ordered that, pending an investigation, 'the striking
of thame be cessit'.[87] This was a pious hope: in a signet letter of 23
July 1483 the king ordered payment of £180 16s. 0d. 'to the werk-
men that wrocht the blac money of oure command'.[88] Since their
expenses were so considerable it may be assumed that the quantity of
black money they had produced was not small. It was doubtless this
money that had contributed to the political crisis of 1482.[89] After
the episode at Lauder brig there was a 'crying down' (*declamatio*) of
the placks with which the name of Cochrane, the king's familiar, was

[82] *Ibid.*, 118, c. 3.
[84] *Ibid.*, 86, c. 12; *E.R.*, IX. lxv.
[86] *A.P.S.*, II. 88–9, c. 1.
[88] *E.R.*, IX. 218–9.

[83] *Ibid.*, 90, c. 5.
[85] *E.R.*, IX. lxv.
[87] *Ibid.*, 105, c. 12.
[89] Pp. 499–500 below.

associated. Nor was the process achieved without considerable inconvenience: in May 1483 the hammermen of Edinburgh complained that they were 'rycht havely [heavily] hurt and put to greit poverty throw the doun cumming of the blak money'.[90] The devalued placks continued to be regarded with suspicion: in the parliament of May 1485 the king commanded that 'nane of his liegis refuse thaim . . . nor rase ther penny worthis hear [higher] na thai wald sell for uther money, gold or silver, under payne of dede and eschete of all ther gudis'.[91] Shortly afterwards it was announced that dearth and inflation had resulted from 'greit quantities of fals counterfatit money plakkis strikin in cunze of lait'. These counterfeit coins, produced both inside and outside the realm, were made 'sa subtellie' that it was 'unpossible to decerne and knaw the trew fra the fals'. Hence in response to the request of the three estates the king had given orders 'to ceiss the courss and passage of all the new plakkis last cunzeit and gar put the samyne to the fire'. From the bullion obtained by their smelting a new penny of fine silver was to be produced 'like the xiiijd. grote'; one of the groats would be given for seven placks, true or counterfeit, if the latter were delivered to special receivers by a certain date.[92]

By this time an ambitious scheme, first mooted in February 1484 and confirmed in May 1485, had been devised for the minting of a new coinage. A 'fyne penny of gold' was to be struck of the same weight and fineness as the English rose noble. There were also to be new silver pennies or groats equal in fineness to the old English groat. Ten of these silver pennies were to be coined from the ounce of silver and each was to be rated at fourteen pence in units of account. The new gold penny would be worth thirty of these silver pennies (or groats). There were also to be gold coins worth twenty groats and ten groats, and it was stipulated that all other money should be 'conformit therfor'.[93] Silver groats and gold pennies called 'unicornys' were certainly being coined by 1487.[94]

The enactments of February 1484 and May 1485 that gave details of the new coinage also declared that the king should appoint a wise man 'that has knaulage in the money' to be warden of the mint and to examine and assay the quality of the coins.[95] This moderate measure seems to have been ignored by the king: in

---

[90] *Edinburgh Burgh Recs.*, I. 47; see also *E.R.*, IX. lxvii.
[91] *A.P.S.*, II. 172, c. 16.   [92] *Ibid.*, 174, c. 1.
[93] *Ibid.*, 166, c. 10; 172, c. 16.   [94] *E.R.*, IX. 548-9.
[95] *A.P.S.*, II. 166, c. 10; 172, c. 16.

January 1488 parliament made more detailed provisions for the organisation of the mint and stipulated that its officials be supervised by the exchequer. For in an indictment of previous practice it was asserted that the whole realm was suffering not only from the activities of counterfeiters but 'throw making of fals money that nowther kepis wecht nor fynace efter the forme of the act of the kingis parliament'; and it was evidently the royal mint that was producing this false money.[96]

An act of May 1474 had somewhat despairingly affirmed that 'the mater of the mone is rycht subtile'.[97] James III can hardly be blamed if he failed to pick his way adroitly through the morass of subtlety. Nonetheless the evidence suggests that in currency matters he added a subtlety of his own and became suspect to parliament by reason of his minting operations. And, just as he seems to have failed to execute the acts for the reformation of law and order, so also he seems to have failed to execute the fairly sensible acts for the conservation and augmentation of stocks of bullion. As early as November 1475 parliament complained of 'the pretermitting [postponement] and sleuth [sloth] that has bene in the execucioune of the actis maid for the in bringing of bulzone . . . and alsa the serching and kepin of the money fra passin furth of the realme'. The king was enjoined to see the acts 'scharply put to execucioune' and to 'deput true and abill serchers'.[98] In June 1478 it was announced that the king 'has grantit now to mak the actis of his parliament . . . be observit and kepit, and . . . be put to scharp execucioune'. In December 1482 the same acts were to be 'put to execucioune'. In February 1484 they were to be 'scharply put to execucioune'. In January 1488 the act regarding 'searching' was re-issued in an extended form that made the illicit export of money by Scotsmen or foreigners a crime punishable in the justice ayre. Once again 'sharp execucioune' was enjoined.[99] There can be little doubt that in this matter, as well as in that of law enforcement, James III constantly failed to fulfil the expectations of his parliaments.

The problem of bullion supplies, and hence of the currency, might not have existed if Scottish exports had been flourishing. Customs duties still remained at the later fourteenth-century level: two marks

[96] *Ibid.*, 182, c. 9. See also c. 10. For details of the mint and the coins it produced see *E.R.*, v. 67; vii. 368–9; ix. lxi–lxviii; and the comprehensive works of I. H. Stewart and R. W. Cochran-Patrick.

[97] *A.P.S.*, ii. 106, c. 4.   [98] *Ibid.*, 112, c. 6.

[99] *Ibid.*, 118, c. 3; 144, c. 8; 166, c. 11; 182, c. 11; 183, c. 13.

(26s. 8d.) on the sack of wool, one mark on the great hundred (120) of woolfells, and four marks on the last (200–240) of hides. In addition a few new duties had been levied, of which the more important were those on the export of woollen cloth and salmon. Cloth, as in the reign of James I, paid an *ad valorem* duty of 2s. in the pound, and an *ad valorem* duty on salmon of 2s. 6d. in the pound was raised in 1466 to 3s., and in 1480 to 4s.[100] During the reign the gross proceeds from the customs perhaps averaged £3,300 a year,[101] but in 1486–7 they were only £2,781 6s. 5½d.,[102] less than one-third of what they had been in 1371. In 1478–9 a high-point was reached when the great customs from over twenty burghs came to £3,887 18s. 2½d. (gross). Almost half of the total was forthcoming from Edinburgh; about one-sixth came from Aberdeen, which was followed in order by Dundee, Berwick, Haddington and Perth.[103] Berwick had apparently regained a modicum of its former prosperity by specialising in the export of salmon, in which it rivalled Aberdeen.[104] A mysterious fishy migration that brought shoals of herring from the Baltic to the Scottish coasts provided a new item of trade : Irvine, the port at which duty was collected on the export of salted herring from the west coast, accounted for thirty-three lasts and duty of £9 18s od.[105] The growing importance of the off-shore fisheries was recognised by an act of May 1471 which encouraged the burghs and the lords spiritual and temporal to construct or acquire ships and boats 'witht nettis . . . for fyschinge', so that there might result 'gret encress of riches to be brocht within the realme of uther cuntreis'.[106] Another commodity—salt—was also beginning to figure among Scottish exports. In 1478–9, 243 chalders of salt were exported from Dysart and 145 from Preston, probably Prestonpans. By 1486 the exports from Dysart doubled, though those from Preston remained about the same.[107] Meanwhile the former staples of Scottish exports—wool, woolfells and hides—had dropped in importance, presumably because of lessened demand abroad. These staple wares were no longer exported in quantity from many burghs, and Edinburgh was unique in continuing to specialise in them : in 1478–9

[100] *E.R.*, IX. lxx, lxxii–lxxiii.   [101] *Ibid.*, lxxv.
[102] *Ibid.*, 536–48. . ,   [103] *Ibid.*, VIII. 620–32.
[104] Berwick exported 80 lasts and 11 barrels, Aberdeen 102 lasts and 10½ barrels (*ibid.*, 620, 631–2). There were twelve barrels in each last; the barrels were of Hamburg measure, each containing 14 gallons (*ibid.*, IX. lxxii–lxxiii). For the salmon trade see Grant, *Social and Economic Development*, p. 316.
[105] *E.R.*, VIII. 621–2.   [106] *A.P.S.*, II. 100, c. 10.
[107] *E.R.*, VIII. 627, 631 ; IX. lxxiv.

wool, hides, woolfells, and similar natural products brought in £1,625 14s. 5½d. (about 90%) of the Edinburgh customs.[108] Most of the remainder was made up from the export of 2,326 dozen pieces of woollen cloth, which paid £139 6s. od. in custom. Dundee, which paid duty £36 16s. od., came next in this line of business, followed by Kirkcudbright (export duties £23 15s. od.), Haddington (£21 17s. 6d.) and Wigtown (£17 1os. od.)[109] The ports of the south-west, long the Cinderellas of trade (or the scarlet women of smuggling) thereby acquired some significance,[110] and it must be presumed that the weaving of cloth had become an important home industry in Galloway. Nonetheless, since most burghs, with the exception of those north of Aberdeen, exported at least some cloth, it would seem that this relatively new development had begun to affect most of Lowland Scotland, though its importance should not be exaggerated.[111] The overall picture of the export trade was one of concentration in Edinburgh, increased diversification in the products exported, but a low general level of exports.

Another aspect was the increased interest in trade shown by the barons and the king. A diplomatic interchange of 1475 shows that Sir John Colquhoun of Luss possessed a ship of his own, and a safe-conduct of 1485 suggests that Lord Lyle was about to embark as trader in a ship of fifty tuns.[112] The Edinburgh customs returns for 1486–7 show that Lord Seton was exporting salt, and Lady Hamilton, the king's sister, was exporting hides. By 1473 her husband was reclaiming land from the tidal reaches of the Forth near his new castle of Craiglyoune; he had already five saltpans in operation and intended to construct others.[113] James himself, whatever his other failings, was not unmindful of his own economic interests : it is significant that the accounts of the treasurer, audited in December 1474, were not only signed by the auditors but bore the king's signature, rapidly scrawled by a hand well used to holding a pen.[114] Not only did the king import luxuries from the Low Countries through Scottish merchants like John Dalrymple,[115] but in 1476 he tried to establish a direct connection with Italy by granting a three-

[108] *Ibid.*, VIII. 629.   [109] *Ibid.*, 623, 624, 625–6, 630.
[110] See A. L. Murray, 'The Customs Accounts of Kirkcudbright, Wigtown and Dumfries, 1434–1560', *Dumfriesshire Trans.*, XL. 136–62.
[111] *E.R.*, IX. lxxi, lxxii–lxxiii.
[112] *Cal. Docs. Scot.*, IV. No. 1429; *Rot. Scot.*, II. 464.
[113] *E.R.*, IX. 547; *R.M.S.*, II. Nos. 1140, 1178.
[114] See the facsimile in *T.A.*, I. 75.
[115] *E.R.*, VII. 31–2; Dunlop, *Bishop Kennedy*, p. 357; Grant, *Social and Economic Development*, pp. 321–2.

year safe-conduct so that Jacob Dini and his associates, merchants of Florence, might be unimpeded by acts of parliament in selling their goods to the lords of council and the king's 'familiars'.[116] James also engaged in trade on his own account: 'the king's hides were sent to France and Flanders for wine, his ships sent to France and Denmark, his woollen cloth exported for saltpetre and for wine, and his merchandise sent to France', while 'the armed merchantmen belonging to the king were employed by turn in trade, in war, and in missions to foreign states'.[117] The barley owed to the king as rent from Orkney was in 1475–6 shipped to Leith, converted into malt, and delivered to the king's ships, presumably for export.[118] In 1475 John Barton, senior member of a seafaring family of Leith, was serving as captain of the king's carvel, probably the famous *Yellow Carvel*;[119] and as early as 1477 James recognised the services of another Leith skipper, Andrew Wood, by giving him a nineteen-year tack of the lands and town of Largo.[120] By 1488 Captain Wood was 'principall servand to the king . . . haveand wages of him, and furnist him and his schipis oftymes to pase quhair he pleissit'.[121] If the economic interests of burgesses, barons and king had once been distinct they were no longer so in the reign of James III.

One consequence was the increased involvement of king and parliament in commercial diplomacy. A breach in trade with Flanders was serious enough to receive the attention of a parliamentary commission in January 1467. The causes can hardly be described as 'more obvious than is usual in this period of obscurity'.[122] For they are not to be explained by Franco-Burgundian animosities and the desire of the Scots to show their loyalty to the French alliance. A letter of James III,[123] which has been tentatively ascribed to 1474, but which more probably refers to the breach in 1467, gives only vague reasons for dissatisfaction with Bruges and other Flemish towns, though it is obvious from the acts of the parliamentary commission in 1467 that the sense of grievance of the Scots was acute. It was enacted that from 1 August 1467 no ships or goods should be sent to the Flemish towns of the Swyn, the Sluys, the Damme, or Bruges, and that all Scots should remove themselves and their goods from these places on pain of banishment from Scotland. Meanwhile the king, on the advice of his council, granted

[116] *R.M.S.*, II. No. 1266.   [117] *E.R.*, VIII. lix.
[118] *Ibid.*, 364.   [119] *Ibid.*, lx.
[120] *Ibid.*, 450; *R.M.S.* II. Nos. 1563, 1720.   [121] Pitscottie, *Historie*, I. 214.
[122] Davidson and Gray, *Staple*, p. 132.
[123] Reproduced in facsimile, *ibid.*, facing p. 136.

'tollerance and sufferance' to Scottish merchants to trade with Middelburg, though 'nocht to remane thar as at a stapele' until the king should see 'quhat fredomes and priviliegis thai sal haf in tym to cum at the place quhar thai sal be staplit'. A mission was to be sent 'in al gudly haste and to bring ansuere agane thar apone'.[124] This mission seems to have been undertaken by Thomas Folkert (Flockhart), former dean of gild of Edinburgh, and Alexander Napier, former and future provost of the burgh, who had recently been knighted.[125] They were appointed by the king on 24 April to negotiate with the magistrates of Middelburg.[126] Presumably until the result was known it was ordained that 'al stapele gudis [were] to remane and to stapele and pas to na merkatis', which seems to mean that an embargo was placed on the export of staple wares. Meanwhile the parliamentary commission also ordained that merchants might continue to trade with La Rochelle, Bordeaux, France and Norway.[127] It is curious that no mention was made of the Baltic or German trade. In the Baltic regions there is certainly evidence of increasing Scottish interest : a German chronicle affirms that twenty-four Scottish ships entered Danzig between 1474 and 1476; by 1475 the Scots maintained an altar in the church of the Benedictines in the city.[128]

The disruption of trade with Flanders in 1467 was not long-lasting. In 1469 the ancient privileges of the Scots were confirmed, and on 31 May 1472 the king ordered Scottish merchants to take their goods to Bruges and not elsewhere.[129] A few days later James issued a commission to Sir Anselm Adournes as conservator of the privileges granted to Scottish merchants by the Dukes of Burgundy. Though settled in Bruges (of which he became burgomaster in 1475)[130] Sir Anselm was of Genoese extraction and had been sent on missions as far as Persia, in the course of which, so James believed, he had reflected credit on Scotland and its king, not only at the papal court and in Christian lands, but among the barbarous nations of Saracens and Turks.[131] An account of these journeys was dedicated to James,[132] who had diverted himself in his youth with Sir John

---

[124] *A.P.S.*, II. 87, cc. 6, 7.
[125] *Edinburgh Burgh Recs.*, I. 258–61. Napier was described as a knight in a charter of February 1467 (*R.M.S.*, II. No. 908).
[126] Facsimile letter of James III, Davidson and Gray, *Staple*, facing p. 136.
[127] *A.P.S.*, II. 87, c. 8.   [128] T. A. Fischer, *Scots in Prussia*, pp. 8–11.
[129] Davidson and Gray, *Staple*, pp. 134 and n. 1, 139.
[130] W. H. Finlayson, *op. cit.*, *S.H.R.*, XXVIII. 195–6, at 196; pp. 419–20 above.
[131] Davidson and Gray, *Staple*, p. 134 and n. 2.
[132] W. H. Finlayson, *op. cit.*, 196.

Mandeville's fanciful book of travels.[133] The king doubtless esteemed someone who had traversed strange lands and was ready to overlook Sir Anselm's championship of the fallen Boyds.[134] The commission granted to him as conservator gave him some jurisdiction (in conjunction with resident Scottish burgesses) over Scottish subjects in the Burgundian dominions, and allowed him as salary a tax on staple wares which 'the provosts, bailies, town councillors and merchants of our realm . . . granted to him with unanimous consent and assent in our parliament by their letters under the common seals of the said burghs of our realm'.[135] This grant, made before the king had reached years of discretion, was revoked in 1476, partly because Sir Anselm was an alien, whereupon the king appointed his familiar esquire, Andrew Woodman, as conservator.[136] In 1483, however, the post was said to be vacant by the death of Sir Anselm (who may have recovered the office in the course of the visit to Scotland that ended in his death) whereupon the conservatorship was bestowed by the king upon Thomas Swift, his familiar servant.[137]

The changes in the conservatorship were accompanied by changes in the site of the staple: by 1477 it had returned from Bruges to Middelburg,[138] possibly as a consequence of the troubles that beset Flanders during and after the over-strenuous career of Charles the Bold, who was killed by the Swiss in January 1477.[139] His successor was Maximilian of Hapsburg, husband of Charles's daughter and heiress. Maximilian was soon to be King of the Romans, and, after 1493, emperor. On assuming control of the Burgundian territories he hastened to reach an understanding with the Scots. In June 1478 parliament was told that letters which were 'rycht hertfull, thankfull and honourable' had arrived from the Duke of Burgundy 'for the keeping of fredome of merchiandis of this realme in time tocum and reformacioune of the scathis that thai haf sustenit in tyme bigaine'. An embassy, to be financed by 'the hale burowis', was to be sent to the duke to renew and confirm the old alliance and 'to purchess uther grettare privilegis gif thai can be gottin in favoure of the merchandis'.[140] The parliamentary commission appointed in

[133] *E.R.*, VII. 500.   [134] Pp. 419-20 above.
[135] *Estaple de Bruges*, cited in Davidson and Gray, *Staple*, p. 134, n. 3.
[136] *R.M.S.*, II. No. 1234.   [137] P. 514 below; *R.M.S.*, II. No. 1548.
[138] Davidson and Gray, *Staple*, p. 135.
[139] It is significant that after 1477 Sir Anselm Adournes was exiled from Bruges as a result of these troubles (W. H. Finlayson, *op. cit.*, *S.H.R.*, XXVIII. 195-6, at 196).   [140] *A.P.S.*, II. 118, c. 4.

March 1479 was again to consider 'the gud of merchandice ande sending to the Duk of Burgunze'.[141] The latter was engaged in warfare with France until the death of his wife in 1482, when he made peace. In the following year Bruges made a successful attempt to woo the Scots away from Middelburg.[142] Nonetheless new causes of friction arose through Maximilian's issue of a letter of marque. This was a rough and ready method of securing redress for some commercial injury: it allowed plunder of the ships and goods of all countrymen of the perpetrator until the original loss had been recovered—a procedure that was all too likely to lead to counter-reprisals. The letter issued by Maximilian had resulted from a sentènce given by the lords of council, who, with the courts of the seaport burghs, and those of the admiral and his deputes, shared jurisdiction over maritime cases.[143] The burgh commissioners hoped that a sealed copy of the transactions of the lords of council would suffice as 'verificacioune of justice' in demonstration that Maximilian's subjects had no cause for complaint, 'quhilk may be distruccioune of the said letter of marque'. This was apparently having serious repercussions on Scottish trade, since to achieve its 'doune putting' parliament decided to send an embassy of one clerk and two burgesses to the King of the Romans. Their expenses were to be paid by 'the hale merchandis of borowis' and the burgh officials were 'to speid the inbringing of the said expenss' on pain of imprisonment.[144]

This was only one example of concerted action initiated by, or imposed upon, the burghs. The parliamentary commission appointed in October 1466 had been given power to 'autorize, ratify and apprufe, or til annull as thai think expedient and profitable, al actis and statutis avisit and commonit in the sessiouns of burowis for the gude of merchiandice'.[145] These 'sessiouns of burowis' were perhaps burgh representatives meeting under the form of the court or 'parliament' of the four burghs. The last allusion to a meeting of this body

[141] *Ibid.*, 122.   [142] Davidson and Gray, *Staple*, p. 135.

[143] See *Scot. Legal Hist.*, pp. 398–9. For maritime cases brought before the lords of council see *A.D.C.*, I. 93, 274–5. The record of a dispute of 1461 involving merchants of Amsterdam and Danzig which was brought before Alexander Napier of Merchiston as admiral-depute of Alexander, Duke of Albany, is given in T. A. Fischer, *Scots in Germany*, pp. 239–41.

[144] *A.P.S.*, II. 178, c. 11. The affair was still unsettled in 1491 and the expenses to which it gave rise were still the subject of dispute in 1496 (Theodora Pagan, *Convention of Royal Burghs*, pp. 18–9).

[145] *A.P.S.*, II. 85, c. 2.

is found in 1507,[146] and the last record of its transactions in 1500. On 10 November in that year the 'court of the parliament of the four burghs' met in the tolbooth of Edinburgh under the presidency of the chamberlain, Lord Home, and issued enactments in favour of the merchants' trade monopoly.[147] Thus if the judicial functions of the court were becoming less necessary or desirable it was nonetheless able to acquire new functions in dealing with topics close to the hearts of the merchants. It is therefore strange that the closing years of the fifteenth century saw a quest for some other type of assembly that would replace, or at least supplement, the ancient one, and also, perhaps, the chamberlain ayre, which fell into desuetude after 1517.[148] In March 1484 a tax payable by seventeen burghs north of Forth was 'modifiit be the commissaris of burghis the tyme of the parliament haldin at Edinburgh'.[149] In the parliament of October 1487 'the haill commissaris of burrowis' also acted jointly in presenting 'actis and statutis' which they desired to have 'ratyfyit and apprevit in this present parliament and to be put to execucioun for . . . the weilfar of merchandis'.[150] Among the statutes which were thereupon ratified by the three estates was one which ordained that

> zerely in tyme tocum certane commissaris of all borowis, baith southe and north, convene . . . anis in ilk zere in the burghe of Inverkethin on the morne efter Sanct James day [26 July] . . . to comoune and trete apoune the welefare of merchandis, the gude rewll and statutis for the commoune proffit of borowis and to provide for remede apoune the scaith and iniuris sustenit within burowis.[151]

It is tempting to regard this act as the foundation charter of the convention of royal burghs (only recently dissolved). But 'no record of any meeting in Inverkeithing is now extant, and the practice of holding annual conventions there, if such a practice ever existed, seems to have been speedily discontinued'. It was not until the mid-sixteenth century that the convention of royal burghs definitely emerged. Meanwhile it remained uncertain what form extra-

[146] Theodora Pagan, *Convention of Royal Burghs*, p. 13.
[147] *Edinburgh Burgh Recs.*, I. 86–7.
[148] Athol Murray, 'The Last Chamberlain Ayre', *S.H.R.*, xxxix. 85.
[149] *Burghs Convention Recs.*, I. 543. The stent roll that was then produced, the earliest extant record of the apportionment of taxation by the burghs, shows that Aberdeen and Dundee were each to pay £26 13s. 4d. They were followed by Perth (£22 4s. 6d.) then by St Andrews and Inverness (each £10 0s. 0d.).
[150] *A.P.S.*, II. 178.   [151] *Ibid.*, 179, c. 17.

parliamentary meetings of burgh commissioners would finally take, and meetings of various types continued to be held.[152]

There was, however, little doubt as to the policies that such meetings were intended to foster, and parliament, which usually met in the tolbooth of Edinburgh, surrounded by the booths of the merchants,[153] could confidently be expected to ratify what had been devised for the welfare of mercantile interests. In 1438, and again in 1499, the magistrates of Edinburgh showed their anxiety to regulate the freighting of ships in the interests of merchants.[154] Thus the parliamentary commission of 1467 passed an act requiring the completion of charter-parties (written contracts between skippers and merchants) which would assure the latter of the safety and careful handling of the goods that they shipped. This act was re-affirmed at the request of 'the haill commissaris of burrowis' in the parliament of October 1487.[155]

More significant, however, was an act of 1467 which ordained that no craftsman should 'use merchandise' unless he renounced his craft.[156] This act was also re-affirmed in October 1487, when provision was made for its execution through 'searchers', who would confiscate to the use of the king the merchandise of the over-ambitious craftsman.[157] When the court of the parliament of the four burghs was held in Edinburgh on 10 November 1500 these acts were re-affirmed and it was ordained that only merchants who were resident burgesses should pass with merchandise to France or Flanders.[158] In 1467 it had also been ordained by parliament that only those who were 'famous and worschipfull' and possessed of at least half a last of goods should be allowed to take their goods abroad for sale.[159] Part of the explanation for this act may have been that in Germany there were so many itinerant Scots of small means that they brought disrepute upon themselves and their nation : passing as pedlars or pilgrims they acted like vagabonds.[160] But the main reason for the acts that were designed to keep craftsmen out of trade was the desire of the established merchants to guard their own

[152] *Burghs Convention Recs.*, I. vii; see also Theodora Pagan, *Convention of Royal Burghs*, pp. 24–5.   [153] *Edinburgh Burgh Recs.*, I. 39.
[154] *Ibid.*, 5–6, 78–9.   [155] *A.P.S.*, II. 87, c. 4; 178, c. 15.
[156] *Ibid.*, 86, c. 2.   [157] *Ibid.*, 178, c. 14.
[158] *Edinburgh Burgh Recs.*, I. 86–7. Copies of this ordinance were to be extracted from 'the book of the acts of the court of the parliament of the four burghs' by each burgh.
[159] *A.P.S.*, II. 87, c. 3.
[160] T. A. Fischer, *Scots in Germany*, pp. 241–2; *Scots in Prussia*, pp. 4–6 and c., n. I.

monopoly and ward off competition at a time when trade was in decline.

In other respects too, the merchant oligarchy that controlled the burghs showed a desire to curb the craftsmen. An act of parliament of November 1469 curtailed the holidays of masons, wrights and other craftsmen. Henceforth they were to abstain from work only on 'gret solempnit festis'; if they showed undue religiosity in abstaining from work they were, somewhat incongruously, to be punished by excommunication.[161] Another more important act of the same parliament complained that in the yearly choosing of alderman (provost), bailies and other burgh officials there was 'gret truble and contensione' caused 'throw multitud and clamor of commonis sympil personis'[162]—who undoubtedly comprised the craftsmen. The latter, it may be assumed, were claiming a share in burgh administration, or at least in burgh elections.

The earliest account of a burgh election is to be found in the surviving burgh records of Aberdeen, which open in 1398 with a notice of the election in the Michaelmas head court of various officials—the alderman, four bailies, four serjeants, and thirteen appraisers of flesh, wine and beer, whose pleasing duty was to test the quality of these commodities. This election is recorded as being made 'with the consent and assent of the whole community'. But it would be rash to assume that this was a 'democratic' election. It must be asked, 'whether, indeed, the "community" of the burgh is not . . . the merchant gild'. Certainly when the records of the Aberdeen gild court book commence in 1441 they show that the burgh council 'was elected by the gild, in the gild, at its regular meeting on the Friday following the Michaelmas head court'.[163] It is at least clear that elections were held each year, as laid down in the old *Leges Burgorum*—in a charter of 1391 there is an allusion to the alderman of Dundee and 'twelve good men of his council chosen yearly'.[164] It is also clear that the burgh court held by the bailies was never displaced by the gild court. But the latter, over which the alderman or provost might preside alongside the dean of gild, was not limited to the regulation of trade and strictly gild business: it might receive accounts and have control over the admission of new burgesses; often the gild and burgh records were kept in the same book by the same clerk, and the officials of the gild were officials of

161 *A.P.S.*, II. 97, c. 15.   162 *Ibid.*, 95, c. 5.
163 *Aberdeen Burgh Recs.*, pp. 21, ciii–civ.   164 *A.P.S.*, I. 577.

the burgh. In Edinburgh there existed not only an ordinary town council, perhaps elected in the burgh court, but a supplementary body called the 'dusane', a body not of twelve but of thirty-two, or even forty-five, which seems in 1453 and 1458 to have been elected, together with provost, dean of gild and treasurer, by the gild brethren in the Michaelmas gild court.[165] In 1463 the dusane was of the usual number of thirty-two, 'quhairof', affirms an early transcriber of the records, 'everie ane stylit be his craft'.[166]

If the dusane was made up on this occasion entirely of craftsmen the circumstance is startling, for those who had been elected to it ten years previously had included merchants of note and consequence such as Adam Cant and John Lamb, respectively former and future dean of gild.[167] Moreover it was the dusane which drew up leets for the election of the burgh officers, as was revealed in an investigation held by the chamberlain and certain lords of council on 6 October 1456. This procedure had, however, been broken by the choice of a bailie whose name had not appeared on the leet.[168] The fact that this led to the intervention of the chamberlain and lords of council indicates that high feelings had been aroused. Thus there are some grounds for supposing that in Edinburgh—which by itself encompassed half the burghal life of Scotland—there had been the 'contensione' in elections of which the act of 1469 complained.

The remedy devised by the act was a subtle one. It was 'thocht expedient' to continue the practice of yearly elections laid down in the *Leges Burgorum*, but the electorate was to be a limited one : the retiring burgh council was to choose the new council; the retiring council, together with the incoming council and with a representative of each craft, was to elect the burgh officers, including the alderman (provost), bailies and dean of gild. This procedure was modified by a further act of May 1474 which stipulated that four 'worthy persounis' of the retiring council should be chosen to sit on the incoming council.[169]

The acts of 1469 and 1474 seem at first to have been observed only in Edinburgh, which probably inspired them : in 1590 the magistrates of Aberdeen would defend their exclusion of craftsmen from the town council by affirming that

[165] *Edinburgh Burgh Recs.*, I. 1, 18. The entry under 3 October 1403 (p. 1) should be dated 1453 : the names of those elected coincide with those of the officials of 1454 (*ibid.*, 258).

[166] *Ibid.*, 20.   [167] Compare *ibid.*, 1–2 and 256–8.

[168] *Ibid.*, 15.   [169] *A.P.S.*, II. 95, c. 5; 107, c. 12.

thair is nocht ane uniforme ordour . . . observit amang the haill burrowes . . . anent the chesing and electing of thair magistratis and officieris, bot dyvers burrowes hes dyvers customes . . . nather yit is the actis of parliament anent the chesing and electing of magistratis universalye observit amangis the haill burrowes.[170]

But sooner or later this legislation did have an influence on most Scottish burghs. Among the acts ratified at the behest of the burgh commissioners in the parliament of October 1487 was one that reaffirmed the measure of 1469 and required that it be 'put to execucioun in tym to com', so that the burgh officers should be chosen from 'the best and worthiest induellaris of the toun' (resident merchants?) and not 'be parcialite nor masterschip, quhilk is undoing of the borowis'.[171] Yet the acts that had been passed tended to aggravate the very abuses that were feared : the act of 1474 could even be interpreted as meaning that *at least* four of the old council should be seated on the new : in theory there was nothing to prevent the old council from re-electing itself *en bloc* as the new. In 1567 the inhabitants of Cupar would complain that

> the auld counsale, having alwayis facultie to elect the new, thay cheis men of thair factioun and swa haldis the publict officis and counsale amangis a certane of particular men fra hand to hand, usand and disponand the common gude of the said burgh at thair plesour.[172]

Such 'parcialite' could be combined with 'masterschip'. For even the greatest burghs looked to the baronage for leadership. Patrick Charteris was provost of Perth in 1447, Andrew Charteris between 1465 and 1473, John Charteris in 1507.[173] In Aberdeen Gilbert Menzies was provost by 1506 and had initiated the thraldom of the burgh to the 'raice of Menzeissis'.[174] In Edinburgh Sir Alexander Napier of Merchiston was frequently provost until at least 1471 and John Napier of Merchiston was provost in 1484.[175] A decision of the burgh council in 1478 that for the 'honour and worschip of the towne' the provost should have a yearly fee of £20 [176] doubtless made the post more attractive and showed the desire of the burgh to have as its head someone who would keep up appearances. On 8

---

[170] *Burghs Convention Recs.*, I. 325–6.   [171] *A.P.S.*, II. 178, c. 14.
[172] *R.P.C.*, I. 582. For a similar complaint of the community of Aberdeen in 1590 see *Burghs Convention Recs.*, I. 312–5.
[173] *R.M.S.*, II. Nos. 400, 896, 1122, 1648, 3107.
[174] *R.P.C.*, IV. 533; *Burghs Convention Recs.*, I. 313; *R.S.S.*, I. No. 1738.
[175] *Edinburgh Burgh Recs.*, I. 258–61, 265.   [176] *Ibid.*, 37.

August 1487 Patrick Hepburn, Lord Hailes, was chosen as provost and appointed James Crichton of Felde (Philde in Perthshire) as his depute 'because the haill towne committit power to his lordschip to cheise his deputes . . . as aft as he sall think expedient'. In 1513, after Flodden, no less a person than Archibald Douglas, Earl of Angus, would be provost.[177]

Whatever the ultimate consequences of the act of 1469 regulating burgh elections the feature that may well have seemed most novel and important was that it allowed each craft to choose one of its members to have a vote in the election of the burgh officers: thus in eschewing the participation of a 'multitud' of 'commonis sympil personis' the measure gave some recognition to the claims of crafts-men and may well have been intended as a concession that would reduce friction within the burghs. This seems, at any rate, to have been the effect in Edinburgh during the rest of the century. Nor is it likely that this was accidental: for the act of 1469 had assumed the distinctiveness of each craft; it had transformed an amorphous multitude, which might have taken the form of a union of *all* crafts-men, comparable to the merchant gild, into a number of separate organisations that were necessarily small and likely to develop sectional interests.

It is striking that such individual craft organisations, which attracted suspicion in the reign of James I,[178] acquired respectability in the second half of the fifteenth century. It came to be recognised that those who exercised a particular craft might pursue certain activities in common, and to some of these activities the burgh authorities could not in decency refuse approval. Thus on 12 January 1451 seventeen skinners of Edinburgh bound themselves to contribute to the upkeep of a chaplainry which they had founded in St Giles Kirk and also of the altar of St Christopher at which the chaplain was to celebrate. At the request of the skinners this obliga-tion was registered 'in the common book of gild of the same burgh'. Thus indirectly the authorities recognised an organisation uniting the skinners, since the upkeep of their religious benefaction re-quired stipulated contributions and an organisation to enforce them. It was also ordained that if any discord should arise among the skinners it was to be submitted to the determination of their brethren 'and to the decreet of the council and dusane of the burgh'.[179] On 13 September 1456 the question of support of an altar

---

[177] *Ibid.*, 52, 277. [178] Pp. 308-9 above. [179] *Edinburgh Burgh Recs.*, I. 9-11.

also figured in a concession made by the provost, bailies and council
in favour of 'the haill craft of the baxteris', so that no baker was to
be made a freeman or burgess 'without the avys and consent of the
maist pairt of the worthiest of the craft'.[180] It was not, however, until
after the act of 1469 had regulated burgh elections that the development and recognition of craft associations—the 'incorporated trades'
of modern time—gained momentum. On 18 February 1473 ten Edinburgh hat-makers compeared in the tolbooth before the provost,
bailies and council 'in judgement sittand' and presented a 'bill of
supplicatioun', requesting that they might choose 'ane deacon
amanges thame for conserveing of the said craft and all guid rewlles
and ordinances'. The magistrates granted this supplication as being
'reasonabill and profitabill' and ratified a number of ordinances that
were thereupon presented. These controlled terms of apprenticeship
and entry to the craft, ostensibly in the interests of maintaining
standards. The stipulation that 'nane of the said craft purches ony
lordschipe incontrair ony pointtis of the said craft' was one that the
magistrates, fearful of the intervention of powerful outsiders, must
have welcomed. Thus the burgh's seal of cause (the seal of the
burgh court) was attached to the documents recording the supplication and ordinances.[181] In this semi-judicial fashion the hat-makers
secured powers of organisation and discipline. Further incorpora-
tions by seal of cause soon followed—the skinners in 1474, the masons
and wrights in 1475, the websters (weavers) in 1476, the hammermen (blacksmiths, goldsmiths, lorimers, cutlers, buckle-makers and
armourers) in 1483, the fleshers (butchers) in 1488, the coopers in
1489.[182] And the process would continue, for, as the cordiners
(leather workers) explained in a supplication for incorporation in
1510, 'multitude but [without] reull makis confusioun'.[183] Thus by
permitting organisation within each individual craft the merchant
oligarchy turned the radicalism of the multitude into the conservatism of the few. By 1490 at least twelve crafts were so respectably
organised that their deacons were associated with the burgh council
in letting the burgh muir.[184]

Whatever the social and economic discords within Edinburgh its
inhabitants were united against the outside world and showed an
aggressive community spirit. From at least 1436 onwards the magistrates often tried, for the 'common proffitt', to purchase in bulk all

[180] Ibid., 14.   [181] Ibid., 26-8.
[182] Ibid., 28-30, 30-2, 33-4, 47-9, 54-6, 57-8.
[183] Ibid., 127.   [184] Ibid., 58.

cargoes of victual, and sometimes timber, that were landed at Leith. Thereafter all inhabitants of the burgh might buy at a favourable price whatever they required from the bulk purchase, on the understanding that what they bought was not to be re-sold.[185] In 1462 it was ordained that the whole community should enter into a mutually profitable conspiracy so that 'na nychtbour . . . tak upon hand to warne ony strangaris of the price of vittuallis in the cuntrey'.[186] Unscrupulous community spirit was particularly aroused in exploiting the rights over the port of Leith which the burgh had obtained from Sir Robert Logan of Restalrig in 1398.[187] In 1428 Edinburgh has also been granted by James I the right to exact tolls upon ships, boats and cargoes for the 'fabrik and reparatioun of the port or herberie of Leith'—a grant which was thereafter several times renewed and confirmed.[188] Edinburgh's stranglehold over its unfortunate port was shown by an ordinance at the close of the century which arranged that 'all nichtbouris and all deikynis with thair craftismen' should be ready to descend upon Leith with the provost and bailies to hold a court 'for reforming of injuries done aganis thair fredome [privilege]' and by another ordinance which in 1482 prohibited the holding of any market in Leith.[189] On 16 November in the same year a royal charter confirmed Edinburgh's control over the port, and another charter of the same date increased the autonomy of the burgh by permitting the provost to be sheriff within its bounds, so that the inhabitants would no longer be subject to the jurisdiction of the 'landward' sheriff.[190]

Despite the pugnacious self-reliance of the Edinburgh burgesses, they, and the other burgesses of the realm, were hard pressed to maintain their status as one of the three estates. While individual burgesses continued to advance themselves, their estate as a whole suffered from the depression in international trade that perhaps left its mark in the 'voide placis' in Edinburgh to which allusion was made in royal letters patent of October 1477.[191] The growing attention that the burgesses paid to collective action perhaps betrayed their unease. It was ominous that they had been omitted from the 'congregation' of lords spiritual and temporal held by Bishop Ken-

---

[185] *Ibid.*, 4–5, 6, 19–20, 59.   [186] *Ibid.*, 19–20.
[187] *Edinburgh City Charters*, No. xx.
[188] *Edinburgh Burgh Recs.*, i. 3–4, 7–8, 14, 25, 43–7; see also pp. 23–4.
[189] *Ibid.*, 46, 50, 59.
[190] *R.M.S.*, ii. Nos. 1525, 1526. The burgesses were to show their gratitude by celebrating a mass each year for the soul of James II.
[191] *Edinburgh Burgh Recs.*, i. 34–6.

nedy in 1464.[192] And though no attempt was made to unseat them from the estates they were tolerated rather than respected, and underwent various snubs. While burgesses were naturally employed in negotiations concerning trade, they were not represented on the 1468 marriage embassy to Denmark [193] nor on the embassy of 1471 that was to mediate between France and Burgundy. This was all the more striking in the latter case since the lords, 'considering the estatis', thought that the embassy should consist of one bishop, one earl, one lord, one knight, one clerk, and one herald.[194] Yet the burgesses contributed one-third of the £3,000 allotted to the expenses of the marriage embassy and one-third of the 3,000 crowns granted for the embassy of mediation.[195] Thereafter they seem to have been unable to pay their way on equal terms with the other two estates, a fact which was all the more obvious since attempts to levy taxation on the basis of a general assessment had been given up : in parliament each estate granted a specific proportion of a tax and made its own arrangements for its collection.[196] In February 1472, when parliament granted £5,000 to the king to send an expedition to Brittany, the clergy and barons were each to pay two-fifths of the contribution and the burghs the remaining one-fifth. When a contribution of 20,000 marks was granted in the parliament of March 1479 for the marriage of the king's younger sister, and when another was granted in the parliament of April 1481 for the victualling of Berwick, the clergy and barons again offered two-fifths each and the burghs the remaining one-fifth. [197]

Taxation was rare and was granted, as shown above, only for extraordinary expenditures on royal marriages, diplomacy, or military preparations. Moreover it may be questioned whether the grants were in every case followed by actual payment to the king : he did not send an expedition to Brittany and his younger sister ended her days in blighted spinsterhood.[198] Taxation may therefore be ignored in any examination of the royal revenues. Their approximate composition c. 1486 has been estimated (too generously) as follows :

[192] P. 407 above.
[193] See *E.R.*, VIII. lxxix–lxxx.
[194] *A.P.S.*, II. 99, c. 2.
[195] *Ibid.*, 90, c. 1 ; 99, c. 2.
[196] Rait, *Parliaments*, p. 491. The clergy had valuation rolls for each diocese and apportioned taxation on a diocesan basis (*A.P.S.*, II. 102–3). In 1468 the barons paid their share of the tax for the marriage embassy on the basis of inquests held by lairds in the sheriffdoms (*ibid.*, 90–1). By 1484 the burghs had their stent roll (p. 445 above).
[197] *A.P.S.*, II. 102, 122, 134.
[198] Pp. 488–9 below.

from crown lands	£10,600	(gross receipts)
from sheriffs	£1,720	(gross receipts)
from customs	£3,300	(gross receipts)
from burgh ferms	£760	(gross receipts)

£16,380 [199]

Even in monetary terms, as well as in purchasing power, the revenues of James III cannot have surpassed those of the crown in the last year of David II's reign. Their composition, as can be seen, had radically altered: the bulk of David's income was provided by the great customs and direct taxation; the bulk of James's income was forthcoming from the crown lands.

The change is explained by the vast additions made to the crown lands since 1424, a process of accretion which by no means abated in the reign of James III. Besides minor or temporary acquisitions he secured the lands of the Boyds, Orkney and Shetland, and the earldom of Ross, and recovered the earldoms of March and Mar by the forfeiture of his brothers.[200]

What the king inherited or acquired he tried to keep; and if his patrimony was depleted from time to time by generous grants it was well understood that these could be revoked, more or less plausibly, if they had been made before he had reached his 'perfect age' of twenty-five years.[201] Thus John Stewart, Lord Darnley, who was recognised as Earl of Lennox in 1473, had his title revoked on 12 January 1476, though it was not until 10 July 1476 that the king proclaimed in parliament a 'general revocation' of all grants prejudicial to the crown.[202] Revocation, whether particular or general, seems the likeliest explanation for many resignations and re-grants of land. Sir William Monypenny, Lord Avondale, Lord Lindsay of the Byres, Sir John Colquhoun of Luss and Archibald Douglas, Earl of Angus, were among those who resigned lands; and it was the king's 'familiars' who sooner or later received grants of these lands.[203] Thus acts of revocation seem to have led to a game of musical chairs

[199] *E.R.*, IX. lxxvi. The figures are criticised by Athol Murray in 'The Comptroller 1425-1488', *S.H.R.*, LII. 1-29.
[200] See *E.R.*, IX, lxix; pp. 480, 485, 516 below.
[201] Prior to 1474 there was some revocation from which a certain apothecary in receipt of an annual fee of £20 was exempted (*E.R.*, VIII. 253).
[202] *H.B.C.*, p. 480; *A.P.S.*, II. 113.
[203] *R.M.S.*, II. Nos. 1202 (Colquhoun); 1213 (Angus); 1264, 1299, 1587, 1627 (Monypenny); 1613, 1632 (Avondale); 1657, 1693 (Lindsay).

between nobles and 'familiars' in which the ultimate losers included some nobles of consequence.

Besides revocation there was another mainstay of the royal patrimony- -annexation. In the parliament of November 1469 the Boyd lands had been annexed to serve as an endowment for royal heirs apparent. In the parliament of February 1472 the earldom of Orkney and the lordship of Shetland were annexed to the crown and were not to be given away save, perhaps, to a legitimate son of the king. In July 1476 a similar arrangement was made regarding the earldom of Ross, and in October 1487 the earldom of March and lordship of Annandale were annexed to the crown.[204]

It was conservation and extension of the crown lands, rather than increases in their value, that led to any rise in the royal revenues from this source, for, on the whole, landed rents seem to have remained more or less unchanged throughout the reign.[205] Alterations seem to have been made not so much in the rents themselves as in the rate and frequency of 'grassums' (usually equal to a year's rent) or in the varying exaction of a similar payment known as 'introitus' on the renewal of a tack.[206] When these payments are taken into consideration there appears a slight downward trend in the cash returns from land : in 1470–71 the chamberlain of Fife accounted for money rents of £598 15s. 10½d. and grassums of £393 8s. 4d.; in 1486–7 the rents had somewhat increased to £632 12s. 1½d. but the grassums were only £190 17s. 6d.[207] Such a trend seems to have been general. Moreover by 1479 the account of the chamberlain of Fife showed arrears of £28 17s. 4d. and by 1487 his arrears had increased to £954 3s. 4d.[208] At the same audit the arrears of Strathearn were given as £486 11s. 2d. and those of Galloway as £236 4s. 6½d.[209] Already in the parliament of February 1484 such arrears had caused concern. It was asserted that 'the kingis malis, rentis and fermez . . . ar haldin fra his hienes, apoune the quhilk his estait and houshald suld be sustenit'. The proposed remedy was that the master of the household (then the Earl of Crawford) and the comptroller (then Thomas Simson of Knockhill, chamberlain of Fife) should investigate the withholding of rents and,

[204] *A.P.S.*, II. 102, 113, 146, 179–80, 187.
[205] G. G. Coulton (*Scottish Abbeys*, p. 138) cites the rental of Coupar Abbey as showing that the rise in rents kept no pace with the fall in money value, and that in some cases there was no rise in rent at all.
[206] *E.R.*, IX. xxxiii–xxxiv.   [207] *Ibid.*, VIII. 92; IX. 509.
[208] *Ibid.*, VIII. 568; IX. 505.   [209] *Ibid.*, IX. 460, 491.

with lords of council, should 'pas and distrenze the officiaris in thai partis'.[210] At least one negligent rent collector was arrested.[211]

With the exception of laxity in rent-collecting towards the end of the reign it would seem that there was careful attention given to the exploitation of the royal lands. The accounts of the *ballivi ad extra*—the bailies, chamberlains and receivers who administered the crown lands—survive in large number and are supplemented towards the end of the reign by detailed rentals periodically drawn up by commissions of assessment appointed by letters under the privy seal.[212] Thus in 1484 the king appointed a commission of twelve persons, headed by the Earl of Argyll and Lord Avondale. A minimum of three of these persons might act, providing that they included the comptroller, who was the key figure in all such commissions since he had general oversight of the king's landed revenues. The commissioners were instructed to set the rents of the royal lands 'that beis fundin richtwisly vaikand, and to prolong and continew takkis of thaim for the space of fyve yeris or within, as salbe sene speidfull to them'.[213] Tacks for five years were generally granted in Galloway, but elsewhere three-year tacks were usual; only exceptionally were longer tacks granted. In Bute and a few other areas there were 'kindly tenants' who did not require to obtain tacks or pay grassums but paid a customary rent.[214]

Grants in feu-ferm seem to have been comparatively rare, though not so rare as has been generally supposed :[215] James III, besides granting a number of tenements in Berwick in feu-ferm to encourage the re-population of the burgh,[216] made at least seventeen other grants[217] and confirmed at least thirteen grants of feu-ferm made by others.[218] Just as significant as feuing in its repercussions upon landholding was the development of an open market in land by the 'new inventiouns of selling of landis be chartir' that were noted by parliament in November 1469.[219] Besides the voluntary sales that resulted there were also compulsory sales under the terms of another act of the same parliament that authorised the apprising

[210] *A.P.S.*, II. 165, c. 6.   [211] *E.R.*, IX. 306–7.

[212] *Ibid.*, xxxiii.   [213] *E.R.*, IX. 603.   [214] *Ibid.*, xxxiv–xxxv.

[215] See Dunlop, *Bishop Kennedy*, p. 344; Grant, *Social and Economic Development*, p. 268.

[216] *R.M.S.*, II. Nos. 1165, 1275, 1280, 1285, 1293.

[217] *Ibid.*, Nos. 1058, 1074, 1141, 1148, 1150, 1152, 1159, 1334, 1387, 1421, 1518, 1545, 1563, 1568, 1718, 1727; *T.A.*, I. 11.

[218] *R.M.S.*, II. Nos. 1029, 1040, 1081, 1204, 1313, 1384, 1393, 1463, 1502, 1508, 1560, 1574, 1688.   [219] *A.P.S.*, II. 94–5, c. 3.

and sale of lands to recover debts.[220(a)] From the combined evidence of the voluntary and compulsory sales of land it would seem that transfers of land took place mainly within the baronial class, partly to the disadvantage of the lords, partly to the advantage of a small group of ecclesiastics, partly to that of some burgesses, for whom an investment in land was a stepping-stone to gentility, very greatly to the advantage of the king and his 'familiars'.[220(b)]

Thus, thanks to various developments, land was no longer a concern only of the barons, trade no longer a concern only of the burgesses; all were consciously engaged in money-making; and the crown, while continuing to act (with or without parliament) as the ultimate regulator of all enterprise, was itself preoccupied with the administration of its own vast landholdings and was engaged in other miscellaneous undertakings. The position of the majority of the population who worked on the land is less clear. It was they, doubtless, who in 1468 spread the 'grete romour' about landlords who used the change in money values as an excuse for raising rents; and it was 'to content the commons' that there was a return to the *status quo*.[221] The evidence that during the reign rents did not rise suggests that a relative shortage of labour prevented rack-renting and allowed the rural population a standard of living high enough to encourage the domestic market.

By change in custom, or by legal enactment, there existed new opportunities for all classes, even for craftsmen. Nonetheless these opportunities became available at a time when the export trade was languishing, the returns from land were not improving, and the variations in the currency were generally exasperating. In such a situation those who fared badly, or hoped to fare better, might well turn their attention to politics, seeking preferment under the crown, or advancement through an opposition that might be rewarding. The church too offered tempting spoil, for it gave few signs of enterprise of its own, and its vast wealth—demonstrated by its ability to pay two-fifths of taxation—made it a possible victim of the enterprise of others.

This was particularly demonstrated in the case of the Benedictine priory of Coldingham, which 'remained one of the richest of

[220(a)] *Ibid.*, 96, c. 12.
[220(b)] Ranald Nicholson, 'Feudal Developments in late Medieval Scotland' *Juridical Review*, April 1973, pt, i. 1–21, at 9–16.
[221] *A.P.S.*, II. 92, c. 1; pp. 434–5 above.

border prizes'.[222] Its position as a dependency of the English priory of Durham had been often threatened since at least 1378 : the priory was coveted by the late Bishop Kennedy, and also, more persistently, by the Benedictines of Dunfermline (whose claims were given lively publicity in Abbot Bower's influential *Scotichronicon*),[223] while the local baronial family of the Homes (sometimes engaged in rivalry among themselves) had vested interests that they were determined to maintain. In Scotland, however, there was at least growing agreement that the connection between Coldingham and Durham had to be broken. The occasion came with the onset of warfare with the Yorkists at the opening of James III's reign : 'by mid-May 1462 the last English monks north of the Tweed had been ejected from Scotland for ever',[224] and in the parliament of October 1466 it was pointedly ordained 'that na Inglis man have na benefice, seculare nor religouss, within the realme'.[225] It was in vain that the Durham monks sought until 1478 to recover their lost priory by litigation in the *curia* : they were by no means alone in finding papal justice more expensive than effective. Meanwhile it seemed that the beneficiary of their failure would be Master Patrick Home, archdeacon of Teviotdale, who in 1461 sought to obtain the priory of Coldingham *in commendam*.[226] In 1464, however, Sir Alexander Home of that Ilk, bailie of Coldingham since 1442, successfully sought the appointment of his son John as prior so that he (Sir Alexander) 'could continue to exploit the very real wealth of the priory in the interests of his own determination to play an aggressive and ambitious role in Scottish and border politics'.[227] This aim was countered in April 1472 when James III successfully petitioned the pope that the priory be suppressed and its revenues united to the royal chapel of St Mary at St Andrews. For over a decade there was stalemate : 'although . . . James never . . . abandoned the plan to exploit Coldingham in his own interests, the Homes proved formidable and eventually successful antagonists'.[228]

In 1472, the year when he staked a claim to Coldingham, James also intervened in the appointment of an Abbot of Dunfermline : although the monks had elected one of their number, the king 'promovit Henry Creychtoun [Crichton], Abbat of Paislay, therto, quha wes preferrit be the paip, through the kingis supplicationis, to the

[222] R. B. Dobson, 'The last English monks on Scottish soil', *S.H.R.*, XLVI. 1–25, at 3.

[223] *Ibid.*; *Chron Bower*, II. 163–5.   [224] R. B. Dobson, *op cit.*, 8.

[225] *A.P.S.*, II. 86, c. 9.   [226] R. B. Dobson, *op. cit.*, 6–7, 25.

[227] *Ibid.*, pp. 13–5.   [228] *Ibid.*, pp. 20–1 ; pp. 523–4 below.

saide abbacye'.[229] This left vacant the abbey of Paisley, to which James secured the appointment of Master Robert Shaw, parson of Minto. Writing a century later, Bishop Lesley singled out the king's intervention at Dunfermline and Paisley as the beginning of the degradation of Scottish monastic life :

> . . . the godlie electiones war frustrate and dekayde, becaus that the court of Rome admittit the princis supplicationis, the rather that thay gat greyt proffeit and sowmes of money thairby; quhairfore the bischoppis durst not conferme thame that wes chosin be the convent, nor thay quha wer electit durst not persew thair own ryght: and sua the abbayis come to secular abussis; the abbottis and pryouris being promovit furth of the court, quha levit courtlyk, secularlye, and voluptuoslye.[230]

Lesley's analysis is open to criticism : there had been lapses in monastic life before the crown's supposedly decisive intervention in 1472—it was not altogether unusual that in 1466 the Prior of Whithorn had been accused of grave charges, including fornication, and had been forced to resign;[231] and as early as 1425 James I had uttered strictures against the Benedictines and Augustinians.[232] Nor was Lesley correct in assuming that prior to 1472 'godlie electiones' had been common, for rights of election had long been frustrated by papal reservations, provisions, and grants *in commendam,* and it was often as the upholder of 'godlie electiones' (which he could manipulate) that James III tried to extend his control of appointments (already considerable in the case of secular benefices) to the monastic benefices as well.

In view of the existing contentions over appointments to these, of which Coldingham provided a notable example, such a development might have proved salutary; but much depended on the use to which the crown put its extended powers of patronage. In the reign of James III the object seems to have been to use the heads of monastic houses in royal administration; it was somewhat novel, though hardly scandalous, that Archibald Crawford, Abbot of Holyrood, and David Lichtoun (or Leighton), Abbot of Arbroath, served successively as treasurer, and that the latter, together with the Abbots of Cambuskenneth and Paisley and the Prior of Pittenweem, were commissioned to assess crown lands.[233]

[229] Lesley, *History,* pp. 39–40.
[231] *Wigtown Charters,* pp. 9–10.
[233] *H.B.C.,* p. 181; *E.R.,* ix. 631, 649.
[230] *Ibid.*
[232] Pp. 298–9 above.

Not without a struggle did the crown wrest a share of ecclesiastical patronage from a reluctant papacy. The contest had begun in October 1466 during the dominance of Lord Boyd, who could count on some popular support in legislating against the malpractices of the *curia*. Patrick Graham, Bishop of St Andrews, was vulnerable since the papacy had granted him the abbey of Paisley *in commendam* after the existing abbot had been deprived for failure to pay a pension to one of the cardinals.[234] Thus the parliament of October 1466 passed (in vague terms) an act against pensions and a more explicit act which threatened any holder of a commend with the loss of his temporality and the penalties of rebellion.[235] When Graham thereupon resigned his commend of Paisley[236] the pope tempted fortune by granting him on 28 April 1467 a commend of the priory of Pittenweem.[237] In the parliament of November 1469 it appeared that James III intended to pursue the ecclesiastical policy of Lord Boyd and to use the Bishop of St Andrews to that end. An act was passed which alluded to an indult (privilege) granted by Nicholas V to the late Bishop Kennedy, whereby the Bishop of St Andrews was permitted to confirm elections in the monastic houses in his diocese. These were named, and included Coldingham and Dunfermline as well as another ten abbeys and three priories. Since this indult was 'to the comoune proffit of the realme' it was to be 'observit and kepit' under pain of treason. The same act also forbade any of the king's lieges to purchase (by papal provision) any benefice to which presentation or confirmation customarily pertained within the realm.[238] It was therefore James's intention to limit papal provisions by insisting upon the right of Scotsmen to nominate to benefices of which they held the patronage, and the right of Scottish monastic chapters to proceed with the 'godlie electiones' esteemed by Bishop Lesley. Thanks to the St Andrews indult local nominations and elections could be locally confirmed and papal patronage could be largely excluded from the most important Scottish diocese.

Much, however, depended upon the attitude of the papacy and upon that of the Bishop of St Andrews, who was thrust willy-nilly into the position of upholder of royal patronage. Paul II responded by announcing that the St Andrews indult had been revoked.[239] In the

[234] R. K. Hannay, *The Scottish Crown and the Papacy*, p. 6.
[235] *A.P.S.*, II. 85, cc. 4 and 5.
[236] R. K. Hannay, *The Scottish Crown and the Papacy*, p. 8.
[237] Leslie J. Macfarlane, 'The Primacy of the Scottish Church, 1472-1521', *Innes Review*, xx. 111-29, at 113.   [238] *A.P.S.*, II. 98, c. 21.
[239] R. K. Hannay, *The Scottish Crown and the Papacy*, p. 8.

parliament of May 1471 no reference was made to the indult but the right of 'fre eleccioune' was re-asserted; no papal collector was to levy taxes on the clergy higher than those customary in the past; there were to be no annexations or unions of benefices, unless for the endowment of collegiate kirks (now the most favoured of ecclesiastical institutions); other annexations and unions made since the king's accession were to be annulled. The restriction upon such appropriations came two centuries too late to have any effect on the structure of the Scottish kirk but was notable as tacitly assuming that parliament could undo what the pope had sanctioned in an area hitherto regarded as fully within his jurisdiction. Cumulatively the measures of May 1471 (which were to be observed on pain of treason) were intended to remedy 'the gret dampnage and skaith dayli donne to al the realme' by resort to the *curia*, 'considering the innowmerable riches that is had out of the realme thar throw'.[240] Using different methods, James III had gone at least as far as James I in challenging papal authority, particularly since the parliament of May 1471 also renewed restrictions on the export of money. He had established a bargaining position which it was doubtless the task of the Abbot of Cambuskenneth to exploit when he was appointed in the following month as the king's procurator and plenipotentiary on a mission to Paul II and the *curia*.[241]

But it was the Bishop of St Andrews who was to win the attention of the *curia*. Graham had business of his own to transact in Rome : he owed at least 3,100 gold florins for his various bulls of provision, and it was doubtless his financial troubles that had brought him into controversy with the monks of his erstwhile commend of Paisley and the dean and chapter of his former bishopric of Brechin, and induced him to contest the bequests made by the late Bishop Kennedy, proceedings which were not likely to endear him either to his colleagues or to the university of St Andrews.[242] Moreover it seems that Graham had gone to seek papal support for a policy that was at variance with that of the crown.[243]

His arrival at Rome must have occurred shortly after the death of Paul II and the election of Sixtus IV, who saw in the presence of the foremost Scottish bishop an opportunity to devise a new policy towards Scotland. Its features showed that Sixtus was either unaware of Scottish conditions or was misled by Graham : on 13 August

[240] *A.P.S.*, II. 99, c. 4.   [241] *R.M.S.*, II. No. 1034.
[242] Leslie J. Macfarlane, *op. cit.*, 113–4; Dunlop, *Bishop Kennedy*, p. 296.
[243] J. Herkless and R. K. Hannay, *Archbishops of St Andrews*, I. 42–3.

1472 a bull was issued erecting the bishopric of St Andrews into an archbishopric with metropolitan authority; henceforth the Bishops of Glasgow, Dunkeld, Aberdeen, Moray, Brechin, Dunblane, Ross, Caithness, Galloway, Argyll, the Isles, and Orkney were to be suffragans who owed obedience to the new archbishop, to whom they were enjoined to show reverence and honour.[244] Sixtus's bull was couched in courteous terms flattering to the Scots, and it took note of current criticisms of undue recourse to the *curia* by hinting that the existence of a metropolitan would reduce the number of appeals to Rome. The bull also recognised political realities by including in the metropolitan's province three bishoprics that had hitherto been technically outside the Scottish kirk : Galloway was removed from the shadowy jurisdiction of the Archbishop of York; the Isles and Orkney from that of the Archbishop of Nidaros, and, so far as Orkney was concerned, this was yet another move that tacitly assumed permanent Scottish control of the Northern Isles.[245] It was perhaps less pleasing that the bull hinted that the Scottish ordinaries (the bishops) had been wont to overstep their power and required to be disciplined by a metropolitan, and also that ecclesiastical cases 'are drawn to a forbidden court [*e.g.* parliament] and dealt with there'. Nothing in the bull alluded to the leading cause of controversy—the disputed control of ecclesiastical patronage—and although the new metropolitan would have powers of confirming elections this had not in other countries proved any obstacle to the exercise of papal control over appointments. Three centuries earlier the erection of St Andrews to archiepiscopal dignity would have been welcomed in Scotland and would have solved obvious problems; by 1472 it was a move that only disturbed vested interests. In the promotion of Patrick Graham the Scottish bishops saw their own demotion, and James III, who does not seem to have been consulted, saw a challenge to the authority over the kirk that he was exerting himself to acquire. News of the outcry in Scotland must have reached Graham, who tactfully remained on the continent until at least September 1473.[246] By that time the pope had injudiciously appointed him legate *a latere* and collector of a tithe to be imposed on the kirk, and had in other ways augmented his powers and privileges, mostly in order that he might raise money in Scotland for a crusade against the Turks. Moreover,

---

[244] Robertson, *Concilia*, I. cx.
[245] It is significant that a few months previously the bishops who granted a tax to James III included those of Orkney and Galloway (*A.P.S.*, II. 102-3).
[246] Leslie J. Macfarlane, *op. cit., Innes Review*, xx. 111-29, at 114.

in direct contradiction of the recent act against unions and annexations, the revenues of the priory of Pittenweem (lately recognised by royal charter as pertaining to the Prior and chapter of St Andrews) [247] together with those of seven parish kirks (including one that was a benefice of John Laing, the treasurer) were granted for the maintenance of the archbishop's household; and Graham was empowered to visit and reform all monasteries, even those of Kelso and Holyrood (the latter held by Archibald Crawford, frequent auditor of exchequer and soon to be treasurer) which had been exempt from such visitations. [248] Finally Graham was granted the abbey of Arbroath *in commendam* for a period of five years. [249]

The opposition to the absent archbishop gathered momentum. In August 1473 the king sent to St Andrews for a chaplain who could divulge 'certane materez anent the bishop', and orders were issued to put an embargo on 'schippis that suld have past to the Bischop of Sanctandros'. [250] In October or November a summons was issued for a 'generale consale twiching the archbischop'. [251] Mention in May 1474 of 'the inbringing of the kingis last taxt grantit be the clergy' may support Bishop Lesley's statement that the bishops had offered the king twelve thousand marks for his help against the archbishop. [252] By February 1474 James had recognosced the temporalities of St Andrews and had sent a notary there to publish an appeal, presumably to the pope, against Graham. [253] After his return to Scotland Graham does not seem to have attended parliament or to have witnessed royal charters. He was evidently in deep disgrace and was not recognised as archbishop.

There is little to support the view that Graham was 'a prelate of singular and primitive virtue' bent upon reform. [253(b)] It was as a great-grandson of Robert III and a nephew of Bishop Kennedy rather than by any personal qualifications that he had obtained the bishopric of St Andrews in 1465 when scarcely thirty years old, despite the fact that there were at that time at least five bishops of greater experience. [254] Although 'there is no evidence to suggest that

[247] *R.M.S.*, II. No. 1039.
[248] J. A. F. Thomson, 'Some New Light on the Elevation of Patrick Graham', *S.H.R.*, XL. 83-8, at 84, 86.
[249] R. K. Hannay, *The Scottish Crown and the Papacy*, pp. 8-9.
[250] *T.A.*, I. 43, 67.   [251] *Ibid.*, 46.
[252] Lesley, *History*, p. 41; *T.A.*, I. 50. The 'taxt' may however have been that of £2,000 offered by the clergy in the parliament of February 1472 to dissuade the king from a personal expedition to Brittany (*A.P.S.*, II. 102-3).
[253] *T.A.*, I. 49; *E.R.*, VIII. 318-9.   [253(b)] Tytler, *History*, I. pt. ii, 206.
[254] Leslie J. Macfarlane, *op. cit., Innes Review*, XX. 111-29, at 113.

he was other than a conscientious and hard-working bishop'[255] Graham played no outstanding part in public administration. At a critical juncture in the relationship between crown and papacy he had associated himself with the latter. But if this sprang from a sincere dislike of James III's growing mastery over the kirk Graham did not demonstrate his opposition straightforwardly, and his stance was weakened by the prolonged pursuit of benefices and privileges that culminated in his appointment as archbishop and legate. Latterly he had alienated both the king and the prelates and was left deserted. He was therefore valueless to the *curia*, and, unable to pay his debts, incurred excommunication in 1475, after which his troubles seem to have brought on a mental breakdown. By September 1476 the pope had been informed that Graham had lost his reason, and in December a papal commission of inquiry was set up under John Huseman, a German canon lawyer. It found that Graham was a 'heretic, schismatic, falsifier, simoniac, person of irregular life, blasphemer and excommunicate', who asserted that he himself was a pope chosen by God for the reformation of the kirk.[256] Graham was therefore deprived of his archbishopric on 9 January 1478, after which he was imprisoned in Inchcolm and Dunfermline, and finally in Lochleven, where he died.[257]

James III (albeit with the support of the prelates) had broken Scotland's first archbishop. The papacy, which had promoted Graham, was further discredited by his fall, and the king was left demonstrably master of the kirk. It now suited James's purposes to recognise the institution of the archbishopric, providing that it would not be bestowed upon anyone who might acquire delusions of grandeur, or upon anyone sufficiently reputable to use it as a possible leader of clerical intransigence. Thus experienced bishops, such as Thomas Spens of Aberdeen, Ninian Spot of Galloway and William Tulloch of Moray, were bypassed, together with John Laing, a civil servant recently promoted to Glasgow. James had detected a 'safe' man in William Scheves, who 'started under the double handicap of illegitimacy and non-baronial parentage'.[258] He had been installed in the archdeaconry of St Andrews by Patrick Graham in 1472, and in 1474 secured papal provision. He was also provost of the collegiate kirk of Crichton, and in 1474 was provided (unsuccessfully) to the

[255] *Ibid.*, p. 114.
[256] J. A. F. Thomson, *op. cit., S.H.R.*, XL. 83–8, at 87–8; *T.A.*, I. li and lii, n. 2.   [257] Lesley, *History*, pp. 42–3.
[258] Leslie J. Macfarlane, *op. cit., Innes Review*, XX. 111–29, at 115.

archdeaconry of Dunblane, and in 1474 (successfully) to the deanery of Dunkeld.[259] He had graduated at St Andrews in 1456 and had worked for another four years in that university before studying medicine and astronomy at Louvain under a teacher of repute.[260] These advanced studies seem to have led to preferment at court. Astronomy included astrology, which was both respectable and fashionable. Whether or not Scheves was court astrologer, he certainly received an annual fee of £20 between 1471 and 1474 for his services as royal physician.[261] In 1474 he was to be found making payments on behalf of the king for the purchase of green ginger, 'certane potigariis' (medicines), velvet, Holland cloth, seventy pair of 'patynnis' (clogs), and the sewing of the royal shirts. It would therefore seem that he had been given some official post, perhaps in the wardrobe alongside a certain Rob Scheves.[262] From 1475 onwards he also acted as auditor of exchequer.[263] It was undoubtedly Scheves's connection with the court rather than his academic and ecclesiastical attainments that won him the archbishopric. Six weeks before Graham's deprivation it had already been settled in the *curia* that Scheves was to be his successor; on 11 February 1478, two days after the deprivation, Scheves was provided to the archbishopric.[264] If the papacy had any doubts about his qualifications they were perhaps put to rest by a bargain whereby Prosper Camogli de' Medici was provided to the bishopric of Caithness in May 1478. The first (and last) Italian to obtain possession of a Scottish bishopric was admitted to the temporalities in 1481 but resigned three years later.[265]

Scheves was consecrated in Holyrood in the spring of 1479 in the presence of the king and nobility and was to hold the archbishopric of St Andrews until his death in 1497.[266] He was never able to win much co-operation from his suffragan bishops, and resentment at the existence of a metropolitan seems to have prevented the holding of a provincial council for several decades.[267] But Scheves acted as a loyal servant of the crown, participating in routine public business in parliament, hearing civil cases as a lord of council, serving as auditor of exchequer, commissioner of crown lands, and latterly as ambas-

[259] Watt, *Fasti*, pp. 89, 105, 307, 350; Leslie J. Macfarlane, *op. cit.*, *Innes Review*, xx. 111-29, at 115, 116.
[260] *Ibid.*, p. 115.   [261] *E.R.*, viii. 120, 190, 253.
[262] *T.A.*, i. xlviii, 18, 21, 23, 28.   [263] *E.R.*, viii. 266, 326, 401.
[264] J. A. F. Thomson, *op. cit.*, *S.H.R.*, xl. 83-8, at 88; Leslie J. Macfarlane, *op. cit.*, *Innes Review*, xx. 111-29, at 116; Watt, *Fasti*, p. 295.
[265] See Cameron, *Apostolic Camera*, pp. xlvii-xlix.
[266] Watt, *Fasti*, p. 295; Lesley, *History*, p. 43.
[267] D. E. Easson, *Gavin Dunbar . . . Archbishop of Glasgow* (1947), p. 59.

E.H.S.—16

sador. Nor did he bring discredit upon his ecclesiastical office, but proved himself 'a cultured and learned man with a genuine love of his country and its history, a conscientious archbishop who late in life turned to theology, a generous benefactor of the university of St Andrews'.[268]

Co-operation between Scheves and James III formed part of a resumed campaign to extend crown control over ecclesiastical patronage. In the parliament of October 1479 all grants and privileges previously bestowed upon the bishopric of St Andrews were confirmed in favour of the new archbishop and his successors. This measure (in an obvious reversal of former policy) particularly included all 'uniounes and annexaciounis of any benefice maid be oure hali faider the pape'.[269] Two charters were issued which formally detailed the privileges that had just been confirmed in parliament.[270] One of these reissued the Golden Charter once granted to Bishop Kennedy.[271] The other professed the king's devotion to St Andrew, patron saint of the realm, and James's singular favour towards Archbishop Scheves; it confirmed a variety of privileges, especially the indult granted to Bishop Kennedy by Nicholas V. This was perhaps the main object of the exercise, for already in the parliament of March 1479 the act of November 1469 ordering the observance of the St Andrews indult had been presented for ratification and confirmation.[272] In the parliament of March 1482, when this indult was again re-affirmed, its provisions were extended to other dioceses 'that hes been in use, consuetude, or possessioune, of confirmatioune of electionis'; and in May 1485 the same matter was again raised.[273] Until 1487, when its function was taken over by a more advantageous indult, the St Andrews indult was one of the twin pillars of the king's ecclesiastical policy.

The other was the claim to rights of patronage *sede vacante*. This claim was re-affirmed in the parliaments of April 1481, March 1482, and also in that of February 1484, when it was decided that the chancellor should write to the pope 'for the defence of our souverane lordis patronage'.[274] Meanwhile, in the parliament of December 1482

---

[268] Leslie J. Macfarlane, *op. cit., Innes Review*, xx. 111–29, at 118. The archbishop's interests may be traced in the surviving books that once belonged to his large collection. See John Durkan and Anthony Ross, *Early Scottish Libraries*, pp. 47–9; John Durkan, 'The Beginnings of Humanism in Scotland', *Innes Review*, IV. 5–24, at 5, 17–9; *T.A.*, I. liii, n. I.

[269] *A.P.S.*, II. 128–9.   [270] *Ibid.*, 193–6.
[271] P. 363 above.   [272] *A.P.S.*, II. 123.
[273] *Ibid.*, 140–1, c. 15; 171–2, cc. 10, 12, 14.
[274] *Ibid.*, 133, c. 7; 141, cc. 16 and 17; 166, c. 9.

it was ordained that the acts against the purchasing of pensions from benefices should be 'put to execucioune'.[275]

To the papacy all this posed a renewed menace. In some notable instances Sixtus IV resisted : in 1483 the Glasgow chapter had elected George Carmichael and the Dunkeld chapter had elected Alexander Inglis, the clerk register, whose archdeaconry of St Andrews was intended to go to the king's 'traist counsallour', Master John Ireland, professor of theology.[276] These proceedings vindicated the right of election which James (for his own purposes) championed. In each case, however, Sixtus IV vindicated the right of papal provision : he annulled the elections, provided George Brown to Dunkeld and translated Robert Blackadder from Aberdeen to Glasgow. This move allowed the pope to translate William Elphinstone from Ross to Aberdeen and to make a provision to Ross.[277] About the same time John Hepburn was provided to the priory of St Andrews.

In the parliament of May 1485 reference was made to these appointments, and while it was announced (in vain) that the king would 'nocht suffre Maister George Broune, nor nane utheris that has presumyt to be promovit to the saide bischopric of Dunkelde contrare our souveran lordis mynde', it was also conceded that Blackadder, Elphinstone and Hepburn were 'thankfull personis to our souverane lord, and of his speciale consale, and . . . admittit be his hienes to ther temperaliteis'.[278] The new pope, Innocent VIII, did not fail to take the hint that there would be no more royal championship of free elections and that papal provisions would be accepted by the king so long as they were made in favour of 'thankfull personis'.

At the outset of his pontificate Innocent was evidently anxious to achieve a settlement with the Scottish crown : by April 1485 James, Bishop of Imola, had arrived in Scotland as legate a latere.[279] The king showed his esteem for the legate 'with royal gifts', taking him with him wherever he went.[280] Imola probably witnessed the proceedings in the parliament of May 1485, where the king publicised his objectives in readiness for a diplomatic confrontation with the papacy. The occasion was provided by preparations to send the customary embassy to Rome to tender Scotland's obedience to the new pope. According to the instructions drawn up in parliament the embassy was to inform Innocent of Scottish grievances and seek a

[275] Ibid., 144, c. 9.   [276] Ibid., 171, c. 8.
[277] Watt, Fasti, pp. 3, 98, 149, 269.   [278] A.P.S., II. 171, c. 8.
[279] J. A. F. Thomson, 'Innocent VIII and the Scottish Church', Innes Review, XIX. 23–31, at 25, n. 17.   [280] Boece, Vitae, p. 52.

multitude of privileges,[281] in particular that the pope concede to the king and his successors a six-month delay before any papal disposition of prelacies or elective benefices so that 'our souverane lordis writing and supplicacioun may be sende for the promocioun of sic personis as is thankful to his hienes . . . sen'[since] all the prelatis of his realme has the first vote in his parlment and of his secrete counsale'.[282] Meanwhile the legate had evidently sent reports that induced the pope to act benignly towards James III, who in the spring of 1486 was presented with the golden rose, a traditional token of special papal regard which had been forwarded from Rome.[283]

It was not until December 1486 that the Scottish embassy, accompanied by the legate and headed by Archbishop Scheves and Bishop Blackadder of Glasgow, arrived in Rome. Despite an altercation on 2 February 1487, when to their disgust the orator of the King of Hungary was given precedence over them,[284] the ambassadors acquired valuable privileges for themselves and their king. It was probably as a result of James's desire to reward Scheves that the pope augmented the latter's dignity on 27 March 1487 by making St Andrews a primatial see with the same rights as Canterbury. As primate of Scotland and *legatus natus* the archbishop was now beyond dispute at the head of the Scottish hierarchy.[285] Much more important was an indult of 20 April 1487 whereby Innocent conceded that he would delay making appointments to cathedral kirks and monasteries with annual revenues exceeding two hundred gold florins until they had remained vacant for eight months; during this period he would await the 'humble supplications' of the king and his successors, 'so that . . . we may the better be able to proceed to these provisions as we shall think expedient, urging our successors that in such provisions they take equal care to observe our practice'.[286]

In one respect—by granting a delay of eight months instead of only six—Innocent had granted more than the parliament of May 1485 had desired; and the advantage to the crown was correspondingly increased since bishoprics and abbacies could be kept vacant somewhat longer while the king drew the revenues of the temporali-

[281] *A.P.S.*, II. 170–2, cc. 5, 6–12, 14.   [282] *Ibid.*, 171, cc. 7, 9.
[283] J. A. F. Thomson, *op. cit.*, *Innes Review*, XIX. 23–31, at 26; Charles Burns, 'Papal Gifts to Scottish Monarchs: the Golden Rose and the Blessed Sword', *Innes Review*, XX. 150–94.   [284] J. A. F. Thomson, *op. cit.*, 26.
[285] Leslie J. Macfarlane, *op. cit.*, *Innes Review*, XX. 111–29, at 116; J. A. F. Thomson, *op. cit.*, 27.
[286] Text in J. Herkless and R. K. Hannay, *Archbishops of St Andrews*, I. 257–8.

ties, exercised the ecclesiastical patronage *sede vacante* that he per-tinaciously claimed, and negotiated to obtain provision of an acceptable new bishop or abbot. But the pope did not bind himself to accept the nominations presented in the king's 'humble supplications'. The efficacy of the indult therefore depended on the current relation-ship between crown and papacy.

This relationship was soon soured : thanks to the troubles that ended in James's downfall the king was suspicious of everyone, in-cluding the pope. In the parliament of January 1488 there were more fulminations about 'impetrations at the court of Rome of bishopricks, abbacyis and uthir beneficis'; the crown's rights *sede vacante* were again re-affirmed, and could be applied, so parliament asserted, in the bishopric of Aberdeen, which was still technically vacant since Bishop Elphinstone's bulls of appointment had not been delivered.[287]

Just as James's position was weakened through political troubles so also for different reasons was that of his protégé, the archbishop, whose 'relationship with his hierarchy, never an easy one, rapidly deteriorated after his primatial appointment'.[288] In February 1474 Thomas Spens, Bishop of Aberdeen, had set a precedent by obtaining exemption from the jurisdiction of Archbishop Graham.[289] In May and June 1488 Bishop Blackadder of Glasgow and Andrew Stewart, Bishop of Moray, respectively obtained bulls exempting them from the primate's jurisdiction.[290] At the end of the reign both primate and king were under attack and the kirk was divided.

While it is evident that the erection of St Andrews to metropolitan and primatial status introduced a new element of discord within the Scottish kirk, this was the result, originally at least, of the initiative of the papacy, not that of the crown. What resulted from James's own forceful intervention in the affairs of the kirk is harder to assess. His acquisition of the indult of 1487 was one that subsequent kings would exploit, and the example that they set was not necessarily one that he himself would have followed. If in his time scandal existed in ecclesiastical high places it was probably no greater than in previous reigns, and in most cases arose from the bitter struggle for benefices, aggravated by the vacillating and mercenary practices of the *curia*. And these it was James's ambition to circumvent. His influence over ecclesiastical appointments was used to promote serviceable men,

[287] *A.P.S.*, II. 183-4, cc. 12, 19.
[288] Leslie J. Macfarlane, *op. cit.*, *Innes Review*, xx. 111-29, at 117.
[289] *Ibid.*, 114.   [290] *Ibid.*, 117.

mostly with administrative experience. Despite his underhand methods in securing appointments those who were appointed had respectable qualifications, or, as in the case of Scheves, proved themselves not unfit for office. It was James, rather than the pope, who furthered the career of William Elphinstone, drawing him from academic life (he was rector of Glasgow University in 1474) to onerous responsibility as 'official' of Lothian, auditor of exchequer and of the parliamentary committee of causes and complaints, and probably securing his provision to the bishopric of Ross. If it was through the initiative of the papacy that Elphinstone was further promoted, its treatment of the best Scottish bishop of the time also illustrates 'how legalistic and inflexible the legitimate processes of the Apostolic Camera could sometimes be . . . to the prejudice of good sense, and vexation of the faithful'. For Elphinstone's difficulties in paying the 'common services' due to the *camera* for his promotion to Aberdeen meant that his bulls of provision were not released for five years, during which he remained unconsecrated bishop of that diocese.[291]

Elphinstone was apparently on familiar terms with the king, who, thanks to the bishop's admonitions (so affirms Boece) displayed an edifying piety in almsgiving, generous gifts to kirks, and personal devotion; for whenever James beheld an image of Christ or the Virgin he would burst into tears and prayer.[292] The king certainly showed favour to a wide variety of ecclesiastical institutions. He confirmed grants made to the Franciscan Observants (now established in seven leading burghs),[293] and bestowed an annuity of twenty-four marks upon the Dominicans of Edinburgh on condition that they celebrated a daily mass for the soul of Queen Margaret.[294] His interest in St Salvator's was shown by his acquisition of the patronage of the college from Lord Kennedy and his kin, who were compensated (perhaps inadequately) in Galloway.[295] It was with royal encouragement that the collegiate kirk of St Duthac was established at Tain.[296] Apart from Tain and the abortive erection of Coldingham as a collegiate kirk, the reign saw the establishment of new collegiate kirks at Guthrie and Restalrig, as well as a 'new erection' at Dalkeith, to which some parish kirks were appropriated.[297] Beside the new kirk of Restalrig James

[291] Leslie J. Macfarlane, 'William Elphinstone, Founder of the University of Aberdeen', *Aberdeen University Review*, xxxix. 1-18, at pp. 6-8.
[292] Boece, *Vitae*, p. 52.   [293] Easson, *Religious Houses*, pp. 109-13.
[294] *R.M.S.*, ii. Nos. 1164, 1434.   [295] *Ibid.*, No. 1128.
[296] *Ibid.*, No. 1694. See also John Durkan, 'The Sanctuary and College of Tain', *Innes Review*, xiii. 147-56.
[297] Easson, *Religious Houses*, pp. 173-88; *Morton Registrum*, ii. No. 230.

built a handsome octagonal chapel to enshrine the relics of St Triduana.[298] In Edinburgh Queen Mary's foundation of Trinity College was followed by the raising of St Giles to collegiate status and its munificent endowment by the burgesses—its provost was to receive the enormous annual pension of 220 marks from the magistrates.[299] Elsewhere the foundation of chaplainries went on apace, particularly in the burgh kirks.[300]

The burgesses devoutly invested not only in the votive masses celebrated by chaplains but also, with more worldly motives, in the exploitation of ecclesiastical revenues. Thus the prominent Edinburgh burgesses Walter Bertram and Patrick Barron each founded a chaplainry in St Giles and each obtained tacks or feus from Henry Crichton, the Abbot of Dunfermline intruded by the king in 1472.[301] Nor was it only the temporalities of the religious houses that were involved in such transactions : Abbot Crichton was following a common practice when, a few months after his appointment, and possibly to help to pay for it, he obtained £450 by granting to a burgess of Linlithgow a nineteen-year tack of the teinds of the parsonage of Stirling.[302] Heavy burgess investment in the mass, coupled with investment in the kirk's spiritualities and temporalities, was an explosive mixture liable to ignite as soon as John Knox pronounced that the mass was idolatry.

[298] David McRoberts, *op. cit.*, *Innes Review*, XIX. 3–14, at 13.
[299] *R.M.S.*, II. No. 1397.
[300] *Ibid.*, Nos. 1157, 1238, 1320, 1328, 1333, 1339, 1392, 1400, 1469, 1544, 1586, 1596, 1628, 1655, 1672, 1692.
[301] *Ibid.*, Nos. 1392, 1544; *Dunfermline Registrum*, Nos. 479, 480, 488.
[302] *Dunfermline Registrum*, Nos. 476, 481; Coulton, *Scottish Abbeys*, pp. 93–4.

16

DOMESTIC AND INTERNATIONAL
POLITICS, 1469–1488

The complexity of James III's reign after 1469, sufficiently illustrated in the surviving records, is hardly made simpler by the surviving narrative sources. John Major, perhaps significantly, ended his consideration of Scottish affairs in 1469, while Hector Boece's *Scotorum Historiae* terminates in 1460. The continuation by the Piedmontese Giovanni Ferreri (Johannes Ferrerius), who from 1531 to 1545 taught in the abbey of Kinloss,[1] is of a later generation and, like the other sixteenth-century writers, Robert Lindsay of Pitscottie, Bishop John Lesley, and George Buchanan, Ferrerius seems uncritically (though not necessarily wrongly) to have accepted popular traditions. Buchanan's work, the least trustworthy of the lot, has even been styled 'little else than a classical romance'.[2] In addition there survives an anonymous chronicle that is useful but all too short. The narrators are thus poor guides through the fields of domestic and international politics where James's attempts to gain his ends met sometimes with success, sometimes with failure, and at length with disaster.

On the whole the international situation favoured Scotland : with the recovery of Berwick the Scots had no further ambitions to be satisfied at the expense of recurrent enmity with England. If peace or an effective truce could be achieved James would be free to assert himself both at home and on the continent, where he hoped to cut a fine figure, particularly by intervening in the disputes between Charles the Bold of Burgundy and Louis XI of France. In the parliament of

[1] John Durkan, *op cit., Innes Review*, IV. 5–24, at 14–6.
[2] Tytler, *History*, I. pt. ii, Notes and Illustrations, p. 388.

May 1471 certain articles concerning France, England and Burgundy were presented, as a result of which it was proposed to send an embassy to 'labour delygently for trety and concorde' betwixt the King of France and the Duke of Burgundy, to both of whom Scotland was bound by 'tender alyans'. The ambassadors, who were to be financed by a grant of 3,000 crowns from the three estates, were to seek 'a convenient place for the mariage of my young lady, our soverane lordis sistir'.[3] What parliament intended was that the king's younger sister, Margaret, should be married in such a way as to reconcile the courts of France and Burgundy. The aim of Louis XI, however, was to attach James to his side by beguiling him with hopes of acquiring the duchy of Brittany, with which James had a tenuous connection through Duchess Isabella, his aunt.[4] This manoeuvre looked likely to succeed: when parliament met in February 1472 there was support for James's project of a 'passage utouthe [outwith] his realm for the recoveryng of his richt of Bertane [Brittany]'. Towards the furnishing of an expedition of six thousand men the three estates made a grant of £5,000, 'of the quhilk the king was content'.[5] But the clergy had some forebodings. They pointed out that the king was still 'in tender age' and as yet had no offspring to maintain the royal succession; if James left the realm it would be 'opyn be apperance to his ald ennemyis of Ingland'; they therefore professed their 'grete tender lufe' for the king to 'induce him to remain at hame' and tried to make their grant towards the proposed expedition conditional upon the king's non-participation.[6]

The argument of the clergy lost some force after the birth of a royal son and heir on 17 March 1473. In the parliament of July in that year James presented a number of articles, the last of which concerned 'the passing of the king'.[7] Probably to enlist support for this scheme James showed favour to a number of nobles before, and during, this parliament,[8] and Sir Alexander Home was made a lord of parliament.[9] But despite James's timely favours the lords announced that they could 'nocht in na wiss gif thare counsale to his passage'. They took it for granted, however, that they could impose no veto if the king were 'uterly determyt to pas'. At any rate he could not do so 'in this sesone' since no preparations had been made.[10] If, nonetheless, the king were 'determit', he should recall a letter which had been sent

---

[3] *A.P.S.*, II. 99, c. 2. [4] P. 347 above. [5] *A.P.S.*, II. 102.
[6] *Ibid.*, 102–3. [7] *Ibid.*, 103, c. 2.
[8] *R.M.S.*, II. Nos. 1111, 1117, 1120, 1126, 1133, 1136, 1147.
[9] *A.P.S.*, II. 103. [10] *Ibid.*, 103, c. 2.

to the King of France (probably one that accepted the latter's terms for a conquest of Brittany) since 'na mater can be convoyit to the honour, worschip and profit of his hienes without cessing of the said letter'.[11]

If parliament failed to dissuade the king from his 'passage' it had an alternative scheme—to convert the 'passage' from a military expedition into one that was diplomatic. It was asserted that the only honourable and acceptable cause for the king's personal intervention overseas was mediation between France and Burgundy, since 'throw the contencioune being betuix the said princis the grettast part of Cristindome is trublit'. Successful mediation would aid resistance to 'the gret ennemy of Cristin faithe', the Great Turk, and would be pleasing to God; it would redound to James's honour and might 'bring him therthrow to his richt, nocht alanerly to the counte of Zanctone bot als of the duchery of Gillire'.[12] Thus James's cupidity was diverted from Brittany both to the French county of Saintonge (in regard to which James I had once received an undertaking from the French)[13] and to the duchy of Guelders, where the duke's son had imprisoned his father, so that, it was confidently asserted, 'the duchery of Gillir be naturall successioune of law and resone pertenis to our soverain lorde',[14] presumably since James had reversionary rights through his mother.

It would be difficult to guess which of the three claims, to Brittany, Saintonge or Guelders, was the most illusory; but the last two were at least the less dangerous and could be raised, so it was thought, in the course of mediation. For, once the letter to Louis XI had been recalled, so parliament advised, James should send an embassy to Burgundy and France to announce his readiness to mediate. If the ambassadors found that Louis refused to deliver Saintonge they were to report this 'injustice and unkyndlyness' to the allied Dukes of Burgundy and Brittany and seek their aid in obtaining Saintonge; the Duke of Burgundy was also to be exhorted to help James secure Guelders. If, however, both Charles and Louis were *each* willing to gratify James (all too naïve a supposition) then the ambassadors should try to have James accepted not merely as mediator but as arbiter.[15]

The prelates craftily pointed out that James's success in this ambitious plan might be furthered if he 'war now in the meyntyme to . . . travel throw his realme and put sic justice and polycy in his awn

[11] *Ibid.*, 103, c. 4.   [12] *Ibid.*, 103, c. 3.   [13] Pp. 289, 393 above.
[14] *A.P.S.*, II. 104, c. 5.   [15] *Ibid.*

realme that the brute [renown] and the fame of him mycht pas in utheris contreis'. Thus James was flatteringly enticed to attend more diligently to the governance of his own kingdom. Thereby, so the prelates continued, 'he mycht be grace of God be callit to gretare thingis than is zit expremit'.[16] This was doubtless a hint that James might eventually be elected emperor. When parliament met in May 1474 it was thought expedient that the king should send an embassy to his father-in-law of Denmark 'to mak and bynde confideracione and alliance with the emperour [Frederick III]'.[17] Thus thanks to the extraordinary wiliness of the lords and prelates in the parliament of July 1473 James's proposed 'passage' was transformed, if not into a diligent pursuit of justice, at least into harmless and inconclusive diplomacy. It was Charles the Bold who won the duchy of Guelders.[18]

Parliament had not only hinted that the king should pay more attention to the execution of justice but had reminded him that continental ambitions could not safely be pursued when the attitude of England was uncertain. That country was recovering from new political troubles. A series of remarkable vicissitudes had begun in August 1469, when Edward IV had become the virtual prisoner of the Earl of Warwick (the Kingmaker). After the king secured his liberty Warwick sailed to France, allied himself with Margaret of Anjou, and invaded England in September 1470. Edward IV fled to the Burgundian dominions. There followed the release and 'readeption' of Henry VI under Warwick's tutelage. The game of musical chairs continued when Edward returned in March 1471 to defeat Warwick and the Lancastrians at Barnet on 13 April and Tewkesbury on 4 May. After the death of Warwick and of Henry's heir, Edward, the capture of Margaret of Anjou, and the murder of Henry, Edward IV resumed his reign.[19]

A few Lancastrian refugees, including the Earl of Oxford and Lords Lovel and Latimer, received Scottish safe-conducts.[20] In May 1471 the Scottish parliament, fearful of a Yorkist invasion, undertook military preparations: it was agreed that prelates and barons should make 'cartis of weir'; it was ordained that the length of spears should be standardised at six ells, and each yeoman who 'can nocht deil witht the bow' was to have 'a gud ax and a targe of leddyr to resist the schot of Ingland'; wappinschaws were to be held; football and golf

---

[16] *Ibid.*, 104, c. 6.   [17] *Ibid.*, 106, c. 3.
[18] E. F. Jacob, *The Fifteenth Century*, p. 572.
[19] *Ibid.*, pp. 555–61, 566–9.   [20] *R.M.S.*, II. Nos. 1017, 1033.

were to be abandoned.[21] By July 1473, however, the 'cartis of were' were evidently not forthcoming, and the barons undertook to 'mak thaim incontinent'.[22] By May 1474 they were still not forthcoming.[23] Since 1471, however, fears of Yorkist hostility had gradually abated. The readeption of Henry VI had been too short-lived for the Scots to have committed themselves to the Warwickian Lancastrians,[24] and the restoration of Edward IV was followed for almost a decade by repeated interchanges of ambassadors, commissioners, envoys and heralds,[25] though their business was not always amicable. In the spring of 1473 Charles the Bold had even intervened to induce the Scottish and English kings to guarantee for at least two years their existing truce, which was supposed to last to 1519.[26]

There followed polite but somewhat cold exchanges of view. On 13 July 1473 James replied to a message of the Earl of Northumberland.[27] The English warden had complained of 'gret attemptatis committit be oure liegis of Liddalisdale uppoun Inglismen aganis the forme of the trewis'. James rejoined by asserting that 'in likwiss oure liegis ar richt complaintewss of Inglismen duelland within Tindaile and Riddisdaile, quhilkis daili makis depredacionis and herschippis upon oure liegis'. Northumberland's pursuivant had also remonstrated 'twiching the resaving of the Erle of Oxinfurde within oure realme'. James admitted that Oxford 'of lang tyme passit had oure saufe conduct'—which was still unexpired—but complained that 'oure rebell and tratoure, Robert Boid, is resett within your toune of Anwik'.[28] Lord Boyd was in fact receiving a yearly pension of two hundred marks from Edward IV;[29] and the forfeited Earl of Douglas, whose annuity had been confirmed during Henry VI's readeption,[30]

---

[21] A.P.S., II. 99–100, cc. 5, 6. [22] Ibid., 105, c. 13.

[23] Ibid., 106, c. 5.

[24] Only one Scottish mission, for which safe-conducts were issued on 13 November 1470 (Rot. Scot., II. 425–6) seems to have been sent during the readeption.

[25] Cal. Docs. Scot., IV. Nos. 1394, 1395, 1397, 1398, 1408, 1409, 1413, 1460; Rot. Scot., II. 429, 430–4, 436–8, 444, 454.

[26] Cal. Docs. Scot., IV. No. 1405; Rot. Scot., II. 436.

[27] Cal. Docs. Scot., IV. No. 1430 (Appendix 1. No. 24). The editor has assigned this document to 1475, but its reference to Oxford, who in 1475 was in prison (E. F. Jacob, Fifteenth Century, p. 572), indicates an earlier date. There can be little doubt that James's letter was written shortly before the meeting of commissioners at Alnwick on 28 September 1473, where the activities of Oxford were again discussed (p. 477 below).

[28] Cal. Docs. Scot., IV. No. 1430 (Appendix 1, No. 24).

[29] Ibid., Nos. 1413, 1415, 1440, 1441. [30] Ibid., No. 1392.

again had it confirmed by Edward IV a few years later, when it was said to amount to £390.[31]

The Scottish parliament of July 1473 was somewhat suspicious of Edward's intentions and noted that he had failed through 'ignorance, reklesnes or malice' to deliver safe-conducts so that Scottish commissioners might come to Alnwick for redress of breaches of the truce.[32] But the safe-conducts had at least been enrolled, if not issued, on 21 April, and English commissioners had been named.[33] When the English and Scottish commissioners at length met at Alnwick on 28 September 1473 they made remarkable progress in approving a schedule for the holding of March Days at a number of places in the Borders and in dealing with outstanding problems. The English again complained of 'the resetting of th'Erle of Oxfurd',[34] who was hovering off the English shores and would soon seize St Michael's Mount in Cornwall.[35] The Scots answered that they had not aided the earl and that his existing safe-conduct, which would expire at Michaelmas, had not been renewed. The siege of St Michael's Mount and the submission of the earl in January 1474[36] removed this cause of dispute. A claim presented by a number of Scottish merchants was the subject of adjudication by the English commissioners at Alnwick, after which full satisfaction was forthcoming from Edward IV, who presented the merchants with silk and woollen cloth to the value of £200 English or £911 8s. od. Scots.[37]

A more serious claim concerned a Scottish vessel described as 'the barge of St Andrews', but more precisely identified as the famous *Salvator* constructed by Bishop Kennedy. Sometime before August 1472 it had been wrecked and plundered near Bamburgh.[38] In the meeting at Alnwick the Scottish claim was referred to the admirals of both kingdoms, though without result, since the parliament of May 1474 arranged that a forthcoming embassy should raise the subject of 'the barge'.[39] By 3 February 1475 the affair was settled when Edward

[31] *Ibid.*, No. 1423.   [32] *A.P.S.*, II. 104–5, c. 10.
[33] *Rot. Scot.*, II. 436–7.
[34] *Cal. Docs. Scot.*, IV. No. 1431 (Appendix 1. No. 25). The editor has mistakenly assigned this document to 1475, but it was signed by the same notables as those who acted as Scottish commissioners at Alnwick in September 1473 (compare *ibid.*, No. 1409). Its contents obviously refer to the conditions of 1473, not those of 1475.
[35] E. F. Jacob, *The Fifteenth Century*, pp. 571–2; *Cal. Docs. Scot.*, IV. Nos. 1406, 1412, 1413.
[36] E. F. Jacob, *The Fifteenth Century*, pp. 571–2.
[37] *Cal. Docs. Scot.*, IV. No. 1412 (Appendix 1, No. 23).
[38] *Rot. Scot.*, II. 434–5; Lesley, *History*, p. 39.
[39] *Cal. Docs. Scot.*, IV. No. 1409; *A.P.S.*, II. 106, c. 2; Lesley, *History*, p. 40.

paid compensation of five hundred marks, English, and received letters of acquittance that James had issued in readiness on 25 October 1474.[40]

The behaviour of the English king in the wake of the Alnwick meeting must have stimulated the confidence of Scots merchants, who obtained English safe-conducts for themselves and their vessels both during the readeption of Henry VI and the restoration of Edward IV; a few licences were also issued to allow English merchants to export goods to Scotland.[41] Thus, at least after the meeting of the commissioners at Alnwick on 28 September 1473, Edward had proved by his actions that he was willing to allow the truce to become a reality. The Scots responded. The parliament of May 1474 thought it expedient to send 'ane honorable ambassat in Ingland' to work for 'gud materis of frendschep and amitie . . . and keping of the pece in tym to cum'.[42]

What parliament had in mind was a marriage alliance. For on 15 June James empowered the ambassadors to propose a match between the king's son and heir and Cecily, Edward's youngest daughter.[43] On 29 July 1474 Edward appointed commissioners to discuss this proposal.[44] The preliminaries were settled, in almost unseemly haste, by indentures drawn up on the following day.[45] Thereafter the business proceeded with suspicious speed. English ambassadors even came to Edinburgh, where they concluded an indenture on 26 October 1474.[46] Its preamble stated that :

> Forasmuche as this noble isle called Grete Britaigne canne not be kepte and mainteigned better in welthe and prosperite than such things to be practized and concluded betwene the kyngs of both reames, England and Scotland, wherby thaye and thair subgetts might be assured to lyve in peas . . . hit hath be agreed . . . that, considered the longe continued troubles betwene the both reames, with grete and mortell werre that hath followed theruppone, for the appesyng . . . of the same . . . a more especiall wey is to be found . . . than only the truste of the trewe . . . that is now, or any other trewe that couthe be devysed betwixt both partees.

The 'more especiall wey' was to be a marriage between James, Duke of Rothesay, and the Lady Cecily. For

[40] *Cal. Docs. Scot.*, IV. Nos. 1414, 1416, 1424; *Rot. Scot.*, II. 445.

[41] *Cal. Docs. Scot.*, IV. Nos. 1389, 1407, 1411, 1433, 1439, 1457; *Rot. Scot.*, II. 426, 427, 432, 438, 440, 443-4, 452, 455.   [42] *A.P.S.*, II. 106, c. 2.

[43] *Rot. Scot.*, II. 443.   [44] *Ibid; Cal Docs. Scot.*, IV. No. 1414.

[45] *Rot. Scot.*, II. 444, 446.   [46] *Ibid.*, 446-50.

the said marriage is thouthe to be the very rote and establisshment of all the love, favour and assistence that the one partie shalle owe to the other.

Thus a formal betrothal was solemnised in the Blackfriars of Edinburgh. The prospective bride and groom did not take part, she being five years of age and he not having reached his second birthday.[47] It was the Earl of Crawford and Lord Scrope who, as proxies, joined hands and plighted troth.[48]

It was stipulated in the indenture of 26 October that the marriage was to follow as soon as the couple were of fit age. Cecily's dower was specified, and her dowry was set at 20,000 marks, English. A first instalment of 2,000 marks was to be paid to James III within three months, and a further two yearly payments of the same amount were to be made, after which the remaining 14,000 marks were to be paid at the rate of 1,000 a year. All instalments above the sum of 2,500 marks were to be returned if the royal marriage for any reason did not take place.[49] This proviso, together with the scheme of extended payments of the dowry, was intended to keep the Scots peaceable. As a further guarantee both kings were to re-affirm the existing truce (to last till 1519) and neither side would aid the traitors and rebels of the other.[50] On 3 November 1474 James ratified the marriage treaty and truce,[51] and on the same day Edward ordered proclamation of the truce to be made throughout England.[52] On 3 February 1475 James acknowledged receipt of the first instalment of 2,000 marks towards the dowry.[53] For a small outlay Edward had neutralised Scotland.

Since at least 1474 the English king had planned an invasion of France, and in July 1474 had allied himself with Duke Charles of Burgundy. Thus 'the new marriage treaty was, next to his own treaty with Charles, the most important advantage which Edward had yet gained over Louis, and the most necessary to the success of an English invasion of France'.[54] James, piqued by his disappointments over Brittany and Saintonge, paid no heed when Edward crossed to France in July 1475 with a large army, which included the Earl of Douglas and Lord Boyd, each of whom led a retinue and received wages of war.[55] Since no effective Burgundian help was forthcoming Edward

[47] *H.B.C.*, pp. 38, 58.
[48] *Foedera*, v. pt. iii, 47–8; *Cal. Docs. Scot.*, iv. No. 1417.
[49] See *Cal. Docs. Scot.*, iv. No. 1420.   [50] *Rot. Scot.*, ii. 447.
[51] *Cal. Docs. Scot.*, iv. No. 1418.   [52] *Ibid.*, No. 1419.
[53] *Ibid.*, No. 1425.   [54] E. F. Jacob, *The Fifteenth Century*, p. 575.
[55] *Cal. Docs. Scot.*, iv. No. 1428.

allowed himself to be bought off by Louis XI. At Picquigny on 29 August 1475 an Anglo-French truce was concluded to last for seven years, and Edward was to receive from Louis an annual pension of 50,000 crowns.[56]

It seems likely that on the eve of his departure for France Edward let slip some information regarding the treaty of London that he had concluded with Earl John of Ross in 1462.[57] Such a move could be represented as evidence of Edward's good faith in implementing the provisions of the marriage treaty of 1474 that bound the English and Scottish kings to aid one another against rebels; more to the point, the information was likely to distract James's attention from France by arousing his ire against MacDonald. On 16 October 1475 Unicorn pursuivant appeared with letters of peremptory summons at the earl's castle of Dingwall (to which he was denied entry) and at the gates cited the earl to compear in parliament at Edinburgh on 1 December to answer for 'tresonable ligis and bandis mad be him with Edvarde, King of Yngland', and other miscellaneous treasons and crimes.[58] When parliament met on 1 December the earl was not there, whereupon Chancellor Avondale presented the case against him, the three estates unanimously adjudged him guilty and the dempster pronounced that the earl had forfeited to the king his life, lands, rents, superiorities and offices.[59] As a result MacDonald 'humyllit himself and come to the kingis will apoun certaine condiciones'.[60]

These were revealed in a parliament at Edinburgh in July 1476. MacDonald, who appeared in person, resigned to the crown the earldom of Ross, the lands of Knapdale and Kintyre, and the sheriffships of Inverness and Nairn. Thereupon the earldom of Ross was at once, with the assent of the three estates, annexed to the crown. The new status of the former earl was clarified when the king created 'John of Islay' a baron, banneret, and lord of parliament, with the title of 'Lord of the Isles', and ordered the heralds to proclaim him as such.[61]

A fuller account of these transactions is given in a charter of 15 July 1476 which was witnessed by many notables.[62] In the same charter MacDonald's remaining territories, presumably at his own request, were entailed to any future legitimate male offspring, failing whom, they were to pass to his illegitimate son, Angus of Islay, and

[56] E. F. Jacob, *The Fifteenth Century*, pp. 575–8.
[57] Pp. 401–2 above.   [58] *A.P.S.*, II. 109–10.
[59] *Ibid.*, 111.   [60] Lesley, *History*, p. 41.
[61] *A.P.S.*, II. 113.   [62] *Ibid.*, 189–90.

the latter's legitimate heirs male. From his remaining lands, which were still considerable, the Lord of the Isles was to render due rights and services to the crown, and, together with his tenants and the inhabitants of his lands, he was to cause to be observed the laws and customs of the realm like other barons, freeholders and lieges of the realm—a tall order.[63] Macdonald's fateful decision to submit upon such terms prevented a civil war in which, aided by geography and can loyalty, he might conceivably have held his own, for James III was no inspiring military leader. But neither, so it would appear, was Macdonald. His submission opened the far north and west to the Lowland influences that were bound to follow, sooner or later, in the wake of crown control.

The events of 1476 had imposed a strain upon the MacDonald hegemony that fatally disrupted its unity and, in the process, led to more disorder. The house of Islay was itself torn with dissension : by March 1478 Elizabeth Livingston, MacDonald's estranged spouse, had informed the pope that her husband was trying to poison her.[64] More important was the attitude of MacDonald's illegitimate son and heir, Angus,[65] who chafed at the truncation of his patrimony and at his father's generous grants to the MacLean, MacLeod and MacNeill vassals of the MacDonalds. And 'when the MacDonalds and heads of their family saw that their chief and family was to be sunk they began to look up to Angus Ogg, the young lord'. A clan seannachie recounts how Angus hounded his father from his lodging, forcing him to spend the night in the shelter of an upturned boat. On the morrow the Lord of the Isles formally laid a curse upon his son.[66]

It was probably the latter who was responsible for raids upon Arran, which was 'laid waste by the Islesmen' in 1477 and 1478.[67] It was Angus's father who had to answer to the government. By 7 April 1478 the Lord of the Isles had been summoned before the king in parliament for harbouring troublemakers.[68] But by December 1478 James had been led to believe in the innocence of the Lord of the Isles and renewed the grant of his lands (with the previous exceptions of Ross, Kintyre and Knapdale).[69] It was probably about this time, and certainly as a result of the quarrel between Angus Og and his

---

[63] *Ibid.*, 190; *R.M.S.*, II. No. 1246; *Highland Papers*, I. 123.
[64] *Highland Papers*, IV. 206–9.
[65] His career is imaginatively recounted by I. F. Grant in *Angus Og of the Isles*.
[66] *Highland Papers*, I. 47–50; Gregory, *Western Highlands*, p. 51.
[67] *E.R.*, VIII. 487–8; *Highland Papers*, I. 51.
[68] *A.P.S.*, II. 115.   [69] *R.M.S.*, II. No. 1410.

father, that the latter appeared unexpectedly at Inveraray with a small retinue and humbly sought the good services of Argyll,[70] whose daughter was wife of Angus Og.[71] The result seems to have been an interview on the Sound of Mull, where father and son had assembled in their galleys with the chief men of the Isles and the Earls of Argyll and Atholl.[72] Instead of pacification both sides resolved to fight. At 'the Bloody Bay' near Tobermory, probably sometime in 1481, the galleys of Angus Og prevailed against those of his father, the Mac-Leods of Lewis and Harris, MacLean of Duart and MacNeill of Barra.[73] Henceforth it was Angus Og who was the effective head of the MacDonalds, and his father became a mere protégé of the crown.

The Earl of Argyll, who would soon be made chancellor, was at least the indirect beneficiary of the troubles that beset the Mac-Donalds after 1475. Nor did he omit to secure his own interests : after the battle of 'the Bloody Bay' the Earl of Atholl 'being provided with boats by Argyle crossed over privately to Isla, where Angus Ogg's lady, daughter of Argyle, was, and apprehended Donald Du, ... a child of three years of age, and committed him prisoner to Inch Chonnil ... where he remained in custody until his hair got grey'.[74] Donald, the son of Angus and therefore, under the tailzie of 15 July 1476, the potential heir to the lordship, was to cause no small trouble when he escaped from Campbell custody.[75]

The feuds that had broken out among the MacDonalds and their vassals in the aftermath of the king's forfeiture of the earldom of Ross were by no means unique : the parliament of March 1479 included 'the gret trubill that is in Ross, Cathness and Suthirlande' as only one feature of 'the gret brek that is now, and apperand to be, in diverss partis of the realme' : Angus was disturbed by feud between the Earl of Buchan and the Earl of Erroll, between the Master of Crawford and Lord Glamis; a feud between Lord Maxwell of Caerlaverock and the laird of Drumlanrig threatened peace in Nithsdale and Annan-dale; Teviotdale was the scene of factious contention between the Rutherfords and Turnbulls, between the sheriff and his uncles and the laird of Cranston.[76] Even more serious than baronial feuds was the estrangement between the king and his brothers, Alexander, Duke of Albany, and John, Earl of Mar. These two, according to Pitscottie,

---

[70] *Highland Papers*, I. 48.   [71] *Ibid.*, 50; *Scots Peerage*, v. 47.

[72] *Highland Papers*, I. 49.

[73] *Ibid.*, 49–50; Gregory, *Western Highlands*, pp. 52–4; I. F. Grant, *Angus Og of the Isles*, pp. 133–5.   [74] *Highland Papers*, I. 50.

[75] P. 545 below.   [76] *A.P.S.*, II. 122.

presented the stirring figures expected of men of their rank, while the king was thought to be 'ane that lovit sollitarnes and desyrit never to heir of weiris nor the fame thairof, but delytit mair in musik and polliecie of beging [architecture] nor he did in the goverment of his realme; for he was wondrous covettous in conquissing of money rather than the heartis of his barrouns, for he delyttit mair in singing and playing upoun instrumentis nor he did in defence of the Bordouris or the ministratioun of justice'.[77]

It is by no means certain that James had no interest in Border defence and wars: although over £750 were paid to the masters of works in 1473, probably for building operations at the royal residences, this sum included expenditure on artillery.[78] Nor did the king altogether neglect fashionable country sports: he collected greyhounds and hawks.[79] But the records certainly have entries that indicate his liking for music: John Broune, lute player, was paid £5 so that he might go overseas to learn his craft; he, or some other luteplayer, went to Bruges and received a solicitous gift of a barrel of salmon from the king.[80] Ferrerius gives the impression that James was something of a dilettante who ignored class boundaries in his patronage not only of scholars but of skilled craftsmen.[81] Pitscottie's allusion to the king's 'conquissing of money' seems to have been well founded: Bishop Elphinstone was reputed to have urged him to eschew avarice;[82] at James's death it was found that his notorious 'blak kist' and other receptacles contained enough treasure to stuff Aladdin's cave, much of it in the form of jewels and ornaments that were doubtless works of art.[83] In addition the king's outlay on clothes and personal accoutrements was surpassed only by that of the queen, and amounted in 1473–4 to £639 0s. 5d.[84] An extravagant court ill suited 'a barane land . . . fertile of folk, with great scantnes of fude'[85] that was racked by famine, inflation and feud.

Together with an expensive court went a high-flown view of royal authority. One significant act of 1469 affirmed that James possessed 'ful jurisdictioune and fre impire within his realme' and that he might therefore create notaries public (hitherto the prerogative of the pope and the emperor); henceforth notaries created by the emperor were to

[77] Pitscottie, Historie, I. 162–3.   [78] T.A., I. 74; see also ibid., ccci.
[79] Ibid., 43, 44, 45, 46.
[80] Ibid., 43, 59, 60, 67; see also E.R., IX. xliv, n. I.
[81] Ferrerius, Continuatio, p. 391.   [82] Boece, Vitae, p. 51.
[83] P. 531 below.   [84] T.A., I. 13–28.
[85] The Harp (printed in Chron. Pluscarden, I. 392–400).

have no authority within Scotland.[86] In the parliament of April 1478 a clerk was accused of 'tresonable usurpacioune' for having legitimated a bastard 'in the name and authorite of the emperoure, contrare to oure souverain lordis croune and majeste riale'.[87] The implication was that the Scottish king was to be regarded as the equal of the emperor. Nor was he beneath the king of France in dignity; for an ineffective act of 1472 ordained that the royal arms should no longer bear the double tressure of fleurs de lys [88] which might heraldically be construed as evidence of a subordinate relationship to the crown of France. Evidently touchy on questions of his dignity and authority, James was described by Polydore Vergil as 'impatient of criticism, quick to make a foolish decision and slow to revoke it'.[89] Already the king had shown his political capriciousness in his attack upon the Boyds in 1469; a decade later he was to give another demonstration in an attack upon his two brothers, whose conventional tastes and extrovert character doubtless won them a popularity that the king resented.

Hitherto Albany and Mar seem to have tactfully avoided the political limelight or to have been deliberately excluded from government. In contrast to the king's uncles, Atholl and Buchan, his brothers seldom attended parliament and hardly ever were mentioned as witnesses to royal charters. Nonetheless, as admiral of Scotland and warden of the East and West March,[90] Albany had important official duties. His lands in Annandale (a den of thieves according to Pitscottie) probably demanded close attention; so also did his lands of the earldom of March where (so Pitscottie avers) the duke manfully resisted the encroachments of the rapacious Lord Home. Finding himself thwarted by Albany (who appears to have maintained a gang of desperadoes that included some renegade Homes),[91] Lord Home concluded a bond with the Hepburns and sought the good services of 'ane new courteour start upe [upstart] callit Couchren, quho had at that tyme great preheminence . . . and credence witht the king'.[92] It was through Cochrane's machinations, so Pitscottie asserts, that a witch (with some accuracy) prophesied to the king that he would be slain by one of the nearest of his kin, whom he took to mean his brothers.[93] In England a member of the Duke of Clarence's household had lately been executed for necromancy and practising with magic

---

[86] *A.P.S.*, II. 95, c. 6.
[88] *Ibid.*, 102.
[90] *R.M.S.*, II. No. 1428.
[92] Pitscottie, *Historie*, I. 163–5.

[87] *Ibid.*, 115.
[89] Mackie, *James IV*, p. 12.
[91] *A.P.S.*, I. 128.
[93] *Ibid.*, 166–7.

arts against Edward IV's life; Clarence himself was then accused by his brother the king of 'unnatural and loathly treason', sentenced to death by an act of attainder, and drowned on 18 February 1478 either in a bath or a butt of malmsey wine.[94] Necromancy and fraternal treason were in the air; and James probably heeded the prognostication of a more professional adept of the occult sciences than a mere witch—Dr Andreas, who had appeared in the Scottish court by 1471, had acquired some repute by correctly prophesying the death of Charles the Bold.[95]

Thus in the spring of 1479 Albany was imprisoned in Edinburgh Castle. He escaped to his own castle of Dunbar, which he garrisoned and munitioned before fleeing to the French court.[96] Probably in December 1479, after Dunbar had fallen, the king's remaining brother, the Earl of Mar, 'wes takin in the nicht in his awin house, had to Cragmillar, and kepit thair at the kings commaund, and wes convict of ane conspiracie be witchecrafte aganis the king; . . . thair wes also mony and divers witches and sorceraris, alsueill men as wemen, suspect of that cryme, convict and burnit for the same at Edinburghe'.[97] A short contemporary chronicle gives a similar account : 'that yer [1479] was mony weches and warlois [warlocks] brint on Crag Gayt; and Jhone, the Erle of Mar, the king's brother, was slayne becaus thai said he favoryt the weches and warlois'.[98] The earl appears to have lost his life, either by accident or design, in a house in the Canongate, while seated in a bath after undergoing the fashionable medical treatment of bleeding : Lesley succinctly remarks that 'they cuttit ane of his vanes and causit him bleid to dead'.[99] Since a charter of July 1480 makes it clear that the earldom of Mar had been forfeited to the crown[100] some sentence must have been passed against the earl; and since there is no surviving record of proceedings against him in parliament this sentence may have been awarded in some extempore court of the royal household of the type that had done to death the sixth Earl of Douglas in 1440.

[94] E. F. Jacob, *The Fifteenth Century*, pp. 579–81.   [95] *E.R.*, VIII. lxviii, n. 2.
[96] Lesley, *History*, p. 43; *E.R.*, VIII. lxx–lxxii; Ferrerius, *Continuatio*, p. 393 v.; short contemporary chronicle appended to the B.M. Royal MSS. 17 DXX of Wyntoun, printed in Pinkerton's *History*, I. 502–4, at 503. Pitscottie's colourful account of the duke's escape from Edinburgh Castle (*Historie*, I. 185–8) may have some factual basis but is inserted out of context.
[97] Lesley, *History*, pp. 43–4. The date of Mar's arrest is given as December 1480 by Lesley but the previous year is much more likely.
[98] B.M. Royal MSS. 17 DXX in Pinkerton, *History*, I. 503.
[99] Lesley, *History*, p. 43; *Pitscottie*, *Historie*, I. 167–8; Ferrerius, *Continuatio*, p. 393 v.   [100] *R.M.S.*, II. No. 1446.

It was possibly news that he was about to be 'justified' by such a court that had prompted Albany to make his escape.[101] Since he was no longer in royal custody, and was unlikely to compear to defend himself, it was safe to institute a public prosecution in parliament. It was apparently in the parliament of October 1479 that the charges against Albany and his partisans were first heard. As was to be expected, none of the accused compeared. In what seems to have been a test case the king obtained a sentence of forfeiture of life, lands, possessions and goods against John Ellem of Buttirdene, captain of Dunbar, and his twenty associates.[102] By contrast the process against Albany was continued until 17 January 1480 with the consent of the three estates 'and at the gret raquest, instance and supplicacioune of thame'. A similar continuation was granted in respect of Patrick Home of Polwarth and other accomplices of Albany.[103] The parliament that was to have been held on 17 January 1480 was continued by special royal precept until 13 March, when it was held by a commission. The commissioners duly summoned Albany, Patrick Home of Polwarth, and twenty others (none of whom compeared) and then continued the processes against them until 4 May. The same procedure was successively followed by another fourteen parliamentary commissions, the last continuation being until 11 March 1482.[104] Since parliament did not meet until a week after that date [105] it would seem that these processes against Albany and his accomplices were deliberately allowed to lapse; at any rate nothing more was heard of them.

What lay behind the repeated adjournments is uncertain. It is possible that the case was kept open as a means of putting pressure upon the fugitive Albany to make a voluntary submission. On the other hand in the case of Ellem of Buttirdene and his accomplices the king had asked for the 'sensment' of parliament, which was willing to condemn those who had held Dunbar against the king. So far as Albany and the others were concerned the 'sensment' of parliament was evidently different and its 'supplicacioune' led to the first adjournment. Afraid to demand sentence, which might have been in favour of Albany, James stubbornly kept the case open for month after month, hoping perhaps for some shift in opinion against the duke. Already, it would seem, James could not count on easy compliance with his wishes and the Albany affair demonstrated the existence of a rift between king and barons.

---

[101] Pitscottie, *Historie*, I. 185.   [102] *A.P.S.*, II. 125–8.
[103] *Ibid.*, 128.   [104] *Ibid.*, 129–36.   [105] *Ibid.*, 136–7.

Meanwhile Albany had received a polite welcome at the French court. On 9 March 1478 the duke had obtained from the 'official' of Lothian a divorce from Catherine Sinclair, daughter of the Earl of Caithness,[106] and on 19 January 1480 he married Anne de la Tour, daughter of the Count of Auvergne and Bouillon—their son, John, would become governor of Scotland in 1515.[107] Louis XI, who may have resented the Scottish king's pretensions to act as mediator between France and Burgundy, probably took sardonic pleasure in sending the scholarly Dr Ireland on an embassy to Scotland to try to achieve a reconciliation between James and Albany. James was also to be induced 'to move weir contrar King Edward of Ingland'.[108] This French request was probably stimulated by a pact of friendship that Edward IV had concluded in August 1480 with Mary and Maximilian of Burgundy; but since Louis XI did not himself wage war against Edward, and continued to pay him the pension of 50,000 crowns promised in the treaty of Picquigny,[109] it would have been impertinent to suggest that the Scots should start a war with England had not warfare already broken out.

For the betrothal of the Scottish heir apparent to Edward's daughter Cecily in October 1474[110] had not led to a lasting improvement in Anglo-Scottish relations. It would be wrong to give the impression that there was 'haggling over the payment of the . . . dowry':[111] up to the spring of 1479 Edward had paid (with occasional slight delay)[112] all that was due; but he was no longer eager to cultivate Scottish friendship after he had extorted the Picquigny settlement from the French.[113] In contrast, James's eagerness for friendship with England increased, as was shown in the somewhat obsequious language of his letters to 'the richt excellent, hie and michty prince, oure derrest cousing and bruthir, the King of Inglande'.[114] Under the impression that he had reached a firm settlement with England James planned to win prestige on the continent by a pilgrimage to St John's shrine at Amiens. Since he feared that a long sea passage would be detrimental to his health he obtained a safe-conduct on 15 May 1476 to pass through England with a train of up to four hundred

[106] *Ibid.*, 283.   [107] *Scots Peerage*, I. 153–4.
[108] Lesley, *History*, p. 44.
[109] E. F. Jacob, *The Fifteenth Century*, pp. 583–4; p. 480 above.
[110] Pp. 478–9 above.   [111] Mackie, *James IV*, p. 9.
[112] See *Cal. Docs. Scot.*, IV. No. 1452, and Appendix 1, Nos. 29, 30.
[113] P. 480 above.
[114] *Cal. Docs. Scot.*, IV. Appendix 1. Nos. 29, 30.

attendants.[115] The application for such a safe-conduct was a hint that
he expected to be invited to the English court; and there can be little
doubt that James hoped also to add to his own renown by intervening
personally in Franco-Burgundian disputes. For some reason the projected pilgrimage was delayed and a second English safe-conduct
was issued on 17 March 1478, this time allowing James to travel with
as many as a thousand attendants.[116] By this time also, James was
deeply engrossed in plans to enhance Anglo-Scottish friendship by
further matrimonial alliances. In the parliament of November 1475
the three estates encouraged the king to make arrangements for the
marriage of his younger sister, Margaret, and offered help in defray-
ing the expenses.[117] Her marriage was one of the matters to be dealt
with by a parliamentary commission appointed in July 1476.[118] By
the following year approaches had been made to Edward IV not only
for a marriage between James's sister and the Duke of Clarence, but
also another between the Duke of Albany (at that time uncontamin-
ated by treason) and Edward's sister, the newly-widowed Duchess of
Burgundy. Edward instructed his ambassador, Master Legh, to
explain that 'aftre the old usaige of this our royalme, noon estat ne
person honnorable communeth of mariage within the yere of their
doole [mourning]' [119]—a point of etiquette that affected the Duchess
of Burgundy, but hardly the Duke of Clarence. Despite Edward's
coldness James persevered with his matrimonial schemes: in June
1478 another parliamentary commission was to discuss the marriage
of his sister (who had lately left the Cistercian nunnery of Haddington to make her début at court)[120] after an embassy to be sent to
England 'in all gudly haist' had reported back with 'hasti ansuere'.[121]
Edward condescended to negotiate for the marriage of his brother-
in-law, Anthony Woodville, Earl Rivers.[122] By 2 February 1479 the
terms of a marriage contract had been worked out: Margaret was to
bring to Earl Rivers a dowry of 4,000 marks (English) but this sum
was to be deducted from forthcoming instalments of the dowry that
Edward owed James in respect of the marriage planned between
Cecily and the Scottish heir apparent.[123] On 23 January 1479 an

[115] *Rot. Scot.*, II. 453.   [116] *Ibid.*, 455.
[117] *A.P.S.*, II. 112, c. 5.   [118] *Ibid.*, 114.
[119] Edward IV—Master Legh, 1477 (B. M. Cotton MSS. Vespasian C. XVI. f.
121, in Pinkerton, *History*, I. 501).
[120] *T.A.*, I. cclxxxvi.   [121] *A.P.S.*, II. 119, c. 12.
[122] *Rot. Scot.*, II. 456. T. Dickson (*T.A.*, I. cclxxxvii) was misled in believing
that these negotiations were authorised on 14 December 1482, the date wrongly
given in *Foedera*, v. pt. iii, 126–7.   [123] *R.M.S.*, II. No. 1417.

English safe-conduct was issued so that Margaret might come to England with up to three hundred attendants for her marriage to Earl Rivers.[124] In the parliament of March 1479 the three estates granted the king a contribution of 20,000 marks (Scots) for the marriage expenses : this sum was to be raised in three equal annual instalments, beginning at midsummer 1479, the clergy and barons each paying a total of 8,000 marks and the burgesses the remaining 4,000.[125] Up to this time there was some point in the sardonic criticism of James's pro-English policy voiced by the author of *The Wallace* : 'till honour ennymis is our haile entent'.[126]

Blind Harry (or whoever wrote in his name) was soon justified in his forebodings. For although James's sister was supposed to be conducted south for her marriage by 16 May 1479[127] she did not set out. On 22 August another safe-conduct was issued so that she might come to the English court for her marriage in November;[128] and on 23 November another safe-conduct was issued so that James might go on his deferred pilgrimage to Amiens.[129] But neither safe-conduct was to be used : it was doubtless about this time that it could no longer be hidden that Margaret was pregnant.

The father of her child (a daughter also named Margaret) was William, third Lord Crichton.[130] He appears to have sought the sanctuary of St Duthac at Tain : despite an intervening pardon for many past 'traitorous actions' he was certainly skulking there on 30 December 1483 when he was cited to answer for new treasons.[131] His affair with the Lady Margaret must have wrecked the pro-English policy that James had patiently pursued for five years just at the time when (in his eyes) it was about to be triumphantly vindicated. Edward's behaviour towards Scotland had since 1474 been correct, though not enthusiastic, and though his reaction to the news of the misconduct of Earl Rivers's betrothed may in private have been one

---

[124] *Cal. Docs. Scot.*, IV. No. 1455.   [125] *A.P.S.*, II. 122.
[126] See Matthew P. McDiarmid, 'The Date of the *Wallace*', S.H.R., XXXIV. 26–31, at 30.   [127] *Cal. Docs. Scot.*, IV. No. 1455.
[128] G. Burnett and T. Dickson (*E.R.*, VIII. lxiii and *T.A.*, I. cclxxxvii) were misled in believing this safe-conduct was issued on 22 August 1482, the date under which it is wrongly recorded in *Foedera*, v. pt. iii, 123. The correct date is given in *Rot. Scot.*, II. 457.   [129] *Rot. Scot.* II. 457.
[130] Full details of the life of James's sister and her daughter are given in *T.A.*, I. Appendix I. cclxxxvi–ccxcii. Since Crichton attended the parliament of October 1479 (*A.P.S.*, II. 124), his liaison with the Lady Margaret cannot at that time have been apparent.   [131] *A.P.S.*, II. 159.

of amusement it must in public have been that of outraged honour. He had ample occasion to make a break with James, whose desire for sincere cordiality was in Edward's view unfashionable and unrewarding. Edward was now plotting with Louis XI against Maximilian of Burgundy, and with Maximilian against Louis,[132] who in return would send Dr Ireland to Scotland to stir up James against Edward.

Dr Ireland, who must have arrived in the spring or early summer of 1480,[133] probably found James smarting under Edward's recriminations over the Lady Margaret. They were evidently sufficiently serious to cause Bishop Spens of Aberdeen, who had always urged peace upon the rulers of Scotland, France, England and Burgundy, to die 'of malancolie' on 15 April 1480.[134] Some fifty Scotsmen resident in England obtained letters of denization between February and September 1480[135] to avoid the misfortune of some of their compatriots whose property was confiscated.[136] The anonymous author of a short contemporary Scottish chronicle laconically remarks that in 1480 'raise ane gret wer betwix Ingland and Scotland; and that yer the Erle of Anguys with gret power of Scots passyt in Ingland, and brynt Balmburgh, and lay thre nytis and thre dais in Ingland'.[137] In retaliation the Duke of Gloucester, who since 1470 had been warden of the English West March,[138] led a raid into Scotland, and at a meeting of the English council in November 1480 it was decided that Edward himself would lead an expedition against the Scots, though he was in fact to leave this business in other hands.[139]

From October 1480 to March 1481 there were intensive preparations in England for the coming campaign : a fleet was assembled, Lord John Howard was appointed king's lieutenant and captain of a force of 3,000 men who were engaged to serve for sixteen weeks; the disinherited Douglas was resuscitated and given 200 marks; shortly

---

[132] E. F. Jacob, *The Fifteenth Century*, pp. 582-4.

[133] He served as one of the lords of council in civil causes for the first time on 15 July 1480 (*A.D.C.*, I. 78).

[134] Lesley, *History*, p. 44; Boece, *Vitae*, pp. 36, 37. As recently as 1477 Spens had been sent on embassy to England (*Rot. Scot.*, II. 454).

[135] *Cal. Docs. Scot.*, IV. Nos. 1462, 1465. The latter entries from the patent roll of 20 Edward IV refer to the year 4 March 1480-3 March 1481, not 1479-80. Somewhat later another score of Scots obtained letters of denization (*ibid.*, Nos. 1468, 1471, 1473).   [136] *Ibid.*, Nos. 1467, 1485.

[137] B.M. Royal MSS. 17 DXX, in Pinkerton, *History*, I. 503.

[138] *Rot. Scot.*, II. 423-4.

[139] E. F. Jacob, *The Fifteenth Century*, pp. 584-5.

afterwards the disinherited Lord Boyd received a gift of £20.[140] While these preparations were being undertaken in the winter of 1480 or the early spring of 1481 Edward issued instructions to his ambassador, Master Legh, that amounted to an ultimatum to the Scottish king : 'upon grete groundes and urgent causes', especially on account of Scottish breaches of the truce, Edward was determined 'to make ayeinst the said Scottes rigorous and cruel werre'. Master Legh (if he saw fit) was to announce that James was illegally occupying Berwick, Coldingham and Roxburgh, 'having no right nor title unto thaym'; that he had neglected to do homage; that Edward 'as soverain of Scotland' intended to see the wronged Douglas restored to his possessions; and that the Prince of Scotland (the Duke of Rothesay) was to be delivered to England by the end of May 'for th' accomplisshement of his said promised mariage'. If all four demands could not at once be met by the Scots Edward would content himself with the delivery of Berwick and the prince to avoid 'th'effusion of Christen blode'. Finally, Master Legh was to accumulate evidence to refute charges in a letter brought by Ross herald in which blame for breach of truce was laid upon the English Borderers.[141]

It was this mission of Ross herald that James had in mind in March 1482 when he gave his own retrospective version of the events that had led to war : he had sent 'his writing' (doubtless the letter to which Edward IV alluded) with a herald and pursuivant to offer redress of breaches of truce on a reciprocal basis, but the herald and pursuivant were 'lang haldin and taryit in Ingland be the revare [robber] Edward, calland him[self] King of Ingland', after which they had been dismissed without answer in word or writing, as an affront to James, whose only desire was to have peace and keep the truce.[142] Bishop Lesley adds that the Scottish envoys were deliberately detained until Edward had despatched 'ane navye of schippis' to the Forth, where they appeared off Leith, Kinghorn and Pittenweem and 'invaidit all the schippis that wes in the Firth, and tuik awaye with thame aucht [eight] greit schippis, bot wes not sufferit to land in ony parte, saffing at Blacknes, quhair they brint the toun and ane greit barge schip wes lyand besyd'.[143] Whether or not the Scottish heralds were purposely detained, Edward's instructions to Master

[140] These entries (*Cal. Docs. Scot.*, IV. Nos. 1463, 1466), wrongly ascribed by Joseph Bain to 1479, were made during the exchequer year 30 September 1480—29 September 1481.
[141] *Ibid.*, No. 1436 (Appendix I, No. 28). This document has been wrongly ascribed by the editor to 1475–6.
[142] *A.P.S.*, II. 138. [143] Lesley, *History*, p. 44.

Legh certainly show that it was not his intention that James's plea for peace should go unanswered. The absence of any reference to Edward's insulting demands in any surviving Scottish source shows either that they were never delivered, or, what is perhaps more likely, that James, who had an overweening sense of his own dignity, was so chagrined that he kept silent about them.

The English naval attack, however, made it clear that war had broken out, and induced James to summon parliament, which seems to have met since October 1479 only in the form of the parliamentary commissions that went through the rigmarole of summoning Albany. When the three estates met in April 1481 they adopted some defensive measures: the acts concerning wappinschaws were to be 'put to dew execucioune' and some attempt was made to standardise the arms used by the host—spears were to be at least five ells in length; and prototype shields in leather and wood were to be sent to each sheriffdom so that they could be copied by those armed with axes rather than with spears or bows; the host was to be called out on eight days warning, and those who assembled were warned not to despoil the countryside; it was announced that the king would repair 'his' castles of Dunbar and Lochmaben and 'stuff' them with victuals and artillery, and all lords with castles on the Borders or on the coast were enjoined to follow the king's example.[144] Special provision was made for the defence of Berwick, which was likely to be the main English objective: the three estates 'for the plesance of the kingis hienes' granted a contribution of 7,000 marks to victual the town; two-fifths would be paid by the beneficed clergy, another two-fifths by 'landit men' (except those who served in person in Berwick) and the remaining one-fifth by the burghs; it was noted that the burgh commissioners (except those of Montrose) had already committed themselves to uphold Berwick.[145] No provision had been made for prolonged warfare—Berwick was to be victualled for only forty days, and the host for only twenty, whereas Lord Howard's three thousand troops were to serve for sixteen weeks.

As it happened, the host had no sooner been assembled in the campaigning season of 1481 than it was dismissed, having accomplished nothing. For, as James angrily explained in the parliament of March 1482, he had assembled 'the hale grete powere of Scotland . . . for the resistence and invasioune of oure ennemyis of Ingland' but had been shown certain papal bulls and monitions and had disbanded his troops in the belief that the English would be similarly

[144] *A.P.S.*, II. 132-3, cc. 1-6.   [145] *Ibid.*, 134.

obedient to papal demands—which they were not, but inflicted upon Scotland 'grete byrnyngis, hereschip and distructioune'.[146] A somewhat fuller picture is given by Lesley, who states that when the Scots host was about to invade England there arrived a messenger of King Edward, sent from a cardinal legate in England;[147] by apostolic authority James was ordered to cease the war on pain of interdict, so that Christian princes might prepare an army against the Turks; James thereupon disbanded his host, but Edward once more sent his fleet to the Forth, where it lay off Inchkeith, though its attacks on the coast were repulsed by local resistance; thereafter the Scottish Borderers raided the English Marches 'and tuik away mony praies of guidis, and distroyit mony townis, and led mony presonouris in Scotland, so that greit trubles and invasiones was betuix the tua realmes all that yeir'.[148]

When a well-attended parliament met in Edinburgh in March 1482 it proceeded with ordinary judicial business[149] and made some enactments dealing with ecclesiastical affairs,[150] but its preoccupation was with the war. James professed his own desire for peace and fulsomely denounced the duplicity, perjury and aggressiveness of the 'Revare Edwarde', who 'throu birnand averice and for fals reif [robbery] and conqueist . . . is aluterly set to continew in this were that he has movit and begunnyne, and be all his powere tendis and schapis to invaid and distroye and . . . to conquest this realme'. This declamation, which was not wholly unfounded, elicited from the three estates a profession of their loyal determination to resist: they would 'remane and abide at the command of his hienes with thare persouns and all thare substance of landis and gudis in the defence of his maste noble persoune, his successioune, realme, and liegis, as thai and thare forbearis has of all tymes done of before'[151]—a profession that was soon to be dramatically belied.

Meanwhile the king and the three estates made preparations for a full-scale war and showed that they had learnt some lessons from the fighting of the previous year. It was thought desirable to win early information (probably by spies) of English invasion plans. Wappinschaws were to be held every fortnight and the host was to be ready to assemble as soon as warned. The royal couriers, whose duty was to convey warning, were accused of slothfulness in the past, and a

[146] *Ibid.*, 138.
[147] The envoy was probably 'Gelicane, the papis messinger', to whom James paid £20 (*E.R.*, IX. 218 n.).
[148] Lesley, *History*, p. 45.
[149] *A.P.S.*, II. 137; 140, c. 14; 141.
[150] *Ibid.*, 140–1, cc. 15, 16, 17.
[151] *Ibid.*, 138–9, cc. 1 and 2.

speedier service was to be organised. Over each stretch of coastline six miles long, and the country up to one mile inland, a captain was to be appointed to lead a *levée en masse* 'for the resisting and inpugnacioune' of English attacks. If the English king sent forces headed by wardens they were to be resisted by the Scottish wardens with corresponding forces; if he led an invasion in person he was to be resisted by the Scottish king in person, at the head of 'the hale body of the realme, to leyf and dee with his hienes in his defence'.[152] At long last the necessity for large-scale payment of troops was recognised : the king offered to maintain at his own expense a garrison of five hundred in Berwick. To this the estates agreed to add a further six hundred troops stationed in Border strongholds. The Berwick garrison was to be in place on 1 June, and the Border garrisons, commanded by six captains, on 1 May. Each captain was to recruit his hundred men by his own choice and was to appoint two deputy captains. He was also to receive wages and disburse them at the daily rate of 2s. 6d. for each spearman and 2s. for each archer. It was stipulated that half of the 'wageouris' should consist of spearmen and the other half of archers.[153] Thus, apart from the Berwick garrison, for which the king paid, the three estates committed themselves to providing £67 10s. 0d. a day, which, over a three-month period, would come to more than £6,000. This heavy expenditure was to be apportioned 'eftir the forme of the ald use and consuetude', the clergy and barons each being responsible for two-fifths, and the burghs for the remaining one-fifth.[154] This apportionment, hardly an old one, thus suddenly acquired venerability.

Despite these intensive preparations for defence there were grounds for unease. It was decided that an embassy from the king and the three estates should be sent to Louis XI and the *parlement* of Paris to seek aid. Whatever part Louis had played in fomenting Anglo-Scottish war it was significant that James's earlier appeals for aid had 'gottin nane answer'.[155] Nor was the relationship between the king and the three estates quite so harmonious as on the surface appeared : in the parliamentary record the profession of loyalty of the three estates was immediately followed by the king's recognition of their 'grete affectioune and hertfull lufe' and his undertaking that with 'gude and trew consale of his prelatis, lordis, and wise discrete persouns', he would cause justice to be impartially administered and apply himself to 'the puttin of gude reull in all partis of his realme

152 *Ibid.*, 139, cc. 4, 5.   153 *Ibid.*, 139–40, cc. 7–10.
154 *Ibid.*, 139–40, c. 7.   155 *Ibid.*, 140, c. 13.

... to the grete disconfort and confounding of his ennemyis and of all fals tratouris and untrew hertis'.[156] The prominent place given to this undertaking, and its wording, suggest that there had been accusations that the king did not follow the counsel of 'wise discrete persouns', that justice and government in general were defective, and that there existed 'untrew hertis' who saw opportunities in the king's resulting unpopularity. Moreover it would seem that the king, perhaps by some rash words, had antagonised his uncles, the Earls of Atholl and Buchan, by raising the question of their 'takin and intrometting ... of the castel of Edinburgh' sometime during the royal minority.[157] On 18 March James seems to have tried to conciliate Atholl by granting him in flattering terms a tailzie of his earldom in favour of heirs male.[158] Four days later, however, Atholl and Buchan obtained from the king in parliament a formal exoneration for their assumption of the custody of the castle.[159] Between the king and his uncles suspicion obviously existed. Already, too, Edward was tampering with the loyalties of various Scots: on 22 June 1481 he had authorised the mayor of Carrickfergus and Patrick Haliburton (a Scots chaplain in his service) to conclude an alliance with two prominent MacDonalds—John, Lord of the Glens of Antrim, and Donald Gorm.[160] To counter this move James seems to have encouraged the ever-restive native Irish: he paid £10 'to ane Ireland man',[161] and he equipped a ship at Ayr to be sent to the Lord of the Isles (who had loyally attended the abortive assembly of the king's host in 1481)[162] for the capture of the traitorous Master Patrick Haliburton.[163] Much more serious was a commission that Edward issued on 22 August 1481 empowering the Duke of Gloucester and the disinherited Douglas to promise lands, lordships and gifts to all Scotsmen who would collaborate with the English.[164] In the parliament of March 1482 Lord Lyle was accused of treasonable correspondence with Douglas but was acquitted by an assize of sixteen barons headed by the Earls of Atholl and Morton,[165] which was doubtless a setback for the king. James was, however, able to rally some support against 'the tratour James of Douglace quhilk is now cummyng to the Bordouris': proclamation was to be made that anyone who slew Douglas

[156] Ibid., 139, c. 3. [157] Ibid., 138.
[158] R.M.S., II. No. 1503. [159] A.P.S., II. 138.
[160] Cal Docs. Scot., IV. No. 1469. George Burnett mistakenly confused the Lord of the Glens with the Lord of the Isles (E.R., IX. xl). [161] E.R., IX. 219 n.
[162] Lesley, History, p. 45. [163] E.R., IX. 211.
[164] Cal. Docs. Scot., IV. No. 1470. [165] A.P.S., II. 137-8.

or delivered him alive should be infeft heritably in lands worth a hundred marks a year and have a cash reward of a thousand marks and assurance of the king's 'lufe and tendernes'. Proportionate rewards were offered for the slaying or capture of Douglas's underlings. At the same time his accomplices, with the exception of Alexander Jardine, Master Patrick Haliburton and Sir Richard Holland (author of *The Buke of the Howlat*) were given twenty-four days' grace to obtain remission and forgiveness for past misdeeds; if they neglected this opportunity they would 'never be ressavit to favouris nor grace'. Probably lest desperation should drive criminals to consort with the enemy a general respite and remission was offered to all (particularly the Borderers) who had committed treason or trespass in the past.[166] So that the wardens might root out the 'untrew persounis' who favoured Douglas, the king revoked all exemptions from the jurisdiction of the warden courts, except in respect of persons in the town and castle of Berwick.[167]

Before long, Scottish malcontents could seek encouragement from a more illustrious patron than Douglas: at the end of April 1482 a Scottish carvel brought the Duke of Albany from France to Southampton, whence he was conducted to London to be installed in the 'Hospice de Erber' at Edward's expense.[168] Disappointed at the failure of Louis XI to secure his restoration Albany was ready to seek the good services of Edward at the price of notable treason: at Fotheringhay Castle on 10 June 1482 the duke, rather prematurely styling himself 'Alexander, King of Scotland', promised that after he had acquired his realm he would do homage to the English king, break the alliance with France, and surrender Berwick within a fortnight of his arrival in Edinburgh.[169] In an indenture of the following day Edward bound himself to aid Albany to obtain the Scottish crown and made it clear that he wanted not only Berwick but much of the Scottish Borders as well. Edward also undertook to grant his daughter Cecily in marriage to 'Alexander, King of Scotland'—if the latter 'can mak hym self clere fra all othir women . . . withyn ane yere next ensuyng'.[170] Although Albany's royal pretensions were, for the time being, to remain secret, he joined Gloucester, who on 12 January had been appointed Edward's lieutenant-general in charge of an expedition against his 'capital enemy', the Scottish king.[171]

---

[166] *Ibid.*, 139, c. 6.   [167] *Ibid.*, 140, c. 12.
[168] *Cal. Docs. Scot.*, IV. No. 1474. E. F. Jacob wrongly states that Albany had arrived in England in April 1481 (*The Fifteenth Century*, p. 585).
[169] *Cal. Docs. Scot.*, IV. No. 1475.   [170] *Ibid.*, No. 1476.
[171] *Rot. Scot.*, II. 458; *Cal. Docs. Scot.*, IV. No. 1474.

Gloucester's initial objective was Berwick. James had tried with some success to restore both the town's prosperity and its Scottish character by granting waste tenements to Scottish clerics and burgesses,[172] and after the outbreak of war he had incurred 'grete cost and expenss ... in the fortifying, strenthing and biggin [construction] of the wallis ... and reperacioune of the castell and stuffing thareof be artilzery'.[173] Throughout the winter of 1481–2 Berwick had been besieged by land and sea; but apart from destroying the newly-built encircling wall the besiegers had hitherto had no success.[174] It was doubtless the renewed threat to Berwick caused by the approach of Gloucester and Albany with a full-scale army that induced James to call out the Scottish host in July 1482 and to lead it in person.

The host assembled on the Burgh Muir of Edinburgh, marched to Soutra, and on the following day to the village of Lauder.[175] A number of lords now had the opportunity for which, according to Pitscottie, they had long planned : discontented with James's methods of government they had realised that 'thay could do nathing mair in this matter quhil [until] they war togither upoun the feildis in campt or battell'—it was when the magnates were gathered in arms and surrounded by their retainers that they stood least in awe of the monarch. Pitscottie even suggests that for this reason the malcontent nobles had deliberately broken the Anglo-Scottish truce so as to bring on war and cause the king to call out the host ;[176] it was certainly the Earl of Angus who had burned Bamburgh,[177] and when the magnates gathered in the kirk of Lauder and chose twenty-four of their number to concert measures against the king it was he who was 'principall of the consall'.[178] The others included the Earls of Huntly, Buchan and Lennox (*rectius* Lord Darnley) and Lords Gray and Lyle.[179] The boldness of their subsequent proceedings can be explained only on the assumption that for one reason or another James had alienated the majority of his nobles.

That the king's alleged lack of interest in military matters was involved may be discounted : his conduct of war measures was not lax; he was commended by parliament for his heavy personal expenditure in the defence of Berwick;[180] he seems to have had an

[172] *R.M.S.*, II. Nos. 1165, 1275, 1280-2, 1293; p. 298, n. 1.
[173] *A.P.S.*, II. 139, c. 7.   [174] Lesley, *History*, p. 45.
[175] Pitscottie, *Historie*, I. 172–3.   [176] *Ibid.*, 171.
[177] P. 490 above.   [178] Pitscottie, *Historie*, I. 173.
[179] These are the names given by Lesley (*History*, p. 48). Pitscottie's list seems unreliable.   [180] *A.P.S.*, II. 139, c. 7.

interest in artillery and during the current warfare spent over £200 on the purchase of iron for the fabrication of bombards and 'serpentines';[181] during the same period he showed concern for naval defence by spending over £300 on the construction of two 'roll bargis' (galleys);[182] finally the fact that James headed his army in person (which according to a recent measure he was not obliged to do, since he was not opposed by Edward in person) disposes of any suggestion of pusillanimity.

It was rather the inadequacies of James's administration that inspired disaffection: a sixteenth-century writer summed up what seems to have been the general opinion when he affirmed that he was not remarkable for his energy as a ruler.[183] In this respect some qualifications are required, for James did not altogether neglect government: the civil service was expanded, and holders of the new posts of director of chancery and receiver-general of the household augmented the civil servant element at exchequer audits, which followed their normal course even during the warfare and baronial disaffection of the summer of 1482.[184] Over government finance James seems to have kept a keen watch, and it was probably in order to prevent the growth of any vested interest in the key office of the comptroller that its holders (invariably clerics or lairds) were changed no less than twelve times between 1470 and 1488, while during most of this period the post of treasurer was held by the Abbots of Holyrood and Arbroath.[185] It is also clear that in some aspects of government, particularly in his contest with the papacy, James pursued his ends pertinaciously. He evidently had a liking for diplomacy and high politics, and, in the royal interest, notably developed the concept of treason and announced that by the common law of the realm the successors to traitors could not inherit their possessions save by royal grace.[186] In the more humdrum affairs of government that most nearly concerned his subjects he was less interested—it is perhaps significant that a note for the purchase of velvet lining for a riding gown was jotted down during parliament.[187]

Although parliament itself probably met as frequently as in previous reigns, the three estates and the king must have experienced some mutual disillusionment, largely because the problems in which they were involved were so intractable. In stubbornly ignoring

---

[181] *T.A.*, I. ccci.
[183] Ferrerius, *Continuatio*, p. 391.
[185] *H.B.C.*, pp. 181, 183–4.
[187] *T.A.*, I. 24.

[182] *E.R.*, IX. 218 n.
[184] *E.R.*, IX. 163–209.
[186] *R.M.S.*, II. No. 1203.

remonstrations on the subject of remissions [188] the king forfeited the goodwill of his subjects. The sale of remissions was not new, but it was unpopular. In *The Harp* [189] one anonymous poet obviously had James II or James III in mind when he declared :

> Bot of a [one] thing all gude men mervalis mair:
> Quhen grete counsale, with thine awn consent,
> Has ordanit strate justice na man to spair,
> Within schort tym thou changis thine entent,
> Sendand a contrair lettir incontinent,
> Chargeand that of that mater mair be nocht;
> Than al the warld murmuris that thou are bocht.

In *The Thre Prestis of Peblis* another anonymous poet satirised James's pliant and mercenary attitude towards justice,[190] and not without cause : between August 1473 and December 1474 the king drew almost £550 as the price of remissions and compositions granted to over sixty persons in respect of offences ranging from the receiving of outlaws to murder.[191] It was typical of the complexity of James's character, and of the consequent complexity of the reign, that the maladministration of justice sprang not only from greed but from clemency.[192] More serious in the immediate context of 1482 was the debasement of the coinage by the issue of the 'black money',[193] a copper coinage, so declared Bishop Lesley, 'unmeit to have course or passage in ony realme, quhairwith the pepill grudgeit, and sua wes the caus of greyt darthe and hunger throughout all the cuntrey'.[194] It was not debasement that caused a shortage of food but rather 'gret distructioun throw the weris . . . of corne and catell',[195] coupled with an English naval blockade which stopped trade ; hence an act of the parliament of March 1482 to attract foreign merchants 'and specially to gar [cause] vittalis be brocht in, sen [since] thar is now skantnes therof'.[196] The issue of a debased coinage was itself an inflationary measure; it coincided with a time of scarcity when prices would naturally be high; the combined effect was doubtless a sudden and extraordinary rise in the price of necessities. Thus a contemporary chronicler narrates that in 1482 'thar was ane gret hungyr and deid in Scotland, for the boll of meill was for four punds; for thar was

---

[188] Pp. 430–1 above.   [189] *Chron. Pluscarden*, I. 392–400.
[190] *The Thre Prestis of Peblis* (S.T.S.), pp. 31–8.
[191] *T.A.*, I. 2–12.   [192] See Boece, *Vitae*, pp. 52–3.
[193] Pp. 436–7 above.   [194] Lesley, *History*, p. 48.
[195] B.M. Royal MSS. 17 DXX in Pinkerton, *History*, I. 503.
[196] *A.P.S.*, II. 141, c. 18.

blak cunye in the realm, strikkin and ordinyt be King James the thred, half-pennys, and three-penny pennys, innumerabill, of coppir ... and mony pur folk deit of hungar'.[197] It was not only the poor who were affected : the Franciscan friars of Dundee had to pawn their books and ecclesiastical furnishings 'to sustain a miserable life';[198] one laird on 10 May 1482 entered into manrent with the Earl of Morton for money in his necessity.[199] According to the Pluscarden chronicler reformation of the coinage was one of the marks of a good ruler;[200] deformation of the coinage was doubtless the mark of a bad one; and by the summer of 1482 the resulting exasperation with James must have been wholesale and led to popular condemnation of all aspects of his government. There can be no doubt that it was James III to whom the poet Robert Henryson alluded in his fable of *The Lion and the Mouse* as a king who

> ... takis no laubour
> To rewll nor steir the land nor justice keip,
> Bot lyis still in lustis, slewth and sleip.[201]

In the same poem the reason why the hunters (the nobility) snare the lion (James) is conveyed in the lines

> The lyone yeid to hunt
> For he had nocht, bot levit on his pray,
> And slew baith tame and wyld as he wes wunt,
> And in the cuntre maid a grit dirray.[202]

A comparison of these two passages shows their incongruity : in the first the king is represented as slothful, in the second as energetically preying upon his tame (Lowland) and wild (Highland) subjects;[203] yet it is true that James could display energy as well as indolence and that some of the nobility had suffered at the hands of a government that in certain respects, particularly in transactions relating to land, was active enough. A sixteenth-century manuscript[204] relates the story that James with his own hands tore up the Earl of Morton's charter and was forced by the nobles to sew it up again. Although

---

[197] B.M. Royal MSS. 17 DXX in Pinkerton, *History*, I. 503.
[198] W. Moir Bryce, *The Scottish Grey Friars*, II. 129-33.
[199] *Morton Registrum*, II. No. 236.   [200] *Chron. Pluscarden*, II. 65.
[201] MacQueen, *Robert Henryson*, pp. 152-3, 170.   [202] *Ibid.*, 171-2.
[203] This was a neat allusion to such events as the forfeiture of the Boyds and the king's acquisition of the earldom of Ross.
[204] Printed in Pinkerton, *History*, II. 501.

this tale is apocryphal it at least symbolises the fear and resentment aroused by the king's tendency to regard the title to land not as indefeasible but subject to constant review and confirmation. There was probably also resentment that advancement to lands and offices, both lay and ecclesiastical, was no longer the natural perquisite of the nobility but had to be earned by drudgery in administration (as in the case of the Earl of Argyll and Lord Avondale) whereas it was forthcoming for others whose origins and talents seemed alike obscure.

These were the men whom Pitscottie styled the king's 'secreit servandis or cubecularis',[205] whom Lesley thought were the 'unworthye vyle persouns' who were the king's 'counsallouris',[206] and whom modern historians have pejoratively designated as 'favourites'.[207] A short contemporary chronicle, with more reticence, described them as members of the king's household;[208] James himself usually called them his 'familiars'. Up to the summer of 1482 this term was applied in official records to over twenty persons, of whom most, including William Roger, were styled familiar esquires,[209] some, including James Hommyl, as familiar servants,[210] and some as familiar clerks,[211] while the group included a number of physicians and apothecaries[212] whom the hypochondriac king retained, besides Thomas Cochrane and Thomas Preston (not styled familiars in the few references made to them in extant records).[213] It has been remarked that 'the names of Cochrane, Leonard, Torphichen, and Roger, . . . conspicuous in the pages of the late sixteenth-century historians, do not appear at all in the lists of witnesses in the Register of the Great Seal; nor do they figure in the sederunts of the Lords of Council'.[214] Certainly none of the familiars, with the exception of John Ross of Montgrenan, prominent as a lord of council in civil

---

[205] Pitscottie, *Historie*, I. 176. [206] Lesley, *History*, pp. 48–9.

[207] Mackie, *James IV*, p. 19.

[208] B.M. Royal MSS. 17 DXX in Pinkerton, *History*, I. 503.

[209] *R.M.S.*, II. No. 1418. See also Nos. 1116, 1119, 1141, 1454, 1475; *E.R.*, IX. 494 n.

[210] *E.R.*, IX. 93–4. See also *R.M.S.*, II. Nos. 1150, 1285, 1341.

[211] *R.M.S.*, II. Nos. 1280, 1357, 1468.

[212] Dr Andrews (*T.A.*, I. 69); Master Conrad (*R.M.S.*, II. No. 1343); Master Thomas Smith (*ibid.*, No. 1357).

[213] R. L. Mackie (*James IV*, p. 15), wrongly follows some narrative sources which give Cochrane's first name as Robert. Lesley (*History*, p. 48) names him Thomas, and there can be no doubt that the Thomas Cochrane alluded to in proceedings before the lords of council (*A.D.C.*, I. 49, 82), was the Cochrane who became notorious. For Preston see *E.R.*, IX. 218.

[214] Mackie, *James IV*, p. 16.

causes [215] and Sir John Colquhoun of Luss, familiar chamberlain of the household, who was killed at the siege of Dunbar in 1479, held any position in government. Torphichen (a fencing-master) and Leonard (a shoemaker) are not even mentioned in any extant record, though it should be borne in mind that the records of the household, as distinct from 'state' records, are no longer extant, and that for James's reign the accounts of the treasurer, full of intimate detail, survive for only 1473–4. Most of the familiars probably had official duties in the royal household, and these are occasionally mentioned : one familiar esquire was a member of the royal guard,[216] William Roger was probably clerk of the spices,[217] and one familiar clerk nicknamed 'Stobo' (perhaps the author of *The Thre Prestis of Peblis*) [218] was a scribe employed in writing letters to the pope and foreign potentates.[219]

The favour in which the king held his familiars was displayed in the grants he bestowed upon them, sometimes to the detriment of the nobility. It was out of reverence for the king (which may mean under royal pressure) that Lord Hamilton granted lands in Lanarkshire to his kinsman, David Hamilton, a familiar esquire.[220] By 1473 another familiar esquire, David Crichton, had supplanted the Earl of Argyll in the custody of Edinburgh Castle, worth two hundred marks a year ;[221] he soon obtained lands resigned by the Earl of Angus, by Robert Lauder of the Bass, and by Sir John Colquhoun of Luss,[222] and had his lands erected as a free barony.[223] In 1473 a quarter of the earldom of Lennox was bestowed in heritage upon another familiar esquire, John Haldane of Rusky, 'as first and principal of the same'.[224] Although this grant reserved the liferent of the whole earldom, which had been conferred in 1471 upon Chancellor Avondale,[225] the latter can hardly have relished Haldane's advancement. Still less can it have pleased Lord Darnley, who was officially recognised as Earl of Lennox in 1473 only to have his title revoked in 1476.[226] James Hommyl, the king's tailor, described more flatteringly as 'familiar servitur and werkman for oure persoun', received miscellaneous small grants from 1473 onwards, and by letters under the privy seal

---

[215] E.g. *A.D.C.*, I. 19, 29, 79.
[216] *R.M.S.*, II. No. 1283.
[217] *E.R.*, VIII. 190.
[218] This is plausibly argued by T. D. Robb in the S.T.S. edition of the poem, pp. xiv–xix.
[219] *R.M.S.*, II. No. 1341.
[220] *Ibid.*, No. 1284.
[221] *E.R.*, VIII. 190, 253.
[222] *R.M.S.*, II. Nos. 1202, 1213, 1299.
[223] *Ibid.*, No. 1356.
[224] *Ibid.*, No. 1116.
[225] *Ibid.*, No. 1018.
[226] *H.B.C.*, p. 480.

was awarded in 1478 a yearly pension of £20 for life.[227] William Roger, a talented musician whose pupils were held in esteem long after his own death,[228] had accompanied an English embassy to Scotland and then entered James's service as a familiar esquire, being rewarded with no less a grant than the barony of Traquair. Aristocratic resentment probably caused this grant to be revoked in 1476, after which Traquair was bestowed in more conventional fashion upon the king's uncle, the Earl of Buchan.[229]

It was Thomas Cochrane, however, whose advancement seems to have been most bitterly resented. Originally an apprentice to a mason, he 'become verie ingeneous into that craft, and bigit [built] money stain house'.[230] Thanks to his skill he was appointed the king's master mason, and in this capacity was probably the architect of the great hall of Stirling Castle. In 1480 he was granted a total of £60 due to the king as a result of litigation before the lords of council, and he was the tenant of lands in Cousland probably conferred by the king and worth £20 a year.[231] Much more striking is the fact that Lesley and Pitscottie state that Cochrane was made Earl of Mar after the death of the king's brother—an event for which Pitscottie held Cochrane responsible.[232] It at least seems that 'the revenues of the earldom were out of the crown's hands during the period when Cochrane is said to have been earl'.[233] If Cochrane was indeed made Earl of Mar, or given its revenues, or even a post of responsibility in administering the earldom, such a step was injudicious in the extreme. For while the talents of James's familiars would be mostly recognised as respectable by modern standards they were not the sort that by fifteenth-century standards were expected to be notably rewarded.

Apart from the disturbance to aristocratic vested interests implied in the advancement of some of James's familiars, a constitutional issue was involved: it was believed, and possibly correctly, that the king's policies and behaviour were influenced by the secret whisperings of his low-born familiars; following counsel that was 'young', not 'wise',[234] he 'keipit him self quietlie, leveing voluptuouslie, and had lychtlyit [scorned] his awin nobill quene, and intertanit ane howir [whore] callit the Daesie, in her place; and . . . causit slay

---

[227] E.R., IX. xlv, 93–4.　　　[228] Ferrerius, Continuatio, p. 395.
[229] R.M.S., II. No. 1418.　　　[230] Pitscottie, Historie, I. 176.
[231] A.D.C., I. 49, 82.
[232] Lesley, History, p. 48; Pitscottie, Historie, I. 166–8.
[233] E.R., IX. xliii–xliv.
[234] See The Thre Prestis of Peblis (S.T.S.), pp. 31, 38.

his awin brodir, the Erle of Mar, and banisd his uther brodir the Duik of Albany',[235] Moreover direct responsibility for the latest disastrous debasement of the coinage was attributed to Cochrane.[236] According to Pitscottie the latter 'grew sa familiear witht . . . the kingis grace that . . . all men that wald have had thair bussienes drest [expedited] . . . come to Couchrin, and maid him forspeiker for them and gaif him large money'.[237] To the anonymous eighteenth-century author of *The Life of Sir Robert* [sic] *Cochran, Prime Minister to King James III of Scotland*,[238] such a situation was natural enough, and the purpose of his fanciful treatise was to satirise Sir Robert Walpole. But to the fifteenth-century Scottish nobility, the situation was novel and unnatural: the court had become the place in which policy was formulated, parliament and council merely the places in which it was publicised; the great lords and officers of state, the king's official councillors, were no longer his real counsellors but had become mere administrators, relegated to such tedious tasks as assessing royal lands, auditing accounts, hearing literally hundreds of cases as auditors of causes and complaints or as lords of council,[239] while the king 'wrocht mair the consaell of his housald, at war bot sympill, na he did of thame that war lordds'.[240] The new breed of courtier had displaced the feudal baron and, thanks to the personal interests of James III, good birth was not by itself a qualification for a place as courtier: 'be this way the kingis grace tint [lost] money of the harttis of the

---

[235] Lesley, *History*, p. 48. The Daesie, together with Lesley's later reference to James as 'taking his plesour of wemen' (*ibid.*, p. 55), would seem to dispose of a recently expressed view (A. J. Stewart, *Falcon: The Autobiography of His Grace James the 4 King of Scots*, pp. 19–20), that the attachment between James and his familiars was homosexual and that this explains what took place at Lauder. There are several allusions to James's lust: in Robert Henryson's fable of *The Lion and the Mouse* it is linked with the vice of sloth (p. 500 above); according to Boece (*Vitae*, p. 51), Bishop Elphinstone urged the king to eschew lust and content himself with Queen Margaret, 'the chastest of women', as 'the consort of a genial couch'; Buchanan, whose veracity may be questioned, relates that James seduced the wife of Lord Crichton and that it was as an act of revenge that Crichton seduced the king's sister. (See P. F. Tytler, *History*, I. pt. ii, Notes and Illustrations, pp. 388–9). In *The Thre Prestis of Peblis* (S.T.S., pp. 39–44), an apocryphal tale of the attempted seduction of a burgess's daughter seems to allude to the amours of James III.

[236] Lesley, *History*, p. 48; Pitscottie, *Historie*, I. 169.

[237] Pitscottie, *Historie*, I. 168–9; Ferrerius, *Continuatio*, p. 395; Lesley, *History*, p. 48.

[238] Published (2nd edn.) in London in 1734.

[239] The sederunts of the lords of council in civil causes (*A.D.C.*, I. 3–79), disprove the view that the nobles were not pulling their weight in the administration of justice.

[240] B.M. Royal MSS. 17 DXX in Pinkerton, *History*, I. 504.

lordis . . . and allso of thair souns and brether that faine wald have
servit the kingis grace bot thai could gett na place for this Couchrin
and his companie'.[241] Thus in the kirk of Lauder an attack upon the
courtiers was planned.

According to a seventeenth-century source some difficulty arose
as to who was to initiate the attack : the mice would fain hang a bell
around the cat that preyed upon them, but which mouse was to bell
the cat? The Earl of Angus, who may not have forgiven the king's
attack upon the Boyd kinsfolk of his wife,[242] is traditionally believed
to have volunteered and thereby became known as Archibald Bell-
the-Cat.[243] Pitscottie gives a colourful account of what followed :
Cochrane, whose accoutrements and campaigning outfit were
ostentatiously impressive, was arrested by Angus and Sir Robert
Douglas, laird of Lochleven ; it may well be believed that the former
snatched the gold chain from the doomed courtier's neck while the
latter grasped the ornate hunting horn that he carried ;[244] certainly
one of the baronial underlings took the opportunity at Lauder to
purloin £146 from one of the Edinburgh custumars.[245] The lynching party probably extemporised a court of some sort : Cochrane and
Thomas Preston were afterwards deemed to have been sentenced to
forfeiture.[246] They, William Roger, and other courtiers, were hanged
from Lauder brig and 'the blak silver' (the coinage attributed to
Cochrane) was 'cryit downe' or devalued. Not all of the courtiers
perished, for the lords 'slew ane part of the king's housald, and other
part thai banysyt'. Among the latter were James Hommyl the tailor,
and John Ramsay, a young courtier of good birth who was spared
at the 'ernist supplicatione' of the king. James himself was taken
back to Edinburgh and on 22 July 1482 was warded in the castle in
the keeping of his uncle of Atholl.[247]

Had the ringleaders of the Lauder conspiracy marched forward
to relieve Berwick their conduct would have been less questionable
and their capacity for leadership more obvious. Instead they allowed
the host to disband and left the country without government and

[241] Pitscottie, *Historie*, I. 170. [242] Pp. 418–9 above.
[243] See Mackie, *James IV*, p. 19. [244] Pitscottie, *Historie*, I. 175.
[245] *E.R.*, IX. 219 n.
[246] *A.D.C.*, I. 82; *R.M.S.*, II. No. 1533. Lesley (*History*, p. 49), states that the
victims were 'convict'.
[247] Pitscottie, *Historie*, I. 175–6; B.M. Royal MSS. 17 DXX in Pinkerton,
History, I. 503; Ferrerius, *Continuatio*, pp. 394v–395v. Lesley (*History*, p. 49)
wrongly states that Hommyl was hanged.

without defence. The opportunity was immediately seized by the Dukes of Gloucester and Albany : leaving the siege of Berwick they marched unopposed upon Edinburgh and encamped outside the town at the beginning of August. It was fortunate for the townsfolk that the mission of the English army was political rather than military : Albany was well placed to turn recent events to his own advantage and to emerge as Alexander IV, vassal of the Yorkists; hence Gloucester's aim was not to defeat the Scots (they had already defeated themselves) but to exact the political rewards of victory. This meant that there had to be negotiations with the Scottish leaders —whoever they were. On 2 August they appeared, not in the form of Bell-the-Cat and his henchmen but in that of Archbishop Scheves, James Livingston, Bishop of Dunkeld, the Earl of Argyll and Chancellor Avondale,[248] who crawled bravely from the wreck of government as a group of moderate royalists. They were hardly the audience to whom Albany had hoped to propound his royal pretensions ; nor, without the participation of James III (which could have been obtained only by a siege of the castle) were they capable of ceding the territories that Edward coveted. Thus Albany seems to have decided to conceal the full scope of his schemes in the hope that he could construct a government that would countenance them : like Henry Bolingbroke in 1399 and Edward of York in 1471 he had ostensibly come back merely to secure his own inheritance.

This was something which Scheves and his party were hardly in a position to withhold, particularly since there was obviously widespread sympathy for the dispossessed duke, and the process of forfeiture against him had not culminated in a sentence. Thus on 2 August 1482 the archbishop and his three colleagues sealed an obligation in which they undertook to obtain remission and restoration for Albany and his adherents if the duke would observe his allegiance to James III.[249] This last provision demonstrated the political acumen of Scheves and his party : if it were broken they were no longer committed to supporting the duke ; nor could Albany refuse to accept this condition without immediately publicising his own designs upon the throne, for which the time was not yet ripe. Gloucester, the watchdog over Yorkist interests, understood Albany's dilemma and contented himself with a written assurance that despite any agreements the latter had made, or might make, with Scottish lords, he would remain true to the treaty of Fotheringhay[250]—a stipulation that explains,

[248] Lesley, *History*, p. 49; *Cal. Docs. Scot.*, IV. No. 1479.
[249] *Cal. Docs. Scot.*, IV. No. 1479.   [250] Mackie, *James IV*, p. 22.

though hardly excuses, Albany's subsequent conduct. In another respect Gloucester showed commendable moderation : instead of sacking and burning Edinburgh he accepted 'only such presentes as the merchantis gentelly offered him and his capitaynes' ;[251] and on 4 August he obtained from Provost Walter Bertram and 'the hale fallowschip of merchandis, burgesses and communite' a bond that committed them to refund the advance instalments of Cecily's dowry if Edward signified his intention to break off the match between his daughter and the Duke of Rothesay.[252] On 27 October Edward duly intimated through Garter king-of-arms that this was his intention.[253]

A truce might have been expected to follow these arrangements, but it suited Albany that the English should continue their efforts to capture Berwick rather than that he should immediately blight his prospects by incurring the odium of yielding the town. Thus Gloucester marched back to resume the siege of Berwick while Albany went through the farcical motion of leading a force as far as the Lammermuirs, supposedly to raise the siege. The defenders of Berwick, who had acquitted themselves well against the English, saw that they had been either betrayed or deserted : the town (though not the castle) seems already to have been lost by 24 August 1482 when they capitulated and 'partit thairfra with bagg and baggages'.[254] By November Edward was making arrangements to provision the town and castle, and in February 1483 he graciously confirmed the charters of the burgesses.[255]

Meanwhile, shortly after his assumption of government, Albany had gone with the archbishop, Chancellor Avondale and the Earl of Argyll, to hold consultation at Stirling with Queen Margaret and the nine-year-old Duke of Rothesay. Probably the suggestion was made that the Queen should use her good offices to induce James III to abdicate in favour of the heir apparent, and that Albany be recognised as governor. The queen's advice was that James must first be set at liberty. It can hardly have been on account of Albany's implementation of this proposal (as Lesley suggests) that Scheves, Argyll and Avondale 'throw gret feir fled into thair awin cuntreyis'.[256] What is more likely is that the duke had disclosed his own hopes of attaining the crown and that this had lost him the support of the influential trio. Thus Albany had to seek other allies.

[251] *Ibid.*, p. 21.   [252] *Cal. Docs. Scot.*, IV. No. 1480.
[253] *Ibid.*, Nos. 1481, 1482, 1483, 1484.
[254] Lesley, *History*, pp. 49-50; *E.R.*, IX. xlii and n. 1.
[255] *Rot. Scot.*, II. 458-60.   [256] Lesley, *History*, p. 50.

Their identity is revealed in the witness list of a charter dated at Edinburgh on 25 August 1482.[257] Avondale had been replaced as chancellor by John Laing, Bishop of Glasgow. Other witnesses, including James Livingston, Bishop of Dunkeld, were probably associated with the new administration less by inclination than by a desire to preserve government. Three witnesses, however—the Earls of Atholl and Buchan and their brother, Andrew Stewart, Bishop elect of Moray (now keeper of the privy seal), formed a special group : they were the king's uncles and one of them, Atholl, had custody of Edinburgh Castle and the imprisoned king. The price of their support for Albany was that Andrew Stewart should be made Archbishop of St Andrews. Probably the king was induced to write to persuade the loyal Scheves to go through the motions of appointing procurators to resign the archbishopric.[258] By 8 November the Edinburgh burgesses had also been induced to pledge their already strained credit to furnish 6,000 gold ducats to finance the promotion of Andrew Stewart at the *curia*, receiving in return a promise of repayment from him, his brothers, and three of their associates.[259] Meanwhile the king was to be released, which meant that he was to be delivered to Albany. This, however, could not be arranged without stratagem since Atholl was under some commitment to the ringleaders of the Lauder conspiracy : although he was a witness to the charter issued by the new administration on 25 August, and to its next recorded charter on 10 October,[260] his honour had to be saved in the interim by a 'siege' of the castle that lasted until Michaelmas (29 September)[261] when, so affirms the credulous Bishop Lesley, its defenders capitulated 'for want of victuallis'.[262]

James, well aware of the part he was expected to play, accompanied his brother in a triumphal procession from the castle to the abbey of Holyrood,[263] 'quhair they remainit ane quhyle in great mirienes'. To publicise Albany's faithful service to the king who had once injured him, two charters were issued on 16 November granting

---

[257] *R.M.S.*, II. No. 1517.

[258] P. 513 below; Lesley, *History*, p. 50; Ferrerius, *Continuatio*, p. 396v. J. Herkless and R. K. Hannay (*Archbishops of St Andrews*, I. 109), criticise Scheves for failing to behave like a second Anselm or Becket; they seem unaware that times had changed and that the issues were different.

[259] *Edinburgh City Charters*, No. liii.

[260] *R.M.S.*, II. Nos. 1517, 1518.

[261] B.M. Royal MSS. 17 DXX, in Pinkerton, *History*, I. 504.

[262] Lesley, *History*, p. 50; Ferrerius, *Continuatio*, p. 396v.

[263] Pitscottie, whose account of this period is hopelessly confused, is probably correct in this detail (*Historie*, I. 182).

to the magistrates of Edinburgh the office of sheriffship within the burgh and strengthening the burgh's control over the vassal town of Leith;[264] these favours were rewards for the support the burgesses had given to the king's 'dearest brother', even exposing their lives to danger, in besieging Edinburgh Castle and restoring James to complete liberty. For the same reason (and to compensate for the losses he had incurred on the king's behalf) Walter Bertram was granted an annual pension of £40 payable during the lifetime of himself and his wife.[265] Albany's exercise in propaganda was not in vain : the heroism of the Edinburgh burgesses was commemorated by Robert Henryson in the fable of *The Lion and the Mouse*; the mice who free the lion (James) trapped by the hunters (the nobility) are the Edinburgh burgesses, and the leading mouse is doubtless Bertram.[266]

Albany's own heroic services had been recognised in a 'great council' in which he was granted the earldom of Mar and the Garioch and was styled in a manner that indicated not only his restoration to all his former lands and offices but his assumption of the post of king's lieutenant-general.[267] To consolidate his position the duke summoned a parliament to meet at Edinburgh. When it assembled on 2 December 1482 Scheves, Argyll and Avondale were notable absentees. It is also striking that in contrast to the previous parliament of March 1482 there was a complete absence of lairds. That these were reckoned to be supporters of the king may be deduced from the announcement continuing parliament to 1 March 1483 but excusing from attendance all persons with an income of less than £100.[268] In other respects, however, the composition of the parliament of December 1482 was perfectly normal, and the attendance much the same as in the parliament that James had held in April 1478.[269] The crucial question that was to be decided by parliament was whether Albany should be recognised as lieutenant-general. The method devised to achieve this goal proceeded from a review of the existing war with England. It was ordained that 'pece be takin with Ingland gif it can be had with honour' : a herald was to be sent to announce the willingness of the Scots to renew the truce

[264] *Edinburgh City Charters*, Nos, liv, lv; p. 452 above.

[265] *E.R.*, IX. 219–20; *R.M.S.*, II. No. 1829.

[266] Equating the mouse with 'the ordinary people of Scotland', John MacQueen (*Robert Henryson*, pp. 170–3), does not detect the more precise allegory.

[267] *R.M.S.*, II. No. 1541. Although the charter is inserted in a position that would indicate a date between 18 and 20 January 1483 the editor rightly states in a footnote that it was probably issued between 29 September and 10 October 1482 (as the witness list suggests).

[268] *A.P.S.*, II. 145.   [269] Compare *ibid.*, 115, 136–7, 142.

and (all too optimistically) the marriage contract between Rothesay and Cecily. If, however, the English were determined to wage war, James professed his readiness to 'defend his realme in honour and freedom'. Next it was announced that 'it accordis nocht to the honoure of his hienes [James] to put his nobile persone daily to dangere'; he should therefore 'speke to his bruther, the Duke of Albany, to tak apone him to be lieutenent generale of the realme . . . and to avise how he sal be supportit to bere the grete charge and costis of the saide office etc.' A further act ordained that the warden courts should be held frequently to punish 'baith tratouris and theyfis', and since Albany was warden of the East and West Marches this measure would have given him the power to suppress whomsoever he deemed to be traitors.[270]

Despite his apparent victory Albany could make no headway in the cross currents of Scottish politics. Those who attended parliament were not all supporters of the duke rather than of the king: the more worldly-wise were aware that James was not a free agent and they had come to fish in troubled waters; the less worldly-wise, deluded by Albany's own propaganda, believed that James was really free, and expected to see him wielding his former authority. Thus Albany had to take his place in parliament as merely foremost of the barons,[271] while, it may be supposed, James sat in state, and, to at least a limited extent, had the chance to influence the proceedings and revive old loyalties. In July exasperation with the king and his familiars was wholesale, but it must have varied greatly in intensity; it is unlikely that every magnate approved of the exploits of Bell-the-Cat; and some may have been shocked into a new loyalty towards James as recollection of his former conduct was replaced by sympathy for his humiliation, and as the months of famine were replaced by better times; for after the king's release 'the victall grew better chaip, for the boll that was for four pounds was than for xxii s. of quhyt silver'.[272] It was a sign of the reviving of James's authority that no outright appointment of Albany as lieutenant-general was made in parliament but that the three estates assumed that it was the king who had to make the appointment. Whether or not the king did, Albany's power was already waning. He appeared for the last time as witness to a royal charter on 25 December;[273] it was Bishop Livingston of Dunkeld, a former associate of Scheves, Argyll and Avondale,

[270] *Ibid.*, pp. 143–4, cc. 1–2, 4.   [271] *Ibid.*, 142.
[272] B.M. Royal MSS. 17 DXX, in Pinkerton, *History*, I. 504.
[273] *R.M.S.*, II. No. 1533.

who became chancellor when Bishop Laing of Glasgow died on 11 January 1483;[274] on the following day Albany issued letters from Dunbar empowering the Earl of Angus, Lord Gray, and Sir James Liddell of Halkerston to go on a mission to Edward IV.[275]

Liddell had already been employed by Albany on a similar mission in the autumn of 1482,[276] but the association of Angus and Gray with the duke was new and must have been formed after the December parliament which Angus attended.[277] Until then, he had been sulking in Tantallon,[278] a residence calculated to inspire any owner with delusions of unique grandeur. In August, when news of Lauder was fresh, when Gloucester's army was at the gates of Edinburgh, and when James was a prisoner, an alliance between Albany and Bell-the-Cat might have been overpowering, and such an alliance must have seemed almost inevitable. But it is clear that the conspiracies of Albany and Bell-the-Cat had been entirely distinct and in no way co-ordinated. Apart from any feeling that Albany had stolen his thunder, Angus must have suspected that the duke had promised Edward to restore the disinherited Douglas. The latter too was a natural ally of Albany, but his restoration would mean not only that Angus would lose the headship of the Douglas 'name' to the senior branch, but would lose the lordship of Douglasdale granted to his father by James II.[279] Thus Albany had either to choose between Angus and Douglas or arrange a settlement between them. This was the belated object of the mission to the English court. On 11 February 1483 Angus, Gray and Liddell signed and sealed a treaty at Westminster with the Earl of Northumberland and other English commissioners. The terms resembled those formerly agreed upon at Fotheringhay and, in addition, bound Albany to assist the restoration of Douglas in accordance with a convention arranged between the latter and Angus; in return Edward would help Albany to acquire the Scottish crown by conquest. On the following day arrangements were made to send Douglas to Scotland.[280]

It was too late. James III's restoration to power may be traced by the appearance as witnesses to his charters of Scheves in January, Argyll in February, and Avondale in March,[281] and the corresponding

[274] H.B.C., p. 175.
[275] Cal. Docs. Scot., IV. No. 1486.
[276] Ibid., No. 1478.
[277] A.P.S., II. 142.
[278] In contrast to Buchan and Atholl he witnessed no royal charters in this period. On 28 September he was in Tantallon (R.M.S., II. No. 1619).
[279] See ibid., No. 774.
[280] Cal. Docs. Scot., IV. Nos. 1489, 1490; Rot. Scot., II. 458.
[281] R.M.S., II. Nos. 1544, 1555, 1563.

disappearance of the king's three uncles. Only one of these, Buchan, dared to join Albany in Dunbar, and a charter issued there by the duke on 21 February [282] suggests that his following had dwindled to a handful of desperate men, including Lord Crichton and James, 'Lord' Boyd, son of the first marriage of the king's sister with the forfeited Earl of Arran, nephew of Angus's wife, Elizabeth Boyd, and grandson and heir of Robert, Lord Boyd, who seems to have died shortly before.[283] By this time also, those who were beneficiaries under charters issued by Angus and his predecessors were obtaining royal confirmations,[284] which suggests that the earl's intrigues in England had become known and were expected to lead to his forfeiture.

The parliament of December 1482 had been continued until 1 March 1483 and duly assembled on that date, when Scheves, Argyll and Avondale were appointed to the committee of the articles. Since James was not yet ready to crush Albany there were successive continuations until 27 June.[285] In the meantime the duke was forced to accept the humiliating terms of an indenture drawn up at Edinburgh on 16 March 1483 and signed and sealed by him at Dunbar three days later.[286] Albany was 'nocht in tyme tocum' to 'use . . . the office of lieutenend generale . . . bot discharge hyme therof now incontinent'. He was to produce to parliament a letter under his seal refuting 'a sclandir and murmur rising in the cuntre' that he had been poisoned while at court.[287] He was to swear never in future to make treasonable leagues with the English king, renounce those that he had already made, deliver letters to this effect that could be displayed to Edward, and use his influence to obtain peace and the marriage alliance. The duke was also to deliver to James letters of manrent promising lifelong loyalty, renounce all bonds that he had made in Scotland, especially those binding him to the king's three uncles, the Earl of Angus, Lords Crichton and Gray, Sir John Douglas (Master of Morton), Alexander Home (nephew of Lord Home), and James Liddell of Halkerston, discharge all of them from their undertakings to Edward, and 'nocht hauld thame in daily houshauld in tyme tocum'. None of these persons, nor the duke himself, was to approach within six miles of the king without special leave. In addition some of Albany's supporters were to be further humiliated : the Master of Morton was to surrender the sheriffship of Edinburgh; Angus was to surrender his offices as justiciar south of Forth, as steward of Kirk-

[282] *Ibid.*, No. 1573.
[284] *R.M.S.*, II. Nos. 1550, 1560.
[286] Text in *A.P.S.*, XII. 31-3.

[283] *Scots Peerage*, V. 145.
[285] *A.P.S.*, II. 145.
[287] See Lesley, *History*, pp. 50-1.

cudbright, and as sheriff of Lanark, as well as his custody of Threave Castle and a lucrative wardship; Buchan was to surrender the chamberlainship (now given to the Earl of Crawford),[288] the wardenship of the Middle March and the custody of Newark Castle; together with Crichton and Liddell, he was also to 'devoid the realme of Scotland and the realme of Ingland' for three years. His brother, Andrew Stewart, Bishop elect of Moray, saw the waning of his hopes of supplanting Scheves in the archbishopric by means of 'the pretendit procuratouris of resignacioune therof that he [Scheves] wes throw force, aw, and dreid, compellit to constitut and mak, as is notourly knawin': instead of supporting Andrew Stewart's ecclesiastical schemes Albany was obliged to bestow his 'hertly favouris and tendirness' upon Scheves.

In return for all the king's demands upon Albany and his followers they received few concessions: the king undertook to regard his brother with 'hertly lufe, favore and tendirnes in tyme tocum' and to grant remissions to him and all adherents whom he named; the names were to be forwarded to the chancellor within twenty days, and Albany was to 'mak faith that thai personis tuke part with him, and that he sal ask remissioune to nane uthir bot to thame that tuke part with hyme'. In these few words, perhaps, may be seen the whole object of the lengthy indenture: for if such a list were ever delivered by Albany it would have given James a chart by which to map his future political course. Nor was the indenture likely to prove any obstacle: the signed and sealed letters of security to be given to Albany depended upon his 'kepand his lauty . . . to oure soverane lord'; and the loyalty of Albany, if not also the good faith of James, proved as lasting as snow in summer. On 17 May 1483 Rothesay herald summoned the duke and Liddell of Halkerston to compear in parliament on 27 June to answer charges of treason.[289] Shortly after this summons, having collected his Whitsuntide rents, Albany fled by sea to England and arranged that an English garrison should be admitted to his castle of Dunbar.[290] The 'parliament' of 27 June was in fact a continuation of that of 1 March and was held by Crawford and Argyll, acting as the king's justiciars. Their duty was simply to continue the processes against Albany and Liddell from day to day until 8 July when the king and the three estates assembled. After the summonses and charges had been rehearsed, John Ross of Mont-

[288] H.B.C., p. 179.   [289] A.P.S., II. 151, 152.
[290] E.R., IX. 427. Lesley's account (History, p. 51), wrongly states that the duke sailed to France.

grenan, the king's advocate, obtained the expected verdict of forfeiture against Albany and Liddell of Halkerston, who tactfully
failed to compear.[291]

Within a year of the twofold threat to his crown that stemmed
from the bitter humiliation of Lauder and Albany's bid for power
James had adroitly mastered his opponents. It may well be believed
that it had been a year when 'thair wes greit thift, reiff and slauchter
in divers partis of the realme, quhilk come be the occasioun of the
diversitye betuix the king and his nobles'.[292] It was probably typical
that Sir Anselm Adournes, one of the more exotic of the king's
familiars, was involved in the faction-fighting (he destroyed the
east mill of Linlithgow)[293] and that he was slain by Alexander Jardine, a henchman of Douglas,[294] while Albany's attempt to restore the
Boyds by granting their former lands in liferent to Lady Hamilton
and in fee to her son by her first marriage, led to the slaying of the
latter by Hugh Montgomery of Eglinton.[295]

For the royalists, at least, there was some reparation of past misfortunes : as a result of litigation before the lords of council Archibald Preston, probably a kinsman of the deceased Thomas Preston,
was installed in the lands of Cousland formerly occupied by the luck-
less Cochrane; and as a result of litigation before the lords auditors
of causes and complaints the widow of Thomas Preston was awarded
substantial sums of money.[296] Of the survivors of the attacks upon the
king's familiars John Haldane had his lands erected into the free
barony of Gleneagles,[297] John Ross of Montgrenan sat once more
as a lord of council in civil causes,[298] James Hommyl resumed his
well-paid sewing of the royal garments,[299] and the young John Ram-

[291] A.P.S., II. 145–52.   [292] Lesley, History, p. 50.

[293] E.R., IX. 400, 460. Adournes held lands near Linlithgow (R.M.S., II. No.
1735).

[294] Adournes was dead by 29 January 1483 (R.M.S., II. No. 1548). Flemish
sources describe his slayer as 'Sander Gardin', whom W. H. Finlayson took to be
the marquis (sic) of Huntly, and whom a critical correspondent took to be Alexander, third son of the first Earl of Huntly (op. cit., S.H.R., XXVIII. 195–6, at 196;
XXIX. 120). There can be little doubt, however, that 'Sander Gardin' was 'Alexander Jarding', a diehard Douglas follower who was excluded from a general
remission offered in the parliament of March 1482 (A.P.S., II. 139, c. 6; p. 496
above).

[295] See Scots Peerage, V. 149–50, where, however, the view that James III
sanctioned the restoration of James Boyd is based upon a misunderstanding of a
royal confirmation (R.M.S., II. No. 1573).

[296] A.D.C., I. 82; A.D.A., pp. 115, 116, 120.   [297] R.M.S., II. No. 1546.
[298] A.D.C., I. 81–118.   [299] E.R., IX. 249.

say, who had had a narrow escape at Lauder, was well rewarded for the risk he had run. Described as a 'familiar esquire of the chamber' he was granted some titbits of land in September 1483.[300] Then on 25 February 1484, with the approval of parliament, he was granted the lordship of Bothwell (revoked from Lord Monypenny) and to this grant some representatives of each estate attached their seals. On the same day they also sealed a grant whereby Ramsay and his mother, Janet Napier (now wife of an Edinburgh burgess),[301] were confirmed as tenants of lands recently awarded to them by the lords of council at the expense of Lord Crichton.[302] After attaining his majority the new Lord Bothwell would figure as ambassador, witness to royal charters, and commissioner for the assessment of crown lands.[303]

Even before the forfeiture of Albany the king had begun to fill the gaps among his familiars, and by the end of the reign their number probably exceeded forty. From the Lauder episode he had at least learnt to exclude the exotic, and to give some heed to good birth. Thus Oliver Sinclair, son of the Earl of Caithness, appeared as a 'familiar knight', as did Sir Patrick Hepburn of Dunsyre who had lately held Berwick Castle against the English;[304] and Alexander Kennedy, son of Lord Kennedy, became an usher of the chamber.[305] In addition, as was pompously announced in a charter of 1484,[306] James was prepared to reward services to the state of a type that the nobility could understand—victory in warfare was particularly mentioned. Already John Dundas of that Ilk, described as 'familiar esquire of the chamber', had obtained the lands of the barony of Bothkennar for helping in the release of the king from Edinburgh Castle,[307] and James, having considered the trusty deeds of his familiar servant, Andrew Wood, both on land and sea, especially his exploits against the English, had rewarded him 'in the time of parliament' by converting his nineteen-year tack of the township of Largo into a grant in feu-ferm.[308]

Further opportunity for the bestowal of rewards and familiarity was forthcoming through the forfeiture of Albany. If the date of a royal charter is to be believed, the Earl of Argyll had already, on 29

[300] R.M.S., II. No. 1565.   [301] Ibid., No. 1591.
[302] A.P.S., II. 153–4; R.M.S., II. No. 1577. Crichton also lost lands through a decreet of the lords auditors of causes and complaints (ibid., No. 1575).
[303] R.M.S., II. Nos. 1666–1722, passim; E.R., IX. 631, 639, 649.
[304] E.R., IX. xlii and n. I.
[305] R.M.S., II. Nos. 1552, 1665, 1718.   [306] Ibid., No. 1590.
[307] Ibid., No. 1539.   [308] Ibid., No. 1563.

April 1483, been granted certain lands forfeited from 'Alexander, onetime Duke of Albany',[309] some two months before sentence of forfeiture was passed on 8 July. Thereafter parliament had appointed a commission of twenty-three ecclesiastics, twenty-three barons, and the representatives of ten burghs, to have power to annex to the crown the lands forfeited from the duke and Liddell of Halkerston, 'sa that thereafter our soveran lord may be avisit how he wil dispone the remanent to the rewarding of his trew liegis that has in tymes bigain done, and sal in tyme tocum do, his hienes gude and trew service'.[310] Portions of Albany's lands were eventually bestowed upon the Earl of Crawford, John Home, familiar esquire of the chamber, the familiar Alexander Home of that Ilk (Master of Home, grandson and heir of Lord Home) and Alexander Bruce, familiar esquire.[311]

Meanwhile the political eccentricities of Scotland had been surpassed by those of England: Edward IV had died on 9 April 1483; his son, the young Edward V, was deposed on 25 June and subsequently perished with his brother in the Tower; the Duke of Gloucester acceded as Richard III on 26 June; and, in the course of the blood-letting that accompanied and followed these events, Lord Hastings was executed on 13 June, Earl Rivers on 23 June, and the Duke of Buckingham on 2 November, while from the spring of 1484 onwards Richard III was expecting an invasion led by Henry Tudor, Earl of Richmond, who was raising forces in France.[312] Thus when Albany reached England after his flight from Dunbar at Whitsuntide 1483 the times were not propitious for a major expedition to reinstate him in Scotland. Instead Douglas was granted an annuity of £200 on 12 February 1484 [313] and was probably given a free hand to co-operate with Albany. The pair descended upon Lochmaben when a fair was being held on 22 July 1484.[314] It had not been forgotten that in the parliament of March 1482 a reward in cash and land had been proffered to anyone who killed or captured Douglas.[315] Inspired by self-interest, if not patriotism, the Borderers rallied. Robert and Edward Crichton, members of the Sanquhar branch of that family, were afterwards favoured with charters for their part in the engagement, while Alexander Kirkpatrick, an old retainer of Douglas, took the earl prisoner and was duly rewarded with lands worth £100

[309] *Ibid.*, No. 1564.   [310] *A.P.S.*, II. 146.
[311] *R.M.S.*, II. Nos. 1571, 1572, 1599, 1638; *E.R.*, x. xl.
[312] E. F. Jacob, *The Fifteenth Century*, pp. 610–28, 639.
[313] *Cal. Docs. Scot.*, IV. Nos. 1494, 1496, 1497.
[314] Lesley, *History*, p. 47; Godscroft, *Douglas and Angus*, pp. 205–6; *E.R.*, IX. 519; *A.P.S.*, II. 173.   [315] *A.P.S.*, II. 139, c. 6.

a year 'to instigate others . . . to perform such services in future times'.[316] James displayed his clemency by sentencing Douglas to no worse fate than confinement in the abbey of Lindores. Albany escaped to France, where in 1485 he jousted in a tournament with the Duke of Orleans (afterwards Louis XII) and was mortally wounded by the splinter of a lance.[317] The last episode in the Anglo-Scottish hostilities that had begun in 1481 was enacted at Dunbar, where the castle was held by the English garrison installed by Albany.[318] Siege operations were conducted ineffectively from time to time, and the defenders had the benefit of some months respite under the terms of the Anglo-Scottish truce of September 1484 [319] before the crown recovered the castle, apparently on 6 December 1485. By 30 June in the following year Lord Bothwell had been granted its custody with an annual fee of £100.[320]

The episode at Lochmaben and the prolonged siege of Dunbar did not prevent Scottish attempts to end the war : Bishop Elphinstone of Aberdeen, who headed Scottish peace missions, was granted safe-conducts by Richard III in November 1483, March, April and August 1484.[321] On 12 September 1484 the bishop, Master Archibald Whitelaw, and another six Scottish envoys were formally received in Nottingham Castle,[322] where they concluded indentures for a three-year truce and a marriage between Rothesay and Anne de la Pole, daughter of the Duke of Suffolk and niece of the English king.[323] Peaceful plotting and counter-plotting could now take the place of open war.

Although the Franco-Scottish alliance was assumed to be in existence during the reign of Louis XI, it does not seem to have been formally renewed, possibly because James was aware of Louis's notorious double-dealing. Latterly there had even been signs of strained relations between France and Scotland : in the Albany-dominated parliament of December 1482 complaint had been made that the goods of Scottish merchants were being requisitioned in France 'be command of the [French] king, as is allegit . . . contrare to the aliance and band betuix the realmes'; Walter Bertram was to

[316] *R.M.S.*, II. Nos. 1594, 1597, 1603; *E.R.*, IX. 519.
[317] Lesley, *History*, pp. 47, 51; *Scots Peerage*, I. 152; *E.R.*, X. lxvii.
[318] Lesley, *History*, p. 51.
[319] *A.P.S.*, II. 146, 165, c. 2; *E.R.*, IX. 288, 432, 434.
[320] *E.R.*, IX. 433, 523.   [321] *Rot. Scot.*, II. 461–2, 464.
[322] See 'Negotiations of the Scottish Commissioners at Nottingham', *Bannatyne Misc. II*, 32–48.
[323] *Cal. Docs. Scot.*, IV. No. 1504; *Foedera*, V. pt. iii, 149–55.

be sent to France to remonstrate. Opposite this entry in the record is a marginal entry : 'this grant contenit in this writing is fulfillit be our soverain lordis lettres direct of before' ;[324] James evidently recognised the futility of remonstrances. The situation seems to have changed with the accession of Charles VIII, who in March 1484 sent to Scotland Bernard Stewart, Sieur d'Aubigny, for a renewal of the Auld Alliance.[325] Its ratification by the two kings was probably accompanied by the enlisting of Scots mercenaries and discussion of their possible employment by Charles to further the fortunes of Henry Tudor, Earl of Richmond.[326] If James had outwardly reconciled himself with Richard III he had also secretly ingratiated himself with the man who would displace the Yorkist from his shaky throne. Although accounts vary as to the number of troops who accompanied Henry on his invasion of England in August 1485 there can be no doubt that they included Frenchmen under the Sieur d'Aubigny and Scots under Alexander Bruce of Earlshall.[327] This 'familiar esquire' would be rewarded by James in February 1486 for the good service he had performed not only within the realm but outside it.[328]

The defeat and death of Richard III at Bosworth on 21 August 1485 brought Henry Tudor to the throne as Henry VII. His coronation was attended by a Scottish delegation that included Bishop Elphinstone and Lord Bothwell. Thereafter 'negotiations between Henry VII and James III were in fact almost continuous'.[329] A remarkable stability existed since neither monarch was by nature aggressive and the internal disaffection that faced each was of comparable dimensions : Henry would soon be troubled by the first Yorkist pretender of his reign—Lambert Simnel—and James by the opposition of the Border barons. Thus Henry made no attempt to hinder James's recovery of Dunbar Castle, and with the conclusion of a three-year truce at London in July 1486[330] amicable counterplotting gave way to an amity that was intended to cover Western Europe. In addition one clause showed that James's hopes of dynastic alliances with England had blossomed afresh : there were to be negotiations for the marriage of his second son, James, Marquess of Ormond,[331] and the Lady Katherine, third daughter of Edward IV

---

[324] *A.P.S.*, II. 144–5, cc. 6, 11.   [325] Mackie, *James IV*, p. 26.
[326] Conway, *Henry VII*, pp. 5–7.
[327] *Ibid.*, pp. 5–7; Mackie, *James IV*, pp. 27–8.   [328] *R.M.S.*, II. No. 1638.
[329] Conway, *Henry VII*, p. 10.   [330] Text in *Rot. Scot.*, II. 473–7.
[331] It is wrongly stated in *H.B.C.*, p. 486, that the creation of this marquessate dated from 29 January 1488 : the title had been bestowed on the king's second son by 23 January 1481 (*R.M.S.*, II. Nos. 1457, 1470).

and sister of Henry's own queen.[332] In the following year English ambassadors came to Edinburgh and concluded an indenture on 28 November 1487.[333] This alluded to 'the grete tendur lufe and kindnes' that the two kings had hitherto displayed to one another, and revealed the sprouting of two additional matrimonial schemes 'for the incressing of mare love and amite' : James himself had been widowed by the death of Queen Margaret in the summer of 1486 ; having paid respect to her memory by trying to have her canonised [334] he was free to seek the hand of Elizabeth Woodville, widow of Edward IV; and it was thought that the Duke of Rothesay might marry one or other of Edward IV's brood of daughters.

One stumbling-block to Anglo-Scottish understanding might thereby be removed : the question of Berwick had caused difficulties in the negotiations for the truce of July 1486,[335] and in November 1487 James, who had won Orkney and Shetland through marriage, made it clear that he expected the proposed marriages to bring 'the finall appeasing and cause of cesing all sic debaitis and controversies as in tyme past has bene for the castell and town of Berwik ... of the quhilk castell and town ... the said King of Scottis desiris alwais deliverance at the finale appeasing of the said mariagis or any of thame'. This weighty matter was probably to be discussed, together with 'uthir gretir intelligencis for the increasing of mare lufe, amyte and tenderness' at a conference to be held by the two kings in person in July 1488 'at sic a place as canne be betwix thame agreit'.[336] For the first time in two hundred years the Scottish and English kings were sincere and like-minded in a desire for peace.

The desire was not shared by some Scottish nobles, particularly those who were powerful on the Borders. They had not rallied to the defence of Berwick when it was in Scottish hands, but now that it was occupied by the English it was fair game for plunder. Hence regardless of truces and the general trend of James's diplomacy they made menacing moves against the town in September 1485, September 1487, and January 1488.[337] The Borderers, so long inured to warfare, sensed that their peculiar power would be shattered if real peace were established : for almost two centuries they had been the bulwark of Scotland and they assumed (as the ballad hero Johnnie Armstrong

[332] Rot. Scot., II. 475. [333] Ibid., 480-2.
[334] Mackie, James IV, p. 34, n. 5. [335] Rot. Scot., II. 475.
[336] Ibid., 480-1. [337] Conway, Henry VII, pp. 8-9, 10, 11.

still did in 1530)[338] that their military services atoned for their lawless insubordination; if military service was no longer in demand the Borderers could no longer be a law unto themselves and their unemployed chiefs would be disregarded. To this consideration the Red Douglas cannot have been blind. He had hastened to win the good graces of the king in March 1484 by founding a chaplainry in St Bride's Kirk for the soul's weal of, among others, James and his queen.[339] This gesture perhaps earned his appointment to the wardenships of the Middle and Eastern (or Southern) Marches.[340] But it did not prevent a decreet of the lords of council on 7 December 1485 as a result of which a few of the titles to annualrents held by Angus were apprised to raise a sum of about £50.[341] Nor did the earl figure as a witness to royal charters.[342] In the background hovered the spectres of the victims of the Lauder lynching : 'no truce could efface the memory of such a deed on either side',[343] especially on that of James III, whose similitude, the lion of Henryson's fable, proudly announced :

> I lat you wit my mycht is merceabill
> And steris [disturbs] none that ar to me prostrat.

Angus and his accomplices were not disposed to prostrate themselves. It was in vain that the poet hoped

> That tressone of this cuntre be exyled
> And Justice ring [reign] and lordes keip thair fey [fealty]

Equally in vain Henryson addressed James in the lines :

> Without mercy Justice is creweltie
> . . . .
> Quhen rigour sittis in the tribunall,
> The equety of law quha may sustene? [344]

Treason, and its punishment, hung heavily over the land.

Lord Crichton provided the first manifestation. In the parliament of October 1483 a decreet of the auditors of causes and com-

---

[338] G. Donaldson, *Scotland: James V to James VII* (1965), p. 50.

[339] *R.M.S.*, II. No. 1586.

[340] In the truce treaty of July 1486 (*Rot. Scot.*, II. 476), Angus is named as warden of the Middle and Southern Marches, Lord Maxwell as warden of the West March.   [341] *R.M.S.*, II. No. 1664.

[342] See p. 527 below.   [343] Conway, *Henry VII*, p. 3.

[344] MacQueen, *Robert Henryson*, pp. 151, 171, 173.

plaints ordered that some of his lands be apprised to satisfy damages of over 540 marks as a result of a spuilzie he had committed upon Lord Borthwick.[345] By decreet of the lords of council on 12 February 1484 more of Crichton's lands were apprised in compensation for £800 in gold and a gold chain obtained by spuilzie committed upon John Ramsay of Bothwell, his mother, Janet Napier, and her burgess husband.[346] Already Crichton had been summoned to answer charges of treason on account of his complicity with Albany. He did not compear when process was led against him in parliament on 19 February 1484; on 24 February he was sentenced, along with forty more obscure persons, to forfeit life, lands, goods, offices and possessions.[347]

One enactment of this parliament urged that before the end of the session the king should receive the great lords and 'put thaim in freindschip and concord or [before] thai depart fra his presens' and that the justiciars should do likewise with 'smallar personis . . . sa that our souverane lordis liegis stand in peax . . . and be obedient to oure souverane lordis autorite'.[348] But the troubles of the last few years made it almost impossible to distinguish between feuds and crimes that were 'ordinary' and those that were political. Some misgiving must have been caused by the advice of the lords of the articles that justice ayres and warden courts should set to work, and that the king should obtain the co-operation of 'certane lordis and hedismenn of the Bordouris . . . for the apprehending . . . of the masterfull trespassouris that ar fugitive fra his lawis'.[349] In the past the king's lavish grants of remission had been unpopular; the members of parliament must have had mixed feelings when it was announced on 24 February that for three years the king would issue no remissions in respect of treason, slaughter, and certain other crimes.[350] The motive was divulged in another act in which the king was urged to cause diligent inquisition to be made to detect those who had partaken in Albany's treason 'and to mak thame be punyst . . . in exemple of all utheris in tym tocum to comytt sa odious crime and offence aganis his majeste'.[351] In the next parliament, in May 1485, James Gifford of Sheriffhall was sentenced for treason for his deliverance of Dunbar Castle to the English,[352] and it was thought expedient that the king should summon lords and 'hedismen' from all parts of the realm to act as a sort of grand jury of presentment that would denounce

[345] *R.M.S.*, II. No. 1575. [346] *Ibid.*, No. 1577.
[347] *A.P.S.*, II. 154–64. [348] *Ibid.*, 165, c. 8. [349] *Ibid.*, 165, c. 3.
[350] *Ibid.*, 165, c. 8. [351] *Ibid.*, 165, c. 3. [352] *Ibid.*, 172–4.

'notour trespassouris', who should be 'takin and justifiit without remissioune'.[353]

It was significant that the following parliament of October 1487, in which the lairds outnumbered the earls and lords,[354] showed obvious deference to the king, who had 'benignly grauntit to thaim all ther desiris and requestis'.[355] At the opening of proceedings James acknowledged that the realm was 'greitlie brokin' through treason and other crimes and through 'default of scharpe executioune of justice and ouer commoun granting of grace and remissiounis'; for the following seven years there would be no more remissions and the guilty would be 'punist extremely'.[356] Thereupon the members of each estate undertook to take oath that they would not support any 'manifest tratouris' or other criminals but would help to 'inquere and gett knaulage of the said trespassouris' and bring them to justice.[357] Thus, according to Bishop Lesley, 'the king begouth to use sharp executione of justice in all partis, quhilk mony culd nocht abyde'.[358]

Their discomfort was increased by spiritual means. For at royal request Sixtus IV issued a bull in May 1484 ordering obedience to the king.[359] This did not mean that James was panic-stricken and abjectly invoking papal support: requests for papal intervention were simply attempts on his part to grasp all available weapons with which to coerce the opposition; far from being cowed he was in aggressive mood, and his approaches to the papacy for support were part and parcel of his general attitude of expecting the papacy to comply with all his wishes. The guarded attitude of the papacy towards James's protests over provisions was diplomatically balanced by its readiness to give political backing. Thus in August 1485 Innocent VIII took note of the recent disputes over ecclesiastical appointments and, more fulsomely, accepted the king's interpretation of recent political troubles: certain nobles had not blushed to stick out their necks against the king, whereupon evils innumerable had ensued; James was exhorted not to withdraw the pardon he had extended to the offenders; excommunication and interdict would be pronounced against all individuals and communities who flouted the royal authority; copies of this admonitory letter were to be posted in every cathedral. Thereupon the Bishop of Imola, the papal legate then in Scotland, fulminated no few excommunications and interdicts.[360] It was perhaps a misfortune for James that the co-

[353] Ibid., 170, c. 4.   [354] Ibid., 175.   [355] Ibid., 176, c. 2.
[356] Ibid., 176, c. 3.   [357] Ibid.   [358] Lesley, History, p. 55.
[359] Mackie, James IV, p. 30.   [360] Ibid., pp. 31–2.

operative legate left Scotland to accompany Archbishop Scheves
on the mission to Rome that resulted in the indult of 1487.[361]

Another consequence of the mission was even more ill-fated for
the king : in the parliament of May 1485 it had been decided that
the envoys should petition for 'ane ereccioun of Coldingahame to
our souverane lordis chapel'[362]—in other words that the revenues
of that Home-ridden establishment, now of uncertain status, be used
for the foundation of a collegiate kirk at Coldingham which would be
an additional royal chapel. This petition, granted by the pope in
April 1487,[363] earned the king the enmity of the Homes, who had
lately been his familiars.[364] By October 1487 their opposition was
obviously so strong that parliament declared that anyone who
obstructed the king's plans for Coldingham would be punished as a
traitor.[365]

When parliament was prorogued to 11 January 1488 the announcement of the agenda for the next session summed up all that the
malcontent nobles found most distasteful : the proposed dynastic
alliances with England, the Coldingham business, and 'the process
of forfatur of the laird of Drumelzier and Edward Hunter'. Warning
was given that any prelate or lord absent from the forthcoming
session (and the Homes were notably absent from the current session)
would incur the king's 'indignacioun and displesance'.[366]

The Homes were nonetheless absent (and so also was Lord
Hailes, their Hepburn associate) when parliament re-assembled on
11 January 1488. And even more obviously than in the previous session the lords were outnumbered by the lairds. The loyalty of the
latter was recognised at the close of parliament on 29 January when
four of them were created lords and one was knighted along with the
heirs of Lords Kennedy and Carlyle. On the same day the king's
second son, James, Marquess of Ormond, was created Duke of
Ross.[367]

The proceedings of this parliament showed that the king had not
relaxed his intention of using judicial machinery to crush political
opponents : it was thought expedient that he should choose two 'gret
justices' from a short leet of four (Lords Bothwell, Lyle, Glamis and
Drummond). Those chosen would act south of Forth, while their
northern counterparts would be the Earls of Huntly and Crawford.
It was also suggested that, once ayres had been arranged, the king

[361] Lesley, *History*, p. 54.   [362] *A.P.S.*, II. 171, c. 7.
[363] Watt, *Fasti*, p. 347.   [364] P. 516 above.
[365] *A.P.S.*, II. 179, c. 19.   [366] *Ibid.*, 180.   [367] *Ibid.*, 180–81.

should send wise lords and persons of his council to act as assessors and counsellors to the justices. Whatever the intrinsic merits of this scheme it was one that entrusted criminal jurisdiction to prominent political figures who had axes to grind. The ordinance was significantly accompanied by an announcement that it was expedient that the ayres previously arranged should be 'dissolvit' and new ones proclaimed in spring.[368] To the king's opponents this change must have seemed ominous. Parliament also went ahead with the agenda formerly arranged. Preparations were made to finance an embassy to England to treat of the proposed royal marriages. It was nothing new that the condition was made that these could not go forward unless the castle and town of Berwick were delivered to the Scots or destroyed :[369] James had stipulated the same condition in the negotiations with the English ambassadors the previous November.[370] Even if the marriages were not agreed upon, the king and his council were empowered to make truces at their discretion; and the Borderers can hardly have relished an enactment that truce-breakers should be punished so 'extremely' that 'throw the terroure and exempill therof sic like trespasses may be forborne in tyme tocum'.[371] Notice was also taken of those persons who had treasonably contravened the act of the previous session regarding Coldingham : the clerical offenders were to be summoned to answer in the church courts and the laymen to be summoned before a parliament to be held in May. Since it was reckoned 'hevy to travale the hale estatis to the said parliament' it was decided that a commission of the estates be appointed 'to have the powere of the hale parliament to procede in the said mater'.[372] Finally, when parliament was continued to 5 May, seventeen ecclesiastics, eighteen barons, three civil servants, and the representatives of twelve burghs were named to sit upon this commission.[373]

It never met. The herald sent to summon the Homes at their stronghold of Fast Castle was 'evill intreitit',[374] and on 2 February James Schaw of Sauchie, keeper of Stirling Castle, whose wife was a Home, released the heir apparent into the hands of the king's opponents.[375]

There can be little doubt that they found it easy to turn the

[368] Ibid., 182, cc. 5, 6, 7.   [369] Ibid., 181–2, cc. 2, 3.
[370] P. 519 above.   [371] A.P.S., ii. 182–3, cc. 4, 14.
[372] Ibid., 182, c. 8.   [373] Ibid., 184.   [374] Pitscottie, Historie, i. 201.
[375] Ibid., 203; Ferrerius, Continuatio, p. 399 v.; A.P.S., ii. 223; R.M.S., ii. No. 3011.

prince's head. The death of Queen Margaret, who in 1478 had been entrusted with his custody,[376] removed an influence that might have prevented his association with his father's adversaries. Whether or not the association already existed, the king suspected that it did; although the Duke of Rothesay was close to fifteen years of age he was apparently kept away from parliament, and it would seem that he was held in Stirling virtually as a prisoner. The elevation of his younger brother (another James) as Duke of Ross was an event that hinted that the Duke of Rothesay was not irreplaceable; and the heir apparent's new associates doubtless did not hesitate to assure him that his father purposed his demotion from the succession—if not worse.[377]

In this crisis the king did not panic but took various steps to secure his position and to show his moderation. Bishop Elphinstone, an admirable choice as mediator, was made chancellor on 18 February 1488 in place of Argyll, whose loyalties may already have been wavering. By the advice of his council the king proclaimed on 21 February that for 'certane ressonable and gret causs' the parliamentary commission that was to sit on 5 May had been dissolved and that a new 'generale parliament' was to be held in its place on 12 May: general precepts of summons would be issued and, in addition, special letters under the signet would be issued to all the prelates and great lords 'to schew and declare to thame the causs of the settin of his said parliament'[378]—an opportunity for the king to publicise his own interpretation of recent events.

For some months both the king and the opposition had doubtless engaged in a quest for support from the papacy and other powers. In the parliament of January 1488 it had been thought expedient that no papal legate or messenger should be allowed entry to Scotland until his business had been ascertained.[379] James probably suspected (though wrongly) that the legate who was on his way (but arrived too late)[380] would co-operate with the opposition rather than with himself. More important was the attitude of England. It has been thought that Henry VII had been alienated from James by the demand for the delivery of Berwick, but this was not necessarily the case: Henry, who paid remarkable attention to finance, had by 1486 'enormously reduced the regular annual cost of keeping the

[376] R.M.S., II. No. 1361.   [377] Pitscottie, Historie, I. 203-4.
[378] A.P.S., II. 184.   [379] Ibid., 183-4, c. 16.
[380] Lesley, History, p. 57; Conway, Henry VII, p. 19.

Marches'[381] and may well have thought that the savings resulting from a stabilised frontier more than balanced the empty prestige of holding Berwick. Elphinstone and Lord Bothwell, James's supporters, had been among those involved in recent negotiations with England, and James's uncle, the Earl of Buchan (now loyal to the king) had visited the English court in December 1487 and returned to Scotland in the following spring having received marks of favour from Henry.[382] His efforts to win English support were seconded by those of Lord Bothwell, who was present at Windsor for the celebration of the feast of St George (23 April).[383] Both Buchan and Bothwell would later be accused of having tried to persuade Henry to invade Scotland in person, and Bothwell was held responsible, with the Bishop of Moray, Lord Forbes, Ross of Montgrenan, and three other royal familiars (including Hommyl the tailor) for the fabrication of a commission empowering the English to break the truce.[384] The supporters of the prince, on the other hand, had not neglected to try to present their case to Henry: they had applied for English safe-conducts for Bishop Blackadder of Glasgow, Bishop Brown of Dunkeld, the Earl of Argyll, Lord Hailes, Lord Lyle, the Master of Darnley and the Master of Home.[385] Since Argyll was evidently styled chancellor in this application it must have been forwarded prior to 21 February 1488 when he was replaced as chancellor by Bishop Elphinstone. Not until early May, when there was a lull in hostilities in Scotland, did Henry issue these safe-conducts, and it is unlikely that they were used. For by then ambassadors had arrived in Scotland to denounce the baronial rising and to declare that the Kings of France and England 'thoucht the same as ane commoun injurie done unto thame selves, and the exampill to be verraye wickit and pernicious'.[386] Thanks to the commission conveyed by Bothwell to the Earl of Northumberland—so it was later alleged—the English had proclaimed war upon the prince's party, some of whom had been plundered and even slain.[387] But this English intervention, possibly on the part of the garrison of Berwick, was on too small a scale to affect the outcome of the insurrection.

It was not until March 1488 that it became indisputable that there *was* an insurrection. Hitherto, it would appear, the prince merely remained at Linlithgow issuing manifestoes[388] with some of

[381] R. L. Storey, *op. cit.*, *E.H.R.*, LXXII. 593–609, at 608.
[382] Conway, *Henry VII*, pp. 16–7.
[383] *Ibid.*, p. 18.   [384] *A.P.S.*, II. 201, 202.
[385] *Rot. Scot.*, II. 485–6.   [386] Lesley, *History*, p. 57.
[387] *A.P.S.*, II. 201.   [388] Pitscottie, *Historie*, I. 203–4.

his new friends, while others frequented the court at Edinburgh and strove for a compromise. Angus even appeared briefly as a witness to royal charters until 7 March, and Argyll remained as a witness until 23 March,[389] when he too left court. This was also the last appearance of the elder statesman Avondale, who seems to have died shortly afterwards.[390] By this time James was virtually beleaguered in Edinburgh Castle, and his efforts at mediation brought only the haughty demand that he abdicate in favour of the prince.[391] A break in the entries in the great seal register after 23 March [392] shows that the king had given up the attempt to carry on normal government from Edinburgh. Leaving his isolated position in the castle he boarded one of Andrew Wood's ships that was ready to sail to Flanders. He was chased on the way to Leith and some of his baggage fell into the hands of his assailants, who used the treasure to hire troops.[393]

It was not in Flanders but in Fife that James disembarked. With the exception of the Campbell territories and those of Lord Gray in Angus and Lord Drummond in Strathearn all of Scotland north of Forth was ready to rally to his side. As he rode towards Aberdeen, the seat of loyal Bishop Elphinstone, he ordered the sheriffs to call out the host.[394] James also visited Lindores to seek the aid of its tragic recluse, the disinherited Douglas. The latter had already, it would seem, rebuffed the advances of the prince's party and is reported to have told James : 'Sir, you have kept me and your black coffer in Stirling too long ; neither of us can do you any good'.[395] At Aberdeen, however, powerful royalist supporters were assembling, as is shown in the witness list to a charter issued there on 16 April.[396] With the backing of 'all the Northt of Scotland' the king took the field.[397] His objective was the rebel headquarters in Linlithgow, and the position that he occupied at Blackness was one that would enable him to receive supplies and reinforcements shipped in by Andrew Wood.

At Blackness skirmishes were interspersed with negotiations for a peaceful settlement. James commissioned Bishop Elphinstone, Huntly, Erroll, Marischal, Glamis and Alexander Lindsay to treat

[389] *R.M.S.*, II. Nos. 1708, 1709, 1717, 1722. The part played by Angus is discussed in Fraser, *Douglas*, II. 82.   [390] *Scots Peerage*, V, 349.
[391] Lesley, *History*, pp. 56-7.   [392] *R.M.S.*, II. 362.
[393] Pitscottie, *Historie*, I. 202, 204; Ferrerius, *Continuatio*, p. 399v.
[394] Pitscottie, *Historie*, I. 202.
[395] Godscroft, *Douglas and Angus*, p. 206; Ferrerius, *Continuatio*, p. 399v.; Lesley, *History*, p. 58.
[396] *Moray Registrum*, p. 234; Conway, *Henry VII*, p. 15.
[397] Ferrerius, *Continuatio*, p. 400; Pitscottie, *Historie*, I. 204.

with the commissioners of the other side—Bishop Blackadder, Angus, Argyll, Hailes and Lyle. They at least agreed upon the points that had to be settled.[398] It was to be arranged 'that the kingis hie honour ... be exaltit', that he should enjoy honour, security and freedom, and that 'thar be prelatis, erlis, lordis and baronis and utheris persouns of wisdomé ... unsuspect to his hienes ... dayly about his nobill persoune to the gud giding of his realme and liegis'—a provision which to the minds of the opposition doubtless meant the dismissal of the king's existing councillors. The remaining items mostly concerned the safeguards and favours expected by the prince and his party. He too was to be surrounded daily by 'wiss lordis and honerabill persouns'. He was to receive from the king 'honerabill sustentaccioune'. He would 'tak in hertlie favoris all ... that has bene with the kingis hienes in consale or uthir service now in this tym of truble'. His own supporters who had in the past 'done displessur to his hienes' would 'mak honerabile and aggreabile amendis ... thar liffis, heretage and honouris except', and they would have the king's 'favoriis and grace ... and hertly forgevinnys'. It was hoped that the personal dissension between lords of each side, especially that between the Earl of Buchan and Lord Lyle, would be set at rest, and consideration was to be given as to 'how my lord prince sall in all tymes tocum be obedient to his faider the king, and how that faiderly luff and tendernes sall at all tymes be had beteux thame etc.'. But although these articles were subscribed by the king he was tempted to repudiate them: 'the saidis articulis wes diverss times grantit to and broken be the perverst counsale of diverss persouns ... quhilkis counsalit and assistit to him in the inbringing of Inglissmen and to the perpetuale subjeccione of the realm'. Shocked by the king's behaviour (so it was later alleged) Huntly, Erroll, Marischal and Glamis left him and, according to one official version, returned home; another official version, anxious to put the best face upon their action, stated that they adhered to the prince 'and his trew opynzoune for the commoune gud of the realme'.[399]

Neither James's shilly-shallying nor his skirmishing did him any good: he had lost valuable supporters and was forced to hand over Buchan, Ruthven and two others as sureties for his observance of the original terms of the pacification.[400] After this he returned to Edinburgh Castle. A resumption of sparse entries in the great seal register from 18 May onwards indicates a partial restoration of

[398] A.P.S., II. 210; R.M.S., II. Nos. 2529, 2530.
[399] A.P.S., II. 201, 202, 210–1.   [400] Ibid., 201.

government.[401] But the character of the entries shows that the situation was far from settled : James was evidently buying support in readiness for a renewed struggle. The most prominent of those favoured was Crawford, whose devoted and heroic service at Blackness was rewarded on 18 May by a grant of the burgh of Montrose and his creation as Duke of Montrose.[402] Ten days later Alexander Cunningham, Lord Kilmaurs, was created Earl of Glencairn. In the case of two other beneficiaries the favours that were bestowed were made conditional upon continuing loyalty [403]—a sad indication that by this time James believed that he could trust no one. In his distraught uncertainty he was persuaded, allegedly by Lord Bothwell, to leave Edinburgh and to make a final attempt to crush the opposition.[404] The ships of Andrew Wood that commanded the Forth allowed him to cross once more to Fife to link up with his northern supporters. A muster took place in Perth, where Lord Lindsay of the Byres presented the king with a great grey charger that could outdistance any horse in Scotland. Once more the whole north rallied to James's support.[405]

On 11 June 1488 the royalist army had passed through Stirling on its way towards the rebel headquarters at Linlithgow when it found that the prince's army had reached the Carron and was advancing to the encounter. The two armies were arrayed for battle on or near the field of Bannockburn,[406] and it was ironic that James had brought with him the sword of Robert Bruce.[407] He had placed himself in the centre battalion of his troops 'witht all the burrowis and commons of Scottland', flanked on one side by the men of Fife and Angus, and on the other by those of Strathearn and Stormont. The rearguard was composed of men from Stirling and the west; and the vanguard consisted of Highlanders under the Earls of Atholl and Huntly. On the opposing side were the men of the Merse, Teviotdale, East Lothian, Liddesdale, Annandale, and parts of Galloway ; and the Homes and Hepburns led the vanguard.[408] It was a confrontation between north and south; and, by a curious reversal of the usual state of affairs, the Highlanders were conspicuous among the king's supporters.[409] Even more striking was the opposition of king and prince. The tragedy of the situation is caught in the lines cited in Pitscottie :

[401] R.M.S., II. Nos. 1723-36.
[402] Ibid., No. 1725.
[403] Ibid., Nos. 1727, 1730.
[404] A.P.S., II. 202, 204.
[405] Pitscottie, Historie, I. 204-5, 206.
[406] Ibid., 205-6; Lesley, History, p. 57.
[407] E.R., X. xxxix; T.A., I. lxxiii.
[408] Pitscottie, Historie, I. 206-7.
[409] See Highland Papers, II. 26-7.

> The civill weir, the battell intestine,
> Nou that the sone with baner bred displayit
> Aganis the fader in battell come arreyit.[410]

The banner that the prince displayed was the royal standard.[411] This audacious assertion of his own kingship demonstrated his determination to unseat his father and was calculated to inspire the insurgents and dismay the royalists.

It certainly had that effect upon the king himself. Perhaps he was 'never hardie nor yeit constant in battell'; perhaps he remembered the old prophesies that he would fall by the hand of his nearest of kin. At any rate he was urged (allegedly by Ross of Montgrenan) to leave the field.[412] Hard fighting at once commenced beside the little Sauchie burn (now the Sauchinford burn) that would eventually give its name to the battle.[413] At length the royalists were forced back to the Tor Wood and as darkness fell took to flight.[414] Some were evidently pursued across Stirling bridge by the prince, who in turn was put to flight and chased by a counter-attack led by Ross of Montgrenan.[415]

In the confusion no one had thought to provide an escort for the king, who fled distractedly on his great grey charger, possibly making for Andrew Wood's ship lying in the Forth. All that was officially known of what afterwards occurred was that he left the field at the beginning of the battle, 'fell into the hands of vile persons and was slain'.[416] Pitscottie, whose great-uncle, David, Lord Lindsay of the Byres, fought for the king at Sauchieburn, is the only writer to give a circumstantial account of the king's death. According to his story the king fell from his charger when it leapt across the Bannock burn. Carried senseless into the nearby mill he regained consciousness and asked for a priest. The miller's wife found a mysterious stranger— 'sum sayis he was the Lord Grayis servand'—who said, 'Heir ame I, ane preist, quhair is the king?' After a few words with the king the supposed priest drew a sword and stabbed him in the heart.[417]

---

[410] Pitscottie, *Historie*, I. 212.   [411] *Ibid.*, 207.   [412] *Ibid.*; *A.P.S.*, II. 204.
[413] Mackie, *James IV*, p. 43, n. 4. The site is discussed by Angus Graham in 'The Battle of Sauchieburn', *S.H.R.*, XXXIX. 89–97.
[414] Pitscottie, *Historie*, I. 208.   [415] *A.P.S.*, II. 204.
[416] *Ibid.*   [417] Pitscottie, *Historie*, I. 209.

17

NEW MONARCHY TRIUMPHANT

It was reported that as a penance for his part in the events that led to the death of his father the new king, James IV, wore an iron belt around his waist.[1] Whatever his remorse it came late rather than early : in October 1488 he endowed masses for his mother alone; not until 1496 did he begin to provide for the weal of his father's soul.[2] For some days, so Pitscottie narrates, it was believed that James III had escaped to Captain Wood's ship. But even before the captain had denied this with 'dispytfull ansueris'[3] the victorious faction had assumed government : on 12 June 1488, the day after Sauchieburn, the new king's peace was proclaimed and a great seal charter was issued in his name.[4] Five days later six of his leading supporters were appointed to take an inventory of his father's treasure in Edinburgh Castle. This hoard, which included not only cash but such venerable relics as the shirt of Robert Bruce, probably yielded the large sum of £24,517 10s. od. mentioned in the first accounts of the new treasurer.[5] Even so, it was believed that this was only a 'small litle parte' of the late king's savings, and in February 1492 secret inquests were ordained in the hope of unearthing the remainder.[6]

The notables appointed to rummage through the late king's treasure were also among those who had been appointed on 15 June to grant tacks of all vacant crown lands. Under the guise of a commission of assessment they were to enjoy unusually far-reaching

---

[1] Pitscottie, *Historie*, I. 217–8; Lesley, *History*, p. 59.
[2] *R.M.S.*, II. Nos. 1783, 2306; *A.P.S.*, XII. 34; *Wigtown Charters*, No. 15; *R.S.S.*, I. No. 2040.
[3] Pitscottie, *Historie*, I. 213–5.
[4] *A.P.S.*, II. 207, c. 4; *R.M.S.*, II. No. 1731.
[5] *T.A.*, I. 79–87, 97, 166–7; *E.R.*, x. 82; *R.M.S.*, II. No. 1820.
[6] *A.P.S.*, II. 230, c. 2. At least one prosecution resulted (*T.A.*, I. lxxi, n. 6).

powers.[7] The intention was probably to make life miserable for members of the defeated party. The commission also gives the earliest indication of the composition of the new government : Colin Campbell, Earl of Argyll, had replaced Bishop Elphinstone as chancellor; Sir William Knollis, Preceptor of the headquarters of the Knights of St John at Torphichen, had replaced the Abbot of Arbroath as treasurer; Patrick Hepburn, Lord Hailes, was master of the household, John Hepburn, Prior of St Andrews, was keeper of the privy seal, and Master William Hepburn was clerk register. Before long, Alexander, Master of Home, who was to succeed his grandfather as second Lord Home in 1490, appeared as chamberlain ; he died in 1506 leaving a son who, as third Lord Home, was almost as influential.[8] No official post was given to Angus, probably because it was recognised that his talents were more destructive than constructive. Although he was to remain influential until the end of the reign, Bell-the-Cat was no politician. It was the Hepburns and the Homes upon whom the new king relied, and to whom he always remained grateful.

The coronation appears to have been sparsely attended,[9] and although an exchequer audit was begun on 7 July,[10] and the lords of council resumed the hearing of civil actions on 12 July,[11] the holding of a parliament was delayed for a few months until the new regime had consolidated its power. Captain Wood was among the majority who, however much they detested the manner of James IV's accession, were at least willing to support him after it had taken place : on 28 July a confirmation was issued of the captain's feu of Largo formerly granted by James III.[12] Some irreconcilables, notably John Ramsay, Lord Bothwell, and Sir John Ross of Montgrenan, had fled to the English court. The danger that they might provoke the intervention of Henry VII was partly allayed by negotiations which culminated in a three-year truce drawn up at Coldstream on 5 October 1488.[13] On the following day the first parliament of the reign opened at Edinburgh.

The attendance demonstrated that the new government had won general acceptance : among the thirty-four ecclesiastical representatives were eight bishops, including such associates of the previous king as Archbishop Scheves and Bishop Elphinstone; the thirty-five

[7] E.R., x. 629–30.
[8] Ibid., xli; xiii. clx–clxii.
[9] Pitscottie, Historie, i. 216–7.
[10] E.R., x. 1–73.
[11] A.D.C., i. 121.
[12] R.M.S., ii. No. 1758.
[13] Conway, Henry VII, pp. 22–6; Rot. Scot., ii. 488–90.

barons included ten earls, headed by Argyll and Angus; and sixteen burghs sent commissioners.[14] On 8 October there was a debate upon the 'causs of the feild of Stervilin in the quhilk umquhile James, King of Scotlande . . . happinnit to be slane'. It was satisfactorily agreed that this mischance was the fault of the defeated party and the 'perverst consale' which had led them astray; the new king and his supporters were completely innocent.[15] More attention seems to have been paid to the punishment of prominent supporters of the late king.[16] Buchan, and possibly some others, came to terms and obtained a royal remission. Bothwell and Montgrenan (still in England) were condemned.[17] In addition some of the statutes passed by parliament inflicted penalties, direct or indirect, upon the defeated party, against whose members the king had conceived 'gret and hie displessur'. All who held heritable office were to lose it for three years; those who held office for life or for a shorter term were to be 'secludit aluterly fra the saidis officis'.[18] It was also ordained that all grants of lands, including those in feu-ferm or blench-ferm, of tailzies, and of offices and dignities, which had been made by James III after 2 February 1488 should be annulled if they were considered prejudicial to the crown.[19] The victorious faction was in no repentant mood, and hardly showed 'statesmanlike moderation',[20] though it did make some concessions, usually in vague terms. It would seem that all lands and houses that had been seized during the civil war were to be restored to the original occupants, while the 'pure unlandit folkis' whose goods had been plundered were to receive recompense from the great men of the defeated party. It was also enacted that the rights of inheritance of the heirs of those who had fallen at Sauchieburn fighting *against* the present king should be safeguarded, while the heirs of those who had fought *for* the present king had their inheritances augmented by a general cancellation of all alienations made by their predecessors.[21] The complex and often imprecise terms of the settlement of 1488 provided ample scope for litigation, though it rarely reached the lords auditors or the lords of council.[22]

It was the business of the parliament of October 1488 not only to settle the conflicts of the past but to outline policy for the future. The perennial problem of justice was to be tackled by securing the

[14] A.P.S., II. 199–200. [15] Ibid., 210–1, c. 15; 269–70.
[16] T.A., I. 92, 93. [17] A.P.S., II. 201–6. [18] Ibid., 207, c. 6.
[19] Ibid., 211, c. 19. A similar act was also passed in February 1490 (ibid., 222–3, c. 25).
[20] Mackie, James IV, p. 46; Rait, Parliaments, pp. 36–9.
[21] A.P.S., II. 207, cc. 4, 5; 211, c. 20. [22] See, however, A.D.A., I. 130.

involvement of king and magnates: James was to attend the ayres accompanied by the justiciar; a number of lords took oath to search for criminals and 'justify' them, and were to compel 'small' lairds to take the same oath; the Earl of Angus was to enforce this act in five sheriffdoms, and similar spheres of influence that covered all Scotland (with the notable exception of the Isles) were mapped out for other magnates. This act, which virtually turned the magnates into local justiciars, was to remain in force until the king was twenty-one.[23] Another act announced that James, now over fifteen years old, was 'of perfitt age to complett the haly band of matrimonze'; an embassy was to be sent abroad to seek as bride 'a nobill prenciss borne and discendit of ane worchepfull houss'. The prospect of an imminent royal marriage was designed not only to titillate loyalty towards the new king but to serve as excuse for a tax to cover the expenses of the matrimonial embassy. In accordance with recent practice one-fifth of the tax was to be raised by the burghs; the clergy would provide two-fifths, so also would the barons and free tenants; the 'commoune pepill' were to be exempt. The total contribution of £5,000 was to be paid before 15 January 1489,[24] by which time parliament, which had been continued to 14 January, would have re-assembled.

The very brief and incomplete record of the parliament of January 1489 reveals two contentious matters. One was an act that the see of Glasgow should become an archbishopric with the same privileges as that of York.[25] This initiative, which was ultimately successful,[26] was a reward for Bishop Blackadder of Glasgow, who from the first had associated himself with the new government,[27] and a spiteful insult to Archbishop Scheves of St Andrews, who had been too closely associated with the old government. A second contentious issue is hinted at in an allusion to the 'displessere' which the Earl of Buchan had aroused in the new king.[28] At this point the record peters out, leaving the nature of Buchan's offence undisclosed. It may have been connected with a surety of 10,000 marks which Buchan, along with Lords Gray and Erskine, had apparently pledged to the king. They were prosecuted for payment on 17 January 1489 before the parliamentary auditors of causes and a decreet was issued for the distraint of their lands.[29] The penalty might have been more

---

[23] A.P.S., II. 208, cc. 8, 9.
[25] Ibid., 212–3, c. 2.
[27] See R.M.S., II. No. 1915.
[29] A.D.A., I. 120.

[24] Ibid., 207, c. 2.
[26] Pp. 557–8 below.
[28] A.P.S., II. 213, c. 5.

severe had the government been aware of the contents of a letter written at Edinburgh on 8 January by Alexander Gordon, Master of Huntly : he reminded Henry VII of the 'threasonable ande cruel slauthir of my soverane lorde and kyng [James III] falsely slayne be a part of his fals and untrew legis', and announced that Buchan would be sent to England to seek help, presumably to overthrow the new government.[30]

It is likely that this plot had been provoked by the government's unwillingness to let bygones be bygones : not content with the settlement of October 1488 it seems to have summoned many supporters of James III to answer charges in a subsequent parliament, probably that of January 1489. This may be inferred from Pitscottie's circumstantial account of the trial (and acquittal) of his great-uncle, David, Lord Lindsay of the Byres.[31] Assuming the 'statesmanlike moderation' of the new government, historians have tried in vain to fit Pitscottie's tale into the context of the parliament of October 1488,[32] even although Lord Lindsay, far from being prosecuted, was then nominated to 'justify' criminals in Fife.[33] A renewed and untimely threat to the supporters of the former king was likely to make them desperate, while some supporters of the new king were equally likely to be driven into disaffection by the way in which rewards were distributed. In January 1490 the custody of Stirling and the keeping of the king's younger brother, John, Earl of Mar, would be entrusted to Alexander Home, the chamberlain.[34] During the first two years of the reign the latter, together with other Homes, profited from twenty-two great seal charters while the Hepburns were the beneficiaries of nine,[35] containing great prizes : John, Prior of St Andrews, became keeper of Falkland; Patrick, Lord Hailes, was granted custody of Edinburgh Castle, the sheriffship of Edinburgh, and the keeping of the heir presumptive, the Duke of Ross; by 10 September 1488, even before the forfeiture of John Ramsay, Lord Bothwell, Hailes had not only been appointed admiral of Scotland but styled Earl of Bothwell.[36] The situation was clarified in the parliament of October 1488 when the lordships of Bothwell and

[30] Text in Pinkerton, *History*, II. 437 (though wrongly assigned to 1491); Conway, *Henry VII*, p. 26.
[31] The 1814 Dalyell edition of Pitscottie (I. 239), gives the date as 10 January 1489, the S.T.S. edition (I. 226), as 10 May 1489. There is no record of a parliament in May, though one did open in Edinburgh on 14 January.
[32] See Mackie, *James IV*, p. 48, n. 3.   [33] *A.P.S.*, II. 208.
[34] *Ibid.*, 211, c. 18; *E.R.*, x. xlviii; *R.M.S.*, II. Nos. 1919, 1946.
[35] *T.A.*, I. lxx, n. 1.
[36] *R.M.S.*, II. Nos. 1732, 1741, 1742, 1774; *A.P.S.*, II. 211, c. 17.

Crichton were erected into the earldom of Bothwell and the new earl was belted.[37] In the following month he was appointed steward of Kirkcudbright and granted the custody of Threave.[38] There was a tendency to forget the vital part played in the drama of 1488 by those who were not Hepburns or Homes; Lord Lyle and the Lennox Stewarts were envious 'that the king wes mare governit be utheris of the factione nor be thame'.[39]

As 'great justiciar of Scotland' Lord Lyle had presided over the treason trials of October 1488.[40] Sir John Stewart of Darnley, who since 1473 had maintained pretensions to the earldom of Lennox,[41] had been recognised as earl in October 1488, and, with his son Matthew, had been granted custody of Dumbarton Castle.[42] Only intense disenchantment with the government could have driven such adherents into open disaffection. In April 1489 heralds were sent to Dumbarton and to Lyle's castle of Duchal, presumably with summonses to answer charges in the parliament that would be held on 26 June. They did not compear but garrisoned their castles and were forfeited along with William, onetime Lord Crichton,[43] already forfeited in the previous reign, whose lands had lately been conferred upon the new Earl of Bothwell. Parliament also put a price on the head of the leading rebels and concerted the military preparations that had been begun at the end of April:[44] the king, with a host levied from south of Forth, was to set siege to Duchal and Lennox's castle of Crookston on 19 July; simultaneously Argyll would besiege Dumbarton with three forces from north of Forth, which would relieve one another at intervals of twenty days.[45] On 10 July 'Mons', the great bombard, was carted from Edinburgh Castle and other guns were hastened westward. By 4 August they were being trundled homeward;[46] Duchal and Crookston had surrendered, though Dumbarton still held out.

While the parliament of June 1489 had supported the king against the rebels it had also sought to reduce the dominance of the Hepburns and Homes by defining the composition of the council in an act that was to remain in force until the next parliament. The council was to be broadly based, although the inclusion of burgesses does not seem to have been contemplated. At least six of the coun-

[37] *A.P.S.*, ii. 205, 206.   [38] *R.M.S.*, ii. No. 1799.
[39] Lesley, *History*, p. 59.   [40] *A.P.S.*, ii. 199.
[41] *E.R.*, x. xlvi.   [42] *R.M.S.*, ii. No. 1794.
[43] *A.P.S.*, ii. 213; 215, c. 11.
[44] *Ibid.*, 215, c. 11; *T.A.*, i. 109, 110, 111, 112, 144, 163.
[45] *A.P.S.*, ii. 214, c. 7.   [46] *T.A.*, i. 117, 123.

cillors were to be in continual attendance upon the king. It was also stipulated that the Earls of Huntly and Crawford should join the council 'quhen thai cum', and that the same applied to all prelates and great barons.[47] This re-modelled council met at Stirling as a 'great council' on 18 September 1489 and restored David Lindsay, Earl of Crawford, to the dukedom of Montrose[48] which he had lost through the act of 1488 that cancelled grants made by James III after 2 February. This restoration was a timely concession to meet a new threat: on 12 September the government was denounced at Aberdeen on the grounds that 'no punishment had been imposed on the treasonable vile persons who put their hands violently on the king's [James III's] most noble person'.[49]

The ringleader of the rising in the north was Lord Forbes. It had been arranged in the parliament of June 1489 that he and the Earl Marischal should join the government forces at Dumbarton in mid-September.[50] Instead they joined the Master of Huntly, adopted as their banner the 'bludy serk' (blood-stained shirt) of James III, and, so the new king announced, made 'certane ligs and bands' with the defenders of Dumbarton.[51] As a result the latter sallied from the castle, burned the town, and drove off the besiegers. Lennox then led a force to join up with the northern insurgents. On the night of 11–12 October he and his men were intercepted and routed by the king and Lord Drummond at Gartalunane near Aberfoyle.[52] A week later the king set out to supervise operations against Dumbarton.[53] Even so, the insurgents were undaunted: despite their rout at 'the feild of the Mos' they sent a manifesto to James denouncing Bishop Blackadder and the Hepburn-Home partisans, who were allegedly exploiting the royal authority and treasure and trying to destroy the king, his brothers, Archbishop Scheves, and 'the haile barownis and nobles of this realme'.[54] The royalist forces in their camp at Dunglass Castle, three miles from Dumbarton, had by this time to be held together by wages contributed by the clergy. It was not until mid-December 1489 that the defenders of Dumbarton capitulated.[55]

The favourable conditions on which they did so were demonstrated when parliament met in February 1490: the Earl of Lennox, his son Matthew, and Lord Lyle, presented a 'lamentable complaint'

[47] *A.P.S.*, II. 215, c. 8.   [48] *Ibid.*, 215–6; *R.M.S.*, II. No. 1895; p. 573 below.
[49] *Aberdeen Council Register*, p. 45.   [50] *A.P.S.*, II. 213; 214–5, c. 7.
[51] *T.A.*, I. lxxxviii, n. 4; Lesley, *History*, p. 59.
[52] *T.A.*, I. xcv, 122; Lesley, *History*, pp. 59–60.
[53] *T.A.*, I. 142.   [54] Sir William Fraser, *Lennox Book* (1874), II. 128–31.
[55] *T.A.*, I. xcv–xcvi.

to the king, alleging that the parliament of June 1489 had not observed 'just and gudely ordoure according to the commoune law' when it had sentenced them to death and forfeiture; the sentence was accordingly annulled and the clerk register was ordered to destroy all record of the process so that 'it be never sene in tyme tocum'; pardon was granted to all persons south of Forth who had been involved in the rising and to over 130 persons who had held Dumbarton Castle against the king and burned the town; all forfeited lands, whether or not they had been granted away by the king, were to be restored.[56]

Although Lord Gordon, Master of Huntly, had taken the field near Dunkeld against royalist forces,[57] the government seems to have overlooked the affair of the 'bludy serk', which simply petered out. An atmosphere of reconciliation seems at last to have prevailed. In January 1489 Henry VII had sought the pope's intervention on behalf of Ross of Montgrenan.[58] By a charter issued at Dunglass in October 1489 he was restored to some of his forfeited lands; by November 1490 he was a royal familiar and received back the lands of Montgrenan which Patrick Home of Fast Castle was induced to resign.[59] Similar consideration was shown towards Sir John Ramsay, onetime Lord Bothwell, who, together with Sir Adam Forman and John Liddell (son of the Laird of Halkerston once forfeited for supporting Albany),[60] had been surreptitiously sent by Henry VII with a boatload of munitions to reinforce the rebels in Dumbarton.[61] Long before he obtained a remission and life pension in 1497 Sir John Ramsay was active about court; he too became a familiar and by 1499 was serving once more on commissions of assessment; in 1510 he would be granted the barony of Balmain.[62] In this case James's clemency was misplaced: Ramsay acted as Henry VII's spy in collaboration with the Earl of Buchan, who proved himself 'a remarkably competent traitor'.[63] By April 1491 the two were privy to an abortive plot to deliver James IV and the Duke of Ross into the hands of Henry VII.[64] Possibly the Earl of Angus was involved. At any rate he alone became an object of suspicion: on 29 July 1491 Lyon king-of-arms was sent to order the earl to ward himself in his

---

[56] *A.P.S.*, II. 213–4, 217–8, 223, c. 26; XII. 33–4; *R.M.S.*, II. No. 1956.
[57] *R.S.S.*, I. Nos. 14, 32.   [58] *T.A.*, I. lxxxii; Conway, *Henry VII*, p. 25.
[59] *R.M.S.*, II. Nos. 1785, 1904, 1989, 2049; see, however, No. 2262.
[60] P. 516 above.   [61] Conway, *Henry VII*, pp. 28–30.
[62] *R.M.S.*, II. Nos. 2348, 2349, 2412, 2453, 2554, 3460; *E.R.*, XI. 432.
[63] Conway, *Henry VII*, pp. 27, 36–7.
[64] *Ibid.*, pp. 36–7; *E.R.*, X. liv and n. 1.

own castle of Tantallon; by October Tantallon was being besieged, blockaded and bombarded. At the end of the year Angus and his son, George Douglas, entered into a pact with Henry VII: they would try to induce James IV to keep the peace with England; if war broke out Henry was not to make peace unless Angus were included; meanwhile if the earl and his son were 'put to that extremytie that they may not, by the eyde and supportacion of the kinges highnes of England, broke or joyse [enjoy] theyr landes and revenues within the roialme of Scotland, ne make their partie good', they would deliver Hermitage Castle to Henry in return for compensation in England.[65] On the same day (29 December 1491) that the envoys of Bell-the-Cat made this agreement in England a complex settlement was initiated in Scotland: as a result of multiple exchanges of lands the Red Douglas lost his hold upon the Borders.[66] Already in 1489 the wardenships of the East and West Marches which he had held had been transferred with the castle of Lochmaben to the Earl of Bothwell for a period of seven years. Thereafter the three wardenships, together with other offices on or near the Borders, seem to have been allotted at the king's pleasure among Hepburns, Homes and Kerrs.[67] And although Angus was appointed chancellor early in 1493 he was replaced by Huntly in 1497.

The king's firm, but moderate, treatment of Bell-the-Cat, the evil genius of his father's reign, epitomises the re-establishment of a monarchy in which the sovereign held undisputed sway. For almost twenty years, at a time when Europe was racked by strife between monarchy and aristocracy, James III had promoted the royal supremacy, and only twice had his authority been overthrown. Unlike Henry Tudor, James IV was not starting a new dynasty which had to make its way in the world but was continuing an ancient one that had already mapped its course. The natural hiatus in personal monarchical rule caused by the new king's minority lasted for only a year or two. The last attempt to hold him in tutelage occurred in the parliament of February 1490, which revoked the exemptions he had granted from the matrimonial tax, hinted that he should not exploit for his own use the revenues of his two brothers, appointed auditors to oversee the accounts of officials, nominated the lords who were to serve on the privy council, and gave them effective powers: it was

---

[65] Fraser, *Douglas*, II. 91; Conway, *Henry VII*, p. 38 and n. 5.
[66] *R.M.S.*, II. Nos. 2072–4, 2092, 2106; *E.R.*, x. lv, n. 3.
[67] *A.P.S.*, II. 214, c. 6; *R.M.S.*, II. Nos. 1874, 1875, 1893, 1921, 2027, 2092, 3406; *R.S.S.*, I. No. 291.

declared that the king had humbled himself to promise that he would be guided by their advice until the next parliament.[68] But these measures had no prolonged effect, the last tremors of Sauchieburn subsided when the parliament of February 1492, in an act 'for the eschewing and cessing of the hevy murmour and voce of the peple', belatedly, and fruitlessly, offered a reward for detection of the slayers of James III.[69] It was the latter's concept of monarchy, not the medieval constitutionalism of the magnates, that James IV would pursue.

A reconstructed court party enhanced his self-assurance. His familiars, eventually more than fifty in number, included six or seven who had served under his father. There were no exotics, though the king's naval interests were revealed in the presence of two sea-dogs—Robert Barton of Over Barnton and Andrew Wood of Largo (who must be carefully distinguished from another familiar, Andrew Wood of Blairton and Fettercairn).[70] Mostly the new familiars were aristocratic, linking the court not only with baronial families but with the ecclesiastical hierarchy. Some of them held office in the royal household.[71] Others acquired administrative responsibilities: George Parklee, Andrew Wood of Largo, and Sir Alexander Mc-Culloch of Myreton, held respectively the custody of Linlithgow, Dunbar and Stirling.[72] On the other hand the list of over a hundred witnesses to great seal charters shows a heavy preponderance of lay and ecclesiastical magnates and a marked absence of familiars.[73] Freed from governmental anxieties and from the more tedious types of administration the familiars were, above all, courtiers and boon companions of the king: James would send a puncheon of wine to the house of John Tyrie, provost of the collegiate kirk of Methven, when he intended to lodge there:[74] he would buy 'daunsing gere' for Thomas Boswell and Patrick Sinclair;[75] he would play 'at the tables' with Robert Colville,[76] and the happy-go-lucky Sir Alexander Mc-Culloch was in constant attendance.[77] Wholly dependent upon royal favour, such men gave social expression to the new monarchy. Although they were rewarded all too generously for their parasitical services they were too conventional to be suspected of malign influence and aroused no controversy.

[68] A.P.S., II. 218, c. 4; 219, c. 8; 220–1, cc. 10–2; Rait, Parliaments, p. 485.
[69] A.P.S., II. 230, c. 3. [70] T.A., I. lxxvi, n.
[71] R.S.S., I. No. 459; see also E.R., XI. 246; XIII. lxxvi–lxxxiv.
[72] R.M.S., II. Nos. 1735, 1743; R.S.S., I. Nos. 672, 978; E.R., XIII. xciii.
[73] R.M.S., II. pp. 848–50.
[74] T.A., I. cii.   [75] Ibid., II. 413.   [76] R.S.S., I. No. 415.

Not only did James avoid the type of favouritism that had brought disrepute upon his father but he also managed to avoid the discredit his father had endured over currency problems. During the reign of James IV the 'inbringing' and 'inhalding' of bullion, together with a new coinage and its defects, drew the attention of the three estates [78] but had no political repercussions. By 26 June 1493, when the king's tutelage was symbolically ended by a sweeping act of revocation that preceded his twenty-first birthday by some nine months,[79] the troubles of James's accession were over and he himself, rather than a coterie of nobles, controlled government. No fresh political troubles had as yet appeared. Only the old troubles of the north and west stood between James and complete mastery of his kingdom. It was natural that he should resume the aggressive attitude of his predecessors towards the tradition of Gaelic autonomy represented by the MacDonalds of Islay.

A foreign observer reported that James IV spoke 'the language of the savages who live in some parts of Scotland and on the islands'.[80] Nor did James despise the music and poetry of the 'savages' : he rewarded players of the clarshach and even Highland bards. In addition his hunts in Glenartney and Glenfinglas,[81] together with many other expeditions, military, devotional and amorous, made him more closely acquainted than his predecessors with many regions of the Highlands and Isles. Yet the Gaelic regions were more than ever regarded as the abode of outlandish folk [82] whose restlessness offended the majesty of the new monarchy. Almost simultaneously, though by no means in co-operation, Henry VII undertook the subjugation of Ireland [83] and James IV began the daunting of the Isles.

In the previous reign the partial forfeiture of John of the Isles had led not to royal supremacy in the Gaelic regions but to increased turmoil. After the battle of the Bloody Bay it was John's illegitimate son, Angus Og, who flouted the government by striving to recover Ross, feuding against the MacKenzies of Kintail, and impoverishing Inverness, where in 1490 he was assassinated by an Irish harper.[84]

[77] *Ibid.*, No. 2430.
[78] *A.P.S.*, II. 208-9, c. 11; 213, c. 1; 215, cc. 9, 10; 221-2, cc. 14, 18; 226, c. 12; 233, c. 10; 234, c. 12; 238, c. 4; 250-1, c. 12; 254, cc. 43, 44; *A.D.C.P.*, p. lx.   [79] *A.P.S.*, II. 236-7, c. 22.
[80] Pedro de Ayala, cited in Brown, *Early Travellers*, p. 38.   [81] *E.R.*, x. lxi.
[82] Major, *History*, pp. 47-50.   [83] Conway, *Henry VII*, ch. III.
[84] *E.R.*, x. lxii, n. 2; Gregory, *Western Highlands*, pp. 52-4; Derick S. Thomson, *op. cit.*, *Trans. Gaelic Soc. of Inverness* (1963), 3-31, at 14; *Highland Papers*, I. 51-2.

Angus's place as ringleader of the insurgent MacDonalds was taken by Alexander of Lochalsh, son of Celestine, half-brother of the Lord of the Isles. Alexander's ally, Farquhar Mackintosh, son of the captain of Clan Chattan, captured and destroyed Inverness Castle and raided Cromarty. The marauders were defeated in 1491 at the battle of Blairnepark by the rival MacKenzies, who now began their rise to prominence, believing that their valuable services to the crown purchased immunity for their own excesses.[85] Eventually both Farquhar Mackintosh and MacKenzie of Kintail were warded in Edinburgh Castle.[86]

In the eyes of the government the root of disorder stretched back to the Isles: the parliamentary commission appointed in May 1491 had been instructed to discuss 'the mater of the Ilis . . . and to provide sua that the kingis lyegis may lif in quiete and peax'.[87] John of the Isles, far from conforming to the eulogistic portrayal composed by his MacMhuirich bard,[88] was either unable or unwilling to control his kinsmen and nominal followers and was merely an obstacle to the forceful policy that the young king intended to initiate. Probably in the parliament of May 1493 the Lord of the Isles was forfeited and his domains were annexed to the crown. John meekly accepted his fate and became a pensioner at court until he died in obscurity.[89]

To assert control over his new acquisitions the king visited Dunstaffnage, and probably the neighbouring Isles, in the late summer of 1493,[90] and in autumn toured the regions around Inverness that had lately been the scene of disorder.[91] Alexander MacDonald of Lochalsh and John MacDonald of Dunivaig and the Glens (alias 'of the Isles' or 'of Islay'), grandson of Donald Balloch and head of the MacDonalds of the south, appear to have been knighted,[92] and the former, some time before he was killed by MacIan of Ardnamurchan, received a promise from the king that all the freeholders of the lordship of the Isles would be infeft in their lands.[93] James

---

[85] Gregory, *Western Highlands*, pp. 56–7, 82; Grant, *Social and Economic Development*, pp. 192–3; *Highland Papers*, II. 24, 30; *E.R.*, x. lvii–lviii.

[86] Gregory, *Western Highlands*, p. 91; *A.D.C.*, II. 94–5.   [87] *A.P.S.*, II. 228.

[88] 'The Red Book of Clanranald', in *Reliquiae Celticae*, II. 259–64.

[89] *E.R.*, x. lix; *T.A.*, I. cxiii, cxviii; Gregory, *Western Highlands*, p. 58. The evidence in *A.D.A.*, I. 177, which has been interpreted as signifying that the Lord of the Isles was *not* forfeited in May 1493 (*Highland Papers*, I. 50, n. 2) is irrelevant since it refers to a transaction of 1490 (*R.M.S.*, II. No. 1969). Some doubt remains, however, whether John of the Isles died at Paisley (*Highland Papers*, I. 50–1) or at Dundee (*T.A.*, II. 354, 357).   [90] *R.M.S.*, II. No. 2171; *E.R.*, XI. 145.

[91] *E.R.*, x. lx–lxi.   [92] *Ibid.*

[93] *R.M.S.*, II. No. 2438; Gregory, *Western Highlands*, pp. 92–3.

was evidently in no hurry to fulfil this undertaking. Although he paid a second visit to the Isles in May 1494 [94] the result does not seem to have been reassuring : on 5 July the lords of the 'Westland', 'Southland', and 'Estland' were summoned to attend the king at Tarbert. The old castle once constructed by Robert I was victualled and garrisoned, and the expense of its renovation was partly met by a tax paid by the prelates.[95] Once more it became a royalist base for military and naval operations in the Isles. Once more, as in the days of Bruce, the crown sought to establish a naval force in the Clyde estuary.[96] The immediate objective of the forces that gathered at Tarbert in July 1494 appears to have been Sir John MacDonald's castle of Dunaverty in south Kintyre.[97] No sooner had a royal garrison been installed than the castle was recaptured and the governor was hanged, reputedly in sight of the royal ships.[98] MacIan of Ardnamurchan probably made his peace with the government by delivering up Sir John MacDonald and some of his sons, who, to the horror of the Ulster annalist, were eventually hanged in Edinburgh.[99]

After Christmas, 1494, there was talk of 'the kingis passing in the Ilis', but the project was delayed until May 1495, when he embarked on the Clyde with the lords of the 'Westland', 'Estland', and 'Southland', and a force of gunners.[100] Captain Andrew Wood had by this time been knighted and commanded the king's ship, the *Flower*. Provisions were sent from many parts of Scotland for the support of the host, which by 18 May appears to have been established at Mingary Castle in Ardnamurchan.[101] The expedition secured the submission of a number of chiefs, who obtained confirmations of their charters between July 1495 and October 1496.[102] In addition James took control of Islay and Tiree, where the comptroller was sent on a commission of assessment.[103] The expenses of the expedition and of the measures undertaken by the king's subordinates after his departure appear to have been met by a heavy 'taxt of the Ilis'.[104] Possibly one of the results was the construction of a new castle at Loch Kilkerran (the present Campbeltown),[105] which became a base

---

[94] *E.R.*, XI. 181.   [95] *T.A.*, I. 215, 237; *E.R.*, X. 407, 451, 478.
[96] *E.R.*, X. 477; *T.A.*, I. 245–54; *R.M.S.*, II. No. 2420; *R.S.S.*, I. No. 448.
[97] *T.A.*, I. 244.   [98] Gregory, *Western Highlands*, p. 89.
[99] *Ibid.*, pp. 89–90; E. Curtis, *Medieval Ireland*, p. 355; Conway, *Henry VII*, p. 96; *T.A.*, I. 238, 239.   [100] *T.A.*, I. 240–2.
[101] *E.R.*, X. 473, 474, 478, 486, 494, 513, 515, 569, 571; *R.M.S.*, II. No. 2253.
[102] *R.M.S.*, II. Nos. 2264, 2281, 2286, 2287, 2327, 2329; *Highland Papers*, I. 242.   [103] *E.R.*, X. 550.   [104] *T.A.*, I. 312, 315.
[105] Gregory, *Western Highlands*, p. 93.

for the king's next three hurried expeditions to the Isles in March, May and August 1498.[106] These were probably occasioned by the utter unworkability of an act of council of 3 October 1496 which declared that any summons issued upon any inhabitant of the lordship of the Isles before 26 April 1497 was to be executed by the chief of his clan. If the latter failed to perform this invidious task he himself was to be proceeded against as if he were the principal defendant in the case. In the summer of 1498 the submission of Alexander Mac-Leod of Dunvegan, Torquil MacLeod of Lewis, Ranald MacAllan of Uist and Eigg, and Angus 'Rewochsoun Makranald' of Eigg, Arisaig and Morar, was marked by the issue of charters granting them the lands they held within the lordship of the Isles.[107]

These last charters, at least, were not affected by the general revocation that the king enacted at Duchal Castle on 16 March 1498, the day before he attained his 'perfect age' of twenty-five.[108] It was presumably to make clear that previous charters were now invalid that letters were entrusted on 20 March to a servant of Lord Gordon 'that passit in Ilis to all the hedis men of the cuntree with the kingis writingis'.[109] To the cowed nobility of the Lowlands the repeated extortion of blackmail for the renewal of charters after a revocation had become common practice. To the chiefs of the Isles it was a novel and insulting infringement of their rights. Most must have been unwilling, if not also unable, to pay the compositions that were expected, and therefore, in the view of the government, became mere tenants-at-will.[110] Nor did the king, pursuing a wild goose chase in quest of international renown, resume his personal intervention in Hebridean affairs. His replacement by the Earl of Argyll was initiated in August 1499 when the latter was granted custody of Tarbert Castle. Much more ominous was the issue on 22 April 1500 of a commission of assessment, of which Argyll was to be an essential member, to grant three-year tacks of all the lands of the lordship of the Isles with the exception of Islay and Kintyre. In all the lands subject to this commission Argyll was to be the king's lieutenant-general with virtually limitless powers for a period of three years.[111] On 11 August 1501 comparable powers were bestowed upon Lord Gordon, who had lately succeeded his father as third Earl of Huntly : he could compel the 'erlis, lordis, baronis and hed kinnysmen' north of the

---

[106] T.A., I. clxiv–clxv, clxvi–clxvii.
[107] R.M.S., II. Nos. 2420, 2424, 2438, 2439.
[108] T.A., I. cxlv, 383; E.R., x. lxvi–lxvii.   [109] T.A., I. 383.
[110] See Gregory, Western Highlands, p. 94.   [111] R.S.S., I. Nos. 413, 513, 520.

Mounth to give 'bandis and oblissingis' to keep the peace, and was to enforce payment of the king's rents in Lochaber.[112] Some months before, the king had granted to Duncan Stewart of Appin certain lands in Glencoe.[113] This may have inspired the MacIans of Glencoe to release Donald Dubh from Argyll's custody in Inchconnel Castle and to convey him to the protection of Torquil MacLeod of Lewis.[114] Donald Dubh was the son of Angus Og by a daughter of Argyll.[115] Although Angus was an illegitimate son of John, the last Lord of the Isles, he had been recognised in a tailzie of 1476 as the rightful heir; and although Donald Dubh was in turn regarded by the government, rightly or wrongly, as an illegitimate son of Angus, he was the representative of the direct line of the Lords of the Isles now that the humiliated John of the Isles had died. It came as a shock to the government to learn that Donald was now in the unreliable hands of Torquil MacLeod, who was summoned before the lords of council in November 1501 but did not compear.[116] To make matters worse, MacKenzie of Kintail and Farquhar Mackintosh contrived to escape from prison. The first, however, was soon slain and Mackintosh (to James's great relief) was soon retaken.[117] Nonetheless, within the next two years it was evident that there was a widespread movement to revive the lordship of the Isles on behalf of Donald Dubh; in the parliament of March 1504 Lauchlan MacLean of Duart was forfeited for the treasonable maintenance of 'Donald, bastard and unlauchtfull sonne of umquhile Anguss of the Ylis, bastard sonne to umquhile Johne of the Ilis . . . for the causatioune of oure soverane lordis liegis to obey to the saide Donalde as Lord of Ylis . . . usurpand oure soverane lordis autorite'.[118] Thereafter summonses for treason proliferated.[119] Nor were royalist forces inactive: in the parliament of March 1504 Huntly undertook to besiege, capture and garrison the castles of Eilean Donan in Loch Alsh and Strome on Loch Carron, 'quhilkis ar rycht necessar for the danting of the Ilis', providing that the king sent a ship with artillery to aid in the sieges. At the same time an incomplete record suggests that separate commands covering the whole of the Highlands and Isles were entrusted

[112] *Ibid.*, Nos. 722, 723.   [113] *R.M.S.*, II. No. 2565.
[114] *E.R.*, XII. lvii; Gregory, *Western Highlands*, p. 100.
[115] He is not to be confused with the Donald Owre mentioned in William Dunbar's poem and the *Treasurer's Accounts*. See J. D. Mackie's review of R. L. Mackie's *King James IV* (*S.H.R.*, XXXVIII. 133–6, at 135).
[116] Mackie, *James IV*, pp. 190–1; *R.S.S.*, I. No. 792 .
[117] *T.A.*, II. xcii.   [118] *A.P.S.*, II. 241, 247–8.
[119] *Ibid.*, 256–66, *passim*.

to Huntly, Crawford, the Earl Marischal and Lord Lovat.[120] Huntly
was also to be consulted about the re-building of Inverlochy Castle,
and Argyll was to look after the masons at work at Dunaverty and
Loch Kilkerran. Finally an inventory was to be taken of the king's
artillery in all parts of the realm.[121] Some, at least, was placed on
board the ships which the king inspected at Dumbarton in April
1504. The flotilla, fitted out by Sir Andrew Wood, accompanied by
Hans Gunnare and Robert Barton, and commanded by James
Hamilton, the new Earl of Arran, set sail in May 1504 and seems to
have bombarded the almost inaccessible castle of Cairn-na-Burgh in
the Treshnish Isles until it was taken and entrusted to Argyll, who for
its custody in the next four years was paid over £400.[122] The novel
demonstration of the powers inherent in naval artillery seems to have
resulted in the submission of MacIan of Ardnamurchan, who was
graciously received at court in November 1504.[123] In May 1505
Lauchlan MacLean of Duart was among the chiefs who received a
five-year respite for their part in supporting Donald Dubh;[124] and in
June 1506 commissioners of assessment met at Dunadd to compose
the feuds of the Isles.[125] The last stronghold of the insurgents was
Torquil MacLeod's castle of Stornoway, which was attacked by
Huntly in the summer of 1506 with a naval squadron based upon
Dumbarton and equipped with guns brought from Edinburgh
Castle.[126] By October 1506 Stornoway had evidently fallen and by
August 1507 Donald Dubh was safely warded in Stirling Castle.[127]

The rising of Donald Dubh had elicited from the parliament of
March 1504 an unwonted show of concern for the betterment of
government in the Highlands and Isles, where 'the pepill ar almaist
gane wilde'. Their misbehaviour was imputed to the 'greit abusioune
of justice' which resulted from the absence of justice ayres, justices
and sheriffs. In future the North Isles were to be served by a justice
and a sheriff based (all too cautiously) at Inverness or Dingwall.
Another justice and sheriff were to serve the South Isles from Tarbert
or Loch Kilkerran (Campbeltown). New sheriffs were also to be
established in Ross and Caithness. These arrangements were based on
the reasoning that the sheriffdom of Inverness was 'oure greit' and
required to be divided so that officers were on hand 'to put gude reule

[120] A.P.S., II. 240.   [121] Ibid., 248.
[122] T.A., II. 428, 429, 431, 433, 434, 435, 442, 446, 448; E.R., XIII. 224.
[123] T.A., III. 103; R.M.S., II. No. 2895.
[124] R.S.S., I. Nos. 1083, 1163, 1174, 1197, 1203, 1208.
[125] E.R., XII. 709–10.   [126] T.A., III. 200, 338, 340, 350.
[127] Ibid., lxxxii, 349.

amang the pepill'. Thus, as Bishop Lesley approvingly remarked, 'it was certanely knowen quhair and in quhat place justice shuld be ministrated in the justice arys and shiriff courtis'.[128] In addition the troubled regions were to be purged of the remnants of ancient Celtic law and be ruled by the king's laws and by 'nane othir lawis'.[129]

The resources of the kirk were to be used to further such ends. During the episcopate of John Campbell, Bishop of the Isles between 1487 and 1510, there was an attempt to turn the ancient abbey of Iona, formerly under the patronage of the MacDonalds, into a bishop's seat that would replace the cathedral on the Isle of Man lost to the English. Nothing definite resulted. But in 1510, when Campbell, a man with local connections, was succeeded by the king's treasurer, George Hepburn, member of that favoured Lowland kin, the king successfully petitioned the pope that the new bishop might hold Arbroath and Iona *in commendam*, so that 'his authority and nobility of race may bind that uncivilised people in devotion to the church'.[130] Similarly there was an attempt, ultimately successful, to suppress the abbey of Saddell, long associated with the MacDonalds, so that its revenues might be diverted to the bishopric of Argyll.[131] In Argyll also, a bishop with local connections (Robert Colquhoun) was succeeded in 1497 by a Lowlander, David Hamilton; since he served among 'wild people' he received royal grants to strengthen his hand, including a grant of ferms in Kintyre to maintain the episcopal castle that had been built there, as well as another grant of the judicial profits of justice ayres and sheriff courts in Argyll, Lorne, Knapdale, Kintyre and Cowal.[132]

From 1507 until the end of the reign an illusory peace settled upon the Highlands and Isles, and, in Bishop Lesley's estimation, they had been thoroughly daunted by the king's firmness.[133] The MacDonalds of the Isles, like the Black Douglases before them, had disappeared as overmighty subjects. But whenever the crown, in the language of James VI, managed to 'beate downe the hornes of proude oppressours',[134] a power vacuum was created that the crown was usually unable to fill. That did not mean that there was no one

[128] *A.P.S.*, II. 241–2, cc. 3, 4, 5; 249, cc. 3, 5; Lesley, *History*, p. 73.

[129] *A.P.S.*, II. 247, c. 27; 252, c. 24.

[130] Watt, *Fasti*, pp. 207–8; Mackie, *James IV*, p. 158; *Highland Papers*, IV. 185; *R.S.S.*, I. No. 184; *R.M.S.*, II. No. 3784.

[131] A. L. Brown, 'The Cistercian Abbey of Saddell, Kintyre', *Innes Review*, XX. 130–7.   [132] *R.S.S.*, I. Nos. 1196, 2369, 3208.

[133] *E.R.*, XIII. xxviii–xxxix; Gregory, *Western Highlands*, pp. 104–5; Lesley, *History*, p. 73.

[134] *The Basilicon Doron of King James VI* (S.T.S.), I. 69.

else who yearned to fill it. Many barons or chiefs who were under-mighty but ambitious began to raise their horns and strive for mastery among themselves. Thus, so the MacMhuirich seannachies recorded, 'there was a great struggle among the Gael for power'.[135]

The struggle took three forms. One of these was shown in the attempts to restore the lordship of the Isles until the death of Donald Dubh in 1545. Another was shown in the ambition of the heads of cadet branches of the MacDonalds to achieve some of the pre-eminence that had formerly belonged to the eldest branch. A third was shown in the strivings of other clans to increase their power and possessions at the expense of all the MacDonalds. Thus the result of the forfeiture of the Lords of the Isles was unusual chaos in the West Highlands and Isles throughout the sixteenth century whenever (and it was more usual than unusual) the crown was afflicted by minorities or other distractions.

Those who came off best in the threefold struggle were not the surviving MacDonalds but the Campbells, the Gordons, and, eventu-ally, the MacKenzies. In so far as they kept on good terms with the Edinburgh government their aggressions at the expense of weaker neighbours were unrestrained; and the latter, dispossessed of their lands, swelled the number of 'broken' clans, notably the MacGregors, whose resentful depredations caused further disorder. The accumula-tion of land and power by the Campbells was particularly spectacu-lar. Sir Duncan Forrester, a Lowland intruder, found it expedient to resign his barony of Skipinch to the Earl of Argyll in 1502.[136] Further territorial expansion was achieved when one Campbell married the heiress of the last Stewart Lord of Lorne [137] and another married the heiress of the Thane of Cawdor.[138] Similar advancement was achieved by Alexander Gordon, third Earl of Huntly. Like Argyll, he received sweeping powers as a commissioner for the assessment of lands,[139] he was granted custody of the castles of Inver-lochy and Inverness,[140] and was generally regarded as the king's chief agent in the northern Highlands and northern Hebrides.[141] In addi-tion the Gordons profited from the afflictions of John, Earl of Suther-land, upon whom a brieve of idiotry had been served in 1494; in 1514 they eventually won the earldom of Sutherland through mar-

[135] 'The Red Book of Clanranald', in *Reliquiae Celticae*, ed. Alexander Mac-Bain and John Kennedy, II. 163.   [136] *R.M.S.*, II. Nos. 2669, 2670.
[137] Gregory, *Western Highlands*, p. 83.   [138] *Highland Papers*, I. 125–7.
[139] E.g. *R.S.S.*, I. No. 1579.   [140] *R.M.S.*, II. Nos. 2950, 3379.
[141] *R.S.S.*, I. No. 1690; Gregory, *Western Highlands*, pp. 105–6.

riage.[142] Thus James IV's intervention in the Highlands and Isles scarcely reduced disorder but made the Campbells and Gordons the crown's indispensable agents in controlling continuing disorder.

This situation might have been avoided had James not been distracted by diplomacy. From the outset of the reign a succession of truces [143] had not concealed the surreptitious hostility that existed between him and Henry VII.[144] Nor did the truces prevent unofficial warfare at sea : in 1489 and 1490 Andrew Wood, commanding the *Yellow Carvel* and the *Flower*, repelled English marauders at the estuaries of the Forth and Tay; a charter of May 1491 allowed him to use English prisoners in building a fortalice at Largo 'to resist and expel those pirates and raiders who have often attacked from the sea' ;[145] and another charter of 1504 alluded to his good service when, on some past occasion, an English fleet and army had tried to capture Dunbar.[146] Injuries inflicted by the English on land and sea were evidently substantial enough for Henry VII to pay a thousand marks and fifty pounds in compensation.[147] The sparse official references to such warfare are supplemented by Pitscottie's circumstantial account of a naval encounter 'verie terrabill to sie', when, in the summer of 1490, Captain Wood captured three English vessels commanded by a certain Stephen Bull.[148]

Anglo-Scottish animosity was a factor that was not ignored when European diplomacy took a new turn after 1494 thanks to the invasions of Italy by Charles VIII and Louis XII of France. Italy became the battleground of Europe, where the new monarchies of France and Spain contended for mastery, while the papacy strove to protect and expand its own territories. In the parliament of May 1491 it had been decided that Scotland's traditional alliance with France should be renewed,[149] and an embassy, which included the seasick poet, William Dunbar, set sail. The result was a ratification on 4 March 1492 of a Franco-Scottish treaty directed against England.[150] It was the aim of the Spanish monarchs, Ferdinand and Isabella, to disrupt the Franco-Scottish alliance and to align Scotland, as well as England, alongside Spain, or at least to prevent the

[142] *T.A.*, I. 238, 239; *A.D.C.*, I. 378, 379; *E.R.*, XIII. cxxxvi.
[143] E.g. *Rot. Scot.*, II. 488, 503–5; *Cal. Docs. Scot.*, IV. Nos. 1545, 1592; *A.P.S.*, II. 220, c. 9; 226, c. 14. [144] Conway, *Henry VII*, p. 32.
[145] *R.M.S.*, II. No. 2040; *A.P.S.*, II. 227. [146] *R.M.S.*, II. No. 2775.
[147] *Cal. Docs. Scot.*, IV. No. 1597; Conway, *Henry VII*, pp. 40–1.
[148] Pitscottie, *Historie*, I. 226–30. [149] *A.P.S.*, II. 224, c. 2.
[150] *T.A.*, I. cix–cx.

Scots from threatening England, so that it had a free hand to engage in their continental schemes. In June 1489 parliament had advised delaying the conclusion of an alliance with France until Spanish envoys arrived in Scotland (with alternative offers).[151] When a Spanish embassy was received at Linlithgow in August 1489 its offers were tantalising enough to win the envoys a 'reward' of six hundred crowns, tactfully secreted in six pairs of gloves. Although some kind of indenture was concluded the ambassadors appear to have exceeded their powers by offering James the hand of an infanta of Spain, while all that the Catholic Monarchs were prepared to offer was an illegitimate daughter of Ferdinand. They reproached their envoys for deluding the Scots, but somewhat inconsistently thought it wise to put off James with false hopes lest he drew closer to the French king.[152]

Whether or not the Scots were deluded, they remained antagonistic towards Henry VII, even after he had reached an understanding with France in the treaty of Étaples of 3 November 1492.[153] It was not apparent to contemporaries that the Wars of the Roses had ended; if English internal dissensions could be revived the Scots might profit, particularly by a recovery of Berwick. Thus Scotland played a part in the schemes of Margaret of York, Dowager Duchess of Burgundy and sister of the late Edward IV. In 1489 and 1490 her emissaries visited the Scottish court, which had already issued safe-conducts to Lord Lovel and all other Englishmen who adopted his Yorkist 'opinion'.[154] James's domestic preoccupations, particularly in the Highlands and Isles, prevented any immediate attachment to the cause of the white rose. But by 1495 this was represented by a likely pretender: Perkin Warbeck, a Flemish impostor,[155] was recognised by Duchess Margaret, and temporarily by Maximilian, King of the Romans, as Richard, Duke of York, the younger of the two sons of Edward IV who had been imprisoned in the Tower by Richard III. In the summer of 1495 the pretender stirred up support in Ireland, and, having failed there,[156] made his way to Scotland. The Scots had already committed themselves to his cause: in July 1495 Bishop Elphinstone and other envoys had asked Maximilian (now emperor designate) to join in an alliance against England; Maximilian's daughter, so they vainly hoped, might marry James, and, in return

---

[151] A.P.S., II. 214, c. 3.   [152] T.A., I. xci–xciii.
[153] Mackie, James IV, pp. 67, 78, 81.
[154] T.A., I. 99, 120, 130; R.M.S., II. Nos. 1738, 1798; Conway, Henry VII, pp. 31, 48.
[155] For his origins and early career see T.A., I. cxxiv–cxxvi.
[156] E. Curtis, Medieval Ireland, pp. 354–5.

for supporting the 'Duke of York', the Scots might regain Berwick.[157] In November 1495 preparations were being made to receive 'Prince Richard of England' at Stirling.[158] Whether or not James took Perkin's pretensions seriously it suited his policy to appear to do so. Perkin was married with great pomp to Lady Catherine Gordon, daughter of the Earl of Huntly. A special contribution was levied to provide the pretender with a yearly allowance of £1,200, and a 'tax of spears' or 'spear silver'—doubtless similar to the old feudal scutage—was exacted to finance military preparations.[159] There was a flurry of diplomatic interchanges as James made ready to invade England, and the courts of England and Spain sought to induce him to change his policy. Robert Blackadder, Archbishop of Glasgow, was twice sent to win concessions (and an infanta) from Ferdinand and Isabella, who at least urged the pope (though in vain) to make Blackadder a cardinal.[160] They also sent Don Pedro de Ayala on an embassy to Scotland in the summer of 1496. Although this likable hidalgo failed to alter James's policy he lingered amiably at court for more than a year, and in his reports to Spain gave an account sometimes shrewd, sometimes flattering, of Scotland and its king.[161] Less flattering accounts of James, together with proposals for the kidnapping of Perkin, were sent to the English court by Sir John Ramsay. He furnished precise details of James's preparations to break the truce and invade England on behalf of the pretender, who had promised to cede Berwick and pay the Scots fifty thousand marks.[162] While Ayala exaggerated Scottish military power Ramsay assessed it more critically and pointed out all too prophetically (though prematurely) how James's 'young adventurousness' could be duly curbed if his invading army were intercepted on its passage back to Scotland.[163]

On 19 September 1496 the host set out from Ellem, crossed the Tweed, and ravaged the valley of the Till. No Englishman would rally to Perkin. James tired of the expedition in a few days. In the following month he went hawking in Perthshire.[164] Early in June 1497 it was the turn of the English to make a foray as far as Duns,[165]

[157] Mackie, *James IV*, pp. 78–9; Conway, *Henry VII*, p. 99.
[158] *T.A.*, I. cxxii–cxxiii.
[159] *Ibid.*, cxxvii; *R.S.S.*, I. No. 405; Lesley, *History*, pp. 63–5.
[160] Mackie, *James IV*, pp. 81–2.
[161] *T.A.*, I. cxxxv; *E.R.*, XI. lviii; Brown, *Early Travellers*, pp. 39–55.
[162] Pinkerton, *History*, II. 437; Conway, *Henry VII*, pp. 99–102.
[163] *T.A.*, I. cxxxvii–cxxxix.   [164] *Ibid.*, cxxxix–cxliii; *E.R.*, XI. lix–lx.
[165] *T.A.*, I. 341; *R.M.S.*, II. Nos. 2362, 2365.

after which James led another brief raid across the Tweed.[166] Perkin was now a nuisance rather than an asset and was allowed to depart with his wife in a Breton ship aptly named the *Cuckoo*. Having sailed from Ayr with Robert Barton in July 1497 he landed first at Cork, then in Cornwall. By October he was Henry's prisoner, and two years later he was executed.[167]

Perkin's departure did not hold back James's preparations for 'the great raid', for which more 'spear silver' was exacted, as well as private contributions from various notables, particularly the abbots. Minstrels played as Mons Meg was trundled from Edinburgh Castle (until its carriage collapsed). The host mustered at Upsetlington on 5 August and vainly assaulted Norham Castle for a week. Only a rebellion that had broken out in Cornwall in May 1497 had prevented an overwhelming concentration of English forces. When Thomas Howard, Earl of Surrey, marched north, James was prepared to fight, but only on chivalric terms : possession of Berwick was to be settled either by a general engagement between the two armies or by a hand-to-hand combat between the two commanders. When Surrey announced that he was not authorised to hazard the town on such terms James 'ffled shamefully and sodeynly with all his company'. To the disappointment of Henry VII five days of foul weather sufficed to disperse Surrey's troops before the Scots could be sufficiently chastised. Thanks to the mediation of Don Pedro, who had helped to amuse James at cards during the siege of Norham, a seven-year truce (later extended) was concluded at Ayton on 30 September 1497.[168]

James was lucky to have been extricated from campaigning so lightly. His preparations had been costly, the results minimal; and service in the host was unpopular.[169] But his personal valour, which aroused the admiration of Don Pedro, left the king with an undiminished conceit of his qualities as a general. A moderate defeat might have given him a grasp of military realities : it was reported to the Spanish court that James had seen 'the ears of the wolf';[170] but he had not seen its jaws. The eagerness of Henry VII to reach a settle-

---

[166] *T.A.*, I. cl–cli.

[167] Conway, *Henry VII*, pp. 109–11; *A.D.C.P.*, p. lx; *T.A.*, I. cli–cliv; *E.R.*, XI. lxi–lxii; Lesley, *History*, pp. 66–7.

[168] Conway, *Henry VII*, pp. 109–14; Mackie, *James IV*, pp. 86–9; *T.A.*, I. cliv–clviii; *E.R.*, XI. lxii–lxiv; Lesley, *History*, pp. 65–6.

[169] A number of remissions were subsequently granted to those who were absent from the host at Ayton (*R.S.S.*, I. Nos. 1956–8, 1961, 1962, 2095, 2100, 2189, 2330).   [170] Mackie, *James IV*, p. 90.

ment left the impression that Scotland's military might was held in awe.

At last, however, James was willing to reach a settlement with Henry, who assuaged the Scottish king's rankled pride when the latest truce was jeopardised by an affray at Norham in the summer of 1498. In November Bishop Fox of Durham was received in private audience at Melrose in his dual capacity as custodian of Norham and close adviser of Henry VII. James made it plain that his prior condition for peace and friendship with England was a marriage between himself and Henry's elder daughter, Margaret, then nine years old.[171]

From the very outset of his reign James had used his own marriage prospects as an asset in internal politics and international diplomacy.[172] He, who quested the hand of an infanta of Spain or an emperor's daughter, can only have been insulted in 1493 when Henry offered him the daughter of the Countess of Wiltshire.[173] Although James pursued his matrimonial quest assiduously he did so with no sense of haste : he had two younger brothers, James, Duke of Ross, and John, Earl of Mar, to assure the succession while he himself dallied with mistresses in a court graced by his aunt, Lady Margaret Stewart, onetime mistress of Lord Crichton. The king's first mistress was Marion Boyd. Their son, Alexander Stewart, born in 1493, was to become Archbishop of St Andrews.[174] The second royal mistress, adopted in 1496, was Margaret Drummond, daughter of Lord Drummond. She and two sisters died suddenly in 1502 after a suspect breakfast.[175] The generosity that James had displayed towards Margaret and her kinsfolk [176] was surpassed by that shown to her rival and successor, Janet Kennedy, daughter of Lord Kennedy. In 1498, it would appear, she was about to be married to Bell-the-Cat, who, having prematurely granted her his lordship of Bothwell, had to content himself with Katherine Stirling.[177] In 1499 the new Lady Bothwell bore a son to the king, who expressed his thankfulness for Janet's 'services' by granting her first the lordship of Menteith, and then, in June 1501, the castle and lands of Darnaway, conveniently

[171] *Ibid.*, pp. 90–2.
[172] E.g. *A.P.S.*, II. 207, c. 2; 224, c. 3; 230, c. 1; 233–4, c. 11.
[173] *Cal. Docs. Scot.*, IV. No. 1588.
[174] Mackie, *James IV*, p. 81; *T.A.*, I. cxxxii–cxxxiii; *E.R.*, XII. xl–xlix.
[175] Mackie, *James IV*, pp. 80–81, 100–101; *T.A.*, I. cxxxii–cxxxiii; II. 358–451, *passim*; Tytler, *History*, I. pt. ii, 394.
[176] *R.M.S.*, II. Nos. 2299, 2311; *R.S.S.*, I. No. 326.
[177] *R.M.S.*, II. Nos. 2434, 2457, 2539; *R.S.S.*, I. No. 258.

sited on the route to St Duthac's shrine. A few days later their son, James Stewart, was created Earl of Moray.[178]

Meanwhile the project discussed at Melrose in November 1498 had been followed by lengthy negotiations that encountered no insuperable obstacle. Henry VII was aware that by marrying his daughter to the Scottish king he might make it possible for James, or his issue, to succeed to the English throne. In such an event, however, so Henry informed his councillors, the greater would draw the less— a Scottish king might win England but he would inevitably make it the predominant partner in a Greater Britain. On 24 January 1502, soon after the bride had attained the nubile age of twelve, the marriage treaty was concluded in London : Margaret Tudor was to receive a dower of lands and castles in Scotland worth £2,000 sterling or £6,000 Scots a year; James was to receive a dowry of £10,000 sterling or £30,000 Scots.[179] The marriage treaty was accompanied by another—the first since 1328—of perpetual peace between Scotland and England.

In the entourage of Bishop Andrew Forman, one of the Scottish negotiators, was the poet William Dunbar, who acknowledged his hospitable reception in the Guildhall by a poem in praise of London, 'the floure of cities all'. In the summer of 1503 he was ready with another poem to celebrate the marriage of 'The Thrissil and the Rose'.[180] Costly preparations had been made in both countries for the northward progress of the royal bride, who was received at Lamberton Kirk by the Archbishop of Glasgow, the Earl of Bothwell and other notables. At Dunbar the guns of the newly rebuilt castle gave a royal salute. At Dalkeith Castle the king, magnificently arrayed in velvet and cloth of gold, first met his bride. Four days later they made their state entry into Edinburgh amid an ostentatious display of religious and secular pageantry. On 8 August the marriage was solemnised in the abbey of Holyrood and there followed five days of festivities in the new palace of Holyroodhouse, where the king belted forty-one knights and created three new earls—Arran, Montrose and Glencairn. Despite James's incredible expenses—each of his two gowns cost more than £600 and the wine bill exceeded £2,000— some of the English guests were not impressed ; the new queen wrote tearfully to her father ; and James paid a discreet visit to St Duthac's

---

[178] R.S.S., I. Nos. 495, 730; R.M.S., II. No. 2585; Lesley, History, p. 81.

[179] Cal. Docs. Scot., IV. No. 1680; R.M.S., II. Nos. 2602-4, 2624; E.R., XII. xlix–liv.

[180] Mackie, James IV, pp. 95-6.

shrine (and Darnaway).[181] In July 1505 he received from Henry the final payment of the queen's dowry.[182] Until Henry's death in 1509 the relationship between Scotland and England was one of friendship and co-operation,[183] and neither country was seriously engaged in continental warfare.

That did not mean that there was any slackening in James's diplomacy, which was addressed not only towards France, Spain, England and the papacy but towards lesser powers with which James had a connection through kinship, commerce, or chivalric ambition. Kinship accounted for James's protective interest in the duchy of Guelders.[184] Both kinship and commerce explained his dealings with Veere and its Van Borselen lords,[185] as well as his support for his uncle, King Hans, who held uneasy sway over Denmark, Norway, and sometimes Sweden.[186] In August 1488 Junker Gerhard, uncle of King Hans and grand-uncle of James, had visited Scotland, possibly as a belated mediator whose mission was rendered unnecessary by Sauchieburn.[187] The parliaments of June 1489, February 1490 and May 1491 approved the sending of an embassy to renew the alliance with Denmark.[188] The successful mission of Sir James Ogilvy of Airlie in 1492 was followed by two return visits of the Danish chancellor,[189] and in 1499 France became a party to the alliance. Thus 'Danish-Scottish relations began to assume an importance in general European politics'.[190] Soon afterwards the troubles of King Hans became so acute that Bishop Lesley wrongly believed that he came in person to Scotland to seek aid.[191] The aid was certainly forthcoming : a tax was levied and in May 1502 there were preparations for 'the

---

[181] *Ibid.*, pp. 102-12; Pitscottie, *Historie*, I. 238-40; Lesley, *History*, pp. 72, 73.

[182] *R.S.S.*, I. No. 1117.   [183] Lesley, *History*, pp. 72, 79.

[184] *Ibid.*, p. 74; *James IV, Letters*, Nos. 71-3, 226, 233, 283, 297; Mackie, *James IV*, pp. 113, 212, 213.

[185] Lesley, *History*, p. 75; *R.M.S.*, II. No. 3165; *James IV, Letters*, Nos. 130, 186, 208, 225.

[186] For the background see the section on Scotland and Denmark in *James IV, Letters*, pp. xxxix-xliii; W. Stanford Reid, 'The Place of Denmark in Scottish Foreign Policy, 1470-1540', *Juridical Review*, LVIII. 183-200; James Dow, 'Skotter in sixteenth-century Scania', *S.H.R.*, XLIV. 34-51; Thorkild L. Christensen, 'Scoto-Danish relations in the sixteenth century', *ibid.*, XLVIII. 80-97, and 'Scots in Denmark in the sixteenth century', *ibid.*, XLIX. 125-45.

[187] He was to pay a second visit in 1497 (*T.A.*, I. lxxvi, cxliv).

[188] *A.P.S.*, II. 214, c. 4; 219, c. 6; 224, c. 4; Mackie, *James IV*, p. 54.

[189] Lesley, *History*, p. 62; *T.A.*, I. cxii, cxviii, and n. 5.

[190] W. Stanford Reid, *op. cit.*, *Juridical Review*, LVIII. 186; *R.S.S.*, I. No. 391.

[191] Lesley, *History*, pp. 72-3.

furnising furth of our soverane lordis armey to pas to Denmark'.[192] An expeditionary force of a few ships and some two thousand men eventually returned, having failed to forestall the fall of Stockholm and the capture of Queen Christina by the insurgent Swedes.[193] Their alliance with Lübeck was likely to maintain a Hanseatic stranglehold upon Baltic trade, to the disadvantage of both Denmark and Scotland. Although James sent no further troops to his uncle's aid his diplomacy helped to achieve the acceptance of a truce by Lübeck in 1507. It scarcely lasted a year. In 1508 James sent one of his new ships, the *Margaret*, commanded by Andrew Barton, to assist King Hans, and in the following year Andrew and his brother Robert were busy in the Baltic.[194] Indirectly both this naval activity and occasional attempts to strengthen the tripartite alliance of Scotland, Denmark and France, would contribute to crisis a few years later.[195] Meanwhile, however, James's far-reaching diplomacy, the growing prestige of his sea-captains, and his own role as peace-maker, combined to give Scotland increasing weight in European politics. The marriage alliance with England had caused no breach with France.[196] From the time of James's marriage until the death of his father-in-law, Scotland had no serious foreign foe and many apparent friends. This favourable situation was recognised by Pope Julius II, who presented James with the golden rose and the sword of state still to be seen in Edinburgh Castle.[197]

James's attitude towards the papacy was the normal one of the age: he was 'quick to exploit, ready to enlist the aid of parliament when necessary, scrupulous about procedures, cautious, but grateful too'.[198] Not only had the papacy failed to learn any lessons from the conciliarist movement but it had altered for the worse since the death of Innocent VIII in 1492. His successor, Roderigo Borgia, who reigned as Alexander VI from 1492 to 1503, was debauched and sinister; and Julius II (1503–1513) was a warrior pope who in 1508 formed the league of Cambrai to despoil the Venetians.[199] The decline in the prestige of the papacy made it less able to resist the chal-

---

[192] *A.D.C.P.*, p. lix; *E.R.*, XII. xxxvii.   [193] See *James IV, Letters*, No. 37.

[194] W. Stanford Reid, *op. cit., Juridical Review*, LVIII. 189–90, and 'Seapower in the Foreign Policy of James IV of Scotland', *Medievalia et Humanistica*, XV. 97–107, at 99, 102–3.   [195] Pp. 595–6 below.

[196] Mackie, *James IV*, pp. 100, 101; Lesley, *History*, pp. 74, 76, 77–8.

[197] Lesley, *History*, pp. 63, 75; Charles Burns, *op. cit., Innes Review*, XX. 150–94.

[198] Leslie J. Macfarlane, *op. cit., Innes Review*, XX. 111–29, at 128–9.

[199] Mackie, *James IV*, p. 202.

lenge of new monarchy. Although Innocent VIII's successors were not bound to observe the terms of the indult granted to James III in 1487 the crown regarded it as a perpetual privilege, and the parliament of June 1493 was prompted to ordain that the king should cause it to 'be observit and kepit, and suffer na promotionis to gang throw in the contrare'.[200] It was nothing new that appointments to the greater benefices were made by papal provision, but this was now set in motion by the crown : 'the really effective transaction . . . came to be the royal nomination with advice of council'.[201] Ever resourceful in legal devices the papacy encouraged the practice of resignation *in favorem*, whereby an incumbent resigned his benefice to a successor, thus avoiding a vacancy in which the king might intervene.[202] But there was nothing to prevent the king from inspiring such a resignation to suit his own purposes. Moreover the parliaments of October 1488, June 1493 and July 1496 saw a wholesale revival of the barratry legislation of James I and of all the legislation of James III that had been designed to safeguard and increase the crown's ecclesiastical patronage, reduce the flow of bullion to the *curia*, and control individual recourse to Rome, the intent being that the crown should enjoy a monopoly of trafficking with the papacy.[203] So long as the latter received the traditional common services and annates it cared little how the traffic was handled : James was even conceded the right to nominate to thirty benefices.[204] The register of the privy seal shows that throughout the reign he made over two hundred nominations or presentations ;[205] and William Dunbar, the poet, was not alone in being granted a pension while waiting until the king provided him with a benefice.[206]

Not only did the crown control many ecclesiastical appointments but it was responsible for a major change in ecclesiastical organisation : the demand for a second archbishopric was motivated partly by a desire for a parity with England, mostly by politics. Although Archbishop Scheves stubbornly opposed the erection of Glasgow as a second archiepiscopal see, the papacy was reluctantly induced to comply : on 9 January 1492 Robert Blackadder was created Archbishop of Glasgow and assigned control as metropolitan, primate and

[200] *A.P.S.*, II. 232, c. 4.
[201] R. K. Hannay, *The Scottish Crown and the Papacy*, p. 10.
[202] See *Wigtown Charters*, Nos. 147 and 197.
[203] *A.P.S.*, II. 209-10, cc. 13, 14; 232-3, cc. 2-9; 237-8, c. 2; R. K. Hannay, *The Scottish Crown and the Papacy*, p. 10.
[204] *R.S.S.*, I. No. 1596.   [205] *Ibid., passim.*
[206] *Ibid.*, Nos. 2018, 2079, 2144, 2119, 2199, 2269, 2302, 2412, 2423.

legatus natus over the sees of Galloway and Argyll and (initially) Dunkeld and Dunblane as well. Wasteful controversy between the two archbishops ensued (to the annoyance of parliament) and the leadership that might have been forthcoming from an effective primacy of St Andrews was undermined.[207]

The sequel to the death of Archbishop Scheves in 1497 demonstrated the trend of affairs. To pursue a cynical scheme of financial chicanery the king secured the appointment of his brother, James, Duke of Ross (about twenty years of age) as the next Archbishop of St Andrews, obtaining in exchange the valuable ducal lands. Whatever the merits of the duke-archbishop he was too young to be consecrated. At his death in 1504 the king stimulated the practice of using the kirk as an employment bureau for the illegitimate sons of the crown and nobility by bestowing the archbishopric upon his eleven-year-old bastard son, Alexander Stewart, which in effect meant that the archbishopric was administered by the crown.[208] The boy-archbishop, like his predecessor, was also nominally made chancellor and was granted one or two rich commendatorships; he (or the crown) thus controlled the abbey of Dunfermline and the priory of Coldingham. These scandalous and demoralising appointments made it clear that the kirk had become a department of state: 'the papacy has been criticised, with some justification, for its failure to resist such abuses, but the role of secular power, which sought them, deserves no less severe criticism'.[209]

When bishops and abbots were increasingly nominated for worldly reasons their spiritual function was bound to suffer. It may be admitted that Bishop Elphinstone presented an unique example of devotion not only to the crown but to the kirk: if he spent three months in Edinburgh on judicial business he passed at least six months a year in his diocese and used royal favour and the profits of government office to promote its welfare.[210] But even Elphinstone could resort to legal chicanery to attain his laudable ends.[211] In his eyes, as in those of James Beaton, second Archbishop of Glasgow, and George Brown, Bishop of Dunkeld, nepotism within the kirk was to

[207] J. A. F. Thomson, *op. cit.*, *Innes Review*, XIX. 23–31, at 30–1; Leslie J. Macfarlane, *op. cit., ibid.*, XX. 111–29, at 117–8.

[208] See *James IV, Letters*, Nos. 20, 21, 24.

[209] J. A. F. Thomson, *op. cit.*, *Innes Review*, XIX. 23–31, at 31. See also Leslie J. Macfarlane, *op. cit., ibid.*, XX. 111–29, at 118–22, 127; *E.R.*, XII. xxxii, xli–xlii; XIII. lxxxvi–xcii.

[210] Leslie J. Macfarlane, *op. cit.*, *Aberdeen University Review*, XXXIX. 1–18, at 9–13; *E.R.*, XI. xxxv–xxxvi; XIII. clix–clx.

[211] See the case of Sir David Lindsay (*A.D.A.*, I. 141).

be accounted a virtue rather than a vice;[212] and it was doubtless thanks to Elphinstone's patronage that his lay kinsfolk received advancement—one presided over the royal nursery, three were royal familiars, and one of these was created a lord of parliament and was expected to lead a hundred spearmen in time of war.[213] More aspersions might be cast against Andrew Forman, Bishop of Moray, apostolic protonotary, commendator of Kelso and Dryburgh, tacksman of Dunbar Mains, keeper of Darnaway, chamberlain of Moray, custumar north of Spey. This talented diplomatist was a Scottish Wolsey 'whose contribution to the wellbeing of the Scottish church can only be considered marginal'.[214] A similar picture is presented by Andrew Stewart, Bishop of Caithness, commendator of Kelso and Fearn, chamberlain of Ross and Ardmannoch, keeper of Dingwall and Redcastle, who served for a time as treasurer and comptroller and dabbled deviously in government finance.[215]

The examples of the duke-archbishop and boy-archbishop of St Andrews, of Bishop Hepburn of the Isles, of Bishop Forman and Bishop Stewart show how ecclesiastics who enjoyed royal favour could expect to be rewarded by the grant of abbeys *in commendam*. This growing practice was a major factor in the decline of monastic life, though the decline was not yet wholesale: while the lords of council were concerned that the abbey of Jedburgh was 'ruinos and hable to failze and fall doune',[216] the priory of Whithorn benefited from royal pilgrimages and in 1508 was at its most flourishing with a complement of twenty-four canons.[217] The interest in gardening shown by one Abbot of Kinloss was counterbalanced by his indulgence in fleshly pleasures; but his successor, Thomas Crystall, was a model of minor virtues.[218] Like the bishops the abbots were increasingly drawn into royal administration: those of Cambuskenneth, Paisley, Dunfermline and Arbroath, together with the commendator of Glenluce, each served as treasurer. The Abbots of Jedburgh, Holyrood, Cambuskenneth, Glenluce, Scone and Dunfermline served alongside the Bishops of Caithness, Dunblane, Argyll, the Isles, Aberdeen, Ross and Moray on commissions for the assessment of crown

[212] Mackie, *James IV*, p. 156; *E.R.*, XIII. clviii–clix; *R.M.S.*, II. Nos. 3667, 3795; Watt, *Fasti, ad indices.*
[213] *R.M.S.*, II. Nos. 2468, 2662, 3128, 3204, 3251, 3875; *R.S.S.*, I. Nos. 388, 799; *E.R.*, XIII. lxxxv.
[214] Leslie J. Macfarlane, *op. cit., Innes Review*, xx. 111–29, at 126; *E.R.*, XIII. clii–clviii.   [215] *E.R.*, XIII. cxlvi–clii; *R.S.S.*, I. No. 1351; *R.M.S.*, II. No. 3758.
[216] *A.D.C.P.*, p. lx. [217] *Wigtown Charters*, pp. 17, 90–1; *R.M.S.*, II. No. 2075.
[218] See Coulton, *Scottish Abbeys*, pp. 120, 148–9, 212.

lands.[219] The Abbot of Lindores was keeper of Linlithgow palace,[220] and Patrick Paniter, the king's chief secretary, obtained the abbey of Cambuskenneth in 1513, as well as a dispensation from assuming canonical garb for a further two years.[221] A hierarchy so closely associated with the crown was ready to comply with the royal wishes even in the matter of taxation, and special contributions levied upon the clergy became increasingly frequent.[222]

One by-product of the close association of kirk and state was an outburst of liturgical and devotional nationalism. Hitherto the Scottish liturgy had closely followed the English 'use of Sarum', and Scottish saints had been neglected. A new spirit was apparent in 1490 when Archbishop Scheves searched at Fordoun for the relics of St Palladius; and Bishop Elphinstone's Aberdeen Breviary of 1509–10, with its list of seventy Scottish saints, the climax to an emphasis on the bygone glories of Scottish Christianity, provided a distinctively national liturgy.[223] It was also typical of the age that the king's exploitation of the kirk was accompanied by religious idealism and assiduous personal devotions. During Lent James was to be found with the zealous Observant Franciscans at Stirling, where he had helped them to establish a house. From the antagonisms of the more worldly Conventuals the Observants were protected by the king : 'Theirs', so he informed the pope, 'is the popular religion ; by their care the salvation of souls here is most diligently advanced, the negligence of others most fully remedied, the sacraments administered, and the word of God spread abroad by the lips of the faithful'.[224]

James's regard for the small band of ascetic evangelists implied no criticism of the more dominant features of contemporary religious life.[225] He made offerings 'to the reliques' at St Andrews and presented a cross enshrined in silver to the altar of St Duthac, who 'divided his reverent regards with . . . the saint of Galloway'.[226] In the course of his frequent pilgrimages to Tain and Whithorn he not only bestowed alms but paid for a 'trental' of masses (thirty) at a time.[227] During the reign the great seal register records confirmations

---

[219] E.R., x. 663, 710, 711; xi. 388, 395–6, 451; xii. 660, 686, 694, 698, 704; xiii. 593.   [220] R.S.S., i. No. 296.

[221] Mackie, James IV, pp. 157–8.   [222] E.g. T.A., iv. 391–3.

[223] David McRoberts, op. cit., Innes Review, xix. 3–14.

[224] A. R. MacEwen, History of the Church in Scotland, i. 364–6; James IV, Letters, Nos. 76, 77; Coulton, Scottish Abbeys, p. 230.

[225] See A. I. Dunlop, op. cit., Scot. Church Hist. Soc. Recs., xv. 153–67, at 167.   [226] T.A., i. cxiv–cxv, cxlvi, clxii.   [227] Ibid., cxlviii–cxlix, clxi.

of the endowment of more than a hundred chaplainries (some of them founded by the king himself),[228] representing an annual outlay of about £1,000 on the salaries of chaplains whose chief duty was a somewhat mechanical celebration of the mass. The new collegiate kirks of Seton (1492), Semple (1504) and St Mary of the Fields, Edinburgh (1512), were surpassed by the King's foundation at Stirling (1501), where James fulfilled his father's fateful ambition of erecting a chapel royal. Its staff, modelled on that of a cathedral, was headed by the Bishop of Galloway and included a chantor, chancellor, treasurer, subdean, sub-chantor, archdeacon and 'official'.[229]

George Vaus, the first 'Bishop of Galloway and the chapel royal' had fathered a son.[230] Although letters of legitimation under the privy seal do not always give the name of the father, there are frequent indications of clerical paternity: one legitimation was issued for the son of a canon of Holyrood, another for the son of a parson of Maybole; chaplains were particularly prolific.[231] Clerical incontinence was nothing new; but the scurrility it aroused [232] was more perilous when the kirk was demoralised, leaderless, beset with incongruities, and worldly. In Paris the scholastic theologian John Major, conciliarist in outlook, expressed misgivings in measured academic language.[233] Lollardy had not been forgotten and may have been reinforced by 'Flemish spirituality' inspired by the Brethren of the Common Life.[234] In 'The Flyting of Dunbar and Kennedie' the poet Walter Kennedy humorously calumniated his opponent with the vituperative terms of 'Lollard laureate' and 'lamp lollardorum'. William Dunbar, far from being a heretic, wrote more seriously that

> The schip of faith tempestuous wind and rane
> Dryvis in the see of Lollerdry that blawis.[235]

Even more striking is John Knox's circumstantial account of a trial held in 1494 when Archbishop Blackadder summoned thirty persons,

[228] R.M.S., II. Nos. 2536, 2549, 2681, 2796, 2903, 3774; A.P.S., II. 267, c. 8.
[229] Watt, Fasti, pp. 335–41; E.R., XII. xxxviii; A.P.S., II. 240, 274; R.M.S., II. Nos. 2760, 3002–3; R.S.S., I. Nos. 1789, 2207; James IV, Letters, Nos. 52, 53.
[230] Wigtown Charters, No. 201.
[231] R.S.S., I. Nos. 1610, 1708, 1946, 2254, 2258, 2335, 2336, 2422.
[232] In his Tabile of Confession William Dunbar wrote of 'Sic pryd of prelattis, hant of harlottis'.
[233] Major, History, p. 136; J. H. Burns, op. cit., S.H.R., XLII. 89–104, at 100.
[234] Durkan, Bishop Turnbull, pp. 40, 44.
[235] William Dunbar, The Praise of Aige.

mostly members of genteel Ayrshire families, to be interrogated before king and council upon thirty-four heretical opinions. These included a denial of transubstantiation, of the Petrine doctrine, of the efficacy of masses, papal indulgences, and adoration of images, as well as an assertion that 'thei which ar called principallis in the church ar thevis and robbaris'. Whether or not the 'Lollards of Kyle' held all these opinions it is clear that their bold spokesman, Adam Reid of Barskimming, questioned the traditional number of the sacraments and had no respect for 'proud prelates'. His witty and cunning ripostes at the expense of the archbishop deprived the proceedings of the gravity necessary for dire punishment, and, so reports Knox, 'the bischop and his band war so dashed out of countenance that the greattest part of the accusatioun was turned to lawchter'.[236] Laurence of Lindores must have turned in his grave.

While most of the changes that affected the kirk were clearly adverse, those that influenced burgh life are more difficult to evaluate. There was a striking increase in the number of burghs.[237] The Earls of Buchan, Huntly, Argyll and Bothwell, Lords Home and Glamis, were each allowed to establish a 'free burgh in barony',[238] and among the score of lairds who obtained the same privilege was Sir Andrew Wood of Largo.[239] Seven monasteries were similarly favoured,[240] and Bishop Elphinstone was responsible for the erection of no less than four baronial burghs.[241] Although some of the new burghs of barony, which were mostly rural, had only a shadowy existence (if any),[242] the attempts to found them testify to a real, or potential, increase in internal trade, from which the feudal superiors hoped to profit. But the new foundations impinged upon the ancient monopolies of the royal burghs: the conflicting privileges claimed both by the old royal burgh of Wigtown and the newly-recognised 'free burgh' of Whithorn (one of the few non-royal burghs whose situation allowed it to participate in overseas trade) led to prolonged recriminations and litigation.[243]

Recriminations also flourished within the burghs, where mer-

---

[236] Knox, *History*, I. 1–2; D. E. Easson, 'The Lollards of Kyle', *Juridical Review*, XLVIII. 123–8; W. Stanford Reid, *op. cit.*, *Church History*, XI. 3–17, at 14–17.　　　[237] See Pryde, *Burghs*, pp. 52–7.

[238] *R.S.S.*, I. Nos. 154, 478; *R.M.S.*, II. Nos. 1864, 1993, 2013, 2064.

[239] *R.M.S.*, II. No. 3880.

[240] *Ibid.*, Nos. 1767, 1944, 2115, 2292, 2336, 2350, 2574.

[241] *Ibid.*, Nos. 2132, 2443, 2492, 2588.

[242] *Wigtown Charters*, p. 6.　　　[243] *Ibid.*, pp. 137–9; Nos. 109–20, *passim*.

chants and craftsmen continued their disputes. There can be no doubt with which side the government sympathised. William Dunbar, in his satire upon Edinburgh, was probably expressing court opinion when he wrote :

> Tailyouris, soutaris and craftis vile
> The fairest of your streets dois fyle.

Fear of tumultuous craftsmen probably underlay the act of May 1491 that forbade bonds or convocations within the burghs, and further acts of June 1493 rejected the fairly liberal policy of the previous reign by resuscitating the punitive legislation of James I : the appointment of deacons by the craftsmen was 'rycht dangerous' and might cause 'greit troubill . . . and convocatioun and rysing of the kingis liegis' ; the craftsmen made statutes of their own for their own profit, which deserved great punishment ; masons and wrights convened to make rules of work, claiming payment on holy days as well as working days, 'or els they sall nocht laubour nor wirk' ; if a craftsman began a job and then, at his own pleasure, left it, no other craftsman would continue the work ; thus all those guilty of devising such rules should be indicted as oppressors of the king's lieges ; meanwhile the craftsmen were not to levy contributions among themselves ; their deacons were to lose office for a year and thereafter confine themselves to criticising the work of their fellow-craftsmen. Another act of June 1496 blamed the craftsmen for rising prices.[244] The merchants consolidated their position both through the court of the four burghs, which in 1500 forbade craftsmen to 'use merchandise or sail in merchandise',[245] and in the parliament of March 1504, where it was enacted that all officers exercising jurisdiction within burghs were to be merchants; the consent not only of the town council but of the merchant gild was to be required for the admission of new burgesses ; both craftsmen and gentlemen burgesses (lairds enrolled as burgesses) were to be prevented from making leagues to usurp the authority of the magistrates.[246] But despite attempts to hold down the craftsmen they continued to organise themselves : in Edinburgh the waulkers and tailors each obtained incorporation under the seal of cause in 1500 ; the surgeons and barbers followed in 1505 (thus initiating the still-flourishing Royal College of

[244] *A.P.S.*, II. 226-7, c. 17; 234, cc. 13, 14; 238, c. 5.
[245] *Burghs Convention Recs.*, I. 505; *Edinburgh Burgh Recs.*, I. 88-9.
[246] *A.P.S.*, II. 252, cc. 25, 29, 31, 32, 35.

Surgeons of Edinburgh), and the cordiners followed in 1510.[247] Nor were the Edinburgh craftsmen content with their share in burgh government: in 1508 they approached the town council, which already included 'ane pairt of the craftismen of the toun', to ask that six or eight craftsmen should sit on the 'daylie counsale of the toun'. As a result this issue was to be referred to parliament.[248]

It was nothing new that parliament concerned itself with the affairs of the burghs, but it was typical of the new monarchy that offences such as regrating and forestalling now became the concern of the privy council, which hoped to prevent the cornering of the market by monopolistic practices and thus avoid a dearth of food supplies.[249] In general the burghs lost something of their independence. In October 1488 they were denied the right to repledge accused burgesses to their own courts (though some burghs subsequently had the privilege confirmed and Stirling even acquired the rare distinction of possessing its own sheriff within the burgh).[250] In the parliament of March 1504, which saw a wholesale reassertion of ancient burghal practices, it was ordained that the commissioners of burghs should be warned to compear when contributions were to be levied so that they might vote as one of the three estates.[251] It may be inferred from this astonishing enactment that taxation had recently been imposed without burghal consent and that the continued existence of a third estate was in jeopardy.

For the burghs were hardly in a flourishing condition. From 1498 onwards they were ravaged by recurring visitations of plague that stilled the clamour of busy markets and made mockery of the naïve pageantry and buffoonery that enlivened their holy days.[252] In 1497 a new pestilence, the 'grandgore'—venereal disease brought to Europe in the ships of Columbus—had also made its appearance: the magistrates of Aberdeen 'for eschewing of the infirmity come out of France and strange partes' ordered the closure of brothels and piously hoped that their sinful inmates would turn to honest work.[253] New financial demands also came with warfare and an exacting government: in 1497 Dundee was stented for 450 crowns to pur-

247 *Edinburgh Burgh Recs.*, I. 80-1, 82-3, 101-4, 127-9.
248 *Ibid.*, 118.
249 *A.D.C.P.*, p. lxiii; *R.S.S.*, I. No. 1568.
250 *A.P.S.*, II. 208, c. 10; *R.M.S.*, II. Nos. 2259, 2605, 3608.
251 *A.P.S.*, II. 252, c. 30.
252 *Edinburgh Burgh Recs.*, I. 72-143, *passim*; Mackie, *James IV*, pp. 150-2.
253 *Edinburgh Burgh Recs.*, I. 71; *Aberdeen Burgh Recs.*, I. 425. See also R. S. Morton, 'Some aspects of the early history of syphilis in Scotland', *British Journal of Venereal Diseases*, XXXVIII. 175-80.

chase exemption from conscription ; some years later its whole community was accused of contempt of royal officials and had to purchase a remission, while in 1511 its burgesses were to be distrained for misdemeanours.[254] Above all, the leading burghs suffered from the continuing trade recession. William Dunbar, full of praise for London, poured scorn upon the poor wares of Edinburgh.

In the backwater of Veere, rather than in the declining city of Bruges or the rising city of Antwerp, Andrew Halyburton, conservator of the staple, carried on small-scale transactions in the traditional commodities of the Netherland trade.[255] The greater enterprise shown in the Baltic had meanwhile spilled over into the interior of Germany, where Scottish traders settled in sizable numbers. They doubtless showed their patriotism by aiding Scottish monks to win control of the Schottenklöster—monasteries founded by Irish monks in the early Middle Ages at a time when the Irish unwarily styled themselves Scots. In 1515 a Scotsman was appointed Abbot of Ratisbon, and by then a score of Scottish traders had settled in that Bavarian city.[256] But their trade can hardly have been with Scotland : it was presumably the lack of opportunity and lucrative wares at home that had induced them to emigrate to a remote land where their expertise was more profitable than in Scotland. Even in depressing times some Scottish merchants enjoyed affluence, but if foreign trade was the life-blood of the burghs the blood was thin.

This is clearly shown in the accounts of the custumars. No new commodities figured in the export trade, and the export of fish, cloth and salt, which had increased during the previous reign, now subsided into stagnation along with that of wool, woolfells and hides. Although the customs duties on these last three products were still levied at the rates introduced by David II, and duties on additional products had meanwhile been imposed, the gross receipts from the great customs during James's reign scarcely averaged £3,000 a year, one-third as much as in 1371 ; Edinburgh scarcely accounted for £2,000, Aberdeen, its nearest rival, for £500. In the troubled conditions of the last year of the reign the total customs receipts were not

[254] *R.S.S.*, I. Nos. 112, 1647; *R.M.S.*, II. No. 3663.
[255] See *The Ledger of Andrew Halyburton*, ed. C. Innes, pp. lxv–lxvi, lxxii; Davidson and Gray, *Staple*, pp. 128–9; *R.S.S.*, I. Nos. 550, 1583; *A.P.S.*, II. 252, cc. 26, 27.
[256] M. Dilworth, 'The First Scottish Monks in Ratisbon', *Innes Review*, XVI. 180–98; T. A. Fischer, *Scots in Germany*, pp. 141–2, 153–4, and *Scots in Prussia*, pp. 235–6.

much more than £2,000.[257] Admittedly some allowance has to be made for a number of grants of exemption from customs duty : it was by this means that the king paid the dowry of his bastard cousin, Margaret Crichton, when she married the Edinburgh merchant, William Todrik.[258] Allowance has also to be made for maladministration in the collection of the customs.[259] With a view to improving returns there were experiments in granting tacks of the right to collect the customs.[260] In October 1510 this practice culminated in a three-year tack whereby Andrew Stewart, Bishop of Caithness, and Thomas Dickson, parson of Turriff, became custumars-general and were to collect the customs of the whole realm for their own profit in return for payment of £4,000 a year into the exchequer.[261] By March 1511 this over-optimistic scheme had to be revised.[262]

In his report on the king's annual revenues Pedro de Ayala had ludicrously estimated the customs receipts at 25,000 ducats (about £20,000), and most of his other estimates were scarcely less exaggerated. Nonetheless he was probably not far off the mark when he affirmed that the king 'is in want of nothing, judging from the manner in which he lives, but he is not able to put money into his strong boxes'.[263] James could not be accused of parsimony in the distribution of his revenues, but perhaps of extortion in their acquisition : save for the difference in the value of money, which raised an artisan's daily wage from the 4d. of the fourteenth century to the princely sum of 12d. in debased coin, it would appear that he had far surpassed the financial achievements of David II. Certainly the sums that the treasurer accounted for were unprecedented : between June 1488 and February 1492 the total (in round figures) came to £31,857; between February 1501 and September 1502 it was £20,709; between September 1502 and February 1505 it was no less than £70,345.[264] The chief contribution to this vast sum was forthcoming from instalments of the queen's dowry amounting to £23,333 6s. 8d. Apart from this non-recurring payment the other

---

[257] E.R., xi. xxviii–xxix, liii. In 1488-9 the customs, including arrears, amounted (in round figures) to £2,890 (ibid., x. 131–45); in 1491-2 they came to £2,464 (ibid., 352–64); in 1494-5 to £2,345 (ibid., 528–39); in 1507-8 to £3,317 (ibid., xiii. 84–96); in 1512–13 to £2,161 (ibid., 569–79).
[258] P. 489 above; R.S.S., i. No. 1219; T.A., i. ccxc; E.R., xii, xxxi–xxxii, 465. For other exemptions see R.S.S., i. Nos. 436, 490, 1335, 1436, 1466, 1494, 2089.   [259] See A.P.S., ii. 234, c. 12; 235, c. 17; R.S.S., i. Nos. 159, 190.
[260] E.R., xii. xxxi; R.S.S., i. No. 1129.
[261] R.S.S., i. No. 2140.   [262] Ibid., No. 2223.
[263] Brown, Early Travellers, p. 43.   [264] T.A., i. 166–8; ii. 19, 196.

main sources of income during the two-and-a-half-year period were as follows.[265]

from prelates	£10,546
	and £320 Flemish
from feudal profits	£7,056
from the sheriffs	£6,944
from judicial profits	£6,083
from compositions for charters	£4,113
from compositions for tacks and feus	£586
from the fees of the great seal	£534

Little information exists as to the revenues forthcoming from the sheriffs, though most was probably derived from their collection of fines imposed in the justice ayres and listed in the rolls of 'estreits' (extracts).[266] The large sums drawn from the prelates[267] must, in part at least, have resulted from taxation. During the reign this was fairly frequently levied for extraordinary purposes; but only the compliant prelates could be relied upon to pay up.[268] On the other hand the sum that the king received from feudal profits (wardships, marriages, reliefs and non-entries) can have represented only the tip of an iceberg: one wardship and marriage was valued at 700 marks in 1501, another at £1,000 in 1511.[269] But the exaction of the crown's feudal rights was chaotic: 'it is evident that both the king and the ward received little . . . and it may be conjectured that the real gainers were the receiver himself, or persons to whom the king gave charges upon the ward estate; in some cases . . . the whole revenue was gifted to a royal favourite'.[270] Indeed this was the normal way in which the crown's vast potential income from wardships, reliefs, non-entries and escheats was disposed of,[271] without ever being subjected to account.

Similarly the profits of justice that the treasurer received in the form of compositions and fines must also have represented the mere tip of an iceberg. For the king acquired immense reward, both in popularity and cash, by responding to the insatiable longing of the three estates for more and better justice. The longing was expressed in repeated enactments dealing with the technicalities of the law and

[265] See *ibid.*, II. 163–96.
[266] See *ibid.* I. lxxix.
[267] *Ibid.*, II. 191–2.
[268] See Mackie, *James IV*, p. 59.
[269] *R.S.S.*, I. No. 661; *R.M.S.*, II. No. 3612.
[270] *E.R.*, XIII. cviii–cxi.
[271] *R.S.S.*, I. *passim.*

its administration,[272] in confused experimentation (hardly successful until the next reign) with the central administration of civil justice in the overlapping supreme courts of lords of council, session and causes,[273] in injunctions that the king should attend the justice ayres, which were to be held in spring and autumn in all parts of the realm,[274] and in another injunction that he should help to compose feuds.[275]

These feuds were the roots of crime, disorder and injustice. Often one magnate and his 'surname' had to be exempted from the jurisdiction of a sheriff or steward who was his rival and with whom he was engaged in 'variance' or 'dedly inimyte'.[276] Surety of £1,000 had to be demanded to keep the peace between Lords Ruthven and Oliphant.[277] In 1508 the rivalry between Crichtons and Maxwells erupted into a spectacular riot at Dumfries.[278] Most deadly of all was the feud which led in 1490 to the burning of six score Murrays in the kirk of Monzievaird by their Drummond foes. James's execution of the Master of Drummond (brother of his future mistress) demonstrated that he was capable of exacting full punishment without respect of rank.[279]

The Borders, where there was 'greit misreule', were the scene of further demonstrations of judicial severity. In August 1504 the king went on 'the raid of Eskdale' in the company of Lord Dacre, warden of the English March, and passed a few weeks in hawking and hanging.[280] Some years later James set off in dead of night for a judicial raid upon Teviotdale and carried out 'Jeddart justice' by bringing his prisoners to the tolbooth of Jedburgh with nooses already hanging around their necks.[281] About the same time the Hepburns, who had been given the task of daunting the ill-disposed Armstrongs, were furnished with letters of fire and sword permitting the wholesale butchery of the malefactors.[282]

---

[272] *A.P.S.*, II. 224, c. 5; 225–6, cc. 8, 9, 11; 227, c. 18; 230, c. 4; 234–5, c. 16; 238–9, c. 6; 250–4, cc. 8–11, 13, 22, 40, 41, 46; *R.S.S.*, I. Nos. 801, 802; *Scot. Legal History*, pp. 21–2; *A.D.C.P.*, pp. xxvii–xxviii.

[273] *A.P.S.*, II. 223, c. 27; 226, c. 16; 248–9, 256–7; *A.D.C.P.*, pp. xxviii–xxxii, lxi; R. K. Hannay, *The College of Justice*, p. 22, and 'On the Foundation of the College of Justice', *S.H.R.* XV. 30–46.

[274] *A.P.S.*, II. 208, c. 8; 218, c. 2; 225, c. 10.   [275] *Ibid.*, 218, c. 3.

[276] *R.S.S.*, I. Nos. 95, 97, 228, 1723, 2307, 2430.   [277] *A.D.A.*, I. 141.

[278] *R.S.S.*, I. Nos. 1745, 1750, 1791; Lesley, *History*, p. 79.

[279] Pitscottie, *Historie*, I. 237; *T.A.*, I. cii–civ; *E.R.*, X. l–lii; *A.D.A.*, I. 150, 151; *R.S.S.*, I. No. 613.

[280] Lesley, *History*, p. 85; *E.R.*, XI. xliii–l; XII. lix; *T.A.*, II. 452–5.

[281] Lesley, *History*, p. 81; *T.A.*, IV. xxiii.

[282] *R.S.S.*, I. Nos. 587, 700, 701, 2165.

But unrestrained severity was exceptional. A more constructive treatment of disorder was to be seen in the 'bands' of the South and Middle Borders (pacts for mutual security) enforced in the parliament of March 1504,[283] and a remunerative treatment of disorder took the form of making compositions and selling respites and remissions. It was for this purpose that the king so often graced the justice ayres, reminding the guilty by his daunting presence that, if need be, the full rigour of the law might be unleashed—as it sometimes was.[284] Also in attendance were the 'lords componitors'—often the Bishops of Aberdeen and Caithness—whose function was to bargain with the guilty and allow them to atone for offences by payment of a composition. Treason against the king's person, arson and rape were, however, generally beyond composition.[285]

The sums involved were considerable: the composition for one remission might well cost £50;[286] as a result of proceedings in a justice ayre at Perth, Lord Drummond owed the king £1,695, which were compounded for 500 marks;[287] in 1511 £1,200 were expected as the remainder of the 'estreats' of three justice ayres of Berwickshire and Lauderdale.[288] The occasional severity of the king not only made offenders all the more eager to purchase remissions but allayed the criticism that his father had incurred by trafficking in them. A proclamation made at Inverness in 1501 announced that the king and his lords had at divers times come north and compounded with all applicants for remissions; many, however, presumed upon the king's clemency; after the forthcoming ayre he would no longer compound for 'commone gret crimes'.[289] This warning was probably intended to stimulate demand and certainly brought no interruption to the profitable traffic: during the reign the privy seal register shows 522 grants of remission. The main categories of crime for which these were granted were manslaughter (182 cases), forthocht felony (88 cases), support of rebels and outlaws (71 cases), theft (69 cases) and oppression (31 cases). General remission was forthcoming for all the inhabitants of Argyll, Bute and the Cumbraes. Specific remissions were granted to many nobles accused of a variety of crimes.

A somewhat different picture emerges in the case of the 168 respites that were purchased to delay legal proceedings for any period ranging from a few weeks to nineteen years. More than one third

[283] *A.P.S.*, II. 248.   [284] *T.A.*, I. lxxix, clxiii; Lesley, *History*, pp. 73–4.
[285] *R.S.S.*, I. Nos. 2154, 2314. The procedure of the justice ayres is outlined in *T.A.*, I. lxxviii–lxxix.
[286] *R.M.S.*, II. No. 3757.   [287] *R.S.S.*, I. No. 1807.
[288] *R.M.S.*, II. No. 3645.   [289] *A.D.C.P.*, p. lix.

of these were granted to persons who wished to go overseas. Study in France accounted for three respites.[290] Pilgrimages to Rome, Compostela and Amiens accounted respectively for the issue of four respites, five respites and eight respites;[291] and a bailie of Peebles hopefully obtained a respite to cover a trip to Jerusalem.[292] Robert Barton significantly obtained five respites to safeguard his interests during his absence on overseas ventures.[293] So far as he was concerned it may be suspected that the real motive was to evade justice. This was the evident motive in some hundred cases where absence overseas could not be pleaded as an excuse.

While the dubious traffic in respites and remissions doubtless furnished a large proportion of the receipts of the treasurer it was the income from crown lands that was the chief source of funds for the second great financial officer, the comptroller. An act of February 1490 sought to protect the king's poor tenants against the oppression of neighbouring lords,[294] but nothing could protect them against commissioners of assessment who imposed unrealistic rents. It was either this or incredible maladministration that resulted in the accumulation of heavy arrears : by 1507 one bailie owed £1,114, and by 1509 Lord Maxwell, steward of Annandale, owed £3,745, which were remitted for a composition of £1,000.[295] Nonetheless, despite arrears, revenues rose in monetary terms, if not in real value : in 1457 the net rents of the lordship of Galloway were £431 ; in 1505 they were £1,026.[296] Ettrick forest, richest jewel in the royal patrimony, provided over £2,500 a year.[297] Altogether, the crown lands furnished the comptroller with more than three times as much as he received from the customs : in the period from September 1508 to August 1509 the total receipts of Sir Duncan Forrester were (in round figures) £13,245, of which £2,412 came from the custumars and £8,993 from the administrators of the crown lands.[298] The gross receipts from these (including arrears) rose from about £8,300 a year in the period from 1488 to 1502 to about £12,300 a year in the period from 1502 to 1513.[299]

Feuing of the crown lands was partly responsible for the in-

[290] R.S.S., I. Nos. 384, 712, 1998.

[291] Ibid., Nos. 212, 221, 485, 1794; 641, 670, 1057, 1424, 1441; 1251, 1257, 1425, 1523, 1545, 1653, 1684, 1840.   [292] Ibid., No. 1821.

[293] Ibid., Nos. 642, 767, 2071, 2371, 2455.

[294] A.P.S., II. 222, c. 22.   [295] E.R., XII. 488; R.S.S., I. No. 1834.

[296] Athol Murray, 'The Crown lands in Galloway, 1455–1543', Dumfriesshire Trans., XXXVII. 9–25, at 22.   [297] E.R., XII. 34, 535; XIII. 524.

[298] Ibid., XIII. 253–4; see also ibid., 115–9.

[299] Compare ibid., X. 249–94; XII. 1–75, 483–589; XIII. 502–64.

creased returns. Up to 1504 James seems to have granted feus on much the same scale as his father. Rapid development was initiated by an act of the parliament of March 1504 which made it clear that the king might grant feus, even from the lands annexed to the crown, providing that there was no diminution in rental, grassums and other duties, and that all freeholders were allowed to do likewise.[300] Often it was stated that a new feu-duty exceeded the old rent (sometimes being twice as much). After 1504 a 'general process set in of converting the royal tenants into feuars; ... feu-ferm became the almost universal tenure of small parcels of lands and a very usual tenure even of larger estates granted by the crown'.[301] The process is clearly seen in the case of the lands of the old earldom of Fife. Until 1508 they were almost always rented on three-year tacks either to individual tacksmen or to joint tenants practising communal farming on the run-rig system. In the rental of March 1510 nearly all the lands were granted in feu.[302] The forest of Ettrick was feued in April 1510, the lordship of Methven in the following month, and the lordship of Stirlingshire in April 1511.[303] Between 1488 and 1513 the great seal register contains scarcely thirty confirmations of feus granted by the king's subjects, but no less than 117 grants of feu by the king, one third of them in favour of familiars. By 1513 the feu-duties accruing to the king from grants recorded in the great seal register amounted to over £3,300 annually, besides large quantities of victuals. It was not yet apparent that the crown's immediate gains would be outweighed by losses when the feu-duties remained unalterable in time of inflation and rising rents.

In many cases the new feu-holders were obliged by the terms of their feu charters to undertake various improvements: one of them was supposed to build a residence of stone and lime, with granary, stable and dove-cot, to plant orchards, gardens and oak trees, to set up beehives and construct bridges.[304] It was improvements such as these that John Major had in mind when he advocated feuing.[305] But if feuing led to improvement it was at the cost of some hardship: 'many tenants could with difficulty pay their rents, still less could they pay the increased feu-duty and had to allow others to take their holdings'.[306] The resulting plight of the poorer rural classes is well illustrated by the poets of the period. Those who were forced off the

[300] *A.P.S.*, II. 244, cc. 30, 31; 253, cc. 36, 37.
[301] Aeneas J. G. Mackay, *E.R.*, XIII. cxix–cxx.   [302] *Ibid.*, cxxi–cxxv.
[303] *Ibid.*, 626–8, 642–3, 649.   [304] *R.M.S.*, II. No. 3643.
[305] Major, *History*, p. 31.   [306] Aeneas J. G. Mackay, *E.R.*, XIII. cxxv, cxxviii.

land could expect no sympathy if they turned to begging (as many seem to have done): in March 1504 parliament revived James I's punitive legislation against mendicancy.[307]

Another act of March 1504 allowed those with an income of less than a hundred marks to absent themselves from parliament unless specially summoned; they were, however, to appoint barons of the shire or 'the maist famouss personis' to act as their procurators and 'to answer for thame'.[308]

This act seems to have aggravated the problem of securing adequate attendance. After the first parliament of the reign [309] attendance regularly dwindled, even in the course of a particular parliament: on 3 February 1506 the sederunt comprised seventeen ecclesiastics, twenty barons, and the commissioners of six burghs; by 16 February there were only eleven ecclesiastics, eleven barons, and two men who represented the burghs.[310] In the brief record of the parliament of May 1509 no sederunt is given, and, apart from the time-honoured affirmation of the privileges of the kirk, the only business done appears to have been the issue of one or two charters and a rescinding of a scheme for division of sheriffdoms.[311] Throughout the reign parliament had become progressively, and farcically, unrepresentative of the political classes. To that extent its authority was bound to be less impressive: in 1504 Logan of Restalrig protested that whatever was concluded by acts or statutes of parliament should not redound to his prejudice.[312] No parliament seems to have been held by James IV after 1509.

The place vacated by parliament was presumably partly filled by the privy council. Although its existing records are copious they take the form of 'a register of judicial decisions in session of council', and since there is 'a remarkable absence of minutes regarding action in public policy' it has been conjectured that a council register devoted to affairs of state has been lost.[313] At any rate there is little information concerning the political activities of the council. The composition of this body was, after 1490, left to the discretion of the king: it was an instrument of his authority, not of the authority of parliament, and could be used as he desired. Ayala reports that James 'lends a willing ear to his counsellors, and decides nothing without

[307] *A.P.S.*, II. 251, c. 14.   [308] *Ibid.*, 244, c. 26; 252, c. 23.
[309] Pp. 532–3 above.   [310] *A.P.S.*, II. 262–3, 266.
[311] *Ibid.*, 267–8, 274–7.   [312] *Ibid.*, 248.
[313] R. K. Hannay, *A.D.C.P.*, pp. vi–vii. A short list of entries concerning public affairs between 1501 and 1513 is given on pp. lix–lxvii.

asking them; but in great matters he acts according to his own judgment'.[314] Nor is it likely that the privy council was consulted on the multitude of small grants made by the king; in these cases all that was required was an expression of his intentions to the appropriate official.

Here lay the importance of the court, which also partly filled the place vacated by parliament. The familiars, the courtiers most regularly in attendance upon the king, were those who could most readily catch the king's ear. It is a testimony to their assiduity and influence that James did not, like his father, garner the resources that he acquired, but distributed them lavishly in gifts of lands, wardships, marriages, reliefs, escheats and life annuities.[315] There was no outcry against this spoils system simply because royal liberality was regarded as a virtue and the circle of beneficiaries was wide: James was indirectly taxing the landholding classes in order to display his generosity to the members of the same classes who were in favour at court.

Certainly the spoils system was not intended to abase the higher nobility, some of whom now decorated the court and pursued 'policy' as well as feuds. The traditional dignity of earl was bestowed more frequently than in the past: Patrick Hepburn had been made Earl of Bothwell in 1488; in 1503 James Hamilton was made Earl of Arran, William Graham was made Earl of Montrose, and Cuthbert Cunningham, grandson of the first Earl of Glencairn who had been killed at Sauchieburn, was restored to that title; in 1507 Hugh Montgomery was made Earl of Eglinton; and in 1509 David Kennedy was made Earl of Cassillis. The less traditional title of duke, however, was evidently to be reserved for members of the royal family: in 1489 David Lindsay had been restored to the dukedom of Montrose, but only for his own lifetime; following his death James blocked the ducal pretensions of the Lindsays by erecting an earldom of Montrose for the Grahams. A regard for ancient nobility and a desire to let bygones be bygones was displayed in the grant of a pension of £200 to the onetime ninth Earl of Douglas until his death in 1491.[316] The only vindictiveness that James showed towards the higher nobility was reserved for George Leslie, second Earl of Rothes, who was outlawed.[317] Yet in 1513, when William Leslie succeeded to the earldom, he was granted back the residue of what the king had seized from his elder brother 'be ressone of recognitioun, alienatioun, fore-

---

[314] Brown, *Early Travellers*, p. 41.
[315] See *R.S.S.*, I. *passim*.
[316] *E.R.*, x. lxii, lxvii.
[317] See Ranald Nicholson, *op. cit., Juridical Review*, April 1973, pt. i. 1–21.

fatour, non-entres of airis or ony uther wais'.[318] Although the power
of the greater nobles had been subordinated to the pre-eminence of
the king they kept their dignity. The deep-seated rancours of the
previous reign had been pacified, and James presided over a dazzling
court that in its pageantry and liberality provided the populace with
the equivalent of bread and circuses.

Even so, there were jarring anomalies between court and country: when evicted peasants were starving James could afford to
devote the customs and burgh maills of Peebles to the 'keping and
feding of herons',[319] to gamble (and lose) £70 in one night on a game
of cards,[320] and to keep his mistresses in a style that was extravagantly
ostentatious. Had his interests been confined solely to a courtly milieu
disaffection might easily have arisen. But this was not the case. In his
devotion to Venus, James did not neglect Mars. Pitscottie approvingly reports his patronage of chivalry. Bishop Lesley tells of one
tournament 'with counterfuting of the round tabill of King Arthour'
when 'ane quha callit himself the wyld knycht' held the field against
French contestants. 'This wyld knycht,' he adds, 'wes the king himself, quha wes vaileyaunt in armeis, and could very well exerce the
same.'[321] Ayala reported in 1498 that James 'loves war so much that
I fear ... the peace will not last long'.[322] The king also appeared to
love justice; his personal activity in its administration blinded his
subjects to its mercenary character and convinced them of the serious-
ness of his vocation as a ruler.[323] His conventional piety and his
occasional retreats into religious seclusion concealed his misuse of the
kirk and gave the impression of high-minded conscientiousness. His
boundless energy, perhaps a sign of psychological insecurity, sent him
galloping over the countryside: Lesley reports (somewhat incredibly)
that in one day he rode alone from Stirling to Elgin via Perth and
Aberdeen, and on the following morning continued to St Duthac's
shrine.[324] No Scottish king knew his country so well; never can the
Scottish people have known a king so intimately. And, as the
treasurer's accounts show, in all the king's progresses there was continual distribution of largesse on a scale appropriate to the status of
the recipients—drink-silver to masons; alms to priests and friars, the
poor, the sick, the deformed, the deranged; gratuities to messengers,
hostesses, huntsmen, ferrymen, fiddlers, falconers, fools, singers (in-

[318] R.S.S., I. No. 2501.   [319] Ibid., No. 1937.   [320] T.A., II. 132.
[321] Pitscottie, Historie, I. 231–2; Lesley, History, p. 78.
[322] Brown, Early Travellers, p. 41.
[323] Lesley, History, pp. 63, 96. For instances of James's meddling with the
course of justice see R.S.S., I. Nos. 813, 1733.   [324] Lesley, History, pp. 75–6.

cluding the maidens of Forres), luters, harpers, guisers, jugglers, and Highland bards.

Thus James acquired, and kept, an easy popularity. Only Sir John Ramsay, shrewd and traitorous, denounced the wilfulness of the king [325] as he moved farther than ever towards the absolutism that had become a possibility since the first stirrings of the new monarchy under James I. The king told Ayala that 'his subjects serve him with their persons and goods . . . exactly as he likes', and, so Ayala thought, James esteemed himself 'as much as though he were lord of the world'.[326] The king's pride was shared by his people; it was doubtless the common opinion of the Scots that Ayala was reporting when he remarked that 'on land they think themselves the most powerful kingdom that exists'.[327] Until 1509 no cloud darkened the horizon.

[325] Conway, *Henry VII*, p. 107.
[326] Brown, *Early Travellers*, pp. 40, 41.   [327] *Ibid.*, p. 48.

18

THE AUREATE AGE AND ITS END

Although Pedro de Ayala noted that the Scots were poor, spending their time in warfare (often among themselves) rather than in profitable work, his account was much more favourable than that of Froissart or Aeneas Sylvius. He affirmed that 'there is as great a difference between the Scotland of old time and the Scotland of today as there is between bad and good',[1] and hinted that James IV was responsible for this advancement. Whether or not, as Ayala claimed, James could speak Latin, French, German, Flemish and Spanish, he was certainly aware of the multifarious changes taking place in Western Europe and was anxious to emulate other rulers in whatever brought renown and prestige. To this end he employed royal patronage with more flamboyance and less discrimination than his father. At court, errant knights, Moorish dancers, a French alchemist and a French dog-fancier, musicians from Italy and from Schleswig, Flemings imported to work in the mint or to cast artillery, rubbed shoulders with William Dunbar, master of the new aureate poetry, John Ireland, the grave theologian, Bishop Elphinstone, intent upon his new university, guisers, tellers of gestes, players of the clarshach, jugglers, tight-rope dancers, and the king's fool; pageantry and buffoonery went hand in hand, and novelty reached its apotheosis in the mock tournament of which a negress was the prize. There was an intermingling and jostling of native and medieval traditions with new importations from a continent swept by cultural and political change and technological innovation.

All the changes of the time are hardly comprised in the term 'renaissance', long battered and misused. For change had not

[1] Brown, *Early Travellers*, pp. 43, 49.

occurred in a void : much was merely the result of development that had been continuous throughout the Middle Ages; even classical learning was not 're-born' but was increasingly viewed through the eyes of Cicero rather than through those of Aquinas and the subsequent scholastics. By studying the unvarnished Greek and Roman originals, so it was thought, man would best develop his higher faculties and perfect himself. The cult of the classical past was a humane study that at best might provide fresh inspiration; at worst the humanist often contented himself with insubstantial imitation. It was this period of continuity, of fusions and juxtapositions, sometimes brilliantly successful, sometimes incongruous, that produced in the groat issued by James III in 1485 'the earliest renaissance coin portrait outside Italy'.[2] But although the coin also depicted the pretensions of James III to imperial authority the idea was conveyed not with the laurel wreath or fillet of a Roman emperor but with the arched crown associated with the medieval emperors.

In architecture, sculpture, painting and the minor arts the continuity of medieval tradition was more obvious than novelty. If the great hall of Stirling Castle, thought to have been designed by Cochrane, was 'the first large-scale building in the whole of Great Britain to display the influences of the renaissance'[3] the influences were to be seen in the application of Italianate motifs rather than in structural innovations. Not even Italianate motifs decorated the large additions made by James IV at Linlithgow : their sober design was in the native 'vernacular' tradition, and the turrets of Holyrood and Falkland, which might well have been mirrored in the Loire,[4] probably date from the succeeding reign.

It was the construction of a *palatium* (a great hall) that made these royal residences 'places' or 'palaces'. In the greater baronial and ecclesiastical establishments there was a similar stress upon halls and comfort rather than upon towers and defence.[5] But the 'policy' sometimes advocated in building licences[6] was still usually expressed by a tower as austere as the landscape. So essential a classical concept as symmetry was avoided in buildings great and small.

Close commercial ties with the Netherlands helped to reinforce an attitude towards the visual arts that was realistic rather than idealistic, as in the beautifully illuminated liturgical books, the finest

[2] David McRoberts, 'Notes on Scoto-Flemish Artistic Contacts', *Innes Review*, x. 91–6, at 92, n. 6.   [3] *Ibid.*
[4] *E.R.*, XII. xxxvii–xxxviii; XIII. xciii–xcvii.
[5] Mackie, *James IV*, pp. 114–6; W. M. Mackenzie, *The Medieval Castle in Scotland*, p. 149.   [6] *R.M.S.*, II. No. 3336.

of which were imported from Flanders.[7] Idealism is certainly to be found in the panels which Hugo van der Goes was commissioned to paint for Trinity College, but the idealism is not the classical, pagan and humane of fifteenth-century Italy but something Gothic, Christian and brooding; religious mysticism is combined with a secular mysticism which depicts the majesty of the new monarchy in the dominance given to the flowing robes and ermine capes of James III, his queen, and the lesser royal figure (often taken to be the youthful James IV but more probably his uncle, the Duke of Albany).[8]

While warfare and iconoclasm have left only vestiges of the art and architecture of the period, neglect has resulted in the loss of much of the literature of the age. Gaelic poetry, dependent upon oral transmission, was particularly perishable. The collection compiled between 1512 and 1526 in the *Book of the Dean of Lismore*[9] probably represents only a small part of the output of the professional bards but shows the variety of their repertoire—Ossianic ballads, elegies, satires, incitements to battle, 'flytings', some moral and didactic verse.[10] Thanks to the political changes initiated by James III and James IV there would be less patronage for the bards in future. Well might the contemporary MacMhuirich declaim :

> Tyrants [the kings] suffered a strong blast from the wise, strong tribe [the MacDonalds], though now they are unhonoured; there is no joy without Clan Donald.[11]

One consequence of declining patronage was the new prominence of Gaelic folk-poetry, the work of amateurs, often talented, but not trained in the bardic tradition.[12]

---

[7] Leslie J. Macfarlane, 'The Book of Hours of James IV and Margaret Tudor', *Innes Review*, XI. 3–21; David McRoberts, 'Dean Brown's Book of Hours', *ibid.*, XIX. 144–67; David McRoberts, *Catalogue of Scottish Medieval Liturgical Books and Fragments* (1953).

[8] David McRoberts, *op. cit.*, *Innes Review*, X. 91–6; David Laing, 'Historical Description of the [Trinity College] Altar-piece . . .', *Proc. Soc. Antiq. Scot.*, III. 8–22, and 'Supplemental Notice', X. 310–24; Conway, *Henry VII*, p. 2.

[9] Published and translated in *Reliquiae Celticae*, ed. Alexander MacBain and John Kennedy, I. 1–109.

[10] Wittig, *Scottish Tradition*, pp. 185–6.

[11] Derick S. Thomson, *op. cit.*, *Transactions of the Gaelic Society of Inverness* (1963), 3–31, at 15.

[12] Derick S. Thomson, 'Scottish Gaelic Folk-Poetry Ante 1650', *Scottish Gaelic Studies*, VIII. 1–17; John MacInnes, 'Gaelic Songs of Mary Macleod', *ibid.*, XI. 3–25.

By contrast the Lowland poets, never professionals, not only developed the folk-poetry that had originated in the ballads but made it a poetry of art, more courtly both in theme and diction. Here too, much has perished : some of the makars (poets) whose deaths were lamented by William Dunbar are nothing more than names, while some works which do survive are of arguable date and authorship : the 'gud gentill Stobo', whose name certainly occurs in official records,[13] cannot with certainty be credited with *The Thre Prestis of Peebles*; and only recently has 'Blind Harry', author of the *Wallace*, acquired verisimilitude.[14] In any case these works, together with Myll's *Spectakle of Luf*, are of minor account [15] in comparison with those of the great trio of makars—Robert Henryson (*floruit* 1480–1490), William Dunbar (*c.* 1460–*c.* 1521) and Gavin Douglas (*c.* 1474–1522), whose achievements have at last begun to attract the attention they deserve.[16] Their themes were not solely native or chivalric but were sometimes inspired by works of classical origin. Their range of expression was extended by their introduction of 'aureate' polysyllabic words of French or Latin origin. New subtleties were discovered in the contrast of homely vernacular words that bespoke byre, broom and heather, with others that evoked a Mediterranean landscape of porticoes, laurels and 'the palm triumphale'.[17]

Many words 'of a decidedly humanistic appearance' were first introduced into the English language by Robert Henryson, who in 1462 was teaching law in Glasgow University and prior to his death was schoolmaster at Dunfermline. But Henryson's humanism (like that of his fellow poets, William Dunbar and Gavin Douglas) was not Italianate : 'he heralds the Northern Renaissance whose continuity with the Middle Ages extended even into the late seventeenth and early eighteenth century—there was no decisive break with the past'.[18] For although Henryson adopted classical motifs he also made impressive use of the ancient technique of alliteration ; in his sonorous Chaucerian stanzas 'gude moralitee' and 'seriositee' were 'hid under

13 *T.A.*, I. xcix–ci; *E.R.*, XI. xxix–xxx.
14 See Matthew P. McDiarmid's introduction to *Harry's Wallace* (S.T.S.).
15 See Wittig, *Scottish Tradition*, pp. 103–30.
16 R. L. Mackie gives an interesting summary of the makars in *James IV*, pp. 171–87. For more specialised works see the Bibliography, pp. 633–4 below.
17 Wittig, *Scottish Tradition*, pp. 62–3, 78–9.
18 MacQueen, *Robert Henryson*, pp. 20–2; *Works of Robert Henryson* (S.T.S.), I. xc. See also John MacQueen, 'Some aspects of the early renaissance in Scotland', *Forum for Modern Language Studies*, III. 201–22, and L. B. Hall, 'An aspect of the renaissance in Gavin Douglas' *Eneados*', *Studies in the Renaissance*, VII. 184–92.

the cloke of poesie'; and the influence of Boethius, so apparent in
The Kingis Quair, re-emerges in *Orpheus and Eurydice*, a Gordian
knot of intricate medieval allegory. Similarly in the satirical *Morall
Fabillis* an explicit *moralitas* (often blatantly naïve) is directed at the
reader who is not versed in allegorical tradition; for those who are
skilled, subtleties abound.

In Henryson's finest poem, *The Testament of Cresseid*, there are
also 'two levels of meaning, the literal and the allegorical . . . but . . .
the figurative sense is solidly based on the literal', for the leprosy with
which the gods have punished Cresseid for her desertion of Troilus
and her subsequent harlotry is 'the visual representation of Cresseid's
invisible sin'.[19] The concluding description of 'the woeful end of this
lusty Cresseid', when her former lover rides past and fails to recognise
her among the lepers is 'one of the most moving things in literature' [20]
and shows the poet's taut control of pathos :

> Than upon him scho kest up baith her enc,
> And with ane blenk it come into his thocht
> That he sumtime hir face befoir had sene
> Bot scho was in sic plye he knew hir nocht,
> Yit than hir luik into his mynd it brocht
> The sweit visage and amorous blenking
> Of fair Cresseid, sumtyme his awin darling.

Although Henryson skilfully used humorous irony it is his serious-
ness, his depth of thought, that is most characteristic. Summing up
the best of medieval morality, but seldom dull or morbid, his work has
a timeless quality. His greatness as a poet—and he ought surely to be
esteemed the greatest of Scottish poets—is seen in his technical
mastery of great themes. Wrestling with the problems of soul and
body, good and evil, he depicts the struggle with conciseness, realism,
directness, and apparent simplicity, sometimes with humour, sometimes with restrained pathos, as in his poignant *Prayer for the Pest*
(Plague) :

> Use derth, O Lord, or seiknes and hungir soir
> And slak thy plaig that is so penetryfe.
> The pepill ar perreist; quha ma remeid thairfor
> Bot thow, O Lord, that for thame lost thy lyfe?

The seeming indifference of the deity to human wretchedness is
also indicated in *The Taill of the Scheip and the Doig*, when the

---

[19] MacQueen, *Robert Henryson*, pp. 64, 91.   [20] *Ibid.*, pp. 88–9.

sheep, representing the 'pure commounis that daylie ar opprest', directs to God the reproachful and unanswered question :

> Seis Thow not this warld owerturnit is,
> As quha wald change gude gold in leid or tyn? [21]

Henryson visualised a benevolent deity :

> ... we may have knawlegeing
> Off God Almychtie be his creatouris
> That he is gude, ffair, wyis and bening.

Like Lorenzo Valla, however, he believed that God's ways are beyond human understanding :

> Nane suld presume be ressoun naturall
> To seirche the secreitis off the Trinitie,
> Bot trow fermelie, and lat all ressoun be. [22]

Coupled with the sensitive observation of time, place and circumstance, and the realism that convincingly transformed countryfolk, burgesses, lawyers and clerks into the likenesses of beasts, went an equally accurate assessment of contemporary wrongs and injustices. [23] Anger inspired by these is veiled in irony, compassion is muted into resignation :

> The sweitest lyfe, thairfor, in this cuntrie
> Is sickernes [security] with small possessioun. [24]

This lesson was not learned by William Dunbar. In his poem *Of Covetyce* he could join in the fashionable practice of decrying extortionate landlords ; in another poem on the even more fashionable theme of the fickleness of fortune he could lament that

> Nane heir bot rich men hes renown
> And pure men ar plukit doun.

But Dunbar himself hankered after lands and riches. Failing to win them he suffered the pangs of a disappointed careerist. In *To the*

---

[21] *Ibid.*, 127–31.
[22] *The Preiching of the Swallow, ibid.*, pp. 153–65.
[23] See M. E. Rowlands, 'Robert Henryson and the Scottish Courts of Law', *Aberdeen University Review*, xxxix. 219–26.
[24] *The Taill of the Uponlandis Mous and the Burges Mous*, MacQueen, *Robert Henryson*, pp. 121–7.

King he pathetically contrasts the high expectations of childhood with the (allegedly) unrewarding outcome of his pursuit of royal patronage :

> I wes in youthe, on nureice kne,
> Cald dandillie, 'bischop', dandillie,
> And quhone that age now dois me greif
> A sempill vicar I can not be.
> . . . .
> How suld I leif and I not landit,
> Nor yit withe benefice am blandit?

This poem may be compared with the lament *Quhen he wes sek* (often misleadingly styled *The Lament for the Makaris*), where the procession of doomed mortals is somehow subordinated to the 'me' that ends the sombre Latin refrain :

> On to the ded gois all estatis,
> Princis, prelotis and potestatis,
> Baith riche and pur of al degre;
> Timor mortis conturbat me.

The 'egocentric attitude' that has been detected in Dunbar [25] is less likable than the broad humanitarian outlook of Henryson but is largely compensated for by versatility in diction, technique and theme. Moreover Dunbar's subjectiveness and his touches of self-revelation, rivalled only by those of François Villon, were something new in literature. For in much medieval writing, even in personal correspondence, there was a reticence and repression of personality which contrasted strongly with the unrepressed public display of emotions by both small and great. In Dunbar there is at least a hint of the humanistic stress upon individual man rather than upon mankind. Yet, unlike most humanists, he had a concept of the individual man that was earthbound rather than sublime ; he eschewed the flattery in which most of them indulged ; and even although he was dependent upon the king for a generous pension of £80 [26] he was not subservient. As a lifelong courtier, however, Dunbar had little empathy with those engaged in the humdrum affairs of simple life and was not loth to expose merchants, craftsmen and peasants to the caustic amusement of the well-bred. Not that he neglected to poke fun at the seamier side of court life, as in *Of the Ladyis Solis-*

[25] Wittig, *Scottish Tradition*, p. 55.   [26] *E.R.*, XIII. cii–cvii.

taris at Court. Moreover the varying moods of the court elicited not only ceremonial pieces such as *The Thrissil and the Rose*, and conventional devotional works such as *Ane Ballat of Our Lady*, but also the whimsical oddities of *The Devillis Inquest* and the scurrility of *The Flyting of Dunbar and Kennedy*, unsurpassed in 'metrical ease, in masterly alliteration, in sumptuousness of ribaldry, in variety of ridicule or in impetuosity of invective'.[27] Thus 'of all the makars, Dunbar is the most accomplished virtuoso, and flits most easily from one plane to another'. He is also 'a virtuoso whose command of an almost inexhaustible variety of metrical forms is such as no English poet possessed until the nineteenth century',[28] while his work 'contains the best examples of a volatile and bizarre fancy controlled by art'.[29] All this provides showy entertainment; but seldom (in contrast to Henryson's compositions) is much demand made upon the reader's intellect or sensibilities.

The subjectivity apparent in Dunbar's work is also a striking feature in that of Gavin Douglas, though it was hardly inspired by disappointed ambition : this third son of Bell-the-Cat obtained the lucrative provostship of St Giles in Edinburgh in 1503 and left it in 1515 only to become Bishop of Dunkeld.[30] It was rather humanistic emulation, a savant's pride of achievement, that led to self-assertion. Sometimes Douglas harangues the reader, sometimes he carries on a dialogue with him, sometimes he loses patience with his supposed literary adversaries, wishes that he could pull their ears, and expostulates : 'O hald your pece, ye verray goddis apis !'[31]

The rather laboured allegorical poem *The Palice of Honour* harks back to the tradition of the *Kingis Quair* but is not uninfluenced by contemporary humanism and has 'Spenser-like passages of impressionistic description'.[32] Douglas's fame, however, rests on *The Eneados*, not only 'one of the great renaissance translations' but 'the most sustained work in Scots poetry, and, considering the scale, the most consistent'.[33] In translating Virgil's *Aeneid* Douglas sought academic precision and adopted high standards of literary criticism : pouring scorn upon the version of Caxton he even found fault with

---

[27] T. F. Henderson, *Scottish Vernacular Literature*, p. 144.
[28] Wittig, *Scottish Tradition*, p. 58.
[29] Douglas Young, 'William Dunbar', *S.H.R.*, xxxviii. 10–9, at 19.
[30] Watt, *Fasti*, p. 357.   [31] Wittig, *Scottish Tradition*, p. 83.
[32] Matthew P. MacDiarmid in review (*S.H.R.*, xlviii. 180–1) of *The Shorter Poems of Gavin Douglas* (S.T.S.). This review also argues that Douglas was not the author of *King Hart*.
[33] Wittig, *Scottish Tradition*, pp. 77, 78.

Chaucer, the idol of the makars.[34] But despite the fidelity of his own version he could not resist the temptation to render specific what Virgil had left in general terms: sometimes the result is cumbrous, sometimes there is increased vigour and colour—one modern poet has daringly affirmed that the translation is better than the original.[35]

It was a translation into a language that Douglas, alone among the makars, called 'Scots' rather than 'Inglis'.[36] The language of the *Eneados* shows the Lowland vernacular at its best, ranging from the rough and guttural suited to rustic themes to the aureate of the more elevated—'the ryall style, clepyt heroycall . . . observand bewte, sentens, and gravite'.[37] In the prologues which he prefaced to each book of the poem Douglas was not tied to an original and was free to unloose his rich vocabulary on whatever themes took his fancy (with some passing reference to the book that was to follow). In these prologues he could expound his views on the Christian symbolism of Roman mythology, discuss the morality of warfare, utter wise saws and pithy proverbs, and, above all, describe the passing seasons not in stilted terms but in 'great nature poems, the first in Scots or English in which landscape is depicted solely for its own sake'. There are no conventional medieval May mornings but 'sharply-defined sense images drawn from a multiple awareness of nature that was to remain unrivalled until the eighteenth century'.[38] The bleakness of a Scottish winter is impressionistically conveyed in the line :

> The wynd maid wayfe the reid weyd on the dyk.

The rare summer days teem with insect life and close with a fiery sunset :

> All byrnand reid gan walxin the evin sky,
> The son enfyrit haill . . .[39]

The combination of scholarly aim, self-assertiveness, diction both rough and mellifluous, and a voluptuous sensitivity to nature, makes Douglas unique.

---

[34] *Ibid.*, p. 77.   [35] *Ibid.*, pp. 79–80.
[36] *Ibid.*, p. 85. Douglas was hardly the first (as Wittig supposed) to think of the Lowland vernacular as a language distinct from English : the *Lament for the Dauphiness* was translated from *lingua Gallicana* into *lingua Scoticana* (*Chron. Pluscarden*, I. 382), and Ayala reported that there was as much difference in the speech of Scots and English as in that of Aragonese and Castilians (Hume Brown, *Early Travellers*, p. 39).   [37] Wittig, *Scottish Tradition*, p. 79.
[38] *Ibid.*, pp. 85–6.   [39] *Ibid.*, pp. 85–90.

The trio of great makars of the aureate age was matched by another of notable scholars—John Ireland (*c.* 1440–*c.* 1496), John Major (*c.* 1469–1550) and Hector Boece (1465–1536).[40] Ireland, a theologian in the conciliarist tradition,[41] had been a prominent teacher at Paris before he entered the service of James III.[42] Besides his theological works in Latin three were composed in the Lowland vernacular; of these the only extant one is *The Meroure of Wyssedome*, presented to James IV in 1490. Ireland apologised (though somewhat vauntingly) that he wrote this work in English rather than in 'the tounge that I knaw better, that is Latin', and claimed that he was ignorant of 'the gret eloquens of Chauceir, na colouris that men uses in this Inglis metir that gret clerkis makis na counte of'.[43] The *Meroure*, which expounds the principles of the Christian faith and offers godly admonitions, is of interest as being the earliest extant sustained composition in Scots prose that is an original work as distinct from translation. It 'achieves an admirably clear expository method that our modern theologians might well emulate'.[44]

The achievements of John Major were more distinguished than those of Ireland. Despite his humble origin as son of an East Lothian countryman he made his way *via* Cambridge to Paris, where in 1493 he began a long and brilliant career in the university. It was a time when Paris attracted a throng of Scottish students, among them Hector Boece, Patrick Paniter and Gavin Douglas. In 1509, at the instance of the influential Douglas, an effort was made (though in vain) to tempt Major back to Scotland with the offer of the treasurership of the Chapel Royal. When he did return in 1518 it was to take up an appointment as principal regent in Glasgow University, after which he moved to St Andrews. There, according to John Knox, possibly one of his students, he was 'a man whose word was reckoned an oracle in matters of religion'.[45]

Major was 'among the last of the schoolmen, the teachers of the

[40] Their works, and those of lesser scholars, are listed by W. Forbes Leith in *Pre-Reformation Scholars in Scotland in the Sixteenth Century* (1915).

[41] J. H. Burns, *op. cit.*, *S.H.R.*, XLII. 89–104.

[42] For his career see the notes to the edition of *The Meroure of Wyssdome* by C. Macpherson and F. Quinn (S.T.S., vol. I, 1926, vol. II, 1965), and review of vol. II by Matthew P. McDiarmid in *S.H.R.*, XLVIII. 179–80.

[43] *Gilbert of the Haye's Prose Manuscript* (S.T.S.), I. lvi.

[44] Matthew P. McDiarmid, *op. cit.*, *S.H.R.*, XLVIII. 179–80, at 179. See also B. Miner, 'John Ireland and the Immaculate Conception', *Innes Review*, XVII. 24–39, and Brother Bonaventure, 'The popular theology of John Ireland', *ibid.*, XLI. 1–22.

[45] See Watt, *Fasti, ad indices*, and the 'Life of the Author', by Aeneas J. G. Mackay, prefixed to the S.H.S. edition of Major's *History*, pp. lxvii–lxviii.

old learning by the rigid scholastic discipline and methods'.[46] His old-fashioned Latin style was decried as 'Sorbonnic' by the humanists, and Melancthon declaimed: 'What waggon-loads of trifles! What pages he fills with dispute whether horsemanship requires a horse, whether the sea was salt when God made it.'[47] But the old learning was capable of application to new themes. Even in Major's theological works, and particularly in the commentary on Book IV of Peter Lombard's *Sentences*, which he published in 1509, there were digressions which showed that the professional academic and one time rustic had a deep interest in the folklore of Scotland and in its social and economic life.[48] As early as 1509 he was a staunch advocate of feuing. By 1521, when he published his *History of Greater Britain*, he had also become an advocate of union between Scotland and England. Like Guicciardini's *History of Italy*, Major's *History* was based on the assumption that a geographical unit, whether peninsula or island, should be treated as an historical unit. Hence for the first time, possibly for the last time, the inter-related histories of Scotland and England were compared, in equal detail, with surprising lack of bias, and with balanced comment. Major showed 'a wonderfully sound historical instinct, distinguishing truth from the fables with which Scottish annals were then encrusted'.[49] To the consternation of his friend, Gavin Douglas, he even rejected the story that the Scottish kings were descended from Scota. Had his *History* become more widely known, European historiography might have jumped forward two hundred years. In that humanistic age Major was damned by his unfashionable Latin style.

Hector Boece of Dundee shared (though naïvely) Major's interest in geography but had an eye for marvels rather than for economics and sociology. His *Lives of the Bishops of Mortlach and Aberdeen* was ingenuous and eulogistic. In his *Histories of the Scots from the Origin of the Race*, published in 1527, he adopted the approach of Livy—colourful narration rather than analysis and interpretation—and a suitably Augustan Latin style. This influential work (a model for that of George Buchanan) wiped out the historiographical advance made by Major.

Like Major, Boece was to have an influence upon university life in Scotland. In 1497 he was summoned from Paris to become regent

[46] Major, *History*, p. xlvi.   [47] *Ibid.*, p. lx.
[48] James Burns, 'The Scotland of John Major', *Innes Review*, II. 65–76.
[49] Aeneas J. G. Mackay, Major's *History*, p. lxxxiv.

master in arts, and eventually principal, of the new university of Aberdeen. This was the brain-child of Bishop Elphinstone, who, with the backing of the king, obtained the necessary papal bull on 10 February 1495. The new university was ostensibly intended to cater for those parts of the kingdom 'separated from the rest . . . by arms of the sea and very high mountains, in which dwell men rude and ignorant of letters, and almost barbarous'.[50] The foundation bull also specifically provided for the instruction of laymen as well as clerics. This novel feature[51] recognised the increased interest of the laity in higher education. A second novelty, which was symptomatic of increasing government intervention in every aspect of national life, was the addition of two of the king's councillors to those masters and scholars, who, under the bishop as ex-officio chancellor, were to formulate the university's constitution.[52] A third novelty was that the faculties at Aberdeen were to include not only arts, theology, canon law and civil law, but medicine. Hitherto this subject had not been altogether neglected in the English and Scottish universities; but Aberdeen was the first of them to aspire to a separate faculty. The king's interest was enlisted and moderate endowment was provided for a doctor of medicine who could be a layman. His precepts were probably less efficacious than those of the craft of surgeons and barbers of Edinburgh, who had a monopoly in the burgh of the sale of the newly invented *aqua vitae* (whisky)—one of the more reliable medicines—as well as the yearly gift of a criminal's corpse 'to mak antomell of, quhairthraw we may haif experience'.[53] By contrast the 'mediciner' of Aberdeen was expected to give instruction after the fashion of Paris—deduction from fanciful theories rather than from practical experience.[54] The courses in theology, arts and canon law were also to be modelled on those of Paris, but an exception was made for civil law, which was to follow the course of Orleans, 'the true source of the great influence exerted by Roman law upon the law of Scotland'.[55] The problems that Elphinstone faced, and surmounted, in providing for the teaching of civil law suggest that he hoped (though in vain) that Aberdeen would develop a strong law school.[56]

[50] *Nat. MSS. Scot.*, III. No. viii. See also Boece, *Vitae*, p. 57.
[51] Leslie J. Macfarlane, *op. cit.*, *Aberdeen University Review*, XXXIX. 1–18, at 11.   [52] *Ibid.*, 14; Rashdall, *Universities*, II. 320.
[53] *Edinburgh Burgh Recs.*, I. 101–4.
[54] *Aberdeen Fasti*, No. 46; *R.M.S.*, II. No. 2358.
[55] John Kirkpatrick, *op. cit.*, *S.H.S. Misc.*, II. 47–102, at 56, 57.
[56] Leslie J. Macfarlane, *op. cit.*, *Aberdeen University Review*, XXXIX. 1–18, at 16; Rashdall, *Universities*, II. 319.

It was some time before the papal bull of 1495 could be fully implemented. For ten years Elphinstone was busy cajoling endowments,[57] while not far from St Machar's Cathedral, where the central tower was nearing completion, rose the crowned tower and chapel of his new college, dedicated to the Virgin, but soon known as King's College. In 1505, when the essential buildings were almost ready for occupation, the constitution of the new establishment was published. As in the case of St Salvator's a collegiate kirk was the nucleus of an academic community. The total foundation of thirty-six members, later augmented to forty-two, can hardly have been as great as the staff of the cathedral, where there were no less than twenty vicars-choral, one of them the eminent musician, John Malison. Initially at least, some of the learned cathedral canons gave instruction in the university,[58] which doubtless also attracted some students who had no bursaries and were not on the foundation. 'From the university of Aberdeen', so Boece could affirm, 'there went out in a short time many men trained in theology, canon law and civil, and very many trained in philosophy'.[59]

Though Scotland now had one more university than England it was a pity that the funds and talents so carefully garnered for Aberdeen had not gone instead to sustain one or other of the two older universities. James III had renewed his father's grant of privileges to Glasgow;[60] Archbishop Blackadder had shown some interest; and reform had been attempted in 1492; but John Major, who disapproved of a 'multitude of universities', opined that Glasgow was 'poorly endowed, and not rich in scholars'.[61] In St Andrews the position was somewhat better. A sort of co-optative professoriate had emerged, and uniform competence, if not specialised brilliance, probably resulted from the 'regenting' system whereby each regent master conducted a group of students through the whole of the arts curriculum.[62] A major source of dispute within the university had been appeased in 1470, when St Salvator's College was induced to renounce the privilege (lately conferred by papal bull) of granting degrees independently of the university.[63] Another source of trouble had been eliminated by the long-delayed suppression of private pedagogies: all save the poorest students or the sons of the local

[57] See R.M.S., II. Nos. 2442, 2570, 3598, 3733; Aberdeen Fasti, pp. 9–52.
[58] Leslie J. Macfarlane, op. cit., Aberdeen University Review, xxxix. 1–18, at 11–7; Aberdeen Fasti, pp. 53–64, 80–108.
[59] Boece, Vitae, p. 91.   [60] R.M.S., II. No. 1095.
[61] Major, History, pp. 28–9; St Andrews Acta, I. xxxviii.
[62] St Andrews Acta, I. cxxi–cxxv.   [63] Ibid., xxix–xxxii.

townsfolk were now obliged to reside either in St Salvator's or in the less flourishing Pedagogy. Alexander Stewart, the boy-archbishop, had thoughts of re-modelling the latter, but in 1512 chose to convert a hospital for elderly women into the new college of St Leonard's for the maintenance of twenty poor clerks, students of arts, and six students of theology.[64] Thus during the reign the university continued to fulfil a modest role : it could number William Dunbar and Gavin Douglas among its graduates, though Douglas was by no means the only graduate who regarded his St Andrews career as a preparation for finer things in the French universities.

The traditional higher education was not the one selected for Alexander Stewart : in 1508 the boy-archbishop was sent to Padua and spent some months at Siena, where he was taught Greek and rhetoric under the tutorship of Erasmus, the leading humanist of the age.[65] Humanism was beginning to affect Scotland. Its possible sources were 'study in Italy, especially at the highly humanist papal court; contact in the Low Countries; and Italian influence coming to Scotland through France'.[66] It is remarkable that as early as 1433 the library at Glasgow Cathedral held a copy of Petrarch's *De Vita Solitaria*.[67] Though such a work was hardly commonplace in fifteenth-century Scottish libraries, where the more traditional scholastic fare abounded,[68] there were personal book collections which hinted at the humanist inclinations of the owners, as in the case of Archibald Whitelaw, tutor of James III and chief secretary between 1462 and 1493. An example of his Ciceronian Latinity survives in the record of negotiations at Nottingham in 1484, when he 'purposyd a oracyon' using no little hyperbole in his flattery of Richard III and going out of his way to explain the meaning of a Greek word.[69] Patrick Paniter, who became chief secretary in 1505 and tutored Alexander Stewart before his trip to Italy,[70] was cast in the same mould. In a Latin of 'Corinthian glitter' he could 'turn a grace-

[64] *R.M.S.*, II. No. 3812; *St Andrews Acta*, I. xliii–xliv; J. Herkless and R. K. Hannay, *The College of St Leonard* (1905).

[65] Lesley, *History*, p. 80; Leslie J. Macfarlane, *op. cit.*, *Innes Review*, xx. 111–29, at 121–2.

[66] Durkan, *Bishop Turnbull*, p. 36.

[67] *Ibid.*, p. 45.

[68] See John Durkan and Anthony Ross, *Early Scottish Libraries*, *passim*, and Anthony Ross, 'Libraries of the Scottish Blackfriars: 1481–1560', *Innes Review*, xx. 3–36.

[69] 'Negotiations of the Scottish Commissioners at Nottingham', *Bannatyne Misc.*, *II*. 41–8; see also Durkan, *Bishop Turnbull*, pp. 43, 56–7, and MacQueen, *Robert Henryson*, pp. 13–5.

[70] Leslie J. Macfarlane, *op. cit.*, *Innes Review*, xx. 111–29, at 121.

ful compliment to a foreign princess, put off the demands of an importunate ally with expressions of deep affection which, seeming to promise everything, promised nothing, throw the cloak of piety over some peculiarly twisted simoniacal transaction, or recite the grievances of merchant or mariner, unaccountably thrust into prison in some foreign port. Sometimes, as when he pleads with the pope to establish peace and concord in Christendom, he reaches real eloquence'.[71] Had his pupil, Alexander Stewart, lived longer, St Andrews, like Cambridge, might have reluctantly given an early welcome to the new learning.

Even in Italy the universities at first resisted the humanist movement. Yet 'it was bound to influence the grammar schools where students received their preliminary training, and in due course infiltrate into university teaching itself'.[72] Little can be certainly known (though much may be inferred) about the condition of the Scottish grammar schools.[73] According to the so-called 'Education Act' issued by the parliament of June 1496 [74] they were at least expected to equip their pupils with 'perfyte Latyne'. The act itself was a statement of educational aspirations: all barons and substantial freeholders, on pain of a £20 fine, were to send their eldest sons and heirs to grammar school from the age of eight or nine; after they had mastered Latin they were to spend three years studying arts or law in the universities. The effectiveness of the act, or the extent to which it corresponded to prevailing conditions, is hard to estimate. In 1501, however, the son and heir of Patrick Home of Fast Castle would obtain leave 'to pas to Parisch to the skulis to lere . . . vertuis and sience'—and to take his wife with him.[75] Several examples may also be found of laymen who had obtained a master's degree;[76] and Henry, Lord Sinclair, can hardly have been altogether unschooled when he besought Gavin Douglas to undertake a translation of Virgil or Homer.[77]

But it was not the aim of the 1496 act to produce aristocratic dilettanti. Its purpose was to inculcate 'knawlege and understanding of the lawis . . . sua that thai that ar schireffis or jugeis ordinaris . . . may have knawlege to do justice'. Thus, it was hoped, 'justice may reigne universalie throw all the realme', and 'the pure pepill sulde

[71] R. L. Mackie in *James IV, Letters*, p. xxxiii.
[72] Durkan, *Bishop Turnbull*, p. 34.
[73] See MacQueen, *Robert Henryson*, pp. 4–12, 15.
[74] *A.P.S.*, II. 238, c. 3. See also Lesley, *History*, p. 63; *St Andrews Acta*, I. xxxix–xl; D. E. Easson, *op. cit.*, *Scot. Church Hist. Soc. Recs.*, VI. 13–26, at 23–4.
[75] *R.S.S.*, I. No. 712.
[76] E.g. *ibid.*, No. 2196.   [77] Mackie, *James IV*, p. 169.

have na neid to seik our soverane lordis principale auditouris for ilk small injure'. The pragmatic attitude towards education was further illustrated by the attitude of the Abbot of Arbroath, who in 1497 was sending some of his monks to university so that 'having learned legal remedies they may frustrate the attacks of certain folk and the sinister machinations which impend against our abbey'.[78]

A practical and utilitarian spirit also inspired the experimentation that the king encouraged. It was probably an apocryphal story that he placed two infants on Inchkeith in the charge of a dumb woman to determine what tongue nature would inspire them to speak.[79] Better attested is the king's patronage of medicine and surgery. One pharmacist, William Fowler, was given exemption from service on inquests and from payment of taxes.[80] John Damian de Falcusis, the 'French leech', fared much better. His vain experiments at Stirling in 1503 in search of the *quinta essencia*—the fifth 'essence' that might transmute base metals into goid—were subsidised by the king,[81] who also made him Abbot of Tongland. The failure of Damian's experiment in flying from the battlements of Stirling inspired one of William Dunbar's satires:

> The air was dirkit with the fowlis
> That come with yawmeris and with yowlis
> With skyrking, skrymming and with scowlis
> To tak him in the tyde.[82]

Bishop Lesley more soberly recounts Damian's explanation that 'thair was sum hen fedderis in the wingis, quhilk . . . covet the mydding and not the skyis'.[83]

In technological advancement the king showed a persistent interest. At his 'instance and request' and for 'the honour and proffit of the realm' a notable initiative was taken by Walter Chepman and Andrew Millar, the first of whom was both a clerk in the secretary's office and a prominent Edinburgh merchant. In 1507 the pair undertook to 'bring hame ane prent . . . and expert men to use the samyne'.[84] Since books printed on the continent were already making their way into Scotland the investment of Chepman and Millar was

---

[78] Coulton, *Scottish Abbeys*, p. 309.   [79] Pitscottie, *Historie*, I. 237.
[80] *R.S.S.*, I. No. 899; see also No. 1343.
[81] *T.A.*, II. 138, 359–62, 374, 402, 422; see also *James IV, Letters*, No. 32.
[82] *The fenyeit Freir of Tungland* (Wittig, *Scottish Tradition*, p. 68).
[83] Lesley, *History*, p. 76.
[84] *R.S.S.*, I. No. 1546; *T.A.*, I. ci; *E.R.*, XI. xxix.

to be safeguarded by prohibiting the export of manuscripts for print-
ting abroad. Meanwhile, it was optimistically hoped, the new printing
press in Edinburgh would be kept busy publishing 'bukis of our
lawis, actis of parliament, croniclis, mess bukis and portuus [brevi-
aries]'. Here, as in much else, there was a utilitarian and nationalist
aim : knowledge of the laws would be disseminated ; chronicles (probably Bower's *Scotichronicon* was intended) would inculcate patriotism; so also would the liturgical works. For the press was to be used
to popularise the developing Scottishness of the kirk :[85] Chepman and
Millar were to print not legends of the saints in general but 'legendis
of Scottis sanctis' as composed by Bishop Elphinstone; and the
liturgical works were to be 'eftir our awin Scottis use', replacing
those modelled upon the English 'use of Sarum'—no 'bukis of Salus-
bery use' were to be 'brocht to be sauld within our realm in tyme
cuming'.[86] Not all of this ambitious publishing programme was
carried out. In 1509 and 1510 appeared the two fine volumes of
Elphinstone's *Aberdeen Breviary*; but tales of chivalry and romance,
Blind Harry's *Wallace*, some of the poems of William Dunbar and
Robert Henryson, provided more profitable printing than acts of
parliament.[87]

Even more obviously than in the case of the printing press royal
and national prestige could be enhanced by technological advance
in the manufacture of artillery and the construction of ships. In
Edinburgh Castle Robert Borthwick, probably aided by Hans Gunnare, George van Erisling and French artificers, was kept busy casting
guns, among them the famous 'Seven Sisters'.[88] Artillery had begun
to revolutionise naval warfare : after a lapse of centuries the warship,
as distinct from the converted merchantman, was beginning to re-
appear ; improved facilities for construction and repair were
required ; a new breed of mariners was beginning to vie for renown
alongside the military élite. Sir Andrew Wood, a mere inhabitant of
Leith, had by-passed burgess-ship in his social rise, was the king's
'familiar knight' by 1495, and by 1513 was just as concerned as any
noble that his surname and arms be preserved to posterity. In all the
typical developments of the age—feuing, tower-building, the erection
of burghs of barony, the foundation of chaplainries, remissions and
respites—he was to be found involved.[89] The three Barton brothers,

[85] See p. 560 above.   [86] *R.S.S.*, I. No. 1546.
[87] Mackie, *James IV*, pp. 170–1.
[88] Pitscottie, *Historie*, I. 259–60; Lesley, *History*, p. 81; *R.M.S.*, II. No. 3546;
R.S.S., I. Nos. 916, 2033; *E.R.*, XIII. clxvii–clxxi; *T.A.*, IV. 276–8.
[89] *R.M.S.*, II. Nos. 2231, 2825, 3880; *E.R.*, XIII. clxxix–clxxxi.

John, Robert and Andrew, bid fair to profit by Wood's example.[90] The need for such men had been demonstrated at the outset of the reign when the depredations of foreign pirates, even in the waters of the Forth, made parliament willingly approve a licence for the fortification of Inchgarvie Isle by John Dundas.[91] King and parliament were also well aware of the potentialities of the new off-shore herring fisheries. These not only increased the kingdom's natural resources[92] but gave employment to men and small vessels that could be pressed into royal service in time of war : both economic and strategic motives lay behind the acts of June 1492 and March 1504 that exhorted burghs and nobles to build fishing boats of at least twenty tuns burthen.[93] In 1505 the king acquired Newhaven (then undeveloped) from Holyrood Abbey, built a pier and dockyard, and in 1511 granted the new port to Edinburgh.[94] In shipbuilding James gave a lead to his subjects. He had inherited a few royal ships from his father ; one or two vessels were purchased, a few others were ordered in the shipyards of Flanders and Brittany; even more significantly timber, tackle and shipwrights were imported from Normandy.[95] The woods of Darnaway were felled for shipbuilding at Leith[96] and those of Fife for the construction of the *Michael* at Newhaven. This vessel, which the French king thought the greatest in Christendom,[97] was reputed to have cost £30,000. Although this, and some other details given by Pitscottie,[98] may be discounted, he was very near the mark in reporting that the crew numbered three hundred.[99]

In 1506 James had informed Louis XII that the creation of a fleet for the protection of Scottish shores was a project of long standing that was close to his heart ; both he and the fleet, so he unctuously affirmed, would be ready to do the bidding of the French king.[100] James showed no intention of using his ships to compete with those of Portugal and Spain in winning the spices of the Indies, the slaves of Africa, the silver of the Americas. Apart from protecting Scotland

[90] See W. Stanford Reid, *Skipper from Leith, passim*; *E.R.*, XIII. clxxxi.
[91] *A.P.S.*, II. 270; *R.M.S.*, II. No. 2038.
[92] See *A.P.S.*, II. 183, c. 15; 209, c. 12; 237, c. 24; *E.R.*, X. 638; *R.S.S.*, I. Nos. 286, 709, 710.
[93] *A.P.S.*, II. 235, c. 20; 251, c. 15.   [94] *R.M.S.*, II. Nos. 2864, 3551.
[95] W. Stanford Reid, *op. cit.*, *Mediaevalia et Humanistica*, XV. 97-107, at 99-101; *E.R.*, XIII. clxxxiv-clxxxvi; *R.S.S.*, I. No. 323; *Lesley, History*, p. 62.
[96] *E.R.*, XIII. clxvi.   [97] *Flodden Papers*, p. 70.
[98] Pitscottie, *Historie*, I. 251-2.
[99] 295 'mariners of the great ship' were paid by the treasurer, mostly at the rate of 35s. a month (*T.A.*, IV. 502-5); see also *E.R.*, XII. xxxv and n.
[100] *James IV, Letters*, No. 42.

the new and costly fleet had four functions : it was an asset in James's complex diplomacy;[101] it proved its worth in the daunting of the Isles; it was used to suppress foreign piracy in the North Sea—in 1506 Andrew Barton, captain of the *Margaret*, sent the king a barrel stuffed with the heads of Dutch freebooters;[102] finally, it could improve James's chances of being accepted as commander of a grand crusade against the Ottoman Turks.

This project, thanks to its long medieval antecedents, had overtones that were quixotic, and the problems it involved were possibly insurmountable. Yet never before did Western Europe stand in greater need of a grand crusade. For while the far corners of the globe were being brought into the service of Europe and Christianity, Christian Europe was itself shrinking : the galleys of Islam swept the Mediterranean; Hungary would soon be lost; and Vienna, besieged in 1529, would not be freed of the Turkish menace until its deliverance by Sobieski in 1683.

The anxiety that James seems to have felt about the Ottoman advance was possibly stimulated by Archbishop Blackadder, who died at Jaffa in 1508 during a pilgrimage to the Holy Land.[103] Firsthand information was also forthcoming from two Greek nobles who visited Scotland, as well as from the laird of Fast Castle, who in 1509 came home after a period in Turkish service in Cairo.[104] In 1510 James outlined to the Marquis of Mantua his hope that 'one army drawn from all nations may be turned against the enemies of Christ'. Alone among the rulers of Europe the Scottish king was prepared to act in the interests of Europe as a whole.[105]

He was not, as has been asserted, a 'moonstruck romantic'.[106] Never blind to his own interests, he had a longer experience of statecraft than most rulers and could rival all of them in deviousness. Yet, having achieved some stability in the relationships that now linked Scotland on honourable terms with France and England, James had no desire to see that stability upset by bickerings in Italian vineyards. The crusading scheme, together with the missions of mediation entrusted to Bishop Forman, might end the international power struggle that became increasingly obnoxious after 1509.

---

[101] W. Stanford Reid, *op. cit.*, *Medievalia et Humanistica*, xv. 97–107.
[102] Lesley, *History*, p. 74.
[103] See David McRoberts, 'Scottish Pilgrims to the Holy Land', *Innes Review*, xx. 80–106.   [104] *T.A.*, II. xxvii; Lesley, *History*, p. 80.
[105] Mackie, *James IV*, p. 205; *James IV, Letters*, Nos. 307, 308, 332, 353, 356, 386, 422, 503, 516.   [106] Mackie, *James IV*, p. 201.

In that year James's astute and pacific father-in-law was succeeded by Henry VIII, an egocentric teenager whose tantrums and
petulance bespoke an inferiority complex. Although he confirmed
the treaty of perpetual peace with Scotland, and in May 1510 made
a treaty with France,[107] Henry was restive and pugnacious. So also
was Julius II. Lately he had humbled Venice with the help of the
French; in 1509 he became implacably committed to expelling them
from Italy, and in October 1511 he concluded a 'Holy League' with
Venice and Ferdinand of Aragon. Henry's adherence to this anti-
French coalition was soon bought when Ferdinand duped him with
the promise of aid towards the recovery of Aquitaine for the English
crown. Meanwhile the question of the royal succession in both England and Scotland must have contributed to the nervousness of their
rulers.[108] James's queen vied with Henry's (Catherine of Aragon) in
natal misfortunes, and the unexpected deaths of James's two brothers
—Mar in 1503 and the duke-archbishop in 1504—brought the Earl
of Arran and the Duke of Albany, absentee and half French, closer
to the throne. But from 1509 until 1516 James's queen was Henry's
heir presumptive. It was hardly tactful that her second son, Arthur
(born in 1509 only to die in 1510) was given the name once borne by
Henry VIII's elder brother, a name that was 'British' rather than
Scottish or English. On 10 April 1512 James's confidence, and
Henry's irritation, must have been increased when Queen Margaret
at last gave birth to a son [109] (the future James V) who escaped infant mortality to inherit his mother's potential claim to the English
crown. Henry's pettiness was displayed in his refusal to transmit to
his sister the bequests made to her by their father.[110]

The two courts had also become estranged over incidents at sea.
The uses to which James intended to put Scottish seapower were not
necessarily those of the naval captains on whom he depended. The
Bartons were pirates whose activities he abetted, particularly by
renewing letters of marque granted to them by James III.[111]
Foreigners who complained to the lords of council were met by judicial procrastination and unhelpfulness. In the spring of 1511 James
again re-issued the letters of marque and Andrew Barton set sail,
finding it difficult to tell the difference between the intended victims
(the Portuguese) and the English. In June he was encountered in the

---

[107] *Ibid.*, p. 200.   [108] *James IV, Letters*, pp. xxxiv–xxxv.
[109] *Ibid.*, Nos. 443, 444.   [110] *Ibid.*, No. 543.
[111] *Edinburgh Burgh Recs.*, I. 119–20; W. Stanford Reid, *Skipper from
Leith*, p. 35.

Downs by the English admiral, Sir Edward Howard, and his brother, Lord Thomas Howard. The *Lion* and the *Jenny Pirwin* were captured and Andrew Barton fell in the engagement. In vain James heatedly demanded that Sir Edward Howard should be arraigned in the warden court for breach of the peace treaty and the death of Andrew Barton. Henry replied with a taunt that it did not become one prince to accuse another of infraction of a treaty merely because justice had been done on a thief or pirate.[112] It was ironic that, independent of the continental power struggle, warfare almost ensued between Scotland and England in 1511 and that Louis XII on 8 November, five days before England entered the Holy League, strove to reconcile James and Henry.[113]

Soon Louis realised his mistake. He had already denounced Julius II as a traitor to Christendom and summoned a general council of the church to meet at Pisa. Louis had no wish to be distracted from the Italian conflict by an English menace to France and hoped to distract the English with a Scottish menace to England. In January 1512 he promised James that vast French assistance for the crusade would be at his disposal a year after the pope should agree to peace with France. In April James was told that Louis would support him in any rightful claim to the English crown. In July James renewed the Franco-Scottish alliance: if either partner were at war with England the other would at once make full-scale war upon the English.[114] It mattered little that the renewed Franco-Scottish alliance was incompatible with the Anglo-Scottish peace treaty that had been renewed in 1509.[115] It was a time when treaties represented little more than wishful thinking: although an English expeditionary force appeared in Guienne in the summer of 1512 and the coasts of Brittany were raided by Sir Edward Howard's fleet, James did not break with England; and at Bayonne the English waited in vain for the aid promised by Ferdinand, who merely used them to distract the French while he seized Navarre and then made a one-year truce. But Ferdinand's temporary defection from the Holy League was counterbalanced by the adherence of Emperor Maximilian, lately the ally of France; and the costly failure in Guienne stung Henry's pride.[116] The expedition planned for the summer of 1513 was one that he meant to command in person.

[112] Mackie, *James IV*, pp. 207–11; *James IV, Letters*, pp. lii–liv.
[113] *Flodden Papers*, No. iv, p. 13.
[114] *James IV, Letters*, pp. liv–lxi; Mackie, *James IV*, pp. 202–7, 213–9.
[115] For a comparison of the terms see Mackie, *James IV*, pp. 98–9, 216–9.
[116] *Ibid.*, pp. 214–25.

What James would do if Henry landed in France was doubtful. In Scotland there had been not only protracted preparations for war but lengthy deliberation on all aspects of the power struggle. In 1511 and 1512 councils had been summoned to discuss relations with France and the pope.[117] James did not commit himself to sending representatives to the Gallican council of Pisa but continued to regard a reconciliation of France and the papacy as his chief diplomatic objective, partly, perhaps, because it might lead to the pope's releasing him from the excommunication he would incur by breaking the peace treaty with England. Meanwhile, it was hoped, Denmark might be aligned with France and Scotland. King Hans would not commit himself to France, responded evasively to the anxious solicitations of his nephew, and eventually sent him some munitions,[118] but not the Danish ships that James hoped to add to his own fleet.[119]

Whilst most of Europe feverishly prepared for a new campaigning season, fresh uncertainties, and hopes, were aroused by the death of Pope Julius. The first tidings of his demise were brought to Scotland by John Barton, whose ship, laden with munitions from France, reached the Forth on 20 March 1513. Eleven days later it sailed back carrying Bishop Forman on a mission to the French and papal courts.[120] Shortly before Forman departed, an English ambassador, Nicholas West, arrived at the Scottish court, where he was to spend an acrimonious and unrewarding three weeks, passing his spare time spying upon the fleet. He strove to obtain a guarantee of Scottish neutrality, even, if possible, a loan of the *Michael*. In return he had nothing to offer. James gave him details of the French king's promise of help for the crusade and explained, 'now you see wherefore I favour the French king and wherefore I am loth to lose him, for if I do I shall never be able to perform my journey'. On 13 April West had to leave for Berwick, having failed to extort from James any definite answer as to whether he would, or would not, remain neutral if Henry invaded France.[121]

Forman would be equally unsuccessful at Rome. The new pope, Leo X, did not offer him the cardinal's hat that Julius II had once hinted at bestowing, but in other respects adhered to the policies of his predecessor and provided the English with letters permitting the excommunication of James if he broke the peace treaty.[122] On the

---

[117] *A.D.C.P.*, pp. vi–vii.   [118] Lesley, *History*, pp. 85–6.
[119] W. Stanford Reid, *op. cit., Juridical Review*, LVIII. 183–200, at 191–3.
[120] Mackie, *James IV*, pp. 230–2.   [121] *Ibid.*, pp. 230–7.
[122] *Ibid.*, pp. 232–3, 236.

way to Rome, however, Forman had transacted important business at the French court, where he presented James's request that Louis should send to Scotland troops, guns, ships and money. Louis was reminded that if Scotland joined in the war France was not to make peace until James had obtained the English crown.[123] James ambitiously hoped to draw the French from their Italian adventures in order to further his own dynastic schemes. If these were successful Scotland and England would be united and he would be free to lead the grand crusade. Louis tactfully twisted James's inordinate requests to his own advantage. In counter-proposals that reached Scotland at the beginning of June he suggested that the Scottish fleet be sent to France, where it would be fully equipped and victualled and a subsidy of 50,000 francs would be paid, then (at some indefinite time) the vessels would be sent back to Scotland with seven French galleys to be used at James's discretion; if James were to invade England as soon as Henry invaded France he would best advance his claim to the English crown.[124] Similar proposals, together with a special request for the *Michael*, had already been put forward by Jehan de la Motte, who in May 1513 acted for the third time as Louis's ambassador at the Scottish court.[125] But James remained uncommitted: on 24 May he wrote to Henry, his 'dearest brothir', to suggest that both Scotland and England become parties to the truce already concluded between France and Aragon; although James also expressed regret that Henry's admiral, Sir Edward Howard, had recently been killed in a naval engagement with the French, he pointedly alluded to the crusade by affirming that the valiant knight's services would have been put to better use in warfare upon the enemies of Christ.[126] Since this appeal had no effect upon Henry, James concluded that he must at least make some moves to disconcert the English and satisfy the French: in June the vessels in the Forth were made ready for war and a mobilisation of sailors was ordered for July.[127]

Early in that month news must have reached Scotland, almost simultaneously, that the French army in Italy had met disaster at Novara on 6 June and that Henry VIII had sailed on 30 June to begin his invasion of France by laying siege to Thérouanne in Artois.[128] Possibly also there arrived a ring from Queen Anne of France and an appeal to James to advance three feet into England for her sake. James's own queen counselled peace. So also did Bishop Elphin-

[123] *Flodden Papers*, No. xvi.　　[124] *Ibid.*, No. xvii.
[125] Mackie, *James IV*, pp. 217–9, 237–9.　[126] *James IV, Letters*, No. 550.
[127] *T.A.*, IV. 413–4, 480, 481, 483.　[128] Mackie, *James IV*, p. 240.

stone, who was shouted down in the council (so Boece asserts) 'because, like a mad old man, he had spoken stupidly and thoughtlessly against the commonweal, against their sacred treaty and ancient league'.[129] The ancient league with France meant much to Bishop Forman : in June Louis XII had begun to put pressure on the chapter of Bourges to accept him as archbishop; Forman eventually obtained this French archbishopric as a reward for persuading James to go to war.[130]

But even at the last moment James played for time : on 24 July the host was summoned to muster at Ellem in Berwickshire;[131] yet when Lyon king-of-arms was despatched to Henry on 26 July he carried a sort of ultimatum, not an outright declaration of war;[132] and although another herald left for Paris on 27 July with the news that the fleet had sailed, the *Michael* and its attendant vessels, nine or eleven in all,[133] had emerged from the Forth to head north, rather than south.

It is inconceivable that the commander of the fleet, the Earl of Arran, no Medina Sidonia but a man formerly entrusted with naval operations in the Hebrides, had disobeyed orders. In 1495, when James was bent upon doing mischief to Henry VII, he had accepted the homage and co-operation of Hugh O'Donnel of Tyrconnel,[134] one of the two great Gaelic chiefs of Ulster. A second Hugh, son and heir of the first, had visited the Scottish court to conclude an offensive and defensive alliance with the king on 25 June 1513. The 'greit Odinle of Ireland', whom James recognised as prince and kinsman, was promised assistance in ships and men. In mid-July he left Edinburgh with a great cannon, another piece of artillery, ammunition, workmen, and eight quarriers 'for undirmynding of wallis'.[135] The *Michael*, which carried at least fourteen gunners, could be used for the same purpose and could disembark a vast complement of troops to enter the breaches in enemy strongholds. Having rounded Cape Wrath and shown the flag in the Hebrides it battered Carrickfergus, the chief English stronghold in Ulster.[136] When the spoil of Carrick-

[129] Boece, *Vitae*, pp. 104–5; Pitscottie, *Historie*, I. 256, 261.
[130] Mackie, *James IV*, p. 277. [131] *T.A.*, IV. 416–7.
[132] *James IV, Letters*, No. 560; Lesley, *History*, pp. 87–91.
[133] Mackie, *James IV*, pp. 242–3.
[134] *R.M.S.*, II. No. 3856; *T.A.*, I. 242; Conway, *Henry VII*, pp. 85–6.
[135] *R.M.S.*, II. No. 3856; *T.A.*, IV. 415–6, 434–5, 527; Lesley, *History*, p. 86; *James IV, Letters*, Nos. 89, 104–6. For the Irish background see E. Curtis, *Medieval Ireland*, p. 362. [136] Pitscottie, *Historie*, I. 256–7.

fergus was carried to Ayr there was still an opportunity to recall the fleet. It sailed on to France. Eventually most of the vessels would come back. But a Scottish fleet would never be re-fashioned: the *Michael*, sold to the French king for 40,000 francs, was left to rot.[137]

Meanwhile, so claims Pitscottie, as James sat in St Michael's Kirk in Linlithgow, 'verie sad and dollarous', a strange man warned him to desist from his projected enterprise then 'vanischit away ... as he had bene ane blink of the sone or ane quhipe of the whirle wind'.[138] But the king's mind remained unaltered. Despite his ambitions he had laboured for three years in the cause of peace. Had Henry VIII shown some signs of goodwill there would have been no war; so long as there was little likelihood of real friendship with England it seemed better to stand by France. Nothing could be farther from the truth than to suppose that this decision was rash and precipitate.

Early in August James had sent his warden, Lord Home, to raid Northumberland. On their withdrawal the booty-laden Scots were ambushed at Milfield between the slopes of Flodden Hill and the river Till, and lost heavily from the fire of English archers concealed among the bracken and thickets. The warden extricated himself with heavy loss, leaving his banner behind him. The humiliation of this 'Ill Raid'[139] probably stimulated the king in his warlike preparations. While contingents of the Scottish army made their way across the bleak Lammermuir hills to muster in the valley of the Whiteadder, preparations were made to send the artillery southwards. On 17 August it made its cumbrous way from Edinburgh Castle. There were seventeen guns in all, 'as goodly guns as have been seen in any realm'.[140] They were drawn on their way by four hundred oxen, and attended by a gang of forty workmen, a crane, powder-carts, and pack animals carrying gunstones.[141] The king, having returned from a devout pilgrimage to the shrine of St Duthac[142] in Ross, set out from Edinburgh on 19 August, probably with the provost and some local contingents that had been mustered on the Burgh Muir.[143] A presage of disaster had occurred on the previous night when some unexplained summons was issued from the Mercat Cross calling on members of the expedition to compear within forty days in the nether

[137] *A.D.C.P.*, pp. 39–40; W. Stanford Reid, *op. cit., Medievalia et Humanistica*, xv. 97–107, at 106–7.

[138] Pitscottie, *Historie*, I. 258–9.   [139] Mackie, *James IV*, p. 246.

[140] 'Trewe Encountre', p. 146.   [141] Mackie, *James IV*, pp. 247–8.

[142] *T.A.*, IV. 419.   [143] Mackie, *James IV*, pp. 247–8.

world.[144] The plague had probably reached Edinburgh,[145] and must have been carried to the host as it mustered at Ellem. On 22 August the Scots forded the Tweed and confronted Norham Castle. On the same day Thérouanne surrendered to Henry VIII. Had the news ever reached James it would have confirmed him in his belief that the threat to France was not to be lightly dismissed. The governor of Norham had boasted that he would hold it against the Scots until Henry came back from France. He held out for only six days.[146] After the capture of Norham the Scots advanced a few miles southward into the valley of the Till. A week was spent in subduing the castles of Etal and Wark. By 4 September, Lady Heron, whose supposed romantic connection with James[147] is probably apocryphal, had surrendered Ford Castle.

At Twizelhaugh on 24 August James had been persuaded to issue an ordinance of a type that seems to have been traditional before some dire engagement : the heirs of any member of the host who might be slain, or die of wounds or disease, would be exempt from payment of the usual feudal casualties.[148] But it was by no means certain that any dire engagement would take place. It may be inferred from James's leisurely proceedings that his strategy was not an ambitious one, that he had no mind to attack Berwick[149] or penetrate deeply into England but was merely engaged in a military demonstration, enough to preserve his credit with the French king but not enough to earn the undying hostility of Henry VIII and render peace-making unduly difficult.

It was not the intention of Thomas Howard, Earl of Surrey, that James should escape so lightly. Before sailing for Calais Henry had entrusted the defence of northern England to the septuagenarian earl.[150] He had worsted James in 1497, escorted his bride to Scotland in 1503, and could well assess the psychology of his opponent. Surrey's well-laid plans for the mobilisation of the northern counties worked well. Despite the downpour of rain that hindered the passage of an army over sodden tracks, he had marched rapidly northward from his base at Pontefract. The English fleet had weathered a storm and arrived in the Tyne in time to land a thousand soldiers and mariners and a number of ships' guns. By 4 September this contingent, led by Surrey's son, Thomas Howard, the new English admiral,

[144] Pitscottie, *Historie*, I. 260–1.   [145] *Edinburgh Burgh Recs.*, I. 141.
[146] Mackie, *James IV*, pp. 249, 256.   [147] Pitscottie, *Historie*, I. 262–4.
[148] *A.P.S.*, II. 278; cf. *R.S.S.*, VII. viii.
[149] See, however, J. D. Mackie, 'The English Army at Flodden', *S.H.S. Misc.* VIII. 35–85, at 37–8.   [150] Mackie, *James IV*, pp. 240–1.

E.H.S.—20*

had reached Alnwick.[151] While the English forces were arrayed there, Surrey engaged in diplomatic exchanges with James, possibly in the belief that he might elude him by slipping back to Scotland only to return when the English army had dispersed; and dispersal was imminent, for if Surrey did not lack men he was certainly short of supplies, notably beer.[152] Thus Rougecroix pursuivant was despatched to inform James that the earl would be prepared to wage battle with him on 9 September. Lest James should pay no heed to this challenge the English admiral added a jibe alluding to his part in the death of Andrew Barton : Howard 'was nowe come in hys awne proper person too be in the vauntgarde of the felde to justifiè the death of the said Andrewe'. On 6 September a reply came by Islay herald to say that James would wait to do battle until noon on 9 September.[153]

For the last few days James had been at Ford Castle, but on 5 September he set fire to it and crossed to the western bank of the Till. The new Scottish encampment was placed between three hills, and the obvious approach, a narrow gulley, was defended by an entrenchment behind which the Scottish artillery was placed.[154] For the Scots to station themselves in a strong fortified camp was a novel practice, which may have owed something to French military advisers and recent experience in the Italian wars.[155] It showed a foresight that displeased the English : the Scots had placed themselves on ground 'like a fortresse or campe' rather than accepting the site of battle thought appropriate by Surrey.[156] But James was not impressed by this chivalric objection. In 1497 he had once challenged Surrey to hand-to-hand combat and the earl had avoided the encounter by chiding the king for his condescension in being willing to fight a mere earl.[157] Now James denied Rougecroix an interview but sent him a message to inform Surrey that 'it beseemeth him not, being an earl, so largely to attempt a great prince'; James would 'take and hold his ground at his own pleasure, and not at the assigning of the Earl of Surrey'.[158]

Diplomacy having failed, Surrey marched alongside the eastern bank of the Till out of range of the Scottish guns and camped for the night. On the morning of 9 September the English once more marched northwards on the eastern side of the Till. As yet, the Scots

---

[151] *Ibid.*, pp. 250–1.   [152] 'Trewe Encountre', p. 147.
[153] *James IV, Letters*, No. 566; Mackie, *James IV*, p. 253.
[154] 'Trewe Encountre', p. 146. See the map in Mackie, *James IV*, p. 258.
[155] Mackenzie, *Flodden*, pp. 72–3.   [156] *James IV, Letters*, No. 566.
[157] M. J. Tucker, *The Life of Thomas Howard, Earl of Surrey* (1964), p. 67.
[158] 'Trewe Encountre', p. 146.

saw no reason to leave their own well-defended camp. Suddenly the
Earl of Surrey with the English rearguard began to ford the river at
Heton, while his son, the admiral, took the vanguard and the artillery
over Twizel bridge, five miles north of the Scottish position and out
of range of the Scottish guns.[159] If the Scots had been watchful there
would probably have been time to contest the passage of the Till.
Had they attacked when the English rearguard and vanguard were
not only divided, but engaged in crossing the river, the English could
hardly have avoided disaster. Why the Scots did not attack at this
point is an enigma. Part of the explanation may be that James had
announced that he would wait to do battle at noon on 9 September;
when noon came and the English forces were seen apparently making
for Berwick, he may have rashly assumed that Surrey was ignominiously declining the prescribed encounter.[160] All too late the Scots
discovered that the enemy had crossed the river and lay between
them and Scotland. Thus the Scots were compelled to make an unexpected volte-face. James hastily moved to the edge of Branxton
Hill near Flodden to deny the high ground to the English.[161] Even
this new position was potentially a strong one. But the Scots had no
time to take much advantage of it. Surrey realised that to make the
most of the initiative he had already won he must make an immediate advance upon the outwitted and flurried Scots. The situation was
one that was calculated to bring out all that was most impetuous in
the character of the Scottish king. Don Pedro de Ayala had made one
serious criticism of James: 'he is not a good captain because he begins to fight before he has given his orders'.[162] The time had come for
coolness and well-considered orders, but James was not the man to
give them. A council of nobles, under the urging of Patrick, Lord
Lindsay, is said to have enjoined him not to venture his own person
in fighting the arthritic Surrey, 'ane old cruikit cairll liand in ane
charieot'. James was infuriated and was not to be dissuaded from
winning knightly renown in the midst of his troops.[163] Sharing the
risks of his men he risked the fortunes of his kingdom.

Personal daring could not make up what had been lost through
carelessness. In face of the enemy the Scots were left with few ad-
vantages. Their numbers were reduced through desertion to perhaps

[159] J. D. Mackie, op. cit., S.H.S. Misc. VIII. 35–85, at 36, 39–40.
[160] Ibid., p. 37; Mackenzie, Flodden, p. 37.
[161] Mackie, James IV, pp. 259–60.
[162] Brown, Early Travellers, p. 40.   [163] Pitscottie, Historie, I. 267–9.

little more than the English total of twenty thousand.[164] Although James had a fine train of artillery, this comprised siege guns of heavy calibre that had battered the walls of Norham, and it is questionable whether all seventeen heavy guns could have been moved to the new position in time.[165] Moreover the skilled foreign gunners had been sent with the fleet to France, leaving in charge the king's secretary, Patrick Paniter.[166] By contrast, the English had guns from their fleet, of smaller calibre than the Scottish culverins, but more numerous and more easily manoeuvred; and they had expert German gunners to use them.[167]

There began an artillery duel that was probably the first in history significantly to affect the outcome of a battle. Although the Scottish artillery made a great noise that at once drove some impressionable English levies to headlong flight,[168] it failed to find the correct range: the heavy gunstones went flying overhead while the opposing artillery quickly found the range of the Scots, killed their master-gunner and silenced their guns.[169] In the past it had been the task of the English archers to goad the Scots into leaving a defensive position; at Flodden strong wind and a heavy shower of rain hindered archery [170] and it was the well-handled English artillery that forced the Scots to attack. Besides, as the Scottish government affirmed some months later, James was 'impatient at the sight of them' [the English] and, 'keeping no order among his men', left his advantageous ground to engage the enemy.[171]

About four in the afternoon of 9 September, on a blustery day of alternate rain and sun, the Scots began to advance. Although at first favoured by the lie of the land they could not gain much impetus. Both sides fought on foot and the wet and slippery ground must have prevented the tightly-packed Scottish battalions from making a headlong charge. Below Branxton Hill the ground levelled out or even rose on the English side. Moreover the Scots relied on their long spears or pikes. In 1481 an act of parliament had attempted to standardise the length of these at seventeen feet six inches. A number had been imported from Veere just before the outbreak of war, and the Scots had probably been trained by French military advisers to use their pikes

---

[164] For estimates of the numbers of the opposing armies see J. D. Mackie, *op. cit., S.H.S. Misc. VIII.* 35–85, at 47–69; Mackenzie, *Flodden*, pp. 45–9; Mackie, *James IV*, pp. 251–2.

[165] J. D. Mackie, *op. cit., S.H.S. Misc. VIII.* 35–85, at 40–1, 42.

[166] *James IV, Letters*, p. xxxi.   [167] Mackie, *James IV*, pp. 263–4, 274–5.

[168] Mackenzie, *Flodden*, p. 77.   [169] Lesley, *History*, pp. 94–5.

[170] 'Trewe Encountre', p. 150.   [171] Mackenzie, *Flodden*, p. 21.

in 'the manner of the Almayns',[172] forming phalanxes comparable to the traditional Scottish schiltrons. Such phalanxes could be irresistible so long as they were not brought to a halt and broken up. But at Flodden the ground was irregular and soft underfoot, and in places even marshy. When it came to hand-to-hand fighting the Scots found their long pikes far less useful than the nine-foot English halberds or bills, which combined an axe-head and spear-head. The pikes were meant for intact formations and were too unwieldy for individual use. As secondary weapons the Scots carried long swords: 'it was finally as swordsmen, not as spearmen, that the Scottish army made its dour disastrous stand at Flodden'.[173] But even the swords were no match for the deadly English bills. The English remarked upon the fine quality of the Scottish armour, against which arrows had been much less effective than usual. But in long-drawn-out fighting heavy armour and heavy swords were cumbersome.

On the Scottish left, the battalion under Lord Home and the Earl of Huntly had soon dispersed the opposing battalion. Further advance was halted by English reinforcements. Thereafter Home and the Scottish Borderers took no further part in the fighting and eventually escaped over the Cheviots with less loss than the other Scottish contingents.[174] On the Scottish right, the Highlanders under the Earls of Lennox and Argyll broke array and were routed by an English attack on the flank and rear. The king, in command of the centre battalion, came within a spear length of the Earl of Surrey only to fall among the slain.[175] This 'shows how desperate the fighting really was and how close James came to victory; . . . for if Surrey were in the rear directing his men, then James very nearly penetrated the entire depth of the English line'.[176] Even after many of the Scots had taken to flight, others remained fighting till nightfall. Long before then, the Scots had been driven from the ground where their king's dead body lay; and the prolongation of the fight merely made the disaster all the worse. The Scottish losses were far greater than the English not only in number but in the rank of the slain. Beside the king fell his illegitimate son, the young Archbishop of St Andrews, whose death led Erasmus to lament: 'What hadst thou to do with fierce Mars . . . thou that wert destined for the Muses and for Christ?'[177] Also among the slain were George Hepburn, Bishop of

[172] *Ibid.*, pp. 71–3.   [173] *Ibid.*, p. 93.
[174] *Ibid.*, pp. 8, 81–2.   [175] *Ibid.*, pp. 84–5.
[176] M. J. Tucker, *The Life of Thomas Howard, Earl of Surrey*, p. 114.
[177] Erasmus, *Adages*, cited in J. Herkless and R. K. Hannay, *The Archbishops of St Andrews*, I. 262.

the Isles, and eight of Scotland's twenty-two earls. Few Scots were admitted to quarter. Once James's pierced body had been recognised it was honourably conveyed to Berwick, finally to Richmond, where it lay in a leaden casket but was never accorded the state funeral that Henry VIII at one time planned for it.[178]

In July 1512 an Edinburgh student at the university of Orleans had written in an elegiac poem :

> Love James the Fourth, O Scotland, with whose aid
> Auspicious Fame will thee to heaven exalt.[179]

Flodden saw the end both of James IV and heavenly exaltation. Sometimes in the past the Scots had suffered a reverse as great as that of 1513 and had quickly recovered ; they did not regard Flodden as an irretrievable disaster ;[180] but the disaster was not retrieved.

[178] *James IV, Letters*, No. 568.
[179] John Kirkpatrick, *op. cit., S.H.S. Misc. II.* 47–102, at 97.
[180] Gordon Donaldson, *Scotland: James V to James VII* (1965), p. 17.

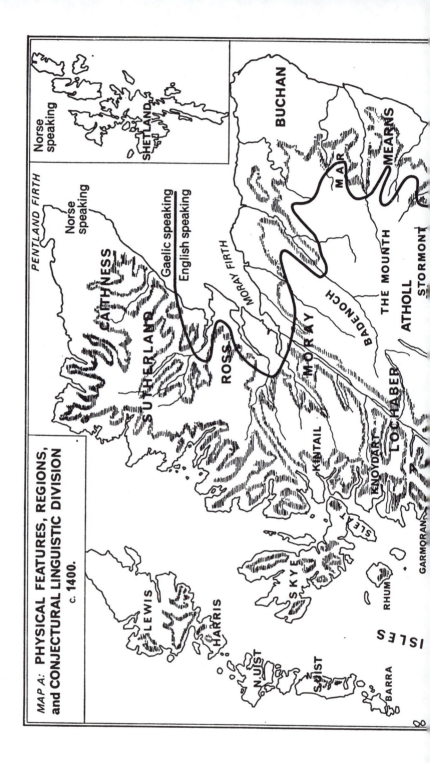

MAP A: **PHYSICAL FEATURES, REGIONS, and CONJECTURAL LINGUISTIC DIVISION** c. 1400.

Gaelic speaking
English speaking

Norse speaking

Norse speaking

SHETLAND

PENTLAND FIRTH

CAITHNESS

SUTHERLAND

ROSS

MORAY FIRTH

MORAY

BADENOCH

KINTAIL

KNOYDART

LOCHABER

SLEAT

GARMORAN

LEWIS

HARRIS

N. UIST

S. UIST

BARRA

SKYE

RHUM

ISLES

MAR

MEARNS

BUCHAN

THE MOUNTH

ATHOLL

STORMONT

8

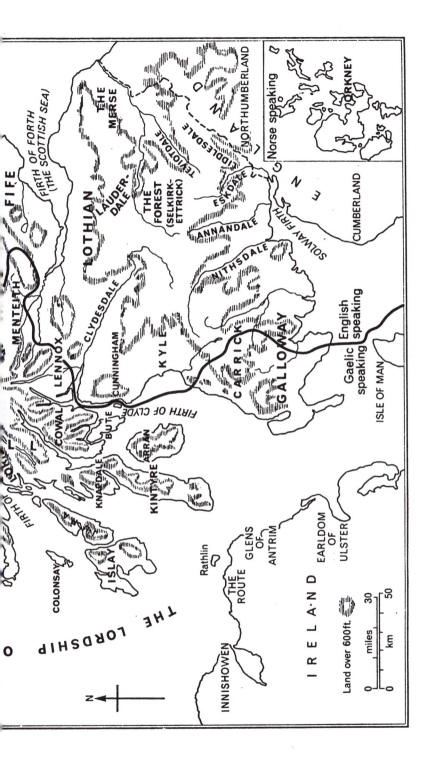

FIFE

FIRTH OF FORTH
(THE SCOTTISH SEA)

THE
MERSE

LOTHIAN

LAUDER-
DALE

THE
FOREST
(SELKIRK-
ETTRICK)

TEVIOTDALE

LIDDLESDALE

NORTHUMBERLAND

ESKDALE

ANNANDALE

NITHSDALE

SOLWAY FIRTH

CUMBERLAND

E N

MENTEITH

CLYDESDALE

LENNOX

CUNNINGHAM

KYLE

CARRICK

GALLOWAY

Gaelic
speaking

English
speaking

ISLE OF MAN

COWAL

BUTE

FIRTH OF CLYDE

KNAPDALE

ARRAN

KINTYRE

COLONSAY

ISLA

THE LORDSHIP O

FIRTH OF

Rathlin

GLENS
OF
ANTRIM

THE
ROUTE

EARLDOM
OF
ULSTER

I R E L A N D

INNISHOWEN

Land over 600ft.

miles   30

km   50

N

Norse speaking

ORKNEY

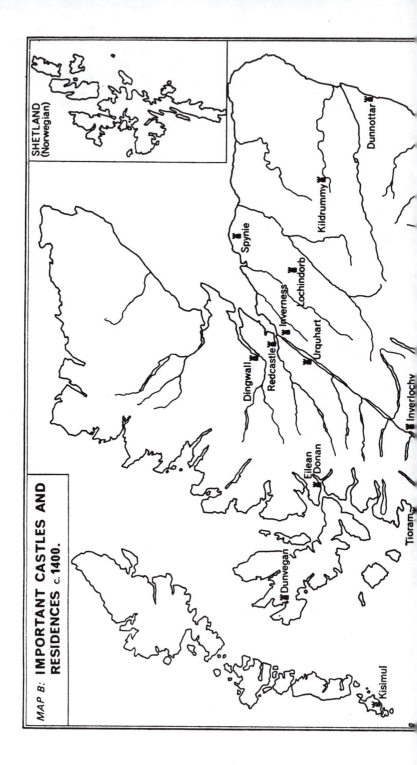

MAP B: **IMPORTANT CASTLES AND RESIDENCES** c. 1400.

SHETLAND
(Norwegian)

Dunnottar

Kildrummy

Spynie

Lochindorb

Inverness

Urquhart

Dingwall

Redcastle

Inverlochy

Eilean
Donan

Tioram

Dunvegan

Kisimul

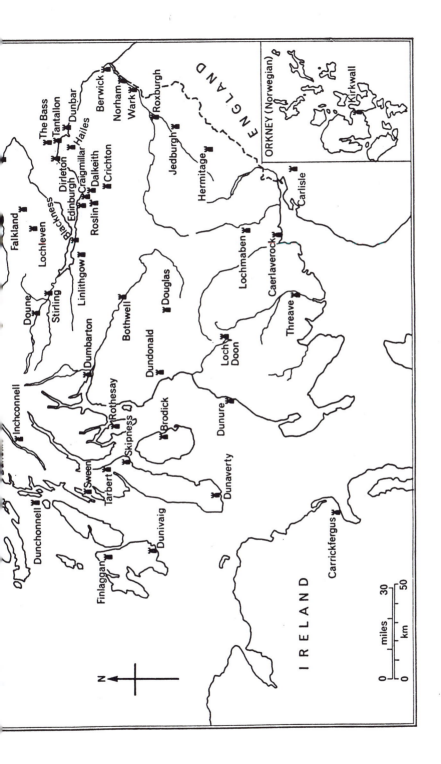

ORKNEY (Norwegian)

Kirkwall

ENGLAND

Berwick
Norham
Wark
Roxburgh
Dunbar
Tantallon
The Bass
Hailes
Dirleton
Craigmillar
Edinburgh
Dalkeith
Roslin
Crichton
Jedburgh
Hermitage
Carlisle
Blackness
Falkland
Lochleven
Linlithgow
Doune
Stirling
Dumbarton
Bothwell
Douglas
Dundonald
Lochmaben
Caerlaverock
Threave
Loch Doon
Inchconnell
Rothesay
Skipness
Brodick
Dunure
Sween
Tarbert
Dunaverty
Dunchonnell
Dunivaig
Finlaggan
Carrickfergus

IRELAND

N

0   miles   30
0   km   50

Inverness

Elgin Banff

Aberdeen

Brechin
Forfar Montrose
Dunkeld Dundee Arbroath
Perth St.Andrews
Cupar Crail
Dunfermline
Stirling Kinghorn
Inverkeithing N. Berwick
Dumbarton Linlithgow Dunbar
Rothesay Glasgow Edinburgh Haddington
Rutherglen
Peebles Berwick
Irvine Lanark (English occupied)
Ayr

Dumfries
Wigtown Kirkcudbright

I R E L A N D E N G L A N D

N

0 miles 50
0 km 100

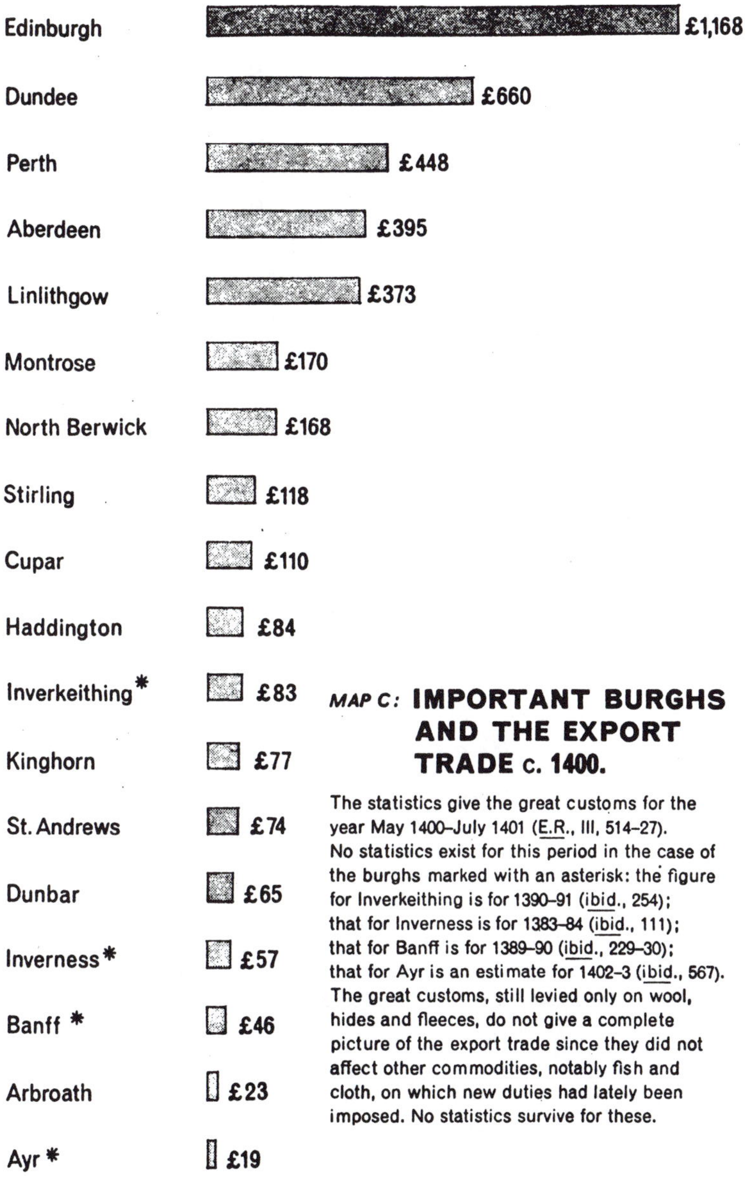

Burgh	Great customs
Edinburgh	£1,168
Dundee	£660
Perth	£448
Aberdeen	£395
Linlithgow	£373
Montrose	£170
North Berwick	£168
Stirling	£118
Cupar	£110
Haddington	£84
Inverkeithing *	£83
Kinghorn	£77
St. Andrews	£74
Dunbar	£65
Inverness *	£57
Banff *	£46
Arbroath	£23
Ayr *	£19

MAP C: **IMPORTANT BURGHS AND THE EXPORT TRADE c. 1400.**

The statistics give the great customs for the year May 1400–July 1401 (E.R., III, 514–27). No statistics exist for this period in the case of the burghs marked with an asterisk: the figure for Inverkeithing is for 1390–91 (ibid., 254); that for Inverness is for 1383–84 (ibid., 111); that for Banff is for 1389–90 (ibid., 229–30); that for Ayr is an estimate for 1402–3 (ibid., 567). The great customs, still levied only on wool, hides and fleeces, do not give a complete picture of the export trade since they did not affect other commodities, notably fish and cloth, on which new duties had lately been imposed. No statistics survive for these.

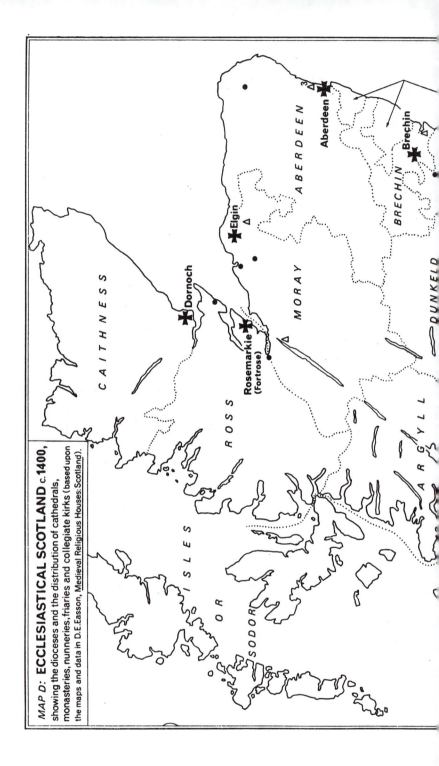

MAP D: **ECCLESIASTICAL SCOTLAND** c.1400, showing the dioceses and the distribution of cathedrals, monasteries, nunneries, friaries and collegiate kirks (based upon the maps and data in D.E.Easson, Medieval Religious Houses: Scotland).

CAITHNESS

Dornoch

Rosemarkie (Fortrose)

Elgin

Dunkeld

Aberdeen

Brechin

ABERDEEN

BRECHIN

MORAY

ROSS

ISLES

OR

SODOR

ARGYLL

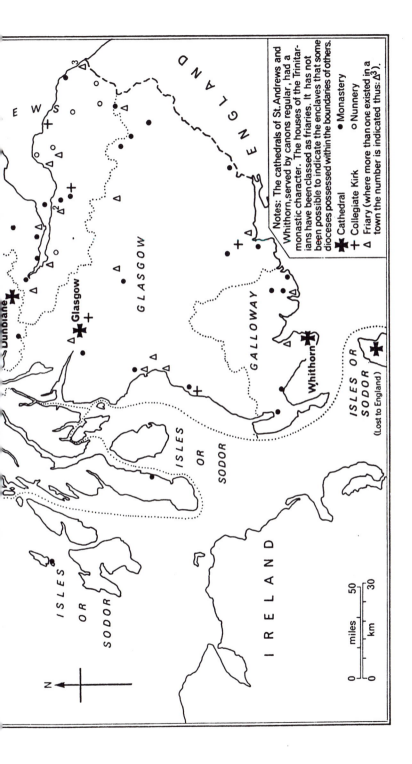

Notes: The cathedrals of St. Andrews and Whithorn, served by canons regular, had a monastic character. The houses of the Trinitarians have been classed as friaries. It has not been possible to indicate the enclaves that some dioceses possessed within the boundaries of others.

✠ Cathedral
✙ Collegiate Kirk
△ Friary (where more than one existed in a town the number is indicated thus: $\triangle^3$).

● Monastery
○ Nunnery

ENGLAND

IRELAND

GLASGOW

GALLOWAY

Dunblane

Glasgow

Whithorn

ISLES OR SODOR
(Lost to England)

ISLES OR SODOR

ISLES OR SODOR

N

miles 0 ... 50
km 0 ... 30

GENEALOGICAL TABLE A: THE ROYAL SUCCESSION 1286–1329

NOTES: Names in capital letters are those of persons who figured in the Great Cause, 1291–92. Persons and dates of minor relevance have been omitted.

E. Earl
d. died
o.s.p. died without offspring
= married

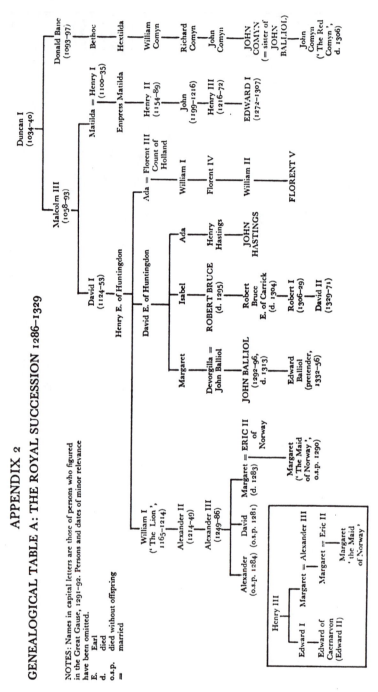

APPENDIX 2

GENEALOGICAL TABLE B: THE ROYAL HOUSE 1329–1437

NOTES: Persons and dates of minor relevance have been omitted.

D.   Duke
E.   Earl
L.   Lord
d.   died
o.s.p.   died without offspring
=   married
~~~   illegitimate descent

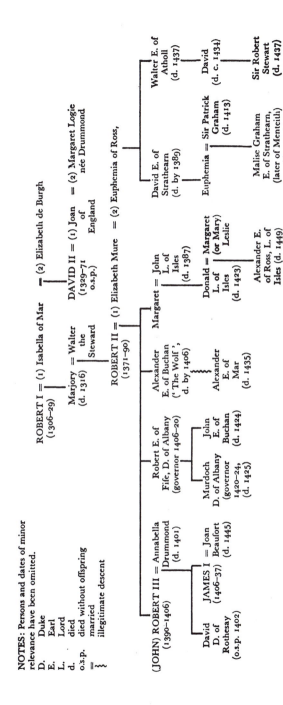

ROBERT I = (1) Isabella of Mar
(1306–29) = (2) Elizabeth de Burgh

Marjory = Walter the Steward
(d. 1316)

DAVID II = (1) Joan of England = (2) Margaret Logie née Drummond
(1329–71 o.s.p.)

ROBERT II = (1) Elizabeth Mure = (2) Euphemia of Ross,
(1371–90)

Walter E. of Atholl (d. 1437)

David (d. c. 1434)

Sir Robert Stewart (d. 1437)

David E. of Strathearn (d. by 1389)

Euphemia = Sir Patrick Graham (d. 1413)

Malise Graham E. of Strathearn, (later of Menteith) (d. 1490)

Margaret = John L. of Isles (d. 1387)

Donald = Margaret (or Mary) Leslie, L. of Isles (d. 1423)

Alexander E. of Ross, L. of Isles (d. 1449)

Alexander E. of Buchan ('The Wolf', d. by 1406)

Alexander E. of Mar (d. 1435)

Robert E. of Fife, D. of Albany (governor 1406–20)

Murdoch D. of Albany (governor 1420–24, (d. 1425)

John E. of Buchan (d. 1424)

(JOHN) ROBERT III = Annabella Drummond (d. 1401)
(1390–1406)

JAMES I = Joan Beaufort (d. 1445)
(1406–37)

David D. of Rothesay (o.s.p. 1402)

APPENDIX 2

GENEALOGICAL TABLE C: THE ROYAL HOUSE 1437–1513

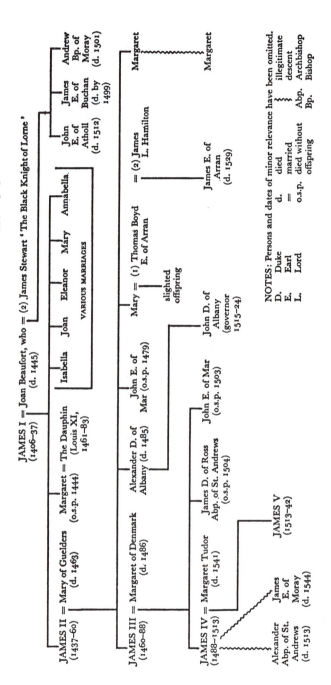

APPENDIX 2

GENEALOGICAL TABLE D: THE HOUSES OF DOUGLAS AND ANGUS 1298–1513

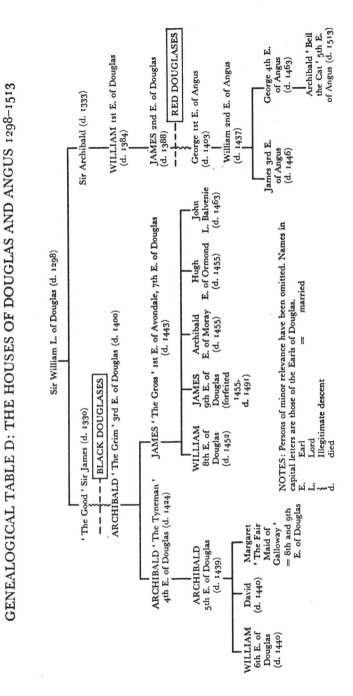

Sir William L. of Douglas (d. 1298)

Sir Archibald (d. 1333)

WILLIAM 1st E. of Douglas (d. 1384)

JAMES 2nd E. of Douglas (d. 1388)

RED DOUGLASES

George 1st E. of Angus (d. 1403)

William 2nd E. of Angus (d. 1437)

James 3rd E. of Angus (d. 1446)

George 4th E. of Angus (d. 1463)

Archibald 'Bell the Cat', 5th E. of Angus (d. 1513)

'The Good' Sir James (d. 1330)

BLACK DOUGLASES

ARCHIBALD 'The Grim', 3rd E. of Douglas (d. 1400)

JAMES 'The Gross', 1st E. of Avondale, 7th E. of Douglas (d. 1443)

ARCHIBALD 'The Tyneman', 4th E. of Douglas (d. 1424)

ARCHIBALD 5th E. of Douglas (d. 1439)

WILLIAM 8th E. of Douglas (d. 1452)

JAMES 9th E. of Douglas (forfeited 1455, d. 1491)

Archibald E. of Moray (d. 1455)

Hugh E. of Ormond (d. 1455)

John L. Balvenie (d. 1463)

David (d. 1440)

Margaret 'The Fair Maid of Galloway' = 8th and 9th E. of Douglas

WILLIAM 6th E. of Douglas (d. 1440)

NOTES: Persons of minor relevance have been omitted. Names in capital letters are those of the Earls of Douglas.

E.   Earl
L.   Lord
 =   married
⌇⌇   Illegitimate descent
d.   died

APPENDIX 2

GENEALOGICAL TABLE E:
THE LORDS OF THE ISLES 1164–1545

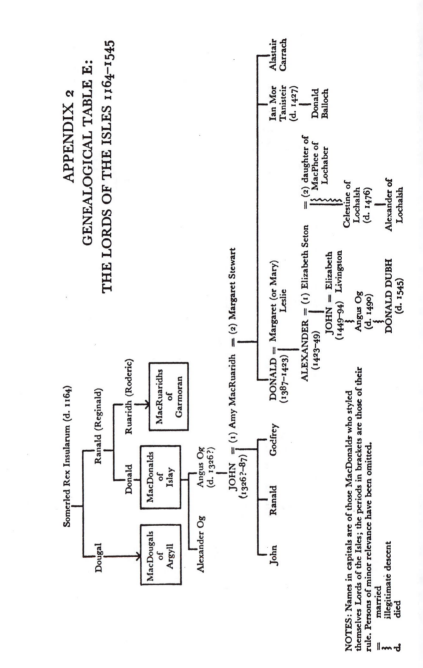

NOTES: Names in capitals are of those MacDonalds who styled themselves Lords of the Isles; the periods in brackets are those of their rule. Persons of minor relevance have been omitted.

= married
〰 illegitimate descent
d. died

BIBLIOGRAPHY

The more specialised books and articles cited in footnotes are in general omitted from the Bibliography. The place of publication is not given except for older and rarer books. Neither date nor place is given for publications of clubs and societies. A list of the abbreviations used in this volume is printed on pp. ix–xvi.

I. GUIDES AND WORKS OF REFERENCE

(a) Guides to Sources

Thanks to the historiographical prominence of Scottish clubs and societies, C. S. Terry, *Catalogue of the Publications of Scottish Historical and kindred Clubs and Societies . . . 1780–1908* (1909) and its continuation to 1927 by C. Matheson (1928) are indispensable. They are supplemented by the *Handlist of Scottish and Welsh Record Publications* by P. Gouldesbrough, A. P. Kup and I. Lewis (Brit. Records Assoc., 1954) and by the official list of government publications in *British National Archives* (H.M.S.O.). M. Livingstone, *A Guide to the Public Records of Scotland* (1905), lists the original records in H.M. Register House, Edinburgh. These are described by J. M. Thomson, *The Public Records of Scotland* (1922). Lists of accessions to the Register House since 1905 are in *S.H.R.* from VOL. XXVI. As a key to the valuable material in the *Historical MSS. Commission Reports*, C. S. Terry, *An Index to the Papers Relating to Scotland* (1908), is no substitute for the indexes to the individual reports. The fullest lists of books are to be found in A. Mitchell and C. G. Cash, *Contribution to the Bibliography of Scottish Topography* (S.H.S.), of which VOL. I is arranged topographically and VOL. II topically; there is a continuation in P. Hancock, *A Bibliography of Books on Scotland, 1916–50* (1960).

Among specialised guides, *Sources and Literature of Scots Law* (Stair Soc.) has much wider scope than its title suggests. Scottish cartularies, with one or two notable exceptions, are listed in G. R. C. Davis, *Medieval Cartularies of Great Britain* (1958). W. R. Scott, *Scottish Economic Literature to 1800* (1911), is continued and supplemented in three articles on the bibliography of Scottish economic history by W. H. Marwick in *Econ. Hist. Rev.*, III. 117–37, 2nd Ser., IV. 376–82 and XVI. 147–54. A related field is covered by G. Donaldson, 'Sources for Scottish agrarian history before the eighteenth century', *Agricultural Hist. Rev.*, VIII. 82–90. H. R. G. Inglis, J. Matheson and C. B. B. Watson provide a guide to *The Early Maps of Scotland* (2nd edn., 1936).

(b) Aids to Study (Biographical)

Scottish biographical information is well represented in the *Dictionary of National Biography*, ed. Sir Leslie Stephen and Sir Sidney Lee (2nd edn., 22 vols., 1959–60), but use should also be made of Robert Chambers, *Biographical Dictionary of Eminent Scotsmen* (3 vols., 1868–70, and other edns.). The *Handbook of British Chronology* (Royal Hist. Soc., 2nd edn.) gives lists of kings, officers of state, bishops, dukes, marquesses and earls. Fuller details of the royal family, together with short notes upon the more dramatic events in each reign, are given in A. H. Dunbar, *Scottish Kings: A Revised Chronology of Scottish History* (2nd edn., 1906). The *Scots Peerage* by J. Balfour Paul (9 vols., 1904–14) deals similarly with the noble families and is replete with genealogical data. It may be supplemented with the help of Margaret Stuart, *Scottish Family History: A Guide to Works of Reference on the History and Genealogy of Scottish Families* (1930); the slighter, but more up-to-date *Scottish Family Histories* (1960) of J. P. S. Ferguson; and George F. Black, *The Surnames of Scotland* (1946). The holders of specific offices are dealt with in G. W. T. Omond, *The Lord Advocates of Scotland* (2 vols., 1883); S. Cowan, *The Lord Chancellors of Scotland* (2 vols., 1911); and J. Herkless and R. K. Hannay, *The Archbishops of St Andrews* (5 vols., 1907–1915). Details of the episcopate as a whole are given in J. Dowden, *The Bishops of Scotland* (1912). The bishops, together with other ecclesiastical dignitaries (but not, save incidentally, members of the monastic and mendicant orders) are conveniently listed in D. E. R. Watt, *Fasti Ecclesiae Scoticanae Medii Aevi* (1969), an invaluable reference work. Lists of the graduates of the three medieval universities are given in *The Early Records of the University of St Andrews* (S.H.S.); *Munimenta Alme Universitatis Glasguensis* (Maitland Club); and *Officers and Graduates of the University and King's College, Aberdeen* (New Spalding Club). Merchants and craftsmen are represented in the *Roll of Edinburgh Burgesses and Guild Brethren, 1406–1700* (Scot. Rec. Soc.).

(c) Aids to Study (Topographical)

The most useful topographical guide is F. H. Groome, *Ordnance Gazetteer of Scotland* (1882–85 and later edns.). Several important works on various subjects are arranged topographically, notably the *Reports* of the Royal Commission on Ancient and Historical Monuments and Constructions of Scotland, which not only give plans of the major medieval buildings but indications of their history. Ian B. Cowan in his outstanding *Parishes of Medieval Scotland* (Scot. Rec. Soc.) lists each parish in alphabetical order and summarises its ecclesiastical history. A useful appendix shows the pattern of appropriation. Lists of burghs of the king, burghs not dependent on the king, and burghs of barony and regality, together with short notes on changes of status, are compiled in G. S. Pryde, *The Burghs of Scotland: A Critical List* (1965). Statistics relating to the establishment, organisation, and relative wealth, of houses of monks, canons, friars, collegiate kirks and hospitals, are arranged in D. E. Easson, *Medieval Religious Houses: Scotland* (1957). This valuable and impressive pioneer work may shortly be replaced by a revised version compiled by Ian B. Cowan. Archdeacon Monro's description of the Western Isles in

1549 has been so well edited by R. W. Munro in *Monro's Western Isles of Scotland and Genealogies of the Clans* (1961) as to become an indispensable guide to the topography and antiquities of the Hebrides.

(d) Aids to Study (Linguistic)

John Jamieson, *An Etymological Dictionary of the Scottish Language*, ed. John Longmuir (5 vols., 1879–87), will be superseded by W. A. Craigie, *A Dictionary of the Older Scottish Tongue* (1931–), of which the first four volumes have appeared.

(e) Aids to Study (Chronological)

A. H. Dunbar, *Scottish Kings* (p. 622 above) deals specifically with the chronology of Scottish history, but the *Handbook of Dates for Students of English History* (Royal Hist. Soc.) has a relevance that extends north of Tweed.

(f) Aids to Study (Sigillography, Heraldry and Numismatics)

These fields are dealt with in the following works: H. Laing, *Descriptive Catalogue of Impressions of Ancient Scottish Seals* (Bannatyne Club) and *Supplemental Catalogue* (1866); J. H. Stevenson and M. Wood, *Scottish Heraldic Seals* (1940); A. Nisbet, *A System of Heraldry* (1816); R. W. Cochran-Patrick, *Records of the Coinage . . . to the Union* (2 vols., 1876); E. Burns, *The Coinage of Scotland* (3 vols., 1887); I. H. Stewart, *The Scottish Coinage* (2nd edn., 1967) and 'Scottish Mints' in *Mints, Dies, and Currency*, ed. R. A. G. Carson (1971), pp. 165–289, which is particularly valuable for the period 1280–1357.

II. PRIMARY SOURCES: RECORDS

(a) Government Records

For practically the whole period the activities of central government are represented in a number of volumes in three essential compendious works: *The Acts of the Parliaments of Scotland*, ed. T. Thomson and C. Innes (12 vols., 1814–75); *Registrum Magni Sigilli Regum Scotorum: the Register of the Great Seal of Scotland*, ed. J. M. Thomson and others (11 vols., 1882–1914); *Rotuli scaccarii regum Scotorum: the Exchequer Rolls of Scotland*, ed. J. Stuart and others (23 vols., 1878–1908). The period does not yet figure in the volumes of the *Regesta Regum Scottorum, 1153–1424*, though those dealing with the *acta* of Robert I and David II may shortly appear. The above works are supplemented for the later fifteenth and early sixteenth century by *Compota thesaurariorum regum Scotorum: Accounts of the Lord High Treasurer of Scotland*, ed. T. Dickson and Sir J. Balfour Paul (1877–); *Registrum secreti sigilli regum Scotorum: the Register of the Privy Seal of Scotland*, ed. M. Livingstone and others (1908–); *The Acts of the Lords of Council in Public Affairs, 1501–1554: Selections from Acta Dominorum Concilii*, ed. R. K. Hannay (1932). Some entries in *The Register of the Privy Council*, ed. J. H. Burton and others (1877–), retrospectively refer to the period prior to 1513.

Civil justice (often involving cases with criminal overtones) is illustrated in *The Acts of the Lords Auditors of Causes and Complaints, 1466–94*, ed. T. Thomson (1839); *The Acts of the Lords of Council in Civil Causes*, ed. T. Thomson and others (1839 and 1918–); and *Acta Dominorum Concilii, 1501–3* (Stair Soc.). Records of criminal justice are printed in R. Pitcairn, *Ancient Criminal Trials in Scotland* [1488–1624] (3 vols., Bannatyne and Maitland Clubs).

Scotland's relationships with other powers are recorded, *passim*, in T. Rymer's *Foedera, Conventiones, Literae etc.* (London, 1704–35; The Hague, 1737–45; London, 1816–69). Relevant records in French archives are printed in A. Teulet, *Inventaire chronologique des documents relatifs à l'histoire de l'Ecosse conservés aux archives du royaume à Paris* (Abbotsford Club). Similar material concerning relations with Norway and Denmark is to be found in *Diplomatarium Norvegicum* (20 vols., Kristiania, 1849–1919). Records of Anglo-Scottish relations are mostly those of the English government. A basic source for practically the whole period is *Rotuli Scotiae*, ed. D. Macpherson and others (2 vols., London, 1814–19). This enrolment is the medieval equivalent of a file upon Scottish affairs maintained by the English government. A similar span of time is also covered by the collection of miscellaneous records summarised and translated in the *Calendar of Documents relating to Scotland*, ed. J. Bain (4 vols., 1881–88). This valuable work, which contains some inaccuracies, is now being revised under the supervision of the Scottish Record Office. In addition the many volumes of *Calendars* of the patent and close rolls preserved in the Public Record Office (H.M.S.O.) include miscellaneous entries relating to Scotland. An indication of the classes of record in the P.R.O. and British Museum in which unprinted material may be found is given in Ranald Nicholson, *Edward III and the Scots* (1965), pp. 258–9.

Anglo-Scottish relations during the wars of independence are particularly illustrated in the following collections: *Documents Illustrative of the History of Scotland 1286–1306*, ed. J. Stevenson (2 vols., 1870); *Documents Illustrative of Sir William Wallace* (Maitland Club); *Documents and Records Illustrating the History of Scotland*, ed. F. Palgrave (London, 1837); *Scotland in 1298*, ed. H. Gough (1888); and E. L. G. Stones, *Anglo-Scottish Relations, 1174–1328* (reprint 1970), which presents the most important documents both in the original language and in translation.

Records of the intensive diplomatic activity during the reign of James IV may be studied in *Flodden Papers* (S.H.S.), *The Letters of James IV* (S.H.S.), and *Letters and Papers, Foreign and Domestic, of the Reign of Henry VIII*, I., ed. J. S. Brewer and R. H. Brodie (1864, 1920).

(b) Ecclesiastical Records

There are no extant Scottish records precisely corresponding to the English episcopal registers: various compilations pertaining to bishoprics, religious houses or collegiate kirks are mainly collections of charters, often under the title of *Liber* or *Registrum*. Most of these have been printed by the Bannatyne Club, others by the Maitland, Abbotsford and Grampian Clubs, S.H.S. and S.B.R.S. The *Copiale Prioratus Sanctiandree*, ed. J. H. Baxter (1930), is a letter-book of Prior Haldenstone of St Andrews and contains valuable material relating to ecclesiastical and political affairs in the late fourteenth and early fifteenth century. A variety of information of judicial, liturgical, social, political and economic significance may be obtained from the following ecclesiastical records: the *St Andrews Formulare* (Stair Soc.); the *Liber Officialis Sancti Andree* (Abbotsford Club); the *Rentale Sancti Andree* (S.H.S.); the *Rentale Dunkeldense* (S.H.S.); the rental books of the diocese of Glasgow and of the abbey of Coupar-Angus (Grampian Club); the *Correspondence, Inventories, Account Rolls and Law Proceedings of the Priory of Coldingham* (Surtees Soc.); the *Breviarium Aberdonense* (Bannatyne Club) and the *Epistolare in Usum Ecclesiae Cathedralis Aberdonensis*, ed. B. McEwen (1924).

Relations between Scotland and the papacy are illustrated in the following collections of records: *Vetera Monumenta Hibernorum et Scotorum Historiam Illustrantia*, ed. A. Theiner (Rome, 1864); the *Calendar of Scottish Supplications to Rome* (3 vols., S.H.S.); the *Calendar of Entries in the Papal Registers relating to Great Britain and Ireland*, ed. W. H. Bliss and others (1893–). In addition microfilmed copies of records in the Vatican Archives (and other continental archives) are held by the Department of Scottish History, the University of Glasgow.

The extant statutes of diocesan synods and provincial councils are collected in *Concilia Scotiae: Ecclesiae Scoticanae Statuta* (Bannatyne Club), translated by David Patrick in *Statutes of the Scottish Church* (S.H.S.).

University records are represented in the following works: *Early Records of the University of St Andrews* (S.H.S.); *Acta Facultatis Artium Universitatis S. Andree, 1413–1588* (S.H.S.); *Munimenta Alme Universitatis Glasguensis* (Maitland Club); and *Fasti Aberdonenses* (Spalding Club).

(c) Burgh Records

Records of burghal law and administration are collected in *Ancient Laws and Customs of the Burghs of Scotland, 1124–1424* and *1424–1707* (S.B.R.S.) and in *Extracts from the Records of the Convention of the Royal Burghs of Scotland*, ed. J. D. Marwick (1870–90). Notable collections of burgh muniments are printed by the Spalding Club and S.H.S. (Aberdeen); by the Ayr and Wigtown Archaeological Assoc. (Ayr); by S.B.R.S. (Edinburgh, Glasgow and Peebles). In addition there are the following useful works: *Charters and Other Writs Illustrating the History of the Royal Burgh of Aberdeen*, ed. P. J. Anderson (1890); *Charters, Writs and Public Documents of the Royal Burgh of Dundee*, ed. W. Hay (1880); *Extracts from the Records of the Royal Burgh of Stirling*, ed. R. Renwick (1884).

(d) Private Muniments

Contents of private charter chests figure largely in the many family histories produced by Sir William Fraser, of which the most important is the *Douglas Book* (4 vols., 1885). Private archives are also represented in the *Reports* of the Royal Commission on Historical Manuscripts (1870–), in the publications of the Spalding and Maitland Clubs and S.R.S. The *Registrum Honoris de Morton* (Bannatyne Club) is of particular significance, as is the *Ledger of Andrew Halyburton*, ed. C. Innes (1867), which records the commercial transactions of a Scottish merchant based in the Netherlands from 1492 to 1503.

Many private collections have in recent years been deposited in the Register House (see lists of accessions in *S.H.R.*), and the National Register of Archives (Scotland) has reports on many which still remain in private custody.

(e) Miscellaneous Records

Some clubs and societies have produced collections of primary sources (both record and narrative) of miscellaneous provenance, as in the case of *Highland Papers* and *Wigtownshire Charters* (S.H.S.) and *Collections for a History of the Shires of Aberdeen and Banff* (Spalding Club). There are also occasional *Miscellany* volumes with no unifying theme, notably those of the Bannatyne Club and S.H.S. Miscellaneous records figure in the *Calendar of the Laing Charters*, ed. J. Anderson (1899). Others are reproduced in facsimile (and transcription) in *Facsimiles of the National Manuscripts of Scotland* (1867–73). The student and general reader will find comprehensive and well-chosen collections from a variety of sources in the *Source Book of Scottish History*, ed. W. Croft Dickinson, Gordon Donaldson and Isabel A. Milne (2nd edn., 3 vols., 1958, reprinted 1963), and in *Scottish Historical Documents*, ed. Gordon Donaldson (1970).

A few protocol books recording deeds drawn up by notaries public are extant for the period prior to 1513. They include those of James Darow, 1469–84 (*Scottish Antiquary*, x–xi); James Young, 1485–1515 (S.R.S.); Cuthbert Simon, 1499–1513 (Grampian Club); John Foular, 1501–28, and Gavin Ros, 1512–32 (S.R.S.).

III. PRIMARY SOURCES: NARRATIVE

(a) Chronicles

These are the chief narrative sources for the period up to the mid-fifteenth century. The few, but essential, Scottish examples are: the chronicles of John of Fordun, ed. and trans. W. F. Skene (1871–72)—discussed on pp. 277–8 above; Andrew of Wyntoun, ed. D. Laing (1872–79)—discussed on p. 278 above; Walter Bower, ed. W. Goodall (Edinburgh, 1759)—discussed on p. 278 above; and the *Auchinleck Chronicle*, ed. T. Thomson (Edinburgh, 1819, 1877)—discussed on p. 328 above. The part played by Scotland in the age of chivalry is illustrated in the works of Froissart (various edns.). Most English chronicles at least touch upon Scottish affairs. Of special importance are the *Vita Edwardi Secundi*, ed. N. Denholm-Young (1957); Thomas Walsingham's *Historia Anglicana*, ed. H. T. Riley (1863); and, above all, two northern works—the *Chronicon de Lanercost* (Maitland Club) and Sir Thomas Gray's *Scalacronica* (Maitland Club).

(b) Poetry

An essential source for the reign of Robert I is Barbour's epic poem *The Bruce* (S.T.S. and various edns.)—discussed on pp. 275–7 above. Wyntoun's *Cronykil* (already mentioned) is poetry of a sort. Blind Harry's *Wallace* (S.T.S.) presents a misleading version of the hero's career but is a pointer to opinion in the time of James III, as is also *The Thre Prestis of Peblis* (S.T.S.). Other poetical works (mostly in S.T.S. edns.) have at least some incidental value as historical sources, particularly in the case of the *Kingis Quair* and the poems of Robert Henryson and William Dunbar.

(c) Early Histories

These, though generally of dubious reliability, often contain material not found elsewhere. The anonymous *Life and Death of King James the First* (Maitland Club)—discussed on p. 286 above—presents a view of James I which differs from that of the chroniclers. John Major's remarkably shrewd *History of Greater Britain* (S.H.S.)—discussed on p. 586 above—is particularly to be valued for its sociological observations. Hector Boece's *Scotorum Historiae* (Paris, 1527), its continuation by John Ferrerius (Paris, 1574)—discussed on pp. 472, 586 above—and George Buchanan's *History of Scotland* (ed. J. Aikman, 1827–30) are humanist works: fact and fancy are artfully and inextricably intermingled; James III almost emerges as a second Tiberius. Bishop Lesley's *History* (Bannatyne Club) is more down-to-earth and makes commendable use of parliamentary records. Robert Lindsay of Pitscottie's highly-coloured and long-winded *Historie* (S.T.S.)—discussed on p. 328 above—does most to fill the gap left by the chroniclers. John Knox's *History of the Reformation* (various edns.) is a source for the history of heresy in the fifteenth century. Traditional histories of the MacDonalds (together with other miscellaneous items relating to the Highlands) are in *Highland Papers* (S.H.S.) and *Reliquiae Celticae*, ed. Alexander MacBain and John Kennedy (1892, 1894).

(d) Travellers' Tales

The impressions of Scotland recorded by foreign visitors are presented entertainingly in P. Hume Brown, *Early Travellers in Scotland* (1891). The report of Pedro de Ayala is an essential source for the reign of James IV.

IV. SECONDARY WORKS

(a) General Histories of Scotland

The histories of J. H. Burton, P. Hume Brown and Andrew Lang have served at least two generations and ought to be laid in honourable rest. P. F. Tytler's *History* (9 vols., 1828–43 and later edns.) and J. Pinkerton's *History ... from the Accession of the House of Stuart to that of Mary* (London, 1797) have appendixes of original documents, some of which are not printed elsewhere. The collections of essays by R. W. Cochran-Patrick—*Mediaeval Scotland* (1892)—and by Cosmo Innes—*Scotland in the Middle Ages* (1860) and *Sketches of Early Scotch History* (1861)—contain interesting oddities. Of the same character, though of greater calibre, is Lord Cooper's *Selected Papers, 1922–1954* (1957). In *The Scottish Nation* (B.B.C. Publications, 1972) the period is covered in four essays by notable medievalists. This useful work has appeared too recently to have influenced the present volume. Treatment of the late medieval period in Rosalind Mitchison, *History of Scotland* (1970), and T. C. Smout, *History of the Scottish People, 1560–1830* (1969), has the merits and defects of impressionist painting; the vignettes in Gordon Donaldson, *Scottish Kings* (1967), are less eye-catching but have more exactitude. Probably the only considerable general history recently written by someone whose main interest and expertise lay in medieval studies is W. Croft Dickinson, *New History of Scotland* (VOL. I, 1961). Partly topical and partly chronological in format its treatment of political and economic history is less commendable than its careful exposition of legal and constitutional developments and its lively appraisal of medieval society, particularly that of the burghs.

Modern Scottish historical scholarship is seen at its best not in works of synthesis but in the articles on a wide range of late medieval topics that appear in the learned periodicals, notably the *S.H.R.* (1903-28, 1947-). Thanks to the absence of up-to-date and large-scale general histories the neglected prefaces of the *Exchequer Rolls* and *Treasurer's Accounts* have a special importance: usually the editors follow the accepted historical view; often, when it conflicts with the records, they introduce necessary modifications.

(b) Political, Military and Diplomatic History

Among the following works those of G. W. S. Barrow, E. W. M. Balfour-Melville, G. Donaldson, A. I. Dunlop, R. L. Mackie, G. Gregory Smith and W. Stanford Reid, as well as *The Scottish Nation*, though primarily devoted to political, military and diplomatic history, also illustrate other branches of history in their respective periods.

1. *1286–1357.* The period of the wars of independence has inspired a number of works which need not be taken too seriously. One exception is E. M. Barron, *The Scottish War of Independence, A Critical Study* (2nd edn., 1934). Designedly contentious it deals in detail with the years from 1295 to 1314 and argues that the struggle for independence was maintained by 'Celtic' Scotland (somewhat loosely defined). Reaction against Celtic romanticism seems to be carried too far in G. W. S. Barrow, *Robert Bruce and the Community of the Realm of Scotland* (1965), where the importance of Lothian appears to be exaggerated, and where a new romanticism centred upon the concept of the community of the realm is certainly inspired in many readers, even if it can hardly be supposed to exist in the austere mind of the author himself. In the half of the book that covers the years between 1286 and 1306 the best possible interpretation is placed upon the sometimes dubious conduct of the future Robert I. Thanks to the recent discovery of a valuable document (see *S.H.R.*, XLIX. 46–59) the dating of the campaigns of 1307 and 1308 is subject to revision. Despite the scholarly ingenuity shown in discussions of the location of Bannockburn the conclusions seem unconvincing. The comparatively thin treatment of the years between 1314 and 1329 is emphasised by omission of a study of the Bruce invasion of Ireland, even although that event permanently affected the balance of power in medieval Britain by turning the English colony in Ireland from an asset to a liability. Nonetheless Professor Barrow's work is undoubtedly outstanding, and hence deserves the application of rigorous standards of criticism: it ought to be read in conjunction with the penetrating review article by A. A. M. Duncan (*S.H.R.*, XLV. 184–201), which, although eulogistic, suggests important modifications of interpretation.

A further few years of the wars of independence (1327–35) are covered in

Ranald Nicholson, *Edward III and the Scots* (1965), a blow-by-blow study of warfare and diplomacy. The remaining years of the wars of independence figure in J. Campbell's essay on 'England, Scotland and the Hundred Years War' in *Europe in the Late Middle Ages*, ed. J. R. Hale and others (1965). The treatment of Anglo-Scottish relations in F. M. Powicke's volume of the Oxford History of England—*The Thirteenth Century 1216-1307* (1953)—is conscientious, though the hero is neither Balliol, Wallace nor Bruce. In the subsequent volume—*The Fourteenth Century 1307-1399* (1959)—May Mc-Kisack seldom lingers north of Tweed. J. Bain, *The Edwards in Scotland, 1296-1377* (1901) may deservedly be neglected.

The importance of the relationship between Scotland and Ireland is shown in G. H. Orpen, *Ireland under the Normans*, VOL. IV (1920), in E. Curtis, *Medieval Ireland* (1938), and in Olive Armstrong, *Edward Bruce's Invasion of Ireland* (1923). J. F. Lydon in his essay in *Historical Studies IV*, ed. G. A. Hayes-McCoy (1963), and in his *Lordship of Ireland in the Later Middle Ages* (1972) stresses exploitation of Ireland as a source of troops and supplies for the campaigns of Edward I and Edward II against the Scots.

The background of the Franco-Scottish alliance of 1295 (and of the last Norwegian interventions in Scottish affairs) is outlined by Ranald Nicholson in *S.H.R.*, XXXVIII. 114-32. In *Les Préliminaires de la Guerre de Cent Ans, 1328-42*, E. Déprez pays some attention to Franco-Scottish relations.

Specialised studies include detailed works on the battle of Bannockburn (see the footnotes to pp. 87-9 above), while the recent 650th anniversary of the Declaration of Arbroath has evoked a number of publications of which the most important are Sir James Fergusson, *The Declaration of Arbroath* (1970), and an essay by A. A. M. Duncan, *The Nation of Scots and the Declaration of Arbroath* (1970), which is particularly valuable because of its sociological approach.

2. *1357-1437*. The later years of the reign of David II are the subject of articles by Bruce Webster ('David II and the Government of Fourteenth-Century Scotland', *T.R.H.S.*, 5th series, XVI. 115-30) and Ranald Nicholson ('David II, the historians and the chroniclers', *S.H.R.*, XLV. 59-78). Both attack the hitherto accepted view that David was an incompetent king under whom there was a decline in government. No detailed modern study exists of politics under Robert II and Robert III, although E. W. M. Balfour-Melville casts backward glances in *James I, King of Scots* (1936). This thorough examination of the reign of the first forceful Stewart king is arranged all too chronologically (though its attention to chronological detail is of value). It is a serviceable factual study founded upon meticulous scholarship rather than a work of interpretation. Anglo-Scottish relations are treated in a similar, though less scholarly, manner in so far as they figure in Sir James Ramsay's *Genesis of Lancaster*, 1307-99 (2 vols., 1913), and his *Lancaster and York* (2 vols., 1892). E. F. Jacob's volume in the Oxford History—*The Fifteenth Century 1399-1485* (1961)—provides (with no few slips and omissions) a background to devious Anglo-Scottish diplomacy and to the increasing interest in France shown by the Scots. This is also outlined in Francisque-Michel, *Les Ecossais en France, les Français en Ecosse* (1862), which may be supplemented by W. Forbes Leith, *The Scots Men-at-arms and Lifeguards in France* (2 vols., 1882), and Louis A. Barbé, *Margaret of Scotland and the Dauphin Louis* (1917).

3. *1437–1488*. Apart from the relevant chapters in *The Scottish Nation* and G. Donaldson, *Scottish Kings*, this period, characterised by strife between new monarchy and old baronage, has elicited only one notable work: Annie I. Dunlop, *The Life and Times of James Kennedy, Bishop of St Andrews* (1950). Despite the clerical character of the hero this book devotes at least as much attention to the politics of the years between 1437 and 1465 as to ecclesiastical affairs. If the author is perhaps mistaken in believing that her bishop moved unsullied through the political morass she has at least shown remarkable skill in describing each feature of the morass and the ways in which its victims were engulfed. Her understanding of fifteenth-century Scotland is unsurpassed, and her work, though not well arranged, and hardly easy reading, reaches the heights of scholarship and will long remain indispensable.

The growing importance of connections between Scotland and Denmark is shown in a number of recent articles (see notes to pp. 413–4, 555 above). Agnes Conway in *Henry VII's Relations with Scotland and Ireland, 1485–1498* (1932) provides an extremely helpful monograph on the particularly complex diplomacy that accompanied the fall of James III and the rise of James IV.

4. *1488–1513*. The accounts of the reign of James IV given by Eric Stair-Kerr and I. A. Taylor are superseded by R. L. Mackie in *King James IV of Scotland* (1958). This vivid and eminently readable work displays a thorough scholarship, sparingly employed, however, in those fields of legal, constitutional and economic history, which, if too assiduously cultivated, bring diminishing returns in readability. Perhaps as a result the interpretation of the personality of James IV seems to lack depth. The view that the king wanted war in 1513 is particularly open to question. James IV's hard-headed exploitation of developments affecting landholding is studied by Ranald Nicholson in 'Feudal Developments in Late Medieval Scotland', *Juridical Review*, April 1973, pt. i 1–21. G. Gregory Smith in *The Days of James IV* (1890) uses extracts from a variety of sources to illustrate the reign. Extra-sensory perception is employed by A. J. Stewart in *Falcon: The Autobiography of His Grace James the 4 King of Scots* (1971).

The account of Anglo-Scottish relations in the Oxford History by J. D. Mackie—*The Earlier Tudors, 1485–1558* (1952)—benefits from the expertise of a scholar well acquainted with the Scottish background who has also contributed to studies of the Flodden campaign. A likely explanation of the disaster is given by W. M. Mackenzie in *The Secret of Flodden* (1931). The naval activity of the period is illustrated in W. Stanford Reid, *Skipper from Leith: the History of Robert Barton of Over Barnton* (1962).

(c) Legal and Constitutional History

James Mackinnon's *Constitutional History of Scotland from Early Times to the Reformation* (1924)—a clear and sensible work which, however, says remarkably little concerning parliament—had the misfortune to be overshadowed by the virtually simultaneous publication of R. S. Rait's *Parliaments of Scotland* (1924). The latter work gives a thorough treatment of all aspects of parliament and related assemblies. Topical in arrangement it fails to convey an overall impression of development—save perhaps that the Scottish parliament was somehow doomed to an inglorious end. It is extremely valuable as a factual study, less so as a work of interpretation. Some of Rait's misconceptions are corrected in A. A. M. Duncan, 'The early parliaments of Scotland', *S.H.R.*, XLV. 36–58.

Studies of the evolution of Scots law and the multiplicity of courts are conveniently summarised in the *Introduction to Scottish Legal History* (Stair Soc.). W. Croft Dickinson's indispensable trilogy—*The Sheriff Court Book of Fife* (S.H.S.), *The Court Book of the Barony of Carnwath* (S.H.S.), and *Early Records of the Burgh of Aberdeen* (S.H.S.)—has earned distinction not so much on account of the records edited but rather by reason of the introductions, which thoroughly describe the courts through which local government was conducted.

More specialised studies include Ian D. Willock, *Origins and Development of the Jury in Scotland* (Stair Soc.); R. K. Hannay, *The College of Justice* (1933); George Neilson, *Trial by Combat* (1890); *The Register of Brieves* (Stair Soc.); A. A. M. Duncan, 'Regiam Majestatem: a reconsideration', *Juridical Review*, N.S., VI. 199–217; and Ranald Nicholson, *op. cit., ibid.,* April 1973, pt. i. 1–21.

The type of law which may be presumed to have existed in the Isles is briefly examined in Mackinnon's *Constitutional History*, and, at greater length, in John Cameron, *Celtic Law* (1937).

(d) Social History

The fullest general survey is C. Rogers, *Social Life in Scotland from Early to Recent Times* (3 vols., Grampian Club). I. F. Grant, *The Social and Economic Development of Scotland before 1603* (1930), shows insight into the characteristics of Scottish society in its rural and clannish setting. James Mackinnon's curiously named *Social and Industrial History of Scotland* (1920) is little more than a brief general history.

Specialised studies include John Warrack, *Domestic Life in Scotland, 1488–1688: A Sketch of the Development of Furniture and Household Usage* (1920); S. Maxwell and R. Hutchison, *Scottish Costume* (1958) and J. T. Dunbar, *History of Highland Dress* (1962).

(e) Economic History

I. F. Grant's work (see above) is less commendable for its treatment of economic history than for its treatment of social history. In the absence of an authoritative general survey the economic history of the period is best learnt from the prefaces to the *Exchequer Rolls* and *Treasurer's Accounts*. One aspect, agrarian history, receives terse treatment in T. B. Franklin, *A History of Scottish Farming* (1952). Another, the organisation of overseas trade through the staple, has mysteriously elicited two impressive works—J. Davidson and A. Gray, *The Scottish Staple at Veere* (1909) and M. P. Rooseboom, *The Scottish Staple in the Netherlands* (1910). Trading connections and Scottish settlement in Germany and the Baltic region are less impressively described by T. A. Fischer in *The Scots in Germany* (1902), *The Scots in Eastern and Western Prussia and Hinterland* (1903), and *The Scots in Sweden* (1907).

(f) Burgh History

A useful general history of this subject is given in W. M. Mackenzie, *The Scottish Burghs* (1949), which may be supplemented by W. Croft Dickinson's introduction to *Early Records of the Burgh of Aberdeen* (S.H.S.). In the introduction to the *Court Book of the Burgh of Kirkintilloch* (S.H.S.), G. S. Pryde discusses the characteristics of burghs of barony in the medieval period. The representative assemblies of the burghs are treated in Theodora Pagan, *The Convention of the Royal Burghs* (1926) and, together with the role of the burgesses in parliament, in J. D. Mackie and G. S. Pryde, *The Estate of Burgesses in the Scots Parliament and its relation to the Convention of the Royal Burghs* (1923).

Among the many works dealing with the history of particular burghs some which deserve mention are A. M. Munro, *Memorials of the . . . Aldermen, Provosts and Lord Provosts of Aberdeen, 1272–1895* (1897); Samuel Cowan, *The Ancient Capital of Scotland* [Perth] (2 vols., 1904); Robert Renwick and Sir John Lindsay, *History of Glasgow* (VOL. I, 1921); and David Robertson and Marguerite Wood, *Castle and Town: Chapters in the History of the Royal Burgh of Edinburgh* (1928). Aspects of the history of Edinburgh are also treated in the publications of the Old Edinburgh Club (1908–).

(g) Ecclesiastical History

Ian B. Cowan's *Parishes* (p. 622 above), D. E. Easson's *Religious Houses* (p. 622 above), D. E. R. Watt's *Fasti* (p. 622 above) and John Dowden's *Bishops* (p. 622 above) conveniently provide essential data.

The general history of the medieval kirk is dealt with at length in A. Bellesheim, *History of the Catholic Church in Scotland* (4 vols., 1887–90); John Cunningham, *The Church History of Scotland* (2 vols., 1882); A. R. MacEwen, *A History of the Church in Scotland* (2 vols., 1913, 1918); and John Dowden, *The Mediaeval Church in Scotland* (1910).

Important aspects of developments on the continent figure in T. S. R. Boase, *Boniface VIII* (1933); G. Mollat, *The Popes at Avignon* (English translation, 1949); Walter Ullmann, *The Origins of the Great Schism* (1948); and John Holland Smith, *The Great Schism* (1970). 'The Conciliarist Tradition in Scotland' is traced by J. H. Burns in *S.H.R.*, XLII. 89–104 and in *Scottish Churchmen and the Council of Basle* (1962), which lists some sixty Scots who were associated with the council. Financial relationships with the papacy are authoritatively explained in the introduction to *The Apostolic Camera and Scottish Benefices*, ed. A. I. Cameron (1934), and their political effects are summarised in R. K. Hannay's essay on 'The Scottish Crown and the Papacy' (Hist. Assoc. of Scotland).

Works on the episcopate include the turgid *Archbishops of St Andrews* of J. Herkless and R. K. Hannay (5 vols., 1907–15); Annie I. Dunlop's *James Kennedy* (see p. 630 above); John Durkan's succinct, but illuminating, *William Turnbull, Bishop of Glasgow* (1951); and Leslie J. Macfarlane, 'William Elphinstone, Founder of the University of Aberdeen' (*Aberdeen University Review*, XXXIX. 1–18)—the forerunner to a substantial biography which may shortly appear.

Various aspects of monastic life are somewhat critically surveyed in G. G. Coulton, *Scottish Abbeys and Social Life* (1933). One of the mendicant orders is well represented in W. Moir Bryce, *The Scottish Greyfriars* (2 vols., 1909). Articles of special importance are: Ian B. Cowan, 'The development of the parochial system in medieval Scotland' in *S.H.R.*, XL. 43–55 and 'Some Aspects of the Appropriation of Parish Churches in Medieval Scotland' in *Scot. Church Hist. Soc. Recs.*, XIII. 203–22; D. E. Easson, 'The Collegiate Churches of Scotland' (*ibid.*, VI. 193–215; VII. 30–47); A. I. Dunlop, 'Remissions and Indulgences in Fifteenth-Century Scotland' (*ibid.*, XV. 153–67); and Donald E. R. Watt, 'University Graduates in Scottish Benefices before 1410' (*ibid.*, XV. 77–88).

Two notable periodicals—the *Records of the Scottish Church History Society* (1923–) and the *Innes Review* (1950–)—are mainly devoted to ecclesiastical history.

(h) Cultural and Intellectual History

There are two works of a general nature: W. G. Blaikie Murdoch, *The Royal Stuarts in their Connection with Art and Letters* (1908); and, more important, John Durkan, 'The Cultural Background in Sixteenth-Century Scotland' in *Innes Review*, X. 382–439.

1. *Art.* Ian Finlay has produced useful studies in *Art in Scotland* (1948), *Scottish Crafts* (1948), and *Scottish Gold and Silver Work* (1956). These may be supplemented by James S. Richardson, *The Medieval Stone Carver in Scotland* (1964), and David McRoberts, 'Notes on Scoto-Flemish Artistic Contacts', *Innes Review*, X. 91–6.

2. *Architecture.* The standard works are D. MacGibbon and T. Ross, *Castellated and Domestic Architecture of Scotland* (5 vols., 1887–92), and *Ecclesiastical Architecture of Scotland* (3 vols., 1896–97). Two expert modern works are Stewart Cruden, *The Scottish Castle* (1960), and John G. Dunbar, *The Historic Architecture of Scotland* (1966). Nigel Tranter, *The Fortified House in Scotland* (5 vols., 1962–70), is more popular in character. In W. M. Mackenzie, *The Mediaeval Castle in Scotland* (1927), the stress is less architectural than social. The *Reports* and *Inventories*, county by county, published by the Royal Commission on Ancient and Historical Monuments are authoritative.

3. *Music.* The standard work is H. G. Farmer, *A History of Music in Scotland* (1947).

4. *Literature.* Useful accounts of Scottish Lowland Literature are to be found in the volumes of the *Oxford History of English Literature*. A lively but hardly comprehensive survey is given in Kurt Wittig, *The Scottish Tradition in Literature* (1958); more restrained accounts are to be found in T. F. Henderson, *Scottish Vernacular Literature* (1898), J. H. Millar, *A Literary History of Scotland* (1903), and A. M. Kinghorn, *The Middle Scots Poets* (1970). R. L. Mackie provides an interesting summary of the makars in his *James IV* (1958), pp. 171–87. Studies of individual authors (mainly poets) will be found in the introductions to the numerous S.T.S. editions. Two important works are J. W. Baxter, *William Dunbar: A Biographical Study* (1952), and John MacQueen, *Robert Henryson: A Study of the Major Narrative Poems* (1967), which has

a wider cultural and historical relevance than the title suggests. J. H. Delargy in his review (*S.H.R.*, XLI. 144–8) of John G. McKay's *More West Highland Tales* (1960) gives a guide to works on Gaelic prose narratives. General surveys of Gaelic literature include N. MacNeill, *The Literature of the Highlanders* (1892, 1929); M. Maclean, *The Literature of the Celts* (1902, 1926) and *The Literature of the Highlands* (1904, 1925).

5. *Libraries and Printing.* The standard works are John Durkan and Anthony Ross, *Early Scottish Libraries* (1961), and H. G. Aldis, *A List of Books printed in Scotland before 1700* (reprint, 1971).

6. *Scholarship.* A. Fleming, *The Medieval Scots Scholar in France* (1952), is hardly an impressive work; and W. Forbes Leith, *Pre-Reformation Scholars in Scotland in the Sixteenth Century* (1915), is little more than a catalogue. Duns Scotus is prominent enough to figure in many works on the history of philosophy. John Major and John Ireland are treated in a number of articles (see notes to pp. 585–6 above). Gaelic scholarship is outlined by D. S. Thomson in 'Gaelic learned orders and literati in medieval Scotland' in *Scottish Studies* XII., 57–78. In a seminal article John Durkan examines 'The Beginnings of Humanism in Scotland' (*Innes Review*, IV. 5–24).

7. *Education.* The standard work on schools, J. Grant, *History of the Burgh and Parish Schools of Scotland* (1876), requires to be supplemented by D. E. Easson's 'The Medieval Church in Scotland and Education' in *Scot. Church Hist. Soc. Recs.* VI. 13–26 and John Durkan's 'Education in the Century of the Reformation' in *Essays on the Scottish Reformation, 1513–1625*, ed. David MacRoberts (1962).

Hastings Rashdall's standard work, *The Universities of Europe in the Middle Ages* (3 vols., 1964), gives due place to the Scottish universities. The three medieval universities are also the subject of the following works: J. M. Anderson, *The University of St Andrews* (1878, 1883); R. G. Cant, *The University of St Andrews* (1946)—both of which may be supplemented by Annie I. Dunlop's helpful introduction to *Acta Facultatis Artium Universitatis S. Andree, 1413–1588* (2 vols., S.H.S.); J. D. Mackie, *The University of Glasgow, 1451–1951* (1954); and R. S. Rait, *The Universities of Aberdeen* (1895).

(i) Regional and Local History

A pertinent study of this branch of history is B. C. Skinner, 'Local history in Scotland: a comment on its status and some recent writing' in *S.H.R.*, XLVII. 160–7. Works dealing with local history are too numerous to mention. The best are usually produced under the auspices of a publishing society, such as the Dumfriesshire and Galloway Natural History and Antiquarian Society (1862–) or the East Lothian Antiquarian and Field Naturalists' Society (1924–). Detailed information is available in the works of A. Mitchell and C. G. Cash, P. Hancock, C. S. Terry, and C. Matheson (see p. 621 above). The following two regions, however, require special mention:

1. *The Borders.* George Ridpath's *Border-history of England and Scotland* (1776) has hardly been superseded. A more readable work is W. R. Kermack, *The Scottish Borders (with Galloway) to 1603* (1967). Thomas I. Rae's excellent *Administration of the Scottish Frontier, 1513–1603* (1966) casts consider-

able light on the earlier period. Denys Hay examines 'Booty in Border Warfare' in *Dumfriesshire Trans.*, XXXI. 145–66.

2. *The Highlands and Isles.* There are few books which deal with this important area other than by way of clan or family histories. Notable exceptions are: W. R. Kermack, *The Scottish Highlands* (1957)—invaluable but all too concise; W. C. Mackenzie, *The Highlands and Isles of Scotland* (1949)—of great value for the sixteenth century, less so for the Middle Ages; and Donald Gregory's rather outmoded *History of the Western Highlands and Isles* (2nd edn., 1881). The introduction, appendices and notes to *Monro's Western Isles of Scotland and Genealogies of the Clans, 1549*, ed. R. W. Munro (1961) comprise an indispensable study of the lordship of the Isles, the downfall of which is portrayed in I. F. Grant, *Angus Og of the Isles* (1969), a work in which facts are supplemented by imaginative improvisations. The relationship between Highlanders and Lowlanders is outlined in Ranald Nicholson, 'Medieval Scotland: One State, Two Cultures' in *Studies in Medieval Culture* IV. (to appear shortly).

(j) Clan and Family Histories

Thanks to the remarkable Scottish propensity for genealogical exhibitionism such works dominate Scottish historiography in number, if not in quality. Guides to this extensive literature are given by J. Balfour Paul, J. P. S. Ferguson, Margaret Stuart and George F. Black (p. 622 above). Some of the best works are those produced by Sir William Fraser, which comprise both edited family records and narrative history. One classic work is still of value—David Hume of Godscroft, *The History of the Houses of Douglas and Angus* (Edinburgh, 1644).

INDEX

Arran, 74, 132, 361, 362, 421, 481, Earls of, *see* Boyd, Thomas *and* Hamilton, James.

Arras, congress of, 290, 297.

Array, commissioners of (English), 48.

Art, 577–8.

Artevelde, Jacques van, 139.

Arthur, King, 104, 276, 574.

'Articles', *and* Committee of the, *and* Lords of the, *see* Parliament, Committees of, of the Articles.

Artillery, 195–6, 292, 370, 372–3, 395, 396, 399, 475–6, 483, 492, 497, 498, 576, 592, 600, 602, 604; naval, 543, 545, 546, 599; *see also* Bombards, Engines of War, 'Mons Meg'.

Arundel, Earl of, *see* Fitzalan, Richard.

Asnières-sur-Oise, truce of, 63, 65.

Assessments (for taxation), 164, 165, 175, 176, 178, 283 *and n*, 453. Commissions and commissioners of, of crown lands, 378, 456, 459, 531–2, 538, 543, 544, 546, 559–60, 570.

Assizes, 18, 190, 210, 287, 310, 312, 419, 427, 429, 495.

Assythment, 210.

Astrology, Astronomy, 465.

Athilmer, John, 333.

Atholl, earldom of, 125, 144, 187, 232, 351, 376. Earls of, *see* Strathbogie, John *and* David of; Douglas, Sir William, of Lothian; Stewart, Robert, Walter *and* John.

Athy, Sir John of, 94–5.

Auchinleck Chronicle, 328.

Auditors, of the Great Cause, 38, 40; of Causes and Complaints, *see* Parliament, Committees of, of Causes and Complaints; of Exchequer, *see* Exchequer, auditors of; of Falsed Dooms, *see* Parliament, Committees of, of Falsed Dooms.

Augustinian Order, 12, 298–9.

Auvergne and Bouillon, Count of, 487.

Avignon, 157, 182–3, 237; *curia* at, 103, 150–2, 190–3; peace conference at (1344), 145. University of, 238, 242.

Avoch Castle, 54, 127, 137.

Avon, River, 332.

Avondale, 369, 375. Earldom of, 357n. Earls of, *see* Douglas, James, William *and* James, 7th, 8th and 9th Earls of Douglas. Lord, *see* Stewart, Andrew.

Ayala, Pedro de, his mission to Scotland, 551–2.

Ayr, 143, 263–4, 361, 419, 495, 552, 600; parliament or council at (1315), 92, 123; merchant gild of, 107; Sandgate of, 253. Dominicans of, 245, 273n.

Ayres, *see* Chamberlain of Scotland, his ayres; Justice ayres.

Ayrshire, 76, 356, 562.

Ayton, 195, 552 *and n*.

'Babylonish Captivity', 190, 237

Badenoch, 72. Lord of, *see* Comyn, John.

Bagimond's Roll, 10.

Bailies, of baronies, 18, 427, 428; of burghs, 17, 23, 109, 210–11, 263, 305, 310, 427, 447, 448; of crown lands, 380, 456; of regalities, 210; of religious houses, 336, 344.

Ballads, 275, 579.

Ballat of our Lady, 583.

Ballet of the Nine Nobles, 276.

Balliol, Alexander, 64. Devorgilla, 11, 13, 35, 39. Edward, son and heir of King John, 47, 62, 132–3, 138, 142–3, 155–6; campaign in Scotland (1332), 124–6; crowned at Scone, 126; flees from Annan, 127; besieges Berwick and is victorious at Halidon, 128–9; cedes southern Scotland, 129–30, 142; campaign of 1335, 131–2; in Perth, 134; in charge of defence of northern

Crichton (*continued*)

Margaret, illegitimate daughter of 3rd Lord Crichton and James III's sister, 489, 566.

Robert, of Sanquhar, 516.

Sir William, chancellor and 1st Lord Crichton, 352, 366, 389; seizes power and executes the Douglas brothers, 328-31; opposed to Black Douglases and Livingstons, 339-42; reconciled, 342; conspires against Douglas, 354-5, 358-9.

William, 3rd Lord Crichton, 489*n*, 504*n*, 512-13, 520-1, 536; his affair with Margaret, sister of James III, 489.

Crichtons, the, 207, 328, 340*n*, 352, 409; their rivalries with the Livingstons, 338-42; their sudden eclipse, 366; their feud with the Maxwells (1508), 568.

Cromarty, 54, 542; sheriffship of, 111.

Crookston Castle, 536.

Crossbowmen, 137.

Crown Lands, the, 313, 402, 531; augmented by Stewart heritage, 211; augmented by James I, 285, 318-19; income from (1433), 319; revenues of, before and after act of annexation of 1455, 378-80; feuing of, under James II, 381; accounts, rents, rentals and assessments of, under James III, 408-9, 456, 459; their extension and conservation under James III, 454-5; receipts of and feuing of, under James IV, 570-1.

Crown, Pleas of the, 19.

Crowners (Coroners), 18, 380, 427.

Croyser, William, archdeacon of Teviotdale, 295-7, 332-3, 335-7.

Crusades, 135, 462, 594, 596, 597; Robert I's interest in, 122; David II's interest in, 174; James IV's interest in, 594; against Lithuanians, 266.

Crusading Tenths, 32-3, 82.

Crystall, Thomas, Abbot of Kinloss, 559.

Culblean, battle of (1335), 132-3, 144.

Cumberland, 32, 35, 136, 145, 146, 197.

Cumbraes, 362, 569.

Cumlaws, 5.

Cumnock, 77; Master Nicholl of, 294.

Cunningham, Alexander, Lord Kilmaurs, 405*n*; Earl of Glencairn, 529.

Cuthbert, restored to earldom of Glencairn (1503), 573.

Cupar, 140, 210, 211, 381, 425; burned (1411), 307; great customs of (*c.* 1394), 213; complaint of inhabitants of (1567), 449; castle of, 72, 135, 138.

Curia (Papal Court), 9, 59, 60, 71, 103, 182-3, 190, 192*n*, 238, 268, 294, 295, 432, 442, 458, 460, 461, 462, 464, 465, 469, 508, 557, 589; *see also* Papacy *and* Popes.

Currency (*see also* coinage), 541; units of, 23.

Customs, the Great, 15, 134, 212, 253, 283-4, 313, 454; under Robert I, 107-8; under David II, 165-6, 176; receipts of, (1371) 177, (1374) 187-8, (1390-1420) 255, 265, (1422-8) 284, (1446, 1449) 349, (1455, 1456) 379, 391, (1479, 1487) 439, (during reign of James IV) 565-6 *and* 566*n*, 570; annexed to crown (1455), 378; tacks of, 566; rates of duty upon, 565; exemptions, pensions and remissions from, 188, 210-11, 255, 566.

Customs, Petty, 14.

Custumars, 23, 107-8, 188, 210-11, 221, 255, 307, 349; custumars-general, 566.

Dacre, Lord, 568.

Dalkeith, 271, 389; 'burgh of barony', 264; castle of, 554; collegiate kirk of, 470.

Dalry, engagement at (1306), 74, 75.

Dalrymple, John, merchant, 440.

E.H.S.—23*

Stewart, David (*continued*)
    duke (1398), 214; appointed lieu-
    tenant (1399), 214-16; jilts Eliza-
    beth Dunbar and marries Marjory
    Douglas, 218-19; as lieutenant,
    ignores expiry of his term of office
    (1402), 220-1; death, 221-2, 256,
    322.
David, son of Earl of Atholl, 321-2.
David, son of James II, 376.
Duncan, of Appin, 545.
Eleanor, daughter of James I, marries
    Duke of Austria, 347.
Euphemia, Countess of Strathearn,
    255-6.
Isabella, daughter of James I, marries
    Duke of Brittany, 347, 473.
Isabella, daughter of Robert II,
    marries Sir James Douglas, 185.
Sir James, the 'Black Knight of
    Lorne', 369; marries Queen Joan,
    329; banished, 341-4.
James, Earl of Buchan, son of above,
    418 *and n*, 482, 484, 495, 503,
    511n, 562; his rôle in 1482-3, 497,
    508, 512; at English court
    (1487-8), 526, 528; plots against
    James IV, 533, 534-5, 538.
James, Earl of Moray, illegitimate
    son of James IV, 554.
James, Marquess of Ormond, Duke
    of Ross and Archbishop of St
    Andrews, second son of James III,
    421, 518 *and n*, 523, 525, 535, 538,
    553, 558, 595.
James, son of Duke Murdoch, 257;
    burns Dumbarton (1425), and
    flees to Ireland, 287, 322.
James, the Steward, 14, 28, 41,
    52-4, 59.
Jean, daughter of Robert II, married
    John Lyon, 189.
Joan, daughter of James I, 'the dumb
    lady', 347.
Sir John, of Darnley, 251, 289.
Sir John, of Darnley, Lord Darnley,
    Earl of Lennox, 454; at Lauder
    (1482), 497, 502; rebels against
    James IV (1489), 536-8.

Stewart, John (*continued*)
    John, 4th Duke of Albany and
    Governor, 487, 595.
John, Earl of Atholl, half-brother of
    James II, 376, 418 *and n*, 482, 484,
    495, 508, 511n, 512, 529.
John, Earl of Buchan, 312-13, 318;
    his designs on Ross, 233, 235-6;
    chamberlain (1408), 254-5; leads
    expedition to France (1419),
    249-50; at Baugé (1421), and
    made constable of France, 251;
    slain at Verneuil (1424), 288.
John, Earl of Carrick, son of Robert
    the Steward, *see* Robert III.
John, Earl of Mar, son of James II,
    376, 397, 482-5 *and n*, 504.
John, Earl of Mar, son of James III,
    421, 535, 553, 595.
John, Lord Lorne and Innermeath,
    401, 406.
Sir John, of Menteith, delivers Wal-
    lace to the English (1305), 68;
    joins Robert I, 81.
John, the Red Stewart of Dun-
    donald, illegitimate son of Robert
    II, 287.
John, another illegitimate son of
    Robert II, 321.
Margaret, Countess of Angus, bears
    son to 1st Earl of Douglas and
    resigns Angus in his favour, 202.
Margaret, daughter of James I, wife
    of Dauphin (later Louis XI), 285,
    289-90, 292, 347.
Margaret, daughter of James II, 397,
    453, 473, 488-90 *and n*, 504n, 553.
Margaret, daughter of Robert the
    Steward, wife of John of the Isles,
    155, 209.
Margaret, Duchess of Touraine,
    widow of 4th Earl of Douglas, 355
    and n, 365.
Mary, daughter of James I, wife of
    Wolfaert van Borselen, 347.
Mary, daughter of James II, 397,
    400, 405, 440, 514; marries Thomas
    Boyd, Earl of Arran (1467), 413;
    in exile with him, 418; returns to